Sketches of Citizens of Baltimore City and Baltimore County, Maryland

Sallie A. Mallick

Taken from
Genealogy and Biography of the Leading Families of the City of Baltimore and Baltimore County, Maryland
Originally Published in 1897

HERITAGE BOOKS
2014

HERITAGE BOOKS
AN IMPRINT OF HERITAGE BOOKS, INC.

Books, CDs, and more—Worldwide

For our listing of thousands of titles see our website
at
www.HeritageBooks.com

Published 2014 by
HERITAGE BOOKS, INC.
Publishing Division
5810 Ruatan Street
Berwyn Heights, Md. 20740

Copyright © 1989 Sallie A. Mallick

Heritage Books by the author:

*Frederick County Militia in the War of 1812:
A Record of Approximately 3,000 of Those Men of Frederick County, Maryland, Who Were Called to Serve in the Defense of Maryland and Washington, D.C.*
Sallie A. Mallick and F. Edward Wright

Sketches of Citizens of Baltimore City and Baltimore County, Maryland

All rights reserved. No part of this book may be reproduced or transmitted in any form or by any means, electronic or mechanical, including photocopying, recording or by any information storage and retrieval system without written permission from the author, except for the inclusion of brief quotations in a review.

International Standard Book Numbers
Paperbound: 978-1-58549-164-3
Clothbound: 978-0-7884-6027-2

INTRODUCTION

This is an abbreviated abstract of the book titled, Genealogy and Biography of the Leading Families of the City of Baltimore and Baltimore County, Maryland. It was published in 1897 by Chapman Publishing Company, New York. This book consists of 1061 pages including portrait photographs of 138 of the 850 personalities described. The publisher's criteria for selection were based on one's willingness to pay for inclusion in the book. Publications like this one were common in the United States in the late 1890's; there were few areas not covered by them.

Although we sometimes belittle these "mug books" as self aggrandizement and replete with errors, nevertheless these can be the source of clues on earlier generations. Because members of the subject's family are usually named along with the names of one or two earlier generations, genealogists will find these books quite valuable.

In the interest of making the pertinent genealogy available to the public I have condensed the book into an abbreviated format and eliminated those portions I thought were insignificant or extraneous. I omitted most of the generalizations about the individual's character. Photographs were also omitted. I have added a complete full-name index replacing the meagre index of the original which included only the names of 850 persons about whom the sketch was written. The biographical data at the end of the paragraph always refers to the accomplishments and affiliations of the subject of the article.

In some instances you find the relationships of individual's difficult to discern. When I was unable to interpret the original writer's meaning [particularly frustrating when dealing with relationships] I retained the exact wording of the original.

Abbreviations used:

Balt. - Baltimore
b. - born
co. - county
d. - died
d/o - daughter of
m. - married [m. (1) = married first to ..., etc.]
s/o - son of
w/o - wife of

Other abbreviations used were the standard ones including those postal abbreviations of the states. The word "subject" refers to the subject of that particular sketch.

Sallie A. Mallick
Westminster, Maryland, 1989

iii

1. ENOCH PRATT - b. 10 Sep. 1808 at North Middleboro, Plymouth Co., MA, d. 17 Sep. 1896, Balt., MD, m. 1 Aug. 1839, Maria Louise Hyde, native of MA, whose ancestors were among first settlers of that state. On her mothers's side Maria is descended from a German family that located in Balt. over 150 years ago. Pratt ancestors were sturdy New Englanders; founder of the family in this country was Phineas Pratt, who arrived in Plymouth in 1623, and d. at Charlestown, MA, in 1680. Mother was descended from Rev. James Keith, who came here from Scotland in 1662. A Republican. Finance commissioner of the city. Founder of the public library that bears his name.

2. JOHN BROOKE BOYLE, M. D. - b. 8 Jan. 1849 in Frederick Co., MD, in same house as father, Hon. John Brooke Boyle. Grandfather was early settler of Frederick Co. Father d. Apr. 1896. Mother, Elizabeth M., d/o John Scott, of Frederick Co., had nine children, seven living: Dr. Daniel Scott of Frederick Co.; Dr. Charles Bruce of Hagerstown, MD; Henry, a farmer of Frederick Co.; Dr. John B.; Norman Bruce of Westminster; Joseph B., postmaster of Westminster; and Mrs. Charles E. Fink, whose husband is states attorney in Carroll Co. John Scott, land owner and farmer. Mother d. 1876. Member of St. Ignatius' Catholic Church. Supports the Democratic party. Physician in Balt.

3. REV. J. FRANK BRYAN - b. in 1870 near Chesterville, Kent Co., MD, s/o Richard and Anna R. (Taylor) Bryan. Paternal grandfather, John Bryan, farmer of the eastern shore, a Democrat but later became a Republican, had two sons, John and Joshua, who were Methodist Episcopal preachers. Father, b. on the eastern shore, farmer near Chesterville, voted Republican, Methodist Episcopalian. Mother, d/o Franklin Taylor, d. in 1884; maternal grandfather in mercantile business in Chesterville, MD, then in Wilmington, DE. Maternal grandmother was a Miss Hayes, aunt of Pres. Rutherford B. Hayes. Richard and Anna had: Benjamin A.; Ida M., w/o Robert Metcalf; Thomas H.; Richard Moffett; Anna R.; and J. Frank. Member of Junior Order of American Mechanics. Pastor of Bethany Methodist Protestant Church, of Balt.

4. HON. WILLIAM H. B. FUSSELBAUGH, of J. - b. 29 Jul. 1854 in Balt., s/o John and Aomanda M. (Reilley) Fusselbaugh. Father, b. in Balt., d. Dec. 1865. Mother, b. in Balt., d. in 1862. Grandfather, William Fusselbaugh, b. in May 1800 in Balt., d. in 1847, m. (1) Mary, d/o Valentine Donovan, of Irish descent. Mary, b. in Balt., d. in 1833. Valentine Donovan, builder and contractor. Grandfather m. (2) Mary Ann O'Laighlin. Great-grandfather, John Henry Fusselbaugh, native of Germany, d. in 1814 in Balt. William m. (1) Miss Alice, d/o B. Shaw and had 1 child, John. Alice, b. in Balt. B. Shaw, captain of the fire department. William m. (2) Miss Laura J., d/o William Hickman, and had two children, Liston P., and Amanda M. Laura, b. in Balt. William Hickman, undertaker. Member of the Hillen Democratic Club of 5th ward, the Landmark Lodge No. 27, A.F.& A.M., the Concordia Chapter, R.A.M., the Crusade Commandery No. 5, K.T., the Boumi Temple of the Mystic Shrine, the Cerneau Consistory, the Balt. Lodge No. 7, B.P.O.E., the Junior American Mechanics, the

Heptosophs and Golden Eagle, and the Knights of Pythias. Attends Methodist Episcopal Church. Ex-member of the state legislature. Interior decorating business man.

5. GEORGE SCHILLING - b. in Oct. 1835 in Sanborn, Kur-Hessen, Germany, s/o Peter Schilling, native of Hessen. Mother d. when George was young. Peter and his 3 sons, George, Michael, who d. in Balt., and Frank, railroad employee living near Pittsburg, PA, sailed 50 days on the Manchester in 1845 to Balt. Father d. in 1853. George m. (1) Mary Henning, who d. in Balt., had 3 children, one surviving is Mrs. Lizzie Wellingfield of Balt.; m. (2) Mary Kettering, had 7 children, 4 surviving are: William H., Frank A., George A., and Mamie; m. (3) Elizabeth Kettering, had 1 child, deceased. Member Oldtown Merchants & Manufacturers' Association, the King David Lodge No. 68 of the Masons, St. John's Chapter, R.A.M., Association of O. Keil, and the Hackman's Union. Belongs to St. Matthew's Lutheran Church. Undertaker and embalmer.

6. JOHN S. ENSOR - b. 28 May 1868 in Towson, MD, only s/o John T. and Caroline (Stokes) Ensor. Father had 4 brothers, 3 living: Andrew of Washington, D.C.; James B., farmer and school commissioner at Belfast; George B., farmer of Harford Co.; other brother d. as an officer in the Confederate army. Father b. in Balt. Mother b. in Philadelphia. John and Caroline had 3 children: John S.; Caroline L., wife of Joseph Clendenin, Jr, sec. and treas. of Balt. Smelting and Refining Co.; and Florence A. Member of Delta Tau Delta, the Junior Order of American Mechanics, and the Independent Order of Odd Fellows. A Republican. Belongs to the Presbyterian Church of Mt. Washington. State's attorney of Balt. Co.

7. SAMUEL REGESTER - b. in 1854 in Balt. Co. on old homestead, Woodlawn, 2nd s/o John and Amanda (Hardy) Regester. Maternal grandfather, Nicholas Hardy of Howard Co, MD. Father, b. in 1823 in Woodlawn, d. in 1896, s/o Samuel and Elizabeth Regester. Samuel came from Talbot Co., MD, in 1805 and was member of Oldtown Quaker Meeting-house. John and Amanda had: Nicholas; Sebastian; John, in dairy business here; Samuel; and Ella, w/o Dr. Louis A. Weigel of Rochester, N.Y. Samuel m. Miss Anna J., d/o Capt. Charles F. Pickering, in the "Sunset State", in 1884. Charles Pickering was in the United States navy. A Republican, then a Democrat. Member of Odd Fellows's, Gordon Lodge No. 114, the Poplar Grove Fishing Club, and the Prospect Gun Club. Lawyer in Balt.

8. MICHAEL PADIAN - b. County Roscommon, Ireland, s/o Richard and Mary (Carliss) Padian. Mother, also native of County Roscommon, d. in 1885. Richard and Mary had: William, in realestate and wholesale liquor business in NY, d. 26 Apr. 1894; James and Peter of NY; Michael; Maria; and Annie and Kate, of NY. Family sailed for America in 1860, settled in the eighth district, Balt. Co., MD. Father was a Catholic and a Democrat. Member of the Catholic Benevolent Legion. A Catholic. A Democrat. An agriculturist.

9. HIS EMINENCE, JAMES CARDINAL GIBBONS - b. 23 Jul. 1834 in Balt. of Catholic parentage. Taken to Ireland when young, on return entered St. Charles College. Ordained to priesthood 30 Jun. 1861. Became Archbishop 3 Oct. 1877. Appointed Cardinal 7 Jun. 1886. Churchman and cardinal.

10. CHARLES BENJAMIN ZIEGLER, M. D. - b. 8 Jul. 1855 in Balt., s/o John M. and Susan A. (Clemmency) Ziegler. 7th generation of a York Co., PA, family founded about 1730 or 1740. Grandfather, Benjamin Ziegler, d. at age 46. Paternal grandmother, Anna M. Pentz, b. York Co. Father, b. York, PA. Maternal grandfather, Charles Clemmency of Talbot Co, MD. Maternal grandmother, Mary A., d/o John Berridge who came to the Eastern Shore from England. Great-grandfather Henry Clemmency was a French soldier who came to America with Lafayette. John and Susan had six children, Charles being the oldest. Charles m. (1) in St. Michael's, Emily I., d/o Edward Tennant, a farmer. Emily d. after 4 months; m. (2) in Balt., Jane, d/o Edward Baker, and had three children: Edith, John E. and Margaret. Jane, b. in Philadelphia. Edward Baker, b. in England, settled first in Philadelphia then Balt., partner in Maryland Meter Works. Member of Medical and Chirurgical Faculty of Maryland, the Clinical Society of Balt., and the Medical and Surgical Society of Balt. Belongs to the Protestant Episcopal Church of Our Saviour. A Democrat. Physician and surgeon.

11. A. A. MORELAND - b. 15 Feb. 1857 at Fells Point, s/o Joseph Foster and Sarah Lund (Johnson) Moreland, he of Philadelphia, PA, and she of Snow Hill, MD. Grandfather, Jabez Moreland, b. in England, d. in Balt. at age 90. Descended on maternal side from Lord Sylva, of England, settler of Snow Hill, d. in MD. After death of Lord Sylva, grandmother came to Fells Point, where she d. Father, a shoemaker, Master Mason and a Baptist. Joseph and Sarah had twelve children, A. A. being the 5th. A. A. m. in Balt., Miss Anna C., d/o Joseph Batty of St. Mary Co., MD, and had 2 children, Alonzo Gordon and Geraldine Cecelia. Anna, b. in Balt. Member Concordia Lodge No. 13, F.& A.M. and the Young Men's 7th Ward Republican Club. A Methodist Episcopal. Businessman.

12. REV. DR. MIECZYSLAW BARABASZ - b. 9 Jul. 1863 in Poland, s/o John and Cecilia Barabasz of Cracow, Austrian Poland. John and Cecilia had 4 children: Mieczyslaw; Julia, w/o Anthony Skretny of MD; Mary and Stephanie, at home. Ordained to priesthood 1886. Rector Holy Rosary Catholic Church, Balt.

13. REV. JOSEPH SKRETNY - b. 23 Oct. 1865 in province of Posen (Poland), s/o Adalbert and Amy Skretny. Ordanied to the holy priesthood 29 Jun. 1890. Pastor of St. Stanislaus. D. 4 Sep. 1897.

14. WILLIAM BISSON - b. 17 Jan. 1851 in Fells Point, s/o William and Martha (Travers) Bisson. Paternal grandparents came from England and d. a month apart in St. Louis. Father, Captain Bisson, b. Isle of Jersey in the English Channel, d. Jun. 1896 at

age 74. Mother, b. in Urbana, Lancaster Co., VA. William and Martha had 6 children, William being the 2nd. William m. in Balt., Miss Sarah Catharine, d/o William Durham of Somerset Co., and had 1 child, Cecelia V. Member of the Marine Engineers' Beneficial Association No. 5 of Balt., LaFayette Lodge No. 111, F.& A.M., the Northwestern Masonic Association, the Shield of Honor and the Home Circle. A Republican. Chief engineer of the Merchants' National Bank building.

15. G. HENRY CHABOT, M. D. - b. 19 Apr. 1861 in Balt., s/o of Lawrence J. and Mary A. (Cole) Chabot of Balt. Father b. Balt. 4 Sep. 1814. Lawrence and Mary, Catholic, had 3 children: William H., d. at twenty-eight; Eleanora, d. in infancy; and G. Henry. G. Henry m. 26 Apr. 1892, Celia R., d/o Thomas and Julia E. Kelly of Balt., and had 2 children: G. H., Jr., d. 17 Aug. 1897, and Julia. Members of Catholic church. Medical practioner at No. 1111 East Preston Street.

16. REV. F. H. O'DONOUGHUE, C. M. - b. Rochester, NY, s/o James and Mary Ann (McAndrew) O'Donoughue, he of Ireland and she of NY. Father, a Catholic and a Democrat, d. 16 Mar. 1895 at age 79. Mother, a Catholic, d. 30 Sep. 1885 at age 65. Ordained to the priesthood 10 Sep. 1876. Rector Immaculate Conception Church, Balt.

17. THE BALTIMORE SUN - partnership of W. M. Swain, Arunah S. Abell, and A. H. Simmons. 1st issue appeared 17 May 1837. Simmons d. 1855, firm became Swain and Abell. Abell took into partnership on 17 May 1887 his three surviving sons: Edwin Franklin, George William and Walter Robert. A. S. Abell d. at his residence in Balt. 19 Apr. 1888. Walter Robert Abell d. 3 Jan. 1891. The Sun was incorporated as the "A. S. Abell Co." on 9 Aug. 1892. George W. Abell d. 1 May 1894.

18. SAMUEL H. TATTERSALL - b. 13 Apr. 1866 in Philadelphia, PA, s/o John and Alice (Lees) Tattersall, natives of England where they married. Parents came to America in 1863, settled in the Quaker city, then in Trenton, NJ. Father, wool manufacturer, member of St. Paul's Episcopal Church in Trenton, the Masons, the Knights of Pythias, the Odd Fellows' society, and a founder of the Sons of St. George in America, was sixty on 18 Sep. 1897. Mother is fifty-nine. John and Alice had: Samuel; Sarah, w/o Joseph Turford of Trenton; and James C. of Trenton. Samuel m. Miss Anna M. Hardy in the Church of the Holy Comforter in Balt. 20 Apr. 1887 and had 4 children, 2 living: Alice M. and Samuel Leslie. Anna was resident of Grantham, England, came to America in the 80's with parents. Members of St. Michael's and All Angels Church. Member of the Concordia Lodge No. 13, A.F. & A.M., the Improved Order Heptasophs, the Royal Arcanum, the American Legion of Honor, the Ancient Order of United Workmen and the Junior Order United American Mechanics. Supreme secretary of the Heptasophs.

19. S. VEIRS MACE, M.D. - b. Jan 1860 in Balt., the 2nd s/o Dr. William H. and Henrietta A. (Johnson) Mace. Father, b. in Balt.,

d. in Mar. 1889, buried in family graveyard. Mother, d/o William H. and Eliza A. (Corrie) Johnson of Talbot Co., MD. William and Henrietta m. in 1853 and had seven children: Elizabeth M., m. Calvin Chestnut of Balt., d. 1890 leaving a son, W. Calvin Chestnut, an attorney in Balt.; William Johnson of Philadelphia; Ella Corrie; Florence Virginia; Charles Ross, lawyer in Balt., a Republican, m. Susan Van Trump; Carville V. and S. Veirs. Mace family is of English origin and founded in Dorchester Co., MD, in 17th century. Grandfather, Dr. Charles Ross Mace, b. in Dorchester Co. S. Veirs m. in 1895, Clara V. Marsh of Frederick Co., MD. Member of Chirurgical Society. A Republican, as are his father and grandfather. Physician and surgeon of Balt. Co.

20. REV. CARL FRITSCH - b. 16 May 1854 in Hesse-Darmstadt, Germany, s/o Rev. Wilhelm and Bertha Fritsch. Wilhelm and Bertha had six sons, all became ministers: eldest son, Edward, in missionary field in Berlin; Frederick, in Offenbach, Germany; John, in Schwartz; Emil, in Grebenau; and Wilhelm, Jr. with mother in Germany. Father, d. in 1891, aged sixty-seven. Carl m. Lydia Fotsch, d/o Rev. Martin Fotsch, of Monroe, Green Co., WI, 4 May 1881, and had three children, Edward, Carl and Leonie. Minister of St. John's Evangelical Lutheran Church, Balt.

21. DONALD McVICAR - b. 21 Mar. 1854 in Argyleshire, Scotland, s/o Alexander and Mary (McInnes) McVicar, both also b. in Argyleshire. Alexander and Mary had five sons and three daughters. Donald m. Mary A. M. Guthrie, of Inverary, Argyleshire in 1877 and had ten children: Alexander G., employed on steamship Dago; William Archibald; Juliet Stewart; Innes Mary; Donald Malcolm; Guthrie James; Charles Morrison; Alice Marion; Lewis Stewart; and Ian Douglas. Came to America, under special contract with Rutherford Stuyvesant, of New Jersey, in 1887. Member of the Masons. Episcopalians. Superintendent of the Bowley's Quarter Ducking Club.

22. HENRY J. HEBB, M. D. - b. 5 Jan. 1842 at Tower Hill, the Hebb family homestead in St. Mary Co., MD, s/o Thomas and Caroline (Wise) Hebb. Brothers William and Thomas Hebb came from England before the Revolution and settled in St. Mary Co. Father, son of William Hebb, both of St. Mary Co., farmers. Maternal grandfather, an Englishman by birth and lineage, came to America before war of 1812, was arrested as a subject of Great Britian during the conflict, deported, but returned after the war and settled in St. Mary Co. Thomas and Caroline had five children: Dr. John W. of Howard Co.; Thomas A. who d. at Front Royal serving Confederate army; surviving sister is Anna, w/o George Duke of Balt. Henry m. (1) Anna A., d/o David Jean, who d. in 1876. He m. (2) Miss Phoebe, d/o John S. Hayes, farmer of Balt. Co., in 1882 and had three children: Henry J., Jr., Elizabeth and Richard. Director of the Home for the Feeble Minded in Owings Mills. Member of the Knight of Pythias. "Wheel-horse" of the Democratic party. Registar of wills for Balt. Co..

23. CAPT. GEORGE ALLEN RAYNOR - b. 1 Dec. 1836 in Freeport, Queens Co., L. I., s/o Allen and Jane A. (Smith) Raynor. Father

and grandfather, both named Allen, were born there and were farmers. Paternal great-grandfather was native of the land that gave to the world Scott and Burns. Mother is eighty-two years old. Allen and Jane had nine children, only two surviving; Elijah, member of 139 New York Volunteer Infantry and killed at Cold Harbor; Captain Henry belonged to same company, d. at Cape Charles City, Va., buried in Freeport, L. I.; Charles B. also belonged to same company and lives in Freeport, L. I. George m. in Norfolk, Va., Miss Sarah, d/o Capt. John Morton, and had three children: George A., Jr., flagman of the Pennsylvania Railroad Co.; James E. T., employed by same steamboat company as father; and Charles B., in the oyster business. Sarah, native of Newberne, NC. Captain of the steamboat Eastern Shore.

24. JACOB DIMMITT NORRIS, M. D. - b. 1 Aug. 1843 near Bel Air, Harford Co., MD, s/o Lloyd A. and Mary Ann (Stansbury) Norris. Family was founded as early as 1690 by Benjamin Norris, a grandson of Sir John Norris, admiral in the British navy. Benjamin's son, John, m. Susannah Bradford. John's son, Aquilla Norris, the great-grandfather of Jacob, was native of Harford Co., where his son, Rhesa M. Norris, was also b. Rhesa, a farmer, m. Susan Dutton, a VA lady, and d. at age eighty. Father also b. near Bel Air, d. at age forty-six. Mother, of Balt. Co., d/o Colonel Stansbury, d. at seventy-two. Both parents devout members of the Methodist Church. Lloyd and Mary had five children: Jacob D.; James H., in the insurance business in Balt.; Susan; Nellie, d. at age thirty-five; and Mary, d. in infancy. Jacob m. Mollie Warfield of Frederick Co. and had four children: Chester, d. at age two; Lester; Hazel; and Jessie. Supports the Democratic party. Commissioner of Franklin Square; chief examiner for Metropolitan Life Insurance Company of New York; surgeon of the Fourth Maryland Regiment of Balt.; member of Balt. Medical & Surgical Society. Medical practitioner in Balt.

25. CHARLES GERALDUS HILL, A. M., M. D. - b. 31 Oct. 1849 in Franklin Co., NC, s/o Maj. Daniel S. and Susan Irving (Toole) Hill. First of this family came to America from England in colonial days and lived in VA and then in NC. Green Hill was member of provincial congress and major in the army. James J., son of Green Hill, was a senator. Charles A., son of James J. and grandfather of Charles G., was b. in NC, m. Rebecca, d/o Col. Nicholas Long, and had seven children. Father b. in GA and d. Aug. 1873. Mother, d/o Geraldus Toole. Maj. Hill and wife had seven daughters and three sons: Louisa, w/o Matthew Davis of NC; Madeline, Mrs. James H. Bess of same state; Susan Rebecca, deceased; Paulina, w/o Rev. John R. Brooks, D. D., of NC; Florence, w/o Garland Jones, of that state; Isabella, w/o Walter Stark, also of that state; Caroline Toole, w/o Harry C. Painter of Balt. Co.; William I., unmarried and lives with brother Charles; D. S., m. Florence Hartman of Balt.; and Charles Geraldus. Charles m. (1) Isabella, d/o Charles Painter, of Balt. Co., and had three children: Charles Irving, student in Balt. Medical College; Dudley S., attending Marston's University School; and Geraldus Toole, also student of that school. He m. (2) Mabel Painter, sister of first wife, and had two children,

Milton P. and Gladys. Member of Medical and Chirurgical Faculty of Maryland, American Medico-Psychological Association, Clinical Society, Neurological Society, the Book and Journal Club, the West Arlington Building, Loan and Savings, the Green Spring Valley Hunt Club, Athenaeum Club of Balt. City, Sharon Lodge of Master Masons, Druic Chapter, Royal Arch Degree, and the Knights Templar, Beauseant Commander. A Democrat. Physician-in-Chief of Mt. Hope Retreat.

26. HARRY E. PETERMAN, M. D. - b. 16 Jul. 1871 in Indiana Co., PA, s/o Jeremiah and Mary (Clark) Peterman, also natives of same county. Father served in 206 PA Infantry in Civil War. Jeremiah and Mary had two daughters and two sons: Eliza, widow of Albert Smith and lives in Indiana Co.; Clara A., w/o John C. Nesbitt, lives in Johnstown, PA; Dr. James H., practicing in Cherry Tree, Grant P. O., PA, and m. Jennie Wilhelm of Indiana Co. Votes the Republican ticket. Member of Westminster Presbyterian Church. Physician at No. 646 West Franklin street.

27. CAPTAIN JOHN RAU - b. 15 Sep. 1828 in Gravinstein, Hesse-Cassel, Germany, s/o John C. and Philipine (Kahler) Rau, both natives of Germany. Father was in Franco-German war, also in Revolutionary war and the war of 1812, d. 1833. John C. and Philipine had five children: the daughter and the eldest son, William, d. in Germany; George D., came to America, became a merchant tailor and d. about 1883; Henry, in business in Balt. John m. Elmira Schluderberg, (family history is given in sketch of William Schluderberg) a native of Germany, 26 Mar. 1854 and had five children: Mary, w/o P. H. Wagoner; William, in postal service in Balt.; Annie, w/o Thomas Roe; Kate, w/o Frederick Heim; and John, in the flour and grocery business. Member of the Odd Fellows' and the Legion of Red Cross; organizer of the Order of Red Men, of Highland. A Republican. Belong to the German Lutheran Reformed Church, of Canton. Retired wheelwright, blacksmith and real estate investor.

28. DR. J. C. HUMMER - b. 10 Oct. 1833, Loudoun Co., VA, s/o Capt. Washington and Martina B. (Fox) Hummer, both of the same county. Father d. at age sixty-five. Mother d. at age eighty-five. Washington and Martina had ten children, four surviving: J. C.; George W. F., living in Washington, DC; Braden E., living in VA; and Annie R. J. C. m. Annie A. Whaley of Loudoun Co., VA, 10 Jun. 1856 and had four children, two surviving: Mrs. Alice A. Cole of Washington and Earnest E. who manufactures the proprietary medicines of his father. Compounded a number of proprietary medicines. Physician at 621 North Carrollton avenue, Balt.

29. WILBUR M. PEARCE, M. D. - b. in 1867 in Balt. Co., s/o Thomas C. and Margretta (Stabler) Pearce. Thomas C. is native of Balt. Co. and s/o William and Mary Ann (Bosley) Pearce also of Balt. Co. Great-grandfather, Daniel Bosley, pioneer of Balt. Co. Margretta was b. near PA line in Balt. Co., a d/o Daniel and Ann (Stabler) Stabler. Thomas C. and Margretta had seven children: Daniel, operates old stock farm of his father; William, d. on farm; Elizabeth, at home; Wilbur M.; Fannie, also at home;

Bosley, d. in childhood; and Adam, at home. Mother, d. in 1889, belonged to Methodist Episcopal Church. Member of Alumni Association of Dickinson College; the Alumni Association of the University of PA; Phi Beta Kappa; Phi Kappa Psi; the Clinical Medical Society; and the Medical and Chirurgial Faculty of MD. Medical practitioner of Balt.

30. REV. JOSEPH A. GALLEN - b. 4 Jul. 1847 in Philadelphia, s/o John and Mary (Campbell) Gallen, natives of Ireland. Father d. in Philadelphia at age seventy-eight. Mother d. at age seventy-five. John and Mary had eight children: James, John, Patricius and Mary are deceased; Mrs. Rose Quinn lives in Philadelphia; Isabella, w/o John P. Lawler, lives in Livermore, CA. Ordained 30 Jun. 1870. Rector of St. Paul's Catholic Church.

31. HON. GEORGE H. MASON, JR. - b. Jul. 1865 in Balt., s/o George H. and Amelia (Roberts) Mason, natives of Balt. Paternal grandfather, E. C. Mason, was born in Bangor, ME. George and Amelia had three sons and a daughter, Rosa Lillian. Member of the Young Men's Republican Club and the Junior Order of United American Mechanics. A Republican. Belongs to Greenmount Avenue Methodist Episcopal Church. Member of the Legislature from the second district of Baltimore.

32. PETER G. ERDMAN - b. 1828 one mile east of the city of Balt. on the Harford road. Peter m. Letitia Waddell, a native of Ireland, and had five sons and five daughters: John G., b. at Harford road homestead in 1852, m. Virginia S. Erdman, a distant relative and the second d/o John G. Erdman, in 1890, had one child, Clarence Elmer; William, b. in the same house in 1857, m. Kate L., eldest d/o George Seipp, of Carroll Co., MD, in 1884 and had one child, William Kenneth; Letitia; Ella; James M.; Mary L., w/o Mr. Reinicker of Balt.; Peter F.; and Harry. Peter d. in May 1896. Politically an independent. A farmer.

33. REV. EPHRAIM L. S. TRESSEL - b. 16 Aug. 1844 in Tuscarawas Co., OH, one of fourteen children of Samuel and Elizabeth (Sparks) Tressel. Father d. in 1873 at the age of fifty-eight. Father and mother were both natives of Tuscarawas Co., OH and lifelong members of the Lutheran Church. Mother is decendant of a long line of Quakers and Baptists in PA. Grandfather, George Tressel, was a native of PA and one of the pioneers of Tuscarawas Co. about 1808. Ephraim m. Amelia, d/o Philip Schmelz, a native of Columbus, 28 Sep. 1869, and had one son, Rev. Walter E. Tressel, who m. Anna E. Nitzen of Balt. and had one child, Walter E., Jr. Pastor of St. Peter's English Lutheran Church on East Fayette street.

34. J. FRANK ROBINSON - b. 11 Feb. 1857 in Easton, Talbot Co., MD, s/o Charles Edward and Mary E. (White) Robinson. Grandfather, Thomas Robinson, a descendant of Scotch ancestors, b. in Talbot Co. Mother, native of Caroline Co. and d/o Joseph White; the White family are heirs of Thomas Eaton, who inherited from Lord Eaton, of England, a large estate in Caroline Co. and also a large fortune in England. Charles and Mary had ten children. J.

Frank m. Clara B., d/o Thomas Evans and a native of Balt., at Easton, 3 Aug. 1880 and had six children: Leah E.; Harry F.; Clara B.; Roger R.; Charles Russell and Ruth. Member of Junior Order United American Mechanics, the Commercial Senate, the Essenic Order, K. of A., the Young Men's Republican Club and the McKinley Club of the fifth ward. A Republican. A Methodist. Justice of the peace in the fifth ward.

35. J. E. HEARD, M. D. - b. 7 Jul. 1850 at his parents home in St. Mary Co., MD, s/o Col. James E. Heard. Grandson of Col. Joseph Heard, an officer in Colonial army during the Revolution. On his mother's side he is the great-grandson of Col. George Dent of the Colonial army and a relative of the family of Mrs. Julia Dent Grant, widow of General Grant. Father, native of MD, a Catholic, d. Mar. 1889, aged seventy-eight. Mother, a d/o William Dent, a Presbyterian, d. 25 Jul. 1897 in St. Mary Co. age seventy-three. James and his wife had ten children: William D. a farmer in St. Mary Co.; Dr. J. E.; Robert, m. Katie Karew, employed at Johns Hopkins Hospital; George H., m. Susie Abell, also employed at Johns Hopkins Hospital; Charles A., teacher in St. Mary Co.; Mills A., m. Cora Yates and lives on a farm in St. Mary Co.; Alice, w/o James A. Jarboe, a farmer of St. Mary Co.; and three children that d. in infancy. J. E. was a policeman in Balt. before he became a doctor in 1882; m. Nina L., d/o John V. Posey, 20 Nov. 1882 and had one child, Roland E. Nina, member of the Episcopal Church of our Savior. Member of the old and the improved Order of Heptasophs, and the Medical and Surgical Association of Balt. Physician at No. 202 Aisquith street.

36. EDWARD PONTNEY IRONS, M. D. - b. 12 Oct. 1824 in Balt., s/o James and Rebecca Irons of MD, one of three children. Father d. in Columbus, AL, at age seventy-two. Mother d. in Balt. in 1829, at thirty years of age. James and Rebecca were both Methodist Episcopal. Edward m. Ann Rebecca, d/o Thomas H. Sewell of Balt., in 1849 and had one daughter, Anna Rowe, who m. (1) Samuel S. Pleasants and had one child, Honor Hampden Pleasants and m. (2) James W. Ramsey of Balt. Member of the Medical and Surgical Association of Balt., the Medical and Chirurgical Faculty of Maryland, and the Masons. A Methodist Episcopalian. Physician at No. 1835 East Baltimore street.

37. COL. WILSON C. NICHOLAS - b. 3 Sep. 1836 in Brooklyn navy yard, Brooklyn, NY, s/o Capt. John Smith and Esther (Stevenson) Nicholas. Founder of Nicholas family in America was Dr. George Nicholas of Lancaster Co., England, who settled in VA at the beginning of the eighteenth century and m. Elizabeth, widow of Maj. Nathaniel Burwell, about 1722; Robert Carter Nicholas, their eldest son, m. Anne, d/o Col. Wilson Cary, in 1754 and their third son, Wilson Cary was b. 31 Jan. 1761 in Williamsburg, VA.; Wilson m. Margaret, d/o John Smith of Balt. in 1783, served as governor of VA and d. 10 Oct. 1820 at Monticello, where he is buried. The Governor and Margaret had: Robert Carter, Wilson Cary, Capt. John Smith, Mary Buchanan, Cary Anne, Jane, Sidney, Sarah Elizabeth and Margaret. Robert Carter, a large planter in LA. Capt. John Smith, b. in 1800 in VA., m. Esther, d/o George

Pitt Stevenson, a merchant of Balt. and had six children: Augusta Campbell, Mrs. Edward De Russy; Cary Anne, unmarried, lives in Balt.; John Smith, a broker in New York City; George Stevenson, merchant in New York; Harry Ingerson, a broker in New York; and Wilson Cary. Capt. John d. 18 Jul. 1865 at his home in NJ. Mary Buchanan m. John Patterson. Cary Anne m. Capt. John Smith, s/o Gen. Samuel Smith. Jane m. Thomas Jefferson Randolph, grandson of Thomas Jefferson. Sidney m. Dabney Carr of Balt. Sarah Elizabeth and Margaret d. unmarried. Col. Wilson was mustered into the Confederate service as a member of the First Maryland Infantry, 22 May 1861. Wilson m. Augusta, d/o Col. Samuel and Ann (White) Moale, Oct. 1866, and had ten children: John Patterson, in business in New York City; Wilson Cary, Jr., helps on family farm; Samuel Moale, employed in Traders' National Bank of Balt.; Mary Patterson, Ann White and Cary Anne at home; George Stevenson and Thomas Jefferson Randolph, attending school in Balt.; and two that d. Father of Col. Samuel Moale, John Moale, was a son of John Moale. Politically favors the Democratic principles. Member of the Masons. Cultivates his estate in the fourth district.

38. HON. WILLIAM FRASER - b. 4 Mar. 1844 in Fochabers, Morayshire, Scotland, s/o William and Margaret (Campbell) Fraser. Family originally from Inverness-shire. Grandfather, Alexander Fraser, b. in Morayshire, a farmer and a Presbyterian, d. at nearly ninety years of age. Father, also of Morayshire, d. at age eighty-four. Mother, b. in Nairnshire, still living at age eighty. William and Margaret had nine children, seven reached years of maturity and William was third born. William m. Miss Marie Ripplemeyer of Balt., d/o C. H. Rippelmeyer, in Balt. and had two children, Dorothy Campbell and Marie Helen. Member of Heptasophs, the Golden Chain, Wilson Post, G. A. R., and the Veteran Organization of the Sixth New York Heavy Artillery. Belongs to the Broadway Presbyterian Church. Florist and landscape gardener.

39. HON. WILMOT JOHNSON - b. in 1820 in Newark, NJ. Wilmot m. Miss Margaret Schuyler of Albany, N. Y., d/o Gen. Stephen Van Rensselaer of Albany, in 1853. Margaret d. 15 Sep. 1897 and is buried in the Van Rensselaer plot in the Rural Cemetery, near Albany. Member of the Maryland Club, the Country Club of Catonsville, the Philadelphia Club, and the Masons. Belongs to the Episcopal Church. A Democrat. Retired business man.

40. REV. AUGUST J. WEISSER - b. 26 Sep. 1852 in Pittsburg, PA, s/o Gabriel and Caroline Weisser. Father spent all his life in the "smoky city" as a watchmaker, a Catholic, d. 9 Jul. 1869 at about seventy-three years. Mother d. 1 Sep. 1870. Gabriel and Caroline had six children: Frank, d. at about thirty-nine years; Anthony, a watchmaker; John, also a watchmaker; Adeline, w/o Joseph Waag; and Philomina, a sister in the Order of Notre Dame. Pastor of St. Anthony's Catholic Church in Gardenville.

41. JAMES H. JARRETT, M. D. - b. 24 Feb. 1832 near Jarrettsville, s/o Luther M. and Julia A. (Scarff) Jarrett. Jarrett

family is of English descent. Grandfather, Jesse Jarrett, born
in Harford Co., m. twice; by first marriage had Asbury and Jesse;
by second marriage had Luther M., b. in Harford Co. in 1804.
Maternal grandfather was Henry Scarff of Harford Co., of English
origin; his son was Joshua H., a commissioner of Harford Co.
Mother, b. 1811 in Harford Co., d. in Jarrettsville in Apr. 1896
at age eighty-five. Luther and Julia had six children: James H.;
William B., merchant in Jarrettsville; Thomas B., merchant and
farmer; Dr. Martin L., physician in Jarrettsville; Joshua W., who
farms the old home place; and Sarah E., m. Benton Nelson, a
farmer, and after his death m. Dr. Frank Cairnes. James m. Julia
A., d/o William Spottswood, of Carlisle, PA., in 1852, and had
four children: Francis W., lives at home and is in business in
Balt.; Dr. J. H. S., practicing in Towson; Emma W., w/o William
A. Lee, a merchant of Towson; and Julia H., living at home.
Julia is a member of the Methodist Church, which the doctor
attends.

42. HARRY SEABREASE - b. in 1876 in Balt., s/o William and Mary
(Miller) Seabrease, both b. in Salzburg, Germany. Father, b. in
1818, came to the United States when about 20 years old, d. 10
Jul. 1894. William and Mary had seven children: Henry, who d.
when about thirty-two; Frank, works for the Traction Car Company;
William, running on the Central Railroad; Edward, works on the
White street-car line; Alphonse, in the transfer business on the
wharfs; Laura, w/o Jack Bland, a glass-blower in Balt. Harry m.
Emma, d/o Charles A. Rogers, of Balt., in 1894. A Democrat.
Member of the Heptasophs. Business man of Baltimore.

43. WALTER R. TOWNSEND - b. 20 Jul. 1857 Porters Bar farm, only
s/o Wilson and Mary L. (Robey) Townsend, he of Balt. and she of
Prince George Co., MD. Father d. in 1893. Grandfather, Mathias
B. Townsend, b. Talbot Co. in 1802. Great-grandfather, Perry
Townsend, b. in Talbot Co., was the first of the family to settle
in Balt. Co. Wilson and Mary had one daughter, Elizabeth T., w/o
James M. Douglas of Balt. Walter m. Cora A. Farmer, of VA, in
1888, and resides at Sunnyside. Cora is a member of the Episcopal Church and he attends. Member of the Royal Arcanum and the
Ancient Order of United Workmen. A Democrat. Attorney-at-law in
general practice at No. 17 St. Paul street.

44. GEORGE A. HARTMAN, M. D. - b. 17 Feb. 1851 in Balt., s/o Dr.
Andrew and Elizabeth Ann (Allen) Hartman. Father, native of
Greencastle, Franklin Co., PA, and on paternal side, of an old PA
family, but his mother was a native of Germany; Lutherans.
Mother, b. in Balt., d/o James Allen also of Balt.; Allen family
from north of Ireland, founded in America by three brothers;
Hugh, James and Dr. Robert William; James was great-grandfather
of subject. Andrew and Elizabeth had seven children, George
being the fifth. George m. Sarah Louise, of Balt., d/o Joseph W.
Abey, in Balt. Member of Balt. Medical Society, the Medical and
Chirurgical Faculty, the Balt. Medical and Surgical Society, the
American Medical Association, the Golden Chain and Royal Arcanum.
Attends the Methodist Episcopal Church. Director of both the
American National Bank and the Economy Savings Bank. A Republi-

can. Physician at No. 1121 North Caroline street.

45. ANDREW J. SAUER, M. D. - b. 2 Nov. 1872 in Balt., s/o Dr. Francis A. and Louisa (Warnecke) Sauer, also of Balt. Father b. 7 Dec. 1847. Mother b. 13 May 1853. The Sauer family came to the United States from England in 1700. Maternal ancestors were Germans. Francis and Louisa had the following children: Linus J., in the drug business; Joseph L., a silversmith; Ambrose C.; William F.; George P.; Margaret H.; and Andrew J. Andrew m. Laura May, eldest d/o Capt. N. C. Ganstar, a wealthy clothier of Balt., in 1895. Member of Catholic Benevolent Legion and the American Catholic League, the Young Men's Literary Society, the Balt. Medical and Surgical Society. Members of the Catholic Church. Physician at No. 222 Foster street.

46. REV. J. F. JENNESS - b. in 1867 in Epping, NH, s/o E. K. and Sarah Augusta (Bartlett) Jenness. Jenness family is among the oldest in NH. Father, b. in NH, became a farmer, a Democrat. Mother, native of Bangor, ME, d/o Daniel Webster Bartlett, contractor and builder. E. K. and Sarah had seven children: Rev. C. K. Jenness of CA; Ida, May, Bessie, Mattie and Althine, at home; and J. F. Pastor of Roland Park Methodist Episcopal Church of Baltimore.

47. JOHN G. JEFFERS, M. D. - b. 14 Jul. 1871 in Balt., s/o George W. and Anna Catherine (Pumphrey) Jeffers, both of MD. George and Anna had three children: John; Anna, w/o Benjamin F. Womack of New York City; and Naomi Emily, at home. Advocates Republican principles. Member of Order of Heptasophs, the Knights of the Ancient Essenic Order, Fraternal Mystic Circle, the Independent Order of Odd Fellows, and the Balt. Medical Association. A Baptist, connected with the Franklin Square Church. Physician at No. 1143 West Franklin street and Assistant surgeon on the staff of the Presbyterian Eye, Ear and Throat Hospital in Baltimore.

48. COL. W. ARMSTRONG JAMES - b. in Richmond, VA, s/o a large planter and slave holder. The Col. m. a d/o Judge Jonathan McCully in Nov. 1877 and had two sons: William M. and Alfred. Wife d. in 1894. Member of the Episcopal Church. In the real estate business at No. 207 St. Paul street.

49. J. CHARLES LINTHICUM - b. 26 Nov. 1867 in Anne Arundel Co., MD, s/o Sweetser and Laura E. (Smith) Linthicum. Father, a farmer, also b. in Anne Arundel Co., a Methodist. Grandfather, William Linthicum, b. in this vicinity in the last century. Mother, d/o James Smith of Anne Arundel Co., a farmer. Sweetser and Laura had nine children: Dr. James S., a druggist in St. Louis; William, a tax clerk in Balt.; Sweetser, Jr., a farmer in Anne Arundel Co.; Dr. G. Milton, of Balt.; Seth Hance, and Wade Hampton, students; Elizabeth V., w/o Joseph K. Benson of Balt.; Annie S., w/o R. Luther Shipley, of Anne Arundel Co., MD; and J. Charles. J. Charles m. Eugenia M., d/o Edward Biden of Balt., in 1893. Eugenia d. in Feb. 1897. Attorney in the Herald building.

50. THEODORE COOKE, M. D. - b. 25 Oct. 1838, s/o Israel and
Arietta (Clark) Cooke. Father, b. in Balt. Co., d. at age eighty
in Jul. 1889. Mother, d/o Henry Clark, a native of MD. Israel
and Arietta had seven children: Mary J., w/o Daniel Cornelius,
and who d. at about sixty years; Theodore; O. A., a physician who
d. in 1888 at age forty-six; Adolphus A., in the mercantile
business in Balt. til his death at age forty-six; O. W., a Balt.
merchant; Edgar S., d. at age twenty-two; and Fannie E. Theodore
m. Sophie, d/o H. W. Webster, M. D., of Balt. in Mar. 1867, and
had three children: Dr. Theodore, Jr., m. Mary, d/o Henry Clark
of Balt. and had a daughter, Virginia M.; Harry Webster, an
attorney in Balt., m. Caroline Stevenson; Sophie, m. Francis H.
Waters, engineer of Balt. and had two children, Francis H. and
Sophie Marguerite who d. 19 Aug. 1897 at age one. Wife, member
of St. Peter's Episcopal Church, d. at age twenty-seven in 1872.
Theodore m. again in 1880, Sarah B., d/o Rev. Sheridan Guiteau,
of Balt., and had one child, Marguerite, who d. at three months.
Member of the Balt. and American Medical Associations, the Medi-
cal and Chirurgical Faculty of Maryland, the Alumni Association
of the University of Maryland, the Knights of Pythias, and the
Civil Service Reform Association. Physician at No. 914 North
Charles street.

51. GEORGE R. GRAHAM, M. D. - b. 28 Jun. 1844, s/o Ellis C. and
Eliza (Gordon) Graham. Father, b. in 1806 in Cecil Co., MD, a
Democrat, d. in 1861 at about age fifty-seven. Mother d. several
years earlier at age forty-three. Ellis and Eliza had eight
children: Mary, w/o Charles LeBaron of Balt.; Ellis, d. at age
fifty-six; Ignatius, d. at age thirty; William J., retired business man of East Balt.; Henry G.; George; Maria, widow of Philip
Ross, of Balt.; and Laura. George m. Hannah, d/o John T.
Brashears, of Balt., in 1869. Hannah, identified with the Methodist Episcopal Church, d. four years after m. at same time as
only child. George m. Ruth, d/o Israel Gosnell, of Carroll Co.,
in 1876. Member of the Grand Army and the Heptasophs. Physician
at No. 725 Columbia avenue.

52. REV. JAMES DONELAN MARR - b. 16 Sep. 1854 in Washington, DC,
s/o James H. and Sarah A. (Stewart) Marr, he of Charles Co., MD,
she of the city of Washington. Father, b. 4 Nov. 1810, employed
by the postoffice in Washington from 1 Jun. 1830 til his death 25
Apr. 1887. Mother b. 27 Mar. 1812, d/o Samuel Stewart. James
and Sarah m. 1 May 1832 and had eleven children, Rev. James Marr
being the youngest. Ordained 22 Dec. 1883. Rector of the Church
of our Lady of Good Counsel of Baltimore.

53. HOLLIDAY H. HAYDEN, M. D. - b. 22 Aug. 1869 in Queen Anne
Co., s/o Isaac and Elizabeth A. (Du Hamel) Hayden, Isaac being a
native of DE. Father d. 5 Aug. 1882 at age fifty-five. Isaac
and Elizabeth had six children: D. F., in business in Centerville; Alfred C., agent and telegraph operator for the Pennsylvania Railroad in Centerville; Sarah C., Lloyd T. and Edward G.,
at home. Member of the Clinical Society of Balt., the Balt.
Medical and Surgical Society, the Medical and Chirurgical Faculty
of Maryland, and the Ancient Essenic Order. Physician and

surgeon at Light and Clement street, South Baltimore.

54. HON. FRANCIS PUTNAM STEVENS - b. 4 Oct. 1842 in Ashburnham, MA, s/o Samuel Small and Martha (Osgood) Stevens. Father d. 1 Dec. 1974 in Balt. On mothers side, connected with Samuel Osgood; also connected with Samuel Stevens, John Putnam, John Osgood and Robert Fletcher, Gen. Israel Putnam, Gen Rufus Putnam and Gen Ebenezer Stevens. All the ancestors were of English lineage. Francis m. Alexina, youngest d/o Alexander J. and Arianna Bouldin, 27 Sep. 1864. Alexina is great-granddaughter of Thomas Sollers and of Thomas Owings. Francis and Alexina had two sons, Francis Alexander and Morris Putnam, both attorneys. Identified with Madison Avenue Methodist Episcopal Church. Attorney in Balt.

55. REV. D. J. RAWLINSON - b. 20 Nov. 1847 in Cambridgeshire, England, s/o David and Rebecca Rawlinson. D. J. m. Sarah A., d/o Joseph Rawlinson, of Cambridge, England, 2 Jan. 1870 and had ten children: Frank Joseph, studying for the ministry; H. J., in the Navy; F. H., ministry student in Balt.; Herbert Howard; Eleanor Annie and Ethel Rose, both at home; Percy, d. at age six, 25 Dec. 1896; another son and two daughters also d. when young. Ordained 30 Nov. 1892, in the First Baptist Church, in Alexandria. Temporarily in charge of the Lee Street Church.

56. CHARLES J. FOX - b. in 1858 in Washington, DC, youngest s/o John and Harriet Damby Fox. Mother, b. in London, d. in 1876 in Balt. Father d. in 1888. John and Harriet had three sons: John Sidney, d. at age nineteen; Henry W., a member of the bar; and Charles J. Charles m. Thomasine M., d/o Robert P. Lamdin, in 1885, and had six children, four surviving: Fannie Dungan, Hazel Annie Bell, John Morris, and Marbury Brewer. Thomasine b. in Balt. A Democrat. In real estate business at No. 210 East Lexington street.

57. JAMES F. H. GORSUCH, M. D. - s/o Luther M. and Sarah E. (Henderson) Gorsuch, of Black Horse, Harford Co., one of ten children. Great-grandfather, Charles Gorsuch, of Charlesboro, received his grant from King George II. James m. Annie Pamelia Riddle, of Long Green, in 1879, who d. in 1892, leaving three children: Gertrude Louisa, Helen Virginia and James Stanley. Member of the Medical and Chirurgical Faculty of Maryland, the Harford Co. Medical Society, and the Balt. Co. Medical Association. Physician at Fork, Balt. County.

58. GEORGE KIRSCHENHOFER - b. 23 Aug. 1842 in Regensburg, Bavaria, Germany, of which place his father and grandfather, both named George, were natives. Father d. at age seventy-seven and grandfather d. at age of ninety-four. Mother, Barbara Bauer Kirschenhofer, b. Sessenbach, Bavaria and d. in 1891 at age seventy-seven. Grandfather, Caspar Bauer, a blacksmith. George and Barbara Kirschenhofer had eight children. George m. Mary, d/o Charles and Fredericka (Dablo) Rheinhart, in Balt. and had six children: Anton, attending Elmhurst College in Ill.; George, wagon-maker; Charles, painter; and Kate, Mary and Fredericka, all

at home. Mary, b. in Lyons, Wayne Co., NY. Member of King David
Lodge, A. F. & A. M., the Ancient Order of United Workmen,
Vorwaerts Turnverein, the Kriegerbund and the Arion Singing Society. A Democrat. Wagon and carriage manufacturer at Eager and
Bond streets.

59. CHARLES H. MITCHELL, M. D. - b. 29 Jul. 1857 in Balt. Co.,
s/o Thomas D. and Harriet (Litzinger) Mitchell. Paternal ancestors were of Scotch and German lineage and early settlers of
Philadelphia where grandfather, Josiah H., was born and reared.
Father, b. Lancaster Co., PA. Mother, d/o Joseph Litzinger, b.
Balt. Co., d. 1878. Thomas and Harriet had five children,
Charles being the only son. Charles m. 2 Oct. 1883 in Reisterstown, Ida R. Parkison, b. Springfield, WV, d/o Rev. Christopher
Parkison, and had two children: Thomas Parkison and Charles
Edwin. Member of the Improved Order of Heptasophs, Pickering
Lodge No. 114, A. F. & A. M., the Shield of Honor, the Medical
and Chirurgical Faculty of Maryland, the Clinical Society of
Balt., the Book and Journal Club and the Alumni Association of
Physicians and Surgeons. Belongs to the Mr. Vernon Methodist
Church. Physician at No. 291 Chestnut avenue.

60. COL. CHARLES B. McCLEAN - b. Cumberland Co., PA, s/o Rev.
Oliver O. and Ann Sophia (Bingham) McClean, natives of Gettysburg, PA, and Emmitsburg, MD, respectively. Grandfather, Charles
McClean, lived in Gettysburg and m. Miss McPherson of same city.
Mother, d/o Judge Charles Bingham. Oliver and Ann had eight
children: William, d. at two years; Ellen, w/o Worrall W. Marks,
of PA; Hannah, d. at eighteen; Mary, w/o Frank B. McCabe;
Jeannette M., w/o John Brusher of Tennessee; Olivia, unmarried
and living in PA; and Sophia, w/o A. W. Porter, a lawyer in
Altoona, Blair Co., PA. Member of the Heptasophs, Knights of
Pythias, Improved Order of Red Men, Ancient Order of United
Workmen and Junior Order United American Mechanics. A Presbyterian and member of the Trinity Church choir. A Democrat.
County surveyor.

61. YOUNG OWENS WILSON - b. 31 Aug. 1826 in Calvert Co., MD, s/o
Rev. T. Wilson. Family came from England about 1700. Young m.
(1) Susan Reece, who d. in 1876 leaving three children: Joseph
R., Mrs. N. O. Berry, and Young Owens. Young m. (2) Mrs. Emily
Reed, b. in Balt. Co., d/o Col. William Hutchins, 14 Nov. 1885.
Member Methodist Episcopal Church South. Young d. 17 Feb. 1897
in Balt. Brick manufacturer and leading business man.

62. JAMES H. SMITH - b. 17 Mar. 1841 in Balt., s/o Henry and
Sarah (Ayler) Smith. Father, b. in north of Ireland, s/o Rev.
Alexander Smith, a Presbyterian clergyman of County Donegal.
Mother, b. in Queen Anne Co., d/o Henry Ayler, a farmer, and d.
in Balt. Co. at age forty-five. Henry and Sarah had four children: James H.; W. O., a bookkeeper; Joseph M., merchant in Balt.;
and Sarah E., of Balt. James m. 27 May 1873, Frances R. Gibson,
b. Harford Co., d/o James F. Gibson, and had two children, Emma
B. and Franklin Howard. Member of the Hamden Presbyterian
Church. Attorney and counselor-at-law at No. 11 East Lexington

street.

63. JAMES S. WOODWARD, M. D. - b. in 1855 in the District of Columbia, s/o James M. and Mary E. (Savage) Woodward, natives of DC, and Balt., respectively. Paternal grandparents, Amon and Julia (Martin) Woodward, both b. in VA, where former's ancestors settled when coming from England. Maternal great-grandfather, George Savage, Sr., came to Balt. from Sligo, Ireland about 1800. George's son, George, b. in Balt. in 1801, m. Susanna S. Chamelon, whose father was from France and mother from Balt. Father d. in Pensacola, FL in 1857 at age thirty-three. James m. Helen Knight Klink, b. in Bloomfield, PA, youngest child of Alexander Klink, in Aug. 1879, and had three children: James S., Alexander, and Edith. Member of the Shield of Honor and the Ancient Order of Foresters. Physician and surgeon of Sparrows Point.

64. MICHAEL GRIFFIN - b. in Ireland. Came to United States when young with parents in 1866, located in Balt., where both parents died. Michael m. Kate Cosgrove, also of Ireland, in Balt., and had five children: John B., Michael T., Mary, Theresa, and Felix. Member of the Golden Chain, the Royal Arcanum, the Heptosophs, the Pimlico Driving Club, the Electric Park and the Gentleman's Driving Club. Liveryman at Centre street and St. Paul, and also at 131 West North avenue.

65. HON. EDWARD F. TOLSON - b. 21 Jul. 1865 in Balt., s/o John A. and Maria (Lambert) Tolson, of Kent Island, MD and Dorchester Co., respectively. Paternal ancestors came to Kent Island from England. Grandfather, John A. Tolson, b. Kent Island, d. Balt.; wife, Rebecca Tolson, b. Kent Island, d. 1892, age ninety-six. Father, d. Mar. 1893, age sixty-six. Mother, d/o Elijah Lambert, who d. in Balt. at age seventy-four. John and Maria had five children. Edward m. Mary E., d/o David Daneker, in Balt., and had one son, Edwin F., Jr. Member of the Columbian Club, Washington Lodge No. 3, A. F. & A. M., and the Golden Chain. A Republican. Wholesale dealer in the oyster packing business on McElderry's wharf.

66. RT. REV. MONSIGNOR EDWARD McCOLGAN, V. G. - b. 1 May 1812 in Co. Donegal, Ireland, s/o Edward and Mary McColgan, who came to America in 1834, settled in Balt. Their sons John, Clarles, Patrick, and James were in mercantile business. Ordained in 1839 by Archbishop Eccleston. Rector of St. Peter's Catholic Church, Balt.

67. JAMES HARVEY STONE - b. 23 Apr. 1821, in Rutland, MA, s/o Harvey and Jerusha (Wheeler) Stone, also of MA. Father d. in New England in 1846, age fifty-four. Grandfather, Jonas Stone, b. in 1752, d. in 1846, was a Revolutionary soldier. James m. Harriet Newell Fusselbaugh, d/o William and Ann (Donovan) Fusselbaugh, of Balt., in 1848, and had seven children: Mary, d. at five years; Harriet, the youngest, d. at one year; Sarah Elizabeth, widow of James R. Seager, a teacher in Balt., and has one child, Harriet; James H., m. Fannie T. Rusk, and had three children, Newell,

Elizabeth and Helen; William F., registrar of the city of Balt., m. Clara S. Roberts, and had three children, Mary, William and Ruth; Maria, d. at three years; John T., m. Clara M., d/o Alban H. and Mary E. Brinton, of Balt., 5 Jan. 1882, and had six children: Harvey, Clarence, Wilmer T., Mary E., Alice M. and Harriet Newell. Members of Monument Street Methodist Episcopal Church. James d. 14 Jan. 1897. Former superintendent of the Chamber of Commerce building.

68. GEORGE C. SHANNON, M. D. - b. 22 Feb. 1864, s/o Rev. Samuel and Deborah M. (Knorr) Shannon, both of PA. Father, b. 1 Aug. 1830, d. 27 Dec. 1896, a minister of the Gospel in the Methodist Episcopal Church, had two brothers, Jared and Joseph. Mother, d/o Captain and Elizabeth Knorr. Grandfather, Jesse Shannon, farmer in Columbia Co., PA, d. at age eighty-three; first wife of Jesse, Anna, d. at age forty-nine, and second wife, Mary, d. about same age; Jesse and Anna had six children; father of Jesse Shannon was native of Emerald Isle. Samuel and Deborah had five children: Thompson Mitchell, d. at about six years; Elizabeth, d. at nine; Mary Luella, w/o William J. Lyons; Edmond L., d. at age twenty-five; and George. George m. 24 Apr. 1889, Nellie R., d/o John R. and Ellen J. Dennison, and had three children: Samuel D., Esther K. and George E. Members of the Whatcoat Methodist Episcopal Church. Member of the Medical and Chirurgical Faculty of Maryland, the Junior Order of United American Mechanics and the Shield of Honor. Votes for the Republican party. In general practice at No. 1442 Presstman street.

69. REV. JOHN J. WICKER - b. 12 Jan. 1866 in Lynchburg, VA, s/o Ambrose and Ann M. (Reed) Wicker. Father, a machinist, a Catholic, native of NC, d. there in 1878. Mother, d/o John O. and Martha W. (Fraser) Reed, father of Martha was General Fraser, who was killed in battle of Saratoga; father of John came to America from Ireland and settled in Campbell Co., VA. Ambrose and Ann had two children: John and Mollie, w/o James A. Litchford, of Campbell Co., VA. John m. Lizzie E., d/o Capt. W. F. Pumphrey, of VA, in Apr. 1892, and had three children: Lizzie Pumphrey, John J., Jr. and James Caldwell. Member of the Junior Order of American Mechanics. Pastor of the Hampden Baptist Church at Roland Park.

70. REV. L. M. ZIMMERMAN, A. M., F. S. - b. 29 Aug. 1863 in Manchester District, s/o Henry and Laah Zimmerman. Ordained 9 Oct. 1887. Member Society of Science, Letters, and Art, of London. Pastor Christ English Lutheran Church of Balt.

71. HON. CHARLES H. MYERS - b. Nov. 1851 in Harford Co., MD, s/o Christian and Mary A. (Myers) Myers, both natives of Washington Co., MD. Paternal grandfather, Abraham Myers, b. in MD, and d. at about ninety-eight. Great-grandfather, also Abraham Myers, b. in Germany and settled in Washington Co., MD, where he d. at about ninety years. Father, an Abolitionist and a Republican, came from Quaker stock, d. in 1887. Mother d. at age seventy-six. Christian and Mary had seven children: Oliver, who lives in Balt.; Nelson, lives near Philadelphia; Stephen, in Balt.;

Samuel, a stone contractor of Balt.; John G., a painter and artist; Isabella (Mrs. Owen); and Charles H. Charles m. Emma C., d/o Otto Pietsch, an Alsatian German, of Balt. and had three children: Otto P., Mary Iola, and Edna C. Otto was a founder of the Hayden Musical Assembly. Member of the American Federation of Labor, the Knights of Pythias, the Granite Cutters' Union, and the Joint Commission of Builders' Exchange and Federation of Labor; a Republican. Chief of the Bureau of Industrial Statistics of MD.

72. REV. A. L. TIMOTHY STIEMKE - b. 24 Aug., 1847, in Washington Co., WI, s/o Charles A. and Wilhelmena (Liesener) Stiemke, natives of Prussia, Germany. Mother d. Sep. 1888, age sixty-eight. Charles and Wilhelmena had eight children, three survive: Rev. Zachariah, d. Oct. 1895, age thirty-five; Edward, a carpenter in Milwaukee; Charles A. of Buffalo; and A. L. T. He m. Anna, d/o Matthias and Margaret Gertrude (Baumann) Schoening, natives of Holstein, Germany and residents of Dakota, 15 Nov. 1874, at Ft. Dodge, IA, and had eight children: Augusta, Henry, Clara, Paul, Martin, Anna, Lydia and Rudolph. Pastor of Emanuel Evangelical Lutheran Church on Caroline street.

73. J. M. TOMPKINS - b. 17 Apr. 1841 in Tremont, Tazewell Co., IL, s/o Coles and Eliza M. (Sidwell) Tompkins. Grandfather, Noah Tompkins, native of Wales, spent later years farming in NY. Father, b. in NY, farmed in IL, near the Mackinaw river til death in 1843. Mother, native of Cecil Co., MD, d/o Joseph Sidwell, who lived in Cecil Co. til death at age sixty-five. Great-grandfather, Levi Sidwell, a member of the Society of Friends, came from Berkshire, England to Cecil Co. before 1730. J. M. m. Margaret Brown, of Alexandria Co., VA, d/o John Brown, in 1867 in Washington, DC. A painter of residence property.

74. HON. WILMOT JOHNSON - b. in 1820 in Newark, NJ, m. Margaret Schuyler, of Albany, NY, d/o Gen. Stephen Van Rensselaer, in 1853; Margaret d. 15 Sep. 1897 in Albany and buried in the Rural cemetery there. Member of Maryland Club, the Country Club of Catonsville, the Philadelphia Club, and the Masonic fraternity. An Episcopalian. A Democrat. Retired business man.

75. JOHN P. SHERWOOD - b. 7 Aug. 1848 in Balt., s/o Henry A. and Eliza J. (Wright) Sherwood, also of Balt. Father d. in Balt. at age forty-seven. Henry and Eliza had six children. John m. Fannie E. Murray, of Balt. and had two children: Irvin and Helen. Member of the Marine Engineers' Beneficial Association No. 5, of Balt. A Catholic. A Democrat. Chief engineer on the Howard, of the Merchants & Miners' Transportation Company.

76. J. FRED GETTEMULLER - b. 18 Apr. 1860 in Balt., one of two children of Herman H. and Annie M. (Kalmey) Gettemuller, both natives of Hanover, Germany, where they were married. Brother is H. J. Gettemuller, a business man of Balt. Herman and Annie came to this country in 1851. Father d. at age seventy-six. Mother d. at age fifty-nine. J. Fred m. Mary Ann Pfau, of Balt., in Balt. and had two daughters: Mabel E. and Eleanore B. Member of

the King David Lodge No. 69, A. F. & A. M.; Adoniram Chapter No. 21, R. A. M.; Monumental Commandery No. 3, K. T.; and Boumi Temple of the Mystic Shrine. A Lutheran. Wholesale and retail dealer in paints, painters' supplies, glass, varnish, etc. at No. 1045 Gay street.

77. GEORGE W. HAMILL, M. D. - b. 16 Oct. 1852, in Balt., one of five children of William J. and Sylvia C. (Hunt) Hamill, he of Balt. Grandfather, Alexander Hamill, was native of County Derry, Ireland, and ancestors were Scotch Presbyterians. Alexander d. at age seventy-eight. Mother, of Welsh descent and from an old PA family. George m. Blanche Newman Grove, of Balt., in Balt., and had two children, Eva Pauline and Blanche Rosalie. Member of Washington Lodge No. 3, A. F. & A. M.; Concordia Chapter No. 1, R. A. M.; Beauseant Commandery No. 8, K. T.; Boumi Temple of the Mystic Shrine; and the Medical and Surgical Society of Balt. An independent Democrat. Physician in Balt.

78. W. GUY TOWNSEND, M. D. - b. 27 Sep. 1864 at Royal Oak, Talbot county, MD, s/o Sylvanus and Anna I. (Bryan) Townsend, he of Talbot Co. and she of Cecil Co. Grandfather, Hon. Richard Townsend, also from Talbot Co. Family is of English origin. Mother, d/o Joel Bryan, also of Cecil Co. Name Bryan comes from the French and was originally Aubrien. Maternal grandmother was also of French lineage and related to General Israel Putnam. Sylvanus and Anna had eight children. Mother d. in 1882. W. Guy m. Sophia M. Duker, of Balt., d/o Otto Duker, in Balt., and had three children: Anna, Guy and Eleanor. Member of the Medical and Chirurgical Faculty of Maryland, the Clinical Society of Maryland, the Balt. Medical Society, the American Medical Institution, the Union League Athletic Club and the Knights of the Ancient Essenic Order. Physician and member of the adjunct faculty of the Balt. Medical College.

79. WILLIAM E. STANSBURY - b. at Union Hall, the family homestead, only s/o William E. and Christiana (Taylor) Stansbury. John E., s/o William, was the father of William E. and grandfather of William E. of this sketch. William Stansbury, a German count, come to the new world some time in the seventeenth century. Father, b. 14 Apr. 1811, d. 27 Mar. 1878, m. Christiana, d/o Elijah Taylor, of Mt. Pleasant, and had four children: Sarah A., Mary Elizabeth, William E., and Alice M. Votes Democratic. Devotes all of his time to the cultivation and improvement of the family homestead, Union Hall.

80. WILLIAM H. KIRWAN - b. 21 Jan. 1848, in Norfolk, VA, s/o William B. and Sarah A. (Shorter) Kirwan, he a native of Somerset Co., MD. Father d. at age fifty-five in Balt. William m. Annabel Rowe, of Balt., and had two children: Nellie R. and William Benjamin. Supports the Democratic party. Clerk of the steamer Avalon.

81. A. PARLETT LLOYD - b. 6 Jan. 1862, in Balt., s/o John H. and Eugenie (MacDonald) Lloyd. Both John H. and his father, John Lloyd, d. at age of thirty-three. Grandfather, John Lloyd, mer-

chant of Baltimore, Whig, m. Miss Taylor, of Dorchester Co., whose mother was a sister of Commodore Decatur. Mother, d/o John MacDonald of Balt., whose ancestors came from Scotland, first settling in Huntingdon Co., PA, and then MD. Father d. in 1863. Mother d. Mar. 1885. The children of John H. and Eugenie were: Benjamin MacDonald, d. in 1877 at age of twenty-one; Mattie, w/o William L. Boyd of Balt.; and Eugenie U., w/o Joseph R. Wilson, of Wilson Brick Company, of Balt. A. Partlett m. Annie E., d/o George J. Loane, 12 Apr. 1882, and had two sons: Henry L. and Eugene D. Mrs. Lloyd is a niece of Robert T. Banks, twice mayor of Balt. Member of the Royal Arcanum and the Order of the Golden Chain. Member of the Balt. bar.

82. HON. GEORGE J. KAUFMAN - b. 14 Jul. 1841 in Germany, s/o John G. and Lena (Kessler) Kaufman. Father, a farmer, d. in 1854 at age forty-five. Mother came to America in 1860 with her five children, first locating in New York, then Balt.; she d. in 1893 at age seventy-seven. George m. Mrs. Jennie Wunder, nee Bien, also of Germany, in Balt. Member of Thomas B. Reed Republican Club, the Masonic Order, the Knights of Pythias, and the Red Men. Belongs to the German Reformed Church. A Republican. Retired stone cutter.

83. CHARLES WILLIAM STOCKETT, M. D. - b. 19 Mar. 1833 in Anne Arundel Co., s/o Joseph Noble and Sophia (Watkins) Stockett. Paternal ancestors were English, being from St. Stephen's parish, Kent Co. Thomas Stockett came to America in 1658 and settled in Anne Arundel Co. Grandfather, Thomas Noble Stockett, M. D., was b. in Anne Arundel Co., and was a surgeon in the American army during the war of the Revolution. Father, also b. in Anne Arundel Co. and m. four times, third wife was mother of Charles. Joseph had sixteen children in all. Sophia, from an old Maryland family, d. 10 Apr. 1839, in Anne Arundel Co. Father d. 21 Dec. 1854. Charles m. Maria E. Duval, of Anne Arundel Co. in 1856, and had twelve children, eight are: Joseph Noble of Balt.; Howard Duval lives in Philadelphia; Jonathan S., Charles William, George S., Robert P., Juliette M. (Mrs. A. W. Robson) and Sophia, all of Balt. Retired physician and surgeon.

84. WALTER H. THORNE - b. 31 May 1851, in Stoke, Somersetshire, England, s/o Henry and Jane (Shoemaker) Thorne. Henry and his father, William, were also from Stoke. Father of William was a captain in the English army. William m. Honor Spracket, and had twelve sons and three daughters: Martha and Harriet, of New Zealand; Betsey; William, a captain; John, a farmer in England; Nathaniel, a farmer; James, horse trainer in England; Samuel, an agriculturist: Christopher, kid glove cutter; Louis, stone and marble cutter; and Henry. William and Honor both d. at age ninety. Henry and Jane, of England, had: Job, an engineer in England; Jane, w/o Joseph Wills, of England, came to America in 1874; Grace, w/o Thomas Wills, settled in New York; Mary, w/o Louis Chant, of VA; Susie, w/o Thomas Boswell, of England; Harriet, w/o Frederick Armstrong, a railroad foreman; Mark, d. in infancy; Mark (2d), d. at age nineteen; Helen, d. at age nine; and Walter Henry. Walter m. Alice, d/o Capt. W. A. and Abbralia

(Hanson) Hogarth, both of English descent, in 1879, and had three children: Alice J. and Walter Henry, who both d. of scarlet fever at age ten and eight, within two weeks of each other; and William Emory. Family inclines to the Episcopalian faith. A Democrat. Contractor for railroad and city work.

85. ISAAC J. MERREY - b. 6 Sep. 1849 in Charleston, Cecil Co., MD, s/o George and Amanda (Lort) Merrey. Grandfather, James Merrey, b. in England, of Scotch descent, came to America and located in Germantown, PA, then Elk Neck, MD, where he d. at age seventy-six. Father, b. Germantown, PA, and d. at Elk Neck, age sixty. Mother, d/o Capt. Joseph Lort, of Elk Neck. George and Amanda had six children, Isaac being the eldest. Isaac m. Mary, d/o James Floyd, in Edenton, NC, and had four children: George E; Florence W.; James F.; and Clifton Lort. Member of Escaville Lodge No. 107, I. O. O. F., La Fayette Lodge No. 7, Independent Order of Mechanics; and Monumental City Lodge No. 12, of the Golden Chain. Belongs to Grace Baptist Churh. A Prohibitionist. Chief engineer of the Chamber of Commerce in Balt.

86. REV. GEORGE MORRISON, D. D. - b. in 1831 in Sweet Air, MD, s/o Rev. George Morrison, Sr. Father, b. at Whitley Creek farm, in Newcastle Co., DE. Family was Scotch, of Norman descent, and founded in American in 1670 by Hans or John Morrison, who settled with Dutch colonists in DE after the treaty of Westphalia. John was father of Hugh, whose son Neal was father of Robert, the great-grandfather of George, whose grandfather was Douglas, of Newcastle Co. George, Sr., m. Elizabeth A. Lovell, in 1823, in Balt., and had: Elizabeth M., who d. in infancy; William Douglas, living in TX; Alexander Martin: George; and Henry, who d. at Sweet Air. George m. Sarah Campbell, d/o Rev. Robert J. Breckenridge, of Lexington, in 1856, in Kentucky. Sarah d. in 1865 in Lexington. George m. (2) Margaret, d/o Joshua and Esther Regester, in Balt., in 1875, and had three children: Esther R., Margaret Lovell, and one who d. in childhood. Wife d. in 1890. Former pastor of the Bethel and Grove Presbyterian Churches.

87. LOUIS ECKELS - b. in 1842 in Prussia, only s/o Powell and Anna (Gray) Eckels. Powell and Anna had a daughter, Margaret, widow of Henry Siebrecht. Louis m. Caroline Lanzer, of Germany, d/o a soldier in the army of that country, in 1866, and had six child-ren: Henry F., Frederick W., August, Philip, William and Mamie. Belonged to Trinity Lutheran Church. Member of the Improved Order of Heptasophs. Wholesale and retail dealer in coal and ice at No. 804 East Eager street.

88. HON. EDWIN J. LAWYER - b. 15 Aug. 1849 at Sunnyside, near Westminster, Carroll Co., MD, s/o William and Susanna (Schaeffer) Lawyer, he a native of Carroll Co., and both of German descent. Paternal great-grandfather, Martin Lawyer, b. in Hanover, Germany, settled in Harford Co., MD, where he reared three sons: Christian, settled in Philadelphia, and has one descendant, Dr. Lawyer; Philip, resident of Lancaster Co., PA, has one descendant, Susan Lawyer, of Adams Co., PA; and Caspar, a farmer of Carroll Co., MD, and d. at age ninety-two. Maternal grandfather,

John Schaeffer, native of this country, and his father, also John, was a farmer in Carroll Co. Father b. 23 Mar. 1811. Edwin m. (1) Mary, of Adams Co., PA, d/o Martin Grove, in Westminster, and had two sons: William and Clarence; Mary, d. in 1891. Edwin m. (2) Martha E. Wagner, of Balt., 1 Sep. 1897. Member of the Masons, the Knights of Pythias, and the Independent Order of Mechanics. A Republican. State Fire Marshall of Maryland.

89. EDWIN GEER, M. D. - b. 9 Feb. 1865 in Wilson Co., NC, s/o Rev. Edwin and Elizabeth M. (Blount) Geer. Father, native of Wilmington, NC, d. in Balt. in Jul. 1880, age sixty-three. Mother, of Washington, Beaufort Co., NC, d/o Thomas H. and Elizabeth Mutter Blount. Edwin and Elizabeth had five children; Sallie, d. at five; Annie, d. at four; Bettie, w/o Capt. George C. Reiter, United States navy, and mother of George C.; and Mary. Member Medical and Chirurgical Faculty of Maryland; the Baltimore Medical Society; the Baltimore Clinical Society; the Medical and Surgical Society of Baltimore and the Journal Club; the Masons, Lafayette Lodge No. 111, A. F. & A. M. Belongs to the Memorial Protestant Episcopal Church. Physician at No. 1614 Bolton street, and the coroner for the southern district of the city.

90. HENRY RECKORD - b. in MA, m. Julia A. Lukens, of MD, in 1852, and had: John H., of Bel Air; Walter P. and William H., b. in Manchester, VA; D. Burnett, Julia A. and Milton H. Son Walter P. m. Lillie R. Chennoworth, and had six children: Grace, Henry, Janet, Raymond, Edward and one d. in infancy. Subject d. in 1888. Identified with the Christian Church. Business man of Balt. Co. and founder of the postoffice named in his honor.

91. JOHN M. STEVENSON, M. D. - b. in Balt., d. 6 Mar. 1888 in Balt. M. Elizabeth Rider in 1877, and had two sons, Allen and H. Burton. Allen, in the grain and coal business at Sherwood, this Co.; H. Burton, physician at Sherwood, m. Margaret, d/o Captain Herman, and had one child. A Mason. Physician and surgeon in Balt.

92. THOMAS V. RICHARDSON - b. 20 Dec. 1851 in Balt. Co., s/o William and Elizabeth A. (Bosley) Richardson. Grandfather, Thomas Richardson, had as children: Penelope, w/o Edward Price; William, the father of Thomas; Jemima A., w/o Zedekiah Masemore; Thomas, who d., leaving three children, T. Monroe, Joshua, and Alberta; Joshua K.; James K., who had two sons; John Pearce, living in New Zealand; Thomas, of Balt. Co.; and John F. Father, b. in tenth district, d. in 1865, as did grandfather. Maternal grandfather, Daniel Bosley. William and Elizabeth had eight children: Mary, w/o W. A. Royston; Emma J., w/o William H. Norris; Rebecca B.; Thomas V.; D. Virginia; two son who d. in infancy; and one daughter who d. at age sixteen. Thomas m. Mary A., d/o Nicholas Parker, in 1892 and had a daughter, Mary E.; a Republican. Leading agriculturist.

93. CHARLES A. CURTIS - b. 30 Apr. 1836 in Frederick Co., MD, s/o John R. and Jane (Livas) Curtis. Descent of English ancestors who settled in MD during the early period of its history.

Father, b. in Frederick Co., d. in 1846. Mother, native of Fred.
Co. John and Jane had nine children: Charles A.; George W., a
manufacturer in Balt. Co.; James A., a farmer in Howard Co.;
Joseph, a cotton manufacturer; Minerva, w/o Adolphus Salfner;
Sarah, deceased w/o C. C. Donger; Mary M., w/o John Hamsen; Jane,
w/o John H. Buxton; and one that d. in infancy. Charles m. Sarah
C. Lewin, of Balt. Co., in 1862, and had six children: William
H., with Western Maryland Railroad in Pikesville; Lillie, w/o
Abraham Greider; Charles Roscoe, who d. at twenty-two; Georgiana
and Ida Frances, who d. in childhood; and Florence C., w/o Joseph
McCullen. A Democrat. Belongs to the Methodist Church. Wheel-
wright and blacksmith on the Reisterstown turnpike, near Pikesville.

94. SYLVESTER JAMES ROCHE - b. 11 Jul. 1858 at Pimblico, s/o
Samuel and Bridget (Dohoney) Roche. Father, b. in County
Wexford, Ireland. Mother also from Ireland. Samuel and Bridget
had six children: Sarah M., w/o David Ormond of Balt. Co.; Ella,
w/o Thomas Kearns, also of Balt. Co.; Patrick T., merchant living
in Pimblico; John J., at home; Samuel F., Jr., carriage manufacturer living in the ninth district; and Sylvester J. Sylvester
m. Johanna Ryan, of Mt. Washington, in 1881, and had seven children: Kittie, Sylvester J., Jr., Mary E., Samuel, N. Annie,
William and Alice. Member Baltimore Building and Loan Association, and Gentlemem's Driving Park. A Democrat. A Catholic.
Engaged in raising fast horses.

95. JAMES C. HARRISON - b. 11 Jan. 1829 in Ellicott City, s/o
William Shipley and Mary (Hargadine) Harrison. Father, b. in
Howard Co., a Democrat, d. in 1870. Mother, a native of Queen
Anne Co., MD. William and Mary had eight children: Mary,
deceased, w/o James Murray; Mary Jane, w/o Emanuel Woodard, of
Howard Co.; Matilda Ann, w/o Louis Wonderer, of France; Eliza,
w/o William Chesgreen; William Henry; Edward H., a painter, d.;
and James. James m. Sarah J., d/o George L. and Esther (Boston)
Trogler, in 1855. Esther is now ninety-seven. James and Sarah
had six children: Mary Ellen, a teacher in Balt.; Olivia G., also
a teacher in Balt.; George L., a painter; J. Arthur, a carpenter;
Sarah and Ann, attending school. A Mason. Identified with the
Presbyterian Church. A carpenter in Govans and the surronunding
country.

96. SARAH R. TAYLOR - Thomas Taylor, b. in England, granted
tract of land in Balt. Co., the deed signed by Lord Baltimore in
1690. Samuel, s/o Thomas, had twelve children: Elijah, the
youngest, b. 12 Oct. 1786 on the Taylor estate; Joseph, the
eldest, b. same place 22 Apr. 1764, m. Sarah Gatch, whose parents
were from Germany; Samuel, the second son, b. 10 Dec. 1765, m.
Miss Thompson and had two children; Richard, the third son, b. 4
Apr. 1767, m. but had no children; Isaac, b. 8 Feb. 1772, m. Miss
Thompson; Mary, b. 8 Mar. 1774, and Rebecca, b. 20 Feb. 1776, d.
unmarried; Mrs. Sarah Baxter, b. 3 Jan. 1778; Hannah, b. 1 Dec.
1779, m. William Scarf and had several children; Jacob, b. 18
Feb. 1782, m. Miss Thompson; and Anna, b. 20 Jan. 1784, m. Mr.
Hale and had several children. Elijah, the father of Sarah, m.

the d/o Jacob Hiss, 17 Oct. 1809, and had nine children: Christiana, the eldest daughter, m. William E. Stansbury; Mary, d. unmarried about 1881; Joseph, never married; Elizabeth, d. single, 1 Aug. 1896; Jacob H., m. Mary C. Muller and had children; Elijah G., m. Miss Lipscomb and had no children; Sarah was the next to the youngest daughter. Active in the work of the Methodist Church that was founded by her ancestors.

97. GEORGE A. BETZOLD - b. 10 Mar. 1875 in Catonsville, s/o Michael and Barbara Betzold. Editor of the Argus, a weekly paper in Catonsville, since the age of nineteen.

98. JUDGE JOHN GONTRUM - b. 21 Jan. 1823 in Hesse-Darmstadt, Germany, s/o Christopher and Anna Maria (Barbara) Gontrum. Father d. in 1846 and mother d. in 1849. Christopher and Anna had three children: John; Peter, a shoemaker, deceased; and Anna Catherine, w/o Henry Haines of Balt. Co. John m. Caroline, d/o Jacob Kinsle, in 1846, and had eleven children: six d. in childhood; Emma, d. at nineteen; Ann Margaret, w/o Robert T. Oyiman; John F., an attorney; Matilda and Ann Catherine, at home. Member Gardenville Lodge No. 114, I. O. O. F., and the Gardeners & Farmers' Beneficial Society. A Democrat. Member of the Lutheran Church. Former judge of the orphans' court.

99. J. ADAM SHUPPERT - b. York Co., PA, s/o John and Mary (Nace) Shuppert, natives of Germany and York Co., respectively. Paternal grandfather, George Shuppert, native of Germany, settled in York Co. about 1847. Father d. at age seventy. J. Adam m. Ella J. Miller, also from York Co., PA, and had three children: Rebecca J., Mary A., and John H., deceased. Ella, devout member of the Reformed Church, d. 4 Feb. 1893, at age thirty. J. Adam m. (2) Catharine Kerl, b. in Balt. Co., and had one child, George Walter. A Democrat. Prosperous agriculturist.

100. LAWRENCE HOFSTETTER - b. in 1823 in Germany, eldest s/o Joseph and Mary Hofstetter. Father m. three times. Joseph and Mary had eight sons: Lawrence; Joseph, a farmer; John, d. in 1896; George, an agriculturist; Frank, in produce business in the city; Edward, lives on Harford road. Lawrence m. Catherine, d/o Valentine and Mary Christina Lutz, 1 Oct. 1846, and had seven children: William Henry, in produce business; George, a farmer in twelfth district; Joseph, in produce business; John; Louisa, w/o Harmon Schone, in the mercantile business; Mary C., w/o Henry Schone, who has a store on Bel Air road; and Annie, at home. Member Gardenville Lodge No. 114, I. O. O. F. Supports the Democratic party. Owns a well-improved garden farm in Gardenville on Furley avenue.

101. THOMAS STANSBURY - Grandfather, Thomas Stansbury, of English descent, but American birth. Father, John, b. Balt. Co., had several children, only Thomas did not go west. Thomas m. Eudocia, d/o William Dawes, of English descent, 9 Jan. 1837, and had son, John Thomas, who d. 14 Apr. 1879, in the prime of young manhood.

102. HON GEORGE YELLOTT - b. 19 Jul. 1819 in the Dulaney Valley, Balt. Co., s/o Capt. John and Rebecca Ridgeley (Coleman) Yellott. Father, b. in England and came to America with parents about the close of the Revolution, d. in Dulaney Valley in 1825. John had a brother, George. Grandfather, John Yellott, had brother Jeremiah who d. in 1805. Maternal grandfather, Rev. John Coleman, of Petersburg, VA. Mothers ancestral history: Cornelius Lyde, of Stanton Neck, England, had eight children, viz.: James, who m. Martha, d/o Andrew Pope, of Bristol; Lionel, who at his death left three children, Sir Lionel Lyde, Samuel and Ann Maria: John, whose children were Roger, Mary, Ann, Elizabeth, Cornelia and Sarah; Cornelius, who left two daughters, Rachel and Mary: Samuel (1st): Samuel (2d); Susanna, w/o Austin Godwin, of Bristol; and Mary, w/o John Birt, of Stepton Mullett, Somersetshire. The children of Austin and Susanna Godwin were named as follows: Nathaniel, who left two daughters, Ann and Mary; Austin, who left five children: Robert, Peter, Henry, Mary and Susanna; Cornelius and Lionel, who d. childless; Lyde, who m. Pleasance, d/o Col. Charles Ridgeley, of MD; Mary, w/o Benjamin Fox, who left two daughter, Susanna and Mary; Ann, w/o John Dixon; Elizabeth, w/o William Hutton; Susanna and Esther, who d. unmarried at ages twenty-two and forty. Six children were b. to Lyde and Pleasance Godwin: Elizabeth, m. Henry Dorsey of Ann Arundel Co. and d. in 1769, leaving a daughter, Elizabeth, w/o John Scott; William first m. Achsah Ridgeley and had one son, William, and then m. Milcah Dorsey, and d. in 1809; Susanna d. unmarried; Rachel Lyde was first w/o Richard Parker of England, and then w/o Jesse Hollingsworth of Balt.: Pleasance m. Rev. John Coleman, and had seven children, six d. young, and one daughter m. John Yellott; and Lyde, M. D., m. Abby Levy of Balt. in 1779, had thirteen children, d. in 1801. Subject of this sketch was eighth of ten children, three who d. in infancy, others were: Jeremiah, a farmer d. 1894; John, a farmer, and father of Maj John I. Yellott, an attorney of Towson; Coleman, member of Balt. bar, d. in 1870; Washington, attorney, d. in 1887. Former judge of the court of appeals.

103. W. GILL SMITH - b. 16 Jul. 1861 in Reisterstown, only child of William B. and Martha (Mays) Smith. Grandfather, Frederick Smith, b. in Germany, settled in York Co., PA, then Balt. in 1840; Frederick and wife lived to be more than eighty years old, and youngest of their eleven children was fifty before there was a death in the family. Mother, one of seven daughters of James Mays, farmer of Balt. Co. W. Gill m. Cornelia, second d/o Samuel E. Parks, a farmer near Towson, in 1886, and had two sons, Harry and Roy. A Democrat. Attorney in Towson.

104. THOMAS E. PEARCE - s/o Josiah S. and Elizabeth A. (Wright) Pearce, natives of Balt. and Harford Counties, MD, respectively. Josiah and Elizabeth had eight children: John, Joseph W., Thomas E., Maggie R., Silas W., Cassie, Ella and Bettie. Father, a lawyer and a Democrat. Grandfather, William Pearce, also b. Balt. Co. Thomas m. Katie M., d/o Henry and Carrie (Buck) Stabler, both natives of Balt. Co.; paternal great-grandfather of Katie was native of England; grandfather, Christian Stabler, b.

in PA; Carrie d. 5 Dec. 1894 at age seventy-two. Thomas and Katie had six children: Virgie, Fannie, Goldie, Thomas C., Beulah and Elmer. A Democrat. Successful and prosperous agriculturist.

105. WILLIAM L. RUSSELL - b. 11 Oct. 1857 in Mobile, AL, s/o Samuel Owens and Ellen (Owens) Russell, natives of AL. Russell family came to America from England in a very early day. Samuel and Ellen had six children: Allen, who d. in childhood; Charles, railroad man in MS; Jennie, w/o William D. Martin, connected with railroad and living in Jackson, TN; Ellen, w/o A. B. Chase, of AL; Delphia Anne, w/o J. A. Wimbish, and lives in Moselle, MS; and William. Father d. in 1870 in MS. Mother d. in 1888. William m. Mrs. Annie M. Granniss, a widow, in 1877, and had three children: Emma May, Millie L. and Annie D. Member the Junior Order of American Mechanics and Division No. 17, Order of Railway Telegraphers, of Balt. Station agent at Arlington and postmaster at Station E.

106. JAMES CRAIG - b. 21 Feb. 1842 in Balt., s/o Dr. John A. and Sarah (Armstrong) Craig. Family founded in America in an early day by Adam Craig, a native of Scotland; John, son of Adam, b. in Cambridge, MD, m. Elizabeth Ennals of Talbot Co. and had two sons William P. and Dr. John A.; William m. Hannah Reeves, and had a daughter, Florence, w/o Allen McClain Hamilton, of New York City; John, father of James, b. in Cambridge, MD, in 1807. John and Sarah, d/o James Armstrong, of Balt., had three children: John A., Margaret, and James: John lives in Fla., m. Fannie Eppes, had three children; Margaret, w/o A. Hamilton Bailey, of Cambridge, MD, had two daughters; James m. Carrie B., d/o George Mathews, of Greensboro, GA, in 1866, and had one child, Mary Armstrong Craig. Retired business man.

107. THOMAS C. BIDDISON - b. 16 Jan. 1841, near Gardenville, s/o John S. and Mary (Forester) Biddison. Grandmother was d/o John L. Burgan, who was b. 18 May 1771, and Elizabeth Burgan, who was b. 8 Dec. 1761 and d. 18 Dec. 1838. Grandfather, Abram Biddison d. while still a young man. Maternal grandfather, James Forester, a native of Scotland. John and Mary had six children: Thomas; Susanna, w/o Charles Hinkel, of Balt.; Lizzie, w/o Capt. Philip Barber, she d. 1863; Martha, w/o John Cugler of Balt.; Alice, w/o Harry Hoy, of twelfth district, Balt. Co.; and Helen, w/o Rev. T. W. Brown of the VA conference. Thomas m. Julia, d/o Gideon McCauley, of Anne Arundel Co., in Sep. 1862, and had eight children: William, police officer in Balt.; Mary, w/o John F. Gontrum lawyer of Towson and Balt.; Susan, w/o Hammond Detricht, in iron business; Bessie, w/o John W. Evans, in the dairy and truck farming business; John S., m. Eva Nichols, and is a lawyer at Towson; Julia, Stella and Thomas, all at home. Member Odd Fellows, Gardenville Lodge No. 114. Attends the Methodist Episcopal church. A Democrat. An auctioneer and farmer.

108. REUBEN STUMP - b. 20 Feb. 1816, s/o Samuel Stump; d. in 1876; m. Margaret, d/o Christopher and Hettie (Smith) Wilson, of Harford Co., in 1854. Christopher and Hettie had eight children, only four survive: Christopher, farmer in Harford Co.; Edward,

farmer in Prince William Co., VA; Mary, w/o David Wilson, owner of Alfred flour mills in Harford Co.; and Margaret. Wilson family originally from England. Reuben and Margaret had seven children: William S., the eldest son, in mercantile business in Woodward, OK; Ellen, the eldest daughter, w/o Dr. Malin Gilkes, of Ludlow, England, and they have two children; Norman, at the home place; Christopher, lives in CO; Alice, w/o J. William Middendorf, a Balt. banker; Reuben, Jr., a machinist, d. in Mexico in 1895; and Ernest, the youngest, a machinist in AL. An Episcopalian. A Democrat. Sea captain and then farmer.

109. ROBERT CORBETT - b. 1 Mar. 1855 in Pikesville, s/o Timothy and Margaret (Rickard) Corbett, natives of Ireland. Father settled in Balt. Co., and d. in 1863. Timothy and Margaret had four children: Margaret, who d. at age twenty; Annie, who d. at nine; Mary, who lives with Robert; and Robert. Robert m. Kate, d/o of John Winand, a distiller, in 1887, and had six children: Robert, Jr., Margaret, Elizabeth, John, Catherine, and Mary. Members of Catholic Church. A Democrat. Store owner in Pikesville.

110. GEORGE WASHINGTON LEISENRING - b. 12 Aug. 1832 in Pottsville, PA, and d. in 1890. George m. Georgiana, b. in Balt., d/o Rev. John G. Morris, D.D., LL.D., and Eliza (Hay) Morris, both natives of York, PA, in 1863, and had five children: Mrs. James P. Leese, of Lutherville; L. Morris, student of University of Pennsylvania; Eliza H., with the Historical Society of Maryland; Mary Helen, and John G. Morris, both at school. Georgiana is one of four children, others being: Annie Hay, deceased, Mrs. M. L. Trowbridge, and Miss M. Hay Morris. Members of the Lutheran Church. Business man in Lutherville and postmaster.

111. COL. LAWRENCE B. McCABE - b. 11 Mar. 1847 in Harve de Grace, Harford Co., MD, s/o Lawrence B. and Rosanna (McFeely) McCabe, natives of Ireland. Father d. in Harve de Grace in 1850, and mother d. in 1891 at age sixty-three. Lawrence and Rosanna had three children: Catherine, the eldest, m. Peter Scully, of Harford Co., and lives in St. Louis, MO; James F., b. in Harve de Grace, m. (1) Gertrude Knight, and had six children, Lawrence P., Gertrude, Cora, James P., Caroline, and Ernest; m. (2) Kate Snowden, of Balt., and had three children, Richard, Catherine and Dorothy. Lawrence m. Ellen, d/o John Keabney, of Cecil Co., MD, in 1877, and had six children: Aileen, Lawrence B., Jr., Mary, John, Patrick, and Henry. Member of the Maryland Club, and the Catholic Club. A Catholic. A Democrat. The largest railroad and city contractor in MD.

112. JOHN W. CROUCH - b. 20 May 1852 in Elk Neck, Cecil Co., MD, s/o John M. and Rebecca L. (Sherwood) Crouch. John and Rebecca had: Mary J., w/o William F. Burroughs, of Cecil Co.; Georgiana, w/o William Brumfield, of Cecil Co.; and John. Mother, a lineal descendant of the Packard family, d. in 1895, age sixty-nine. Father was native of Elk Neck, and d. in 1873. John and Rebecca were both Methodist Episcopal. Subject m. (1) Anna, d/o Capt. William Manly, of Cecil Co., in 1874, and had six children: four

d. in infancy; Robert M. and Helen F.; Anna d. in 1889. Subject m. (2) Margaret P., d/o Joshua and Anna P. League, of Chase, on 1 Oct. 1890 and had two children, Frank T. and Anna R. Member of Pennsylvania Railroad Relief Fund, and trustee of public schools of Chase. Belongs to the Methodist Episcopal Church. Station agent at Chase for the Philadelphia, Wilmington & Baltimore Railroad.

113. JOHN A. IMWOLD - b. 29 Oct. 1847 on farm in the ninth district, s/o John B. and Catherine (Weltner) Imwold. Father b. 15 Jun. 1817 in Germany, came to America at 18, a farmer, d. in 1873. Mother d. in 1894. John B. and Catherine had nine children: Henry, the eldest, m. Anna Kaiser, of Balt.; Charles F., m. Carrie Leonard, of Cincinnati, OH, d/o John Leonard, on 26 Sep. 1874; Samuel, the third son, d. young; Adaline, m. Henry Weltner, and d. in 1873; Caroline W., w/o Frderick Kramer, lives in New York City, has one child; Samuel G., in farming and dairy business in Balt. Co., m. Mary Anderson; Catherine, w/o Samuel Graham; and Frank, the youngest, in business in Balt. Member of the Shield of Honor and the Junior Order of American Mechanics.

114. FREDERICK VON KAPFF - b. 8 Jan. 1854 in Balt., s/o J. F. C. and Anne Donnell (Smith) von Kapff. Grandfather, Bernard von Kapff, native of Germany, m. Hester H. Didier, of Balt., and had seven children: Eliza M., w/o Henry Rodewald; Henry C.; Henrietta, w/o Gen. John Bankard; Jane Mary, w/o Diedrich Motts, of New York; John B. and Amelia, d. in infancy; and J. F. C., the youngest. Mother, was first president of the Maryland Society of Colonial Dames. Maternal grandfather, Samuel W. Smith, whose grandfather was John Smith, b. in Ireland in 1722 and came to Balt. in 1760; great-grandfather, Hon. Robert Smith, whose brother was Gen. Samuel Smith. J. F. C. and Anne had four children: Bernard, who d. unmarried at age thirty; Samuel W., d. young; Eleanor Donnell, w/o James W. Wilson, of Balt.; and Frederick. Frederick m. Annie S., d/o George Brown, in 1877. Member of the Sons of the Revolution. Identified with the Episcopal Church.

115. GEORGE BROWN - b. 25 Feb. 1828 in Balt., s/o Robert Patterson and Jane Shields (Wilson) Brown. Father, b. 13 Oct. 1799 in Balt., s/o Dr. George Brown, native of Ireland. Dr. George m. Rosa Davidson and had eight children. George m. Sarah C. Sharp, of Boston, Mass, and had four children: Robert P., of Balt.; Mary L.; Grace, w/o P. L. C. Ficcher, of Balt.; and Annie S., w/o Frederick von Kapff. George d. in 1874.

116. CONRAD REICH - b. in 1863 in Corehesen, Germany, s/o John and Magdalena (Voltz) Reich, natives of Germany. Father, came to America in 1885, d. in Balt. Co. in 1891. John and Magdalena had three children: Mary, w/o Harry Schmidt, a sea captain; Barbara, w/o George W. Balard, a wheelwright; and Conrad. Conrad m. Maggie, of Balt. Co., d/o George Frederick, in 1896. Members of the Lutheran Church. A Republican. Prosperous farmer of the twelfth district.

117. JACKSON WILSON - b. in 1821 in the tenth district, s/o James and Mary (McClung) Wilson. Father b. in same district in 1782. Grandfather, Robert Wilson, b. in north of Ireland, came to America with two brothers, Andrew and Michael; Michael settled in VA. Mother d. when Jackson was small child and father d. in 1844. Jackson m. Amanda Curtis in 1844 and had five children: James Henry, physician of Fowblesburg; John C., m. Miss Foard, of Long Green Valley; Sarah, w/o Thomas Elliott, of the seventh district; Mary Permelia, at home; and Eugenia, w/o Charles Weakley, of the tenth district. An Episcolapian. A Democrat. An agriculturist.

118. WILLIAM J. PARLETT - b. 13 Apr. 1839 in Balt. Co., s/o Thomas and Massey (Woolf) Parlett. Parlett family orginally came from England. Father b. in Balt. Co. Thomas and Massey had seven children. William m. Anna R., d/o Charles Amos, of Balt. Co., 21 Dec. 1865, and had eleven children: Minnie E.; Gertrude; W. Howard; John T.; Elizabeth A.; Ada F.; May M.; James G.; Julia A.; Morris H. and Grace L. Anna's siblings are: Mrs. Laura J. Clark, Benjamin F., George W., Izah, Eliza A. and John W. Grandfather of Charles Amos, William, was one of the founders of the Quaker faith in Harford Co. William d. 2 Jun. 1896 in the city. Members of the Govanstown Methodist Episcopal Church.

119. MRS. ELIZABETH CARMAN - b. in Harford Co., MD, d/o Elisha and Rebecca (Grafton) Karr. Father, native of England, settled in Chester, then Harford Co., where he d. at age seventy-nine. Paternal grandmother, Hannah Perry Karr, was sister of Commodore Perry. Maternal grandparents, John H. and Elizabeth (Hanna) Grafton, natives of Harford Co., had five children: Rebecca; Elizabeth; Mary Ann; Delia, w/o Charles Welsh, had five children and d. at age eighty-two; and John Hanna. Mother, b, in Harford Co., had four children: Elizabeth; Mary, w/o Robert Royston; Hannah, w/o William Talbert; and Harry, m. Jennie McKenzie of Balt., had one son, Harry, and d. at age twenty-six. Elizabeth m. Elisha Carman in 1859 and had six children: William H., eldest, grocer in Balt.; Harry Lee, engineer on B. & O. Railroad, m. Ida Collins, d/o Lieutenant Collins, and had one son, Roy R.; Perry, superintendent of Balt. Co. almshouse; Stanley C., at home; Clarence Grafton, student; and Carrie May, the youngest, at home.

120. GEORGE M. FULTZ - b. York Co., PA, s/o John and Nancy (Meyers) Fultz, he of MD and she of York Co. John and Mary had four children: Catharine, Lucetta, George M. and John. Grandfather, George Fultz, native of MD, a carpenter. George m. Sarah J. Cross, of Balt., and had one son, Rev. Charles E., who m. Frances L. Cooper, of Balt. Co. and had four children: Edna M., Jennie M., George C. and Nellie M. Member Middletown Lodge No. 92, I. O. O. F., and Spicer Post No. 43, G. A. R. Belongs to the Methodist Episcopal Church. A Republican. Former superintendent of the Rockdale paper mills, substantial agriculturist of the sixth district.

121. JAMES BRIAN - b. in 1848 at the homestead, Raven's Outlet,

in the twelfth district, s/o Nicholas M. and Alexina (Stansbury) Brian. Grandfather, James Brian, first to live in twelfth district. Mother, cousin of Abraham and Darius Stansbury. Nicholas and Alexina had two sons, James, and Stansbury, who lives in Cowenton, MD. James m. Sallie S. Clark, of Talbot Co., MD, in 1882. Sallie is a member of the Holy Comforter Episcopal Church. A Reupblican. Proprietor of an agricultural establishment at Middle River and freight agent for the Phildelphia, Wilmington & Baltimore Railroad, also postmaster.

122. ALBERT A. BLAKENEY - b. 28 Sep. 1850 in Lutherville, north of Towson, s/o John D. and Sarah (Gaunt) Blakeney. Father, native of Balt. Co., carpenter and builder, d. in 1863 during service in Civil war. Mother, b. in England, was left with seven small children. Grandfather, Abel Blakeney, mechanic, made coffin George Washington was buried in. Maternal grandfather, John Gaunt, b. in England, builder and contractor, had contract for Baltimore court-house. Member of Odd Fellows, Red Men and the Masonic order. A Presbyterian. A Republican. President of the board of county commissioners.

123. JOHN W. BLAKENEY - b. 1858 in Balt. City, s/o John D. and Sarah (Gaunt) Blakeney; lives in Franklinville; member of Pickering Lodge No. 146, A. F. & A. M., at Baltimore. In charge of the repair department of the Franklinville duck mills, owned by A. A. Blakeney & Co.

124. WASHINGTON STEVENSON - b. 22 Feb. 1830, s/o Joshua and Isabella (Baltes) Stevenson. Grandfather, Josias Stevenson, b. on family farm, Fellowship Place, near Towson, m. Urath Stevenson, a second cousin, and had four children. Father, b. on homestead, m. Isabella, d/o Ferdinand and Isabella (Fisher) Baltes and had four children: Urath, lives on homeplace; Josias, d. at twelve; Washington; and Edmond, d. unmarried at thirty-seven. Washington m. Anna W., d/o Benjamin W. Gatch, of Norfolk, VA, 2 Jun. 1865 and had five children; Thomas G.; John W., d. at seventeen; Charles Lee, d. in childhood; Annie Belle, and Martha Lee, both at home. Washington d. 19 Sep. 1895 at age sixty-five. A Democrat. Gave his attention to agricultural work.

125. DUANE H. RICE - b. 19 Jan. 1845 in Dover, Windham Co., VT, s/o George Emory and Eliza Ann (Millis) Rice. Great-grandfather, Daniel Rice, b. in Hardwick, MA, 5 Aug., 1755, m. Sallie Ball of New Bedford, MA, on 19 Jun. 1782, and had nine children: Daniel, settled in PA; Susan, w/o Cyril Lawton, lived in Washington Co., NY; Hazelton; Ephraim, grandfather of Duane; David; Sallie; Perez; Asher and Melintha. Hazelton m. Rhoda Stone and had six children, Hiram, Nancy, Melintha, Sallie, Hazelton, and Lewis: Hiram m. Maria Cross and had two children, Alonzo and Melina and lived in Chester, VT; Nancy m. Levi Snow, of Somerset, and had five children, Henriette, Fayette, Annette, Jeannette and Juliet; Melintha, m. Oliver Pike, of Somerset, and had two children, Maria and Lewis; Sallie m. James Alger, of Worcester, MA, and had five children; Hazelton m. Esther Smith and had two children, both deceased, and lived in West Brattleboro, VT. Ephraim, b. 20

Feb. 1792 in Somerset, m. Virtue, d/o Joab and Jennie Johnson, of Dover, VT., 11 Sep. 1814, and had twelve children: Elvira; George, b. 11 Dec 1819 and d. 1 Jan. 1820; George Emory; David Hazelton; Ephraim Emerson, Hosea Johnson, Arvilla Lucretia, Levi Henry, Chester Curtis, Sherman Delos, William Clark and a son who d. in infancy. Elvira, b. 18 May 1816 at Brattleboro, m. A. H. Pike 11 Dec. 1834 and d. 16 Jan. 1844, and had: Philetus, d. a few days before mother; Lomira G., m. John Reed, of Sunderland, VT, who d. leaving a daughter who d. young, a son who lives in Hartford, CT, and son, William, lives in Chicago; Viola A., m. Russell Willard, and had five children, live in SD; and Elmira B., m. Calvin Weld, machinist of Brattleboro, had three children: George Emory, b. 14 Nov. 1820, at Somerset, VT, m. Eliza Ann Millis, of Montague, MA, 31 Mar. 1844, and had nine children: Duane H.; Ellen A., w/o William L. Barnes, blacksmith of Jamaica, VT; Justina E. w/o Edwin A. Fessenden, had Cora J., now w/o George E. McLaughlin of Balt.; Henry E., employed by Rice Brothers; Abbie V., w/o A. K. V. Hull, lives in Balt.; and Lewis Clark, partner of Rice Brothers, m. and has son, Duane Ridgely; and three who d. young. Duane m. Sarah R., d/o George W. McCubbins, of Balt. Co., in 1868, and had three children: Florence A., Maude E., and one who d. Member of Landmark Masonic Lodge of Baltimore, a Knight Templar. Director of Towson National Bank. Half-interest in Rice Brothers.

126. CHARLES G. WHEELER - b. 14 Feb. 1818, s/o Benjamin and Malinda (Gorsuch) Wheeler. Father, b. in fifth district, a blacksmith near Cockeysville, a Democrat, and member of the Methodist Episcopal Church. Mother, sister of "Uncle Charley" Gorsuch. Benjamin and Malinda had seven children: Charles G.; Thomas, of eighth district; Salica; Belinda; Sallie and two who d. Charles m. Mary Gild, of the eighth district, d/o Dr. Gild, about 1857, and had eight children: Ella, of Balt.; Edward, has store in Shawan; Grafton, at home; Kate, of Balt.; Julia w/o Edward Mathews; Lillie, of Balt.; Lizzie, of Balt.; and one who d. Mary d. 1 Feb. 1888. A Methodist. A Democrat. Owner of Eastern View farm.

127. WILLIAM W. HARE - b. in 1844 in the fifth district, s/o William F. Hare. Father, also b. in fifth district, m. (1) Mary Frank and had ten children, m. (2) Annie Bolinger and had two children. Father is seventy-five and a Democrat. William m. Mary, d/o William Curtis, in 1866, and had nine children: Emory, at home; Jennie, w/o George Keiser, of Cockeysville; and John, Milton, Virgil, Royden, Lee, Harry and Lawrence, all at home. Member of the Shield of Honor. Supports Democratic party. Belongs to the Episcopal Church. General merchant in Phoenix.

128. EDWARD RIDER - b. 19 May 1819 near Cockeysville, MD. Father, native of England, came the America at age ten, a Baptist, d. 25 Nov. 1876, age seventy-six. Mother, Rachael, d/o John Gorsuch, b. in Balt. Co., a Baptist, d. 23 Mar. 1888, had twelve children: Richard, d. at eleven; John G., deceased, had son, Howard; Dr. William G., physician, deceased; Abram, William J., and Harrison, deceased, were farmers; Thomas, carpenter and

builder; Sarah Jane, d. at seventeen; Mary, w/o Alexander Worley, had son, John; Angeline, w/o William R. Foster, of Sherwood; Elizabeth, widow of Dr. John M. Stevenson; and Edward. Edward m. Rebecca S., d/o George McConkey, in Mar. 1855, and had eight children; Mary, widow of Rev. John S. M. Haslup, Methodist minister, is preesident of Maryland State Temperance Society; Dr. William B., of Balt.; Eliza and Anna R., of Balt.; Rachael, w/o Rev. Edwin Mowbray, Methodist minister at Hereford, MD; Florence and Ella, at home; and Edward, Jr. Edward d. 31 Jan. 1897. Member Mt. Moriah Lodge, at Towson, and the Independent Order of Odd Fellows. A Henry Clay Whig, became a Democrat, then a Republican. A Methodist. Successful financial and keen business man.

129. ALEXANDER McCORMICK - b. 14 Jul. 1841 in the twelfth district, on farm adjoining one he now owns, s/o Alexander and Maria K. (Rhodes) McCormick, natives of Glasgow, Scotland, and Sheffield, England, respectively. Father came to America at age twenty-one and settled in twelfth district, a farmer and a Republican, d. in 1887. Mother, d/o William Rhodes, a weaver and dyer, came to Balt. Co. as a young girl. Alexander and Maria had six sons: William J., a truck farmer; Charles J. and Nelson F., at the old home farm; Joseph and Samuel, d. in boyhood; and Alexander. Alexander m. Martha A., d/o George Councilman, 31 Jan. 1863; George, b. in 1802 on family farm, a farmer, d. 13 Jul. 1897; grandfather, George Councilman, Sr., b. same farm, which was taken up by the family from Lord Baltimore in 1632; all descendants are interred in the family burying ground. Alexander and Martha had six children: Dr. George Carvill, employed by the Maryland Steel Company at Sparrows Point; Thomas A., carpenter and builder; R. Howard, lives with father; Harry Clifton, conductor on Sparrows Point Railroad; William Clarence and Edward S., d. of typhoid fever in Oct. 1893. Member Baltimore County Grange, the Locust Grove Grange, Patrons of Husbandry, the Garden Lodge No. 114, I. O. O. F., Sharon Encampment No. 28, and the Fullerton Building & Loan Association. Belongs to the Methodist Episcopal Church. A Republican. Well-known florist and farmer of the twelfth district.

130. RICHARD E. TIDINGS - b. 26 Aug. 1833 in the city of Balt., s/o William Henry and Anna (Randall) Tidings. Father, native of Annapolis, a contractor and builder. William and Anna had two sons: Richard E., and Dr. Edwin R., who practiced in Towson, never m., and d. at thirty-three; Richard was taken in by his aunt, Mrs. Sarah A. Bounds, when orphaned at an early age. Richard m. Henrietta, d/o James and Eliza Mann, in 1885, also orphaned when very young and taken in by Mrs. Bounds. Member of Odd Fellows and Mt. Zion Lodge No. 87. A Democrat. Magistrate for eight years.

131. ALBERT J. B. ALMONY - b. 13 Jun. 1834 in Balt. Co., s/o Henry D. and Eliza (Bell) Almony, also natives of Balt. Co. Henry and Eliza had eight children: Albert J. B., William H., Charles., Ephraim B.; Catherine and Kezia, deceased; John W. and Franklin T. Great-grandfather, John Almony, native of England, supposed to have been stolen when a child of four and brought to

America, before the Revolutionary war, and reared in VA; m. a wealthy Scotch lady in England. Grandfather, William Almony, b. in Balt. Albert m. Mrs. Johanna Hoshall, nee Hampshire (formerly w/o Nelson Hoshall), of Balt. Co., when thirty-four; she is member of United Brethren Church; she had son, Clarence M. Hoshall, by first marriage. A Democrat. Traveling salesman of fertilizers, and identified with agricultural interests.

132. JOHN SMITH - b. in Germany, m. Katherine Behler, in 1848, and had four children: Mary; John W.; William H.; and Ella M., who m. Dixon Conley, of Manor, Balt. Co. and had one child. John W., b. in Harford Co., m. Ida, d/o Jackson Curry, in Balt. Co., in 1889, and had five children, John Jackson, William R., Wallace, Mary and Harry. John d. 16 Feb. 1894. A Democrat. County commissioner for Balt. Co. from 1888 to 1892, prominent farmer.

133. GEORGE J. BING - b. 22 Aug. 1869 in twelfth district, s/o Conrad and Mary (Smith) Bing, natives of Germany. Father d. in twelfth district in May 1871. Conrad and Mary also had five daughters: Mary, unmarried and at home; Lizzie, widow of Conrad Kratz; Katie, w/o Henry F. Siech; Sophia, at home; and Caroline, deceased. Member of Council No. 100, Junior Order American Mechanics, and Lauraville Building & Loan Assoc. Favors the Republican party. Raises garden produce for his stall in Lexington market.

134. THOMAS H. TAYLOR - b. 19 Nov. 1839 at Mt. Prospect, Balt. Co., s/o Wilkerson and Rebecca Taylor. Mt. Prospect, one of the oldest estates in this county; old parchment hangs on the wall describing original grant of land, signed by Lord Baltimore, conveying in Balt. Co., fifteen hundred acres of land to Richard Taylor, native of England. Taylor family originated in England; Thomas, s/o Richard Taylor, m. Sarah Price, and had Richard, b. at Mt. Prospect; next in line was Thomas, b. near Towson, m. Ruth, d/o Thomas Stansbury, and had Wilkerson, b. same place, 2 May 1804; Wilkerson m. Rebecca, d/o Caleb Stansbury, of Carroll Co., 28 Jul. 1836, and had three children: Elizabeth Ruth, b. 12 Apr. 1838, and d. 24 Aug. 1863; Thomas H.; and Caleb Stansbury, b. 15 Nov. 1840; Wilkerson d. 7 Jun. 1872. C. S. Taylor m. Eleanor, d/o Robert Moore, 10 Jun. 1869, had four children: Elizabeth Ruth; Robert Moore, last male representative; Annie McEldowney and Eliza Marsh. C. S. d. 22 Feb. 1886. Devoted entire life to farming.

135. J. ALBERT FITE - b. Balt. Co., s/o William and Achsah (Owens) Fite. Grandfather, Jacob Fite, native of Germany, came to America and settled in Balt. Father, b. in Balt., d. in 1886, age eighty-three. Maternal grandfather, Israel Owens. William and Achsah had thirteen children: Henry, Israel, Annie, Annie(2d), Oliver, and Emma died in infancy; Laura, w/o R. P. Choate; Elizabeth R., deceased; Sarah A., widow of Dr. George W. Bailey, lives in Balt.; Georgiana, w/o William C. Odell, farmer in second district; and William E., farmer also in second district. Member in Shiloh Lodge No. 111, I. O. O. F., at Granite.

A Democrat. Engages in general farm pursuits.

136. ATTWOOD BLUNT - b. 26 Jan. 1824 near Goshen, Montgomery Co., MD, s/o Samuel and Harriet W. Blunt. Attwood m. Amanda F. W. Offutt in 1852 and had fourteen children: Maria, widow of S. Francis Miller, of Ellicott City; Albert S., at home; Bradley T. D., of Atlanta, GA; Amanda, Attwood, Sarah, William; Harriet W., Alexander W., Elizabeth, Eleanor, Samuel, Agnus and one unnamed d. in infancy. Member of the Grange. A Democrat. Farming has been his principal occupation.

137. MAJ. WILLIAM L. KENLY - b. 31 Mar. 1833 in Balt., s/o Edward and Maria (Reese) Kenly. Maternal ancestors came from Wales to MD in a very early day; grandfather, Thomas Reese, was a Balt. merchant. Great-grandfather, Rev. Daniel Kenly, a Presbyterian minister, came from Scotland and settled in Harford Co., MD. Grandfather, Richard Kenly, b. in Harford Co., m. Miss Ward, had four children: Daniel, Richard, Edward, and Fannie. Father, b. in Harford Co., and mother attended Quaker Church, and had large family, living: George Tyson, m. Priscilla, d/o Colonel Watkins, had seven sons; John Reese, lawyer, d., unmarried, 20 Dec. 1892; Martha Emily, unmarried and lives in Balt.; Annie M., w/o Benjamin Hynson, d. in 1892, had one daughter; and William L. William m. Elizabeth Marion Hook, 12 Jun. 1861, and had: Guy, d. Balt. at twenty-three; William Lacy, in army; Ritchie G., assistant engineer for Northern Central Railroad; Edward Marion, resident engineer on the Lynchburg & Durham Railroad; George T., assistant engineer of the Gilford Reservoir Company; Maria Reese, Laura Hook and Roberta Martin, at home. Member of the Grand Army of the Republic, Royal Arcanum, Military Order Loyal Legion, American Society of Civil Engineers and the Society of the Army of the Potomac. In the service of the water works company.

138. NEWTON D. R. ALLEN - b. 11 Jul. 1857, York Co., PA, s/o Louis and Sarah Allen. Father, b. 12 Jul. 1816, York Co. Grandfather, Robert Allen, b. in Balt.; great-grandfather, Peter, b. in Scotland, settled in VA; wife of Robert was member of an old Quaker family. Father left Quakers and identified with the Methodist Episcopal Church. Mother, Sarah Parvin, d/o of Daniel Rowe, b. Lancaster Co., PA. Louis and Sarah had five children: three d. in infancy; Amy, d. at eighteen; and Newton D. R. Newton m. Rosa Heathcote, of Balt. Co., 28 Aug. 1889, had three children; Herschel, Wendell DeWitt, and Sarah Ruth. Rosa, member of a York Co. family that came from England. Member of the Knights of Pythias, and the Junior Order of American Mechanics. Belongs to the Prespyterian Church, but attends the Methodist Episcopal Church. County surveyor.

139. SAMUEL COLLINGS - b. 11 Jan. 1826 in Balt., s/o William and Matilda (Royston) Collings. Father, b. Chestertown, Kent Co., MD, d. in Balt. in 1836. Mother, of Scotch descent, d/o a Revolutionary soldier. Two sons of William and Matilda, William and Henry, are in meat business in Balt. Samuel m. Eliza Hamill, b. in MD, ancestors from north of Ireland, in 1850, and had ten children: Annie, w/o C. B. Taylor, of Lutherville, who is with

the IRS in Balt.; C. Harris, in the coal business in Balt.; Samuel, Jr., in business with father; Lydia, w/o W. W. Boyse, connected with C. Garris Collings in the coal business; William S., at home; and three who d. in infancy. Member of the Odd Fellows, Beaver Dam Lodge. A butcher.

140. JAMES MORGAN DAVIS - b. 8 Mar. 1823 in London, England, s/o James Morgan and Elizabeth (Griffiths) Davis. Father, b. in Wales, a farmer and dairyman. James and Elizabeth both d. when son was young, taken in by her brother, William Griffiths; came to U. S. in 1842. James m. Eleanor, d/o William Waddell, of Balt. Co., in 1852, and had: Morgan James, m. Ida Wilson, d/o business man of Brooklyn, NY, had three children, connected with the Mechanics National Bank of Balt.; Letitia, m. Samuel G. Crocker, merchant of Balt., and had six children; Elizabeth, d. young; William Griffiths, also d. young; George Gibson, youngest, also with Mechanics National Bank of Balt., m. Grace, d/o Charles Wesley Goddess, of Balt. Member Methodist Episcopal Church. Voted with the Prohibition party. Farmer and dairyman.

141. HON. JESSE N. DAILY - s/o Jesse and Elizabeth (Masemore) Daily, natives of Harford and Balt. Counties, respectively. Jesse and Elizabeth had seven children: Jesse N.; Mary E., at home; Susan F., w/o J. Frank Palmer, merchant in Balt. Co.; and four who d. when quite young. Jesse m. Lydia S., d/o Daniel S. Wilson, farmer of sixth district, 24 Dec. 1875, had eight children: Dora E., m. Jacob N. Wilhelm, 16 Dec. 1896; Belle V., Grace, Jesse W., Emma S., Harry N., Florence L. and Viola D., at home. A Democrat. Recording clerk for Balt. Co. and a millwright of the sixth district.

142. H. LOUIS NAYLOR, M. D. - b. 20 Sep. 1839 in Prince George Co., MD, s/o James and Mary (Perrie) Naylor. Great-grandfather, Joshua S. Naylor, b. in England, came to America with William Penn; grandfather, James, native of Charles Co., MD; father, James of J., b. Prince George Co., in 1804, was a Whig then a Democrat. Mother, d/o Hugh Perrie, of Prince George Co., of French-Huguenot ancestry. James and Mary had six children: Maggie, m. John Nicholas, of Annapolis, d. soon after marriage; Thomas K., farmer and planter in Prince George Co.; Julia, m. William Townsend, of P. G. Co.; Llewellyn, m. Miss Townsend of P. G. Co.; Susan, widow of Joseph Benson Townsend and lives in P. G. Co. H. Louis m. Margaret, d/o Samuel Brady, in 1869, and had four children: Mary Helen, Martha W., Bertha Perrie and Henry A. Margaret d. in 1888. Louis m. (2) Mary S., d/o A. B. Mudge, of Balt., and had one child, Louis Hastings. Member of the Medical and Chirurgical Faculty of Maryland, the Clinical Society of Baltimore, the Baltimore County Medical Association, the Masons, the Odd Fellows, and the Knights of Pythias. Physician in the third district.

143. ZEPHANIAH POTEET - b. 8 Apr. 1834 in the eighth district, s/o Rev. Thomas and Susannah (Pearse) Poteet. Poteet family originally from France, settled in Harford Co., MD. Maternal grandfather, Richard Pearse, came to Balt. Co. in last century.

Father, a Baptist, d. in 1843, and mother d. in 1869. Thomas and Susannah had: Mary J., w/o Nicholas T. Hutchins, of Carroll's Manor, tenth district; Susan, w/o Nicholas Parker, also of tenth district; and Zephaniah. Zephaniah m. Emily, d/o Commodore Junius J. Boyle (who d. in 1871), 9 Jun. 1870. Emily d. in 1881. A Mason and member of the Mystic Circle No. 109, in Balt. A Democrat. Agriculturist of the eighth district.

144. CAPT. HENRY WILHELM - b. 17 May 1836 in the sixth district, s/o Peter B. and Elizabeth (Kone) Wilhelm. Great-grandfather Wilhelm came to America from Germany during the Revolution. Grandfather, Henry Wilhelm, b. in sixth district. Peter and Elizabeth had nine children, seven being: George W., Jeremiah, Daniel W., Caroline, Julia A., Mary E., and Henry. Henry m. Chloe, d/o Enoch and Susan (Macabee) Dorsey, of the sixth district, in 1868, and had two children, Carrie and May, both deceased. Chloe was next to youngest in family of seven children. Member of Charity Lodge No. 134, A. F. & A. M., of Parkton; Wilson Post No. 1, G. A. R., of Baltimore; Middletown Lodge No. 92, I. O. O. F., of Middletown; Eklo Council No. 134, J. O. A. M. of Eklo; and Summit Grange No. 164, of Middletown. A Republican. Retired from general farming.

145. MRS. T. ELLEN TALBOTT - father, Amon, and grandfather, James Bosley, b. and d. in Balt. Co. Father d. in 1838, mother d. several years later. T. Ellen m. Edward C. Talbott, of Balt. Co., in 1841, and had seven children: two living, Hon. J. Fred C. Talbott, m. Laura Bell, d/o John G. Cockey, pres. of Towson National Bank; and Mary Elizabeth, widow of John G. Bosley, mother of Laura Talbott; two deceased daughters: Eliza M., w/o Ebenezer Strahan, mother of Nellie, w/o Montgomery Corkran, of Lutherville, who has two children, Edna Brown and Frank; and Rebecca, w/o George Glass, d. at home in VA, leaving one child, Edward Talbott. Identified with the Episcopal Church.

146. T. CHALMERS PEEBLES, M. D. - b. 22 Jun. 1843, in Dublin, Ireland,, s/o Dr. John and Anna (Ballingham) Peebles, natives of Dublin and County Antrim, respectively. John and Anna had twelve children: William B., A.B., M.B., T.C., m. an English lady, lives in Ireland; John, T.C.D., d. in north of Ireland; T. Chalmers; other children d. when young. T. Chalmers m. Lizzie, d/o Rt.- Rev. George D. Cummins, D.D. (d. in 1875 in Lutherville), had two children: Maud, w/o Dr. L. Gibbons, of Roland Park; and Florence. Lizzie d. in 1890. T. Chalmers m. (2) Mabel, d/o E. Waldo Cutler, of Cutler Bros., Boston, and had son, Waldo Cutler Peebles. Member of the Medical and Chirurgical Faculty of Maryland, and the Baltimore County Association. Connected with the Reformed Episcopal Church.

147. FREDERICK M. KETCHUM - b. 31 Aug. 1866, Balt. City, s/o Frederick M. and Charlotte M. (Martin) Ketchum. Maternal grandfather, Capt. Isaac Martin. Father, b. in Birmingham, CT, d. 3 Oct. 1870 in Balt. Frederick m. Kate H., d/o George Carter, in 1886 and had three children: Frederick M., Jr., Kate Helen, and Elmer Leroy. Member of the Masonic order and the Golden Chain.

A Democrat. Rising young business man.

148. GEORGE S. ENSOR - b. 2 Jun. 1822 in the eighth district, s/o John and Nellie (Smith) Ensor. Father and grandfather, George, also b. in eighth district. Great-grandfather, George, b. in England, settled in Balt. Co. Father, a Democrat and member of the Bosley Methodist Church, d. in 1857. Mother, d/o Andrew Smith, mother of eleven children, d. in 1860. George m. Delilah, d/o John Ensor, of eighth district, 18 Nov. 1847, and had five children: Orick M.; Howard; Josephine, w/o J. M. Fowble, Jr., of the eighth district; John C. and Rachel. Supports the Democratic party. Successfully engaged in agricultural pursuits in the eighth district.

149. WILLIAM MILLER ELLICOTT - b. 30 Sep. 1807, Balt. City, s/o Thomas and Mary (Miller) Ellicott. First Ellicott came from England and settled in Bucks Co., PA, about 1730. Grandfather was one of the founders of Ellicott Mills. Decendent of the Fox, Evans, and Ellicott families. William m. Sarah, d/o Thomas and Ann Poultney, 11 Nov. 1829, and had eight children: Thomas P., William M., Lindley, Mary M., Nancy P., David B., Sarah P., and Charles L. Thomas P. and David B., work with father on Spears wharf, in Balt. Charles L. lives in Harford Co. Business man of Balt.

150. WILLIAM BOWEN of S. - b. 18 Oct. 1828 near Towson, s/o Solomon and Sarah (Coale) Bowen. Father also b. in Towson. Great-grandfather, Solomon Bowen, came from England prior to the Revolution, to land deeded to him by the king of England. Grandfather, William Bowen, b. in Towson, m. Elizabeth Athington, and had ten children: Elijah, eldest, farmer in Balt. Co.; William, also farmer; John; Ruth, w/o Captain Carroll; Temperance, w/o William J. Perine; Polly, d. in childhood; and Solomon of W., who m. Sarah Coale, and had nine children: John, d. young; Elizabeth, m. a lieutenant in army; Emily, w/o Jacob Wisner, had fifteen children; John N. Wesley, lawyer in Balt.; James P., m. Susie Ann Bishop; Temperance, w/o John Goodwin; Joseph G., a mason; Alexander P., a blacksmith, m. Julia Jackson; and William of S. William m. (1) Sarah E. Van Horn, had three children: Grace E., d. in girlhood; John E., m. Rebecca Bayne; and Benjamin W., farmer and policeman in Towson. Sarah d. in 1867. William m. (2) Sophronia Helen, d/o Henry Webb; other children of Henry Webb: Henry, Euphemia, Mary Ann, Sarah Jane, Cornelius Harrison, Jacob J. and Josephine I. Sophronia had two children by previous marriage to William Van Horn: William H. Van Horn, m. Zoe Everest, and Cornelius L., a miller, m. Clara L. Hobourg. Member of the Odd Felows and Towson Lodge, F. & A. M. Owner and occupant of a farm near Towson.

151. R. PERCY SMITH, M. D. - b. 24 Aug. 1867 in Dunkirk, Calvert Co., MD, s/o Dr. John S. and Ruth E. (Owens) Smith, natives of Calvert and Anne Arundel Counties, MD, respectively. John and Ruth had: Gertrude, w/o Thomas I. Graham, of internal revenue department of Balt.; Eleanor O., w/o Dr. William L. Smith, of Jarrettsville, Harford Co., MD; R. Percy; and Dr. Allen W., of

Balt. Member of the Maryland State Medical Association, the Baltimore County Medical Society, and the American Medical Association. A Presbyterian. A Democrat. Physician in Balt. Co.

152. JUDGE THOMAS G. RUTLEDGE - b. 28 Sep. 1822 in the seventh district, s/o Thomas and Elizabeth (Howard) Rutledge, he of Balt. Co., she of York Co., PA. Father, b. 9 Aug. 1759, m. five times, granted patent at Balt. for five hundred acres in the seventh district 17 Jan. 1787. Thomas m. at twenty-two, Rebecca J. Fife, of York Co., and had nine children: Rufus F., m. and in realestate business in Balt.; Elizabeth A., w/o Silas W. Hazeltine, music teacher in Balt.; John F., deceased; Mary L., w/o Thomas J. Meades; Sarah G., w/o John V. Slade, lives at Corbitt; Leah S., w/o William W. Ratcliffe, of Balt.; and three who d. in infancy. Rebecca, member of the Methodist Episcopal Church, d. 16 Feb. 1896, age seventy-two; son, John F., conductor on the Northern Central Railroad, d. at same time, both buried on Feb. 18. Member of the Mt. Moriah Lodge No. 116, A. F. & A. M., of Towson. A Democrat. Retired.

153. NORRIS B. PARRISH - b. 22 Jan. 1822, in the seventh district, s/o Edward and Clemantha (Hughes) Parrish, he of Balt. Co. and she of Harford Co., MD. Edward and Clemantha had two children: Edward, the younger, d. at three. Father was a farmer. Grandfather, also Edward Parrish, also farmer in Balt. Co. Norris m. Elizabeth O. Lytle, of Balt. Co., at age twenty-two, and had five children: Edward M., an agriculturist, m. Sabra E. Henderson, of Harford Co. and had seven children; Thomas L., an agriculturist, m. Maggie B. Wallace, of Harford Co. and had three children; Nicholas M., real-estate dealer of Balt., m. Laura Henderson, of Harford Co. and had one child; and two who d. in infancy. Supports Prohibition party. Members of the Methodist Episcopal Church. Thorough and skillful farmer.

154. JOSEPH SHAUL - b. 18 Jul. 1828 in the fifth district, s/o Noah and Rachel (Wisner) Shaul, of the fifth district. Grandfather, Joseph Shaul, came from England with brother, John, settled in fifth district, and accumulated over seventeen hundred acres of land. Noah and Rachel had six children: Julia A., Nancy; Reason W., deceased; Joseph, Benjamin L. and Rachel F. Joseph m. Emma V., d/o Elisha Ebaugh, when about forty, and had five children: Bessie O., Joseph W., Estella, Rachel and Clay. Energetic and enterprising farmer.

155. JOHN G. BOOTH - b. 14 Mar. 1831 in Chester Co., PA, s/o Walter and Rachel (Dance) Booth, both b. reared and m. in Chester Co. Paternal grandparents, John and Katherine (Knox) Booth, b. and m. in County Derry, Ireland, located in Chester Co., PA, had three sons, Walter, John and William, and several daughters. Walter and Rachel had: John G.; Walter F., d. unmarried in 1857, age fifty-seven; and Emma A., w/o Charles M. Jessop, all of Balt. Co. John m. Eliza Matthews, sister of Col. D. M. Matthews, 29 Aug. 1859, and had eight children: J. Albert; Harry W., living in Balt.; Edward M., Mary M., and Clara B., all at home; Robert, who d. at seventeen; and two who d. in early childhood. Members of

the Presbyterian Church. An old-line Whig. Prosperous farmer of the eleventh district.

156. WILLIAM M. HEILIG - b. 5 Jul. 1855 in Middletown, PA, s/o Rev. William M. and Mary (Carl) Heilig. Father, b. 1813 in Philadelphia, a Lutheran, d. in Oct. 1888, age seventy-five. Mother, b. Abbottstown, PA, of an old PA family, of good Revolutionary stock, and of German extraction, d. in MD in 1863. William and Mary had six children: John C., business man of Butte, MT; Addie, w/o R. J. Hastings, works for the North Central Railroad; May V., w/o a civil engineer in Balt.; Clara W., w/o D. H. Hastings, of Butte, MT; Charles, lives in South America; and William. Member of the Royal Arcanum and the Junior Order of American Mechanics. A Lutheran. A Republican. Owns general merchandise store in Lutherville and is postmaster.

157. GEORGE CHILCOAT - b. 12 Apr. 1826 in the eighth district s/o George and Matilda Chilcoat. Father, b. on the Western Run, in the eighth district, of English origin, a farmer, m. Mrs. Matilda (Matthews) Wainwright, and had six children: Aquilla; George; Matilda, widow of George Towney, lives in Balt.; and Rachel, w/o H. S. Wheeler of Balt.; and two who d. George and Matilda both d. in 1875. George m. Elizabeth Josephine, d/o Dr. Louis Griffith of the eighth district, on 3 Oct. 1854, and had following: Edward, farmer; Mary, lives in Balt.; Louis, at home; Ella, of Balt.; William, of Harford Co.; Anna, at home; Theodore and George, of Balt.; Ada, w/o Dr. Edwin K. Ballard, of Balt., and mother of Wilson Turner and Donald Duncan; and Marion and Samuel, at home. A Republican. General farmer.

158. COL. CHARLES B. ROGERS - b. in 1850 in Balt., s/o Nathan and Eunice (Butler) Rogers. Children of Nathan and Eunice: Nathan, d. in San Francisco, leaving three children; William Hay, d. in Bodie, NV, leaving four children; John Power, d. unmarried, near Greenville, MS; James Power, d. near Buckeystown, MD, leaving three children; Eliza Butler, d. unmarried; Emily Butler, widow of James W. Williams, and mother of three children, Nathan Rogers, James Wright, and Dorsey McCubbin; Eunice Butler, widow of Marcus B. Bayly, d. in 1895, leaving two sons, Nathan Rogers and John Frederick; Samuel Butler, killed in Confederate service in 1864, unmarried; Charles Butler, unmarried. Father, b. in north of Ireland, of Presbyterian parents, in 1801, came to United States in 1813, d. 1858, age fifty-seven. Grandparents, Thomas and Annie (Hay) Rogers; Thomas, s/o Nathaniel, from Milford, in County Donegal, Ireland, and Annie from Castle Dromboe, near Ramelton, same county. Great-grandparents, Alexander and Margaret (Power) Hay. 2 great-grandparents, William and Eleanor (Patterson) Hay; family of Hay went to Ireland from Scotland about 1432. Eunice, d. in 1894, age eighty-five. Grandfather, Samuel Butler, b. 1763 in Boston, s/o Alford and Eunice (West) Butler, came to Balt. in 1794. Grandmother, Maria Frederica (Brune) Butler, d/o Thomas Brune and Wilhelmina Sophia Von Freinsein, of Germany, near Oldenburg; Maria, her sister Wilhelmina, and brother Thomas, came to Balt. in 1795. Great-grandmother, Eunice West, b. 1744 in Boston, d.

Boston 1804, d/o John West; Eunice, great-granddaughter of Rev. John Cotton, of Boston. Great-grandfather, Alford Butler, a Sandimarian minister, lived to be ninety-four; Alford, s/o Alford and Hannah (Robinson) Butler, he b. 1699 in Boston, d. there in 1763. Alford m. (1) Mercy Tay, no children; Alford m. (2) Hannah, direct descendant of Rev. John Robinson, of Leyden. Alford Butler, Sr., s/o Peter and Elizabeth (Brown) Butler; Peter b. 1640 in Boston and d. 1699, ship owner and trader; Elizabeth, d/o Abraham Brown, ship owner and trader; Peter, s/o Peter and Mary (Alford) Butler; this Peter Butler's name also written Pierce, b. about 1600 in Ireland, of the Cahier branch of Ormond Butlers; Peter Butler, not a Puritan, came to New England with brother, James, in own ship; Mary Alford, of Charlestown, d/o Hon. William Alford, of England. Superintendent of public instruction for Balt. Co. since 1888.

159. RICHARD GUNDRY - b. 14 Oct. on Hampstead Heath, England, s/o Rev. Jonathan Gundry, Baptist minister. Graduated medical department of Harvard University 1851. Richard m. Martha M. Fitzharris, of Dayton, in 1858. Richard d. 23 Apr. 1891. Member Maryland Historical Society, the Harvard Association of Medicine, and the University Club. Former medical superintendent of the Maryland Hospital for the Insane, in Catonsville.

160. JOHN W. WRIGHT - b. 3 Feb. 1823 in Harford Co., s/o William and Amelia (Smithson) Wright, of Balt. Co. and Harford Co., respectively. William and Amelia had thirteen children: Daniel S., John W., William, Joshua W., Johanna, Sarah A., Elizabeth, Mary, Emily, and four who d. young. Great-grandfather, native of Scotland, prior to the Revolutionary war, settled in Balt. Co., where grandfather, Blouis Wright, was born. John m. Mary J. Peters, of Balt., at about twenty-eight years, and had two children, both d. in infancy. Mary d. in 1855, age thirty-six. John m. (2) Mary E., d/o Ezekiel R. and Mary A. (Webb) Herbert, all of York Co., in 1867. Mary E., granddaughter of Gideon Herbert, is a Methodist Protestant. A Prohibitionist. Retired Balt. City police officer.

161. REV. WILLIAM EDWIN ROBERTSON - b. 9 Apr. 1864 near Chase City, Mecklenburg Co., VA, s/o Reps Osborne and Rosa J. (Richards) Robertson. Father, b. 9 Mar. 1831, Charlotte Co., VA, s/o Capt. Charles Henry and Margaret Frances (Osborne) Robertson. Paternal grandfather, also of Charlotte Co., s/o Henry and Martha (Crenshaw) Robertson; Henry, s/o Brooks, a grandson of Henry, Sr., and a great-grandson of Christopher Robertson. Christopher, native of Scotland, settled in VA, in the beginning of the eighteenth century; Christopher had land deeded to him in Prince George and Surry Counties in 1722. Paternal grandmother, d/o Reps Osborne, of Charlotte Co. Reps Robertson m. Rosa Richardson 8 Nov. 1854; Rosa, d/o Capt. John Young and Ann Bedford (Jeffress) Richards, b. 21 Nov. 1835, d. 9 Oct. 1865. Maternal grandmother, d/o Capt. Jennings M. and Margaret Bedford (Moseley) Jeffress, granddaughter of Hilary, Sr., and Ann (Bedford) Mosely, of Charlotte Co.; Jennings, s/o Thomas Jeffress, of Nottoway Co., VA. Father of Capt. John Richards was Rev. William Richards, b.

Essex Co., VA 1763; Mary, w/o William, d/o Edward and Edith
(Gunn) Hogan; father of William, John Richards, b. England, d.
before 1773; mother of William, Millicence, d/o Smith Young.
Reps m. Mary H. Wallace 29 Jan. 1867. Reps had following: Emmett
Henry, b. 26 Aug. 1855, business man in Dallas, TX, m. Lenora
Seegar, d. 23 Jun. 1890 leaving one child; Margaret B., b. 18
Sep. 1857, m. William J. Hatch, merchant and banker in TX; John
Young, b. 3 Nov. 1859, m. Augusta Weil, of Dallas; Mary L., d. in
childhood; Grayson Woods, m. Oneida Barnes, of VA; Anna F., w/o
Edward Rider Foster, of Sherwood, MD; Deanie M. w/o Dr. Allen
Mason, of Clarksville, VA; Rosa, d. young; Mortimer O., in real-
estate in Dallas; Hallie C. and George, at home; and William
Edwin. Subject m. Rosa L., d/o L. L. Perry, of Orange, VA, 19
Jul. 1892, and had three children: William Edwin, Jr., b. 30 Apr.
1893; Richards Osborne, b. 22 Oct. 1894; and Rosa Perry, b. 11
Aug. 1896. Pastor of the Calvary Baptist Church of Towson.

162. GEORGE HOFSTETTER - b. 1835 on the Hofstetter farm in the
twelfth district. George m. Elizabeth Gunther in 1862, and had
ten children: John, married, in business in the city; Harmon and
Aug., work at home; Kate and Henry, at home; and five who d.
quite young. Member of the Gardenville Lodge No. 114, I. O. O.
F., and the Farmers and Gardeners' Association. A Lutheran. A
Democrat. Engaged in farming in the twelfth district.

163. JOHN G. MORRIS, D.D., LL.D. - b. 14 Nov. 1803 in York, PA,
s/o Dr. John Morris. John m. Eliza Hay, of York, PA, in 1827,
and had four children: Annie Hay, deceased; Mrs. M. L. Trowbridge
of Balt.; Mrs. G. Morris Leisenring of Lutherville; and Miss M.
Hay Morris of Balt. Eliza d. in 1875, age sixty-eight. John d.
10 Oct. 1895, in Lutherville. A Lutheran. One of the most
prominent members of the Lutheran Church in the U. S.

164. PHILIP GEBB - b. 3 Feb. 1828, Hesse-Darmstadt, Germany, s/o
George and Charlotte (Cook) Gebb, also of Germany. Father came
to America in 1846 and d. in 1851. George and Charlotte had
seven children, some being: George, the eldest, d. at fifty-
three; Henry, farmer in the twelfth district; Conrad, in business
in Balt.; Wilhelmena, m. (1) John Williams, m. (2) Henry Moss of
Balt., and had six children; Mary, m. Julian Brent, of Balt., had
five children. Came to United States at age eighteen. Philip m.
Margaret Calbfleish, of Germany, in 1862, and had two children:
Amelia, w/o Alfred Stuven, business man in Towson; and Elizabeth,
deceased. Margaret d. in 1894. Member of the New Jerusalem
Church. A Democrat. An influential farmer of the ninth district.

165. JOSHUA F. C. WORTHINGTON - b. 27 Dec. 1840 in the second
district, s/o John and Penelope C. D. G. (Cockey) Worthington.
Father, s/o John Worthington, the half-brother of Rezin
Worthington. John and Penelope had five children: Elizabeth,
deceased; Mary A. C., m. (1) Noah H. Worthington, m. (2) Napoleon
Dorsey, of Howard Co., MD; Thomas and Noah C., deceased; and
Joshua F. C. Father d. 1862, age sixty-nine. Mother d. 1841.
Joshua m. (1) Blanche Nicholas, in 1868, who d.; m. (2) Mary D.,

d/o John W. S. Offutt, of Montgomery Co., MD, in 1882, and had two children, Norah and Mamie O. Member Shiloh Lodge No. 111, I. O. O. F., of Granite. Engaged in general farming in the second district.

166. H. J. COSKERY - b. 24 Jul. 1841 near Powhatan, Balt. Co., s/o Felix S. Coskery, M.D. H. J. m. Elizabeth, d/o Morris Sitler, of Balt. in 1865, and had eight children: Harry M., Arthur B., Paul, Elizabeth, Lawrence, Campbell, Allen and Claude. Proprietor of a drug store in Catonsville and a prescription druggist.

167. ROBERT M. DENISON - b. 29 Nov. 1813 in Balt. City, s/o Edward and Elizabeth (Wilson) Denison. Father, b. Nottingham, England, came to United States at age twenty, d. at age sixty-five, a Democrat. Edward m. Elizabeth, d/o Maj. James Armstrong Wilson, and had one child, Robert. Ancestors, being Protestants, moved from France to England. Robert m. Mary, d/o Charles R. Carroll, of Balt., in 1865, and had four children: Robert M. and Charles Carroll, at home; Mary Carroll, w/o Charles Frick, of Balt.; and Rebecca Carroll, w/o H. M. Warfield, of Balt. Mary d. in 1870. Pew-holder in the Grace Episcopal Church. Supports the Democratic party. Retired, now interested in raising thorough-bred horses.

168. HARRY V. SHIPLEY - b. 27 Feb. 1860 in the eigth district, s/o V. T. and Charlotte (Bennett) Shipley. Three brothers came to America and settled in Balt., Carroll and Howard Counties. Grandfather, John F. Shipley, connected with Northern Central Railroad. Maternal grandfather, Levi T. Bennett, of Carroll Co. V. T. and Charlotte had as children: Howard B., of Balt.; Harry V.; E. C.; and Ella M., w/o George C. Duncan, of Cockeysville. Father, a Democrat and member of the Methodist Episcopal Church, d. Feb. 1891. Harry m. Dora, d/o Brice Shipley, of Carroll Co., 13 Feb. 1883, and had four children: Walter V., Brice, Roger and Harry B. Member of the Mt. Moriah Lodge No. 116, A. F. & A. M., of Towson, and the Epworth Methodist Episcopal Church, of Cockeysville. Brother, E. C., b. 25 Jan. 1869 in the eighth district, m. Sarah, d/o George Hubbard, of the eighth district, 15 Nov. 1892, and had one child, Alan H. Operates farm and manages a lime kiln.

169. JOHN E. ENSOR - b. 23 Jan. 1852 in the eighth district, s/o John H. and Elizabeth (Ensor) Ensor. Father, b. 18 May 1822, same area. 2 great-grandfather, Abraham Ensor, of England, purchased property from Lord Baltimore. Great-grandfather, John Ensor. Grandfather, Luke G. Ensor, b. in eighth district, a carpenter, Democrat, member of Baptist Church at Black Rock. Luke m. Sarah, d/o Daily Ensor, and had: John H.; Ruth Ann, widow of George Ensor, of eighth district; Rachel, widow of Shadrach Streett, of Balt.; Thomas, of Whitehall; George H.; and Mrs. Thomas Burns, of the seventh district. Sarah d. in 1841, Luke d. in 1851. Maternal grandfather, John B. Ensor. John and Elizabeth had thirteen children: Luke, of Balt.; John E.; William, living near John; Joseph, living near William; Eliza, of

Balt.; and Delila, of Forrest Chick, NJ. John m. Mary E., d/o William Gorsuch, in Oct. 1874, and had: Elizabeth A., and William P., at home; John H., of New Windsor, Frederick Co., MD; Abram B., James V., Alexander R., Lawrence E., and Thomas R., all at home. A Democrat. A Baptist. Enterprising and progressive faarmer in the eight district.

170. JOHN I. ANDERSON - b. 15 Sep. 1835 near Towson, s/o Isaac and Elizabeth (Williams) Anderson. Father, b. 28 Sep. 1799 in Glen Arm, Balt. Co., orphaned when young, taken in by Robert Williams, became a blacksmith, a founder of Trinity Methodist Episcopal Church, m. Elizabeth, d/o Robert WIlliams, 20 May 1824, had six children: Mary, Robert, William, Isaac T., and John D., all d. in childhood, and John I. Mother, b. 7 Apr. 1798 in Wales. John m. (1) Elizabeth Cadwallander, d/o a minister, and had eleven children: Isaac C., d. at twelve; William T., conductor on railroad; John F., a clerk at Union depot, m. Laura Herring; James H., contractor in Balt. city and county; Charles E., machinist; George O., clerk with Northern Central Railroad Company; Sargeant H., florist; Morris W., farmer; Elizabeth B., deceased; Jesse E., clerk in hardware store; and Lydia E., d. in girlhood. Elizabeth d. 1884. John m. (2) Abbie, d/o John Brody, 1 Dec. 1886. Member Odd Fellows'. Retired from agriculture.

171. JOHN T. MALLONEE - b. 22 Sep. 1827 in the fourth district, s/o Hezekiah and Keturah (Tipton) Malonee. Grandfather, John Mallonee, native of France, settled in Balt. Co. before Revolutionary war, m. Sallie Bond, English lady, had ten children, some being: Shade, Lewis, Josiah, John and Hezekiah. Father, b. 14 Jul. 1799 in Balt. Co., a wheelwright. Hezekiah and Katurah had ten children: Sarah Ann, d. 1862; Mary Jane, widow of John G. Kelly, of Balt., John T., William, d. 1090; Lewis, wheelwright living in Balt.; Hezekiah, d. in boyhood; George, builder and contractor in Balt.; Ephraim, farmer in Balt. Co.; Thomas W., blacksmith, deceased; and one d. in infancy. John m. Eliza A. Bickingham, of Carroll Co., in Dec. 1861, had seven children: Thomas O., farmer; Anna B.; John Ephraim and Hezekiah Tipton (twins), John m. Gertrude Turbert of Balt. Co.; Wallace W.; Emma Florence, schoolteacher; and one infant who d. Eliza d. in 1891. Members of the Methodist Church. A Mason. A Democrat. Lessee and operator of a farm in the third district.

172. A. C. SMINK, M. D. - b. 17 Dec. 1875 in Hebbville, Balt. Co., s/o Adolphus and Mary J. (Schaible) Smink. Graduated medical department of the University of Maryland in 1896. Rising physician of the second district.

173. WILLIAM D. BOND - b. in 1863 in Balt., s/o Josiah and Caroline V. (Wells) Bond. Father, Balt. Co. farmer, a Republican, m. Caroline V. Wells, d/o farmer of Balt. Co., had twelve children: Charles C., Balt. merchant, d. 1893; William D., d. in infancy; Bertie and Eugene d. in childhood; Joseph, lives in twelfth district; Mary L., w/o Jerome H. Schubert, blacksmith of Balt.; Florence E., schoolteacher in Balt.; Emma, w/o William Dorrett, Balt. Co. farmer; Sadie, unmarried and at home; Edward,

farms with brother; Walter, at school; and William D., named for brother who d. William m. Annie L., d/o James Sewell, and granddaughter of Colonel Sewell, of Harford Co., MD, in 1886 and had two children: William Sewell and Irving Monroe. Member of the Railway Telegraphy, the Junior Order of American Mechanics and the Order of Columbus. Agent of the Lehigh Valley Railroad at Towson.

174. LOUIS J. ROBERTS - b. 12 Jun. 1829 in Balt. Co., only child of Louis and Susan (Cole) Roberts. Father, native of Cecil Co., MD. Maternal grandfather, Samuel Cole, of Balt. Co. Louis m. Annie E., d/o Nicholas Cornelius, business man of Balt. city, in Balt., 6 Dec. 1853, and had four children: Robert R., d. 1887; George B., manages home farm, a Methodist, m. Florence E., d/o John W. Bartlett, of Lovettsville, VA. in Dec. 1886, had two children; Mary L., m. Franck Havenner, Methodist minister of Balt., had two children; and Wilber S., manager Aetna Life Insurance Company, m. Mary F. Taylor, of Balt., had three children. Annie d. 27 Sep. 1889. Member of the Methodist Church. Farmer of the ninth district.

175. REV. GEORGE W. EBELING, Ph. D. - b. 13 Dec. 1821 in Germany. Came to America in 1852, settled in Balt., then Catonsville. George m. Maria Keidel, sister of Henry, Charles and Lewis Keidel, 28 Apr. 1853, had four children: Wilhelm; Herman, professor at Oxford; Henry, deceased, leaving a daughter, Flora; and Mary. A Lutheran. Pastor of the Lutheran Church in Catonsville.

176. WILLIAM ENSOR - b. 31 Aug. 1826 in Balt. city, s/o Luke and Rachel (Ensor) Ensor, he of Balt. city, she of Balt. Co. Both grandfathers came here from England. William m. Julia A., d/o Noah and Rachel (Wiser) Shaul, of the fifth district, in Oct. 1850, and had four children: Noah F., Luke E., Peter W. and Anna R., all m. and live near parents. Noah and Rachel Shaul, of Balt. Co., had six children: Julia A., Reason W., Joseph, Benjamin, Nancy and Rachel. Grandfather of Julia, Dr. Joseph Shaul, b. Germany, settled in the fifth district before the Revolutionary war. Member of the Odd Fellows' Society. Supports the Republican ticket. Agriculturist in the seventh district.

177. STEPHEN HAVEN WILSON - b. 24 Apr. 1838 in the eleventh district, s/o Robert S. and Frances Howard (Sadley) Wilson. Paternal grandfather, Stephen Wilson, of Balt., d. in 1794. Great-grandfather, native of Ireland, a pioneer of Balt. Father, b. Balt., a farmer, m. Frances Howard, d/o Thomas and Elizabeth (Howard) Sadley, and granddaughter of Thomas Gassaway Howard. Stephen m. Mary E., d/o David King, M.D., of Balt., and had three children: two d. in infancy, and Francis Howard. David King, s/o Abraham and Elizabeth King. Live on King homestead, patent signed by Lord Baltimore. Liberal in politics and religion.

178. GEORGE WESLEY GOODWIN - b. 20 Sep. 1866 in Balt. city, s/o James and Eliza Jane (Bamber) Goodwin. Father, b. 1 Oct. 1818 in MD, a Republican, d. 27 Jul. 1887. Mother, b. in Warren, Balt.

Co., where her father settled from England. James and Eliza had six children: George W.; Charles Thomas, a fireman on the Baltimore & Ohio Railroad, m. Mary E. Froelich; Bertha Frost, Mary Blanche, Hannah Elnora and James Herbert, at home. George m. Florence Holbrook Layton, d/o James Holbrook and Emma Jane (Chiveral) Layton, in 1887, had three children: Layton Wesley, Etta Jet and James Roland. Layton family originally from England, came to MD from VA; James, a Democrat, and Emma, had ten children: Florence Holbrook; Edward C., painter; Bertha Cordelia, w/o Timothy Rogers, of Norfolk, VA; Robert Henry, farmer in VA; James Frederick, George Franklin and William Herdman, at home. Members of the Episcopal Church at Canton. Favors the Republican party. Chief engineer of the Sheppard asylum, in Balt.

179. JOHN LIST - b. 14 Jan. 1821 in Utenheim, Germany, s/o J. Philip and Anna Elizabeth (Bauer) List, both of Germany. Father, b. 17 Mar. 1777, settled in Balt. 5 Sep. 1835, shoemaker. Children of J. Philip and Anna: Christopher, went west; J. Adams, Balt. business man til death; Elizabeth, w/o Matthew Shibley, had large family; Jacob, m. Elizabeth England Shoemaker, had six children. John m. Catherine Bing, b. in Germany, in 1849, and had nine children: Katie, d. in childhood; Elizabeth, m. Frederick Schwartz, Balt. business man, had ten children; John P., deceased, m. Elizabeth Baumgartner, five living children; Mary, w/o Henry Schultz, Balt. baker, had five children; Louisa, w/o Charles Schultz, had one daughter; Anna, w/o William Kammer, Balt. baker, had seven children; and Rosa, w/o Frederick Richard, Balt. baker, had four children. Lutherans. Prominent business man of the ninth district.

180. CHARLES H. PRICE - b. 24 Oct. 1850 in eighth district, s/o Samuel M. and Catherine Price. Father, b. same place in 1815, farmer, d. 3 Mar. 1893. Mother, b. Balt. Co., is eighty-two (1897), had three children, two d. Charles m. Anna R., d/o George Matthew, farmer of Balt. Co., in 1884. A Republican. Members of the Society of Friends. Life devoted to agricultural pursuits.

181. JOSIAH S. BOWEN, M. D. - b. 1 Mar. 1832 in Balt. Co., s/o Wilks and Elizabeth (Taylor) Bowen, also of Balt. Co. Father, a Democrat. Wilks and Elizabeth had two children: Josiah, and Elizabeth Marcella, now living in Waverly, MD. Grandfather, Josiah Bowen, b. in ninth district. Subject m. (1) Martha Slack, d. soon afterward, then m. (2) Adeline Pratt, d/o Truman Belt, of Balt. Co., had three children: Wilks, Josiah S., Jr., and Rebecca, all students. Member of the Baltimore County Medical Society. A Mason, and connected with the Knights of Pythias. A Democrat. He is a Methodist, she belongs to the Episcopal Church. Physician at Mt. Washington.

182. COL. BENJAMIN F. TAYLOR - b. 13 Nov. 1840 in city of Balt., s/o Robert and Esther A. (LeCompte) Taylor. Grandfather, Robert Taylor, of Dublin, came to America just before the Revolutionary war. Father, b. in Sep. 1782, on the Hillen road in Balt. Co., m. twice; by first marriage Robert had nine children: Thomas

Wesley, George W., Nathan, Robert Alexander, James J., and 4 who d. young; by second marriage Robert had Benjamin F. Benjamin m. Mary J., d/o Joseph E. Cator, of Harford Co., 3 Feb. 1869, and had three children: Joseph C. LeCompte, Caroline Cator and Martha Adele. Members in the Episcopal Church. Member of the Baltimore County Grange. A Republican.

183. ISAAC KING - b. in 1811 in Chester Co., PA, s/o Temple King, of same county. Paternal grandfather, Eli King, b. in PA, probably of Irish extraction. Isaac m. Jemima Pierson in 1836, and had following: Esther A., deceased, w/o Luke Brown, of Balt. Co., had seven children living; Sarah, w/o John Fishbaugh, of same county, had three children living; Mary, w/o Ephraim Gilbert, of Harford Co., MD; Matilda, w/o Amos Debendoffer, of Balt.; Rachel, w/o Joseph Seitz, of York county, had eleven children; Isaac, at home; Thomas, of West Chester, PA, m. Emma Morgan, had six children; Joshua M., m. Isabella V. Carmady, have one living child, Joshua McKinley; and Jemima E. Settled in Balt. Co. in 1849. Conducted tavern for thirty years.

184. GEORGE B. DUBBS - b. 11 Jun. 1843 in Hanover, PA, s/o Jesse and Caroline (Baum) Dubbs. Father, also b. Hanover, family living there many generations, a Democrat, and member of the German Reformed Church, d. 1887. Jesse m. Caroline, d/o Peter Baum, of PA, had eleven children: Lavina, w/o Samuel Anthey, of PA; Daniel, of Jefferson; Angeline, w/o Jacob Meekley, of Clear Rock, PA; George B., William, of Hanover, PA; Sarah, John, Stambaugh, Miller, Warren, and Ellen, w/o Levi Bayley, of Clear Rock, PA. Mother d. 1892. George m. Lucy Ann, d/o Daniel Roser, of PA, in 1868, and had four children: Daniel, Henry, Elmira and Lilly May. A Democrat. Member of the Presbyterian Church. Thorough and systematic agriculturist.

185. WILLIAM ROWEN MAYES - b. in 1824, in the tenth district, s/o Jeremiah Mayes, also of the tenth district. William m. Margaret A., d/o Jeremiah Mayes, and had: Elizabeth, w/o David Michaels; William McGee, at home; Thomas T., of Philopolis; Nanny, w/o William C. Brooks; and Bertha S., w/o John R. Griffin, of Hereford, Balt. Co. A Democrat. Member of the Methodist Episcopal Church. William d. 22 Jul. 1874. Leading farmer of the eighth district.

186. JAMES L. GEMMILL - b. in York county, PA, s/o John and Mary (Smith) Gemmill, also of York Co. Paternal grandfather, a farmer in York Co. John and Mary had ten children, only two now living, James and Sarah L., widow of William T. Thompson, York Co. farmer. James m. Sarah J. Freeland, of Balt. Co., and had seven children: Margaret, Agnes J., Martha E., James Stephen, and William T., and two who d. when young; James Stephen, m. Lula Bowman, of Delaware, and had two children: Vernon A. and Gladys E. Member of the Independent Order of Red Men, in Freeland. A Republican. Member of the Zion Church (Methodist Protestant). Postmaster at Freeland, in the seventh district.

187. CHRISTIAN A. HELWIG - b. in 1861 in Balt., s/o Godfried and

Theresa (Tames) Helwig. Father came to United States from
Germany when twenty-five, m. Theresa Tames, also b. in Germany,
and had six children; Barbara, d. at sixteen; Lizzie M., w/o L.
W. Kehs, Balt. business man; Annie M., at home; Louis G., wholesale grocer with Christian; William, d. in boyhood, and
Christian. Christian m. Maggie, d/o William A. Hall, of Balt.,
in 1889, and had two children, Albert M. and Vernon Hall. Manufacturer of groceries and all kinds of spices at No. 1209 East
North avenue.

188. JOHN B. WAILES - b. 4 May 1861 in Calvert Co., MD, s/o John
P. and Mary H. (Beckett) Wailes, also b. in Calvert Co. Maternal
grandfather, Capt. John Beckett. John and Mary had six children:
Mary B., w/o J. Warfield; Susie, w/o S. B. Warfield; Elizabeth,
w/o Samuel Burkhead; Joseph C., Balt. store owner; Thomas, Balt.
dairy man; and John B. John m. Annie M., d/o Joshua Shipley, of
Howard Co., MD, in 1885 and had five children: John Shipley,
Annie Shipley; Joseph B., who d. in childhood; Theodore Cook and
Edwin Early. Member of the Independent Order of Heptasophs.
Votes Democratic ticket. Owns large general store in Arlington.

189. JOHN H. SPARKS - b. 7 Jun. 1846 in Balt. Co., s/o Elijah B.
and Elizabeth (Anderson) Sparks. Father, b. 17 Oct. 1807 in
Balt. Co., a saddler. Elijah and Elizabeth had ten children:
William, killed in Civil war; Elmira, w/o Lewis Dawson, Balt. Co.
farmer, had five children; Ann Rebecca, w/o Jacob E. Lowe; Alice
J., w/o Joseph Hartman; Rachel E., w/o Artemus Sullivan, Balt.
Co. farmer; Bettie, w/o James C. Bosley, had three children; and
John H. Edward A. Sparks, brother of Elijah, m. Elizabeth, d/o
Richard Clark, of Balt. John m. Lavinia, d/o George Lucas
Anderson, in Feb. 1874. Members of the Methodist Church. A
blacksmith and machinist.

190. COL. DENNIS M. MATTHEWS - b. in 1831 in Balt. Co., s/o Amos
and Ellen (Marsh) Matthews, also b. and m. in same county.
Paternal great-grandfather probably b. in England. Grandfather,
Mordecai Matthews, native of Balt. Co., member of the Society of
Friends, had six children. Amos and Ellen had seven children:
Dennis M.; Eliza, w/o John G. Booth, of the eleventh district;
Joshua M.; Temperance, w/o Samuel Gover, formerly of Loudoun Co.,
VA, now of Washinginton; Mary, Ellen and Bell. Dennis m. Hattie
Aldridge, of WV, in 1875, and had five children: Eleanor M.,
Andrew Aldridge, Clyde V., J. Marsh and James G. Members of the
Protestant Episcopal Church in Long Green. A Democrat. Leading
agriculturist of the tenth district.

191. EDWARD E. DUNNING - b. 7 Jun. 1861 in Balt. Co., s/o John
and Margaret A. (Jackson) Dunning. Father, s/o John and
Elizabeth Dunning, b. in York Co., PA, m. Margaret A., d/o
William Jackson, of Towson, had five children: Edward E.;
Margaret E., w/o George Hess, of Balt.; John M.; Robert S. carpenter and builder in Balt. Co.; and Arthur G., employed by
Towson Express. Father d. in 1856. Edward m. Lulu, d/o John
Waugh, of Balt., in 1890, and had three children: Norris W.,
Edward Waugh and Beverly W. Members of the Methodist Church.

Engaged in the oil business in Towson.

192. JOHN A. CRAIG, M. D. - b. in 1807 in Cambridge, MD. For first marriage see sketch of son James. John m. (2) Sallie, d/o John Henry and Sarah D. (Lawrence) Keene and granddaughter of Dr. Samuel Yerbury and Sarah (Goldsborough) Keene, in St. Paul's Protestant Episcopal Church of Baltimore in 1868, had two children: Lawrence Ennels, b. 3 Aug. 1869 at Ravenswood, Balt. Co., d. at twenty; and William Pinkney, b. 9 Dec. 1874 in same place, named for uncle, William Pinkney Craig, namesake of William Pinkney. Samuel and Sarah Keene had four children, John Henry, eldest, b. in 1806 in Talbot Co., MD. John Henry and Sarah Keene had ten children: Ann Hall, d. in infancy; Elizabeth Dorsey, d. when young; John Henry, m. Frances Cook, of New York City; Robert Goldsborough, m. Abigail Patterson Bresee, member of the Balt. bar; Jane, William C. and Charles Ridout d. when young; Mary Hollingsworth and Laura Eleanor are unmarried; and Sallie. John d. 10 Dec. 1893 at Ravenswood, in Balt. Co.

193. GEORGE SACK - b. 6 May 1834 in Germany s/o Adam and Johanna (Kukel) Sack. Father, b. in Mar. 1808 in Germany, came to America in 1854. Adam and Johanna had four sons: George; Charles, came to United States in 1862, m., settled in Missouri, a wheelwright; Ernest, a builder, m. Mary Radecke; and Frederick, came to Balt. with father. George m. Beate, d/o Adam and Christiana Rau, native German, had seven children: Charles, m. Mamie Schaferman; Helen, w/o William Ziegler, Balt. grocer, have three children; Amelia, w/o Frederick Hill, have three children; Ernest, carpenter and builder, m. Mary Walsh and have two children; Maggie, at home; John, m.; and Lizzie. Member of the Algemeiner Arbeiter Kranken Unterstetzung Verein. A Lutheran. Contractor, builder, and runs a lumber yard.

194. HERMAN B. L. EVERDING - b. 9 Dec. 1844 in Germany, s/o Herman H. C. and Catherine E. (Honneman) Everding, also b. Germany. Father, b. 1812, brought wife and son to America in 1845, settled in Balt., a Democrat, member of the Independent Order of Odd Fellows, a Lutheran, d. in 1878. Member of the Knights of the Golden Eagle. A Democrat. A Presbyterian. Real-estate owner and business man of Govanstown.

195. PETER B. HOFFMAN - b. in May 1844 in the sixth district; m. Catherine, d/o David S. H. and Annie (Smith) Williams, 31 Dec. 1865. Catherine b. in sixth district. Member of the Independent Order of Odd Fellows, Middletown Lodge No. 92, and A. C. Spicer Post No. 43, at Middletown. Retired paper manufacuturer.

196. SAMUEL E. LLOYD, D. V. S. - b. 6 Nov. 1874 in Govanstown, s/o Josiah E. and Anna (Erdman) Lloyd. Father, b. Philadelphia. Josiah and Anna had four children: Madison E., Balt. lawyer; Samuel E.; Lillie and Anna, at home. Great-grandfather Lloyd, b. in Wales, came to United States as a young man. Member of the Junior Order of American Mechanics. Leading veterinary surgeon of Balt. Co.

197. WILLIAM F. BLAND, M. D. - b. 17 Sep. 1827 in King and Queen Co., VA, s/o Robert and Mary Ann (Boyd) Bland. Grandfather, Robert Bland, native of King and Queen Co., VA. Father, also b. there, a farmer, member of the Methodist Episcopal Church South. Maternal grandfather, John Boyd, of King and Queen Co. Robert and Mary m. 3 Nov. 1826 and had: William F.; John R., d. leaving two children, C. T. and Mary O. Garrett; Mary C., w/o Thomas K. Savage; Dr. James E.; Lucy M.; Virginia B., w/o Dr. Alexander D. Grubb; Benjamin F.; and four who d. in infancy. All except William live in VA. Mother d. 6 Feb. 1863 and father d. 31 Jan. 1871. William m. Louisa A., d/o Dr. James T. Boyd, 16 Nov. 1852, and had six children: four d. in infancy; William Boyd, d. 21 Feb. 1897, leaving wife and six children; Thomas Jackson, M.D., physician in Martinsburg, W.VA., d. 16 Nov. 1895, leaving wife and son. Members of the Methodist Episcopal Church South. A Democrat. Retired from professional practice, now general farmer and dairy man.

198. R. OLIVER PRICE - b. in 1840 in the tenth district, s/o Edward R. and Penelope H. (Richardson) Price. Grandfather, Zachariah Price, native of Balt. Co., had as children: Skelton, Samuel, Jarrett, William, Edward R., and Mrs. Susan Amos. Maternal grandfather, Thomas Richardson. Edward and Penelope had: Mary, d. unmarried; William T., lives in tenth district; Sarah A., w/o Eli Matthews, had one son, Harry, living in Monkton; R. Oliver; J. Richardson, of tenth district; Charles W., d. in early manhood; and Susan A., w/o J. Marion Royston, of Phoenix, MD. Mother d. in 1869, father d. in 1877, were members of the Methodist Episcopal Church. R. Oliver m. Ella, d/o Wesley Royston, Sr. (who d. in 1893), and had six children, Charles M., Bertha C., Mary R., Penelope R., Alice A. and Elmer W., all at home. Members of the Methodist Episcopal Church at Clymalaria. General farmer in the tenth district.

199. WILLIAM D. HOFFMAN - b. in 1826 in the sixth district, s/o William D. and Susan (Hoffman) Hoffman, he of Frederick Co., MD, and she of the sixth district of Balt. Co. William and Susan had eleven children: Hannah, lives in Ohio; Jane, William D., Johanna, Elizabeth, Sarah, Eliza, Peter B., and three who d. Grandfather, George F. Hoffman, native of Hanover, Germany, came to America just before the Revolution, m. Mary McElvaine, of PA, whose father's forefathers were Scotchmen. Paternal great-grand-father, William Hoffman, from Germany settled near Philadelphia in 1769. Subject m. (1) Susan Hildebrand, of Carroll Co., at age twenty-two, but she d; m. (2) Elizabeth Armacost, of Carroll Co., and had: Lucinda, Johanna, Salema, Joseph, George and Susie. He is Baptist, she is Methodist Episcopal. Member of the Masons and the Odd Fellows. A Democrat. Retired from the paper business.

200. HON. WESLEY R. WHITAKER - b. 19 Nov. 1860 in Harford Co., MD, s/o Lloyd D. and Elizabeth (Stansbury) Whitaker. Father, b. in Balt. City in 1812, d. in 1876, a Republican. Maternal grand-father, Isaac Stansbury, miller in Harford Co.; see William E. Stansbury sketch for more. Lloyd and Elizabeth had six children: Thomas, lives with Wesley; Isaac, d. at twenty-seven; Elizabeth

and Martha, d. in girlhood; Eugenia, w/o Harry McCreary, lives on East Monument street, Balt.; and Wesley. Wesley m. Bertha M., d/o Bartina Cannon, of Balt. in 1884, had six children: Lloyd D., Addie E., John E., Bertie, Joseph and Bertha Jennie. Member of the Junior Order of American Mechanics. A Baptist. A Republican. Real-estate business man.

201. EDWARD WILLIAMS ALTVATER, M. D. - b. 11 Oct. 1836 in the city of Balt., s/o Garrett and Louisa (Williams) Altvater. Garrett, b. in Balt., m. Louisa, d/o Baruch Williams, and niece of Commodore Joshua Barney Williams, and had seven children: John, deceased; Garrett, of Balt.; Louisa, w/o William Woodland; Morris; Frances and Baruch, deceased; and Edward. Paternal grandfather, John H. Altvater, of Germany came to America, m. Ann, d/o Col. Job Garrettson. Father d. in 1887. Edward m. Cassandra Woodland in 1869, had four children: Louisa, w/o Dr. Newberry A. S. Kiser, and d. in 1895, leaving two children, Allen and Mary; May Josephine, w/o Walter Chapman, of the eleventh district; Edward, deceased; and George Barney, d. in infancy. Cassandra d. in 1884. Edward m. (2) Annie, d/o the late Dr. George Airey. Identified with St. John's Episcopal Church. Member of the Baltimore County Medical Association. Physician at Upper Falls, Balt. Co.

202. THE WILSON FAMILY - first represented in Balt. Co. by Benjamin K. Wilson, native of England, settled in Calvert Co., then Balt. Co. Benjamin had four sons: two, Benjamin and Henry, b. and reared in Balt. Co., and m. daughters of William Washington, and were farmers. Benjamin, had two children, Benjamin and Sarah. Sarah d. unmarried, and Benjamin m. Sarah, d/o Lyde Goodwin, and had five children: Goodwin, William W., Elizabeth, Rebecca and Caleb. William W. m. Mary, d/o John E. Reese; Mary d. sixteen years after m.; William identified with Episcopal Church.

203. E. TYSON WARE - b. 9 Nov. 1834 in Towson, s/o Nathan and Eliza C. (Barron) Ware. Ware family came from England at a very early day. Grandfather, Capt. Robert Ware, a farmer, m. Miss Gladden and had large family. Nathan, b. in 1801, a Mason, a Methodist, m. Eliza C., d/o Prescott and Julia (Ridgley) Barron, in 1828, and had: Caroline L., w/o A. H. Green; Valverda A. P., m. sister of his brother-in-law, Mr. Green; Julia B., w/o William H. Green, brother of A. H.; Charles R., m. Miss Flarity; Wallace T. and little sister, Fannie, burned to death in 1853; Robert P., went to Ohio, m. Miss Hanson; Randolph R., m. Miss Owens and lives in MD; Nathan H., Jr., lives in Ohio, m. Miss Price; William B., m Ida Ridgley; E. Tyson; and Eleanor L., w/o Samuel Pinkerton. Julia was d/o Capt. Charles Ridgley. E. Tyson m. Laura V., d/o William Coe, in 1870, had one child, Eliza V. A Mason and a member of the Ancient Order of United Workmen. A Republican. Has a coal business in Towson.

204. JOSHUA F. COCKEY - b. in 1840 in Balt. Co., s/o Joshua F. and Henrietta (Worthington) Cockey. Father d. in 1891 at ninety-one, and mother d. in 1880. Joshua and Henrietta had four child-

ren: Joshua F., Jr.; Mrs. Comfort Morrison; Mrs. Fannie Offutt; and Annie, w/o Adam D. Talbott, deceased. Subject m. (1) Sarah J., d/o William Denmead, of Balt. Co., in 1868, had four children: Comfort, w/o Warren Sadler, of Cockeysville; Joshua F.; Albert, deceased; and John Thomas. Joshua m. (2) Anna Buchanan, d/o Clement and Mary Ridgely Bussey (d/o Thomas D. Cockey), 22 Oct. 1896. President of the National Bank of Cockeysville.

205. EDWARD J. HERRMANN - b. 26 Mar. 1860 in the city of Balt., s/o Peter and Mary (Hart) Herrmann, both of Germany. Peter, b. in Bavaria, settled in Balt. at twenty-one, and Mary had seven children: Edward J.; John P., d. in Dec. 1896; Mary, w/o John N. Downs; Tina, w/o Philip P. Hintz, of Balt.; Kate, w/o George W. Collenberg; Elizabeth, w/o Julius Reckwart; and Albert, grocer in Balt. Edward m. Amelia Naimaster, of Golden Ring, in 1882, and had six children: Emma A., Walter, Frederick, Albert, Ruth and Tabitha. Member of the Independent Order of Odd Fellows and the Encampment of Patriarch Militant Uniformed Rank of Odd Fellows. Conducts large general store at Golden Ring, and is postmaster of the place.

206. J. MORRIS and JAMES W. BALDWIN - J. Morris b. in 1818, James b. in 1820 in Balt. county, sons of John Baldwin. John also had Elizabeth, w/o Joshua H. Scarff, and Mary A. Family of English extraction. Grandfather, William Baldwin, came to MD from PA, had four sons: John, Silas, James and Samuel; only John and Silas had families. John was old-line Whig and old-school Baptist. J. Morris m. Sarah E., d/o Washington Hanway, of Harford Co., in 1853, had three children: Ella L., w/o Dr. John S. Green; Charles W. and Ida J., at home; Sarah d. in 1883. Attend Presbyterian Church. James W. never m. Extensive farmers of the eleventh district.

207. SOLOMON COLUMBUS ALLEN - b. in 1844 in the twelfth district, s/o James and Ann Allen, also of Balt. Co. Solomon m. Amanda Cornes, of Balt. Co., in 1866, and had eleven children: William, Charles, Sarah, Annie, Samuel, George, Maria, Matilda, Catherine, two who d. William, Charles and Annie are m. Member of the Independent Order of Odd Fellows. Progressive and enterprising farmer of the eleventh district.

208. JOHN S. OGIER - b. 8 Jan. 1832 in city of Balt., s/o John and Elizabeth (Hargest) Ogier. Father, b. island of Guernsey, in the bay of St. Michael, s/o John and Mary Ogier, came to America at nine years. John and Elizabeth had thirteen children: James H., farmer, d. in 1885; Mary J., deceased, w/o Henry Snyder of Balt.; Andrew C., farmer in CA., d.; Isabella N., m. William N. Edwards, Jr. and d. in CA; George, farmer in Balt.; Martha and Annie, deceased; John S.; and other children d. in infancy. John m. Mary Elizabeth, d/o Joshua Burgan, of Balt. Co., in 1853, and had thirteen children: Mary Elizabeth, d. at sixteen; John B., Myrtle Helen and Edna B., d. in childhood; James Edwin, d. at twenty-seven; Harry Clinton, d. in youth; Charles Stewart, owns ranch in CA; Fannie Estelle, w/o Jacob K. Nicholson, Jr. of Balt.; George B., Balt. business man; India Belle, Emma Lillie

and Florence Virginia, at home. Supports the Republican party. Retired from farming and gardening business.

209. THOMAS KURTZ - b. 20 Dec. 1841 in Berks Co., PA, s/o John Kurtz. Father, native of Berks Co., a miller, of German extraction. Thomas m. Catherine Leutz, of the eighth district in 1876, and had three children: Sherman L., William F. and Harriet C. Thomas d. 29 Aug. 1895. A Democrat. A Presbyterian. Member of the Masonic lodge at Towson. Conducted store at Oregon, Balt. Co.

210. JOHN W. IGLEHART - b. 23 Sep. 1843 in Anne Arundel Co., s/o John W. and Matilda (Davidson) Iglehart, of same county. Family from Germany, represented in MD since latter part of the sixteenth century. John m. Helen, d/o David McCullough and Margaret (Sellman) Brogden, and had six children: Helen, Elizabeth, Mary Eleanor, two who d. of diphtheria when young, and a son d. in infancy. Votes Democratic. Member of the Episcopal Church. Superintendent of Mr. Bonaparte's property in the eleventh district.

211. JUDGE LUTHER TIMANUS - b. 25 Jul. 1825 in the second district, s/o Jacob and Jane (McCullough) Timanus. Great-grandfather, John J. Timanus, b. in Switzerland, settled in DE, a farmer, had three sons. Grandfather, Jacob Timanus, had five sons, George, Charles, John, Jesse, and Jacob, Jr. Jacob, Jr., b. in second district of Balt. Co., a stone mason, m. (1) Jane McCullough, of Cecil Co., MD, had four children: William J., d. in 1869; Israel, d. in 1892; Louisa, w/o Isaac Strawbridge and d. in 1891, and Ann, Mrs. Mansfield, who d. in 1894. Jacob m. (2) Margaret, d/o Richard Mansfield, b. in England, and had ten children: Luther; Richard H, retired to Clyde, Ohio; Mary J. d, in infancy; Selena, w/o William Harvey Hordey, and d. 19 Oct. 1866; Ethan, farmer of the second district; Andrew, lives in Balt.; George, d. at four; Nathan, d. at twenty-one; John J., Methodist minister in Philadelphia; and Mrs. Mary Berry, d. in 1888. Luther m. Mary F., d/o John S. George, in 1861 and had eight children: George E., merchandiser in Balt.; Clara V., w/o C. Frank Emmert; Florence, m. Mr. Cox and d in 1896; Ernest L., at home; Fannie, w/o Wallace Russell; Ella G., wife of Emory Cox; John J., surveyor of Balt. Co.; and Mollie. Member of the Methodist Church. Former judge of the orphans' court of Balt. Co.

212. JULIUS W. KNOX - b. 15 Jul. 1834 in Balt. Co., s/o Peter and Ernestine (DeMaree) Knox. Father, b. in Germany, first settled in Washington, D.C., then Balt. Co., member of the Odd Fellows, m. Ernestine DeMaree, b. at Friedricksthal, near Carlsruh, Baden, Germany, in 1830, and had four children: Julius W.; Sophia P., w/o Charles F. Heszler, teacher in Balt.; Charles H., farmer, m. Susan Erdman and had six children; and one child d. in infancy. Name was formerly spell Knoch. Julius m. Sophia Reuter, of Balt. Co., in 1861, and had ten children; Louis Peter, raises horses; Charles R.; William, in business with Louis; Teresa, artist, Hazel, vocalist; and five who d. Member of the Odd Fellows and the Gordon Beneficial Society. Belongs to the

Methodist Episcopal Church. Agruculturist of the ninth district.

213. JOHN BARRON, M. D. - b. 16 Mar. 1843 in the city of Clonnell, Ireland, s/o Dr. Thomas Francis and Mary (O'Connor) Barron. Father, b. in White Church, same county, came to United States 4 Jun. 1845, settled in Balt. Paternal grandfather, Edward F. Barron, a lawyer, and son-in-law of Julian O'Connor. Thomas and Mary had seven children: Edward T., m. Mary Whelan, had eight children; Thomas Francis, veterinary surgeon in Balt.; Mary Barron, w/o George S. Duering; Andrew, d. in infancy; Margaret d. at twenty-five; and Catherine, d. at eighteen. John m. (1) Helen, d/o Colonel Leonard of Philadelphia, PA, in 1868 and had son, John T., living in Philadelphia; Helen d. in 1880. John m. (2) Elizabeth M., d/o Col. M. V. Codd, and had: Marie; Julian Paul, d. young; Catherine, William Julian P. and Elizabeth Ann. Member of the Medical and Chirurgical Faculty of Maryland, the American Medical Congress and the East Baltimore Medical and Surgical Association. Physician in Govans, Balt. Co.

214. CHARLES EDWARD THOMAS - b. 21 Aug. 1855 in the eighth district, s/o George Thomas and Martha (Cox) Thomas. Paternal grandfather, b. in Germany, settled in eighth district. Father, b. Balt. Co., farmer, m. Martha, d/o John and Susan (Gill) Cox, he of English ancestry, and had: Charles; George Albert and Ruth Anna, d. in childhood; and Laura, w/o Samuel Cockey, lives in eighth district. Father d. in 1859, age thirty-three. Charles m. Carrie, d/o John G. and Annie Stieber, of Balt. Co., and had six children: Edna Agnes, Benjamin Marvin, Bessie Jennie, Seabrook Stieber, Virginia M., and Charles Edward. Members of the Towson Baptist Church. Substantial and enterprising business man of Towson.

215. DANIEL S. WILHELM - b. in 1861, in the sixth district, s/o Joshua and Elizabeth (Zencker) Wilhelm, of the same district. Joshua and Elizabeth had: Daniel S.; Samuel, railroad agent at Glencoe; William, of Balt.; Jennie, w/o George Bowen; and Ella, w/o Mark Bowen, of MD. Paternal grandfather, Daniel Wilhelm, paper manufacturer of sixth district. Father, agriculturist. Daniel m. Tacie Morris, of Harford Co., in fall of 1882, and had four children: Edith, Cora, Webster and Charles. Member of the Monkton Lodge, K. P. Agriculturist of Glencoe, tenth district.

216. JACOB FREUND - b. 24 Apr. 1822 in Germany. Mother d. when he was three, father d. when he was ten. Left Germany at sixteen, landed in Philadelphia, settled in Balt. Jacob m. Magdelena Zehner in 1856, and had eleven children: Mary, Lewis, John W. and Louisa living; seven d. Connected with the Lutheran Church. A Democrat. Successful harness dealer in Catonsville.

217. CHARLES H. KNOX - b. 15 Feb. 1843 in Govanstown, Balt. Co., s/o John P. and Annstina (Demeree) Knox, of Germany. Father came to the United States at about twenty years, settled in Balt. Co., in florist's business then dairy business at Fairmount, had three children: Charles; Julius W., in produce business in ninth district; and Sophia, w/o Prof. Charles F. Heszler, teacher in Balt.

Father, member of the Farmers and Gardeners' Association, d. in 1879 on his farm. Charles m. Susanna, d/o Mathias Erdman, 28 Dec. 1870, had six children: John W., Stevenson Arthur, Winchester, Eugene, Lulu and Bessie. Member of Corinthian Lodge of Odd Fellows in Baltimore. Connected with the Methodist Protestant Church. Engaged in agricultural pursuits at the old Knox homestead, Araba Deserter.

218. THOMAS R. JENIFER - b. 19 Mar. 1854, Balt. Co., s/o Daniel and Elizabeth (Risteau) Jenifer. Paternal great-grandfather, Daniel Jenifer, b. Charles Co. in 1725, of English lineage; first of family came from St. Thomas in early days of colonies. Father, b. 27 Sep. 1815 in Charles Co., d. 4 Aug. 1890, had brothers: Thomas, physician in Charles Co.; Walter, d. 2 Feb. 1878; John, lived in St. Helena, AR; and Daniel, of St. Thomas, physician, d. in 1843 in Fredericksburg, VA. Grandfather, Daniel, b. 15 Apr. 1791 in Charles Co., d. 18 Dec. 1855; Dr. Daniel Jenifer m. Sarah, d/o Dr. James Craig; Dr. Craig, b. in 1730 in Dumfries, Scotland. 2 great-grandfather, Daniel Jenifer, m. Elizabeth Tripp, d/o John and Marion (Maxwell) Campbell; John, s/o James Campbell of Argyleshire, Scotland, settled in VA in 1754, then Charles Co., MD. Mother, Elizabeth, b. Balt. Co., d/o Dr. Thomas C. and Ann B. Risteau, he a French Huguenot. Elizabeth m. Daniel in 1848 at age eighteen, and had twelve children: Walter H., d. at two; Emily B., d. at four; Nannie C., d. at eighteen; one d. in infancy; Eliza Campbell, w/o John H. Mitchell, attorney in Charles Co.; Mary R., w/o Hugh Mitchell, d. in 1885; Marion, w/o Dr. H. T. Harrison, s/o Rev. Peyton Harrison of VA; Bettie, d. 30 Jul. 1889; Daniel, d. 8 Oct. 1889; John B. Morris, d. 24 Feb. in Carroll Co., MD; Florence C., lives with Thomas. Thomas m. Margaret A., d/o Robert Moore, of Balt., in 1877, and had six children: T. C. Risteau, Robert Moore, Charles W., Daniel, of St. Thomas, H. Courtney and Eleanor T. Member of Mt. Moriah Lodge of Masons at Towson, the Odd Fellows and the Junior Order of American Mechanics. A Democrat. Extensively engaged in farming and stock-raising and has the largest lime kilns in the county, at Loch Raven, four miles east of Towson.

219. EMANUEL W. HERMAN - b. 30 Apr. 1871 in Wrightsville, York Co., PA, s/o Emanuel and Sallie M. (Weiser) Herman. Father, also of York Co., m. Sallie M., d/o Daniel Weiser, merchant of York, and had four children: Emanuel W.; Margaret, w/o H. Burton Stevenson, of Sherwood, MD; Grace, and Sarah, deceased. Emanuel m. Elizabeth I., d/o Dr. and Mrs. George Y. Boal, of Baden, Beaver Co., PA. Member of John Eager Howard Lodge No. 55, Junior Order of American Mechanics. Belongs to St. Paul's Lutheran Church at Lutherville. A Republican. Lawyer in Towson.

220. JOSHUA G. BOSLEY - b. 2 Dec. 1850 in the eighth district, s/o Joseph and Martha (Gorsuch) Bosley. Father, and grandfather, Daniel Bosley, also b. eighth district. Great-grandfather, Joseph Bosley. Father, a Methodist Episcopal, and a Democrat, m. Martha, d/o Captain Gorsuch of the eight district, and had eight children: Thomas C., lives in eighth district; Eleanor G., living with brother Daniel W.; M. Louisa, w/o Charles Zepp, of VA;

Joshua G.; Josephine, w/o F. P Goodwin, of fourth district; M. Rebecca, w/o Frank Scott, of Butler; and Daniel W., of eighth district. Joshua m. Bertha Brown, of Balt. City, in Jan., 1881, and had one child, Mary E. A Democrat. Lawyer in Towson and farmer of the eighth district.

221. CHRISTIAN DICKMYER - b. in Germany, s/o Frederick and Dorothy (Hardin) Dickmyer. Christian came to America at twenty-five; m. Barbara Baker, of Balt. Co., MD, in York Co., PA, and had six children: Anna, deceased; Dorothy; Wilhelmina; Eleanora, deceased; Frederick and Henry. A Democrat. Member of the Reformed Church. Farmer, road supervisor and school director.

222. THOMAS C. BUSSEY, M. D. - b. near Bentleys Springs, in the seventh district. Brother of Dr. B. F. Bussey (see sketch). Physician in Texas, in the eighth district.

223. RICHARD C. FRANCIS - b. in 1827 in the eleventh district, s/o Thomas and Priscilla (Chenoweth) Francis. Grandfather, Samuel Francis, b. in England, one of five brothers who came to America settling in Balt. Co. Father, b. in Balt. Co., m. Priscilla, d/o Richard and Elizabeth (Burton) Chenoweth, and had eight children: Elizabeth, widow of Benjamin Coe; Thomas, d. in the eleventh district leaving wife and son, George W.; Maria, unmarried; Priscilla, w/o John Wittle, had two children, Sarah and Mary; Sarah Eliza, m. Daniel C. Gray, both deceased, had four children; Richard C.; Mary J. w/o Augustus Clark; and Charles, d. in Balt. Co. leaving seven children. Richard m. Ellen, d/o Jacob and Ellen Stover, of Balt. Co., in 1852, and had nine children: John C.; R. Lewis, d. in Kansas City, MO; Samuel, Thomas, Robert, Ellen, Florence; and Edwin and Grace, d. in infancy. Grandfather of Ellen, Jacob Stover, had cannery in Harford Co. A farm manager.

224. JUDGE HENRY WALTER - b. 14 Feb. 1831 in Hesse-Darmstadt, Germany, s/o Ludwig and Margaret (Volker) Walter. Father, b. 24 Dec. 1805, same place, sailed for United States 31 Dec. 1846, settling in Balt. City. Mother, d/o Martin Volker, also of Germany, d. in 1860. Ludwig and Margaret had: Henry Walter; Conrad, never m.; John, tailor, lives in eleventh district; and Lewis, m. Minnie Jones, of Balt. and had one daughter. Ludwig d. in Germany. Henry m. Elizabeth Anna Langkam, b. in Germany, in 1856, and had ten children: Lewis, blacksmith, m. Anna B. Latz; John W., carpenter, m. Anna Jasper; George, farmer, m. Anna Smith; Harry, machinist, m. Sena Wright; William F.; Edward; Mary W., w/o John W. Richards, farmer; Anna, w/o William H. Theill, Balt. machininst; Sophia, d. in 1891; Emma, at home. A Democrat. Member of the Evangelical Lutheran Church. Magistrate.

225. ABRAHAM S. BALDWIN, M. D. - b. 4 Jul. 1825 in Harford Co., MD, s/o Silas and Charlotte (Streett) Baldwin, also of Harford. Grandfather, William Baldwin, of Bucks Co., PA, moved to Harford Co., m. Miss Garrison, had three sons, John, Silas and James. Silas, farmer in Harford, m. Charlotte, d/o Col. John Streett, and had eight children: William, d. in 1895, leaving son, Dr. Silas

Baldwin of Balt.; John S.; Thomas and Silas, deceased; Abraham S.; St. Clair, of Harford Co.; Martha E. and Mary E. Abraham m. Ma Elizabeth Streett, 12 Jun. 1866, and had six children: Emma, w/o James H. Quinby, living near Bel Air; Clarence, on the home farm; Alice, Olivia, Elizabeth and Blanche, at home. Member of the Odd Fellows, and the Baltimore County Medical Association. Belongs to the Episcopal Church. A Democrat. Physician in Balt. Co.

226. JOHN CHILCOAT - b. in 1822 in the eighth district, s/o John and Elizabeth (Ensor) Chilcoat. Family founded here in 1727 by brothers John and James of England. Father, b. in the eighth district, m. Elizabeth, d/o George Ensor, of the eighth district, and had: Ensor, lives in Woodbury, MD; George, of Balt.; and John. John m. Mary, d/o William Brooks, of Belfast, MD, in 1848, and had six children; Elizabeth, w/o S. H. Miller, of the seventh district; Thomas, at home; Julia, w/o W. O. Ensor, of Western Run, eighth district; George B., of Belfast, m. Ruth Brooks, d/o Charles Brooks, of Belfast, 27 Apr. 1887 and had one child, Charles; Mollie, w/o I. H. Caruther, of Belfast; and two d. John d. in 1889, was energetic and progressive farmer of the eighth district.

227. WILLIAM L. BEYER - b. 25 Jul. 1859 in Upper Falls, in the eleventh district, s/o Charles A. and Mary A. (Carter) Beyer. Father, b. in Bavaria, Germany, crossed the ocean in 1843, settled in Long Green Valley, eleventh district, a shoemaker, m. Mary A. Carter of Balt., and had five children: Sarah R., w/o Thomas Proctor, of Balt.; William L.; George L, Balt. merchant; and two sons who d. William m. Mary E., d/o Jacob Frederick, in 1882, and had four children: William L, Marguerite A., Mary Ethel and Howard W, who d. in infancy. Members of the Methodist Episcopal Church. Identified with the Shield of Honor at Phoenix, the Improved Order of Red Men and the Independent Order of Mechanics at Baltimore. A Republican. Superintendent of the Mt. Vernon Co. in Phoenix.

228. HON. BENJAMIN N. PAYNE - b. in Harford Co., s/o Benjamin and Jemima (Cathcart) Payne. Father, native of Harford Co., an agriculturist, m. Jemima, d/o William Cathcart, and had ten children: Alice, w/o Edward Norris; Mary, w/o Robert McClung, had eight children; Charlotte, w/o Jesse Risten, tailor of Harford Co.; Willimina, w/o Zenus Hughes, farmer; Josiah, physician in Black Horse, Harford Co., m. Amanda Hutchinson, had two children; John, in the army; and Benjamin. Benjamin m. Mary Cathcart in 1828 and had six children: Jemima C., Harry B., Lillie C., William, Nettie A., and Frank H. Jemima C., m. Nelson Cooper, 12 Nov. 1850, lived in Towson, he d. in 1894; Harry, lives in Chicago, m. Sophia C. Cox, had two children: Lillie, w/o John D. Roe, had daughter, Bessie Payne Roe; William, lives in Utah, m. Mary Thomas, had one child, Ruth; Nettie, at home; Frank, druggist; Benjamin, a farmer, d. in 1885. Member of the Odd Fellows' lodge of Towson. Former judge of the orphans court. a Democrat.

229. GEORGE V. BOWEN - b. 19 Jul. 1848 near Towson, MD, s/o

William and Mary Ann Bowen. Grandfather, Benjamin Bowen, b. 1766, same place, farmer, m. Temperance Ensor, had William, b. 30 Jan. 1805. William, m. Mary Ann Bowen and had six children: Ann Maria, deceased; Frances, d. in infancy; Rebecca Jemima; Charles Wesley, d. in infancy; Laura Isabella, d. at eight; and George V., the youngest. George m. Mary Frances, d/o Joseph and Ruth Ann (Fussell) Gorsuch, of Balt. Co., 3 May 1870; other children of Joseph and Ruth: John R., m. Fannie Getz, lives in Philadelphia; Clara F., w/o Robert Wilson; Ruth Ann, w/o Harry Phipps, of Towson, had two children, Elizabeth J., and Joseph F. who d. in infancy; and Alice E., at home. William and Mary Ann had thirteen children: Charles B., at home; Clara Belle, d. in infancy; John Franklin, m. Ida House, had one child; Annette Stitt, w/o J. Maurice Watkins; Edgar Howard, d. young; William Rice, at home; Laura V., d. in infancy; George C. and Joseph Gorsuch, at home; Walter, d. in childhood; Minnie P. and Robert H., students; and Julia, d. in infancy. George d. 21 Oct. 1896. Member of Odd Fellows' lodge in Towson, John E. Howard Lodge, and the Junior Order of American Mechanics. A Methodist. Devoted his attention to agriculture.

230. HENRY THOMAS - b. 2 Aug. 1813 in Germany, s/o John and Julia (Wolf) Thomas, also of Germany. Came to America in 1837. John and Julia had four children: Henry, and John; Lewis and Caroline, deceased. Brother John, came to Balt. in 1836, m. Margaret E. Ruhl, of Germany, and had: William, Capt. John, Mary A. and Julia A. Henry m., at age twenty-four, Susan Schrader, b. in Germany, and had: Henry S., Rudolph, Mary, Millie, Lizzie and Louisa. Henry S., m. Caroline Sharman in 1868 and had: Harvey, Harry, and Sarah, w/o Harvey Keeney of York Co., PA. Susan d. in 1885, age sixty-one. A Lutheran. A Democrat. Retired harness maker and farmer.

231. UPTON S. BRADY - s/o Samuel and Helen (Slingluff) Brady. Grandfather, Samuel Brady, Sr., m. Ann Mary Proctor Stansbury, and had eight children: Samuel, Jr.; Benjamin F., moved to CA; John W. S., in oil business in Balt.; Jefferson, killed during the Civil war; Thomas S., farmer; Mary, w/o C. C. Sadler; Martha A., w/o Richard H. Woollen; and Margaret, w/o Dr. H. L. Naylor who is deceased. Father, b. in Balt., m. Helen, d/o Upton Slingluff, in 1872, and had four children: Mary P., Samuel P., Bessie and Upton S. Father d. in 1891. A Mason in Mt. Moriah Lodge at Towson. A Democrat. Manages and supervised family estate.

232. REV. THOMAS HENRY WRIGHT - b. 8 Jan. 1840, s/o Robert J. and Elizabeth Ann (Wilhelm) Wright. Great-grandfather, John Wright, b. in England, passenger in the Mayflower, settled in VA, then Harford Co., MD. Grandfather, Thomas Wright, a miller, m. Rachel Jemmison, of Harford Co., and had seven children: John, a miller, m. Anna Tate, and had five children; Thomas, a miller, m. Selina Morrison, had six children; Richard, farmer, m. Anna Price and had eight children, live in York Co., PA; Martha, m. David Krout, live in IA, he d. in Libby prison; Sarah, w/o James Norris, of Harford Co., had large family; Rachel, at home; and

Robert J. Father, b. 25 Aug. 1815 in Harford Co., m. Elizabeth Ann, d/o Henry Wilhelm, in 1836, and had seven children: Catherine, w/o Nathan Ensor, live in TX, had large family; Mary, w/o A. M. Sandborn, of Laconia, NH, has son George, a Baptist minister; Robert, b. 18 Mar. 1843; Sophronia, w/o David Wilhelm; Anna, w/o George Frederick, had five children; and Sylvester, d. at four. Methodists. Thomas m. Maggie A., d/o Elisha Jones, of York Co., PA, and had: Harry Ellsworth, Mary O., Callie G., Ella M., Pearl L. and Mabel D. Harry, m. d/o Judge Sales, had three children, live in San Jose, CA. Mary, w/o B. R. Brown, of Fond Grove, d in 1896 leaving two children. Callie, w/o Elmer B. D. Forest, live near San Jose, CA. Ella, w/o Dr. Hawkins, of Fond Grove. Pearl and Mabel, at home. Pastor of the Methodist Protestant Church of Towson.

233. WILLIAM PARKS - b. 7 Jun. 1826 in the eighth district, s/o John and Margaret (Swartz) Parks. Grandfather, Peter Parks, of England, d. in Balt. Co., age ninety-one. Father, m. Margaret Swartz, of PA, and had: Peter, of the eighth district; William; Adeline, w/o Robert Price; Penelope, w/o Edward Griffith; John and Charles, of the eighth district. Father d. in 1887, mother d. in 1891. William m. Charcillia C. O., d/o John F. Shipley, of the eighth district, about 1858, and had six children: J. Linwood; May, w/o J. T. Kelly; Florence, w/o James B. Crother; William G.; and Effie and Blanch, at home. A Democrat. A Methodist. In business as lime burner.

234. THOMAS J. MILLER - b. in 1846 in the seventh district, s/o Samuel and Mary (Howard) Miller. Father, b. in York Co., PA, m. Mary in York Co., and had: Hattie H.; Thomas J.; E. Olivia, w/o Dr. J. S. Miller, of York, PA, and d. Jun. 1894; and Ida E., w/o William T. Bond, a Balt. business man, and had Mary Melletta. Father, member of the Independent Order of Odd Fellows, and a Republican, d. in 1894, mother d. in 1896. Thomas m. Victoria, d/o Judge John B. Holmes, and had two children: S. Elmer, business man in Monkton; and Mabel F. A Republican. Progressive and energetic farmer of the tenth district.

235. JOHN S. BALDWIN - b. 1818 in Harford Co., MD, s/o Silas and Charlotte (Streett) Baldwin, also of Harford. Paternal grandfather, William Baldwin, native of Bucks Co., PA, m. Miss Garrison, and had three sons, John, Silas and James. Father, b. on homestead in Harford Co., m. d/o Col. John Streett, of Deer Creek, Harford Co., and had: William, d. in 1895, leaving one son, Dr. Silas Baldwin, of Balt.; John S.; Thomas and Silas, deceased; Abraham S., M. D., of Baldwin; St. Clair, of Harford Co.; Martha E. and Mary E. John m. Rachel C., d/o Elisha and Mary (Divers) Bull, and had eight children: Mary, Lottie and R. Cora, d. in childhood; Charles A., Silas E., Thomas C., John R. and Harry W. Charles A., physician in Smithsburg, Washington Co., MD, d. there leaving Leon, Rachel C., Charles and Amy. Thomas C., physician in Stewartstown, York Co., PA. John R., lives in Harford Co., m. and has John R., Jr., and Rachel E. Harry W., m. and had Harry Streett and Mary Margaret. Mother d. in 1890. Member of the Episcopal Church. A Democrat. Pros-

perous farmer of the eleventh district.

236. JESSE DAILY - b. 6 Jun. 1817 in the seventh district, s/o Jesse and Susan (Tracy) Daily, of same district. Grandfather, Jacob Daily, farmer. Jesse and Susan had five children, two living, Jesse and Susan. Father, soldier in war of 1812, a farmer. Jesse m. Elizabeth Masmore, of Balt. Co., and had seven children, two living: Mary Elizabeth, at home; and Jesse N., m. Miss Wilson of the sixth district and had eight children, one is a son Jesse. Member of Middletown Lodge No. 92, I.O.O.F. A Democrat. A Baptist. A millwright and farmer.

237. JOHN M. STEVENSON, M. D. - b. in the city of Balt.; m. Elizabeth Rider, sister of Edward Rider, and had two sons, Allen and H. Burton. Allen, in grain and coal business at Rider, Balt. Co.; H. Burton, physician at Rider, m. Margaret Herman, and had John Metzgel. A Knight Templar Mason. John d. 6 Mar. 1888. Skillful physician and surgeon in Balt.

238. THE WATKINS FAMILY - Samuel M. Watkins had son, John, whose son, John, Jr., was father of John (3d), b. in Balt. Co. in 1802. John B. Watkins, son of John (3d) and Minerva (Slade) Watkins, b. same county in 1838. John B. m. Clara A., d/o John O. Bagley, and sister of Dr. Bagley of Bagley, Harford Co., in 1869, and had four children: Samuel, merchant at Baldwin; Harry Guyton, John and Charles Beale. Family of Clara came to Harford Co. from England in 1783. John B., a Democrat, an Episcopalian, proprietor of a general mercantile store at Baldwin.

239. EDWARD F. JENKINS - b. in 1816 in Balt., s/o Edward and Ann (Spaulding) Jenkins. Edward and Ann had: William Spaulding, Austin, Alfred, Edward F., Thomas Meredith, Charity A., Mary L., Ellen and Harriet. Edward m. Sarah Catherine, d/o Josiah and Elizabeth (Hillen) Jenkins. Josiah and Elizabeth had: John Hillen, Ann, George, Michael, Sarah, Ellen, Thomas and William (who d. in infancy) and Josiah. Edward and Sarah had: Mary Josephine, Annie M., Clara, Mary Augusta, Edward F., and Bessie, all deceased, and Helen, who m. Henry J. Lilly and had: Mary Josephine Jenkins, Edward Joseph Jenkins, Mary Loretta, Austin Jenkins, Mary Edith, George Cromwell and Margaret Jenkins. Edward d. in Aug. 1891 at seventy-three. Retired from the mercantile business in Balt.

240. G. ALBERT MAYS - 21 Sep. 1852 in the seventh district, s/o John P. and Martha E. (Mellor) Mays, also of Balt. Co. John and Martha had: Sarah R., Rachel A., G. Albert, and John F. and William, deceased. Paternal grandfather, John Mays, of English descent. Mark Mellor, maternal grandfather, b. on the Merrie Isle, located in Balt. Co. before the Revolution. G. Albert m. Elizabeth A., d/o William and Harriet (Almony) Sterling, also of seventh district, when twenty-seven, and had: John P., William M., Sterling, Mellor and Mary. A Democrat. Member of the Methodist Episcopal Church. Leading farmer and dairyman of the seventh district.

241. HENRY KNOEBEL - b. 25 Jan. 1841, in city of Balt., s/o Henry and Anna (Riecke) Knoebel. Father, b. in Westphalia, Germany, settled in Balt. in 1834, d. 19 Oct. 1870. Henry m. Anna, d/o John Mueller (of Germany), 13 Oct. 1864 and had: Henry W.; Annie, w/o Joseph Dilworth; and Catherine E., w/o Jesse Dilworth. Henry, b. 9 Oct. 1865, m. Mary, d/o Edward Graefe, 11 Mar. 1891, and had, Henry. Member of the I.O.O.F., and Bethany Lodge of Glen Arm. A Democrat. Proprietor of a general store at the station called Knoebel.

242. GEORGE F. WINEHOLT - b. 7 Oct. 1839 in York Co., PA, s/o Zachariah and Catharine (Hindle) Wineholt, also of York Co. Paternal grandfather, George F. Wineholt, Sr., farmer of York Co. Great-grandfather, George Wineholt, b. Hanover, Germany. George m. Lizzie McCou, of York Co., at twenty-four, and had Leander J. who m. Lizzie Doster, of Balt. Co., and had five children, three living: Nellie, Irwin and George G. Member of the Red Men, Conowingo Tribe No. 74, of Freeland, MD. A Democrat. A Lutheran. Retired from the Northern Central Railroad.

243. JOHN A. BOSLEY - b. in 1808 at Dulaneys Valley in the eighth district, s/o William Bosley of England. Father, youngest s/o Earl of Stafford. John m. Catherine Elizabeth Stansbury, and had: Catherine E., m. (1) Robert McGraham, m. (2) and widowed by Ed L. Venderbury, lives at Balt.; and Mrs. A. D. Brown, of Timonium. Catherine d. in 1848. John d. in Balt. in 1848. Member Baltimore County bar. Eminent and successful lawyer of Balt.

244. THOMAS WRIGHT - b. 29 Aug. 1811, s/o Thomas and Lydia Wright, of England. Father had brothers Robert, Thomas and John. Thomas and Lydia had: Robert, m. Sarah Holland; Ann, w/o Samuel Buckley, of England and had six children; Mary, m. Mr. Frazier; Mrs. Ellen McGee, had two children; John, b. in Balt. Co., m. d/o Robert Jenkins, d. leaving four children; and Thomas. Thomas m. Mary Ann, d/o John B. Wyman. Mary Ann d. 13 Jan. 1896 at eighty-two years. Member of the Methodist Episcopal Church. President and superintendent in family bleaching works company.

245. THOMAS WRIGHT of R. - b. 31 Jan. 1831 in the city of Balt., s/o Robert and Sarah (Holland) Wright. Robert and Sarah had: Robert, m. Mary E. Pierce, of Balt. Co.; Lydia A., w/o Thomas Hook, of Balt. Co.; Rachel, d. in 1839; Mary Ann, d. unmarried; Elizabeth, w/o R. C. McGinn; and Thomas. Thomas m. Frances S. Hall, in 1869, and had: Thomas C., d. at fifteen; Robert E.; Helen E., at home at Brooklandville; John A.; and Frank H., at home. Identified with the Wright bleaching works.

246. EDWARD GRAEFE - b. in 1829 in Muhlhausen, Tueringen, Prussia, crossed the Atlantic in Aug. 1853. Edward m. Caroline Meisner, and had four children: Edward, farmer; Mary, w/o Henry Knoebel; Charles, works for B. & O. Railroad; and William, of Balt. Edward m.(2) Mollie Bomme, in 1873, and had: Henry, Frederick and Minnie. Retired cabinet-maker.

247. ROBERT DILWORTH - b. in the north of Ireland, came to

America at three years. Father, Anthony Dilworth, settled in Lancaster Co., PA, then Kingsville, MD, had: George, of rKingsville; John, of Balt.; Robert; William, of Kingsville; and Susan, w/o William Dilworth, lives near Balt. Robert m. Mary Ramsey, of Lancaster Co., PA, and had: Albert, of Balt.; Harry; Jesse, of Balt.; Joseph; Lillie; Florence; and Robert, who d. in childhood. Son, Harry W., m. Carrie, d/o John G. Holland, in 1892, and had one child, Paul. Member of the I.O.O.F. A Republican. Agriculturist.

248. HENRY T. RITTER - b. 2 Apr. 1827 in the third district, s/o Jacob and Margaret A. (Bell) Ritter. Grandfather, Thomas Ritter, b. near Pikesville; great-grandfather, Thomas Ritter, b. in Germany, settled in Balt. county, farmer. Father, b. in third district, m. Margaret A. Bell, of Balt. Co. and granddaughter of John Bell. Henry m. Alice Dovall, and had: Jacob, plasterer, m. Ida Dempsey; Letitia Alice, m. George Sentz, d. leaving five children; and Margaret, w/o John Earl. Alice d. in 1884. Henry m. (2) Mrs. Martha Smith. An Episcopalian. Blacksmith and merchant near Brooklandville.

249. HON. JAMES A. GARY - s/o James S. Gary, from MA, came to MD when James A. was six. Father established the Alberton cotton mills, d. in 1863. James A. had son, E. Stanley. Identified with the Merchants & Manufacturers' Association, the Citizens' Bank, the Savings Bank of Baltimore, the American Fire Insurance Company, the Consolidated Gas Company, and the Baltimore Trust & Guarantee Company. A Republican. Postmaster-general in President McKinley's cabinet.

250. JOHN DEAVER LUCAS - b. 28 Dec. 1831 in the city of Balt., s/o James Lucas, b. 10 May 1795 in Balt. First of the Lucas family to cross the ocean was Basil, who settled in MD in 1704, his son, Capt. Thomas Lucas, b. 30 Mar. 1712, his son Thomas, b. in England and became a Methodist minister and m. Mary Chamberlain 3 Feb. 1762. John, s/o Thomas and grandfather of John Deaver, b. in 1764. Subject m. Sarah E., d/o Reuben and Susan Thompson, 30 Apr. 1862; Reuben, only s/o an only son, b. in NJ, a sea captain; Reuben m. Susan Bowen Jean, whose mother was a Bowen and grandmother a Percy. John and Sarah had five children: John A. and Ernest N., d. when quite young; George L., m. Mollie M. Dillehunt, had two children; Mary Vickery, w/o Smith Fancher Turner, had one child; and Emma B., at home. John d. 4 Mar. 1893. Keen business man of Balt.

251. HENRY L. BOWEN - b. 11 Nov. 1830 near Towson, s/o John and Loretta (Aulther) Bowen. Grandfather, William Bowen, b. near Towson. Father, b. same place in 1800. Other children of William were: Solomon, d. a young man; Mrs. Ruth Carroll, descendants live in the city of Balt.; and Elizabeth, w/o William Lee, farmer in Balt. Co. Mother, b. near Towson, d/o Jacob Aulther of Germany; her father and only brother, William, were farmers. Some of the eleven children of John and Loretta were: Gerand, mechanic in Towson; Fernandis, gardener of Catonsville; Ann Maria, w/o John Bonsaw, mechanic in Balt., d.; Celia Ann, w/o

John Wesley German, of Towson. Henry m. Mary Ann Parks, of Balt. Co., 15 Sep. 1860, and had three children: Ella, d. in girlhood; Harriet Loretta; and Mary, an artist. Mary Ann d. in Sep. of 1869. Member of the Mt. Moriah Lodge, the Phoenix Royal Arch Chapter and Maryland Commandery No. 1, K.T. A Methodist. Gives his attention to the development and sale of his real-estate interests.

252. HON. WILLIAM PINKNEY WHYTE - b. 9 Aug. 1824. Maternal grandfather, William Pinkney, held many government and diplomatic postions. Held many government positions, some being state comptroller of the treasury, senator, governor, and attorney-general of the state.

253. PHINEAS HARTLEY - b. in 1868 in the second district, s/o Phineas and Deborah (Cornthwait) Hartley. Father, native of same district. Grandfather came to second district from Bucks Co., PA, in early manhood. Phineas and Deborah had six children: Joseph, of Balt.; Samuel, farmer in the eleventh district; Phineas, Wilbur, Elizabeth and Annie. Phineas, Sr., d. in 1894. Member of the Odd Fellows' Society. A Republican. Ancetors were members of the Society of Friends. Conducts grist and sawmill, and is proprietor of a general store.

254. ALBERT M. BROWN - b. in 1825 in Balt., s/o Garrett and Mary (Fenby) Brown, he of Harford Co., MD, and she of England. Grandfather, Thomas Brown, b. in Harford Co. Garrett and Mary had: Thomas H., Alexander E., George F., William H., Albert M., Septimus and Charles E. Albert m. Ellen, d/o Robert Howard, of County Wicklow, Ireland, in 1852, and had: Garrett; Mary H.; Ellen, w/o Charles Hall, of Rossville, Balt. Co.; Percy Howard, of New Orleans; Fletcher S. and Alberta. Son, Garrett, b. in 1853 in Balt., m. Julia Poole of Philadelphia, PA, in 1894. A Democrat. A Presbyterian. Albert d. 25 Oct. 1880. Retired dry-goods merchant in the city.

255. HARRISON HOLLIDAY EMICH - b. in 1862 at Reistertown, Balt. Co., s/o Henry F. and Mary Sophia (Hiser) Emich, he of the city of Balt. and she of Owings Mills. Father, a harness-maker, had one brother, Nicholas. Henry and Sophia had: Harrison, and Nannie Hiser, d. at eighteen. Harrison m. Charlotte C., d/o Joseph Passano, of Balt. in Apr. of 1887, and had: Nannie R., Harris C. and Charles C. Member of Sharon Lodge, A.F.&A.M., the Mt. Zion Lodge of Odd Fellows, and Arlington Council, Junior Order of American Mechanics. Belongs to the Methodist Episcopal Church South. A Democrat. A harness-maker, with stores in Arlington, Pikesville, and Pimlico.

256. THOMAS G. BLOOM - b. in 1863 in Balt. Co., s/o David and Melinda (Albert) Bloom. Father, Balt. Co. farmer, d. in 1892, age fifth-seven. David and Melinda had seven children: Thomas; Mary, w/o William Smith, of Balt. Co.; Isaac, contractor in the city; Ida, w/o Thomas Bailey; Maggie M,; Jennie, w/o Frank Most; and Edith, at home. Thomas m. Emma Plowman, of Balt. in 1886 and had a son, Millard P. Attends Methodist Episcopal Church.

Connected with the State Mutual Assurance Company and the Junior
Order of American Mechanics. Former carpenter, now has general
store in Mt. Washington.

257. WILLIAM MOORE ISAAC - b. 12 Mar. 1834 on a farm in Anne
Arundel Co., now Howard Co., s/o Zedekiah Moore and Mary R.
(Ware) Issac. Father, b. in same county 12 Jul. 1808, d. in
Ellicott City in 1892, had three brothers: Thomas J., a mechanic
who d. at eighty-three; Andrew J., is eighty; and George W., a
blacksmith, d. at eighty-five. Grandfather, John Isaac, b. in
Anne Arundel Co. in 1777, a millwright and farmer, m. Elizabeth
Moore. Mother, b. 12 May 1811, in Balt. Co., now Carroll Co.,
d/o Elias and Mary Ware. Elias d. at age seventy-eight; Elias
and Mary had three sons: Elias, Jr., Henry and Asbury. Zedekiah
and Mary had: Martha Ann, of Balt.; Gertrude, w/o Benjamin C.
Sunderland, of Howard Co.; and William. William m. Ella
Phillips, of Harrisonville, 29 Sep. 1859, and had: Amy P.; Mary
W.; Eleanor; Randolph Moore and Zedekiah Howard, of the Balt. Co.
bar. Member of Mt. Moriah Lodge of Masons at Towson, the
Maryland Commandery No. 1, K.T., the Odd Fellows. A Democrat.
Raised Methodist, connected with the Protestant Episcopal Church.
Held many offices, including furst comptroller of the United
States treasury at Washington, deputy in the fifth auditor's
office, deputy registrar of wills for Balt. Co., deputy clerk for
Balt. Co., president of the school board, clerk of Balt. Co.,
chief deputy United States marshal for the district of MD.

258. HON. WILLIAM H. CURTIS - b. in 1836 at My Lady's Manor, s/o
John S. Curtis. Traces ancestry back to Daniel Curtis, who came
from England a few years before the Revolutionary war and settled
in city of Balt., moved to the country, had two sons: Joseph,
drifted westward, and William Curtis, b. at My Lady's Manor, m.
Miss Sheppard, lived in the tenth district, had: Rachel, John S.,
Levi, Nancy, Elizabeth, Eli, William, Thomas and Eliza. Father,
b. in 1795 in Balt. Co., m. Miss Anderson, had six children:
Amanda, w/o Jackson Wilson; May; ELiza, w/o John Pierson; Charles
H. C.; Matilda, w/o William Prince; and William H. Great-grandfather lived to be over one hundred years, the grandfather,
ninety-nine, and the father, eighty. William m. Annie Gunther,
and had: Estelle, w/o Howard Marshall, of Sweet Air, MD; Roscoe
C. and Luella. Member of the Independent Order of Odd Fellows.
A Republican. Elected to state legislature in 1875.

259. JOHN W. HARRISON, M. D. - b. 11 Feb. 1869 in Prince George
Co., VA, s/o William H. and Annie A. (Boisseau) Harrison, of same
county. Grandfather, Richard M. Harrison, b. same county;
distant relative of President William H. Harrison. William and
Annie also had two daughters, who live in VA. John m. Fannie R.,
d/o John T. Gwyn, in 1891, and had three children: Mary Carrey,
Annie B. and William H. Member of the Episcopal Church. Physician of the twelfth district.

260. JUDGE W. W. JOHNSON - b. in Bay View, Cecil Co., MD, s/o H.
C. and Rachel (Moore) Johnson, he of Bay View, she of Elk Neck,
Cecil Co. Paternal grandfather, Jethro Johnson, manufactured

woolen goods. Father, owned the Providence Woolen Mills, at Bay View. H. C. and Rachel had three children: W. W.; Rev. H. S., Methodist Episcopal minister, in Powell Co., MD; and Julia, at home. W. W. m. Laura, d/o Adam and Emma Oesterla, of Balt., and had two children: W. W., Jr., and Gladys M. Member of the Junior Order of American Mechanics, No. 148, and the Catonsville Hose Company. A Republican. Justice of the peace for District No. 1, and station agent for the Philadelphia, Wilmington & Baltimore Railroad, at Catonsville.

261. JOHN T. B. PARLETT - b. 11 Apr. 1828 in Balt. Co., s/o Moses and Temperance Parlett. Father and grandfather, William, b. same place. Great-grandfather, William Parlett, Sr., m. a French lady. Moses m. Temperance Kidd, nee Bosley, and had two children: William J. B., m. Elizabeth Bond, and had seven children, three living, John T. B., Margaret and Matilda; and John T. B. Father, a farmer, d. in 1847, mother d. in 1871, aged eighty-three. John m. Mary J., d/o Frederick and Elizabeth (Oler) Smith, of Balt. Co., in 1852, and had no children. Frederick and Elizabeth had: Susan, w/o William Hiss; James, d. wealthy and unmarried; Jacob, farmer in Texas, MD, m. Margaret Parlett and had two children; Mary, w/o John Burton; Elizabeth, w/o William Price, and had seven children; George A., farmer, m. Margaret Knox in 1852 and had four children, had five more by second marriage; Frederick J., farmer, m. Louisa Waddell, had three children; William, farmer, m. Martha Mayze; John T., m. Charlotte Parlett and had six children; Ann Rebecca, w/o Elijah Clinton; and Oliver S., m. Rebecca Wooder, has one child. Members of St. Andrew's Episcopal Church. John d. at age fifty-seven. Former treasurer of Balt. Co. and county commissioner.

262. GEORGE B. B. COALE - b. 28 Jul. 1851 near Ruxton, s/o Samuel W. and Emma (Bowen) Coale. Grandfather, William Coale, came from England, farmer in Balt. Co., m. Elizabeth Bowen, b. in Balt. Co., d/o John Bowen. Father, a farmer, b. 5 May 1805 in same house as George, m. Emma, d/o John M. Bowen, of Balt. Co., and had ten children: Elizabeth Ann, w/o William A. Lee, had ten children; Charles H., m. Myra Lee and had eight children; John W., d. at twenty-four; Samuel Amos and Mary Emma, d. in childhood; Laura V., w/o Joseph Ross, had four children; Boscomb R. and Grace M., d. quite young; and George B. B. Father, connected with Hunt's Methodist Episcopal Church, d. at home in Jan., 1880. George m. Zipporah A., d/o Capt. McLane Bush, 25 Jan. 1883, and had four children: George H.; Samuel Carroll; Jessie E., d in childhood; and Ellen Isabel. Capt. Bush, of eastern MD, an old sea captian. A Methodist.

263. GEORGE J. FASTIE - b. 13 Aug. 1835 in Balt., s/o George and Mary (Walter) Fastie. Father, b. in Holland, m. Mary Walter, and had five children: George J.; Julia; John, d. unmarried; Theodore; and Washington, of Balt., m. and had three children, Howard, Arthur and Maud. George m. Eliza Gamphor, of Germany, in Jun. 1861, and had seven children: Annie, w/o John C. Eichner, of Balt.; Minnie; Ida; Lillie; William F.; and two who d. in infancy. Members of the Lutheran Church. A Democrat.

264. JOHN FELTER - b. in Oct. 1855 near Frankfort, Germany, s/o George and Catherine Felter. John m. Irene, d/o Leonard Hartzell, of Balt., 21 Nov. 1884, and had: Helen C., George L., John C. and Robert E. John is a Methodist and Irene is a Catholic. Member of the Masons, Heptasophs and Red Men. A Democrat. General contractor.

265. FRANCIS S. ERDMAN - b. 15 Aug. 1842 on Harford road, Balt., s/o John and Mary A. (Hoddinott) Erdman. Father, b. near same place, a blacksmith, then farmer, d. in 1876, age seventy-three. Grandfather, Peter Erdman, b. in Germany, settled in Balt. Co., had nine children. Mother, b. in England, d/o Simon Hoddinott, a locksmith. John and Mary had eight children: Peter G., farmer, d. in May 1897, leaving a large family; John, Jr., of Balt.; Frederick, in produce business in the city; Gottlieb H. and Charles are farmers in Balt. Co.; Henry L., lives in Canton, OH; Barbara E., m. Jacob Lamley and d. at forty-eight; and Francis S. Francis m. Mary A. Graves, whose father was from St. Mary's Co., MD, and had three children: Rose, Harry S., and one who d. in boyhood. Member of the Waverly Lodge No. 123, A.F.& A.M., the Ancient Order of United Workmen and the Corinthian Lodge No. 10, I.O.O.F. A Methodist Protestant, wife belongs to the Universalist Church. A Democrat. In meat business in winter and farms in summer.

266. ELI GAMBRILL - b. in the ninth district, s/o John and Abigail (Green) Gambrill, he of Anne Arundel Co. and she of Balt. John and Abigail had twelve children: Elizabeth, w/o Richard Hook; Nelson, d. in Balt.; Juliet, w/o Henry Leef; William, d. in Balt. Co.; Augustus, of Howard Co.; Miriam, w/o Thomas Davis, of Philadelphia, where she d.; John, d. in CA; Eli; Mrs. Adaline Ward, of Balt.; Elmira, w/o Thomas Thompson, of Balt.; Louisa, d in childhood; and B. Franklin, d. in VA, leaving a family. Eli m. Hester Ann, d/o Isaiah Baker, and had six children: Alice, w/o W. Henry Harrison Edwards, of Wilmington, DE.; Melville, of Havre de Grace, Harford Co.; Robert; Ella, w/o William Billingsley, farmer; Elizabeth, w/o John Billingsley; and Edward, contractor and builder. Members of the Methodist Episcopal Church South. A Democrat. Leading farmer of Germantown.

267. ALBERT OTTO - b. 1 Mar. 1859 in Lauraville, s/o John W. and Barbara (Sastler) Otto. Father, b. in Germany, a Democart, d. in 1877. Grandfather, a confectioner in Balt. Mother, b. in Germany, d. in 1894. John and Barbara had six children: Henry, of the twelfth district; John, lived on Bel Air road, d. in Mar., 1897; Albert; Leonard, farmer in VA; Sophia, single, lives with Albert; and Lizzie, w/o Jaco Krash, farmer in the twelfth district. Connected with the Methodist Episcopal Church South. A Prohibitionist. Raises smaller fruits and vegetables for his stand at Lexington market.

268. PETER LINK - b. 18 Jan. 1836 in Hesse, Germany. Came to Balt. at age sixteen. Peter m. Mary Lownan and had Kate, w/o Edward Hahn. Member of the Odd Fellows' lodge. A Lutheran.

Progressive and enterprising business man of the city.

269. ALFRED CROSSMORE - b. in 1825 in Harford Co., s/o William and Mary (Staggers) Crossmore, he of PA, she of France. Paternal grandfather, b. in Germany, m. in Philadelphia, moved to Muncy, PA, son William b. there. Father, a tanner. William and Mary lived in Harford Co., had seven children: John, d. in Cecil Co., leaving a family; William, d.; George, d. in CA; Alfred; Theodore, d. in Balt. Co., leaving a family; Jacob, d. leaving a family in PA; and Oliver, d. leaving a son, William, of Balt. Alfred m. Martha, d/o James Hawkins, in 1855 and had six children: Alice; Jennie, w/o Rev. J. F. Gray, Methodist Episcopal minister of Balt. Co.; Cornelia, Carrie; William, merchant of Upper Falls, MD; and Wade H. Member of the Washington Lodge, I.O.O.F. Supports Democratic party. Owns canning factory.

270. JOSEPH SNYDER - b. Dec. 1839 in Germany. Mother d. when Joseph was very young. Came to America with father and grandparents. Grandfather, John Snyder. Joseph m. Annie Waters in 1860 and had three children: Joseph H., Mary A. and Catherine. Joseph m. (2) Elizabeth Fisher, and had: Josephine, Mary L., John and Helen. Supports Republican party. Member of the Catholic Church, of which Father Jordan is pastor. Iron worker on the corner of Elliott street and Bouldin avenue.

271. N. R. GERRY, M. D. - b. 25 Jun. 1832 in Rowlandsville, Cecil Co., MD. N. R. m. Margaret E. Fusting, 8 Sep. 1858, and had seven children: Agnes; Joseph P., d.; Philip; James L., attorney in Chicago; Charles F.; Lillie A., teacher in Washington; and C. N. R., a student. Physician of Catonsville.

272. HENRY HOEN - b. in Westerwald, Germany, s/o Gerhardt Hoen. Father, came to MD in 1843, returned to Germany, and d. Henry m. Mary Glynn, in 1849 and had: George; Mary, w/o Charles Muller; Josephine, w/o Herman Muller; Alma, w/o William Buckles; and John, traveling salesman. Henry d. in Mar. 1893. Wife and children members of the Catholic Church. Retired proprietor of a printing and lithographing establishment in Balt.

273. CHARLES S. GRANT - b. 25 Dec. 1840 in Aberdeen, Scotland. Charles m. Isabella Middletown, and had six children: William M., Isabella R., Charles S., Jr., Archibald, Jane A. and Mary L. Member of the Odd Fellows' Lodge No. 111, of Granite. A Presbyterian. General manager of the Filford Waterville Granite Company, at Granite.

274. WILLIAM A. LEE - b. in 1857 at Govanstown, s/o J. Wesley Lee. Father, native of same county, postmaster of Towson. William m. Emma W., d/o Dr. James H. Jarrett, in 1881, and had four children: James H., Martin L,., Julia A. and Marguerite. Member of the Independent Order of Odd Fellows and the Junior Order of American Mechanics. A Democrat. Proprietor of J. W. Lee & Son.

275. FRANCIS ADY - b. in Harford Co., s/o Solomon Ady. Francis

m. Caroline Wheeler and had two children in Harford Co., Christiana and Francis M., moved to Parkville, Balt. Co., and had: Benjamin W.; Elizabeth, w/o George T. Thompson, and lives in Philadelphia; Henrietta, d.; Jennie M., w/o Samuel W. Brinker, of Easton, PA; and William H. Benjamin, lives in Long Green Valley, a Democrat, m. Annie E., d/o Thomas Parlett, in 1880 and had six children: Francis H., Laura, Bessie, Annie E., Benjamin W. and Cassandra M. Francis, proprietor of a hotel at Cub Hill, d. at home on 7 May 1865.

276. JAMES H. S. JARRETT, M. D. - b. 29 Nov. 1860 at Jarrettsville, Harford Co., MD, s/o Hon. J. H. Jarrett, M.D. James m. Lillie, d/o George B. and Emma Catherine (Brooke) Lessig, of Pottstown, PA, 26 Jan. 1893, and had a son, Brooke Lessig. Member of the Medical & Chirurgical Faculty of the State of Maryland, the American Medical Association and the Baltimore County Medical Society. Physician of Towson.

277. EUGENE F. RAPHEL - b. 6 Oct. 1845 in the eleventh district, s/o Stephen Joseph and Mary A. (McAtee) Raphel. Grandfather, Stephen Raphel, b. in Marseilles, France, came to Harford Co. in 1792, naturalized in 1795, had sons, Stephen, and Amedee, located in Havana, Cuba. Father, Stephen Joseph Raphel, b. in 1789 on the Island of Ste. Lucie, s/o Stephen and Elizabeth (Fressenjat) Raphel, m. Mary A. , d/o Capt. Henry and Teresa (Wheeler) McAtee, of Harford Co. Henry and Teresa were m. in 1799 and had: Ignatius, George I., Lewis, Sylvester, Clement, Mary A., Teresa and Elizabeth A. Teresa, d/o Ignatius Wheeler. Captain Henry's father, George McAtee, m Elizabeth, d/o William Hamilton, of Charles Co., MD in 1760 and had: Henry, b. 1769; Jane, b. 1771; Clement, b. 1773; George and Mary, went to KY; Henrietta Maria, b. 1776, m. Benjamin Wheeler, had several children; Ann, b. 1777; Samuel b. 1778; Leonard, b. 1780, m. Julia, sister of Hamilton Morgan; Mary Ann, b. 1782, m. Francis I. Wheeler; Sarah, b. 1784, m. John Butler; Francis and George. Stephen and Elizabeth had six children: Stephane, lives in Lourdes, France; Stephen Amedee, m., lives in Kansas City, KS; Anna Teresa, now Sister Josephine in the Convent of the Visitation at Frederick, MD; Henry, d. in Havana; Joseph Alexis, m. Miss Zell in Havana and d. at Bordeauz, France; and Eugene Fressenjat. Eugene m. Janet Braden, of Loudoun Co., VA, about 1870, and had eight children: Noble, Eugene, Alexis, Florence, Henry, Janet and two who d. in infancy. A Democrat. A Catholic. Farmer of the eleventh district.

278. HORATIO BURTON - b. in Balt. Co., s/o John Burton. Horatio m. Sarah J., d/o James Woolf, about 1840, and had eight children: James A., of Balt.; Eliza R., w/o Isaiah S. Watkins and lives in the eleventh district; Horatio, Jr., b. 4 Mar. 1848, a Democrat; Edmond A., of Balt. Co.; Oliver, lives in Denver, CO; C. Owen, lives in Balt.; Harry; and Uriah, who d. in infancy. Horatio d. 11 Jul. 1889; wife d. 8 Mar. 1861. Business man of Balt.

279. JOHN W. BURTON - b. 15 Apr. 1822 in the eleventh district, s/o James and Ellen (Watkins) Burton. Great-grandfather, James Burton, came to MD from England. Grandfather, John Burton, of

Balt. Co., had son, James. John m. Eliza R., d/o James Woolf and granddaughter of James Woolf, Sr., who came to Balt. from England. John and Eliza had five children: James Woolf, physician, d. in 1881; George Henry, farmer; Robert, pharmacist in Philadelphia; Charles, farmer; and John Eugene, attorney in Towson. Member of the Methodist Episcopal Church. A Democrat.

280. MRS. MARGARET I. H. WEBSTER - b. in Brooklyn, NY, d/o William and Sophia Suter (Holland) Lee, he a native of ME, she of England. William d. in 1850; Sophia d. in 1844 in New York. Margaret m. in 1845, Henry Elliott Browne, attorney of New York City, and had Holland Lee Browne. Henry d. in New York City in 1850. Margaret m. (2) Dr. George W. Webster, of Balt. Co., in 1855, had three children, all d. Grandfather of the late Dr. Webster, Joseph Thornburgh. Member of the Episcopal Church.

281. THOMAS ARMACOST - b. in the seventh district, s/o Melchor and Elizabeth (Foster) Armacost, he of Carroll Co. and she of Balt. Co. Paternal grandfather, b. in Germany, came to America with parents. Thomas m. Lizzie Hoffman, also of Balt. Co., and had six children: Emory, Grace, William M., Carrie, Johnnie and Edna Pear. A Democrat. Agriculturist of the seventh district.

282. RICHARD F. GUNDRY, M. D. - b. 21 Apr. 1866 in Dayton, OH, s/o Dr. and Mrs. Richard Gundry, Sr. Richard m. Catherina A. Hines, of Kent Co., 29 Oct. 1895. Member of the Athenia Club, the Country Club, of Catonsville, the Baltimore Neurological Society, the Clinical Society of Maryland, the American Medico-Psychological Society, and the Medical and Chirurgical Faculty of Maryland. With mother, established the Richard Gundry Home for treatment of private patients with mental diseases.

283. HON. ELI SCOTT - b. 22 Jun. 1830 in the eighth district near Cockeysville, s/o Eli and Elizabeth (Cole) Scott. Grandfather, Thomas, b. in Balt. Co., a farmer, member of the Quaker Church. Father, b. in 1795, on Western Run, near Cockeysville, a Quaker turned Baptist, had brother John who lived to ninety-three. Mother, d/o Abram Cole, farmer near Black Rock Baptist meeting house, b. in 1792 and d. at sixty-nine. Eli and Elizabeth had twelve children, some: Eleanor R., lived with daughter in East Orange, NJ, d. in Dec. of 1896, widow of Joseph Gist, a Balt. merchant; Thomas M., deceased, farmer; Abram C.; Eliza, m. Harvey Merriman, both d.; Cecilia A., m. Dr. John Bracken, of OH, where both d.; Elizabeth Ann, m. John M. Wells, of Wellsburg, WV, both d. in Balt.; Arianna H.; Ruth C., m. William Barnes, of Wellsburg, WV, moved to St. Louis, both d.; Sarah C., m. Richard Mathews, d. in Balt.; Julia D., widow of Campbell Starr, of Wellsburg, WV, lives in East Orange, NJ; Lewis C., Balt. business man til d. Eli m. Mrs. Alberta (Richstein) Clifford, widow of John Clifford, and d/o George Richstein, in 1854; Richstein family of German ancestry. Alberta identified with the German Reformed Church, and Eli with the Old School Baptist Church. First a Whig, then a Republican. Chief judge of the orphans' court of Balt. Co.

284. W. A. SLADE - b. 20 Jan. 1831 in the tenth district; m. Belinda T. Slade, in 1861, and had one son, H. M., a physician in Reisterstown. A Democrat. An Episcopalian. Ex-sheriff of the county and ex-postmaster at Reisterstown.

285. CAPT. WILLIAM F. VEASEY - b. in 1836 in Somerset Co., MD, s/o William H. and Sarah (Richards) Veasey. Grandfather, James Veasey, b. in Newtown, MD. Father, b. in Worcester Co. in 1808, d. in Jan. of 1867 at Pocomoke. Mother, b. in Somerset Co., d/o Joseph Richards, d. in 1846. William and Sarah had: Isaac N., owns a vessel at Pocomoke; Thomas J., agent for the Baltimore, Chesapeake & Atlantic Railroad Company; William F.; and Mrs. Elizabeth Bonovel, of Pocomoke. William m. (1) Laura Coston, b. and d. in Somerset, MD. William m. (2) Emily Dryden, also of Somerset and had five children: H. James, quartermaster on the Tivoli; Austin Henry, on the same boat; Marion T., Sadie and Louise. Member of the Heptasophs, the Ancient Order of United Workmen and the Royal Arcanum, all of Salisbury. Commander of the Tivoli.

286. GEORGE W. WHITE - b. 7 Nov. 1865 in the twelfth district, s/o William and Mary M. (Barber) White. Father, agriculturist, b. in Ireland, m. Mary, of Balt. Co., and had six children: Mary E., w/o Lambert R. McDonald; Dora, w/o Charles P. Ehrhardt, farmer; Alice w/o William Ehrhardt, produce dealer in Balt.; Emma S., w/o John S. Martell; Kate, w/o Aaron H. Foard; and George W. George m. Stella Fuller, in 1891, and had: Ethel, Georgia and Milton. Member of the Lauraville Council No. 100, Junior Order of American Mechanics. Belongs to the Methodist Episcopal Church. A Republican. Cultivates and manages a farm in the twelfth district.

287. CAPT. WILLIAM H. PORTER - b. 6 Jul. 1850 in Balt., s/o William F. and Amanda (Alexander) Porter. Father, b. on the eastern shore. Mother, native of Balt. William and Amanda had: William H.; Rose, of Cincinnati, OH; Alberta, w/o Peter Wehr, of Portland, OR; Mary E., w/o Lee Smith, of Cincinnati; and Emma, w/o James White, Balt. Co. florist. Both parents d. when William was young. William m. Emma S. Jacob, of Balt., 29 Dec. 1875, and had five children: Elizabeth J, Rose, Emma, Mary and William F. Both parents of Emma b. on the eastern shore. Member of the American Legion of Honor. A Republican. Master of the Virginia, belonging to the Bay Line.

288. JOHN SCOTT - b. 13 Dec. 1851 in Balt., s/o William J. and Mary A. (McCormick) Scott. Father, b. in Balt., a carpenter and builder, d. in Balt. 11 Sep. 1897, aged seventy-two. Grandfather, William Scott, Sr., b. in the north of Ireland, settled in Balt., d. at eighty-four. Mother, b. in Ireland, d. in 1893, aged fifty-eight. William and Mary had seven children. John m. (1) Elizabeth, d/o Thomas Bell of Balt., in Waverly, MD; Elizabeth d. in 1892; Thomas Bell d. in 1897; John and Elizabeth had six children: Annie, Jennie, Mary, Ella, Laura and Daisy. John m. (2) Annie, d/o Henry Norman, of Balt. Member of the Northern Central Building & Loan Association. A Republican.

Foreman of the freight car repair department of the Northern Central Railroad.

289. EDWARD J. RUTTER - b. 4 Apr. 1872 in the city of Balt., s/o Edward J. and Harriet Rebecca (Norwood) Rutter. Father, of Balt. Co., farmer, and contractor, d. 11 Mar. 1872, a Democrat, member of the Methodist Episcopal Church. Grandfather, Edward J. Rutter, d. 6 Mar. 1844. Mother, b. 15 Jul. 1846 in Balt. Co., d/o Giles Norwood. Edward and Harriet had four children; Edward; Harry, d. at eighteen; and Isabella Alexander and Maud, d. of scarlet fever. Father d. about a month before b. of Edward. Member of the Towson Lodge of Odd Fellows. A Democrat. Partner with William E. Stansbury in the livery business.

290. JOHN S. GREEN, M. D. - b. 12 Sep. 1856 in Harford Co., MD, s/o Joshua R. and Sarah R.(Rankin) Green. Paternal grandfather, Elisha Green. Father from tenth district, mother from the eleventh. Joshua and Sarah had seven children: Moses, John S., Mary E. (m. and left two children); R. Corville, Sarah R., Lillie May and Joshua R. Father d. 1 May 1892. John m. Eleanor L. Baldwin, in 1883, and had: Ida May, d.; Edith R., Maurice B., Eleanor L., Charles H., John S and Mary E. Member of the Independent Order of Odd Fellows. A Presbyterian. A Democrat. Physician at Long Green.

291. WILLIAM MARSHALL DAVIS - b. 12 Jan. 1827 in Balt. Co., s/o Joseph and Mary (Mask) Davis. Father, of Lancaster Co., PA, a miller. Grandfather, Jesse Davis, of English descent, settled in Balt. Co. Mother, of Balt. and of English descent. Joseph d. at age sixty-nine, Mary d. in 1895. Joseph and Mary had seven children: Thomas and Joseph P., served in the Civil war; Charles, lives in Cecil Co., MD. William m. Caroline A. Davis, in 1850, in Petersburg, VA and had one child, Warren W., an engineer on the Northern Central Railroad. Caroline d. in 1857. William m. (2) Georgiana Buckingham, of Balt. City. Member of Columbia Lodge, I.O.O.F., the Warren Lodge, A.F. & A.M., the Knight Templar Commandery. Belongs to the Emanuel Methodist Episcopal Church. Foreman of the machine shops of the Northern Central Railroad.

292. WILLIAM KLUTH - b. in 1854 in Germany, s/o Frederick and Elizabeth (Hak) Kluth, also of Germany. Mother d. in 1894. Other children of Frederick and Elizabeth were: Tena, d. at twenty-five; two sons d. in Germany; Frederick, d. at thirty-six; Herman, business man of Balt.; Mina, w/o Charles Liebnow; Augusta, w/o Peter Brooks; and Lizzie, w/o Lewis Trone. William m. Augusta Walther, of Balt., and had five children: Emma, William, Charles, Frederick and Harry. Member of the Cedar Conclave No. 6 and the Good Brother at Catonsville. A Democrat. A Lutheran. A wheelwright with a general carriage and horseshoeing shop in Arlington.

293. HON. GEORGE W. WARRENBERGER - b. 22 Feb. 1850, in Balt., s/o Peter M. and Catherine (Fisher) Warrenberger, he of Switzerland, and she of Balt. Peter and Catherine had nine children.

Father d. 13 Sep. 1896 in Balt. Father and mother of Peter d. at eighty-six and eighty-four. George m. Susan, d/o William A. Trumbo, 20 Apr. 1881, in Balt., and had five children: Ella, Albert, Clara, Mabel and George W., Jr. Member of the Methodist Episcopal Church. A Republican. In charge of the stock department of Day, Jones & Co., and served on the state legislature from the sixteenth ward of the third district. Also member of the city council from the sixteenth ward.

294. GEORGE F. CLARKE - b. in Balt., s/o Martin and Jane (Farrell) Clarke. Father b. in County Mayo, Ireland, a grocer, d. in May 1881. Mother d. 21 Sep. 1891. Martin and Jane had seven children. George m. Cecelia G., d/o Thomas King, in Balt., and had one child, M. Manly. Member of the Shield of Honor, the Heptasophs, the Benevolent Protective Order of Elks, and the Catholic Benevolent Legion. A Democrat. Proprietor of family undertaking business at No. 1707 Bank street.

295. NATHANIEL P. CORBIN - b. in 1823 in the ninth district, s/o William W. and Rebecca (Hancock) Corbin. Paternal grandfather, William W., b. in Balt. Co., s/o William Corbin, b. in England. Father, b. in 1789 in Balt. Co., a farmer, m. Miss Hancock, descendant of John Hancock. Nathaniel m. Rachel F., d/o George Evans, of Balt. in Dec. 1846. Rachel d. in Nov. of 1892. A Republican. Judge of election of the district, and an agriculturist.

296. ANDREW BROWN - b. 16 Mar. 1827 in County Fermanagh, Ireland, s/o Edward and Mary (Crawford) Brown, of the same county. Grandfather, John Brown, lived near Belfast, Ireland, moved to County Fermanagh. Maternal grandfather, Andrew Crawford, a carpenter. Edward, Mary and eleven children left Liverpool in 1837 on the Chieftain, arrived at Balt. after eight weeks. Edward d. at sixty-eight, as did Mary; buried in Greenmount Cemetery, Balt. Andrew m. Jane B., d/o John and Elizabeth (Holmes) Stewart, of Hollywood, County Down, Ireland, on 16 Mar. 1848, in Balt. and had: Mary E., w/o W. Stewart, of Balt.; Mrs. Margaret F. Mallory, of Balt.; Edward, d. in Balt. at seventeen; John H., civil engineer in Balt.; Mrs. Jennie Ennis, of Philadelphia; Sallie, w/o Thomas T. Boswell, of Balt.; Andrew J.; and William Stewart, merchant in Balt. Grandfather of Jane, John Stewart, Sr., farmer in Ireland. John, a merchant tailor, and Elizabeth Stewart brought family the United States in 1835 on the Edwin and settled in Balt., where both d. John and Elizabeth had eight children, Jane being the fourth. Member of the Royal Arch Masons, the St. John's Lodge No. 34, A.F.& A.M., and the Phoenix Chapter No. 7, R.A.M.. Belongs to the Trinity Episcopal Church. A Democrat. Contractor in bridge and vessel building.

297. EDWARD EVERETT HARGEST - b. 1 Nov. 1864 in Balt., s/o Thomas and Urith Ann (Leach) Hargest. Father, native of Balt., farmer, a Republican. Thomas and Urith had nine children: Thomas Jefferson, farmer in Balt. Co.; William Henry Harrison, farmer; George Washington, Balt. business man; Andrew Jackson, of Balt.

city; Edward E.; Charles Francis Marion, farmer; James Monroe, business man in the city; Mary Elizabeth, w/o James D. Robb; and Catherine E., Mrs. E. Tupper Robb. Edward m. Augusta Wistland, of Balt., in 1892. Member of the Methodist Church. Member of the firm of Hargest & Fitzsimmons, proprietors of the horseshoeing shop at Arlington.

298. J. PERRCY WADE, M. D. - b. in 1868 in VA, s/o John J. and Mary A. (Chapman) Wade. Paternal grandfather, planter of VA. Father, b. in VA, lawyer, m. Mary A., d/o Gen. A. A. Chapman, and had: William A., attorney of Balt.; Dr. James T.; George B., of Balt.; Walter S., of Birmingham, AL; H. B., of Balt. and J. Percy. Member of the Medical and Chirurgical Faculty of Baltimore, the Medical and Surgical Society, the American Medico and Psychological Society, the American Medical Society, the Maryland Neurological Society, and the Alumni Association of the College of Physician and Surgeons. A Presbyterian. Superintendent of the Maryland Hospital for the Insane, near Catonsville.

299. CAPT. DANIEL M. DAVIS - b. 22 Sep. 1842 in Stafford Co., VA, s/o James L. and Salina (Brown) Davis, also of the Old Dominion. Great-grandfather, b. in Wales, came to VA. Brown family of Scotch-Irish descent. Grandfather, John Brown, VA planter. Father, b. 1809 in VA, where he d. in 1878. Mother d. a young woman. James and Salina had three children. Daniel m. Sarah Bates in Fredericksburg, and had eight children: Florence, Minnie, Winnie; Charles, a business man in Fredericksburg; William, deals in tinware and stoves in Fredericksburg; John, Daniel M., Jr. and Walter. Sarah d. in 1891 in Fredericksburg. Member of the Fredericksvurg Lodge No. 4, the Myrtle Lodge No. 50, I.O.O.F., of Fredericksburg, and with Morey Camp at Fredericksburg, Confederate Volunteers of America. A Democrat. Belongs to the Baptist Church of Fredericksburg. Master of the Essex, on the Weems line, considers Balt. his headquarters, but makes his home in Fredericksburg, VA.

300. JAMES GILMORE - b. 25 May 1853 in Balt., s/o James and Nancy (Campbell) Gilmore. Father, b. in Ireland, moved to England, then America, first in St. Mary Co., MD, then Balt. Mother, native of Balt. Co. Half-sister of James is Elizabeth, Mrs. John Richards, deceased. James m. Agnes Virginia Young in 1875, and had one son, John Campbell. Agnes, on her maternal side, related to the Colgates. Member of the Masonic Order, the Independent Order of Odd Fellows, the Red Men, the Heptasophs, and the Shield of Honor. A Democrat.

301. GEORGE S. CHAIMS, LL. B., M. D. - b. 13 Jamuary 1864 in Austria, s/o Morris and Rachel (Backman) Chaims, also of Austria; both families are old German. George came to America in 1881 via Bremen to Balt. George m. Cecelia Katter, of Russia, in Russia, and had six children: Mary, Morris, Sadie, Clara, Lizzie and Charles. Member of the Alumni Society of the Baltimore University School of Medicine. Physician at No. 246 South Broadway. Chief of clinic and assistant to the professor of gynecology in the Baltimore University School of Medicine.

302. R. H. REICHE, M. D. - b. in 1837 in Lippestadt, Westphalia, s/o Christian and Caroline (von Sommer) Reiche. Mother, d/o a baron of Westphalia. Father, an architect and contractor. Caroline and Christian both d. in Germany. R. H. m. Emily, d/o William B. Duvall, of Balt., 17 Jan. 1877 in St. John's Episcopal Church, by Rev. M. Johnston, and had six children, five being: Fannie, Carolina, Emily, Mary and Louise. A Knight of Honor, Knight of the Golden Chain and Knight of the Golden Eagle. Belongs to St. John's Episcopal Church. A Democrat. Physician and surgeon at Waverly.

303. CAPT. A. C. NICKLE - b. in 1832 in Burlington Co., NJ, s/o John and Lydia (Lippincott) Nickle, both of NJ. Father, of German descent, mother of English. John and Lydia had twelve children, A.C. being the seventh. Both parents d. in DE. A. C. m. Clarinda, d/o Capt. Jesse N. Braddock, in CT, and had seven children. Member of the Mt. Olive Lodge No. 52, A.F.&A.M. of Connecticut, the Rescue Harbor M. & P. Association. A Republican.

304. BENJAMIN F. GROVE - b. 12 Sep. 1860 in the city of Balt., s/o Lewis Jewett and Frances (Gaskins) Grove. Grandfather, Jacob, farmer in PA. Father, physician of Balt., a Democrat, m. Frances Gaskins of VA, had six children: Alice, m. Andrew Ensor and d. at thirty-two; Emma Jane, m. Daniel Little, of Balt.; Fannie, d. in infancy; Fannie Anne, w/o John Davis; Charles, d. in boyhood; and Benjamin F. Father d. in 1876. Benjamin m. Alberta, d/o Jesse and Elesbeth Fisher, of Balt. in Aug. 1882, and had six children; John Edgar, Leonard Ellsworth, Howard, Herbert, Jesse and Beulah. Member of the Junior Order of American Mechanics. A Republican. Leading contractor and builder of Arlington.

305. WILLIAM H. O'DONNELL - b. 22 Feb. 1843 in Morestown, Ireland, s/o Patrick F. and Bridget (Burns) O'Donnell, natives of the same place. William m. Sarah Mulvahill, of Salem, NJ, and had eight children: John, William, Frank, Mamie, Thomas, Joseph, James and Ella. Member of St. Mary's Catholic Church and the Catholic Benevolent Legion. A Democrat. Chief engineer of the Richmond, one of the largest and best steamers of the Weems line.

306. CHRISTOPHER E. FITZSIMMONS - b. 19 Jan. 1861 in Balt., s/o Christopher and Bridget (Rogers) Fitzsimmons, of West Meath and Roscommon, Ireland, respectively. Christopher and Bridget had six children: Thomas Joseph, d. at twenty-three; William Henry, d. in his youth; John Francis, lives in Balt.; Michael P., a tailor in Washington, D.C.; Mary Elizabeth, at home; and Christopher. Christopher m. Mary Murphy, of Balt. in 1885, and had five children: Ella, Thomas, Gertrude; Bessie, d. in infancy, and Edward. A Democrat. Horse-shoer, in business with Mr. Hargest in Arlington.

307. GEORGE PETER QUICK - b. 13 Dec. 1824 in Hesse-Darmstadt, Germany. George and wife had five children: George, m., farmer; Edward, m., works on home farm; Louisa, w/o Lewis Glacher; Jacob,

at home; and one who d. Members of the Gardenville Lutheran Church. Politically an independent. In farming and market-gardening business in the twelfth district.

308. MATTHEW RICHMOND - b. 12 May 1862 in County Antrim, Ireland, s/o Daniel and Eliza (Sterling) Richmond. Father, b. on same farm, agriculturist, Presbyterian, d. in 1885. Daniel and Eliza had: Matthew, Daniel, Mary, and Mrs. Robert McElroy of Philadelphia, PA. Matthew m. Annie, d/o Samuel Richmond, in 1884 and had four children: Bessie, Samuel, Mattie and Mabel. Attends the Methodist Episcopal Church. A Democrat. Florist and gardening business.

309. JOSHUA HAMMOND - b. in Harford Co., MD, s/o Dominick and Amanda (Ayres) Hammond. Father, b. in England in 1829, m. Amanda in Harford Co. in 1840, had four children: Joshua; Francis, Balt. business man; Sarah Elizabeth, w/o Thomas Burton; and Martha Ellen, w/o James Bowen. Joshua m. Augusta, d/o Isaac Ledley, of Upper Falls, in 1869 and had seven children: J. Dominick; Minnie, w/o William S. Crossmore; Ella M.; Edward Clinton, Roscoe, Claude and Frank. Members of the Methodist Episcopal Church. A Republican. Butcher in Upper Falls.

310. CHRISTOPHER SLADE - b. 12 Jun. 1825 in the seventh district, s/o Christopher and Delilah (Creighton) Slade, also of Balt. Co. Christopher and Delilah had seven children: Asbury, d.; William; Christ; Abraham; Creighton; John T., d.; and Ann. Great-grandfather, Ezekiel Slade, of England, settled in MD in the colonial days. Grandfather, Abraham Slade, b. in Harford Co., had sons, Christopher, John and Abraham. Christopher m. Maria E. Carlin, 8 Feb. 1853, of Balt. Co., and had eleven children: William, Zipporah, Columbus C., Mary, Asbury, John R., Bettie W. and Carl, still living. A Democrat. General farming and dairy business.

311. J. K. CULLEN - b. 9 Oct. 1869 in Dover, DE, s/o Capt. Hezekiah and Margaret (Kimmey) Cullen. Grandfather, John W. Cullen, b. in DE, farmer and merchant. Father, tanner and currier, lives in Camden, DE. Hezekiah and Margaret had three children, J. K., being the second. Member of the Alumni Association of the Philadelphia College of Pharmacy. Conducts one of the leading drug stores of Catonsville.

312. CAPT. WILLIAM C. GEOGHEGAN - b. 20 Dec. 1838 in Dorchester Co., MD, s/o Stewart K. and Susan A. (Travers) Geoghegan. Mother, member of the Methodist Church, d. in 1847, age thirty-five. Father is eighty-six in 1897. William m. Celone Chaney, of Balt., 12 May 1862, and had three children: Charles M., first mate of the Potomac; Roberta and William, at home. Member of the Rescue Harbor No. 14, Pilots' Association of Baltimore, and Hiram Lodge No. 107, A.F.&A.M. Belongs to the Methodist Church. A Democrat. Master of the steamer Potomac, of the Weems line.

313. JOHN H. GRIMES, M. D. - b. 24 Sep. 1842 in Carroll Co., MD, s/o George Washington and Eliza (Buffington) Grimes. Grand-

father, Elias Grimes, b. in Carroll Co., of Scotch lineage.
Maternal grandfather, Abraham Buffington, of English descent.
Eliza d. at age seventy-five. George and Eliza had five children: Elias Oliver, merchant of Westminster, MD; Dr. John H.;
Margaret, w/o Dr. Russell, of VA; Franklin A., merchant of Yolo
Co., CA; and William S., farmer, d in Carroll Co., MD. John m.
Mary M., d/o Samuel Butler, of Balt., in Oct. 1874, and had three
children: S. Butler, Robert Harold; and Charlotte B., d. at
sixteen. Samuel Butler, a ship builder and owner of large yard
on the wharf. Member of the Medical and Chirurgical Faculty of
Maryland. a Democrat. Oldest physician located in North Balt.

314. WILLIAM SLADE - b. 30 Sep. 1822 in Balt. Co., s/o
Christopher and Delilah (Creighton) Slade, and brother of
Christopher Slade (which see). William m. Julia P., d/o Thomas
and Charity (McComas) Lytle, of Balt., and had three children,
all d.: Lida A., w/o John B. Pearce, of Balt. Co., had three
children; Marion F., d. at four; and Ella, d. at sixteen. Thomas
Lytle, of Balt. Co. and Charity of Harford Co. Children of John
B. and Lida A. Pearce: Dr. William H. physician of Balt., m. Anna
Tillman, of Cumberland, MD; Ella S., w/o Rev. Edward Hays; and
Charles M., m. Stella Payne. Members of the Methodist Episcopal
Church. A Democrat. Former member of the Maryland Legislature.

315. CHARLES H. A. MEYER - b. 27 Oct. 1860 in Bremen, Germany,
s/o John D. and Fredericka (Fechter) Meyer. Paternal grandfather, Albert G. Meyer, in hotel business in Germany. Maternal
grandfather, Capt. C. H. Fechter, commander of the clipper
Shakespeare, d. in NY in 1877, age sixty-five. Charles was
oldest of seven children; brother Albert G., second officer for
the North German Lloyd Company, and brother John F., mate on an
American schooner. Came to New York with maternal grandfather in
1876. Charles m. Lottie E., d/o James Lipp, of Balt. City, and
had five children: Edith, Carl, Lottie, John and one d. Member
of the Alumni Association of the College of Pharmacy, the Medical
and Chirurgical Faculty of Maryland, the National Union and
Shield of Honor, and the Harmonica Lodge, Vorwaerts Turnverein.
A Republican. A Lutheran. Physician at No. 1033 North Caroline
street.

316. HENRY HOECK - b. 29 Aug. 1853 on Gay street, Balt., s/o
Henry and Catherine (Roth) Hoeck, Sr. Father, b. in Bavaria,
Germany, cabinet-maker, m. Catherine, d/o Joseph Roth of Germany,
and had: John, undertaker, d. 28 Feb. 1897; Henry; Joseph and
Catherine, both d. in Balt. Father d. in 1894, age seventy-five,
mother d. in 1872, age forty-nine. Henry m. Maggie, d/o John
Burier, a brick mason, in Balt., and had five children: Henry,
Kate, Joseph, John and Margaretta. Member of the Heptasophs,
Spaulding Legion of Honor No. 45, and the Calumet Club. Belongs
to the St. James' Catholic Church. A Democrat. Cabinet-maker
and undertaker at No. 1301 Central avenue, and has a livery barn
at No. 932 Sterling street.

317. GEORGE F. TAYLOR, M. D. - b. 17 Aug. 1855 in Balt., s/o
Jesse and Elizabeth (Church) Taylor. Father, b. York Co., PA,

wheelwright, a Methodist Episcopal, d. in 1889, age seventy-six. Jesse m. Elizabeth J., d/o John and Jane (Hall) Church, of Balt., and had five children; Rev. Jesse Church, Protestant Episcopal minister at Lewes, DE; Edvina V., d.; George F.; and two others who d. John Chruch, Balt. shoe merchant, m. Jane Hall, of one of the oldest Anne Arundel Co. families; father of Jane, Nathaniel Hall, grandson of "Long" John Hall, who was over seven feet tall. George m. Mary Janet, d/o THomas McGill, in Washington, D.C., 19 Dec. 1882, and had two children: Herbert Douglass; and George McGill, d. at eight months. Member of the Medical and Chirurgical Faculty of Maryland, the Alumni Society of the College of Physicians and Surgeons, the Medical and Surgical Society of Baltimore, the Clinical Society, and the American Medical Association. Belongs to the Knights of Phythias and the Junior Order of American Mechanics. A Democrat. Physician at No. 1254 North Broadway.

318. DANIEL W. CAMERON - b. 10 Sep. 1811 in Balt. Co., s/o Hugh and Sarah (Walker) Cameron, he of Georgetown, D.C., she of Balt. Co. Paternal grandfather, b. in Scotland, settled in MD. Maternal grandfather, Daniel Walker, b. Balt. Co., of German descent. Father, farmer, had following: William, Daniel W., James, Elizabeth and Evaline. Nephew, George H. Cameron, s/o James Cameron, m. Mary Shunk, of York Co., PA. Member of the Independent Order of Odd Fellows. Operates mill and farm.

319. CHARLES L. MATTFELDT, M. D. - b. 14 Jan. 1867 in the city of Balt. Charles m. Wilhelmina Schwiensburg, in 1890, and had one daughter, May. Member of the University of Maryland Medical Society, the Balt. Co. Medical Society, Maryland Medical and Chirurgical Faculty, the Public Health Association, the Catonsville Building Association, the Catonsville Fire Company, and the Odd Fellows' Providence Lodge No. 116 and Encampment No. 4. A Lutheran. A Republican. Physician of Catonsville.

320. GEORGE W. ELLIOTT - b. 1 May 1828 in the seventh district, s/o Abraham and Margaret (Cunningham) Elliott. Paternal great-grandfather came to America from England. Grandfather, George Elliott, b. in Balt. Co., farmer. Abraham and Margaret had ten children, five still living: Keziah, Robert, Elizabeth, George W. and Abraham J. George m. Eliza E. Hicks, of Balt. Co., and had one daughter, S. Florence, who m. Charles H. Mays, of Balt. Co., and had two children: John E. and Walter H. Member of the Methodist Episcopal Church. A Democrat. Has general merchandising store in Hereford.

321. FRANK W. SCHUESSLER, M. D. - b. 8 Sep. 1866 in Bavaria, Germany, s/o Frank Joseph and Louisa (Noe) Schuessler, of Germany. Frank m. Ida M., d/o Henry and Mary Lang, 9 Dec. 1891, and had one son, Herbert Franklin. Member of the Legion of the Red Cross, the Foresters, the Sons of Liberty and the Heptasophs. Physician in Canton.

322. GEORGE H. HUTTON - b. in 1821 in Richmond, VA, s/o George H. and Emily Hutton, Sr. Father, b. in Scotland, settled in VA,

buried in St. John's Cemetery, on Church Hill, Richmond. Mother d. when George was six, buried in Richmond. Sister, Julia, w/o Anderson Moore, of Manchester, VA, and mother of three children, d. in Mar. of 1897. George m. Mildred Blackburn in Richmond, 5 Jun. 1855, and had ten children: George H., in business with father; Robert E., Methodist Episcopal minister and head of electrical plant in Lexington, VA; Rose B., w/o Joseph R. Chapman, of Brooklyn, NY; M. Dora, at home; Dovie. w/o William A. Carlton, of Balt.; Giralda, at home; and four who d. Members of the Harford Avenue Methodist Episcopal Church. A Republican. Has a plant for the manufacture of material for carriages at the corner of Harford and Central avenues.

323. GEORGE F. CORSE, M. D. - b. 8 Dec. 1839 near Gardenville, s/o William and Deborah (Sinclair) Corse. Father, of Harford Co., a tanner, a Republican, d. at home 1869. Mother, d/o Robert Sinclair, Sr. William and Deborah had: George F.; Robert; William J.; Frank E.; Mary W., w/o Edward S. Campbell, of Philadelphia; Caroline, at home; Susan, w/o Maj. E. C. Gilbreath, of the U.S. army; Hettie S., w/o Dr. E. W. Janney; Annie C., w/o Calvin Conrad, of Phihladelphia; and Lucy C., w/o Prof. B. F. Betts, of Philadelphia. George m. Sarah, d/o James L. and Elizabeth M. Sutton, 13 Nov. 1866, and had: Laura S., w/o Oliver J. Matthews, Balt. merchant; Carrie, w/o Allen L. Carter, s/o Dr. Carter, of WV; and Ella S. Member of the Medico-Chirurgical Association of Baltimore. Belongs to the Quaker Church. Physician in Gardenville and the city of Baltimore.

324. WESLEY A. and J. MARION ROYSTON - sons of Wesley and Mary (Fuller) Royston. Wesley A., b. in 1837 in the tenth district, m. Mary C., d/o William Richardson, and had four children: William A., deceased; Augusta, w/o William Smith, of the tenth district; Mary E.,; and Blanche, w/o William Shelly, of the tenth district. J. Marion, b. in 1842 in Balt. Co., m. Susie, d/o Edward R. Price, in 1871, and had five children: Edward Price, Clara L., Horace Wesley, Cora Estelle and Emma Grace. Paternal grandparents, John and Ruth (McClung) Royston, of the tenth district, had eleven children: John, m., lives in the sixth district; Robert, d., leaving children; William, lives in the eleventh district; Caleb, children live in Balt. Co.; Joshua, Balt. merchant; Thomas, d. in Balt. Co., family lives elsewhere; Ruth, Elizabeth, Margaret, Mary and Wesley. Father, youngest of family, m. Mary, d/o William Fuller who was killed by his slaves in the tenth district, and had: Alice, widow of Robert Wilson; George R., of Balt.; Cecelia, w/o Desman Carter, of Balt.; Clara, w/o Eli Matthews, of the seventh district; Wesley A.; Mary Ellen, w/o Oliver Price, of the tenth district; Joshua Marion; Emma, d. in childhood; and Frederika, w/o Rev. Curtis C. Griffith, a Methodist Episcopal minister at Hagerstown, MD. Methodist Episcopals. Democrats. Farmers.

325. JAMES G. KANE - b. in 1849 in County Antrim, Ireland, s/o James and Frances (Getty) Kane. James and Frances had four children: Mary A., w/o Dr. William H. Tolson, of Balt.; Robert J., Balt. business man; James G.; and one who d. in infancy.

Came to Balt. in 1851. Father d. 16 Jan. 1885 in Long Green Valley. James m. Lenore, d/o Lorenzo Patterson, in 1884, and had five children: Allen; Irving; Wallace, d. in childhood; Frances and Marjorie. Member of the Chestnut Grove Presbyterian Church. A Republican. Engaged in farming and the dairy business.

326. EDWARD A. MONTGOMERY - b. in 1873 in Creswell, Harford Co., MD, s/o Acal and Harriet A. (Wells) Montgomery, of the same county. Father, b. in same house, a carpenter, settled near Upper Falls, in the eleventh district, is now (1897) sixty-nine years of age. Grandfather, Issac Montgomery, nephew of General Montgomery of Revolutionary fame. Acal and Harriet had eleven children: William B., carpenter in Baltilmore; Henry, carpenter, d. 19 Mar. 1888; Elijah B., m. Sarah Andrews, had three children; Sadie, w/o Robert Francis, farmer of Balt. Co.; Birkhead E., business man in Hamilton, NJ; Annie, w/o Henry Cloman, of Anne Arundel Co.; Katie, d. in girlhood; Eliza E., w/o Henry Vogts, a blacksmith of Harford Co.; May, at home; James L. Edward m. Mary E. Lamley, of Balt. in 1896. Member of the Gardeners' Club. A Lutheran. Edward and James L. are Republicans, Elijah a Democrat. Possessor of one of the largest florist establishments, located on Erdman avenue.

327. WILLIAM J. FERGUSON - b. 28 Mar. 1854 in Balt., s/o Adam and Elizabeth (Campbell) Ferguson. Father, b. in Edinburgh, Scotland, as was grandfather, Adam, a chemist. Father, d. 1855 in Balt., age thirty-five, a Presbyterian. Mother, b. in Edinburgh, d. in Balt. at age forty-nine. William m. Emma J., d/o Charles Turner, of Balt., and had six children: Mamie, Edna, Ethel, William J., Oliver and Harry. Charles Turner, carpenter and stair builder. Member of Clydesdale Lodge of Glasgow, and Cassia Lodge No. 45, A.F.&A.M., of Balt. A Republican. Machinist and inventor.

328. JAMES B. YOUNG - b. 27 Jan. 1857 in the sixth district, s/o Joseph and Rachel (Walker) Young, also of the sixth district. Joseph and Rachel had six children: Amanda, Joseph, Daniel, James B., Ariel B. and Sallie. Grandfather, John Young, of VA, paper manufacturer in the sixth district of Balt. Co. James m. Dora C. Finney, of York Co., PA, and had six children: Pearl, Bessie, Mabel, Ruth, Beulah and James M. A Republican. Attends Mt. Zion Methodist Protestant Church. Junior member of the firm of D. & J. B. Young, paper manufacturers of the sixth district.

329. ROSS BOND - b. 14 Oct. 1830 in the seventh district, s/o George and Jemima (Pocock) Bond, also of Balt. Grandfather, Edward Bond, b. in England, settled in Balt. Co. before the American Revolution, a farmer, had seven children, those living: Ross, and Mrs. Harriet Smith of Atchison Co., KS. Ross m. Mary Jane d/o Abraham and Jane (Markey) McDonald, of Balt. Co., and had six children: Smith B., Jane E., Virrena J., Mollie C. R., John R. and Lottie A. A Democrat. Farmer in the seventh district.

330. EDWARD N. BRUSH, M. D. - b. 23 Apr. 1852 in Glenwood, Erie Co., NY s/o Nathaniel H. and Myra (Warren) Brush, he of New York

state and she of Pittsfield, MA. Col. Nathaniel Brush and Gen. John Brush, members of same family; family was among the first settlers of Southold, L.I. Father, d. in 1870. Edwrad m. Delia A., d/o Hon. E. S. Hawley of Buffalo, in 1879, and had three children, Lavinia, Nathaniel and Florence. Member of the American Neurological Association, the Neurological Societies of Philadelphia and Baltimore, the American Medical Association, the Medical and Chirurgical Faculty of Maryland, a fellow of the College of Physicians of Philadelphia, and of the New York State Medical Association. Professor of psychiatry in the Womenn's Medical College of Baltimore. Superintendent of Sheppard asylum for the insane near Towson.

331. JOSEPH P. BURNETT - b. in 1861 in Balt. City, s/o Solomon and Mary M. (Chason) Burnett, also of the city. Mother is of French descent. Solomon and Mary had six children, Joseph being the first. Joseph m. Lizzie, d/o James Onion, in Balt., and had two children, Helen and Grace. Member of Marine Engineers, Benevolent Association, the Junior Order of Americna Mechanics, the Shield of Honor and the Legion of the Red Cross. A Democrat. Chief engineer for the Central Street Railway Company of Balt.

332. ALBERT A. MILLER - b. in 1820 in Austria, s/o Nimrod and Anna Miller. Parents first settled in Cincinnati, OH, moved to Balt. Co. in 1830. Nimrod and Anna had several children d. in infancy, and John, d. in PA. Albert m. Elizabeth Steinfelt in 1844 and had twelve children: Edward, d. in infancy; Joseph, of Balt.; John; Mary, w/o Frederick Weber, of Catonsville, MD; Albert, at home; Franklin and Margaret (twins), the former deceased; Charles, of Balt.; Herman; Annie, w/o John Snyder; Stephen and Leonard J. A Whig, then a Democrat. Communicants of the Catholic Church. Farmer.

333. JOHN W. SPARKS - b. 7 Nov. 1845 in Gloucester Co., NJ, s/o Benjamin D. and Elizabeth (Pew) Sparks. Mother, b. in DE, close to the MD line, d. in 1866. Father, b. in NJ, a ship builder, then in the commission business in Philadelphia, a Democrat. Children of Benjamin: Edward E., d.; Benjamin R., lives in Camden, NJ, in the wholesale fish business in Philadelphia; David H., soldier; Margaret P., Mathida P., C. Anna, Hannah Elizabeth and Mary Louisa. John m. Mary M., d/o Isaac Way, native of Harford Co., in Jan. 1868, and had four children: Benjamin I., m. Leah Z., d/o John Merritt, and had two daughters, Caroline Matilda and Mary Melvina; William E., m. Anna Elizabeth, d/o Benjamin G. Todd, and had one child, Sarah Ethel; Sarah Elizabeth and Mary Martha. Identified with the Methodist Episcopal Church. A Democrat. Farmer of the twelfth district.

333. FRANK J. FLANNERY, M. D. - b. 10 May 1858 in Balt. City, s/o John and Mary (Gleason) Flannery. John, b. in Ireland, a Democrat, m. Mary Gleason, b. in Ireland, and had four children: Frank J., M.D.; Thomas J., Balt. business man; Mamie E., at home; and Loretta. Grandfather, Frank Flannery, contractor. Subject m. Ella, d/o Judge Henry Brannon, of WV, in 1883, and had one child, Ella. Connected with the Clinical and Alumni Association

of Maryland and Virginia. Member of the Baltimore County Medical Society, the Neurological Association of Baltimore, the Golden Chain and several benevolent associations. Resident physician of Mt. Hope Retreat.

334. BENJAMIN FRANKLIN GROFF - b. in 1834 in Lancaster Co., PA. First of family in America was Johannes Graf, exiled from native principality on the borders of Switzerland, fled to Alsace, then America, took up large tract of land, Earl Township,, in Lancaster Co., PA; at death of Johannes, property divided among his six sons, and they left it to their children; Mennonites in faith. Abraham Groff, great-grandson of Johannes, b. in Lancaster Co., PA, in 1772, had seven children. Benjamin m. Elizabeth A., d/o William and Rachael (Baldwin) Denmead, and had four children: Mary Ray and Clara Denmead, at home; William Denmead, student; and Guy B., b. 10 Oct. 1875. Benjamin d. 27 Oct. 1895. A Republican. Carried on a general mercantile business.

335. J. WESLEY JACKSON - b. 3 Oct. 1837 in My Lady's Manor, in the tenth district, s/o Thomas and Julia Ann (Murray) Jackson. Grandfather, Elisha Jackson, farmer in Balt. Co., d. at age seventy-six. Maternal grandfather, Col. William Murray, merchant, member of the Methodist Episcopal Church, commissioner of Carroll Co., d. at age ninety-one. Father and mother both b. in Balt. Co., MD. Father d. at his farm, Becenia Cambria, age eighty-three, and mother d. at seventy. Thomas and Julia had six children. J. Wesley m. Emily J., d/o Robert Royston, farmer of Balt. Co., and had three children; Robert Royston, with the Philadelphia, Wilmington & Baltimore Transfer Company; Thomas D., in business with father; and John H. B., bookkeeper for S. Register & Son. Member of the Funeral Directors' Association of Baltimore, the Benjamin Franklin Lodge No. 97, A.F.&A.M., of Baltimore, and Oriental Lodge No. 6, I.O.A.M. Belongs to the Madison Square Methodist Episcopal Church. Leading undertaker and embalmer of Balt.

336. HENRY T. RENNOLDS, M. D. - b. 8 Jan. 1844 in the city of Balt., s/o Lindsay H. and Mary (Carter) Rennolds, of Essex Co., VA, and Balt., respectively. Paternal grandfather, planter, belonged to one of the F.F.V.'s, descent from English ancestors among the first settlers of VA. Father, an architect, member of the Independent Order of Odd Fellows, a Methodist, d. at age sixty-three. Mother, of English descent, d. at age sixty-three. Lindsay and Mary had four children: Virginia R., Mrs. Cable, of Balt.; William Lindsay, member of Mosby's cavalry, d. in Houston, TX, about 1887; Mary L., Mrs. Nutwell, d. in Balt.; and Dr. Henry T. Henry m. Georgia, d/o George Grape, in Balt. Member of the Medical and Surgical Society of Baltimore, the Medical and Chirurgical Faculty of Maryland, the American Medical Association, the Clinical Society of Baltimore. A Republican. Belongs to the Methodist Episcopal Church. Physician to the Kelson Orphan Asylum and in private practice.

337. JUSTUS MARTELL - b. 8 Mar. 1839 in Balt., s/o Peter and

Catherine (Miller) Martell. Father, grocer then agriculturist, a Whig then Democrat, d. 25 Sep. 1862, aged sixty-four. Mother d. 11 Jul. 1886. Peter and Catherine had eight children: Peter H., framer; Charles, in dairy business on North Point road; Alexander H., d. at twenty-two; Margaret, widow of William Smith; Mrs. Louisa Davis is a widow; Elizabeth, m. Charles Lerch; Mary, w/o William Craig and lives at Buckeystown, Frederick Co., MD.; and Justus. Justus m. Lucinda, d/o Isaac Way, of Harford Co., 27 Apr. 1860, and had nine children: J. Scott, farmer in the twelfth district; Sarah C., w/o James Johnson, and had three children; Alexander Harrison, motorman on the City and Suburban Railway; Mary Martha, w/o William Ritter; and five boys d. in childhood. Lucinda d. 12 Sep. 1895. Justus m. (2) Ella S. Havern, of North Point, in Apr. 1896. A Democrat. He identified with the Evangelical Lutheran Church, she a Methodist. Engaged in farming in the twelfth district.

338. FRANCIS JAMES DE SHIELDS - b. 9 May 1845 near Princess Anne, in Somerset Co., MD, s/o James A. and Charlotte (DeShields) DeShields. Originally French Huguenots, went to England, then America, three brothers settling in Somerset Co., MD. Grandfather, James W. DeShields, b. in Somerset, a farmer. Father, b. at the head of Wetipquen Creek, d. at Snow Hill, on the Pocomoke, aged seventy-nine. Mother, also of Somerset Co., d. there at forty-four. Haste W. DeShields, father of Charlotte, a cabinet maker. James and Charlotte had two sons, Francis and Erastus S., dentist of Snow Hill. Francis m. Harriett, d/o James Broughton, of Balt., at Temperanceville, Accomac Co., VA, and had one child, Frances M. Member of the Royal Arcanum Lodge and Evergreen Lodge No. 153, A.F.& A.M., of Snow Hill. An Episcopalian, belonging to the Church of the Messiah. A Democrat. Chief engineer of the Enoch Pratt.

339. CAPT. JOHN H. LYNCH - b. in 1831 in Balt., s/o Joseph and Ellen (Stone) Lynch, of Balt. Co. Father, a contractor, d. in 1852, aged fifty-two; mother d. at eighty-three. Joseph and Ellen had eight children: Joshua, John H., Joseph, James, George and Lewis, and the others d. John m. Frances R., d/o George Ensor, of Balt., in 1852, and had seven children; Richard H., bookkeeper and manager of the Martindale Commercial Agency for Maryland and Delaware, m. Jennie Vernon, d/o Rev. Holly Smith, and had three children, Edmund, Frances and Vernon; Alice R., m. E. D. Wyke, Balt. business man; John T., magistrate for the twelfth district, m. Sarah Parsons, and had two children, Howard and Richard; Ella May, w/o Dr. William S. Gibson, and had one child, William L.; John E., d. in infancy; Joseph M., d. at four; and Laura, d. at six. Member in the Young Men's Christian Association, and the Independent Order of Odd Fellows. Superintendent of the Boys' Home Society of Baltimore.

340. JOHN R. REESE - b. 15 Dec. 1823 near Westminster, in Frederick Co., s/o Andrew and Rebecca (Roop) Reese. Andrew and Rebecca had two sons, David, d. 17 Mar. 1895, and John. Father d. in 1826. John m. Elizabeth Roop, in 1850, and had six children: Charles A., Frances D., Mary L., John B., and two who d. A

Republican. Leading and successful farmer and dairyman of the fourth district.

341. BENJAMIN COLLISON - b. 31 Mar. 1864 in Anne Arundel Co., s/o Nicholas and Susan (Elbinder) Collison, of Dorchester Co. Nicholas and Susan had ten children: Thomas E., sailor; Mary Elizabeth, w/o John R. Lee; Sarah C., w/o Thomas E. Petty, a sea captain; Nicholas George, Jr., sailor; Susan L. B., w/o Benjamin R. Brown, farmer, miller and merchant; Annie M., w/o Frank B. Brashares; David W., farmer in Anne Arundel Co.; Laura P., w/o Thomas K. Dawson; George and Benjamin. Benjamin m. Elizabeth Davis, of Anne Arundel Co., in 1885, and had four children: Myrtle C., Ruby S., Roy A. and Paul G. Members of the Methodist Episcopal Church. Farmer of the third district.

342. JOHN L. HUDSON - b. 7 Dec. 1824 near Swedesboro, in Gloucester Co., NJ, s/o William and Sarah (Lewis) Hudson, of the same state. Father, b. in Cumberland Co., farmer, d. at ninety-three, had two brothers who lived to ninety-two and eighty-six. Mother d. at sixty. Grandfather, John Lewis, shoemaker, of German descent, d. in NJ at fifty-two. Paternal grandfather, John L. Hudson, also of NJ, farmer, belongs to same family as Hendrick Hudson. William and Sarah had five children. John m. Mary A. Armstrong, of Salem Co., in NJ, and had: Clarkson, chief engineer on the tug PHiladelphia; Lewis, chief engineer on the Emma Giles; Susan, d.; and Mrs. Sarah Allen, of NJ. Sarah d. in NJ. John m. (2) Elizabeth Allen, of Cumberland Co., NJ, and had three children: Mrs. Elizabeth Mount, of Camden, NJ; William, bookkeeper for the Tolchester line; and Calvin, chief engineer on the Easton. Member of the Marine Engineers' Benevolent Association No. 5, of Baltimore, and the Enterprise Lodge No. 139, I.O.O.F., of Bridgeport, NJ. A Republican. Marine engineer in DE and Chesapeake Bay.

343. PHILIP WATTS - b. 14 Feb. 1841 in the third district, s/o Benjamin and Rachel (Waggoner) Watts. Edward Watts, b. in England in 1691, among first of the familty to come to America. John, son of Edward, b. 5 Dec. 1722 in Balt. Co., large planter, m. (1) Ann Boddy, m. (2) Sarah Stansbury, d. in 1767. Rev. Nathaniel Watts, son of John and Sarah Watts, b. 1 Jul. 1764, at North Point, Balt. Co., a Methodist minister, m. Rebecca Stansbury (b. 19 Feb. 1766 at North Point, d. 8 Septmeber 1826), d. 2 Oct. 1848. Benjamin, son of Nathaniel, b. 21 Apr. 1803 in the third district, architect and builder, m. Rachael Waggoner, (b. 3 Apr. 1811, d. 6 Mar. 1885), d. 12 Jan. 1890. Philip m. Katharine Louisa Mettam, in 1868, and had five children: Mattie Adele; Albert Sydney, architect; Philip Bartley, Balt. Lawyer; Ruth A. and Lister Turner, at home. Katharine, b. 9 Oct. 1848, in Pikesville, d/o Joseph and Ruth (Barker) Mettam. Joseph Mettam b. 27 Mar. 1805 at Mt. Sorrel, Derbyshire, England, pastor of the Baptist Church at Pikesville, d. 1 Feb. 1888; Ruth, b. 16 Aug. 1803 in Chesterfield, Derbyshire, England, d. 20 Aug. 1897 at Pikesville. Rev. Joseph Mettam, s/o Joseph Mettam, b. 5 Nov. 1780 in Brimington, England and d. 4 Nov. 1834; wife of Joseph, Rebecca Rudkin, b. 1776 in England and d. 4 Mar. 1859 in Phila-

delphia. Joseph Mettam, Sr., s/o Joseph and Sarah (Greaves) Mettam, both of England, he b. 1 Aug. 1753; his father, Robert, b. in 1724 in England, d. in 1796, m. (1) Rosamond Greaves who d. 18 Nov. 1768, m. (2) Mary Greaves who d. 16 Jan. 1794; parents of Robert were George de Brimington and Mary (Walsh) Mettam, he b. in 1681; father of George was Robert b. in 1645 and d. in 1699, wife Alice Mettam; father of Robert was Robert, Sr., b. in 1579.

344. OGDEN A. KIRKLAND - b. 20 Sep. 1835 in Norwich, Mass. s/o Samuel Maxwell and Ann L. (Knight) Kirkland. First of family settled in Saybrook, CT, about 1640. Great-uncle, Dr. John Thornton Kirkland, president of Harvard College. Father, also b. in Norwich, farmer, d. 1846. Mother d. in 1887. Samuel and Ann had five children. Ogden m. Elizabeth, d/o Col. G. W. Green, of DE, 23 Jun. 1875, and had three children: Mary Clara, Margaret Calvert and Bessie Green. Member of the Sons of the Revolution, the Atheneum Social Club, and the Catholic Club. Director in the Marine National Bank, Fireman's Insurance Company, and Baltimore City Passenger Railway, and president of the Maryland Building and Loan Association. Engaged in the auction business, real-estate and court business.

345. RICHARD EMORY WARFIELD - b. 11 Aug. 1855 at Manor Glen, near the Harford Co. line, s/o Henry M. and Anna (Emory) Warfield. Grandfather, Daniel Warfield. Henry and Daniel both of Howard Co., MD. Father, a merchant, Democrat, m. Anna, d/o Richard Emory, of Manor Glen, and had seven children: Richard Emory; S. Davies, postmaster of Balt.; Henry M., of Balt., manager of the Royal Insurance Company of Liverpool; and four deceased. Father d. in 1885. Richard m. Betty, d/o Solomon Davies, 19 Apr. 1881, and had two children: Douglas Robinson and Henry Mactier. Betty is great grand niece of President Monroe. Member of the Heptasophs, the Royal Arcanum and Golden Chain. A Democrat. An Episcopalian. Assistant manager of the consolidated departments of Balt. and Philadelphia of the Royal Insurance Company of Liverpool.

346. JOSHUA P. CLARK - b. in 1833 in Alloway, Salem Co., NJ, s/o Archibald and Rosanna (Emmel) Clark. Maternal grandfather, John Emmel, farmer of Salem Co., of German descent. Archibald and Rosanna had three children: Joshua P., a sister, and a brother who d. Joshua m. Hannah Garrison, of Atlantic Co., NJ, in 1860, and had four children: Isaac, farmer in VA; John Wesley, blacksmith in Salem; Wilbur, printer in Salem; and Harry, lives in Salem. Hannah d. in Salem 1 Feb. 1890. A Methodist. A Prohibitionist. Chief engineer of the Tangier.

347. JAMES FRANK SHENTON - b. in 1856 in Golden Hill, Dorchester Co., MD, s/o Moses and Mary (Slocum) Shenton. Father and grandfather, William Shenton, both b. came local. Mother, b. in Dorchester Co., d. at age fifty-five. Moses and Mary had ten children. James m. Kate, d/o Gottlieb Forester, of Balt., in Balt. in 1866. Kate d. after three years. James m. (2) Fannie, d/o Caleb Taylor, of Balt., and had two children, William Franklin and Harry Worth. Member of Concordia Lodge No. 24,

K.P., the Marine Engineers' Association, and the Shield of Honor. A Democrat. An Episcopalian. Chief engineer of the Central Savings Bank building.

348. WILLIAM T. HACKETT - b. in 1838 in Cecil Co., MD, s/o Joseph P. and Henrietta (Pennington) Hackett. Maternal grandfather, Col. H. Pennington. Paternal grandfather, William T. Hackett, a Methodist Episcopal. Father, a Methodist, farmer, d. in 1846. Joseph and Henrietta had six children: Cecelia Maryland, d. at fifteen; William T.; John P. farmer of the twelfth district; and three sons who d. William m. Elizabeth McDonald in 1861 and had eleven children: William P., farmer; Mary Kate, w/o William Littleton; Reese, m. Charles Jewell, of Balt.; James M., m.; Stella, Emma, Charles, Edith; and three who d. Member of the Grange and the Ancient Order of United Workmen. Methodist Episcopal. Farmer of the twelfth district.

349. JOHN J. CARR - b. 7 Jan. 1867 in Weston, Somerset Co., NJ, s/o John and Mary (Shehan) Carr, of same place. Father, farmer, d. at sixty-seven. Subject m. Sarah Gaines, of Balt., and had three children: Julia, John and Robert. Member of the Marine Engineers' Benevolent Association No. 5 of Baltimore. A Democrat. Chief engineer on the Chesapeake, of the WHeeler transportation line of Balt.

350. WILLIAM F. SIMERING - b. 1 Jan. 1847 in Balt., s/o William and Sophia (Rush) Simering. Paternal grandfather, a machinist, b. in England, settled in Balt., m. a German lady. Father, b. in Balt., a machinist, m. Sophia Rush, of Balt., had thirteen children. Father d. past the age of forty-eight. Mother d. at fifty-two. Frederick Rush, father of Sophia, b. in France, settled in Balt., a merchant tailor. William m. Annie, d/o Thomas and Elizabeth Chittener, in Baltimore and had three children: John Thomas, shirt cutter; Annie Elizabeth, at home; and William F., apprentice iron moulder. Thomas Chittener, locksmith. Member of the Marine Engineers' Benevolent Association No 5, of Baltimore. A Republican. Chief engineer of the Tred Avon,of the Baltimore, Chesapeake & Atlantic Company.

351. ELISHA BROWN - b. 18 Feb. 1820 in the fifth district, s/o Thomas and Mary (Gittinger) Brown. Father, b. near Hampstead, MD, m. Mary Gittinger, and had four children: Elizabeth, d., Elisha; and Sarah and Mary, both d. Elisha m. Nancy, d/o Henry Algire, of the fifth district, and had two children: William J., farmer in the fifth district; and Mary, w/o William E. Benson. A Republican. A Lutheran. Farmer of the fifth district.

352. WILLIAM L. RUSSELL, M. D. - b. 7 Mar. 1835 at Peru, St. Mary Co., MD, s/o Thomas and Elizabeth (Combs) Russell. Grandfather, Thomas Russell, Sr., lived whole life in Balt. Father, b. in Balt., a shoemaker, m. in St. Mary Co., Elizabeth Combs. David Jones, father of mother of Elizabeth. Nathaniel Combs, father of Elizabeth, b. in St. Mary Co., of English parentage, farmer, blacksmith, carpenter, mechanic, member of the Methodist Episcopal Church in St. Mary Co., rest of family Catholic.

Thomas and Elizabeth had four children: William L.; Thomas
Nathaniel, ship builder of Balt.; Isabel Marion, w/o Capt. John
Abbott, of Balt.; and Charles Wesley, boat captain, lives in
Balt. William m. Cecelia, d/o John W. and Almira (Cowles) Hall
at the parsonage of Rev. A. F. Nelville Rolfe, a Protestant
Episcopal clergyman of Balt., 10 Jul. 1862, and had eight children: Willie Nathaniel, in the drug business in Balt.; Frank
Donaldson, in the drug business; Mary; and five who have d.
Founder of the Hall family in America was John Hall, known as
"Long John" Hall since he was nearly seven feet tall, b. in
England, a farmer; Nathaniel Hall, grandson of John and great-
grandfather of Cecelia, m. Sarah Marriott, and had son Nathaniel,
b. in 1787, grandfather of Cecelia; great-grandfather d. from
scurvy in the service; grandfather, m. Delila, d/o Nathan and
Sarah (Hancock) Williams, and d. in Balt. in 1862; John W. Hall,
father of Cecelia, native of Anne Arundel Co., MD, superintendent
of the Methodist Episcopal Sunday-school on Caroline street,
Balt.; mother of Cecelia, Almira, d/o William and Margaret (Hall)
Cowles, he of CT and she of Balt.; John W. and Almira Hall had
eight children, five still living: Cecelia; William A., book-
keeper at Gaults; John W., receiver for the Baltimore Street
Passenger Railroad; Mrs. Almira Hebron and Mrs. Emily Harrison,
both of Balt.; Almira d. when Cecelia quite young; John m. (2)
Caroline T. Cox, and had two children: Delila J., w/o Rev.
Charles A. York, of Balt.; and Caroline G., w/o La Fayette
Stewart of Balt. Member of the Royal Arcanum. An Episcopalian.
Physician and surgeon of Balt.

353. REV. J. E. DUNN - b. in Lone Green Valley, Balt. Co.
Ordained 23 Dec. 1882, at the Cathedral in Balt. by his eminence,
Cardinal Gibbons. Pastor of St. Mark's Catholic Church at
Catonsville.

354. J. A. BADEN, M. D. - b. 26 Jan. 1833 in Calvert Co., MD,
s/o Jeremiah and Elizabeth (Greenwell) Baden, he of Calvert and
she of St. Mary Counties. Paternal grandfather, Jeremiah, and
father, Jeremiah, b. in Calvert Co. Badens came to America from
Wiltshire, England. Father, d. at age twenty-nine. Maternal
grandfather, Thomas Greenwell, b. in St. Mary Co., a planter.
Elizabeth d. at age eighty-one. J. A. m. Maria C., d/o James R.
Thompson, in St. Mary Co., and had one child: Richard. Member of
Calvert Lodge, Order of the Golden Chain, and the Royal Arcanum.
A Democrat. An Episcopalian. Physician at No. 2105 North
Calvert street.

355. WILLIAM F. HENRY - b. 22 Nov. 1854 in Balt., s/o John B.
and Emma C. (Wiegand) Henry, also of Balt. Father, of Scotch and
French descent, a pattern maker. Mother, of German extraction,
m. (2) J. L. Forrest who d. in Balt. William m. A. C. Atkinson,
of Queen Anne County, Md, and had: Ora, WIlliam, Martha, Lucy,
James and Katie. Member of the Marine Engineers' Benevolent
Association and the American Legion of Honor. A Democrat.
Attends the Baptist Church. Chief engineer on the B. S. Ford, of
the Chester River Steamboat Company.

356. JAMES H. WILSON, M. D. - b. 17 Dec. 1844 in the tenth district. James m. Sally A. Slade, in 1872, and had two children: Beryl G. and Olive. Member of the Ionic Lodge, A.F.&A.M., of Reisterstown. Belongs to the Episcopal Church. A Democrat. Physician and surgeon of the fourth district.

357. PERCY STANSBURY, M. D. - b. 10 Feb. 1860 in Balt., s/o Nathaniel and Hannah A. (Waddell) Stansbury. Great-grandfather, Tobias Stansbury, b. in England, crossed the Atlantic and settled in Patapsco Neck, MD, with his three brothers, Hammond, Nathaniel and Darius. Grandfather, Rev. Tobias Stansbury, b. at North Point, a Methodist Episcopal minister, cousin of Gen. John E. Stansbury, m. Arcana Sollers 10 Dec. 1799, d. at age seventy-four. Father, Nathaniel, b. in 1804 at North Point, a planter, m. cousin Catharine, d/o Darius Stansbury, 11 May 1827, and had four children; after death of Catharine, m. 2 Hannah A., d/o Capt. Henry M. and Ann Maria (Mondur) Waddell, 10 Oct. 1850, and had four sons: Frank P., Balt. business man; Charles B. and William Mondur, of Balt.; and Percy. Father d. in Balt. in 1872, member of the Methodist Episcopal Church and a Whig. Member of the Alumni Association of the Baltimore University of Medicine, of the Seventh Ward Democratic Club, and the William Tell Lodge, K. P. Attends the Methodist Episcopal Church. Physician and surgeon at No. 1422 East Preston street.

358. PETER G. ZOUCK - b. 31 May 1846 in what was then Zoucks-ville, but is now Trenton, Balt. Co. Peter m. Mary E. Myers of Hanover, PA on 12 Mar. 1872, and had seven children: Mary E.; H. Blanche; Harry M., d. in Dec., 1893; George P., Edith E., Rebecca N., and one who d. in infancy. Member of the Masonic lodge of Reisterstown. A Prohibitionist. A Lutheran. In the lime and lumber business at Cavetown, has a grain and feed store and coal yard at Glyndon, and Senior member of the firm of Zouck & Stern, wire strap manufacturers at No. 318 North Front street, Baltimore

359. A. WASHINGTON GORE - b. 14 Oct. 1827 in Balt. Co., s/o Elijah Gore. Grandfather, George Gore, and father, Elijah Gore, also b. same place. A. Washington m. Martha J. Neel, in 1865, and had five children: Katie, w/o Edward Graves, conducts large bakery in Washington, D.C.; Mary Belle; Charles W., Hugh C., and Albert. Members of the Methodist Episcopal Church of Reisters-town. Farmer of the fourth district.

360. I. T. UHRICH - b. 18 May 1849 in Halifax, Cauphin Co., PA. I. T. m. Martha Lovell, and had four children: Annie, Lizzie, Nettie M. and Mary. Member of the Junior Order of American Mechanics. A Methodist. A Republican. Engaged in both the saw and grist mill business in Reisterstown.

361. JAMES M. CRAIGHILL, M. D. - b. in 1857 in Georgetown, DC, s/o Gen. William P. and Mary A. (Morsell) Craighill, he of Charlestown, WV, and she of Georgetown, DC. Father, b. 1 Jul. 1833, attended West Point, member of the American Society of Civil Engineers. Grandfather, William Nathaniel Craighill, b. in Charlestown, WV, of Scotch descent. Maternal grandfather, Judge

James S. Morsell, b. in Calvert Co., MD, attorney and judge, of French extraction, d. in 1869 at age ninety-five. William and Mary had seven children, three servive: William E., captain of engineers in the U.S. army; Nathaniel R., professor of mechanical ingineering in the University of North Carolina; and James. James m. Anne F., b. near Culpepper, VA and d/o John F. Berry, in Georgetown, DC, and had one child, Annie. Member of the Medical and Chirurgical Faculty of Maryland, the Clinical Society of Baltimore, the Gynecological and Obstetrical Society, and the Maryland Bicycle Club. Physician of Balt.

362. D. HALLOWELL TWINING - b. in 1828 in Bucks Co., PA, s/o Isaac and Ann (Hallowell) Twining. First of Twining family to come to America settled in MA by 1640. Father, s/o of David Twining, b. in Bucks Co., descended of Quakers, father of following children: David Hallowell; Martha; Horace B., m. Fannie Ashton of Harford Co., had two children, Albert and Mary; Isaac, of TX; Frank, chemist in Philadelphia, d. leaving one son, Robert B.; Caroline, w/o William Bartleson, of Harford Co.; and Barclay, killed at Bull Run. D. Hallowell m. Alice P., d/o Joseph and Sarah Baynes, of Balt. in 1865, and had four children: Joseph, farmer in Harford Co.; Isaac, at home; and two d. in infancy. Alice d. of consumption in 1876. Favors Republican principles. Farmer of the eleventh district.

363. REV. EDWARD HUBER - b. 22 Jun. 1845 in Canton Thurgau, Switzerland, near the Rhine, s/o John Ulrich and Margaretta Huber. Family settled in Milwaukee. Father d. of blood poisoning, in 1871, aged fifty-six; mother d. in 1879, aged fifty-nine. Edward m. Louisa Cordes, 6 Oct. 1870, by Rev. Joseph Hartman, in Chicago, and had six children: Emma. teacher; Frederick, at school; Louisa; Ulrich; and Edward, d. at thirteen. Pastor of St. Matthew's German Evangelical Lutheran Church.

364. EDWARD REYNOLDS - b. at Sherwood Forest, in the eleventh district, s/o Thomas and Rachel (Weems) Reynolds. Father, the fifth generation b. on the old homestead in Calvert Co., MD. Edward Reynolds, crossed Atlantic in 1680, from Ireland; Thomas, s/o Edward, had son Edward, who had son Joseph, eldest of nineteen children; Thomas, son of Joseph, eldest of eight children, m. Rachel Weems, and had two children, Harriet and Edward. Father d. when Edward was six. Edward m. Helen, d/o W. A. Dunnington, of Balt. in 1874, and had three children: Helen Dunnington, Sarah Brice and William Augustus. A Democrat. Farmer and real-estate dealer of the eleventh district.

365. FREDERICK G. HOENER, M. D. - s/o Frederick W. A. and Lizzie W. (Weege) Hoener. Father, b. in Germany, d. in Balt. at age eighty-one. Frederick m. Katie Anna, d/o Christopher Dering, of Balt. and had one child, Mattie. Member of the Physio-Medical Association, the Waverly Lodge of the Masonic fraternity, and Druid Chapter No. 28, R.A.M. Lutherans. Physician at No. 112 South Broadway.

366. JOHN W. INGHAM - b. in the sixth district of Balt. Co., s/o

John and Sarah (Price) Ingham, he of England, and she of Balt. Co. Father, left England in 1819, at twelve years, with father, also John, settled in Balt. Co. John and Sarah had twelve children: four d. in infancy, five now living: Anna R., Emily, Henrietta, Lucy S. and John W. John m. Sereptha J. McCullough, of Balt. Co., and had seven children: Virginia B., Milton W., Alberta E., CHarles W., Erma, Mary and Grace. Independent in politics. Agriculturist of the sixth district.

367. JAMES N. FREDERICK - b. 9 Oct. 1849 in the seventh district, s/o Morris and Hannah (Norris) Frederick, also of same county. More on family in next sketch of brother, George. James m. Jennie Hunter of the seventh district; more on Hunter family in sketch of Thomas Hunter. Member of the Knights of Phthias, the Knights of the Golden Eagle, and the Junior Order of American Mechanics. A Republican. Agruculturist and county commissioner of Balt. Co.

368. GEORGE FREDERICK - b. 19 Sep. 1839 in the seventh district, s/o Morris and Hannah (Norris) Frederick, also of same county. Morris and Hannah had seven children: Ann M.; John T., d. in southern prison during the Civil war; George; James N. and three d. in infancy. Great-grandfather, John Frederick, a German, crossed the Atlantic, settled in Balt. Co., MD, a farmer, had sons: Aquilla, Stephen, and Benjamin, grandfather of George. George m. Frances, d/o Thomas and Nancy (Mathews) Cooper, of Balt. Co., and had six children: Silas C., physician of Wilmington, DE; Francis D., at school; and four d. in infancy. A Republican. General and dairy farmer.

369. WILLIAM A. BELL - b. 15 Nov. 1854 in Balt. s/o Capt. George and Martha (Rothen) Bell, both of Dorchester Co., MD. Father, owner and master of a schooner, drowned near Ballers wharf, in the port of Balt., when William was six. Mother, d/o Benjamin Rothen who d in Balt. aged ninety-two. Martha m. (2) a Mr. Pulk, who was lost at sea; George and Martha had a son and a daughter. Martha and Mr. Pulk had a daughter. William m. Hester, d/o John Bromwell, of Dorchester Co., MD, in Balt., and had two children: Percy B. and William Morris. Member of the South Baltimore Station Methodist Episcopal Church. A Prohibitionist. Chief engineer for the Union Soap Company, of Balt.

370. REV. J. P. DEAN - b. 9 Dec. 1822 near Chaptico, St. Mary Co., MD. J. P. m. Margaret Beckley, in 1854, and had one son, John L. B., who d. at age twenty-three. J. P. m. (2) Catherine E. Ducker. Methodist Episcopal.

371. ALFRED LOWE - b. 18 May 1805 in the fourth district, s/o Nicholas Lowe, Jr, b. in same neighborhood. Grandfather, Nicholas Lowe, Sr., b. in England. Father, m. Keturah Baker, and had eight children: Merab, Amos, Jeremiah, Ralph, Asenath, Jane, Alfred and one who d. in infancy. Father d. at age sixty-five, when Alfred was fourteen. A Baptist. Farmer.

372. REISTER RUSSELL - b. 25 Oct. 1844 in Westmoreland Co., PA,

s/o Dr. A. H. and Susan (Kephart) Russell, he of PA, she of
Carroll, MD. Maternal grandmother, Margaret Reister, belonged to
family that founded Reisterstown. Dr. and Mrs. Russell had five
children: George, retired in PA; Elizabeth; William; Reister; and
Susan, w/o James S. Whitmore, of Pittsburg, PA. Father d. at
about forty-seven, mother is eighty-four. Reister m. Julia C.,
d/o Henry Ducker, of Reisterstown in 1871 and had eight children:
Walter, d.; Henry H., in business with father; Reister K., at
school; James S., d. in 1896; Edith, d. in infancy; Raymond;
Jeremiah D. and Grace. Member of the Golden Chain of Reisterstown and the Henry Clay Lodge No. 81, I.O.O.F., of Reisterstown.
A Republican. A Lutheran. Owns a large general store in
Reisterstown.

373. JESSE HOSHALL - b. 14 Jul. 1825 in the sixth district, s/o
Jesse and Elizabeth (Gill) Hoshall, also of Balt. Co. Jesse and
Elizabeth had ten children, of who two d. in infancy. Grand-
father, Jesse Hoshall, b. in Holland, came to America at seven-
teen, m. Ellen Hurst, of England. Jesse m. Sarah A. Kroh, of
Balt. Co. and had five children: Frederick R.; Minnie B.; Jesse
M.; and Florence S. and Elizabeth O., who d. Member of the
Middletown Lodge No. 92, I.O.O.F. of Middletown, MD and the
Grange. A Democrat. A Baptist. Farmer of the sixth district.

374. CHARLES AKEHURST - b. 11 Jan. 1828 in Sussex, England, near
London, s/o Henry and Louisa (Delves) Akehurst. Henry and Louisa
had six children: Charles, Mary, Emma, Louisa, Henry and James.
Father, a farmer. Charles m. Amanda Bevans, and had seven child-
ren: Elizabeth, w/o Samuel Shanklin; Edward; David; George W. T.;
Louisa, w/o Ira Thomas; Emily and Mary J. Members of Camp Chapel
Methodist Episcopal Church. Prohibitionists. Florist of the
eleventh district.

375. GEORGE W. WISNER - b. 8 Nov. 1803 in the fifth district,
s/o Christian and Annie (Storms) Wisner. Father, b. in same
district, s/o Mathias Wisner, of Germany. Mathias had eight
children: John, Isaac, Abraham, Christian and Mathias, others d.
in childhood. Christian and Annie had ten children: Susan,
Katie, Nancy, Mary, Margaret, Joshua, Mathias, George W., Henry
and Christopher. George m. Rachel Armacost, in 1850 and had four
children: Ruth A., w/o Jesse Benson of the fifth district; John
H.; Sarah I., w/o Andrew Scoville; and Rachel, deceased. Wife,
Rachel, d. 15 Dec. 1896. Member of the United Brethren Church.
Farmer of the fifth district.

376. JOSEPH GILL - b. 17 Dec. 1835 in the eighth district; m.
Florence E. Hutchins, b. 20 Dec. 1846 in Catonsville, Balt. Co.,
27 Sep. 1877, and had: Robert O., b. in 1881, d. 26 May 1881;
Agnes Rebecca, b. 10 Jul. 1882; Stanley H., b. 1 Feb. 1885; and
Julia Edna, b. 18 Oct. 1888. A Democrat. Wife is member of the
Methodist Episcopal Church. Farmer of the fifth district.

377. ALEXANDER J. DIEDRICH - b. 12 Apr. 1863 in Balt., s/o
Martin and Sophie M. (Wittie) Diedrich. Grandfather, Albert
Diedrich, came from Germany to Balt., returned to Germany and d.

there. Father, b. in northern Germany, came to Balt. at eighteen. Mother, b. in Germany, d. in Balt. at thirty-three. Alexander m. Emma Langhenry, of Balt. in 1885, and had three children: Millard, Annie and Menno. Member of the Columbia Brotherhood of Engineers and the Shield of Honor. Attends the Lutheran Church. Chief engineeer of the Herald building in Balt.

378. ANDREW J. GILL - b. 12 Nov. 1829 in the eighth district, s/o George W. and Rebecca (Ensor) Gill. John Gill, came from England, located on Chestnut Ridge, in the fourth district, Balt. Co. Nicholas, s/o John and great-grandfather of Andrew. Grandfather, Stephen Gill. Father, also b. on same farm in eighth district, farmer, d. at age seventy-six. George and Rebecca had: Andrew J.; Stephen and John G., both d.; Joseph, farmer of the fifth district; Nicholas A., lawyer of Balt.; and Harrison and Samuel, both d. Andrew m. Mrs. K. C. Read, formerly Catherine A. Wheeler, of Harford Co., in 1889. Communicants of the Catholic Church. Farmer and business man of the fifth district.

379. EPHRAIM J. TRIPLETT - b. 7 Jul. 1822, in the fourth district, s/o Edward and Elizabeth (Parker) Triplett. Father m. (1) Margaret Ware, had two children, Elizabeth and Ellen; m. (2) Elizabeth and had eleven children. Paternal grandfather, John Triplett. Ephraim m. Elizabeth Lowe and had: Clarence W. and Elmire V., d.; Raymond W., Emma L., Amos, Elizabeth, Ernest, Mary, Jefferson and Ollie E. A Democrat. Farmer of the fourth district.

380. JAMES TAYLOR - b. 3 Sep. 1835 in Balt. Co., s/o William Taylor. Grandfather, Edmund Taylor, spent whole life in England. Father, b. near Manchester, England, came to Balt. Co. as a young man, m. Jane Gartberry, of England, both d. in Woodberry, William being nearly eighty years old. James married 2 times and had at least seven children with the first. James m. Mary, d/o James Williams, of Scotland, and had nine children: James, d. in childhood; Walter E., blacksmith in Wilmington, DE; Mrs. Virginia M. Thompson, of Balt.; William A., car builder, d. 30 May 1894; James W., employed in the Northern Central car shops; Effie E., d. 3 Mar. 1893; Thomas F., twin brother of Effie, a tinner at Wilmington, DE; Annie L. and Harry C., at home. Mary d. in 1895. Foreman of the passenger car shops of the Northern Central Railroad of Balt.

381. REV. HUGH H. ACKLER - b. 22 Sep. 1869 in Balt., s/o William F. and Margaret A. Ackler. Father, b. in Balt. in 1836, a banker, had five children: Hugh H.; William F., Jr., employed by the Western Maryland Railroad Company; Margaret A., w/o Rev. C. A. Hufnagel, of the Evangelical Lutheran Church at Randallstown, now deceased; Mary; and Robert. Hugh m. Louise T., d/o Theodore Collenberg, of Balt., on 5 Dec. 1895, and had one child. Pastor of the Faith Evangelical Lutheran Church of Balt.

382. GEORGE B. JOHNSON - b. 19 Dec. 1821 near Randallstown, s/o Elijah and Hannah (Barnett) Johnson. Father, b. on the Severn river, s/o Elijah Johnson, Sr. Maternal grandfather, George

Barnett. George m. Elizabeth Beckley, and had: Philip G., Edward A., Mary E.; George H., deceased; Elmer, Annie, and one who d. in infancy. Member of the Independent Order of Odd Fellows. Methodist Episcopalian. Tiller of the soil and dairyman of the fourth district.

383. WILLIAM H. BENDLER - b. about half a century ago in Chicago. William m. Minnie Burk (b. in Germany), and had three children: Sophia, w/o Mr. Haslup, Balt. hardware merchant; Lizzie, w/o Mr. Schetlich, music dealer of Balt.; and William Bendler, Jr., proprietor of father's music store at No. 335 Gay street. William d. in 1895.

384. MRS. CATHARINE REIER - b. in Germany, came to America at age twenty-two, settling in Balt.; m. Conrad Reier, a shoemaker in the city, and had four children: Adam; Dora, w/o William Prigel, lives in Kansas City, MO; Antoine, farmer near Greenwood; and one who d. After death of Conrad, Catharine moved to eleventh district, m. Adam Reier, merchant tailor and brother of Conrad, and had four children: George, carriage builder in Balt.; Annie, d. in infancy; Minnie, w/o William Grover, of the eleventh district; and Henry, at home. Conrad was member of the Independent Orer of the Odd Fellows and the Inproved Order of Red Men; Conrad d. in 1876. Son Adam, b. in the eleventh district in 1859, m. Mary E., d/o George and Eleanora Stiegler, of Harford Co. on 20 Apr. 1885, and had seven children: Henry, Eleanor, Adam, Carl, Marie, Conrad and Paul. A Lutheran. Postmistress at Greenwood, in the eleventh district.

385. IRVING MILLER, M. D. - b. 5 Mar. 1858 in Kent Co., MD, s/o William T. and Elizabeth (Aldridge) Miller. Grandfather, William Miller, farmer of same county, of Scotch descent. Father, William T., b. in Kent Co., farmer, m. Elizabeth, d/o John Aldridge, of Cecil Co. John Aldridge, b. in England, became farmer of Elk Neck, Cecil Co. William and Elizabeth had four children. Irving m. Miss Knotts, d/o William H. Knotts, of Balt., in Balt., and had one daughter, Bessie. Member of the Masons. Physician specializing gynecological surgery.

386. CAPT. HENRY W. LUCAS - b. 1 Jan. 1862 in Anne Arundel Co., MD, s/o William and Lucia Lucas. Father, b. in Gloucester Co., VA, now seventy-two years of age. Mother, b. in Anne Arundel Co. Henry m. Sophia Lerch, of Anne Arundel Co., and had one son, Edward. Member of the Center Lodge No. 108, A.F.& A.M., of Balt. With the Baltimore, Chesapeake & Atlantic Steamboat Company.

387. WILLIAM B. ORAM - b. 16 Jul. 1848 in the city of Balt., s/o James D. and Olivia A. (Williams) Oram. Mother, d/o Richard and Mary Williams. Grandfather, John Oram, native of NJ. Father, b. 22 Jul. 1817 in Balt. Co., a painter. James and Olivia had four children: John W., d. in boyhood; Mary L. and James F., d. young; and William B. William m. Eleanor, d/o Richard and Mary Hipkins, in 1873, and had three children: Nellie Olivia, Margaret A. and Franklin H. Richard and Mary Hipkins d. when Eleanor was a small child. Member of the Maryland Lodge No. 11, I.O.O.F.

Attend the Methodist Episcopal Church. Politically an independent. Raises cereals and several varieties of fruit.

388. JOHN W. GIBSON - b. 7 Jan. 1862 in Queen Anne Co., MD. John m. Annie K., d/o John T. and Martha (Bryan) Norman, of Queen Anne Co., in 1890, and had two children, John Norman and Estelle. Member of the Evangelical Church. Chief engineer of the Record building.

389. ALBERT F. PHILBIN - b. in 1856 in Hanover, York Co., PA, s/o Francis and Magdelene Philbin. Father, b. in Ireland, came to America with two brothers, located in Balt., d. at age sixty-eight. Mother, b. in Germany, came to Balt. when young, d. at age sixty-one. Albert, only child of Francis and Magdelene. Albert m. Katie C., d/o Captain Roche, of Balt. Member of the Heptasophs, the Catholic Benevolent Legion, and the Foresters of America. Belongs to St. Vincent de Paul Society of Corpus Christi parish of the Catholic Church. A Democrat. Undertaker at No. 1711 Maryland avenue.

390. EDWIN WELLS ROUSE - b. in Apr., 1845 near Easton, in Talbot Co., MD, s/o Francis W. and Susan (Wells) Rouse. Name was originally spell La Rue, of French extraction. Grandfather Rouse, b. and d. on the eastern shore, a farmer. Father, native of Talbot Co., carpenter, d. in MS. Mother, b. in Balt. of English parentage, only one of five children b. in America. Francis and Susan had: Edwin Wells; Francis W., connected with Bailey, Banks & Biddle, of Philadelphia; and Fannie C., Mrs. C. J. Weiner, of Balt. Susan m. (2) and raised a second family. Members of the Methodist Episcopal Church. Edwin m. Mary G. Hoffman, and had two children: Francis W., tinner; and Mrs. Hattie M. Martin, of Balt. After death of Mary, Edwin m. (2) Ann R., d/o Richard Chenowith, of Balt. Co., and had one son, Edwin Wells, Jr. Member of the Masons, Corinthian Lodge, A.F.&A.M., the Concordia Chapter, R.A.M., the Concordia Council, the Monumental Commander, K.R., the Bonnie Temple, Ancient Arabic Order of the Mystic Shrine, the Alpha Lodge, Royal Arcanum, the Zetha Lodge, Heptasophs, and the Pennsylvania Relief Association. Attends the Methodist Episcopal Church. A Democrat. Foreman of the tin and sheet iron department of the Northern Central Railroad works.

391. LEVI FERGUSON - b. in 1824 at Unionville, in the eleventh district, s/o Levi and Elizabeth (Barton) Ferguson. Maternal grandfather, Asa Barton, s/o Captain Barton. Father, and grandfather, William Ferguson, both b. in Prince Geroge Co. Levi and Elizabeth had three children: David B., farmer in the eleventh district; Elizabeth, w/o Milton Dance, of Dulaneys Valley, had three children, only one living, Mary E., w/o Harry Patterson, of Balt. Co.; and Levi. Levi m. Keziah B., d/o Charles Jessop, but she d. in 1892. Member of the Methodist Episcopal Church South. A Democrat. Farmer and fruit grower of the eleventh district.

392. JOSEPH M. COALE - b. in Jan. 1830 in Balt. Co., s/o Philemon and Hettie (Bowen) Coale. Grandfather, William Coale, b. in England, farmer, d. at age ninety-four, his wife at ninety-

three. Parents of grandmother were natives of Normandy. Father d. at age eighty; mother d. age eighty-eight. Philemon m. previously and had three children, all deceased. Philemon and Hettie had twelve children, Joseph being the only boy. Joseph m. Louisa E. Greble, of Balt., in Balt., and had three children: Frank W., secretary of Coale's Muffler and Safety-valve Company; Joseph, manager of the Maryland Brass Company; and Walter I., student of Maryland Art Institute. Joseph m. (2) Mary L., d/o Frank Rodenmeyer, of Balt. Member of the Master Mechanics Association of the United States and Canada. A Republican. Master mechanic of the Northern Central Railroad shops.

393. GEORGE W. WEBSTER - b. in Balt. in 1838, s/o Henry and Anna (Lewis) Webster. Father d. at age seventy-four. Father had two wives, both named Anna Lewis, and had seven children by each; George was the third child and second son of the first marriage. George m. Mary E. Feffel, of Balt., and had five children: George W. and John H., of Balt.: Clara Olivia, Bertha May and Emma Elizabeth, d. Member of the Independent Order of Mechanics and the Third District Prohibiton League of Maryland. A Prohibitionist. Belongs to the Methodist Protestant Church. Chief engineer of the Bell Telephone building in Balt.

394. HON. WILLIAM BOND - b. 27 Nov. 1843 in Balt., s/o William and Theresa (Heiser) Bond. Father, manufacturer of fireworks in Balt., d. about the time of the breaking out of the Civil war. Mother, b. in Germany, d. in Balt. in 1876. William and Theresa had eight children. William m. Elizabeth Grunewald, of Balt., in 1872 and had four children: Charlotte, William C., Harry and Porter Terry. Member of the Grand Army of the Republic and the Patriotic Order Sons of America. Associate judge of the orphans' court of Balt. Co.

395. DARBY BELT - b. 18 Mar. 1819 in the fifth district, s/o Leonard and Catherine (Almock) Belt. Father, of Balt., m. Catherine and had eleven children: Caroline, widow of Joshua Cullison of the fifth district; Leonard, d.; William, lives in Woodberry; Jackson and Thomas, d.; Darby; Charles, d,; Amos, lives in Balt.; Elijah; John, d.; and Ephraim, d. in infancy. Father, shoemaker, d. in the fifth district in 1829. Mother d. at age of fifty-eight. Darby m. Mary W. Cullison, in 1844 and had two children: Keziah Cordelia, d. at twelve; and George W., m. Mary J. Gill and had eight children: Henry E., Nolan E.; Vesta I., d.; Denton O., Mary F., Bayard O., Goldo F., and Alva G., d. Mary d. 16 Apr. 1892 at age seventy-four years, six months and thirteen days. Member of the Methodist Episcopal Church. A Republican. Carpenter and undertaker of the fifth district.

396. JOHNZEY E. MYERS - b. 3 Feb. 1831 in the fifth district, s/o Samuel and Elizabeth (Earhart) Myers. Samuel, of PA, and Elizabeth had: George, Polly, Rachel, Elizabeth, Daniel, Harriet, Laura, Jane, Martha, Johnzey E. and Sarah. Johnzey m. Susan Wilfe and had two daughters: Ida M. and Esther V. Member of the Trenton Lodge No. 33, I.O.M. A Democrat. Agriculturist of the fifth district.

397. C. G. W. MACGILL, M. D. - b. 10 May 1833 in Hagerstown, MD, s/o Dr. Charles Macgill. Father, physician in Hagerstown. C. G. m. Louisa Thompson, d/o John H. and Eugenia (Morgan) McEndree, of Shepherdstown, Jefferson Co., VA, 27 Sep. 1859, and had seven children, five living: Eugenia, w/o G. T. M. Gibson, of Balt.: Mary Ragan, w/o E. Stanley Gary, only son of Hon. James A. Gary, of Balt.; Louisa R.; J. Charles, physician with father; and Margie, w/o Norman James, of Catonsville. Member of the Catonsville Country Coub, the Maryland Medical and Chirurgical Faculty, and the Baltimore Merchants' Club. A Democrat. Belongs to St. Timothy's Episcopal Church of Catonsville. Physician in Catonsville, and president of the First National Bank of Catonsville.

398. GEORGE B. TITTER - b. 10 Oct. 1862 near Chesapeake City, Cecil Co., MD, s/o Isaac and Eliza (Annison) Titter. Paternal grandfather came from England, a farmer and merchant of Newcastle, DE. Mother, d/o John Annison, both of Cecil Co.; John, carpenter, contractor and merchant of Chesapeake City, of English descent and m. Miss Wolford, of French lineage; John d. at age sixty-eight. George m. Tillie B. Peterson, of Delaware City, in Chesapeake City, and had one son, Milton. Member of the Odd Fellows' Society, joined Bohemia Lodge of Cheapeake City at age twenty-one, the Marine Engineers' Benevolent Association No. 5, of Balt. Belongs to the South Baltimore Station Methodist Episcopal Church. Chief engineer on the Choptank, a vessel of the Baltimore, Chesapeake & Atlantic Railroad Company's line.

399. EDWARD C. JAMISON - b. in 1869 in Balt., s/o Charles E. and Ellen (Ferguson) Jamison. Father, b. same place, d. at age fifty-two; mother b. in Edinburgh, Scotland (see brother, W. J. Ferguson). Paternal grandfather, of Scotch descent, d. in Balt. Charles and Ellen had four children. Member of the Friendship Lodge No. 7, I.O.O.F. A Republican. A Presbyterian. Chief engineer of the Diamond Ice Plant on the corner of East York and William streets.

400. J. B. SAUNDERS, M. D. - b. 25 Apr. 1864 in Balt., s/o James S. and Mary A. (Macklin) Saunders. Great-grandfather, Captain Saunders, b. in Cecil Co., MD, m. a Balt. lady. Grandfather, Abram Saunders, b. in Balt. Father, b. in Balt., a machinist and engineer. Mother, d/o John Macklin, b. in Balt. of Irish parentage. James and Mary had five children: John T. and James, both d.; J. B.; Mary E., assistant principal of School No. 20; and one who d. young. Member of the Medical and Chirurgical Faculty, the Baltimore Medical and Surgical Society, the Clinical Society, the Maryland Pilgrims' Association, is archan of Clifton Conclave, Improved Order of Heptasophs, the St. Lee's Council No. 19, president of St. Ignatius Branch of Catholic Friends, and secretary of the League of the Sacred Heart. Belongs to St. Ignatius Catholic Church. A Democrat. Physician of Balt.

401. STEPHEN S. MERRITT - b. in 1854 in Anne Arundel Co., s/o John and Eliza C. (Stewart) Merritt. Father, native of Anne Arundel Co., a Democrat, d. in Balt. Co. in 1864. Mother, d/o

Stephen Stewart, sister of C. J. Stewart. Stephen m. Aberilla C.
Graves, in 1881, and had six children: Maggie, Stephen, Boyd,
Abbie, Lillie and Levering. Member of the Shield of Honor.
Attends the Methodist Episcopal Church South. A Democrat.
Agriculturist of the twelfth district.

402. CAPT. JAMES R. CORKRIN - b. 9 May 1844, in Balt., s/o Capt.
William H. and Sarah A. (Patterson) Corkrin. Father, native of
Dorchester Co., MD, lives in Balt., is eighty-three. Mother,
native of Dorchester Co., d. at age seventy-three. William and
Sarah had two children, James R. and Charlesanna, w/o John R.
Collison. James m. Sarah A. Cochran, of Balt., and had four
children: James R., Jr.; George Cowell; Kittie Iola; and William
H., d. near Salisbury, MD, at age twenty-one. Master of the
Joppa, belonging to the Baltimore, Chesapeake & Atlantic line.

403. SAMUEL E. MCCREADY - b. 27 Aug. 1853, in Balt., s/o George
McCready. Father, native of St. Mary County, MD. Samuel m. (1)
Marilla Green, of Balt., and had three children: John E.,
Margaret E. and Marcella; Samuel m. (2) Sarah J. McCall, of Balt.
and had two children: Mary E., deceased; and Lillian. A Demo-
crat. Chief engineer on the Chowan, of the Baltimore, Chesapeake
& Atlantic Railroad Company.

404. A. S. ATKINSON, M. D. - b. 3 Sep. 1870 in Balt., s/o W. G.
and Kate (Gogel) Atkinson, he of Balt. and she of Harrisburg, PA.
Maternal grandparents, Charles and Jane (Smedley) Gogel. Smedley
family first to settle in Chester Co., PA. Paternal grandfather,
an Englishman, located in Balt., m. Araminta Waters. A Republican. Physician and surgeon of Balt.

405. HENRY C. BOWMAN - b. in 1844 five miles north of Balt., s/o
John and Catherine (Markeret) Bowman, both of PA. Father, b. in
Lancaster Co., d. at eighty-four at home in Balt. Mother d. in
Balt. at age seventy-five. John and Catherine were both Lutheran
and had fourteen children. Henry m. (1) Sarah Roberts, of
England, who d. in Balt., leaving a son, Elwood E. Henry m. (2)
Nannie R. Robinson, of VA, and had three children: Charles,
Anneda and Anna. Member of the Master Plumbers' Association of
Baltimore. Attends the Emanuel Methodist Episcopal Church. Pro-
prietor of a plumbing establishment at No. 328 North Howard
street.

406. REV. THOMAS GORSUCH of C. - b. in Harford county, near Bel
Air road, s/o Charles and Ann (Meredith) Gorsuch. Descendant of
English ancestors who settled in America at a very early day.
Grandfather, Charles Gorsuch, farmer. Father, b. at Fork, Balt.
Co., an old-line Whig, d. at Black Horse, in Harford Co., over
ninety years old. Mother, b. in Balt. Co., near the PA line, d/o
Thomas Meredith, she d. in Harford Co., aged eighty-five.
Charles and Ann had ten children: Wesley, d. in Ohio in 1897,
aged eighty-five; Susan, w/o Archibald Henderson, of Black Horse;
Luther, d. in Balt.; Sarah Ann, widow of John Buckwater, of IN;
Joseph, a widower, living in Balt.; Ellen, w/o Thomas Walker,
deceased; Mrs. Mary E. Smith, of New Market, MD; Nicholas and

Thomas. Thomas m. Ann T., d/o Benjamin Gatch, 2 May 1847, and had one daughter, Bettie, w/o James H. Cole. Ann d. 6 Jan. 1890. Thomas m. (2) Mary E. Stansbury, three years later; Mary is niece of Elijah Stansbury. A thirty-second degree Mason, and an Odd Fellow. A Republican.

407. A. VON DER WETTERN - b. 5 Feb. 1842 in Burgdorf, Hanover, Germany, s/o William and Caroline (Wiemack) Von der Wettern. Father and grandfather, both William, both of same province. Father d. at age sixty-four. Mother, b. in Hanover, Germany, d/o Hon. Henry Wiemack, d. at age sixty-eight. William and Caroline had seven children. Brother, William, living on Saratoga street, Balt. Subject m. Dora, d/o Heinrich and Mina (Muller) Buchholz, 1 Apr. 1866, and had nine children: Erna, w/o Mr. Becker, of Balt.; Tillie, at home; Otto; Mrs. Frieda Atkinson, of Balt. and five who d. Dora, b. in Germany. Heinrich and Mina also natives of Germany, he d. at age fifty-six and she at eighty-three. Heinrich and Mina had nine children; sister of Dora is w/o Charles Naslle, pharmacist of Balt.; brother is Henry, in Burgdorf; another brother is Frederick, d. in Germany. Member of the Germanic Lodge No. 160, A.F.&A.M., the Schellsgen Lodge, I.O.O.F., and the Kregerbuen. A Republican. Has dyeing and cleaning establishment at No. 570 Gay street.

408. THOMAS J. VAN BUSKIRK - b. 23 Nov. 1849 in Chesapeake City, Cecil Co., MD, s/o Thomas J. Van Buskirk, Sr. Father, b. in York Co., PA, a farmer, d. in Chesapeake City at age sixty-two, a Republican. Thomas m. Panola Morris, of Cecilton, MD and had three children: Elma, Blanche W. and Panola M. Member of the Marine Engineers' Benevolent Association No. 5, of Baltimore, and Banner Lodge No. 5, A.O.U.W. Belong to the Methodist Episcopal Church. A Republican. Chief engineer of the Joppa, belonging to the Baltimore, Chesapeake & Atlantic Railroad Company.

409. THOMAS DOWELL - b. 25 Feb. 1836 near Alexandria, in Prince William Co., VA, s/o Jesse and Sarah (Murphy) Dowell. Father, of Scotch descent, d. when Thomas was one year old. Mother, b. in VA, d/o Hedgeman Murphy. Jesse and Sarah had four children. Thomas m. Jane Kedwell, of Fairfax, VA, in Alexandria, VA, and had: Samuel, blacksmith;; Virginia, d; and Mrs. Catherine Johnson, of Baltimore. Jane d. in Fairfax. Thomas m. (2) Mrs. Eliza (Wilhelm) Schwartz, of York, in York. Emanuel Wilhelm, father of Eliza. Member of Zeredetha Lodge No. 451, F.&A.M., of York, PA, Herman Lodge No. 342, I.O.O.F., and the Pennsylvania Railroad Relief Association. A Republican. Foreman of the blacksmith department of the Northern Central Railroad Company.

410. ALFRED FOWBLE - b. 29 Oct. 1844 in the fifth district, s/o Joshua V. and Charlotte (Gill) Fowble. Grandfather, Nelcor Fowble, m. Miss Wher, and had: Milliker, Jacob, Peter; Penelope, w/o Judge Joshua F. Cockey; Sevena, w/o Conrad Ebaugh; Kate, w/o George Algere; Mary, w/o Henry Algere; Margaret, w/o Elijah Benson; Joshua; Susan, w/o William Herton; John and Thomas. Father, b. 16 Oct. 1804 in the same home, m. Charlotte, b. 26 Nov. 1802 and d/o Capt. Stephen Gill, and had seven children:

Phoebe, w/o Jacob Hoshall, of the sixth district, Balt. Co.;
Stephen M., killed in 1867; Louisa, w/o Thomas Cole, of the
fourth district; John T., lives near Fairview, m. Miss Gill;
Rebecca, w/o Elijah T. Benson; Sarvena J., w/o George A. Smith,
of the ninth district; and Alfred. Father d. 15 Feb. 1883, and
mother d. 9 Feb. 1877. Alfred m. Florence G. Cole, of Balt., 28
Nov. 1867, and had seven children: Irene, b. 1 Sep. 1868; Wilbur
H., b. 12 Dec. 1870; Selina, b. 14 Apr. 1874; Charlotte G., b. 5
Feb. 1877; Joseph I., b. 20 Sep. 1881; Florence T., b. 29 Nov.
1882; and Joshua A., b. 26 Apr. 1885. Irene is w/o Frank
Millenner. Florence d. 11 Nov. 1886. Alfred m. (2) Mary C.
Bixler, teacher in Balt. Co., 9 Sep. 1896. Member of the Junior
Order of American Mechanics. A Democrat. Agriculturist of the
fifth district.

411. RICHARD THOMAS MORAN - b. 2 Mar. 1840 in Balt., s/o Richard
G. Moran. Father, b. in Charles Co., MD, a blacksmith, then
steamboat engineer, is now eighty-two, a Democrat, and a
Catholic. Mother, b. in Kent Co., MD, a Catholic, is now
seventy-six. Richard and wife had four children. Subject m.
Alice A. McNeir, of Balt., and had fourteen children, eight
living: Florence, w/o Vincent Roach, Balt. attorney; Blanche, w/o
John A. Cordori; Richard Thomas, engineer; William J., carpenter;
James Avan Gibbons, electrical engineer; Edwin, Ira and Alice, at
home; Laura d. at fourteen, and five others d. in infancy.
Member of the Marine Engineers' Benevolent Association No. 5, of
Balt., and the Moranville Council No. 21, Catholic Benevolent
Legion, of Balt. Communicants of the Catholic Church. A Demo-
crat. Chief engineer of the Lancaster, belonging to the Weems
Steamboat Company.

412. FREDERICK DECKER - b. in Dec. 1834 in Konigsberg, Hesse
Darmstadt, Germany, s/o Matthias and Louisa Decker, also of
Germany. Father, a butcher, a Lutheran, d. when Frederick was
ten. Mother d. at age fifty-four. Matthias and Louisa had
fourteen children, two came to America, Frederick and Charles,
live in Balt. Frederick m. Margaret, d/o Henrick Deitrich,
Balt. merchant tailor, in Balt., and had three children:
Frederick William and Charles C., in partnership with father; and
Mrs. Mary L. Schuckhardt. Margaret, b. in Hesse-Darmstadt,
Germany. Member of the King David Lodge, A.F.&A.M., the Inde-
pendent Order of Odd Fellows, the Turnverein and Harmonica
Society. A Lutheran. A Democrat. Engaged in contracting and
building under the name of Frederick Decker & Sons.

413. HARRY R. TITTER - b. in 1865 in Chesapeake City, MD, s/o
Isaac and Eliza (Annison) Titter. Father, b. near Wilmington,
DE, d. at seventy-four near Chesapeake City. Mother, b. in
Chesapeake City; Isaac and Eliza had eight children, five
living: George and Edward, engineers; Curtis and John, farmers;
and Harry, the youngest. Member of the Junior Order of American
Mechanics and the Marine Engineers' Beneficial Association No.
13, of Philadelphia. A Democrat. Inclines to the Methodist
Episcopal Church. Chief engineer of the Octorara.

414. WILLIAM CLOUD - b. 14 Oct. 1849 in Balt., s/o Benjamin and Isabel (Kelley) Cloud, he of Sugartown, Chester Co., PA, and she of Balt. Father d. at age fifty-six. Mother d. in 1896 at age eighty-three. Benjamin and Isabel had six children, William being the third. William m. Mrs. Sarah J. Hall, d/o Andrew and Elizabeth Hunter, of Balt., in Balt. Member of the Ancient Order of United Workmen, and Wilson Post, G.A.R. Identified with the Republican party. Proprietor of William Cloud's marine railway and yards at Hughes and Covington streets.

415. RICHARD C. TRACEY - b. 30 Nov. 1823, at Black Rock Mills in the fifth district, s/o Jonathan Tracey. Father, merchandiser and miller at Black Rock Mills, then farmer. Richard m. Mary A. Price in 1849, and had seven children: Laura V., d.; Florence, w/o Wesley Ports, of the fifth district; C. Melvin, d. in 1873; Samuel J., farmer in the fifth district; George C., has a hotel in Towson; and R. W. Price and Emory C., agriculturists in the fifth district. After death of Mary, m. (2) Charlotte C. Fowble, in 1876. Charlotte d. in 1891. A Democrat. A Methodist. Retired general farmer.

416. S. HOWARD COLE - b. 17 May 1830, in the eighth district, Balt. Co.; m. (1) Emily Shaw in 1857, and had five children: William P., farmer and sheriff of Balt. Co.; Lewis S., warden at the jail; George H., lives in NC; Frank, telegraph operator; and Mary F., at home. After death of first wife, m. (2) Eleanor Shaw, sister of his first wife, in 1874. Attends the Baptist Church. Supports the Democratic party. Farmer in the fifth district.

417. ROBERT M. HURTT - b. in 1847 in Kent Co., MD, s/o Charles R. and Sarah E. (Hurtt) Hurtt. Mother, b. on the eastern shore, distant blood relative of Charles. Father, b. in MD, farmer, Democrat, d. in 1887. Hurtt family established in America when six brothers came from England in 1640 and settled on the eastern shore. Robert is only suvivor of six sons of Charles and Sarah. Robert m. Mary E. Spangler, of Williamsport, MD, in 1872, and had nine children: Annie E., Emma G., Charles R., Martha, William N., Mary L., Edward W., Linda E. and Mabel. A Democrat. Agriculturist in the twelfth district.

418. REGINALD BOWIE - b. 14 Dec. 1854 in Prince George Co., MD, s/o Walter William Wims and Adaline (Snowden) Bowie. Father, b. in Prince George Co., attorney, Democrat, d. at age seventy-eight. Mother, b. in Prince George Co., member of the Episcopal Church, d. in Balt. at age fifty-four. Walter and Adaline had eleven children; Henry B., Balt. lumber man; Amelia, w/o Thomas W. Welch; Ada, w/o Professor Morrice, of the Philadelphia City College; Robert A., civil engineer in TN; Mary, w/o Thomas Franklin, civil engineer in TX; Reginald; Walter, a lawyer, killed in the war; and four others who d. when young. Reginald m. Blanche Crouch, of Kent Co., MD, and had three children: Clarence K., Cecelia and Mary B. Connected with the Baptist Church. Chief engineer of the postoffice building of Balt.

419. JOHN N. KUNKEL - b. in Sep. 1831, in Gailbach, Bavaria, Germany, s/o John Adam and Anna M. (Christ) Kunkel. Father, b. 3 Sep. 1800 in Rosbach, farmer and weaver, d. in 1836. Mother, b. 23 Jul. 1801, m. (2) Nicholas Kunkel, brother of John, had two children, one survives, Casper, a baker in Philadelphia. Anna d. in Brightsburg, PA, 27 Jul. 1887. John m. Mary Rosina, d/o Anton Kerchner, of Wilmington, DE, in Nov. 1859 in Balt., and had nine children: Frederick J., b. in Balt. 23 Sep. 1860, in the wagon business with father; Mary R., b. 6 Sep. 1863, lives in Wilmington, NC; John A., b. 5 Aug. 1866, helps father in business; Nicholas A., b. 17 Jun. 1868, helps father in business; Francis F., b. 9 Jul. 1870, studying for the priesthood in Paris, France; Mary Theresa, b. 14 Aug. 1871, w/o P. J. Ward, of Philadelphia; Margaret, b. 1 Dec. 1874, now in the Josephinum Convent, Chicago; William F., b. 4 Dec. 1878, helps father in business; and Joseph A., b. 10 Dec. 1882, student at Calvert Hall College. Member of the Catholic Benevolent Legion No. 63, the St. Vincent de Paul Society and the Young Catholic's Friend Society. Attends Holy Cross Catholic Church. A Democrat. Proprietor of the Monumental wagon works of Balt.

420. JOHN T. GRACE - b. 10 Sep. 1855 in the twelfth district, s/o John and Mary (Bond) Grace. Father, b. at Back River Neck in the twelfth district, farmer, a Democrat, d. in 1895. Grandfather, Aaron Boyer Grace, native of the twelfth district, farmer. Mother, Mary, d/o William Bond. John and Mary had eleven children: John T.; Joseph A., of the twelfth district; Carval James, fisherman; George Washington; Sarah, w/o William Lynch, grandson of Patrick Lynch; Mary Margaret, w/o Lee McGowen, a s/o Harry McGowen; others d. John m. Mary Alice, d/o James Wilkinson, in 1879. James lived at Middle River Neck for many years; mother of Mary was d/o Moses Galloway. Member of the Shield of Honor. Attends the Methodist Episcopal Church. A Democrat. Farmer of the twelfth district.

421. WILLIAM H. EHLERS - b. 9 Mar. 1834 in the city of Balt., s/o Lewis Ehlers. Father, merchandiser, had ten children, six surviving: William H.; Justus Henry, of the second district; Louisa, w/o John Oussler, farmer; Amelia, w/o Oliver Holbrook; and Lewis, assistant superintendent of the Loudoun Park cemetery. William m. Sarah R., d/o John K. Harvey, in 1856, had four children, all d. in infancy. A Democrat. Farmer of the fifth district.

422. JOSEPH F. SHIMANEK - b. 24 Nov. 1851 in Lashan Desfours, s/o Joseph and Frances (Pech) Shimanek. Father, b. in Lashen Desfours, a blacksmith. Mother, of the same locality, d. in Feb. 1897. Children of Joseph and Frances: John, eldest, employed by McShane & Co., of Balt.; Wenceslaus, came to America, but returned to old country; Anton, blacksmith; Mary, widow of Joseph Barooh, of Balt.; Caroline, w/o Joseph Klima, of Balt. Joseph m. Annie Kalal, of Balt., in 1877, and had six children: Joseph, student at Loyola College; Mary, Annie, Francis, Wenceslaus and Lizzie. Member of the Catholic Knighthood. Belongs to the St. Wenceslaus Catholic Church. A Democrat. Manufacturer of

carriages and wagons at the northwest corner of Ashland avenue and Chapel street.

423. EDWARD E. MACKENZIE, M. D. - b. 19 Aug. 1858 in Balt., s/o Thomas and Elenora I. (Brevitt) Mackenzie, he of Calvert Co., she of Balt. Father, proprietor of large hardware store on Balt. street, d. in 1866. Mother, d/o Joseph Brevitt, M.D. of Balt., member of the Society of Friends, d. in 1880. Thomas had four children by his first marriage, two survive, Cosmo T. and Colin B., live in Balt. and engaged in hardware business, and six by marriage to Elenora: Thomas, Balt. attorney; Catherine, widow of Edwin W. Brevitt; Elenora B., w/o Rev. Ogle Marbury of Howard Co., MD, both deceased; Mary E. T. and Cassandra, of Balt.; and Edward E. Member of the Medical and Chirurgical Faculty of Maryland. Physician and surgeon at northwest corner of Biddle and Eutaw streets.

424. AUGUST KAHLER - b. 12 Jan. 1854 in the twelfth district, s/o Jacob and Christina (Otis) Kahler, of Germany. Father, settled in Balt. Co., farmer, d. in 1882. Mother, came to United States in girhood, d. in 1894, aged eighty-four. Jacob and Christina had six children: Charles, proprietor of saloon on the Philadelphia road at Collington; Jacob, farmer in the twelfth district; August; and a daughter, d. in childhood. August m. Mary, d/o Joseph Klein, of the twelfth district, in 1875, and had eleven children: Mary, w/o William Diegel, of Balt. Co.; Charles, employed on the Balt. & Ohio Railroad; Jack, Ricka, George, Joseph, Kate, Maggie, John, August, Jr., and Annie. A Democrat. Proprietor of a hotel in the twelfth district.

425. WILLIAM F. HENGST, M. D. - b. 13 Sep. 1853 in Balt., s/o Rev. Benjamin and Mary A. (Dunkle) Hengst, he of York Co. and she of Union Co., PA. Paternal great-grandfather, Michael Hengst, b. in York Co., s/o a German who came to America as a soldier in the Hessian troops during the Revolution. Grandfather, Samuel Hengst. Father, minister in the Evangelical Association, now seventy, lives in York, PA. Mother, d. in Balt. age age fifty-two. Maternal grandfather, Martin Dunkle, b. in Union Co., PA, grandson of a Swiss who came to America. Benjamin and Mary had five children: Charles D., d. in Balt.; John Edwin, druggist in Balt.; William F.; Louis Alfred, employed on the Pennsylvania Railroad; and Anne Leah, m. and lives in Williamsport, PA. William m. Martha L. Feast, d/o Zaccheus Durham of Balt., in Balt. 7 Aug. 1884. Physician and surgeon at No. 2032 North Calvert street.

426. JOSHUA F. BENSON - b. 14 Dec. 1821 near Mt. Carmel in the fifth district, s/o Elijah and Peggy (Fowler) Benson, also of the fifth district. Paternal grandfather, James Benson, b. in York Co., PA, came to Balt. Co., MD, as early as 1790, d. in 1832, aged seventy-three. Elijah and Peggy had: Sylvania, widow of Benjamin Jackson, of Hampstead, MD; James, lives in Darke Co., OH; Melchor A., farmer of the fifth district; Margaret, w/o Thomas Miller, of the fifth district; Elijah, of the fifth district; and John W., of Glyndon. Father d. at age forty-two,

and mother d. at age seventy-three. Joshua m. Hannah A. Miller, in 1856, and had five children: Ida V., w/o W. Frank Mitchell, Towson attorney; R. Seymour; E. Belle; Annie G. and Lillian. Connected with the Methodist Episcopal Church. Farmer of the fifth district.

427. FRANK M. LEE - b. in the eighth district, s/o Thomas Jefferson and Cassandra O. (Nisbet) Lee. Members of the Lee family came to America from Ditchley, England, in the early seventeenth century, locating in MA. Name originally spelled Leigh. Great-grandfather and grandfather, both William Lee, and natives of the old Bay State. Grandfather, counsul to Bordeaux, France, d. in Roxbury, MA, 29 Feb. 1840, at age sixty-eight, and buried in vault at King's Chapel, Boston. Father, b. 7 Aug. 1808, in Bordeaux, France, m. Cassandra O., d/o Judge Alexander and Mary C. Nisbet, and had four children: Alexander Nisbet Lee, d. in fall of 1879; Susan Palfrey Lee; Thomas Nisbet Lee, d. in 1878; and Frank M. Lee. Father d. in 1892, mother in 1890. First of Nisbet family to come to America, was Rev. Charles Nisbet, D.D., of Haddington, Scotland, third s/o William Nisbet, passenger on the Clyde, landing in Philadelphia, 9 Jun. 1785; Dr. Nesbit m. Anne, d/o Thomas Tweedie of Quarter, Scotland, in 1766; Alexander Nisbet, second son of Dr. and Anne Nisbet, lawyer then judge in Balt., m. Mary, d/o John Owings, and great-granddaughter of Col. Richard Colgate. Engaged in the manufacture of lime and quarrying of stone, and a farmer.

428. REV. WILLIAM W. BARNES - b. 26 Jun. 1861 near Barton, Allegany Co., MD, s/o John and Nancy (Shaw) Barnes, he of Allegany Co., and she of WV. Father, school teacher, then farmer, a Republican, is seventy-eight. Family of mother, Scotch-Irish stock, Presbyterian faith, among first settlers of WV. Mother d. in 1874. John and Nancy had five children: Henrietta, widow of James Goodwin; Nettie, w/o Albion Coles, of Norfolk, VA; Mamie, single, lives in Allegany Co.; Clara, w/o Herman Creutzberg, of Norfolk, VA; and William W. William m. Alice Lynn, d/o Dr. D. A. Cox of Hanpstead in 1886, and had two daughters: Flossie M. and Helen Lynn. Member of the Masons, and the Junior Order of American Mechanics. Pastor of the Canton Methodist Episcopal Church of Baltimore.

429. CAPT. HENRY W. MYERS - b. 29 Nov. 1828 in Hanover, Germany, s/o Lewis and Sophia Myers. Father, native of Germany, brought family to America in 1835, a miller, d. in Philadelphia. Mother d. in Balt. Lewis and Sophia had three children: Mrs. Louisa Vonder Haff, d. in Holland, leaving four children, Henry, Peter, Sophia and Louisa; Henry W.; and Fred. Henry m. Melvina, d/o Charles Aburn, of Balt., in Balt., and had three children: Charles Evers, Mabel, and John, who d. at three years. Father of Charles Aburn, English, founder of one of the old families in Balt. Melvina d. in Mar. 1886. Member of the Rescue Harbor No. 14, Masters and Pilots' Association, and the Revenue Masonic Relief Association. Belongs to the Lutheran Church. Captain, in the government service.

430. JOHN J. WIGHT - b. 18 Dec. 1820 in Balt., s/o William J. and Margaret (Howard) Wight. Father, b. near Woodstock, MD, moved to Balt. in 1805, in lumber business, an Episcopalian, a Democrat, m. Margaret Howard of Balt. and had three children, d. in 1865. Grandfather, Richard Wight, came to Balt. Co. from Northampton, Mass. John m. Amelia, d/o Alpheus Hyatt, of Balt., 18 Dec. 1844, and had: William H., farmer in the eight district; John H., president of the Sherwood Distilling Company of Balt.; James, conducts a store in Cockeysville; Margaret, deceased w/o George Morris Bond of Balt.; and Alpheus, has stone quarry in Balt. Supports the Democratic principles.

431. HAROLD BIRD - b. 25 Mar. 1857 in Wilmington, Del, s/o Dr. Clark Bird, of Washington, D.C. Harold m. Mrs. Eleanor L. Luard, d/o Capt. William and Elizabeth (Thompson) Assheton, he of Lancashire and she of Yorkshire, England, and had two children: Harold Assheton and Helen Wilson Bird. Capt. Assheton settled in Fauquier Co., VA on coming to America, and had six children: Walter, lives in Washington, D.C.; William Herbert, m. Juliet Wheelwright of Balt., and lives in VA; Ronald, owns large farm in Prince George Co.; William, Balt. business man, lives in Howard Co.; Eleanor; and Evelyn, w/o Edward Wade Calton; d. at age sixty-four, wife d. at age seventy-one. Eleanor, m. at age eighteen, Montague Luard, who d. in Washington, D.C., leaving two sons, William Sidney and Lawrence Shirley. Episcopalians. Engaged in the bicycle business in Balt.

432. HUGH HASSON - b. in Dec. 1830 , in Belfast, County Antrim, Ireland, s/o Charles and Isabel (Shannon) Hasson. Father, native of County Kerry, Ireland, sailed in 1838, with wife and three sons, Malcolm, Charles, and Hugh, on the Napoleon, of Belfast, landing in Quebec, settled first in Norristown, Montgomery Co., PA, then Balt. Co. MD, d. at about forty-three. Grandfather, Joseph Hasson, b. in County Kerry, Ireland, carder in a cotton mill, moved to Scotland. Mother, b. in Lairn, near Belfast, Ireland, d/o Hugh Shannon, a butcher. Isabel, had twelve brothers, d. in Balt. at age sixty-seven. Charles and Isabel had eight children: three daughters d. in Belfast, Ireland; two sons d. in Glasgow, Scotland. Hugh m. Ann Steener Beck, b. in Suksoldenburg, Germany, and had six children, three now living: Annie, at home; Hugh, with the Pennsylvania Railroad; and Alice, at home; Joseph, d. at age twenty-seven; Edward, d. at twenty-seven; and Mary, d. at seventeen. Ann d. in Balt., and Hugh m. (2) Ellen Dowd of VA, in Balt. Member of the Warren Lodge No. 71, I.O.O.F., and the Pennsylvania Relief Association. Attends the Methodist Episcopal Church. Employed by the Northern Central Railroad.

433. CAPT. J. H. TRUITT - b. in 1833 in Kent Co., Del, s/o Elisha and Mary (Rutledge) Truitt. Father, native of Sussex Co., DE, d. at age of forty-four, Grandfather, John Truitt, a farmer, also of Sussex Co. Family is of English lineage. Mother, native of Kent Co., d/o John and Mary (Jester) Rutledge, of the same state and farmers, d. at age forty-four. Elisha and Mary had nine children. J. H. m. Rebecca, d/o Asa Mattson, in Swedesboro,

NJ, and had one child, Bertha; Asa Mattson, steamboat captain. Member of the Independent Order of Odd Fellows. Belongs to the Wesley Chapel Methodist Episcopal Church. A Republican. Captain of the Louisa, a steamer of the Tolchester line.

434. C. ROSS MACE - b. 17 Sep. 1868 in the twelfth district, s/o Dr. William H. and Henrietta M. (Johnson) Mace. For history of Mace family see sketch of Dr. S. V. Mace. C. Ross m. Sue N., d/o Samuel N. Van Trump of Wilmington, DE, in 1849, and had two children, Rebecca Newbold and William Ross. Sue, b. in Balt. Co., MD. A Republican. Member of the Balt. bar.

435. PHILIP J. KRACH - b. in 1848 in the ninth district, s/o George Caspar and Barbara (Kausmall) Krach, of Germany. Father, farmer in the twelfth district, a Republican, d. in Mar. 1897, age eighty-four. George and Barbara had: John J., manager for a Balt. Co. lawyer; George C., farmer; August, lives on the Bel Air road; Leonard, farmer on same road; Mary, w/o Julius Deckart, of same district; Barbara, w/o John Otto; and Philip J. Philip m. Elizabeth Otto, and had seven children: John P., lives at Gardenville; George C., d. at two; Robert T., Jacob P., Lillie, Ernest and Mary at home. Member of the Gardenville Lodge No. 114, I.O.O.F., and the Junior Order of American Mechanics. Belongs to the Gardenville Lutheran Church. A Republican. Farmer of the twelfth district.

436. SQUIRE W. C. SPARKS - b. 3 Mar. 1827 in the tenth district; m. Susan Hoover, in 1848 and had nine children: Mary E., Emma F., Theodore E., George A., Walter H.; William H., Francis M., Sarah M., all d., and one d. in infancy. Supports the Prohibition party. Agriculturist of the fifth district.

437. GEORGE L. STANSBURY - b. 19 Mar. 1852 at General's Point, s/o Darius and Mary J. Stansbury. Maternal grandfather, contractor and builder in Balt. Paternal grandfather, George Stansbury, lived on same farm, which has been in the possession of the family for over two centuries. Darius and Mary had four children: two boys, deceased; George L. and Mrs. Charles E. Lynch. Father, b. in 1804, same place, d. in 1879, mother d. in 1869. George m. Mary S., d/o Joshua Lynch, in 1880, and had two children, Charles E. and Mary E. Joshua Lynch, lived on the lower part of the Patapsco Neck. Attends the Methodist Episcopal Church. A Prohibitionist. Owner of General's Point.

438. JOSEPH ALOFF - b. 19 Mar. 1840 in the city of Balt., s/o Wentling and Margaret (Beall) Aloff. Wentling and Margaret had six children: Pelina, w/o John Bigerman; Mary, m. (1) George Ort, m. (2) John Thorn; Margaret, w/o George Beacham, of Canton; Catherine, lives in Hampton, IL; Joseph; and another son. Father, farmer, d in 1842. Joseph m. Bernadena Boklage, 10 Sep. 1867, and had one daughter, Elizabeth B. Identified with the Sacred Heart Church. A Democrat. Superintendent of the Sacred Heart cemetery, in the twelfth district.

439. GEORGE ISRAEL GERMAN - s/o Joseph and Mary A. (Lauder)

German. Father, b. in Balt. Co., s/o early settlers, a Methodist, m. Mary A. Lauder and had twelve children: Joseph, eldest, never m., farmer of this area; Emory, also farmer of this area; Thomas, farmer and market gardener in Anne Arundel Co.; John Wesley, Balt. druggist; Christian, never m. lives with brother Israel, engaged in farming and the dairy business; Solomon, Methodist minister in Balt. Co., m. Mary Harrington and has two children; Theodore, m. Rosa Ray, lives on old homestead; Rachel and Mary, never m., also live on old home farm; and George. George m. Elizabeth A., d/o James Foreman, 28 Apr. 1868, and had ten children: Clara, d. in childhood; Mary Elizabeth and Annie, at home; Lilian May, d.; Charles S., carpenter and contractor; George Edwin, helps manage farm; Edith, at school; James Oscar, Randolph and Joseph, at school.

440. MILTON H. WAGONER - b. 22 Apr. 1856 in Westminster, Carroll Co., s/o Frederick and Mary A. (Blubaugh) Wagoner, of Adams Co., PA. Grandfather, Jacob Wagoner. Father, framer, tanner and huckster in vicinity of Gettysburg, then Carroll Co., where he d. in Jan. 1856. Youngest of eight children b. to Frederick and Mary. Milton m. C. V., d/o J. W. Armstrong, of Balt., and had three children: Mildred, Carroll, and an infant. Member of the Free and Accepted Masons, the Ancient Order of United Workmen, the Knights of the Golden Chain, and Balt. Lodge of the Order of Elks. A Republican. Treasurer of Armstrong, Denny & Co., undertakers and embalmers, at Nos. 715 and 717 Light street.

441. HENRY S. COOPER - b. 29 Jan. 1839 at Beckleysville, in the fifth district, s/o Henry and Barbara (Shaver) Cooper. Paternal grandfather, William Cooper, of York county, PA, first of the family in Balt. Co., d. in PA over seventy years old. Father, b. at Beckleysville, also d. there at forty-five. Henry and Barbara had six children: Abraham S., lives in Trenton, MD; Margaret, widow of Theodore Ottawaco; William S., lives on a farm near Black Rock, MD; Henry S.; Elizabeth, deceased w/o John Morris; and Samuel S., has farm near West Liberty, in the seventh district. Henry m. Diana, of the fifth district, and d/o Shedwick Kemp, in 1860, and had six children: Emma S., w/o Charles Rice; Shedwick, lives in the fifth district; Laura M., w/o T. C. Sparks, of the sixth district; Henry Richard, farmer in Carroll Co., MD; Abraham B.,d.; and Samuel W., at home. Diana d. in 1876. Henry m. (2) Mrs. Mary E. Rupp, d/o George Armacost, and granddaughter of Adam Armacost who d. in 1857. George Armacost and wife, Susanna Hager, had eight children: Mary E.; Lucinda, d.,; Margaret, w/o Joseph Miller; John Adam, lives in Carroll Co., MD; Amos H., lives in Carroll Co., MD; Susan, w/o Howard Kemp, of Carroll Co.; Keziah Myers, lives in Trenton, in the fifth district; and Georgia A., w/o Elijah Armacost. Member of Daniel Jacob Lodge, I.O.O.F., and Trenton Lodge No. 33, I.O.M. Supports the Prohibition party. Belongs to the Methodist Episcopal Church. Agriculturist of the fifth district.

442. JOHN H. TAMES - b. in 1848 in the twelfth district, s/o John and Annie Catherine (Geller) Tames. Father, a shoemaker and later in general mercantile business, then in the general mercan-

tile business, and old-line Whig, d. in 1887, age seventy-one.
Mother, now seventy-three year old (1897). John and Annie had:
John H.; Charles, partner of John, m. Sallie Dodd of Balt. Co.,
and had one daughter; George W., farmer in Harford Co.; Samuel,
worked for John til death, 8 May 1897; Mrs. Susie Richards;
Amelia, w/o William Hammock of Balt.; and Kate, d. at twenty.
Democrat. Butcher, then engaged in general mercantile business
on the Harford road in 1887.

443. G. W. ALER LOCKARD - b. 8 Oct. 1872, in the second district, s/o William and Roxana (Aler) Lockard. Maternal grandfather, George Washington Aler, b. at Fourteen Mile House, in the fourth district, the grandson of the progenitor of the family in America, who was a native of Germany located in PA. Great-grandfather, George W., lived in the fourth district. George Washington Aler, maternal grandfather, m. Elizabeth, d/o Edward and Catherine (Ware) Triplett, and had six children: George E., d. in 1868; Reuben A., d. at age two; Roxana; John M., d. in 1864; Eliza J., d. in infancy; and Pauline, d. at nine. Edward Triplett, a blacksmith, member of the Methodist Episcopal Church, affiliated with the Odd Fellows', d. in Nov. 1889, aged seventy-six. Catherine Triplett, d. in Aug. 1881, aged sixty-eight. Member of the Junior Order of American Mechanics. Farmer of the second district.

444. J. H. WISNER - b. 17 Mar. 1852 near Newton in the fifth district. J. H. m. Janey A., d/o John Armacost in Oct. 1884, and had four children: George H., Rachel B., John Arthur and Nellie J. Member of the Mt. Zion United Brethern Church. A Democrat. Agriculturist of the fifth district.

445. CAPT. TOLBART STEPHEN ILER - b. 22 Oct. 1820 in Bohemia Manor, Cecil Co., MD, s/o Capt. John Highland and Sarah (Pennington) Iler, also of Cecil Co. Grandfather, Capt. Stephen Iler, of Cecil county, master of a schooner, d. at Harlan Point. Mother, d/o Squire Robert Pennington, d. at eighty-four years. John and Sarah had four children: John, seaman, headquarterd in New Orleans; Sarah R., d. in Chesapeake City, w/o Jeremiah Malster, and mother of William T. Malster; George Washington Iler, seaman, went to New Orleans; and Tolbart Stephen. Tolbart m. (1) Mary Ann, d/o Samuel Sampson a master builder at Philadelphia, had daughter, Mary Ann, w/o George R. Cross of Balt.; m. (2) Margaret Ann, b. in Cecil Co. d/o William Hudson a farmer, and had two children: William Tolbart, grocer in Philadelphia, d. there at age twenty-seven; and Maggie, w/o R. B. Jones, of Balt. Old-line Democrat. A Presbyterian. Oldest master now sailing the bay. master of the steamer General Cadwallader.

446. JOHN F. WEYLER - b. 8 Feb. 1844 in Montgomery Co., MD. Parents came to Montgomery Co. from Wurtemberg. John m. Louisa, of Balt. and d/o Charles Hillen. Charles, a farmer on Bel Air road. Warden of the Maryland penitentiary.

447. JOSEPH HEBRANK - b. in 1848 in Lancaster Co., PA, s/o Henry and Teresa (Traig) Hebrank, also of PA. Father, a stone-mason,

Democrat, a Catholic. Henry and Teresa had: Joseph; Henry, lives in Harrisburg, PA; Michael, employed by the Northern Central Railroad Company; Max, with the Pennsylvania Railroad Company; Mary, unmarried and at home; Annie, w/o L. J. Willinger; Christina, d. in girlhood; Lena, w/o John Gray, lives in Lancaster, PA; and Sophia, w/o Francis Dotterweich. Joseph m. Bernidene Willinger, in 1872, and had twelve children: Lizzie, at home; Joseph, blinded by diphtheria; Sierlies; and Mary, b. 11 Sep. 1897; three d. at one time from diphtheria; five d. in childhood. Member of the Catholic Benevolent Legion. A Democrat. A Catholic. Member of the firm Willinger & Hebrank.

448. HENRY CARROLL WINCHESTER - b. 22 Jan. 1855, s/o Alexander and Sarah Jane (Carroll) Winchester. Father, s/o Samuel Winchester, b. in Balt., believer in Democracy. Alexander m. Sarah Jane Carroll and had large family: Elizabeth Carroll, w/o Richard Irwin Manning of South Carolina s/o General Manning; Fannie Mactier, w/o George Brown s/o Alexander Brown; Samuel Mactier, m. Lilla de Ford, Balt. business man, d. in 1878, quite young; Harriet Sterrett, w/o Rev. John S. Jones, of Philadelphia and mother of two children, Elizabeth H. and Margaret Carroll; and Henry Carroll. Henry m. Fannie Albert, d/o James Ray and Jennie (Albert) Hosmer, in 1882, and had one son, Henry Carroll, Jr. James Ray Hosmer, b. in New York City, a lawyer, m. Martha Jane, d/o Augustus James Albert, of Balt. in 1858, and had one daughter, Fannie Albert. James Ray m. (2) Ethel Bayard, and had two children.

449. JOHN F. MURRAY - b. in 1848 near Patapsco Neck in the twelfth district, s/o John and Elizabeth (Wilson) Murray, he of Middle River, MD, and she of Stafford Co., VA. Sister, Annie M., m. Joseph Carver of Havre de Grace, and a half-sister, Eliza, widow of George L. Lynch. John m. Martha J. Fenton, of PA, in 1877, and had four children: Elizabeth G., Mary O., Carrie C. and John F., Jr.. Attends the Methodist Episcopal Church. Agruculturist of the twelfth district.

450. CHARLES G. GROVER - b. 19 August 1826 in Oldtown, Balt., s/o Charles and Susanna (Stewart) Grover. Father, native of Marietta, PA, a carpenter, then in lumber business, d. at age seventy-two. Mother, b. in Balt., d. at age seventy. Grandfather, Robert Stewart, of Scotch descent, a stonecutter and contractor. Charles and Susanna had three children: Agnes, w/o Charles House, d. in Balt.; William, killed at eighteen; and Charles G. Charles m. Sarah Bond, of Balt., and had five children, three survive; Agnes, at home; Mrs. Margaret Fleming, of Balt.; and William, in business with father. Member of the Harmony Lodge No. 6, I.O.O.F., and Jerusalem Encampment. Attends the Presbyterian Church. Wholesale and retail coal dealer at No. 926 Monument street.

451. JOHN L. STONE - b. 16 Feb. 1850 in Westminster, Carroll Co., MD, s/o William H. and Marcella (Butler) Stone, both b. in Carroll Co., she near Mt. Airy. Paternal grandfather, Jacob H. Stone, b. in Germany, came to America, located in Carroll County,

a farmer. Butler family of English origin, founded in America by the great-grandfather. Grandfather, John Butler, b. in Carroll Co., farmer, m. Miss Leatherwood, also of English descent. Father, manufactured lime at Westminster, now sixty-eight. Mother d. in 1895. William and Marcella had nine children, four d.. John m. Ellen Eppler, at Marysville, near Harrisburg, PA, in 1875. Ellen, b. in Harrisburg; father of Ellen, Herman Eppler, had ten children. Member of the Landmark Lodge No. 127, A.F.& A.M., The Shield of Honor, the Junior Order of American Mechanics, the Baltimore Coal Exchange, the Seventh Ward Republican Association, and the Columbian Club. Belongs to the First Reformed Church. Wholesale and retail dealer in coal at the corner of Gay street and Sinclair avenue.

452. CALVIN T. HUDSON - b. 5 Dec. 1865 in Pedricktown, NJ, s/o John L. Hudson, Sr., (see his sketch). Calvin m. May Bailey, of Balt., and had a daughter, Mazie, aged seven. Member of the Independent Order of Heptasophs and the Marine Engineers' Beneficial Association No. 5. A Republican. Chief engineer on the steamer Easton, of the Wheeler Transportation Company, of Balt.

453. EDWARD R. DIGGS - b. in Balt., s/o Charles F. Diggs. Edward m. Mary W., d/o Robert D. Child, in Oct. 1896. Secretary and treasurer of the Baltimore High Grade Brick Company.

454. CASPAR WENIG - b. 14 Jul. 1821 in Saxony, Germany. Came to America when twenty-seven, first settled in New York, the Balt. in 1853. Caspar m. Amelia Nickerson, in Balt. Amelia d. about one year after the marriage. Caspar m. (2) Eva Mathyas in 1855. Has one son, George Wenig, manager of father's farm, m. Lena, d/o Martin Homburg, in 1896. Member of the Independent Order of Odd Fellows. A Republican. Former grocer on Alexander street.

455. CHARLES W. STANSBURY - b. in 1854 in the twelfth district, s/o Richard C. and Mary (Bond) Stansbury, also of Balt. Co. Maternal grandfather, Joseph Bond, farmer in the twelfth district. Father, also farmer in the twelfth district, d. in 1857. Richard and Mary had four children: Sarah, m. Thomas Hamilton, of Balt. and d. three years ago, all her children d. in childhood; Mary, m. George Hamilton, clerk in the Maryland Meter Works of Baltimore; Charles; and a son who d. young. Charles m. Annie E., d/o Joseph L. and Elizabeth (Boon) Harley, in 1880, and had three children: Elmer, Charles Vernon and Annie Louise. Member of the Grange. A Democrat. Belongs to the Methodist Episcopal Church. Business man of the twelfth district.

456. WORTHINGTON LUKE JONES - b. 4 Feb. 1857 in Frederick Co., MD, s/o Josiah and Mary Jones. Father, native of MD, d. in Balt. in 1881. Josiah and Mary had eleven children: William, railroad man living in Cincinnati; Charles, lives in Cincinnati, in the bicycle business; Bertie, lives in Chillicothe, IL, a railroad man; Taylor, d.; Helen; Nettie, w/o Harry Martindale, lives in Balt.; and Worthington. Worthington m. Alice Elizabeth, d/o Martin and Eliza M. (Hoffman) Cook in 1879, and had one son, Benson. Martin Cook came to America from Germany with his

parents at age three. Members of the Episcopal Church. Engaged in general farming and the dairy business in the ninth district.

457. JOHN BUSHROD SCHWATKA, M. D. - b. 19 Feb. 1861 in Chesterville, Kent Co., MD, s/o John A and Rachel (Sanders) Schwatka. Grandfather, John Schwatka, b. in Balt. in 1810, a blacksmith and wheelwright, d. at seventy-five. Great-grandfather, August Schwatka, b. in Bortien, Germany, came to America and settled in Balt. in 1796, a machinist. Father, b. in Chesterville, a wheelwright, m. Rachel, d/o Bushrod and Emily (Moffett) Sanders, and had two children, John Bushrod and William H., physician of Balt.; Rachel, b. in Kent Co.; great-grandfather Sanders, clergyman in the Methodist Episcopal Church. John m. Margaret G. Cooper, of Philadelphia, in Kent Co., 6 Oct. 1885, and had three children: John Bushrod, Jr., William H. and Margaret V. Cooper family, of PA, Quaker lineage, settled at Attleboro. Member of the Cassia Lodge No. 45, A.F.&A.M., the St. John's Chapter No. 19, R.A.M., the Concordia Council No. 1, R.&S. M., the Crusade Commandery No. 5, K.T., and Boumi Temple, Ancient Arabic Order, Nobles of the Mystic Shrine. Professor of anatomy in the Baltimore University School of Medicine.

458. EDWARD D. PRESTON - b. in 1843 in the southern part of the city of Balt., s/o William and Elizabeth (Auld) Preston. Grandfather, Edmond Preston, b. in VT. Father, also b. in the Green Mountain state, a blacksmith, member of the Wesley chapel Methodist Episcopal Church, a Whig, d. in 1863. Mother, Elizabeth, d/o Dawson and Susan Auld, of Talbot county, MD, d. in 1874, age sixty-two. Edward m. Rachel, d/o Francis and Hannah Dunn, in Balt. in 1861, and had nine children; Mary R., Elizabeth, Susan R. and Bertie; three children d. in infancy; Ellen at eight and George C., d. in 1893, age twenty-six. Member of the Odd Fellows and the Masonic order. Belongs to the Methodist Episcopal Church South. Builder and contractor of Balt.

459. E. A. MUNOZ, M. D. - b. 21 Mar. 1863 in Cuba, s/o Antonio Munoz. Old Cuban family that traces its ancestry back nine hundred years or more to the days of the Castilians and their progenitors, the Moors. Father, Antonio, and grandfather, Joseph Munoz, both b. in Cuba, and both d. when comparatively young. Mother, recent widow, came to America with son in 1870. Member of the Officers' Association of the Fifth Regiment, the alumni of the Baltimore University School of Medicine, and the Medical and Chirurgical Faculty of Maryland. A Democrat. Physician at the corner of Guilford and La Fayette avenue.

460. JOHN S. LONGNECKER - b. 1 Feb. 1854 in the fourth district, s/o David S. and Ann (Bachman) Longnecker. Father, b. near Strasburg, in Lancaster Co., PA. Grandfather, David Longnecker, Sr., located in Dulaneys Valley, a farmer, d. in Towson at seventy-five. Children of David, Sr., were: John H.; Lizzie, widow of Col. James Miller; Emma, widow of Augustus Hamilton; and David S. David, Jr., m. Ann Bachman, of Lancaster, and had four children: Edwin B., d. in 1886; one who d. in infancy; John S.; and Annie S., b. in 1863, lives in Glyndon, MD. John m. Betsy

Scott, of the eighth district, on 23 Nov. 1879, and had three
children; John G., Frank and Mabel. Member of the Golden Chain.
Belongs to the Methodist Episcopal Church. A Republican. Dairyman and general farmer of the fourth district.

461. JOHN T. FOWBLE - b. 10 Oct. 1835 in the fifth district.
John m. Eliza, d/o Richard Gill, in 1870, and had four children:
Maggie, w/o William J. Nolte, of the fourth district; Elmo, at
home; Sevena, d.; and Ollie E., at home. A Democrat. Agriculturist of the fourth district.

462. H. F. MILLER & SON - Henry F. Miller, b. 29 Nov. 1837 in
Hesse-Cassel, Germany, s/o George Miller. Father, a paper manu-
facturer, d. when Henry was eleven. Mother, a widow, came to
America with two sons and one daughter in 1848, locating in
Pittsburg, PA. H. F. m. Martha E., b. in Hamburg, Germany, d/o
John Loewer an oil merchant in the fatherland, in Cincinnati, and
had six children: Nellie L.; George; Bertha A., Mrs. R. T.
Wegner, of New York City; Lydia L., Mrs. R. J. W. Hamill, of
Balt.; Sarah S. and Lily M. Member of the Baptist Benevolent
organization of the United States. A Republican. Son, George
Miller, b. 16 Aug. 1865 in Rochester, NY, member of the Baptist
Benevolent Association of the United States, the Baptist Young
People's Union of America, the Maryland Baptist Union Associa-
tion, the First Baptist Church, and the Young Men's Christian
Association. A Republican. Manufacturers of tin boxes at Oak
and Twenty-sixth streets.

463. WILLIAM J. GREEN - b. in 1866 at Twin Oaks, in the twelfth
district, s/o Josiah and Eleanor (Stansbury) Green, both b. in
twelfth district. Grandfather, Abram Stansbury, b. at Twin Oaks,
and d. at Twin Oaks in 1897 age ninety. Father, in the clothing
business in Balt., had brother, Vincent Green. William m. Laura
V., d/o Jacob Schunk, farmer of the twelfth distict, in 1893 and
had two children, Eleanor Ruth and Lillian. Member of the
Grange. Belongs to the Methodist Episcopal Church. Votes Democratic.

464. THOMAS WHEELER - b. 5 September 1843 in York, PA, s/o
Joseph and Martha (Thompson) Wheeler. Of English lineage.
Paternal grandfather, farmer at Rider's Switch, in Balt. Co.
Father, b. at Rider's Switch, a railroad man, d. in Balt. at age
sixty-four, on 15 Apr. 1865. Mother, native of Balt. Co., d. at
age seventy-three. Joseph and Martha had nine children, Thomas
being the fifth. Had brothers Joseph and Charles, fought for the
union during the Civil war. Thomas m. Laura J. Mackenhamer, of
Balt., and had seven children: Ida Grace; Clarence E., machinist;
William E, a tinsmith; Joseph Lewis, works for the Maryland Meter
Works; George Thompson; Harry Howen and Elsie May. Member of the
Morley Lodge No. 107, I.O.O.F., the Camp No. 16, Patriotic Order
Sons of America, and the Pennsylvania Relief Association. A
Republican. A Methodist Protestant. Foreman of the coppersmith
and steam-fitting department of the Northern Central Railroad
Company, in Balt.

465. JAMES H. CALLIS - b. in the city of Balt., s/o Daniel and Anna (Tucker) Callis. Father, b. in Mathews Co., VA, m. Anna Tucker, b. in Ann Arundel Co., and had four children. Grandfather, George Callis. Mother, d/o Zachariah Tucker a farmer, d. in Balt. aged seventy-five. James m. Susan Bell, of Balt., and had eight children, five living; James, master bricklayer; Charles, carpenter; Thomas, muscian; Harry, clerk; all live in Balt., and Mrs. Newton Kinley, lives in Frederick Co., MD. Member of the Franklin Lodge of Odd Fellows. A Republican. Connected with the Broadway Methodist Episcopal Church. Oldest coal dealer in Balt., with yards at No. 1528 East Baltimore street.

466. WILLIAM C. BROOKS - b. 27 Apr. 1861 near Belfast in the eighth district, s/o Charles and Mary P. (Goodwin) Brooks. Father, farmer, b. same place, a Democrat, a Methodist Episcopalian, m. Mary P. Goodwin, of Carroll Co., and had three children: Benjamin, has the old homestead at Belfast; Ruth T., w/o George R. Chilcoat, of Belfast; and William C. Grandfather, William Brooks, farmer, b. in Balt. Co. Ancestors from England. William m. Nannie E., d/o Rowan Mays of the eighth district, and had five children: Allen G., Margaret, William, Landon and Helen. Member of the Shield of Honor. A Democrat. Belongs to the Methodist Epicopal Church. Undertaker and dealer in monuments.

467. GEORGE TYSON KENLY - b. in 1814 in Balt., s/o Edward and Maria (Reese) Kenly; (see Maj. William L. Kenly). George m. Priscilla, d/o Col. Gassaway and Ellemora Bowie (Claggett) Watkins, and had following: Edward G., president of the Motor & Heater Company of Baltimore; John R., general manager of the Atlantic Coast Line Railroad, lives in Wilmington, NC; Davis L., farmer in Hagerstown, MD; Douglas C., connected with the Cash Register Company of New York; William W., general manager of the United States Motor Supply Company of New York City; and Albert C., general freight agent of Balt. for the Atlantic Coast Line Railroad. Priscilla d. 16 May 1893. Member of the Episcopal Church. Treasurer of the Chamber of Commerce in Balt.

468. WILLIAM W. RADCLIFFE - b. 28 Feb. 1853 in Howard Co., MD, s/o Samuel J. and Martha Ann (Gosnell) Radcliffe. Father, b. in England, left an orphan at an early age, came to the United States, settled on the Patapsco river, near Thistle, about 1832, a farmer and a painter, member of the Odd Fellows' Lodge and the Knights of Pythias, a Democrat. Mother, b. in Howard Co., MD. Samuel and Martha had eight chihldren: Samuel E., contractor; George Worth, merchant; Charles C., painter; Thomas Brent, printer, all of Ellicott City; Ella, widow of Beil Helm; Annie M., w/o George E. Johnson, of Ellicott City; and Carrie, d. William m. Leah Susan, d/o Thomas G. and Rebecca J. Rutledge, 16 Oct. 1878, and had three children: Rutledge Winfield, Aleda Grace and William Austin, all at home. Member of the Shield of Honor and the Odd Fellows. A Presbyterian. A Democrat. Leading cola merchant, and dealer in grain and feed, at No. 1800 West Pratt street.

469. ARTHUR CHENOWETH - b. 18 Nov. 1833, in the eighth distict, s/o William and Amy (Davis) Chenoweth. Grandfather, Richard, b. in Balt. Co., m. Ellen Ascue, 14 Nov. 1779, and had: Sarah E.; Jemima, w/o a merchant in Balt.; Mrs. Mary Stone, husband a farmer and miller; Arthur, William and Joshua. Father, b. 9 May 1791 in the fourth district, a farmer, m. 16 Sep. 1813, Amy Davis and had eleven children: Rixton, PA business man; John, farmer; Horace, mail contractor; Robert, connected with the Baltimore & Ohio Railroad; William, farmer; George, farmer; Absalom B., miller; Mary w/o Charles Hilyard, carpenter and builder; Richard, police in Balt.; David; and Arthur. Father d. in 1853. Arthur m. Harriet, d/o James and Ellen (Dixon) Jones, 10 Jan. 1861, and had nine children: Mary Florence, w/o Joseph J. Davis; William, m. Edna Shipley of Balt. Co., lives at Pikesville, a painter; Louis N., a carpenter; and six who d. when young. Member of the Odd Fellows, the Knights of Pythias, the Junior Order of American Mechanics, the Grange, and the Masons. Belongs to the Methodist Episcopal church. Superintendent of the Dunbarton estate, in the third district

470. ALLEN D. SPENCER - b. in 1836 at Newport, Campbell Co., KY, s/o William and Eliza R. (Kellum) Spencer. Family founded on the eastern shore by great-grandfather, who came from England, a farmer and merchandiser. Father, b. in Worcester Co., MD, m. Eliza R., d/o Custes Kellum, both b. in Bellehaven, VA, and had six children: Allen, others d. in early life. Father, a shoe-maker, d. in KY. Mother, m. two more times, had two children, both deceased, d. in Snow Hill, MD, at age of ninety-two. Allen m. Priscilla, d/o James King, in Pokomoke City, MD and had six children: Ella I., at home; Mrs. Jennie McKey, of Snow Hill; Allen D., with the Southern Electric Light Company of Baltimore; and John, William and James, all at home. Priscilla, b. near Princess Anne, member of the Methodist Episcopal Church. Member of the Mt. Vernon Lodge of Baltimore. A Democrat. Chief engineer of the Maggie, of the Baltimore, Chesapeake & Atlantic Railroad Company.

471. ELISHA WEBB - b. 16 Jun. 1844, in DE, s/o James Webb. Father, also native of DE, a ship carpenter, age eighty-three. Lives in Philadelphia, with son. Member of the Marine Engineers' Beneficial Association. A Republican. Senior member of the firm of Elisha Webb & Son, manufacturers and dealers in steamship ranges, cabooses and general galley equipment, ship lamps and lanterns, and steamship, railway and engineers' supplies at No. 142 South Delaware avenue, Philadelphia, PA. Chief engineer of the Ericsson, of the Ericsson Steamboat line.

472. WILLIAM FITZELL - b. 22 May 1841 in Ireland, s/o John and Rebecca (Buck) Fitzell, both of Ireland. John and Rebecca, m. in Ireland, 17 Mar. 1840, came to America, located in NJ, then near Owings Mills, in Balt. Co., MD, then Hampton, and finally in the twelfth district. Father, a farmer, a Democrat. John and Rebecca had eleven children: George, MD farmer, d.; Rebecca, m. James A. Jones; John, farmer in the twelfth district; James, farmer, d.; Thomas R., farmer in the twelfth district, moved to

NC; Richard, farmer in NC; Samuel, d. at eighteen; Annie, m. John Campbell, of Balt. Co.; Mollie, m. Joseph Petezold, grocer at Sparrows Point; and Lizzie, m. August Bussie, farmer in Balt. Co. William m. Mary A. Holderman, of Philadelphia, PA, in 1880. Members of the Methodist Episcopal Church. Had been a Democrat, but supported the Republican party in the presidential election of 1896.

473. JOHN E. PRICHARD, M. D. - b. 13 Feb. 1830 in Wales, s/o Henry E. and Elizabeth (Owen) Prichard. Family of Henry, a native of England, lived in one place for over ten generations. Henry m. Elizabeth Owen, an English lady, came to America in 1840, settled in Lewis Co., NY, d. in 1872. Elizabeth d. shortly after coming to America. Henry and Elizabeth also had a daughter, Magdaline, m/ Andrew Radley, and had three children. John m. Mary, d/o Thomas Jones, of Albany, NY, in 1857, and had one child, Mary, w/o Frederick Bell, of Albany, NY. Mary d. in 1858. John m. (2) Emma Jenkins, in 1863, and had three children: Harry F., furnace builder; Hugh J., d. in 1897, on his twenty-eight birthday; and John W., worked in the copper works of Canton. Member of the Masonic order and the Royal Arcanum. A Republican. Attends the Episcopal Church. Physician in Canton.

474. JOHN D. C. DUNCAN - b. 29 Apr. 1829, near Cockeysville, s/o William and Ellen (Litsinger) Duncan. Father, b. in the north of Ireland, of Scotch descent, came to American, settling in Balt. Co., MD, in 1818, a mason, a Democrat, a Presbyterian, d. in 1885. Mother, d/o Joseph Litsinger, family of German origin, d. in 1883. William and Ellen twelve children, following survive: John D. C.; Charles H., lives in Oil City, PA; Eliza, widow of F. I. Wheeler, of Montgomery Co., MD; Dr. James A., physician in Pittsburg, PA; Martha, w/o Henry Whitaker, of Harford Co., MD; Clara, w/o Joseph Shamburger, of York, PA; George H., of Balt.; and Jackson L., Methodist minister of Hagerstown, MD. John m. Catherine E., d/o Charles Jones, 29 Mar. 1854, and had six children: Frank I., lives in Lutherville, MD; Dr. Edward M., physician in Govanstown; George C., lives in Cockeysville; Albert E., of Cockeysville; and Nellie F. and Bettie B., at home. A Democrat. Attends the Methodist Church. Retired from general merchandising.

475. WILLIAM CORSE - b. in 1804 in Harford Co., MD, s/o John and Susan (Coale) Corse. William m. Deborah S., d/o Robert Sinclair, Sr., in 1831, and had eleven children: Mary W., m. Edward S. Campbell, Philadelphia lawyer; Carrie D., at home; Robert S., m. Rachel S. Norris, lives in Owings Mills; George F., M.D., in another sketch; Esther S., m. Dr. E. W. Janney, of Loudoun Co., VA; Susan C., m. Maj. E. C. Gilbreath, officer in the regular army; Dr. William J., in the nursery business; Annie C., m. Calvin Conard, of Philadelphia; Frank E., in the nursery business with brother, m. Sallie H. Mathews, d/o John D. Mathews; Lucy C., m. Dr. B. F. Betts, of Philadelphia; and Henry C., d. at three years and ten months. Robert Sinclair, a nurseryman, d. 27 Oct. 1853, age eighty-two. Esther, w/o Robert, d. in Feb. 1853, age eighty-three. Deborah b. in Balt. A Republican. William d. 8

Mar. 1869, age sixty-five. Had nursery business which is now in the hands of sons, William and Frank.

476. CAPT. WILLIAM HENRY H. PERRY - b. 8 Feb. 1841 in Caroline Co., MD, s/o William and Nancy (Waddell) Perry, also of Caroline Co. William and Nancy had: William Henry Harrison; Charles, soldier and farmer, d. in Caroline Co.; David F., farmer near Preston; Sarah A., d.; and Georgia and Mary, live at Pottstown, PA. Father, member of the Methodist Episcopal Church, farmer, d. in 1870. Grandfather, Nathan Perry, of English descent, member of the Methodist Episcopal Church. William m. Fannie, d/o Willis Wright, 3 Apr. 1872, and had two children: Harry Oscar, merchant tailor in Balt.; and Georgia Alice. Fannie b. at Choptank. Member of the Masons, and the Masters and Pilots' Association. A Republican. Members of the Methodist Episcopal Church. Skipper of the Easton.

477. EDWIN D. SELBY - b. 11 Jul. 1840 in Freedom, Carroll Co., MD. Edwin m. Celia Moneymaker, 20 Aug. 1863, and had four children, only two living: Mary E., w/o W. S. Tipton; and Celia, w/o Joseph F. Eline. Member of the Odd Fellows' lodge of Reisterstown. Supports the Democratic principles. Undertaker of Reisterstown, and manufacturer of tombstones and monuments.

478. GEORGE H. BUDEKE - b. 12 May 1846 in Hamilton, N.C., s/o Henry and Clara (Huckelmann) Budeke. Father, b. in Hanover, Germany, settled in Balt. in 1837, then moved to Hamilton, NC in 1846, d. in 1858, age forty-two. Mother, also b. in Germany, d. in Balt. in 1880, age sixty-four. Henry and Clara had five children. George m. Wilhelmina Grothaus, of Balt., in Balt. After Wilhelmina d., George m. (2) Julia Wahl, b. and d. in Balt. George had five children, two living, George Milton and Anthony Wahl. Member of the Second Ward Young Men's Progressive Democratic Club, the East Baltimore Business Men's Association, the Royal Arcanum, the Okeil Society, and Morley Lodge, I.O.O.F. Dealer in paints, oils and painters' supplies at No. 418 South Broadway.

479. FRADUS A. ROBINSON - b. 12 Aug. 1844 in Elkton, Cecil Co., MD, s/o William and Julia (Aldridge) Robinson, also of same county. Father, a sailor, s/o a farmer, d. in Elkton, age sixty-four. Mother d. at sixty-eight. William and Julia had eleven children, six living: Fradus A.; William, chief engineer at Sparrows Point; John, chief engineer, lives at Wilmington, DE; Nicholas, stationary engineer in Chester, PA; and Harry, engineer in Philadelphia. Fradus m. Mattie Randall, of Philadelphia, in Philadelphia. Mattie d. in Philadelphia. Fradus m. (2) Beulah, d/o William Brock, in Balt., and had three children, Beulah, Leslie and Burke. Beulah, b. in Balt., d. in Camden. Fradus m. (3) Louise Peltier, of Palmyre, NJ. Member of the Marine Engineers' Beneficial Association No. 13, of Philadelphia. Belongs to the Methodist Episcopal Church of Camden. Chief engineer of the steamboat Anthony Groves, Jr.

480. JAMES GARDNER - b. in Oct. 1860 in Balt., s/o Joseph and

Sarah (Johnson) Gardner. Paternal grandfather, native of the north of Ireland, came to America, settled in the Lackawanna Valley, PA, moved to the Shenandoah Valley. Father, b. near Scranton, PA, m. Sarah Johnson, and had five children. Sarah, b. on the eastern shore, of English ancestry, d. in Balt. James m. Rosa , d/o William Amey, of Balt., in Balt., and had two children, Arthur and Myrtle. Member of the Marine Engineers' Association No. 5, the Columbian Brotherhood of Steam Engineers and the Heptasophs. Identified with the Republican party. Chief engineer at Hotel Rennert.

481. CHARLES E. BELT - b. 26 Jul. 1852 in New Windsor, Carroll Co., MD, s/o Leonard and Sarah A. (Gilbert) Belt. Father, b. in Carroll Co., killed between two passenger coaches in 1896, age sixty-eight, member of the Masons. Mother, b. in Carroll Co., d/o David Gilbert, d. in Balt. Leonard and Sarah had ten children, Charles being the oldest. Charles m. Lizzie, d/o Daniel Battenfield, in Balt., and had one child, Irene. Lizzie b. in Balt. Member of the Mechanics Lodge No. 15, I.O.O.F. Belongs to the Grace English Lutheran Church. Chief engineer and custodian of the Baltimore & Ohio Central building.

482. JOHN C. JIMISON - b. 15 Jan. 1847 in Newcastle Co., DE, s/o Absalom and Jane E. (Mirch) Jimison, of the same state. Father, d. in Newcastle Co. at age thirty-five, when John was an infant. Mother, d. at age seventy-three. Absalom and Jane had four sons. John m. Matilda Stephenson, of Philadelphia, in 1873, and had two sons: Samuel T., traveling salesman; and John C., oiler on the Anthony Groves. Matilda d. in 1882. John m. (2) Mary Wortche, of Balt. in 1886, and had two children: Howard W. and Elizabeth W., known as Elsie, both at home. Member of the Eureka Lodge No. 12, K. P., of Philadelphia, the Hancock Lodge No. 2, Shield of Honor, and the Marine Engineers' Beneficial Association No. 13, of Philadelphia. Attends the English Lutheran Church. Chief engineer on the General Cadwalader, of the Ericsson line.

483. J. CALVIN SCHOFIELD - b. 11 Aug. 1864 in Birmingham, Huntingdon Co., PA, s/o William and Catherine J. (Wall) Schofield, he of Belfast, Ireland, and she of PA. Father, came to the United States in 1851, settled in Pittsburg, PA, a Republican. Mother, Catherine, d/o John Wall, a distiller in Bucks Co., PA, and granddaughter of a distiller who settled in Bucks Co. in 1796. William and Catherine had seven children: J. Calvin; William H., in the harness business in Tyrone, Blair Co., PA; James F., M.D., physician of Huntingdon Co., PA; Robert K., M.D., lives in Birmingham, PA; Edward, Myrtle and Zella, all at school. J. Calvin m. Carrie M., d/o George W. Rever, of Balt. Co., in 1892. Member of the Orders of Red Cross and Heptasophs. Attends the German Lutheran Church. A Democrat. Physician and surgeon of Orangeville.

484. CHRISTOPH GISSEL - b. in Frankfort-on-the-Main, Germany, s/o Paul and Maggie (Steinmaer) Gissel. Father, carpenter and builder, spent whole life in same place, d. at age seventy-five. Mother, b. in Steinbach, Frankfort. Paul and Maggie had seven

children, Christoph only one to come to America. Left Germany in 1852, for London, sailed to New York, settled in Balt. Christoph m. Mary Sophia Hempel, b. in Hessen, Germany, in Balt. Member of the King David Lodge No. 168, A.F.&A.M., the Odd Fellows' society, and the Independent Order of Red Men. A Republican. Belongs to St. Matthew's Lutheran Church. Retired contractor and builder.

485. SAMUEL RICHMOND - b. 9 Apr. 1824 in County Antrim, Ireland, s/o Daniel and Mattie (Walker) Richmond, of the same county. Father, a farmer, d. in Ireland, age fifty-two. Mother, d. in Ireland, age eighty-eight. Daniel and Mattie had nine children, only Samuel and Matthew surviving. Came to America in 1847, settled in Balt. Co. Samuel m. Eliza Ann Bell, b. in County Down, Ireland, in 1848, and had twelve children: Daniel Walker, m. May Wright, and had four sons; Mattie, w/o Samuel Shipley, of Balt.; Belle, at home; Mary, m. and lives in Balt.; Ella, w/o D. R. Holmes, of Balt.; Annie, m. Matthew Richmond, a florist; Lillie, m. Edward Holden, of Balt.; Agnes, w/o Robert Brodie, of Balt. Co.; John, d. at age thirty-six; and three who d. in childhood. A Democrat. A Presbyterian.

486. JOHN A. NEEL - b. 30 Apr. 1844 in Lancaster Co., PA, s/o Hugh and Mary (Neeper) Neel. Hugh and Mary had six children: John A.; Thomas, d. in 1857; Samuel, lives in Christian Co., IL; Martha J., w/o A. W. Fore, farmer in the fourth district; Rebecca S.; and Joseph. Father d. in 1866, age sixty-six. John m. Mary E. Ducker, 21 Jun. 1877. A Prohibitionist. Members of the Lutheran Church. General farmer and dairy man of the fourth district.

487. ALBERT V. TUTTLE - b. 10 Nov. 1866 in Balt. City, s/o Charles and Rebecca (Hall) Tuttle. Grandfather, Alfred Tuttle, printer for the Baltimore Sun. Father, b. in Newark, NJ, a tailor in Balt., m. Rebecca Hall, b. in Snow Hill, and had nine children. Father d. in 1880; mother is now sixty-nine. Albert m. Bertha, d/o Nicholas Rupp, of Balt., in Balt., and had one son, Albert Vinton, Jr. Member of the Clifton Wheelmen's Club. A Democrat. Teaches all styles of dancing at Patterson Hall, No. 1000 Broadway.

488. MARCELLUS WOODWARD - b. 1 Dec. 1843 in Pickston (now Randolph), ME. Marcellus m. Emma, d/o Anderson B. King, in Worcester, MA, and had two children: Joseph M., student; and Meddie, d. at age ten, in 1893. Emma lived near Monmouth, ME before marriage. Universalists. Chief engineer of the steamer Fairfax, on the Merchants and Miners' Steamboat line.

489. CAPT. J. D. JOHNSON - b. in 1855 in Balt., s/o John and Maggie (Houck) Johnson. Father, b. in Germany, a carpenter, d. in 1856, age thirty-five. Mother, b. in Wurtemberg, Germany, lives in Balt. J. D. m. Lizzie L., d/o Peter Zimmerman, in Balt., and had: William, Maggie, Edward, Lizzie, Mary, Lena and James, living; John, Henry, George, Daisy and Emma (twins), Katie and Frederick, deceased. Member of Valiant Lodge No. 63, K. P.

Attends the Lutheran Church on Eastern avenue. Commands the Defender, the largest dredge in the country.

490. CAPT. W. W. MATTHEWS - b. 9 Jan. 1834 in Balt., s/o Stephen and Maria (Banam) Matthews. Father, b. in Worcester Co., MD, lost at sea with his ship. Mother, b. in Worcester Co., d. in early womanhood. W. W. m. Priscilla, d/o Peter Johnson, 25 May 1871, near Pocomoke City, and had: Alonzo and Leroy, printers; and Willietta Montrue, at home. Priscilla b. in Pocomoke City. Member of the Order of the Golden Chain. A Democrat. Captain of the steamer Tangier, is the oldest master in the employ of the Baltimore, Chesapeake & Atlantic Steamboat Company

491. CAPT. GRIFFIN D. RICE - b. in 1846 in Northumberland Co., VA, s/o J. B. and Elizabeth (Lampkin) Rice. J. B. and Elizabeth had eleven children, Griffin being the first. Father, b. in Northumberland Co., farmer, d. at age fifty. Grandfather, Richard Rice, a Virginian, descendent of Scotch ancestors. Mother, d/o Griffin Lampkin, descended from English ancestors. Griffin m. Essie Roberts, in 1885 and had two children. Essie, b. in Northampton, VA, d. in Balt. Master of the Meteor.

492. COL. VICTOR HOLMES - b. on the Belmore farm in the tenth district, s/o Gabriel Holmes. Father, b. in one of the northern counties of Ireland, came to American, settled in Balt. Co., had seven children: James, d. unmarried; Jane, w/o Nathan Kane, of Harford Co.; William, d. unmarried; Temperance, w/o James Boyd, of Balt.; Elizabeth, w/o Robert Crawford, of VA; John G., and Victor. Victor m. Elizabeth, d/o Maj. Dixon Stansbury, and had one daughter, Griselda. Griselda, m. Thomas Lane Emory, and had three children; Bessie, w/o Charles Robbins Lord, Balt. business man; Mary Rogers; and Richard, b. 24 Mar. 1870 in the tenth district, general manager of the Baltimore Traction Company, member of the Royal Arcanum. A Democrat. Family identified with the Episcopal Church. Victor d.

493. DAVID GREGG McINTOSH - b. 16 Mar. 1836 at Society Hill, SC, s/o James H. and Martha Jamison (Gregg) McIntosh. Great-grandfather, John McIntosh, settled near Society Hill about 1756. John and younger brother, Alexander, left Scotland, among early pioneers who settled on the upper waters of the Great Pee Dee, in what was called the Welch Neck. John left five sons, eldest being, Capt. Alexander McIntosh. Youngest son of John, James, m. Margaret Lucas, whose son, James H., m. Martha Jamison, d/o David and Athalinda Gregg, and had eight children, David being next to the eldest. Grandfather, John Gregg, moved from the north of Scotland to Londonderry, Ireland, then to America, settling near the Pee Dee where he was granted thirteen hundred and fifty acres. John Gregg had seven children, the eldest, James, m. Mary Wilson, of Williamsburg, and had nine children, the second son being David; David, left three daughters, the eldest being Martha Jamison, and a son, the late Right Reverend Alexander Gregg of TX. David m. Virginia Johnson, d/o Gen. James W. Pegram and Virginia Johnson, in the fall of 1865, and had three children: Virginia, d. in 1896; Mrs. William Waller Morton, of Richmond;

and David G. McIntosh, Jr. Virginia was sister of Gen. John
Pegram and Col William I. Pegram. A Democrat. Attorney.

494. DAVID W. JONES, M. D. - b. 16 Feb. 1862 in Merthyr-Tydvil,
Wales, s/o John W. and Mary (Reese) Jones, also of Wales. John
and Mary came to America about 1866, settled in Scranton, PA.
Father, a miner, accidentally killed, in 1889. John and Mary had
twelve children. David m. Elizabeth, d/o Frederick and Hanna
Kindervatter, in 1891, and had one child, Elizabeth. Elizabeth,
b. in Balt., d. soon after birth of daughter. Member of the
Masons. A Republican. Physician in Canton.

495. PROF. BERNARD PURCELL MUSE, M. D. - b. 23 Jan. 1868 in
Essex Co., VA, s/o S. W. and Mary Louise (Purcell) Muse, both of
VA. Family moved to Balt. in 1870. Father, a traveling sales-
man, is now fifty-six, and mother is fifty-two. S. W. and Mary
identified with the Brantley Baptist Church, of Balt. Bernard m.
Florence, d/o Dr. William H. Sunderland, 21 Apr. 1891, in Green-
briar Co., WV, and had two children, Marie Lorena and Samuel
William, Jr. Florence, b. in Balt., member of the Methodist
Episcopal Church South. Member of the Masonic order, the
Improved Order of Heptasophs, and the Baltimore Medical and
Surgical Society. Identified with the Brantley Baptist Church.
Physician and surgeon at No. 1002 Edmondson avenue.

496. CAPT. JOHN RHODES - b. 8 Jul. 1845, in Devonshire, England.
Not liking study, ran away from home at age twelve, became a
cabin boy on a sailing-vessel. John m. Mary Nelson, of Balt., 2
Oct. 1877, and had two daughter: Matilda E., d. in 1883, aged
nearly six, and Bessie C., at home. A Republican. Master of the
dredge Pugh, of the Moore Dredge Company, of Mobile, AL.

497. GEORGE W. EFFORD - b. 18 May 1860 in Richmond Co. VA, s/o
Zachariah and Margaret (Roberts) Efford. Father d. when George
was six months old. Mother, b. on the eastern shore, of English
descent. Grandfather, Thomas Roberts, farmer, d. at age eighty-
eight. Zachariah and Margaret had nine children. George m.
Mollie, d/o Capt. William Pines, in Balt., and had three children: Alice, Charles and Harry. Mollie b. in VA. William Pines,
farmer and oysterman in VA. Member of the Junior Order of United
American Mechanics, Washington lodge of Masons and the Marine
Engineers' Beneficial Association. A Republican. Chief engineer
of the Rock Creek Steamboat Company.

498. PROF. J. W. C. CUDDY, A. M., M. D. - b. 7 Apr. 1840 in
Balt. Co., s/o John P. and Ruth C. (Billingsley) Cuddy, also of
Balt. Co. Father, farmer, Methodist Episcopal, m. Ruth in 1832,
and had four children: Sarah E., eldest, never m., still at home;
Rev. James B., member of the Central Pennsylvania Methodist
Episcopal Conference, d. in 1874 at age thirty-eight; Rebecca, m.
John F. Heisse, d. at age forty-two, had six chilldren, three
being, Rev. J. Fred Heisse, Edwin W., Mrs. Belle Wolfe; and J. W.
C. J. W. C. m. Laura C., d/o Andrew Graham, 17 Mar. 1863, and
had two children: John Preston, d. in infancy, and Clarence
Eugene, a commercial man of Chicago. Andrew Graham, b. in

Paisley, Scotland. Laura, member of the Presbyterian Church, and the Women's Relief Corps, d. of neuralgia of the heart on 3 Nov. 1894, age fifty-four. Professor of theory and practice of medicine in the Baltimore University School of Medicine, with office at No. 506 North Carrolton avenue.

499. FRANK LONG - b. 31 Jan. 1847 at Beaver Dam (now Cockeysville) in the eighth district, s/o George and Regina (Ahern) Long. Father, b. in Saxony, Germany, came to America in 1828, settled in Balt. Co., a farmer and later contractor, d. at age sixty-eight. Mother, also b. in Saxony, came to America in 1832, a Lutheran. George and Regina had six children: William, in business with father; Frank: John, a contractor, d. at forty-two; George, d. at thirty; Caroline, Mrs. Conrad Kisner, of Balt.; and Rebecca, d. at age three. Frank m. Mary Singel, b. in Balt., in 1870, and had fourteen children, those surviving: George, helps father in contracting business; Conrad; Lizzie, w/o Edward Way, of Canton; Katie; Lina, Annie, Michael, Rose and William. Member of the Independent Order of American Mechanics, the Heptasophs, the Sons of Liberty and the American Legion of Honor. First a Democrat, then a Republican. Belongs to the German Evangelical Lutheran Church of Canton. Engaged in general contracting at Canton.

500. THOMAS A. CROSS - b. in 1864 near Upper Marlborough, Prince George Co., MD, s/o Thomas A. and Arabella (Duvall) Cross. Great-grandfather, Col. Joseph Cross. Grandfather, Fielder Cross, b. in Prince George Co., a planter, owner of Locust Grove. Father, b. at Locust Grove, d. in 1864. Mother, b. in same neighborhood, d/o Dennis Duvall, a planter, d. in 1876. Thomas and Arabella had four children: Joseph, farmer in Prince George Co.; Henry Winter Davis, of Balt.; Mrs. Dr. F. K. Slingluff; and Thomas A. Member of the Episcopal Church. A Democrat. Chief electrical engineer of the Traction Company of Baltimore.

501. DANIEL M. HOFFMAN - b. in 1860 in Balt., s/o Charles E. and Mary E. A. (Myers) Hoffman. On coming to America the Hoffman family settled in PA. Aaron Hoffman and his father, John, b. in PA. Aaron moved to MD. Charles E., b. in 1833 in Balt., son of Aaron, m. Mary E. A. Myers of Balt., and had seven children: Daniel; Naomi, w/o Samuel Murphy; George M., farmer in Balt. Co.; Rosalba, m. Michael Strohmer, Balt. business man; William S., business man in Catonsville; Mary, w/o Henry Fish; and Mattie, w/o William Gutherige, who d. 15 Aug. 1897. Daniel m. Mary Hardin, and had two children, Charles E. and Lillie M. Mary d in 1890. Daniel m. (2) Nellie Gutherige, and had a daughter. Member of the Junior Order of American Mechanics. Belongs to the Methodist Episcopal Church. A Democrat. Proprietor of a general store on Main street, Arlington.

502. CAPT. WILLIAM H. STARK - b. 6 May 1848 in Balt., s/o Henry and Honora (Luce) Stark, both b. in Ireland. Paternal grandfather, moved from France to Ireland, a farmer. Maternal grandfather, William Luce, officer in British army. Henry and Honora had thriteen children. William m. Ella Elizabeth, d/o Capt. J.

Turner, in Balt., and had one child, Maggie May, m. and lives in Balt. Ella, b. in Balt. Capt. Turner, in the fish business. Member of the Captains and Pilots' Beneficial Association, the Naval Veterans' Association, the Calumet Club, and the Burnside Post of the Grand Army of the Potomac. Belong to St. Vincent's Catholic Church. A Democrat. Captain of the Atlantic.

503. HENRY MEISNER - b. 20 Nov. 1840 in Balt., s/o John and Agnes (Michau) Meisner, he of Alsfeld, Hesse-Darmstadt, and she of Saxony, Germany. Great-great-grandfather, Christopher Meisner, and grandfather, veterinary surgeons. Father, veterinary surgeon, blacksmith and horseshoer, came to America at age twenty-one, settled in Balt., d. at age fifty-one. Mother, d. at age of fifty-five. Maternal grandfather, Henry Michau, came to America, settled in Balt., conducted restaurant there. John and Agnes had seven children, Henry the eldest. Henry m. Caroline Luther, in Balt., and had four children: Harry Albert, veterinary surgeon in Balt.; Minnie Florence and Carrie, at home; and one who d. Caroline, b. in Balt. Member of the Germania Lodge No. 160, A.F.&A.M.; a Democrat. Blacksmith and manufacturer of carriages and wagons at Nos. 1106, 1110 and 1112 East Madison street.

504. SAMUEL PARKER BOSLEY - b. 21 Feb. 1840, s/o John H. and Elizabeth (Parker) Bosley. Grandfather, Daniel, a sea merchant, s/o Zebulon Bosley, m. Sarah, d/o Rev. John Hagerty, of Prince George Co., MD. John and Elizabeth had three children: George, Sarah Ann and Samuel Parker. Samuel m. Georgie, d/o William and Elizabeth (Smith) Price, 23 Jan. 1873, and had: Edgar Winthrop and E. Stanton, law students; Georgie Price, Elizabeth, Mary Parker and Orville Mason, at home in Towson. Georgie, b. in the eighth district, 10 Nov. 1850, one of seven children. William Price, grandfather of Georgie, b. in Lincolnshire, England, 17 Jun. 1776, eldest of nine children, came to America in 1816, on ship he met Elizabeth Jones, an English lady, m. her in Balt. in 1817; William and Elizabeth had two sons: George, b. 24 Sep. 1818, an unmarried farmer; and William, b. in 1820 in Balt.; William m. Elizabeth, d/o Frederick Smith, of Balt. Co.; William d. 14 Spetember 1891, age seventy-one. Member of the Independent Order of Odd Fellows and the Ancient Order of United Workmen. He was Methodist, she is Episcopalian. Samuel d. at home, 19 Nov. 1889. Member of the Balt. Co. bar.

505. CAPT. JOHN W. GRACE - b. 3 May 1845 in Cecil Co., MD, s/o E. P. and Mary (Mainley) Grace, also of that county. Father, farmer, now lives with children in Balt. E. P. and Mary had three sons: William, pilot of the Ericsson; John W.; and E. M., Balt. merchant. Mother d. in 1849. Paternal grandfather, William Grace, b. in Cecil Co., farmer. Maternal grandfather, William Mainley, native of Cecil Co., merchant and innkeeper. John m. Wilhelmina, d/o Absalom Hyland, in Cecil Co., and had two children, Mary A. and Wallace Eugene. Wilhelmina, b. in Cecil Co. Members of the Madison Square Episcopal Church. A Democrat. Captain of the Ericsson

506. CLARENCE NICHOLS, M. D. - b. 29 Nov. 1868 at Gilpins Point, Caroline Co., s/o John and Mary Ellen (Webster) Nichols. Father, b. 24 Dec. 1819, in Caroline Co., s/o Edward and Mary (Stack) Nichols, both of Caroline Co. Father, m. (1) Mary Ellen Stack, and had one son, Frank; m. (2) Mary Ellen Elliott, and had a son, John, living in Delaware; m. (3) Mary Ellen Webster, b. 6 Oct. 1835, and had six children: Flora, w/o R. H. Stevens, of East Newmarket; Alpheus, farmer in Queen Anne Co., MD; Winfield, farmer in Dorchester Co.; Harry, d. at twenty-seven; Clarence; and Annie, d. at sixteen. John Webster, father of Mary Ellen, b. in 1800, an old settler of East Newmarket, Dorchester Co., MD; John d. in 1873, age fifty-five. Clarence m. Edith, d/o Capt. Thomas J. Seward, in Cambridge, MD, 28 Nov. 1893. Edith, b. in Dorchester Co.; Capt. Seward, in transportation business on the Chesapeake and the sea, a merchant resident of Hudson. Member of the American Institute of Hoemopathy and the Maryland State Homeopathic Medical Society, and the Journal Club. Belongs to the Methodist Episcopal Church. Physician and surgeon at No. 1439 East Eager street.

507. THOMAS J. YOUNG - b. 1 Sep. 1849 in Philadelphia, PA, s/o James and Margaret (Hoyt) Young, he of Balt., MD, and she of Winchester, VA. Paternal grandfather, John Andrew McKay Young, b. in St. Andrews, Scotland, a sea captain, spent last years in Balt. Mother, d/o Thomas Hoyt, a Virginian who settled in Balt., d. in Philadelphia when Thomas was five. Father, d. at Piedmont, VA, when Thomas was three. James and Margaret had ten children, only two living, Mrs. Elizabeth Reinhart, of Balt., and Thomas, the youngest. Taken in by uncle, William Brayton, of Hartford, Washington Co., NY. Thomas m. (1) Susan Meekins, in Balt., and had two children: William, a machinist, now electrician on the Potomac; and Laura, at home. Susan, b. and d. in Balt. Thomas m. (2) Mary E. Robbins, b. in Balt. Member of the Knights of the Golden Chain and the Marine Engineers' Beneficial Association No. 5, of Baltimore. An Episcopalian, belonging to the Advent Church of Baltimore. A Democrat. Chief engineer of the Potomac.

508. GEORGE H. EVERHART, M. D. - b. 20 Feb. 1867 in Shrewsbury, PA, s/o George Philip and Mary (Hauer) Everhart. Founder of the family in America was Paulus Everhart, resident of Paltz, Wurtemberg, sailed from Rotterdam in the ship Phoenix, landed at Philadelphia 2 Oct. 1744, located in Germantown, six miles northwest of Philadelphia, purchased land grant from Lord Baltimore of about five square miles between Dugg Hill and Manchester and settled there. Paulus and wife had three daughters and a son; George Everhart, Sr., the son, b. 11 Aug. 1745, in Germantown, PA, a carpenter, m. Eve Elizabeth Zacahrias, and had five children, George, David, Mary M., Elizabeth and Rachel; Eve, b. 12 Feb. 1749, near Pipe creek, in what is now Carroll Co., MD, and d. 12 Jul. 1830; George, a member of the German Reformed Church, d. 13 Apr. 1835; George Everhart, Jr., b. 10 Nov. 1771, on the homestead, m. Elizabeth, d/o Philip Weaver, in 1796, and had nine children, one named George, the grandfather of George H.; Elizabeth, b. 5 Jan. 1778, d. 5 Mar. 1868, her husband d. in Manchester, 4 Jul. 1857. George, the grandfather, b. in Jan.,

1800, on the homestead, m. Catherine, d/o Col John A. Shower, 19 Apr. 1829, and had eleven children; first of the Shower family in America was John Schauer, b. in Zweibrucken, in Rhenish Bavaria, Germany, a blacksmith, settled near Philadelphia, then Carroll Co., MD; eldest son, Col. John Adams Shower, b. 2 Jan. 1774, on father's homestead, m. Anna Elizabeth Troxel, of Emmitsburg, MD, had a daughter, Catherine; Anna d. 13 Feb. 1854 at age eighty; John d. 27 Aug. 1833. Third son of George and Catherine, George Philip Everhart, b. 11 Mar. 1840, m. Mary, d/o Daniel J. and Henrietta (Warner) Hauer; Daniel, b. in 1802 in Frederick Co., MD, s/o Jacob Hauer, m. Henrietta, d/o Henry Warner, of Balt. in 1824; Henrietta d. in 1893. Jacob, came from Alsace, Germany in the eighteenth century, m. Catherine Shellman; family name originally Van Wachter, of Holland-Dutch origin. George m. Mary Almeda, d/o E. H. Fitzgerald, 24 Jun. 1891 in Shrewsbury, PA; Mary, b. in DE; E. H., a merchant of Shrewsbury. Member of the Ancient Order of United Workmen, the Clinical Medical Society, the Medical and Chirurgical Faculty of Maryland. A Republican. Belongs to the Grace Episcopal Church. Physician at No. 100 West Twenty-fifth street.

509. EDGAR ALLEN POE - b. in 1809 in Boston, Mass, s/o David Poe. Father, of Italian descent, disowned by family because he m. a beautiful English actress, came to America. Orphaned at age of three and adopted by wealthy VA people. Edgar m. Virginia Clemm, a cousin, when about twenty-five. Edgar d. in Oct. 1849 in Balt. A poet.

510. MARTIN V. RUDOLPH - b. in 1839 in Balt., s/o Martin and Mary (McNorton) Rudolph, he of Balt., she of county Antrim, Ireland. Grandfather, John Harmon Rudolph, b. in Hesse-Cassel, Germany, settled in Balt. in 1787, a Lutheran, d. at age seventy-nine. Father, a Democrat, d. in 1856, age fifty-four. Mother, came to Balt. at two years, d. in 1871, age fifty-eight. Martin and Mary had fifteen children, Martin the next to the eldest. Martin m. Elizabeth Woods, in Balt., and had eight children: Harmon; Mrs. Virginia Adler; Martin; Harry; Lawrence; Joseph; William and Lizzie. Elizabeth, b. and d. in Balt. Member of the Marine Engineers' Beneficial Association No. 5. A Democrat. Identified with St. Mary's Catholic Church. Chief engineer of the Virginia.

511. BERNHARD DIETZ - b. 12 Feb. 1846 in Weisenburg, Alsace, Germany, s/o Bernhard Dietz, Sr., also of same province. Mother d. when Bernhard was quite small. Father, married again, came to America in 1855, sailed from Havre, France, landed in New York, settled in Balt., moved to Lancaster Co., PA, in 1858, d. in 1871, age fifty-four. Bernhard m. Mary Oler, in Lancaster, PA, and had a daughter, Annie M. Mary, b. at Maintz, on the Rhine, Germany. Member of the Heptasophs, the German Benefit Association, and the Fifth Ward Republican Association. Belongs to St. Matthew's Lutheran Church. Engaged in the manufacture of printers' rollers and roller composition, located at the corner of Grand and Mercer streets.

512. MAJ. WALLER A. DONALDSON - b. 17 Jun. 1827 in Chester, England, s/o Waller A. and Maria (Fillmore) Donaldson. Grandfather, a piano manufacturer. Father, b. in Dublin, a piano manufacturer, then actor, playwright, author and musician, d. in England at age eighty-four. Mother, d/o Rev. Fillmore, of Northumberland County, England, d. in 1855. Waller and Maria had thirteen children: Joseph H., d. making a night attack on Charleston tryng to run the blockade; Fred R., d. in Boston two years after the war; Theodore, engraver in New York City; two sisters live in England. Subject m. Susan H., d/o George W. Lewis, in 1866, in the Arch Street Theatre, of Philadelphia, and had nine children: Walter A., New York City attorney; William E., with the weather bureau in Omaha, NE; Joseph H. and Lewis, of Balt.: Fred, conductor on a street railway in Toledo, OH; Mrs. Nellie Brennan, of Newark, N.J.; Frances; Esther M. and Margaret, at home. Member of the Dodge Post No. 54, G.A.R., the Union Veteran Legion. A Republican. A Catholic. Superintendent of the United States National Cemetery, in Loudoun Park.

513. CAPT. MASON W. GOURLEY - b. 15 Nov. 1858 in Balt., s/o Capt. James and Mariette (Weaver) Gourley. Father, b. in Ireland, brought to America by parents when nine, settled in Balt., later Prince George Co., MD. Mason m. Annie E. Gibson, of Balt., and had three children: Sadie Smith, James David and Helen. Member of the Lee Lodge, A.F.& A.M., of Fredericksburg. A Democrat. A Presbyterian. Master of the steamer Richmond.

514. RADECKE BROTHERS - sons of Dietrich Harmon and Sophia M. (Wedeman) Radecke, of Germany. Father, came to United States, settled in Balt., had a large box factory, sold factory to oldest son, John, and in 1878 gave management of his farm to sons, Henry and Philip. Father, a Democrat, d. in 1886. Mother is now eight-eight. Dietrich and Sophia had nine children: Annie C. w/o Otto Duker; Harmon H., a carpenter; Sophia A., d. single in 1892; Margaret A., widow of Charles Gunther; Mary w/o Ernest Sack, of Balt.; Louisa, w/o George Stoll; and Philip, m. Mary C. Lutz, and had two children, William and Sophia, a Democrat. Henry and brothers, confirmed when boys in the Zion Lutheran Church, on Gay street.

515. FREDERICK NEIDHARDT - b. 22 Apr. 1848 in Waverly, ninth district, s/o George and Mary (Woolf) Neidhardt. Father, b. in Germany, came to America at thirty-five, settled in Balt., moved to Lauraville, a farmer, a founder of the Gardenville Lutheran Church, d. 28 Jul. 1891, age seventy-seven. Mother, b. in Germany. George and Mary had three children: Frederick; John, farmer in the twelfth district; and Catherine, w/o Edward Hofstetter, farmer in the ninth district. Frederick m. Sophia C., d/o John Reuter, in Jun. 1873, and had six children: Annie Elizabeth, w/o John P. Krach, a fireman at Gardenville; John F. Carpenter, Theresa, Cynthia M., Annie Estella and Katie M., at home. Member of the Gardenville Lodge No. 114, I.O.O.F. A Democrat. A Lutheran. Owner of a truck farm on the Harford road in the twelfth district.

516. ROBERT J. PADGETT - b. 26 Jul. 1833 in Mechanicstown, now Thurmont, Frederick Co., MD, s/o Richard and Mary (Weller) Padgett. Paternal grandfather, b. in England, came to America and settled at the Padgett Manor near Frederick, MD. Father, b. in Frederick Co., d. at Mechanicsville in 1835. Mother, b. in Frederick Co., d/o Jacob Weller; Jacob, came from PA, belonged to an old New York family. Richard and Mary had five children: William, d. in Balt.; Mary, d. in early life; Richard, d. at fifteen; Robert J.; and a daughter, d. in childhood. Padgett family affiliated with the Whig party. Mary, m. (2) James Flaharty, d. in 1844. Robert m. Ann J., d/o Robert and Eliza Hamill, in Balt., and had five children: Robert J., contractor of Balt.; Lillie May; William R., in business with father; Mrs. Nora Latrobe Laine, of Balt.; and Grace M. Ann, b. in Philadelphia. Robert and Eliza Hamill, from Ireland. Member of the Oyster Exchange. A Democrat. Connected with the Holy Innocents Episcopal Church. Wholesale and retail dealer in fish, oysters and produce at No. 810 Hillen street.

517. WILLIAM E. HUFFER - b. 31 Aug. 1843 in Frederick Co., MD, s/o Joseph L. and Catherine (Mullindore) Huffer. First of family in America was grandfather, John Huffer, of Germany, a farmer in Washington Co. Father, b. 9 Oct. 1800 in Pleasant Valley, Washington Co., a farmer in Frederick Co., a Republican, d. at eighty-two. John Mullindore, father of Catherine, lived to be one hundred and one. Joseph and Catherine had eight children: David, eldest, farmer in Frederick Co.; John, farmer in Washington Co.; Eliza, w/o William Ramesburg, farmer in Washington Co.; J. Dawson, farmer in Frederick Co.; Jacob M. and George C., farmers in Frederick Co. William m. Annie, d/o Daniel Swomley, of Frederick Co., in 1872, and had one son, Daniel N., in the United States army. Annie d. in 1896. A Republican. Engaged in the contracting business.

518. CHARLES M. WOLF - b. 15 Feb. in Germany, s/o Mitchell and Susan (Hettinger) Wolf. Parents came to the United States in 1878. From a large family, most still in Germany; Lewis, Christian and John are farmers in the old country; a son of John came to America; Jacob, came to America in young manhood; George came in the early '70s. Charles m. Fredericka Leilleck, of Balt. Co., 8 May 1884 and had three children: Edward, student; Mary and George. Attends the Lutheran Church. Farmer residing about five miles from Towson.

519. HON. MURRAY VANDIVER - b. 14 Septmeber 1845, s/o Hon. Robert R. and Mary (Russell) Vandiver. Family founded in America by Jacob Van der Weer, who came here in 1655, settled in DE. Father, b. 22 Jul. 1805 at the old Delaware homestead, moved to Harford Co., a contractor, d. in 1885, age eighty-one. Mother, b. in 1810, d/o Thomas Russell, d. in 1886, age seventy-six. Mother of Mary, member of the Murray family, which was among the first English settlers of Cecil Co. Robert and Mary had seven children: George T., prisoner of war at Point Lookout in 1864, exchanged, d. a few years later; Robert R., Jr., attorney in Cecil and Harford Counties, d. in Dec. 1884; Jacob, Martha, Alice

and Ellen. Murray m. Annie, d/o Henry Clayton, at Philadelphia, 23 Jun. 1886, and had two children: Robert M. and Dorothy. Annie, b. in Tamaqua, PA. Henry Clayton, civil engineer, d. at thirty-two. Member of the Susquehanna Lodge No. 130, A.F.&A.M. A Democrat. Collector of internal revenue for Maryland.

520. J. CLEMENT CLARK, M. D. - b. in 1858 near Easton, in Talbot Co., MD, s/o Clement S. and Ann E. (Mobray) Clark. Father, farmer at Kingston, d. in 1858. Mother, b. in Federalsburg, Caroline Co., MD, d/o Capt. Joseph Mobray. Clement and Ann had two children: J. B., editor of the Sussex Journal, of Georgetown, DE; and J. Clement. After death of Clement, Ann m. Colonel Douglas, of Preston; Colonel Douglas d. in 1887. J. Clement m. Mary, b. in Balt. Co., d/o Robert and Laura (Tyson) Greer, in Caroline Co.; member of the Nanticoke Lodge, A.F.&A.M., Easton Chapter, R.A.M., and Chesapeake Commandery, K.T., at Easton. Attends the Methodist Episcopal Church. First assistant physician at the Maryland Hospital for the Insane, at Catonsville.

521. BENNET F. BUSSEY, M. D. - b. at Bentleys Springs, Balt. Co., s/o Clement and Mary R. (Cockey) Bussey. A family of Harford Co. for many generations, of French extraction. Great-grandfather, Henry Greene Bussey. Father, b. in Hickory, Harford Co., a Roman Catholic, a Democrat, d. in Balt. Co. in 1874. Mother, d/o Thomas D. Cockey of Thomas, of Cool Spring. Clement and Mary had: Rachel A.; Thomas C. Bussey, M. D., physician of Texas, Balt. Co.; Sallie E.; Robert H., attorney of Cockeysville; Bennet F.; Anna V., w/o Joshua F. Cockey, of Cockeysville; Charles R., school teacher; and Fannie Julia, w/o H. B. McGlone, of Timonium. Division surgeon for the Northern Central Railroad.

522. CAPT. CHARLES W. NELSON - b. 2 Apr. 1852 in East Baltimore, s/o Charles and Mary Elizabeth (Hirschmann) Nelson. Of Scotch descent. Grandfather, Capt. Charles Nelson. Father, b. in Wilmington, Del., reared on the ocean. Mother, b. in Prussia, came to Balt. with parents in girlhood. Charles and Mary have seven children: Charles W.; George W., lives in Savannah, captain of a dredge; Joseph, captain of the dredge Patapsco, in Balt.; William, with Rittenhouse Moore Dredging Company, of Mobile; and Joseph, member of the Baltimore Fire Department. Charles m. Pauline, d/o August May, in Balt. in 1875, and had five children: Charles W., George W., Frederick, Gardner and Pauline May. Member of the Benevolent and Protective Order of Elks No. 7, and the Hiram Lodge No. 10, F.&A.M., of Washington, D.C. A Democrat. Pauline is member of the English Lutheran Church. Manager of the Baltimore Dredging Compamy.

523. H. J. GETTEMULLER - b. in 1849, s/o Herman and Anna Maria (Kalmey) Gettemuller, both of Hanover, Germany. The family came to America in 1851. Herman and Anna had three children; H. J.; J. F., of Balt.; and one who d. young. Father, in the transfer business in Balt., d. in 1894. Mother d. about 1889. H. J. m. Amelia Merle, in Balt., and had six children: Mrs. Anna Rettberg, d. leaving a daughter, Amelia, adopted by H. J.; Herman, in business with father; Fred and William, at school; Bertha; and

Mamie, deceased. Member of the King David Lodge No. 68, F.&A.M.,
St. John's Chapter, R.A.M., Monumental Commandery No. 3, K.T.,
Shiller Lodge No. 28, K.P., the Oldtown Merchants' Improvement
Society, and the Oldtown Insurance Company. Belongs to St.
Matthew's Lutheran Church. Conducts wholesale and retail paint
establishment in the business center of the city.

524. HON. GEORGE E. LYNCH - b. 12 Sep. 1851 near Pikesville, s/o
George and Margaret (Wilson) Lynch. Grandfather, Hugh Lynch, b.
in Ireland, came to America in 1765. Benjamin, another son of
Hugh. Father, b. in 1799 in Balt. Co., m. Margaret, d/o Philip
Wilson, and had: George; William, d.; and John W., merchant in
San Francisco, CA. Margaret, b. in Balt. Co.; Philip Wilson,
manager of the Powhatan cotton factory in Balt. Co. George m.
Anna, d/o John S. George, of Balt. Co., in 1880, and had two
children, Ross and Blanche. Member of the Junior Order of
American Mechanics and the Knights of Pythias. A Republican.
Associate judge of the orphans' court of Balt. Co.

525. CAPT. W. J. BOHANNON - b. 4 Mar. 1849 in Westville, Mathews
Co., VA, s/o Joseph and Jane Patterson (Ainslie) Bohannon.
Great-grandfather, Joseph Bohannon, b. in England, came to
America with two brothers, locating in eastern VA, then Kentucky.
Grandfather, Joseph Bohannon, b. in VA, a ship builder, d. at age
sixty-two. Brother of Joseph, Lieut. Cornelius Bohannon, killed
at Bunker Hill. Father, b. in VA, in 1808, a merchant tailor at
Westville, d. in 1893. Mother, b. on East Pratt street in Balt.,
moved with her father, Rev. Peter Ainslie, to Richmond, VA.
Peter Ainslie, b. in Edinburg, Scotland, a Presbyterian preacher,
joined the Baptist Church in Balt., then joined the Disciples
Church. Peter drowned in the Mattoponi river, in VA, during the
ice-flow. Mother d. in Jul. 1896, on her eighty-third birthday.
Joseph and Jane had: Mrs. Eliza Tallman, of Powhatan Co., VA;
Mrs. Anna B. Barker, of Murfreesboro, TN; Joseph Edgar, banker of
Falmouth, KY; Mrs. Kate Williams, of Balt.; Hon. Christopher A.,
an attorney, d. in Richmond; Wickliffe J., and Mrs. Alice
Williams, of Mathews Co., VA. W. J. m. Columbia Bray, of York
Co., VA, in Mathews Co., VA, and had two children who d. in early
life. Member of the Mystic Circle No. 109, A.F.&A.M., of Balt.,
the Jerusalem Chapter No. 9, R.A.M., the Royal Arcanum, Golden
Chain, Heptasophs, and Rescue Harbor No. 14. A Democrat.
Organizer of the Disciples Church on Calhoun street. Captain of
the Alabama.

526. ALOYSIUS X. WHITEFORD, M. D. - b. in 1848 in Balt. Co., s/o
William and Mary A. (Willingham) Whiteford, also of same county.
Father, merchant in Balt. City, d. in Aug. 1867. William and
Mary had nine children: Aloysius; William T., priest in the
Jesuit order, d. in 1883 at Georgetown University, of Washington,
D.C.; Charles R., physician in Balt. Co., d. in 1889; Robert A.,
cattle dealer in Balt. Co., d in 1889; James V., deputy sheriff
of Harford Co., d. in 1889; John M., Balt. business man.
Aloysius m. Annie K. Dieter in 1877, and had three children: Dr.
Lingart I., May Irene and William T. G. A Democrat. Attends St.
Mary's Catholic Church, Govanstown. Physician at Parkville, on

the Harford road.

527. CAPT. WESLEY THOMAS - b. in Jul. 1849 near Cambridge, Dorchester Co., MD, s/o William and Sarah (Warfield) Thomas, of the same county. Father, farmer, d. at Pinepoint, at age fifty-nine, Wesley being only four years old. Mother, d. at sixty-seven. Wesley m. Mary E. Roberts, in Balt., and had five children: Howard, Grace, Harry, Bruce and Fletcher. Mary, b. in Balt. Captain of the Ida, of the Baltimore, Chesapeake & Atlantic Railroad Company.

528. GEORGE J. KURTZ - b. 4 Jul. 1826 in Philadelphia, PA, s/o John Jacob and Nettie A. (Ottison) Kurtz. Father, b. in 1796 at Stuttgart, Wurtemberg, Germany, a merchant tailor. At eighteen, sailed for America, ship wrecked in a severe storm, picked up by a Norwegian pilot boat, and taken to Bergen, Norway, worked at his trade and m. Nettie A. Ottison. Left Norway in 1822, landed in Philadelphia. John and Nettie had five children, George being the third, and the only one living. Father d. in Balt. in 1880, and mother d. at age ninety, both active in the Lutheran Church. George m. Eliza Hays in Balt., and had five children: Alice J., now Mrs. Laib, of Balt.; Isabelle, d. at twenty-four; Harry J., d. at seven; France P., d at thirty-one; and Anna V., at home. Eliza, b. in Balt., d. in 1885. Member of Zion Lutheran Church. A Democrat. Carriage maker at No. 417 North Paca street.

529. JOHN A. RIDDEL - b. in 1800 in Balt., of English descent. John m. Sarah Ann, d/o Hezekiah and Ellen Harp, in 1847, and had three children: William W., m.; Mary Ellen, at home; and Margaret, w/o William J. Cooper, of Balt. Co. Member of the Sons of Liberty. Attended Christ Church. A Republican. John d. in May 1873, at age seventy-three. Ran a commissions business in Balt.

530. J. HENRY FISHER - b. 26 Aug. 1850 in Balt., s/o Frederick and Margaret Mary (Miller) Fisher. Paternal grandfather, b. in Germany, founded family in America. Father, b. in Baden, Germany, located in Balt., a foundryman, d. at age sixty-one. Mother, b. in Bavaria, also d. J. Henry m. Augusta Guenther, of Balt. and had two sons, J. Henry, Jr., and Charles. Member of the Corinthian Lodge, F.&A.M., the Adoniram Chapter, R.A.M., the Monumental Commandery, K.T., the Baltimore Consistory, S.P.R.S., the Bournie Temple of the Mystic Shrine, the Balt. Lodge No. 7, B.P.O.E., the Reliance Lodge No. 12, K.P., the Baltimore Council, Junior Order United American Mechanics and the Turnverein. Belongs to St. Stephen's Lutheran Church. Has a cigar box factory at Nos. 14 and 16 West Barre street.

531. ANDREW HARVEY - b. 12 Apr. 1826 in the second district of Cecil Co. Andrew m. Mary Latchford in 1853, and had eight children, six living: Alice, widow of Wesley Stinchcomb; Andrew E.; William G.; Annie E., m. V. Hance Ward; Minnie, w/o Rev. George W. Bounds; and Merrill, at home. A Republican. Belongs to the Methodist Church. Agriculturist is the second district.

532. PETER H. MORGAN - b. in 1844 in St. Mary Co., MD, s/o Charles and Mary (Hayden) Morgan. Father, b. in same county, farmer, had brothers: George W., Thomas, and George H. Mother's father and family lived in St. Mary Co. for many generations. Charles and Mary had: Benjamin H.; William R., a teacher; George H.; Julia, m. Mr. Fowler, and had several children; May, w/o Capt. J. Guyther; Lettie, m. Mr. Dillahey; Elizabeth, a sister of charity; and Peter. Mother d. when Peter was eight. Peter m. Jennie Sword in 1865, and had two children: Robert L., in business with father; and a son who d. in early life. Member of the Order of Heptasophs, and the Catholic Benevolent Legion. A Democrat. Attends St. Martin's Church. Conducts a general roofing business.

533. WILLIAM R. BECK - b. in 1852 in Rock Hall, Kent Co., MD., s/o Lemuel and Margaret (Coleman) Beck. Father, b. at same place, owner of a schooner. Mother, b. at Rock Hall, d/o Thomas Coleman, d. at Rock Hall about thirty years ago. Paternal grandfather, Elijah Beck, also of Rock Hall, school teacher. Lemuel and Margaret had six children, three living: William; Edward L., oysterman at Rock Hall; and Mary, w/o James Ashley, seaman. William m. Elizabeth, d/o Capt. Thomas Blades, in Philadelphia in 1882. Elizabeth, b. at Snow Hill, MD. Member of the Shield of Honor No. 13, of Baltimore, the Clyde Relief Association and Marine Engineers' Beneficial Association, Division No. 13, of Philadelphia. Attends Bethany Methodist Episcopal Church. A Republican. Chief engineer of the Bluefields.

534. WILLIAM J. HISS - b. on the old homestead in the twelfth district, s/o William and Susannah (Smith) Hiss. Great-great-grandfather, Valentine Hiss, b. in Germany, came to America in the beginning of the seventeenth century, settled in Balt. Jacob Hiss, b. 16 May 1762 in Balt. county, m. Elizabeth Gatch, and had sixteen children: Christiana; Jesse, m. Miss Mellimony; Mary, m. Henry Crow; Elizabeth, never m.; Philip, m. Sally, d/o William Rogers, of Balt.; Jacob, m. Susan Huss; Ann Elizabeth Lee and Thomas, d., unmarried; Joseph, m. Susan Brown; Ellen G., never m.; Nicholas; Hester Ann, unmarried; and Providence, m. Dr. Williams. Father, b. 9 Dec. 1801, on old homestead, m. Susannah Smith, 17 Dec. 1850, and had three children: Mary, w/o Nathaniel J. H. Duncan; Bettie S., d at seventeen; and William J. Agriculturist of the twelfth district.

536. DR. D. CAMERON SUTHERLAND - b. 11 Dec. 1859 in Richmond, s/o Samuel and Martha E. (Rison) Sutherland. Father, b. in Orange Co., NY, a gunmaker, d. 10 Jun. 1876. Mother, b. in Chesterfield Co., VA, d. 4 Feb. 1887, age seventy-four. Samuel and Martha had twelve children: Laura M., m. Lieutenant Mills, C.S.A., who d. at New Orleans, and had two children, m. (2) Edward Buckley, of Birmingham, England, and had two children, m. (3) Sir Major Henry Holland and lives at Herndon, near London, England; Dr. J. B., Balt. dentist; Carlton M., lives in Santa Rosa, CA; A. B., lives in Richmond, VA; Samuel W, lives in AZ; Sallie, w/o John Graham, of Balt.; M. H., lives in Denver, CO; D. Cameron; Albion, traveling salesman; and three who d. in early

childhood. D. Cameron m. Kate S., d/o Capt. James G. Armacost, of Balt., in Aug. 1883, and had five children: Anna D., d. at six; Sadie V.; D. Cameron; Catherine and Edward Paul. Dentist at No. 1118 East Monument street.

536. W. T. HAUGHEY - b. 22 Apr. 1844 in the fourth district, s/o Homer K. Haughey. Father, merchandiser in Reisterstown. W. T. m. Williametta Kemp in 1885, and had one child, Edith. Member of the Ionic Lodge No. 145, A.F.&A.M., of Reisterstown. Belongs to the Methodist Church. A Democrat. General merchandiser in Glyndon.

537. H. LOUIS SCHMIDT - b. 25 Dec. 1847 in Sachsen, Prussia, Germany, s/o Adam Schmidt. Father, farmer, wood worker, lumber yard owner, d. in Prussia at age sixty-five. Mother d. some years after. Children of Adam Schmidt: Georgianna, m., lives in Germany; Lecetta, d. at twenty-six; H. Louis; August, lives in Germany; Julius, d. in 1895, age forty-two; Frederick, d. in Germany at twenty-six; and Alvan, lives in Balt., works for Louis. Came to America at seventeen. H. Louis m. Fredericka Henrietta Lintner, b. in Germany, 15 May 1877, and had five children: Katie; Minnie, d. at fifteen; Jennie, Tillie and Anna. Fredericka, a Lutheran, b. 24 May 1852, of German parents, d. 27 Jan. 1892. Mother of Fredericka d. in Germany, father in America. Member of the Independent Order of Odd Fellows, the Kinghts of Pythias and Independent Order of Mechanics. Contractor in Balt.

538. ROBERT J. HENRY, M. D. - b. 16 Aug. 1845 in Elkridge, Howard Co., MD, s/o Dr. Samuel H. Henry. Direct descendant on the paternal side of Patrick and John Henry, on the maternal side of the Ellicott family, mother being the d/o John Ellicott. Great-grandfather, John Henry, b. in England, crossed the Atlantic in latter part of the eighteenth century, settled on the eastern shore. Father, b. on the eastern shore, in 1843, moved to Howard Co., had three children: Robert J.; Edward E., resident of Glyndon; and Mary S. E., w/o W. R. Sturgeon, a farmer. Robert m. Fannie Anderson in 1868, and had four children: Robert S., dentist of Decatur, AL; George A., mechanic in Reisterstown, MD; Joseph E., electircal engineer in Balt.; and Camilla L., at home. Fannie d. in 1893. Robert m. (2) Maggie Humrichause, of Balt., 31 Mar. 1896. Member of the Gosnell Post No. 39, G.A.R., Department of Maryland, at Glyndon. An Episcopalian. Physician and surgeon of Glyndon.

539. R. H. BUSHEY - b. in Jul. 1842 on Prince Edward Island, s/o Simon and Mary (Fogarty) Bushey, also of the island. Paternal grandfather, b. at Harbor Bushia, Nova Scotia. Great-grandfather, b. in France, name was spelled Bushia. Father, moved his family to Bath, ME, lost at sea off the coast of Nova Scotia in 1858. Mother, raised eight of their ten children, d. at Bath, ME. Father of Mary, Dr. Fogarty, surgeon in the English navy. R. H. m. Rachel, d/o Dr. Isaac Harris, in Balt., and had one child; Clara, Mrs. Rohrbaugh, of Manchester, MD. Rachel, b. in Trenton, NJ, d. in Balt. R. H. m. (2) Lena , d/o Henry Wortche,

and had one child, Florence. Lena, b. in Balt. Member of the
Independent Lodge No. 77, I.O.O.F., Wilson Post, G.A.R., the
Marine Engineers' Beneficial Association No. 5, of Balt. A
Republican. Attends the William Street Methodist Church. Chief
engineer of the Baltimore, Chesapeake & Atlantic Railroad.

540. WILLIAM H. ORTH - b. 17 Jul. 1851 in Balt., s/o George P.
and Elizabeth (Schwartz) Orth, he of Nidau, Hesse-Darmstadt,
Germany, she of Frankfort-on-the Main, Germany. Paternal grandfather, tanner, crossed the Atlantic to Balt., located near
Hanover, York Co., PA. Maternal grandfather, merchant tailor,
came to America, settled in Balt. Orth family from Austria.
Father, first of the Orth family to come to America, settled in
Balt. in 1826, upholsterer and paperhanger, d. in Jan. 1893, at
nearly eighty years of age. Mother, settled in Balt. in 1833,
still living, age seventy. George and Elizabeth had four children: G. F., in business with William, d. in Balt.; Mrs. Mary E.
Sickle, of Balt.; William H.; and J. P., bookkeeper in Balt.
William m. Miss A. M., d/o Frederick Kramer, in Balt. A.M., b.
in Balt. Frederick, b. in Hesse-Cassel, Germany, a jeweler, came
to Balt. at age nine, d. 30 Nov., 1895, aged sixty-two. Wife of
Frederick, Mary A. (Kuszmaul) Kramer, b. in Balt., d/o Laurence
Kuszmaul, b. in Derdinger Koenig Kreist, Wurtemberg, Germany.
Laurence, m. Sophia Kline, who is now eighty-three. Member of
the Joppa Lodge No. 132, F.&A.M. A Democrat. Belongs to the
Third English Lutheran Church. Paperhanger and decorator at No.
548 North Gay street.

541. CAPT. H. CROCKETT - b. in 1840 in Salisbury, MD, s/o Capt.
John and Minna (Parks) Crockett. Father, b. in same locality, of
Scotch descent, d. at seventy-five. Mother, b. in Salisbury, d/o
Capt. William Parks, d. in early life. John and Minna had eight
children, three still living; one is Josephus, retired sea captain, lives in Oxford, MD. Subject m. Virginia, d/o John Cross,
and had four children: Marvin H., Myrtle Virginia, Elsie and
Ellery. Virginia, b. in Prince George Co.; John Cross, b. in St.
Mary Co., a farmer; wife of John, Betsy A., b. in St. Mary Co.,
d/o Judge Albey,a school teacher and justice of the peace. John,
m. twice, by 1 had one child, by 2 had nine children, Mrs.
Crockett the fourth. Members of the Baptist Church. A Republican. Commander of the Lancaster, of the Weems Steamboat Company.

542. REV. CHARLES DAMER - b. 16 Jan. 1843 in Balt., s/o
Sebastian A. and Anna Mary (Vogt) Damer, natives of Germany.
Father, came to America in the early thirty's, a huckster, d. in
1873, age seventy-one. Mother, d. in 1890, age seventy-nine
years and six months. Sebastian and Anna, devout members of the
Catholic Church, had four children: Charles; Anna, w/o Henry
Drinkaus, of Balt.; Elenore, Mrs. John J. Knell, d. in 1889, age
forty-two; and one d. in infancy. Rector of the Holy Cross
Church, Balt. Ordained 30 June 1869.

543. REV. JOHN S. M. WITKE - b. 27 Dec. 1863 in Sandow, Germany,
s/o Samuel and Martha (Goercke) Witke. Father, b. 19 May 1832 in
Silesia, Germany, lives on the river Oder, in Silesia, m. (1)

Emma Quistorp who d. 19 Nov., 1861, m. (2) Martha Goercke, b. in
Germany 1 Feb. 1837. Samuel and Martha had eight children, three
still living: Peter, book-binder, and artist; Rev. James, pastor
of St. Paul's Lutheran Church, in Bridgeport, Conn; and Rev.
John. Came to America in Jun. 1885. John m. Matilda M.
Munkenbeck, 1 Dec. 1886. Ceremony performed by Samuel Witke.
Matilda, born in Philadelphia, d/o John and Christiana
Munkenbeck, from Germany, business man of the Quaker City.
Maternal grandfather, Maurice Goercke, Lutheran minister in
Pomeria and Berlin. Pastor of St. Luke's German Lutheran Church.

544. AUGUSTUS A. CLEWELL, M. D. - b. 8 Nov., 1845 in Salem, N C,
s/o David and Dorothy (Schultz) Clewell, also of Salem. Father,
had bookstore in Salem, a Whig, d. in 1862. Mother, now eighty-
two. David and Dorothy had: Frank, d. soon after the Civil war;
Anna, m. Dr. J. W. Booth, of central NC; Edward, a printer, in
Chicago; Rev. John H., Moravian minister, in Salem; Margaret E.,
w/o Capt. R. A. Jenkins, of Salem. Augustus m. Mary A. Palmer,
of Louisville, KY, 24 Apr. 1871, and had one daughter, Mary A.,
at home. Wife, d. in 1882. Augustus m. (2) Christina Kesmodel,
of Balt., and had one child that d. in infancy. Member of the
St. John's Lodge No. 34, A.F.&A.M., and the Medical and Chirurgical Faculty of Maryland. A Democrat. A Lutheran. Physician at
No. 1741 Harford avenue.

545. J. F. BATTY - b. 26 Nov., 1866 in Balt., s/o Joseph W. and
Annie C. (Lynch) Batty, he of St. Mary Co., MD, and she of
Washington, DC. Paternal grandfather, George Batty, machinist
and millwright, b. in Manchester, England, settled first in St.
Mary Co., then Balt. Maternal grandfather, Joshua Lynch, black-
smith, d. in Atlanta, GA. Father, marine engineer. Joseph and
Annie had five children: Annie C., Mrs. Moreland, of Balt.; J.
F.; George J., cigar maker, d. in 1896; Ella M., Mrs. Hax, of
Balt.; and Walter L. Subject m. Annie M. Wooden, of Balt., and
had one child, J. F., Jr. Member of the Royal Arcanum, the
Junior Order of United American Mechanics, and the Marine
Engineers' Beneficial Association, of Baltimore. A Republican.
Belongs to the Methodist Episcopal Church. Machinist, draftsman
and engineer. Chief engineer of the Danville.

546. A. EDWARD F. GREMPLER, M. D. - b. 17 Sep. 1865 in Balt.,
s/o Dr. Karl and Doretta (Myers) Grempler, both of Germany. Karl
and Doretta, m. in Ohio, moved to Balt., had nine children:
Gustav, barber; Godfrey J., dentist; Louisa, w/o William V. D.
Wettern; Edward; Clara, w/o William F. Burns, owner of a creamery
in Frederick, MD; Karl, superintendent of a farm at Owing's
Mills; Henry, carpenter and builder; William, student; and Paul,
works in a commission house. Father, a dentist, b. sixty-three
years ago in Breslau, a Lutheran. Mother, b. in Hanover, a
Lutheran, d. in 1888, about fifty-two years old. Subject m.
Grace, d/o Jacob Deems, of Balt., 16 Jun. 1889, and had three
children, Walter Edward, Grace C. and Karl Frederick. Member of
the Magnolia Lodge No. 6, Shield of Honor, the Spring Garden
Conclave of Heptasophs, the Knights of the Ancient Essenic Order,
the Uncle Brazie Verein (a German secret society), the Pride of

Baltimore Council No. 14, Daughters of America, the Patapsco Council No. 58, Junior Order of American Mechanics, the King David's Lodge No. 68, A.F.&A.M., and Maryland Lodge No. 22, of the Golden Chain. Also belongs to the Southwest Baltimore Business Men's Association, the Young Men's Republican Club of Baltimore City and the Young Men's Club of his own ward. Coroner for the western district of Baltimore.

547. SHADRACH D. SPARKS - b. at Sparks Station in the eighth district, s/o Laban Sparks. Father, also b. same place. Grandfather, Thomas Sparks. Family founded by English emigrants during the seventeenth century; Capt. John Sparks, first located in VA, then MD, present at wedding of Pocahontas. Father, m. a Miss Green. Shadrach m. Susannah, d/o Richard B. Stewart, 6 Sep. 1865, and had five children: S. G., lives at Sparrows Point; Richard B., of Balt.; Laban, Balt. attorney; Reverdy B., of Oil City, PA; and Annie E., at home. A Republican. Member of the Methodist Episcopal Church. Agriculturist. Shadrach d. 17 May 1879.

548. FRANCIS SCOTT KEY - b. in Frederick Co., MD. An attorney. Author of "The Star Spangled Banner". Subject d. 11 Jan. 1848, interred in Frederick Co..

549. JUDGE GEORGE T. LEECH - b. 20 Mar. 1847 in Balt., s/o George F. and Mary A. (Ross) Leech. Grandfather, Thomas Leech, native of Cecil Co., MD, a hatter at North East, PA. Father of Thomas, came to America from the north of Ireland with his parents, locating in Lancaster, PA, Scotch-Irish Presbyterians, moved to Cecil Co., MD. Father, b. in Balt., cigar-maker, d. in 1881, age sixty-four. Mother, b. in Pocomoke City, MD, d. in 1054, leaving two children, George T. and Mrs. Ruth Elliott, of Balt. George m. Susan S. Stevens, of Rock Hall, Kent Co., MD, in Balt., and had four children: Clara E., now Mrs. Morrison; Mrs. Blanche Yeatman, of Balt.; G. Eddie, of Balt.; and Wilbur R. S. Member of Cassia Lodge No. 45, A.F.&A.M., Dushane Post No. 3, G.A.R., and the Elcelsior Lodge No. 13, of the Shield of Honor. A Republican. An ordained local minister in the Jefferson Street Methodist Episcopal Church. Magistrate at large for the city.

550. REV. THOMAS C. EASSON - b. in Forfarshire, Scotland, s/o John and Isabella (Wood) Easson, also b. same place. John and Isabella had seven children, all b. in same shire: Thomas Chalmers and Alexander, a business man in Chicago only ones to come to America. Came to America in 1888, went to Omaha, Neb. Came to Balt. in 1895. Pastor of the Presbyterian Church at Sweet Air.

551. WILLIAM H. SCHWATKA, M. D. - b. 7 Jan. 1863 in Chesterville, Kent county, MD, s/o John A. and Rachel R. E. (Sanders) Schwatka. First of the name came from Germany more than two hundred years ago. Grandfather, b. in Balt., a wheelwright. Father, a wheelwright, b. in Chesterville. Mother, b. in Kent Co., d/o a farmer. Maternal ancestors of Rachel, the Moffitts, old family of eastern shore. Paternal ancestors of Rachel,

Sanders, came to MD from England nearly two hundred years ago. John and Rachel had two sons: William, and John B., professor of anatomy in the Baltimore University. Williwm m. Rosa P., d/o George Travers, in Oct. 1895, and had one son, John Bushrod Herdman. Rosa, b. in Balt. Member of the Medical and Surgical Society, and the Knights Templar. A Democrat. Physician at No. 2429 Fait avenue.

552. HENRY LE BRUN - b. in 1825 in Balt., s/o Ambrose Le Brun. Father, b. in France, came to Balt., d. 5 Mar. 1855, had: Louis, lives in Canton; Josephine, widow of Julian Martin; two sons who d. long ago; and Henry. Henry m. Mary J. Marquett in 1852, and had five children: Joseph; John A.; Nicholas Deshields; Mary Elizabeth and Annie. After death of first wife, Henry m. (2) Mrs. Julia A. Randall, and had two children: Emma, w/o John H. Golden, of Florida, and George, at home, m. Annie D. Brinkmyer in 1896. A Republican. Members of the Methodist Church of Canton. Agriculturist of the twelfth district.

553. JAMES A. FAIRBANKS - b. 10 Jun. 1820 in Brandon, VT. Came to Balt. in 1845. James m. Almeda J. Oursler in 1851; Almeda d. in 1879. Agriculturist of the second district.

554. JAMES W. OFFUTT - b. 9 Oct. 1840 in the second district, s/o Lemuel Offutt. Father, b. in KY, settled in Balt. Co. in early manhood, a farmer, had three children: Amanda, w/o Atwood Blunt, a farmer; Elizabeth, w/o Dr. Thomas Z. Offutt, of the second district; and James. James m. (1) Agnes Hewitt in 1858 and had four children: Lemuel, attorney in Towson; Lillian, m. Francis S. Kemp, lives at Harrisonville; Delia, w/o Wallace Wade, merchant of Granite; and Mary E., m. William Ridgley, lives at Glenwood, Howard Co. James m. (2) Elizabeth Frances Cockey, of Cockeysville, in 1873, and had two children, James F. and Dorsey W., both at home. A Democrat. James d. 5 Jan. 1895. Judge of the orphans' court at time of death.

555. JOHN G. SCHWIND - b. 4 Aug. 1848 in Wurzburg, Bavaria, Germany, s/o Philip and Mary (Unger) Schwind. Father, b. 9 Nov., 1824, a contractor, came to America in 1851, settled in Balt., a Catholic, d. there 27 Mar. 1890. Mother, b. 11 Nov. 1824, d. 26 Mar. 1867. Philip and Mary had five children. Philip m. (2) Mary Fisher, and had five children. John m. Johanna Otta, of Harz Mountain, Germany, in 1873. Member of the Catholic Benevolent Legion, and the Golden Chain. Contractor for stone work at No. 209 East Fayette street.

556. CAPT. WILLIAM J. SKINNER - b. 3 Jun. 1840 in Dorcheter Co., MD, s/o William and Eliza (Salisbury) Skinner. Father, b. in Dorchester Co., as was grandfather, Zachariah Skinner, a ship builder. Grandfather, moved to Balt., returned to Dorchester Co., d. there at ninety. James, a son of Zachariah, d. in Dorchester Co., in 1887. Mother, b. near Denton, Caroline Co., MD, d/o Matthew and Eliza Salisbury. Matthew, farmer, d. at eighty. William and Eliza had sixteen children: William, the eldest, Thomas and John only living sons. Mother, d. at thirty-eight.

William m. Mary V. Jones, of Dorchester Co., in 1863, and had one child, S. Irene, w/o Dr. Miles, of Somerset Co., MD. Mary d. in Balt. William m. (2) Louisa Valiant, b. on the eastern shore, and d. in Balt. William m. (3) Blanche E. Schmidt, of Balt., and had one child, Clifford Scott, b. 10 Sept 1893 and d. 10 Jul. 1894. Member of the Royal Arcanum and Heptasophs. Belongs to the Seventh Baptist Church. Captain of the Gaston.

557. REV. JAMES P. HOLDEN - b. 20 Nov. 1855 in Balt., s/o William and Anne (Scallan) Holden, natives of County Wexford, Ireland. Father, came to America in 1852, settled in Balt. William and Anne had seven children. Mother and father, both about seventy years of age. Rector of St. Jerome's Church in Balt. Ordained by Archbishop Gibbons in 1880.

558. MARTIN W. BROWN - b. 5 Aug. 1863 in Cambridge, Dorchester Co., MD, s/o John and Helen (Martin) Brown, he of Kittery, ME, and she of Cambridge, MD. Maternal grandfather, John Martin, farmer in MD. Paternal grandfather, Captain Brown, in the China and East India trade, on a voyage, he and all on board were lost. Father, civil engineer, d. in Florida during yellow fever epidemic, age sixty-two. Mother, lives in Norfolk, VA. Martin m. Carrie Michener, in Philadelphia. Carrie, b. in Philadelphia. Member of the Brotherhood of Locomotive Engineers, Division No. 45, of Phihladelphia, and the Marine Engineers' Benevolent Association No. 33, of New York City. An Episccopalian. Chief engineer on the Charlotte of the York River line.

559. GEORGE M. D. NICE - b. 12 Oct. 1849 in Balt., s/o John H. and Mary E. (Cave) Nice. Father, b. at Easton, a tinner, d. in Sep. 1862 from having leg shot off at battle of Bull Run. Mother, b. in England, d/o James and Mary Cave, came to America with parents at seven, settled in Fells Point. James Cave d. 5 Sep. 1847. John and Mary had nine children: Emma E., w/o James H. Murdock, of Annapolis, MD; George M. D.; and seven d. in infancy. George m. Maggie Jane Sullivan, of Caroline Co., MD in 1871, and had four children: John H., d. at twenty-three; Maggie, w/o Alfred W. Thomas; Sadie and George V. Member of the Masons, Highland Lodge No. 184, the Zeta Conclave No. 6, Improved Order of Heptasophs, the Fairmount Council No. 63, Junior Order United American Mechanics, and the Pioneer American Club of Baltimore. A Republican. Belongs to the Abbott Memorial Presbyterian Church. Magistrate

560. DAVID B. MEEK - b. in 1823 in Anne Arrundel Co., s/o David B. and Betsey (Harmon) Meek, he of England and she of Anne Arnudel Co. Father, came to America as a boy with parents, settled in Anne Arundel Co., a farmer, d. at age fifty-five, when David was small. David and Betsey had four children: John, wheelwright in Frederick Co., MD; David B.; Ann, widow of Samuel Owens, lives in Laurel, Prince George Co.; and Louisa, d. single, age sixty. David m. Ruth Burnett, of Anne Arundel Co., in 1844, and had: Emma Melvina, w/o Lee Gregwire; John S., farmer in Anne Arundel Co.; William D., m., farmer in the twelfth district; and Ida, w/o Charles T. Harley. Belongs to the Methodist Episcopal

Church. A Democrat. Farmer of the twelfth district.

561. CHARLES H. McCOMAS - b. in 1863 at Blackhorse, Harford Co., MD, s/o Joshua and Rebecca Jane (Maul) McComas. Father, b. in Harford Co., a wheelwright, d. 1 Nov. 1896. Mother, d/o Upton R. and Mary J. (Norris) Maul. Maternal grandfather, manufacturer of spades, then had mercantile establishment in Harford Co., d. in Harford Co. Paternal grandfather, George McComas, wheelwright in Harford Co. Joshua and Rebecca had six children: George Upton, eldest, physician of New Canton, IL; William M., contractor and builder at Quincy, IL; Charles H.; Marion E., machinist and blacksmith of Plainfield, IL; James B., clerk in Balt. postoffice; and Mary Edith, lives with mother in New Canton, IL. Charles m. Edith M., d/o John B. and Virginia Burnham in 1889, and had two children, Elva and Clarence B. A Republican. Members of Hunt's Methodist Church at Sherwood. Station agent at Ruxton.

562. CAPT. SETH S. ULLRICH, M. D. - b. 18 May 1858 in Louisiana, s/o John H. and Leah C. (Stevens) Ullrich, he of Germany and she of PA. Ullrich family prominent in Nuremberg, where great-grandfather d. at one hundred and five. Father came to America in 1847, now seventy-four. Paternal grandfather, killed 4 Jul. 1874. Mother, d. in 1894 at sixty-six. John and Leah had three sons, Seth the youngest. Seth m. Caroline E., d/o J. J. and Frances Boyd, of Baltimore, 26 Jun. 1895. Member of St. John's Chapter No. 19, Crusade Commandery No. 5, K. T., Boumi Temple, Mystic Shrine, the Independent Order of Odd Fellows, the Junior Order of American Mechanics and the Daughters of Liberty. A Democrat. An Episcopalian. Surgeon for the Baltimore & Ohio Railroad and assistant surgeon of the Fourth Regiment of Maryland National Guard.

563. REV. ASBURY ROBERTS REILEY - b. 29 Apr. 1829 in Liberytown, Frederick Co., MD, s/o Rev. James and Eleanor (Ewing) Reiley. Descendant of Irish ancestors who came to America at an early period, located in PA. Father, b. in PA, thirty-four years a Methodist Episcopal minister. Mother, d. 1 Nov. 1886. James and Eleanor had Asbury and Tobias, a minister. Maternal grandfather, Alexander Ewing, a Presbyterian, then Methodist. Alexander had: Eleanor; James, a minister; and Esther, w/o Rev. Tobias Reiley. Asbury m. Julia A. Lowe, in Shrewsbury, PA. Pastor of Kingsley Methodist Episcopal Church, Cumberland, MD.

564. CAPT. SAMUEL CHARLES - b. 11 Aug. 1864 in Dorchester Co., MD, s/o James H. and Mary E., (Mills) Charles, also of same county. Father, carpenter and builder, d. in Beulah at age sixty. Mother, d. at forty-three. Paternal grandfather, Michael Charles, lived in Dorchester Co., of English descent, a farmer. Maternal grandfather, also farmer. James and Mary had six children, Samuel, the eldest; brother, James L., first officer on the Josephine Thompson. Samuel m. Allie Rue, in Auburn, NJ, in 1892, and had one child, William Lawrence. Allie, b. in Auburn. Attends Lafayette Street Methodist Episcopal Church. Master of the Alsenborn.

565. J. ZACHARY TAYLOR, M. D. - b. 29 Aug. 1848 in Somerset Co., MD, s/o Dr. John Wesley and Mary Wesley (Waters) Taylor. Mother, a Methodist Protestant, cousin of Rev. Francis Waters, D.D., d. in 1877, age sixty-three. Maternal grandmother, member of the Bevans family. Maternal great-grandmother, a Miss Custis. Father, a physician, member of the Methodist Episcopal Church, d. in 1865, age fifty-three. John and Mary had eleven children, four living: Virginia, widow of Levin Bounds, lives in Balt.; Rosa E., m. N. R. Hearn, lives in Wicomico Co., MD; Mary, widow of Andrew J. Crawford, lives in Quantico, MD; and J. Zachary, the youngest. Subject m. H. E., d/o William M. Evans, of Deals Island, MD, in 1877, and had four children: Paul, Pearl, Page and Frances. Member of the Masons, the Heptasophs, and the Junior Order of American Mechanics. A Democrat. A Methodist. Physician at No. 13 West Saratoga street.

566. REV. JOHN HOERR - b. 7 Nov. 1843 in Pittsburg, PA, s/o Alexander and Margaret Hoerr. Father, tailor, cooper, distiller, b. 22 Jan. 1800, d. in 1881. Mother, d. in Feb. 1890, age eighty. Alexander and Margaret, members of the German Evangelical Lutheran Church, had eight children, five still live near or in Pittsburg. John m. Margaret, d/o Gebhardt and Rose Naumann, 16 Feb. 1865, and had twelve children: Anna Margaret, assistant matron of the orphanage at Germantown, PA; Rev. J. H. W., pastor of the Lutheran Church at Columbiana, OH, m. Erma Gabel; Emma Louisa, w/o L. W. Wagner, of Balt., and had three children, Margaret, Carl and John; Dora Mary; Frederick C. C., student; William A., with the Baltimore & Ohio Railroad, at Wilmington, DE; Margaret J. R.; Lucy Augusta; John P. M.; Ella M.; Martin Louis and Henry Alexander. Gebhardt and Rose, Germans, lived in Allegany Co., PA. Pastor of St. Mark's German Evangelical Lutheran Church.

567. JOHN COWAN - b. 6 Mar. 1847 near Pikesville, s/o Joshua and Jane (Arnold) Cowan. Father, b. in 1811, on same place as son, a contractor and builder, d. there in 1882. Paternal grandfather, William Cowan, b. in Balt., one of twenty-four children. Great-grandfather, Fielding Cowan, b. in England, founder of family in America. Mother, d/o William and Charlotte Arnold, who came to this county from Ireland. Joshua and Jane had eight children: William; James S., lives in San Francisco, CA; Annie, w/o George Evans; Sophia J., Mrs. J. Hughes, d. in 1896; and three d. in childhood. John m. Kate, d/o Nicholas and Mary Himes, descendant of German ancestors, in 1869, and had five children: Beulah, the eldest, w/o Rev. Charles E. Guthrie; James, William, Charles D. and Martha L., at home. Member of the Masons, the Improved Order of Red Men, the Independent Order of Odd Fellows, the Golden Chain and Knights of Pythias. A Republican. Belongs to the Methodist Church. Contractor and builder with his city office on Madison street.

568. FREDERICK E. FOOS - b. in 1858 in Balt., s/o William and Elizabeth (Ohn) Foos, both b. in Germany. Father, a machinist, came to United States in 1846, now seventy-seven. William and

135

Elizabeth had five children: Frederick; Christian, in the fruit packing business in Balt.; William, manufacturer of confectionery in Balt.; and Bertha, w/o George Heinz, of Balt.; and one who d. Member of the National Confectioners' Association of the United States. A Republican. Member of the United Brethren's denomination. Engaged in the manufacture of confectionery at Nos. 1505-1507 West Baltimore street.

569. WILLIAM WILKINSON - b. in Apr., 1829 at Bengies, in the twelfth district, s/o Samuel and Temperance (Carback) Wilkinson. Father, b. at Middle River, a Democrat, d. in Balt. in 1869, age seventy-three. Mother, d/o Rev. John Carback, of the Methodist Episcopal Church. Sameul and Temperance, had six children: James, green grocer in Balt., d. in Dec. 1895; Samuel J., business man of Chicago, IL. William m. Narcissa, d/o Dr. J. and Elizabeth (Sickles) Gregg, of New York, in 1855, and had nine children: Elizabeth, w/o Christopher Chapman, of VA; Temperance, w/o Andrew C. Jackson; Samuel J., at home; Susan L., d. when young; Nina, d. in childhood; William, m., lives at home; Emeline Rebecca, now Mrs. Robinson; James H., at home; and Mrs. Narcissa May Robinson. Dr. Gregg, physician in PA, later twelfth district, Balt. Co., MD, a Democrat, d. in 1861, leaving four sons, two in New York, one in Cumberland, Co., PA and one in Balt. Co., MD. Members of the Methodist Episcopal Church. A Democrat. Superintendent of the Carroll Island Club.

570. JUDGE PETER SAHM - b. 27 Jan. 1834 in Bavaria. Orphaned at a very early age, brought up by grandparents, who came to America in 1836, locating in Frederick. Grandfather, a weaver in Germany, had wood-sawing business in Frederick, d. at eighty-six. grandmother, over eighty when she d. Peter m. Mary A. B. Maught, 25 Mar. 1858, and had seven children, six d. in infancy or childhood, one son, now in general auditor's office of the Baltimore & Ohio Railroad. Member of the blue lodge of the Masons, in Frederick. He is a Lutheran, wife an Episcopalian. Magistrate in Balt.

571. GEORGE PEABODY - b. 18 Feb. 1795 in the village of South Danvers (now Peabody), MA. Peabody Institute, his gift to Balt. George d. 4 Nov. 1869. Started banking house of George Peabody & Co., in London.

572. W. F. GODWIN, M. D. - b. 30 Sep. 1840 in Milford, Kent Co., DE. Subject m. Annie, d/o Daniel B. Banks, of Balt., and had six children: Anna, Sarah, Margaret, Rebecca W., Frank and Alice. Frank, accidentally killed in 1896. Member of the Masons. A Methodist. Retired physician and surgeon.

573. JOHN WILLCOX JENKINS - s/o Mark Willcox and Ann Maria (Jenkins) Jenkins. Thomas Jenkins, first of the name in America, b. in Wales, settled at White Palins, St. Mary Co., MD, had six children: Edward, William, George, Elizabeth, Ann and Mary. Of these, William Jenkins, b. in 1663 in St. Mary Co., had as children: Ignatius, Henry, William, Thomas Courtney, James, Michael, Jane and Mary A.. Michael Jenkins, b. in St. Mary Co., moved to

Balt. with brother Thomas C. settled at Joppa about 1735; Michael
m. Charity A. Wheeler in 1761 and had: Thomas C., b. in Feb.
1765; William, b. in Feb. 1767; Mary, b. in Aug. 1769; Ann, b. in
Jan. 1772; Edward, b. in Mar. 1774; Ignatius, b. in Mar. 1776;
Michael b. in Feb. 1778; Josias, b. in Mar. 1781; and Elizabeth,
b. in Dec. 1784. William Jenkins, m. (1) Ann Hillen, d. leaving
one daughter; m. (2) Ellen Willcox, and had: Thomas Courtney,
Mark Willcox, Edward, James Willcox, Joseph Willcox, William and
Eleanor. Mark Willcox Jenkins, m. Ann Maria, d/o Capt. Josias
Jenkins, and had: John W., Elizabeth Hillen, William, Rebecca
Hillen, Michael; and Ann Ellen, m. James W. Barroll and had two
children, Elizabeth and Frederick. John m. Alice Julia, d/o
Commodore T. Darrah Shaw, of the United States navy, and had six
children: John Hillen, Eugene, Albin, Mark Willcox, Arthur and
Elizabeth. John H. m. Rebecca, d/o Henry C. Smith, of Balt. and
had, Henry C. S. and Elsie H., who are the tenth generation of
the Jenkins family on Maryland soil, which can be verified by
reference to Will book I, folio 228, in the office of register of
wills in Balt. A Roman Catholic. Farmer of the eleventh district.

574. GEORGE VALENTINE - b. 8 Aug. 1834 in Chester Co., PA, s/o
George and Mary (Downing) Valentine. Valentine family emigrated
from England to America early in the settlement of this country,
Quakers. Thomas Valentine, moved from England to Ireland.
Robert, son of Thomas, came to America, bought land under William
Penn's purchase. Robert brought his son, Robert, Jr., b. in
Chester Co., England and minister in the Quaker Church. George
Valentine, son of Robert, Jr., b. in Chester Co., PA, m. Mary,
d/o Jacob Downing, and had six children, George being the
youngest. George m. Emily T. Jacobs, of Chester Co., PA, and had
four daughters. Retired from the iron business.

575. WILLIAM T. FOSTER - b. 1 Oct. 1826 in Richmond, VA.
William m. Angeline, d/o Edward Rider, Sr., 8 Jun. 1852, and had
six children: Charles Taylor and Edward Rider, m. and live in
Balt.; Annie; William R., the eldest, d. in early manhood; and
two d. in childhood. Identified with the Prohibiton party.
Members of the Sater's Baptist Church. Retired from the grocery
business.

576. AUGUST WEIS - b. 9 Oct. 1843 in Philadelphia, PA, s/o
Conrad and Catherine (Fisher) Weis, both b. in Germany. Father,
came to America a young man, established brewery in Philadelphia,
then came to Balt. and established brewery here, a Democrat, d.
in 1852. Conrad and Catherine had five children: Henry, a baker
in Balt.; Margaret, w/o John Felter, of Balt. Co.; Louisa, w/o
William Carl; Elizabeth, w/o John Long, of Balt. Co.; and August.
August m. Margaret Nitzel, of Balt. Co., in 1862, and had four
children: Robert, d. at twelve; Elizabeth, w/o George Allen,
conductor on the Baltimore & Ohio Railroad; Catherine, w/o George
Tracy, farmer of Balt. Co.; and Ida, w/o John Lawson, of Balt.
Margaret, d. in 1876. August m. (2) Elizabeth Nitzel, sister of
Margaret, and had five children: Augustus E., grain and feed
merchant of Canton; Lillie; Robert; Lulu and Jennetta. Member of

the Knights of Pythias. A Democrat. Practically retired from business, owning a feed store and restaurant in Canton.

577. REV. MATTHEW O'KEEFE - b. 11 May 1828 in Waterford, Ireland. Arrived in Balt. July 1852. Pastor of St. Francis' Catholic Church, at Towson.

578. B. F. PRICE, M. D. - b. 4 Jul. 1835 in the fifth district. Subject m. Mary Harshberger, of Balt., and had: Mamie, Ella, Betty, Mattie, Thomas, William, Annie and Nora. Thomas is a physician in Glyndon, MD. Physician and surgeon in the fifth district.

579. F. DORSEY MITCHELL, M. D. - b. 29 May 1825 in Washington Co., MD, s/o Alexander and Amelia (Carr) Mitchell, also of same county. Alexander and Amelia had five children, F. Dorsey only one living. Paternal grandfather, Dr. Alexander Mitchell, b. in Edinburgh, Scotland, came to America with two brothers, also doctors. Alexander settled in Washington Co., MD., Spencer in Washington, D.C., and the other went to the East Indies. Maternal grandfather, Col. John Carr, b. in Washington Co. F. Dorsey m. Mary E., d/o Maj. David G. and Elizabeth L. (Davis) Yost, he of VA, and she of PA, and had six children: Emily C.; Dr. Clarence L., d.; Dr. Alexander R. and Dr. Frederick G., twins; Elizabeth, d.; and Mary V., at home. Emily C. m. George R. Mowell, of Glencoe, Balt. Co.; Dr. Frederick G., located in Balt. Co., m. only daughter of the late Dickinson Gorsuch. Maj. David Yost, Hagerstown attorney; John Davis, maternal grandfather of Mary Yost, civil engineer, s/o Thomas and Ann Davis, of Marlborough, England, b. 30 Apr. 1770, came to America in 1793, m. Mary Whitelock a cousin of Dolly Madison; John Davis d. in Aug. 1864, age ninety-six. A Democrat. In the real-estate business.

580. PATRICK SINNOTT - b. in County Wexford, Ireland, came to New York, then Balt. Co. Patrick m. Bridget, d/o John Carroll, and had three children: John T. and Robert P., at home; and Catherine, w/o Michael B. Sweeney, of Balt. A Democrat. Farmer of the twelfth district.

581. JOHN R. LEMMERT - b. 9 July 1860 in Balt., s/o George and Anna (Knoefler) Lemmert, natives of Germany. Father came to America about 1852, settled in Balt. Mother, identified with the Green Street Methodist Episcopal CHurch, d. in Dec. 1893, age sixty-three. George and Anna had five children: Bertha, d. in childhood; Emma, w/o Henry Monkenmeyer, of Balt.; Caroline, m. George Immler, in business with John; John R.; and August, jeweler in Balt. John m. Johannetta, d/o Lewis Fernsner, of Balt. 12 Jan. 1887, and had one child, Ruth. Identified with the Second English Lutheran Church. Proprietor of a draper and tailor's establishment at No. 14 Fayette street.

582. CAPT. W. C. ALMY - b. 18 May 1859 at Portsmouth, VA, s/o Holder and Frances (Baker) Almy. Name originally spelled Almond by ancestors in Wales, who left France to escape proscription.

William Almy, first of name in America, came from England with Govenor Winthrop, brought family over on 2 Jun. 1632, which included: William Almond, aged thirty-four; Audry Almond, his wife, thirty-two; Annis Almy, eight years; Christopher Elmie, three years - their children. William was member of the Society of Friends. William Almy, b. in England in 1601, d. 28 Feb. 1677, Audry, b. in 1603, d. in 1676. William and Audry had five children: "Christopher was born in England in 1632, and died Jan. 30, 1713. He married Elizabeth Cornell, a native of Portsmouth, R.I., who died in 1708. Of their nine children, William was born Oct. 27, 1665, and died Jul. 6, 1747. For his first wife he wedded Deborah Cook, of Portsmouth, by whom he had nine children, and after her death married Hope Boeden. His son William was born Oct. 3, 1707, and died in 1778. He had married, Feb. 10. 1730, Patience Allen, of Tiverton, R.I., by whom he had four children. Of these Joseph was born in 1742, and died in 1786. In 1763 he married Sarah Brown, and of their nine children, Holder was born May 24, 1764. He wedded Deborah Cook, of Tiverton, in 1785, and had eight children, of whom William was born Jan. 24, 1796, and died Aug. 5, 1866. His wife, who bore the maiden name of Eliza Wilcox, was born Oct. 7, 1795, and died Frebruary 16, 1879." Father, Holder Almy, s/o William and Eliza (Wilcox) Almy, b. 4 May 1830, a Republican, d. 25 Sep., 1887. Holder m. Frances, native of Cape Cod and d/o Barnabas Baker. Bakers of English descent. Subject m. Ada Wright, of Balt. and had four children. Member of the Masons, the Knights of Pythias and the Heptasophs. Belongs to the McKendry Methodist Episcopal Church South, at Norfolk, VA. Master of the Georgia, of the Baltimore Steam Packet Company.

583. WILLIAM P. COLE - b. 18 May 1859 in the eighth district, s/o S. Howard and Emily (Shaul) Cole. Great-grandfather, Abram Cole, lived in Balt. Lewis R., son of Abram, b. about 1790, farmer, d. at eighty-six. Father, b. in Balt. Co., farmer, had sister, Pamelia F., m. John Bacon, father of Lewis M. Bacon. Mother, d/o Samuel Shaul, b. in Balt. Co., had sister, Sophia, w/o Levi K. Bowen. Mother, d. in middle age. S. Howard and Emily had five children: William P.; Frank, telegraph operator; Lewis S., warden of Balt. Co. jail; George, with Jackson Lumber Company in NC; and Fannie, with father. William m. Estella, d/o George Stocksdale, 25 Nov. 1885, and had four children, William P., Jr., J. Irving, Edith and Helen. Estella, b. in Carroll Co., MD. Member of the Mt. Moriah Lodge of Masons at Towson and Ridgely Encampment of Odd Fellows. A Democrat. Sheriff of Balt. Co.

584. GEORGE W. YELLOTT - b. 23 May 1845. George m. Nannie E., d/o Henry W. Gittings, and had seven children. A Democrat. Member of Trinity Protestant Episcopal Church, Treasurer and collector of taxes for Balt. Co.

585. REV. GEORGE WILLIAM DEVINE - b. 24 Nov. 1843 in County Roscommon, Ireland. Came to America as a child with his parents. Ordained by Bishop Becker, 29 Jun. 1871. Rector of St. John's Catholic Church.

586. ALFRED B. GILES, M. D. - b. 18 Aug. 1858 in Balt., s/o Judge William Fell and Catherine W. (Donaldson) Giles. Maternal grandfather, Dr. William Donaldson, a founder of University of Maryland in 1807, d. in 1835, age fifty-seven. Mother, identified with Grace Protestant Episcopal Church, d. in 1873, about fifty-five. William and Catherine (his second wife) had: Donaldson, d. at thirty-four; Stewart, d. at seventeen at the Virginia Military Institute, at Lexington, VA; Catherine W., single; and Alfred B. William had m. (1) Sarah Wilson, and had William F., Jr., a Balitmore attorney. Alfred m. Georgia C., d/o Captain George W. Bennett, in 1887, and had one child, George Stewart. Member of the Medical and Chirurgical Faculty of Maryland. Physician at No. 1340 Aisquith street.

587. ALEXANDER R. MITCHELL, M. D. - b. in the seventh district. Alexander m. Edith Stockton Conway, of Balt., and had four children, Alexander, Jennie S., Mary D. and Josephine. Member of the State Board of Health, the Baltimore County Medical Association, and Hereford Lodge No. 89, I.O.O.F., of Hereford. A Democrat. An Episcopalian. Physician of the seventh district.

588. WILLIAM H. PORTER - b. in 1844 in Balt., s/o Hugh and Sophia E. (Ross) Porter, also of same city. Father of Scotch descent, mother of German descent. Paternal grandfather, James Porter, b. in the land of hills and heather, came to America, settled in Balt., a stone cutter and contractor. Father, also stone cutter and contractor, d. in Balt., age seventy-five. Mother d. at age seventy-six. Hugh and Sophia had eight children, four now living. William m. Mary , d/o James Glen, in Balt., and had two children: William, in business with father; and Horace, at home. Mary, b. in Scotland, member of the Lutheran Church. James Glen, an engineer of Balt. Member of the Junior Order of United American Mechanics. A Republican. Senior member of the firm of William H. Porter & Son, contractors and builders.

589. GEORGE W. STARR - b. 4 Jul. 1836 in Indianapolis, IN, s/o George W. and Mary A. (Scharf) Starr, Sr. Father, b. in Balt. in 1818, a plasterer, a Democrat, master of King David's Lodge of the Masonic order in 1856, an Episcopalian, d. in 1886, age seventy-nine. Grandfather, Henry Starr, b. in Balt. Maternal grandfather, George Scharf, contractor for plaster-work, b. in Balt. Mother, d. in 1891. George and Mary had seven children: William H., plasterer in Hartford, CT; Charles Howard; Mary Virginia, d.; Eliza Ann, w/o Thomas B. Simpson, of Balt.; two sons d. in childhood. George m. Mary Ellen, d/o Nicholas Lutz, a painter, in 1868, and had four children: Harry Lee, in business with father; Charles Howard, telegraph operator; two daughters d. when young. Attends the Episcopal Church. Engaged in plastering and fresco work with office at No. 960 North Howard street.

590. GEORGE W. KENNARD - b. 17 Dec. 1846 in Balt., s/o Richard and Catherine (White) Kennard. Father, also of Balt., block maker, a Whig, d. at age seventy-four. Mother, also of Balt., member of the Methodist Episcopal Church, d. at seventy-four.

Richard and Catherine had ten children, still living are: John R., Catherine, Henrietta and George W. George m. Mary J. Barton of Balt., and had two children: John R. and William W. Member of the Royal Arcanum and the Marine Engineers' Beneficial Association No. 5, of Baltimore. A Republican. Chief engineer of the Chatham, belonging to the Merchants & Miners' Transportation Company.

591. E. MADISON MITCHELL - b. 27 Nov. 1846 in Harford Co., s/o John and Eliza (Silver) Mitchell, Sr. Father, b. 10 May 1799, near Havre de Grace, spent entire life in Harford Co., d. at ninety-two. Mother d. at sixty-nine. Grandmother, Sarah Mitchell, d. at seventy-seven. E. Madison m. Virginia E., d/o John Hughes, and had one daughter, Henrietta H. Virginia d. in Feb. 1891. Subject m. (2) Mary V. Gibney, of Balt. in Jan. 1894. Member of the Maryland Lodge, I.O.O.F., of Baltimore, the Doric Lodge, F.&A.M., Druid Chapter, R.A.M., and Beauseant Commandery, K.T., all of Balt. Independent Republican. A Presbyterian. Undertaker and funeral director at corner of North avenue and Oak street, and No. 1201 West Fayette street

592. JAMES B. LYNCH - b. in 1857 at Sandy Plains, Patapsco Neck, twelfth district, s/o William and Catherine (Buck) Lynch. Father, b. on family homestead in twelfth district, a Democrat, farmer. William and Catherine had six children: Edwin; James B.; William P. Grandfather, Patrick Lynch, b. old homestead, farmer. James m. Wilhelmina, d/o William G. Langdon, in 1890, and had two children, Charles Edwin and Helen Virginia. Member of the Shield of Honor. A Democrat. Attends the Methodist Episcopal Church. Farmer at the Patapsco Neck, twelfth district.

593. HARRY G. PRENTISS, M. D. - b. 2 May 1858 in Balt., s/o Capt. H. G. and Susanna (Kahlor) Prentiss. Paternal grandparents, natives of England, settled in MA. Father, b. in Marblehead, Mass., a merchant-marine, member of the Masons, d. aboard ship, of yellow fever in 1873. Mother, d. in Jul. 1896, age seventy-two. Susanna, m. (1) Mr. Yerkes, and had three children. H. G. and Susanna had three children. Mother of Susanna, Elizabeth, from the Faucett family. Harry m. Annette, d/o Alexander Aitken, of Balt., 5 Mar. 1888, and had one child, Annette. Member of the Baltimore Medical and Surgical Society. A Democrat. Attends St. Thomas' Episcopal Church. Physician of vaccination for the twenty-second ward.

594. THOMAS RICHARDS - b. 25 Sep. 1843 in Swansea, Wales, s/o David and Mary (Williams) Richards, he of Swansea and she of Prembra, Wales. Father, d. in 1873 at sixty-five. Mother, d. at fifty-eight. David and Mary had four children: David, d. when young; Rachel, w/o Enoch Matthews, had three children, d.; Mary, w/o William Roach, lives in Wales; and Thomas. Came to America in 1868. Thomas m. Annie, d/o John and Catherine Morris, of Wales, in 1870, and had one son, David John, who m. Elizabeth Dittman. Annie came to America at six. A Republican. Foreman of the refining department of the Baltimore Electric Copper Works.

595. ROBERT H. JONES - b. in Sep. 1850 in Balt., s/o R. B. and Elizabeth (Sheldon) Jones. Father, b. in Worcester Co., MD, a farmer, then blacksmith, a Republican, now seventy-eight. Mother, b. on Staten Island, d. in Balt. Maternal grandfather, J. M. Sheldon, from the state of New York. Maternal grandmother, Miss Barnes, of New York state, sister of Judge Barnes. R. B. and Elizabeth had four children, R. H. the eldest. Robert m. Margaret Catherine, d/o Solomon Marshall of VA, in Balt., and had five children: Estella; Edgar, engineer of Emerson's yacht, the Nydia; Howard, Milton and Sidney. Member of Mt. Vernon Lodge No. 151, A.F.&A.M., and the Marine Engineers' Beneficial Association of Baltimore. Chief engineer of the vessel Sue.

596. JOHN B. FAIRALL - b. 27 Dec. 1837 in Anne Arundel Co., MD, s/o Alfred and Achsah (Mallanee) Fairall, also of same county. Seventh of eleven children. John m. Margaret E. Baldwin, of Laurel, in 1862, and had eight children: Mollie Edith, w/o Milton C. Davis, of Balt.; Annie R., w/o William H. Harrison; Effie E., student; and five d. in early years. Member of the Masons, the Odd Fellows and the Shield of Honor. A Republican. Attends the Methodist Church. Superintendent of the No. 4 mill of the Mount Vernon Milling Company.

597. CHARLES T. HARLEY - s/o Joseph L. and Elizabeth A. (Boone) Harley. Father, b. in MD, connected with treasury department at Washington, DC. Mother, b. in Anne Arundel Co., MD, d. at home in 1894. Joseph and Elizabeth had five children: Joseph, eldest, d. at twenty-one; William M., works with father; Harry F., farmer; and Annie E., w/o Charles W. Stansbury. Charles m. Ida L., d/o David Meek, of Balt. Co., in 1875. Ida is identified with the Methodist Episcopal Church. A Republican. Farmer of the twelfth district.

598. JOHN J. CAIN - b. 23 Jan. 1860 in Balt., s/o John and Mary (Harvey) Cain. John and Mary had eight children. Subject m. Kate Sullivan, and had three children, Kate, Mary and John. Member of the Marine Engineers' Beneficial Association No. 5, of Baltimore. A Democrat. Chief engineer of the Baltimore.

599. ROBERT G. RANKIN, M. D. - b. in Oct. 1828 in York Co., PA, s/o Moses and Sarah (Gemmell) Rankin. Third generation descendant of an Irishman, who emigrated to America and settled in PA. Father, b. in York Co., PA, teacher, then in mercantile business, then farmer, d. at seventy-six. Mother, b. in York Co., PA, descendant of Scotch ancestors and d/o Robert Gemmell, d. in Balt. at sixty. Moses and Sarah had five children, Robert the youngest. Robert m. Margaret, d/o Elisha Green, in Balt. Co., and had four children: Moses E., lives in Pittsburg; Mary M., w/o Rev. A. W. Rudisill, missionary in India; Robert G., insurance man in Philadelphia; and Luella L., of Balt. Robert m. (2) Phoebe V., d/o Rev. John Green, of Balt. Rev. Green, Methodist Episcopal minister. Robert d. 26 Sep. 1897. Physician at No. 811 Jefferson street before death.

600. JOHN T. BUCKLEY - b. in Balt., s/o John Buckley. Father,

lived in Balt. over fifty years, in dairy business. Subject m. Ella V., d/o John and Ella Lee, of VA, in 1886, and had one son, John Lee. Contractor and builder with office at No. 127 Richmond street.

601. CAPT. JOHN MOORE - b. near Elkton, Cecil Co., MD, s/o George and Julia (Wilson) Moore, natives of same county. Father, farmer, d. at thirty-nine. Paternal grandfather, Alexander Moore, b. in Ireland came to America at eight, settling in Cecil Co., MD, d. there at sixty. George and Julia had five children, John the eldest. Julia m. (2) Mr. Hart, and had four sons. Mother, d. in 1876, age sixty-five. John m. Mary, d/o Robert Thackery in Cecil Co., and had two children: Harry E., clerks for the Buckman Fruit Company, and Bertha, Mrs. Grimell, lives in Balt. Members of the Methodist Episcopal Church. A Republican. Captain of the Josephine Thompson.

602. PROF. F. D. MORRISON - b. 30 Sep. 1837 near Bel Air, MD, s/o Mansel and Susan E. (Morris) Morrison. Morrison family founded in America by three brothers from Scotland, settled in Delaware Co., PA, in 1736. In 1882, Emmor Morrison, came from native Delaware to MD, settled in Harford Co.; Emmor m. Margaret Davis, of PA, descendant of Welsh ancestry and a Quakeress; Emmor adopted the Quaker faith. Mansel E., s/o Emmor and Margaret, b. in Delaware Co., Pa, in 1812, farmer in Harford Co., d. at sixty-three. Mother of Harford Co. Maternal grandfather, William Morris, also b. Harford Co. First of Morris family in America was Anthony Morris, of London, later an importer in Philadelphia; next in line, William and Israel, b. in Philadelphia; Israel, great-grandfather of F. D., settled near Bel Air; father of Mrs. Morrison, d. at seventy-five, had son Dr. William Hugh Morris, physician of Richmond who d. at eighty. Mansel and Susan had five children: Geroge C., d. in TX; J. Ralph, of Harrisburg, PA; Mrs. Jane A. Buck, of Louisiana; and Florence, of Balt. Subject m. Mary A., d/o Samuel Patrick, of NH, in MA, and had one son, George Clarence, an attorney of Balt. Member of St. Michael's Episcopal Church. Superintendent of the Maryland School for the Blind and the Maryland School for the Colored Blind and Deaf.

603. CHARLES CURTIS HANDY - b. in 1830 in Balt., s/o Edward Henry and Margaret (Greaner) Handy. Grandfather, Capt. Isaac Handy, b. in Scotland, emigrated with eight of his brothers, settled in Somerset Co., MD. Father, b. in Somerset Co., in 1799, d. at seventy-nine, buried in Loudoun Park cemetery. Mother, d/o Daniel Greaner, and sister of William Greaner. Edward and Margaret had seven children: Edward J., d. about twenty years ago; William G., in Mt. Hope hospital; Laura, w/o William Cannon, of Washington, DC; Emma J., widow of Mr. Burton; Amelia, d., w/o William Burton. Charles m. Rachel J. Mathews in 1860, and had eight children: Charles E., d. in 1897; William R., m., deputy-warden in the city jail; Harry J. and Clarence, employed in Balt. & Ohio car shops; Maggie May and Estella Curtis, at home. A Democrat. Former police sergeant of Balt.

604. CHARLES B. BEAL - b. in Balt., s/o Alexander and Ellen

(Milburn) Beal, both of St. Mary Co., MD. Father d. at sixty-three. Alexander and Ellen had twelve children, four living: Charles B., youngest. Charles m. Sallie Forest in Balt., and had four children: Nell, Harry,, Lindsey and Alexander. Sallie, native of NJ, d/o John Forest now deceased. A Democrat. Chief engineer of the steamer Westmoreland.

605. REV. CHARLES E. GUTHRIE - b. 26 May 1867 in Terra Alta, WV, s/o George and Nancy (Dawson) Guthrie. Father, b. in IN, a saddler, moved to WV, d. in 1881. Mother, d/o Francis and Leah Dawson, he former merchant in Garrett Co., MD. George and Nancy had four sons: Sherman, business man in Parkersburg, WV; William , manager for Methodist Printing and Book Concern in Balt.; and Wade is salesman in Balt. Charles m. Beulah, d/o John Cowan, in 1891 and had three children, Freedom, Eleanor and Philip. Member of the Sharon Lodge No. 82, A.F.&A.M. Minister at Columbia Avenue Methodist Episcopal Church of Baltimore.

606. JACOB J. GROSS - b. 12 Feb. 1852 in Harford Co., MD. Jacob m. Ella M., d/o James Todd, b. in Balt. Co., 20 Nov. 1879, and had seven children: Jacob Harvey, Harry Archer, Helen V., Maud Alberta, Edgar Allen, James Percy, d. at nine months; and Ella M. James Todd, bookkeeper. Member of the Grange. A Republican. Supervisor of roads of the twelfth district.

607. LEE COHEN, M. D. - b. 13 Dec. 1873 in Halifax, ND, s/o Joseph and Elizabeth (Kershbaum) Cohen, both of Germany. Father, settled in Philadelphia, in mercantile business, moved to NC. Joseph and Elizabeth had seven children: Sol and William, commercial travelers; Edwin, manager of store in IN; Della, w/o Leopold Walnau; Johan, w/o M. L. Jacobs; Minoli, at home; and Lee, the youngest. Licensed physician in NC, MI and MD. Resident physician of the Bay View Asylum.

608. GEORGE THOMAS BIDDISON - deceased, b. in 1819 in Long Green, Balt. Co. George m. Rebecca d/o Samuel Wilkinson, in 1852, and had nine children: Elizabeth Ann, w/o John Edwards, farmer of the twelfth district; Temperance Rebecca, w/o Phillip Edwards, farmer in the twelfth district; Mary Ellen, w/o William Wilkinson; Samuel J., m Alice Hand of Balt., lives on part of the old homestead; William, m. Clara Schultz of Balt. Co., lives on part of the home farm; Benjamin, m. Florence Earl, of Balt. Co., lives on home farm; and three who d. Samuel Wilkinson, farmer of the twelfth district. Rebecca, b. in the twelfth district, has twenty-five grandchildren and four great-grandchildren. Member of the Methodist Episcopal Church. George d. five years ago. Agriculturist of the twelfth district.

609. JOHN A, CODORI - b. in France. Came to America, settling in with uncle, Nicholas Codori, in Gettysburg, PA, learned the butcher's business, came to Balt. John m. Catherine, d/o Bernard and Catherine (O'Reilly) Cassidy, in St. John's Catholic Church of Balt. Catherine, b. in Ireland, came to America at one with parents, both from County Monaghan. Bernard, grocer in Balt., d. in Mar. 1893, and wife d. in Balt. in Oct. 1895. Bernard and

Catherine had: Catherine, Mrs. Margaret Rice, burned to death with her two children, Mary and Frank; Francis, real-estate dealer of Balt.; Rev. Joseph H., pastor at St. John's Church, at Westminster, MD; and Charles B., butcher in Balt. A Democrat. John d. 13 Jun. 1894. Retired butcher at the Bel Air and Central market.

610. JOHN H. WILHELM - b. in 1870 in Balt., s/o William and Rebecca (Feltman) Wilhelm, natives of Germany. Grandfather, William, Sr., came to the United States in middle life. Father, came here in early life, learned the butcher trade. William and Rebecca had nine children, John being the fourth. John m. Laura R., d/o John G. Hammel, in Balt. in 1896. Laura, b. in York Co., PA. John Hammel, conductor on the Northern Central Railroad. Attends the Calvert Street Reformed Church. Engaged in the meat business at Nos. 1040-1042 Hillen street.

611. REV. J. WYNNE JONES - b. 13 Jan. 1845 in Buford, Wales, s/o Jenkin and Elizabeth Jones, both b. in Wales. Family came to America in 1854, settled in WI. Elizabeth d. in WI in 1880, Jenkin d. at home of son in 1894. Jenkin and Elizabeth, ardent Presbyterians, had five children: two d. in Wales; Helen, d. in Balt., in Sep. 1884; Thomas, merchant of Minneapolis, MN; and J. Wynne. Subject m. Annie H. Harvey, of Princeton, in 1876, and had four children: Harvey Llewellyn, student; Helena May and Charlotte Abbott, at school; and Edith Wynne. Pastor of the Abbott Memorial Presbyterian Church.

612. REV. WILLIAM E. BARTLETT - b. in Balt., s/o John Milton and Sarah Ann (Turner) Bartlett, also of Balt. Father, succeeded his father in wholesale drug business, d. 1 Oct. 1872, age fifty-two. Mother, d. 29 Sep. 1855, age thirty-six. Maternal grandfather, Joseph Turner, lumber dealer in Balt., had six children, only one living, Mrs. William B. Webb, of Philadelphia. John and Sarah, members of the Society of Friends, had seven children: Mary, Mrs. L. W. Abraham, of Port Deposit, MD, d. at forty; Dr. Joseph T., succeeded father in drug business, became a doctor, d. 3 Feb. 1883, age thirty-six; Rebecca T., m. Jonathan P. Bartlett, lives in Easton, MD; John M., in the drug business, d. in San Francisco in 1894, age forty-four; Sallie A., m. (1) Dr. Henry Sherwood, m. (2) William E. Willston, of Easton, MD. Father, m. (2) Mary Inlows, and had two children. Ordained by Cardinal Patrazi, 25 May 1872, in the Church of St. John Lateran. Rector of St. Ann's Catholic Church.

613. JOHN H. GROSS - b. 28 Aug. 1850, s/o George and Elizabeth (Lutz) Gross. Father, b. in France, came to America a small boy, settled in Harford Co., became a farmer and local preacher in the Methodist Episcopal Church, d. in Balt. Co. in 1878, a Republican. Mother, is now seventy-five, lives with John. George and Elizabeth had seven children: John H.; Jacob, farmer in Balt. Co.; George W., machinist at Sparrows Point; Joseph, in the dairy business; Mary Ellen, m. James E. Taylor, d. several years ago, leaving three children; Julia, m., lives in Balt.; and Maggie, w/o James Taylor, carpenter and builder at Sparrows Point. John

m. Carrie M., d/o Frederick Kroeber, in 1881, and had six children: Howard Milton, Frederick Raymond, Walter Kroeber, Elsie Augusta, John Henry, and one d. Carrie b. in Balt. Frederick Kroeber, grocer and feed merchant of Balt. Member of the Grange. A Republican. Farmer of the twelfth district.

614. WILLIAM H. HYMAN - b. 4 Aug. 1866, s/o George W. and Abbie (Wentworth) Hyman. Hyman family of German lineage. Wentworths of English ancestry. Father, a s/o Christopher, lifelong resident of Balt., d. in 1885, age thirty-nine. Mother, b. in Balt., d/o Thomas Wentworth, lives with William. Thomas Wentworth, d. in Balt., age ninety-six. George and Abbie had six children, William being the eldest. William m. Susie, d/o James Bibby, in Balt., and had two children, Lillian Gertrude and George W. Susie, b. in Dorchester Co., MD. James Bibby, farmer in Dorchester Co. Member of the Shield of Honor, and the Marine Engineers' Beneficial Association No. 5, of Baltimore. First assistant engineer of the steamer Charlotte.

615. CAPT. CHARLES E. FOWLER - b. near Dover, DE, s/o William and Lydia (Laocompt) Fowler. French ancestors on both sides. Father, b. same place, became master of a vessel, d. when Charles was one. Mother, b. in Kent Co., DE. Charles m. Annie, d/o Henry Jones, in Balt., and had five children: Mrs. Lydia Cook, lives in Balt.; Mrs. Edith Duffield, lives in NJ; Charles Henry, in a wholesale drug firm; William Arnold, helps father on boat; and Vera Rose, at home. Annie, b. in Dorchester Co., MD. Henry Jones, ship builder in Dorchester Co., retired in Balt. Member of the Knights of Pythias and the Knights of the Golden Chain. Attends the Methodist Episcopal Church. Captain of the Anthony Groves.

616. JOHN ADAM ELGERT - b. in 1829 in Germany, s/o Henry and Henrietta (Simon) Elgert. Father, freight shipper in Germany, d. en route to America in 1866. Mother, with husband at death, came to Balt. Co., d. in twelfth district in 1883, age sixty-eight. Henry and Henrietta had nine children, four living: Charles, in grocery business on Frederick road; Lillie, w/o Nicholas Max; Elizabeth, w/o George Weaver; and John Adam. John m. Kunigunchen Lang, of Germany, in 1853, and had eleven children: seven d. in early childhood; Kate and Lizzie d. at eighteen; Maggie, w/o Charles Wing; and Andrew L. C., engineer on the Baltimore & Ohio Railroad. Member of the Knights of Pythias. A Democrat. Belongs to the Brotherhood Barkman Presbyterian Church. In the restaurant business.

617. ROBERT WRIGHT PRICE, M. D. - b. 11 Nov. 1869, s/o Joseph R. and Mary (Ringgold) Price. Name dates to eleventh century, a powerful chieftain of Wales. Father, b. in Queen Anne Co. Mother, d/o Thomas C. Ringgold, b. on Kent Island, MD, descendant of the Lord of the Manor of Huntingfields. Joseph and Mary had six children, Robert being the third. Robert m. Lina Amelia, d/o B. F. Mann, in the winter of 1888, and had two children, Robert Harry and Joseph Richardson. B. F. Mann, of PA. In general practice at No. 1425 East Preston street.

618. GEN. NATHAN TOWSON - b. 22 Jan. 1784 in Towson, MD, one of twelve children. Served in the war of 1812 and the Mexican war. Nathan d. in Washington, DC in 1854.

619. JOHN THOMAS LYNCH - b. 19 Sep. 1964 in Balt., s/o John H. and Frances (Ensor) Lynch. Father, b. in same city 19 Sep. 1831, a Republican. John and Frances had four children: Richard H.; Alice, w/o Edwin C. White, of Balt.; Ella May, w/o Dr. William Gibson, of the United States navy, lives in Washington, DC; and John T. Lynch family originally came from Wales. John m. Sarah Elizabeth, d/o Joseph Parsons, in 1887, and had two sons, Howard Milton and Richard Hardesty. Joseph Parsons, boat builder in Balt. Member of the Junior Order of American Mechanics. A Republican. Belongs to the Methodist Episcopal Church. Former contractor and builder, now magistrate.

620. CAPT. JOHN A. MONTELIUS - b. about 1861 in Slite, Island of Gottland, Sweden, s/o Capt. John L. and Olivia (Alquist) Montelius. Great-grandfather, Rt.-Rev. Montelius, bishop in Vermdon-Roslagen Co., Sweden. Grandfather, of that village, blacksmith, farrier. Father, b. on the Island of Gottland in the Baltic, followed the sea. Mother, b. in the county of Ruthe, on the Island of Gottland, d/o Hon. Batel Alquist. John and Olivia had six children, John being the oldest. Sailed for Belgium in 1878, then Philadelphia. John m. Maggie, d/o Washington Ratcliffe, in Balt. Maggie, b. in Balt. Member of the Rescue Harbor No. 14, Masters and Pilots' Association, of Baltimore, the Red Men and the Royal Arcanum. Commander of the Chatham, of the Merchants & Miners' Transportation Company.

621. GEORGE H. SPRAGUE - b. 9 Feb. 1842 in Balt., s/o George and Eliza (Curton) Spraque, he of New Enqland, she of Balt. Father, came to Balt. a young man, stricken with paralysis on pilot boat at Old Point in 1865, sent home, d. two days later. Mother, d. in 1876, age fifty-six. George and Eliza had eight children: George; Louis, pilot on the Chesapeake bay; James, engineer on a tug for the Baltimore & Ohio Railroad; Helen and Reese, both live in Balt.; and Aggie and two others d. George m. Jennie, d/o Walter and Mary Smith, in South Amboy, NJ, and had three children: George W., father's assistant engineer on the Martha Stevens; Walter, d. in childhood; and Arthur A., fireman on the revenue cutter Windham. Jennie, b. in South Amboy. Walter Smith, railroad engineer. Member of the Shield of Honor and the Marine Engineers' Beneficial Association, Division No. 5. Chief engineer of the Martha Stevens.

622. CORINNA J. WISE, M. D. - b. in Sunbury, Northumberland Co., PA, d/o George and Sarah A. (Lavenburg) Wise. Father and grandfather, both of same county. Grandfather, Henry A. Wise, sheriff, now eighty-seven, lives in Toledo. Father, came to Balt. in 1886. Mother, b. in Orwigsburg, PA, d/o Daniel Lavenburg. Daniel, a harness-maker, d. in Washington. George and Sarah had nine children, Corinna being the second born, six still living. Member of the Episcopal Church. Physician at No. 908 Gorsuch avenue, in Waverly.

623. JOHN MARION WATTS - b. in 1833, in Harford Co., MD, s/o Benjamin P. and Mary A. (Magness) Watts. First of family in America was grandfather, an Englishman, settled in the twelfth district, at North Point. Father, b. near North Point, became farmer and miller in Harford Co., an old-line Whig, then Democrat, d. in Balt. John m. Harriet V., d/o of Captain Perry, of Charleston, VA, in 1855, and had five children: Catherine, d. at sixteen; Samuel, Bushard M. and Walter D., in coal business in Balt.; and one who d. Harriet was a niece of George Washington. Member of the Knights of Honor. A Democrat. Attends the Presbyterian Church. In the painting business.

624. E. L. LUMBERSON - b. 27 Sep. 1844 in Balt., s/o John and Margaret (Newcomer) Lumberson. Father, b. 11 May 1806 in Knoxville, TN, came to Balt. about 1836, member of the Improved Order of Red Men, the Odd Fellows, and the Association of the war of 1812, a Methodist Episcopalian. Grandfather, Philip Lumberson, b. in PA, moved to TN, d. in GA. John and Margaret had five children: Mary, d. young; Emeline; John, d. in Balt.; E. L. and Catherine. Mother d. in Oct. 1878. Subject m. Naomi, d/o John Reese. Member of the Marine Engineers' Beneficial Association No. 5, and the Ancient Order United Workmen. A Republican. Attends the Methodist Episcopal Church. Engineer in the service of the Bay line.

625. JOHN W. HUGHES - b. 27 Apr. 1836 in the twelfth district, s/o Henry and Elizabeth (Carback) Hughes, of the same area. Father, farmer and gardener, and old-line Whig. Grandfather, John Carback, farmer, and local preacher in the Methodist Episcopal Church. Henry and Elizabeth had ten children: William James, farmer on Middle river; William Henry, works at the Steelton Compamy at Sparrows Point; Elisha H., fisherman; Sophia J. and Elizabeth Ann, d.; Ann, w/o William Morrow; Melvina, w/o John Demsey, lives in CA; and Frances Ann, w/o Edward Maddock, lives on Middle river. John m. Louisa Wood, 6 Sep. 1859, and had three children: John Henry, m., fisherman, lives in the twelfth district; Elizabeth, w/o John Fowler, in coal business in Balt.; and James Wesley, fisherman in the twelfth district. A Democrat turned Republican. Identified with the Methodist Episcopal Church. Gardener and farmer in the twelfth district.

626. CAPT. GEORGE C. LEWIS - b. 8 Oct. 1836 in Kent Co., MD. Family came to Balt. when George was eleven, father, d. two years later. George m. Henrietta J. Pierce. of Balt., and had two children: George S., and Julia Etta. Henrietta d. 25 Dec. 1891. Member of the Corinthian Lodge No. 93, A.F.&A.M., of Baltimore and the Senior Order of American Mehanics No. 2. A Republican. Belongs to the Methodist Episcopal Church. Master of the Alsenborn, of the New York & Baltimore Transportation line.

627. GEORGE W. GENGNAGEL - b. in 1854 in Balt., s/o Jacob and Julia (Buhler) Gengnagel, both b. in Germany. Father, butcher in Balt., d. in 1886, age seventy-two. George and Julia had four children: Jacob, was a butcher in Highland, now lives in San Francisco, CA; Henry, d. at twenty-seven; George W., and Mrs.

Kolbe. George m. Sophia, d/o Theodore and Margaret Maasch, in
1877, and had three children: Jacob, father's assistant; Theodore
E., now sixteen, and George, fourteen. Sophia, b. in Balt.
Member of the Masons, and the Butchers' Beneficial Association.
Attends the Zion Church. Engaged in the wholesale and reatil
butcher business at the corner of Gough and Third streets.

628. THOMAS M. BUTLER - b. 9 Aug. 1840 in Salem, NJ. Thomas m.
Sarah Butler, of Fairfax, VA, and had one daughter, Beulah.
Supports the Prohibition party. A Methodist. Chief engineer on
the steamer Pocomoke, of the Baltimore, Chesapeake & Atlantic
Railroad Steamboat Company.

629. CHARLES H. S. BRANNAN - b. 1 Jun. 1837 in Balt., s/o
William and Sarah R. (Boon) Brannan. Grandfather, pioneer farmer
of Balt. Co., a blacksmith. Father, b. in MD, blacksmith, d. at
about sixty. Mother, b. in London, England, d/o Rev. Ringrose, a
Baptist minister, m. (1) Mr. Boon, and m. (2) William Brannan,
and d. at age eight. William and Sarah had: William, d. in
childhood; and Charles H. S. Mr. Boon and Sarah had four children.
Charles m. Margaret M., d/o Capt. Isaac Dixon, in Balt.,
and had seven children: Mrs. Maggie Mattox, of Balt.; Charles H.,
day inspector at the custom-house; John B., Edith, Martin C.,
Clarence W. and Harry N. Margaret, b. in Talbot Co. A Democrat.
Attends St. Mary's Episcopal Church. Solicitor for the York
River line of steamboats.

630. SAMUEL A JEWELL - b. 12 May 1863 at Locust Grove, Kent Co.,
s/o Samuel R. and Ruthess Jewell. Samuel and Ruthess had nine
children, Samuel being the second. See sketch of William E.
Jewell. Samuel m. Gertrude, d/o Zachariah Elder, in Balt., and
had one child, Mary Irene. Gertrude b. in Balt. Zachariah, agent
for powder firm. Member of the Marine Engineers' Beneficial
Association No. 5. Chief engineer on the William Woodward of the
New York & Baltimore Transportation Company.

631. JUDGE WILLIAM GELL GILES - b. 8 Apr. 1807 in Harford Co.,
MD, s/o Jacob Washington and Martha (Phillips) Giles. Phillips
family originally belonged to the Society of Friends. William
admitted to the bar in 1829. A Democrat. A Presbyterian.
William d. 21 Mar. 1879. Former judge of the district court.

632. WILLIAM F. DE HARENDT - b. 3 Dec. 1865 in Switzerland, s/o
Frederick and Wilhelmina (Miller) de Harendt. Descended from an
honored French family. Grandfather, Frederick de Harendt, Sr.,
b. in France, farmer and manufacturer of wine. Father, also b.
in France, manufacturer and dealer in lumber at Berne, Switzerland, d. at forty-two. Mother, b. in Zurich, Switzerland, lives
in Berne. Frederick and Wilhelmina had seven children, William
being the fifth and the only one in America. Member of the Odd
Fellows' lodge at Passaic, N.J., the Heptasophs, and Passaic
Lodge No. 72, Order of Red Men. A Republican. A Lutheran.
Machinist and electrician at the corner of Gay and Lexington
streets.

633. CAPT. EDMUND T. LEONARD - b. 22 Apr. 1837 in Easton, MD, s/o Robert and Arianna (Vickers) Leonard. Grandfather, Joshua Leonard, and father, natives of same locality, masters and proprietors of numerous boats. Maternal grandfather, Clement Vickers, b. in Dorchester Co., MD. Edmund m. Annie, d/o Robert Larrimore, in 1862, and had six children: E. T., Jr., Robert Hall, Howard E., Clifford B., Annie Nora and Helen E. Annie, b. in Centerville, MD, member of the Episcopal Church. Member of the Royal Arcanum. Master of the steamer Avalon, of the Baltimore, Chesapeake & Atlantic Railway.

634. WILLIAM H. BLOCK, M. D. - b. 13 Oct. 1873 in Bremen, Germany, s/o Edward and Mary (Dallam) Block, he of Germany, she of Balt. Paternal grandfather, lumber dealer in Germany, d. in Breman. Father and mother m. in Balt., bridal tour to Germany. Maternal grandfather, Samuel Dallam, wholesale merchant in Balt., d. early, Mary reared by uncle, John Murphy, of Balt. Edward and Mary had five children: William H.; Charles E., lives in Grand Rapids, MI; Emily D., w/o John F. Schipper, of NY; Marie R., at home; and Bernard. A Democrat. Member of St. Peter's Protestant Episcopal Church. Resident physician of the Home for Incurables, in addition to a general practice.

635. CAPT. AUGUSTINE D. BRANFORD - b. in Williston, Caroline Co., MD, s/o Capt. Thomas and Elizabeth (Liden) Branford. Paternal grandfather, of English ancestors, b. in DE, moved to MD. Father, d. at sixty-four. Mother, b. near Farmington, DE, d. Augustine m. Martha, d/o James B. Calloway, in Williston, MD, and had a daughter, Lulu. James Calloway, master of a schooner. A Democrat. Member of the Methodist Episcopal Church South. Master of the Chesapeake, of the Wheeler line.

636. REV. ALFRED BRADFORD LEESON - b. 13 Jul. 1849 in London, England, s/o Richard and Catherine Bradford, of England. Shortly after graduating the General Theologicaal Seminary at New York in 1873, ordained to the Ministry of the Protestant Episcopal Church by Bishop Potter, of New York. Returned to England, became a convert to the Catholic faith. Ordained in 1878 by Bishop (now Cardinal) Vaughan. Rector of St. Monica's Catholic Church.

637. HENRY A. REPSON - b. in 1864 in Balt., s/o Peter and Minnie (Quatmann) Repson. Father, also b. in Balt., ship carpenter, then superintendent of schools, Republican, of German parentage. Paternal grandfather, b. in Germany, came to Balt., a contractor. Mother, b. in Germany, lived in Balt. from an early age. Maternal grandfather, jeweler in Balt. Peter and Minnie had five children: Jennie, m. John Forstburg, Balt. contractor; Rosa, w/o Frank Huart, engineer in Balt.; Kate and Minnie, at home; and Henry. Henry m. Mamie, d/o Charles J. Hagen, 30 Nov. 1892, in Balt. Charles, a barber. Mamie, identified with the English Lutheran Church. Member of the Junior Order of United American Mechanics. A Republican. Engaged in the photographic business, and proprietor of a gallery at No. 508 South Broadway.

638. REV. EDWARD L. QUADE - b. 29 Dec. 1869 in West Prussia, s/o

Michael and Anna (Klawitter) Quade. Father, wheelwright, d. in native land. Mother, came to America 7 Aug. 1875, settled in Cincinnati, a Catholic, d. in 1889, age fifty-three. Michael and Anna had nine children, four d. in childhood, others came to America with mother: Anna, lives in cincinnati; August, mechanic, manager of coal yard in Cincinnati; Agnes, sister of charity; Edward; and one d. in United States. Ordained 19 Jun. 1896. Rector of St. Peter Claver's Catholic Church.

639. CAPT. WILLIAM KENNEDY - b. 10 Feb. 1801 in Philadelphia, s/o John Kennedy. Father, b. on the Isle of Man, came to America a young man, settled in Philadelphia. William m. Mary A. Jenkins, of Balt. A Catholic. Through his generosity was erected the church on York road, where lie the bodies of himself and wife, their daughter and son-in-law, Col. William M. Boone. William d. 4 Oct. 1873; wife d. 19 Mar. 1873, age seventy-four. Organized the Mt. Vernon Cotton Duck Company.

640. HORACE F. COWAN, D. D. S. - b. 20 May 1854 in Balt., s/o Dr. William L. and Elizabeth (Clark) Cowan. Father, dental surgeon in Balt., d. when Horace was young. Mother, d/o Lemuel B. Clark, of NJ, b. in England, an Episcopalian, d. in 1893, age ninety-two. William, of Irish ancestry. William and Elizabeth had six children: Mary, m. Winfield Scott, had two children, Laura and Gretchen; Charles, d. in 1890, single, age forty; William, of Brooklyn, NY, master of the navy yard, m. (1) Jane Polk, m. (2) Mary, d/o Samuel Cross, of Washington, D.C.; Lemuel C., killed at Sitka. Horace m. Rebecca S., d/o James S. B. Hammett, of St. Mary Co., MD, in 1887. James, d. 27 Aug. 1877, age seventy-seven. Identified with the Episcopal Church. Dentist and surgeon of Balt.

641. DAVID H. DANEKER - b. 20 Sep. 1837 in Balt., s/o Henry B. and Sarah (Crouch) Daneker, both of Balt. Paternal grandfather, Charles W. Daneker, b. at Wurtemberg, Germany, a baker, came to America, settled at Falls Point, m. Elizabeth Coppenhaver, b. at Hanovertown, VA, 16 Aug. 1778; Charles and Elizabeth had: John Jacob, Charles William, Mary Barbara and Henry Baker. Father, tin and sheet iron maker, a Presbyterian, d. at age fifty-two. Mother, d/o David and Margaret (Davis) Crouch, he b. in Cecil Co., moved to Balt. Henry and Sarah had five children. David m. Elizabeth, d/o Thomas H. and Elizabeth (Graham) Meekins, in Balt., and had five children: Ida, Mrs. Burke, d. in Balt.; Mary E., w/o E. F. Tolson; Henry W. D.; Sallie; India; and David George, killed in 1886, age nine. Elizabeth, b. in Dorchester Co., granddaughter of William Meekins, who came from England. Member of the Knights of Pythias, and the Golden Chain. A Republican. Attends the Methodist Episcopal Church. Assessor of the fifteenth ward.

642. ADAM LAUMANN - b. 5 Dec. 1843 in Messel, Hesse-Darmstadt, Germany, s/o Henry and Barbara (Wengel) Laumann. Father, b. same place, landed at Corner's wharf 12 Jul. 1852, merchant tailor, d. 2 Nov. 1861, age sixty-one. Grandfather, Henry Laumann, Sr., wheelwright. Mother, d. 5 Oct. 1884. Henry and Barbara had:

Simon, puddler of Balt.; Elizabeth, d.; Mrs. Susan Kastner, widow, lives in Balt., and Adam. Adam m. Elizabeth, d/o Jacob and Magdelene (Speismocher) Dannenfelser, in Balt., in 1866, and had eight children: Henry W., member of city council; Mrs. Barbara Jacobson, of Balt.; Mrs. Susanna Carroll, of Balt.; George S., works for same firm as father; and Annie, Mary, Louis D. and Adam, Jr., at home. Elizabeth, b. in Rhen Beryne Einzeldum, Germany. Jacob Dannenfelser, farmer, d. in early life. Paternal grandfather of Elizabeth, Jacob Dannenfelser, farmer. Mother of Elizabeth, brought four of her fifteen children to America in 1857, settled in Balt., d. 31 Mar. 1866, age sixty-three. Member of Steuben Lodge No. 87, K.P., the Uniformed Rank, Knights of Pythias, Friendship Lodge No. 7, I.O.O.F., the Mohawk Tribe of Red Men, and the Sons of Liberty. Belongs to the First German Evangelical Church of Baltimore. A Republican. Superintendent of the routes of the Cochran-Oler Ice Company.

643. HENRY J. HELLEN - b. in Sep. 1824, near Dover, DE, s/o Capt. John H. and Caroline (Porter) Hellen. Family of English origin. Father, b. in same state, followed the sea, d. at Snow Hill, Caroline Co., MD, at thirty. Mother, b. in Georgetown, DC, d. in Balt. at fifty. Henry m. Margaret J., d/o Daniel B. and Sarah (Hollingsworth) Wilcox, and had six children: Joseph H. a mason and contractor of Balt.; George E., contractor in stone and marble cutting in Balt.; Charles Loudon, in same business in N.Y. City; Mrs. Caroline Dennis, of Balt.; Mrs. Mary A. Woods, of Balt.; and Mrs. Sarah Dailey, d. in Balt. Member of Independence Lodge No. 77, I.O.O.F. A Republican. Attends the Fayette Street Methodist Episcopal Church. Superintendent of the Loudon Park cemetery.

644. MAJ. THOMAS B. GATCH - b. 21 May 1841 in Balt. Co., s/o Nicholas and Anna Maria (Merryman) Gatch. Father, b. on family estate in Balt. Co., farmer. Nicholas and Anna had two children: Thomas, and Eleanor M., who m. Alfred Ray of Montgomery Co., MD. Nicholas Gatch, s/o Benjamin and Elizabeth (Taylor) Gatch. Father of Benjamin, Godfrey Gatch, came to America from Germany in 1717. Maternal grandfather, John Merryman. Thomas m. Josephine Forrester in Sep. 1868, and had: Frank Ray, m. Olivia Evans; Harry L, single, runs fathers farm; Nicholas B., police officer; Joseph A., John M., Belle Xenia, Benjamin W., Arthur C. Turner, Ashby Fred Albert, Gordon G. and Eleanor M. Member of the Methodist Episcopal Church. A Democrat. Deputy clerk of the Balt. Co. court, at the county-seat, Towson.

645. CHARLES E. MORGAN - b. 4 Jan. 1852 in the first district of Cecil Co., s/o Charles H. Morgan, also of that county. Father, farmer, d. at sixty-seven. Charles m. Laura V. Della, of Balt., and had four children: Charles E., Jr.; Cora E., attending college; and Laura V. and Emily O., at home. Member of the Marine Engineers' Beneficial Association. Belongs to the Methodist Protestant Church. Chief engineer of the Essex, of the Weems Steamboat line.

646. JAMES S. ALLISON - b. in Dec. 1853 in Balt., s/o James S.

and Mary (Baxley) Allison. Father, b. in York Co., PA, moved to Govanstown, Balt. Co., MD, with his father, d. at seventy. Mother, b. in Balt., d/o Francis and Eliza (Wickersham) Baxley, he of Balt. and she of England, d. when James was six. James and Mary had three children. Subject m. Margaretta L., d/o Edward Beans, and had six children: Lillian, Ella, Frank, Amy, Edgar and James. Margaretta, b. in Balt. A Republican. Member of the East Baltimore Methodist Episcopal Church. Manager of the Balt. store of Isaac A. Sheppard & Co.

647. JOHN WESLEY CARBACK - b. in 1843 in the twelfth district, s/o Elisha and Cassie (Wilkinson) Carback. Elisha and Carrie had two children: John, and Elizabeth, w/o George York, farmer of the twelfth district. Father, farmer, d. before the Civil war. Grandfather, John Carback, farmer and local preacher in the Methodist Episcopal Church. Subject m. Elizabeth Ann Razer, of Kent Co., MD, and had one child, Annie. Member of the Knights of Pythias and Sons of Temperance. A Republican. Belongs to the Prince Grove Methodist Episcopal Church. Farmer of the twelfth district.

648. GEORGE J. ROCHE - b. in 1832 in Balt., s/o George J. and Maria (Moore) Roche. Father, b. in Balt., painter, old-line Whig, d. in 1852. Grandfather, Edward Roche. Mother, d. in 1863. George and Maria had nine children. Subject m. Annie J., d/o Benjamin and Elizabeth Jones, in 1854, and had five children: Annie M., w/o Charles R. Beck, Balt. chemist; George Benjamin, in business with father; Harry S., employee of the Pennsylvania Live Stock Insurance Company; William L., clerk with the United States Express Company; and one who d. Annie identified with the Catholic Church. A Republican. Painter with shop Calvert street.

649. DR. DAVID C. MOSELEY - b. in 1830 in Boston, Mass, s/o Isaac and Almira (Farnsworth) Moseley. Father, silver-plater, then farmer, d. at eighty. Isaac and Almira had five children: David C.; T. Benton; Almira, w/o J. S. Emery; Lydia, w/o J. S. Gordon, of Methuen, MA; and one who d. David m. Elmira Hardy, in 1848, and had two children: Ella Etta and Eugene C. Elmira, b. Andover, MA, d. in 1865. David m. (2) Elizabeth Rattel, b. in Ashtabula, OH. Member of the Washington Lodge, K. of P., in Winchester, VA, and the Madison Lodge, I.O.O.F., of VA. Veterinary surgeon in Balt.

650. JAMES R. ANDRE, M. D. - b. 8 Sep. 1823 in Sussex Co., DE. Father, farmer, member of the Reformed Church, d. at eighty-one. Mother, Sarah, d. in 1839. Maternal grandfather, Thomas Watkins, emigrated from Wales when Sarah was six. Paternal family consisted of six children. William E., brother, lives in Washington, DC. James m. Margaret, d/o John McCrone, in Wilmington, DE, 29 Dec. 1857, and had two children, Loma M., and Delaware Clayton. Member of the Knights of Honor, and the Germania Lodge. James and children attend the Episcopal Church, wife attends the Baptist Church. Physician and surgeon at No. 1123 East Baltimore street.

651. BENJAMIN R. & JOSHUA E. BENSON, M. D. - Benjamin, b. 6 Jan. 1854 in Balt. Co., and Joshua b. 7 Sep. 1860, sons of Rev. Joshua L. and Rachel J. (Miller) Benson, of Balt. Maternal grandfather, Robert Miller, d. in Mar. 1896. Father, farmer, miller, and merchandiser, local preacher in the Methodist Episcopal Church. Benjamin m. Mary E. A., d/o Amos Armacost, of Carroll Co., MD, in 1877, and had six children: Carroll P., Beulah M., Benjamin R. Jr., Clarence I., Emory W., and Mattie E. Member of the Shield of Honor. Identified with the Methodist Episcopal Church. Physician in Cockeysville. Joshua m. (1) Annie N. Cross, of Ashland, Balt. Co., in Dec. 1884, and had two children, Edna Luella and Cullom Stewart. Annie d. in Nov. 1890. Joshua m. (2) Katie Cobert Hayes, in Nov. 1891, and had two children, Edward Hayes and Helen Levering. Methodist Episcopal. Prohibitionist. Physician in Cockeysville.

652. HENRY PFROM - b. in 1844 in Hessen, Germany, s/o John M. and Elizabeth (Eper) Pfrom, both b. in same place. Family came to America in 1864, settled in ninth district of Balt. Co. Father d. in 1868, mother d. in 1896, age eighty-four. John and Elizabeth had four children: Andrew, butcher, d. in 1865; John Martin, Cincinnati business man; Henry; and Annie, w/o John Martin Reese, of Highland. Henry m. Catherine Hohhenghorst in 1870, and had four children: John Martin Henry; Annie C., w/o Henry Wischhusen; Sophia; and Lillie, in school. Member of the Shield of Honor and the Independent Order of Heptasophs. A Democrat. Attends the Reformed Lutheran Church, of Canton. Wholesale and retail dealer in pork, in Highland.

653. REV. WILLIAM BATZ - b. in 1862 in Buffalo, N.Y., s/o Philip Daniel and Philipine (Hassinger) Batz. Father, b. in Germany, came to America at eighteen, locating in Buffalo, a Republican, d. in 1887 in Buffalo. Mother, b. in Germany, came to America at fourteen with parents. Maternal grandfather, Jacob Hassinger, hat dealer of Buffalo. Brothers of Philipine, William and Philip. Philip and Philipine had seven children: Henry, d. at twenty-six; Valentine, with mother; Philip, in Buffalo; Louisa, w/o Henry Dietschler, of Buffalo; Elizabeth, w/o Louis Umphrey; William; and one son who d. in infancy. William m. Augusta, d/o Frederick Eigenraug, in 1888, and had two children, Bertha and Hilda. Augusta, b. in Balt. Member of the Improved Order of Heptasophs. Pastor of the German United Evangelical Church of Canton.

654. CHRISTIAN SCHMEISER - b. in 1860 in Balt., s/o John and Rosa (Dohler) Schmeiser, both of Germany. Father, came to America in early manhood, settled in Balt., a farmer, a Democrat. Mother, came to America as a girl with parents. John and Rosa had five children: Henry, cigar dealer in Balt.; George, in live stock business; Lizzie, w/o Otto Rach, of Balt.; Mary M., w/o Andrew Herget, plumber of Canton; and Christian. Christian m. Maggie Boltz in Dec. of 1887, and had four children: Mary, John, Lula and Reda. Members of the Canton Lutheran Church. Wholesale and retail butcher in Highlandtown.

655. FRANK HEINLE - b. in 1866 in Balt., s/o Michael and Elizabeth (Decker) Heinle. Father, farmer, a Democrat, d. in 1893. Maternal grandfather, Frank Decker, tailor of Balt. Michael and Elizabeth had: Michael and Joseph, work on home farm; John, farmer of the twelfth district; Agnes, m. Daniel Leidshuh, farmer in the twelfth district; Mary, w/o John Councilman; and Kate, w/o George Miller, in dairy business in Balt. Frank m. Tracy, d/o John Selig, in 1896. John Selig, blacksmith of Balt. Members of the Sacred Heart Catholic Church of Highlandtown. Identified with the Catholic Benevolent Legion. A Democrat. Manager of his late father's farm in the twelfth district.

656. WILLIAM JAMES HUGHES - b. 22 Mar. 1828 in the twelfth district, s/o Henry and Elizabeth (Carback) Hughes. Father, b. in Balt. Co., farmer, old-line Whig, d. in 1855. Mother d. 8 Feb. 1875. Henry had two brothers, Thomas and James. Father of Elizabeth, prominent Methodist minister in the twelfth district. Henry and Elizabeth had nine children: William; Jane, d., w/o John Lynch; Elizabeth, w/o William Gillespie; John W., lives at Back River Neck; William Henry, living at Steelton; Elisha H., of Back River Neck; Martha Ann, w/o William Morrow; Frances A., w./o Edward E. Maddock, of Balt. Co.; and Amanda, w/o John Demsey. William m. Margaret Ann McBurney, of Balt. Co., and had four sons: William C., living at Chase Station; Charles D., on father's farm; Thomas H., fisherman; and Alexander, superintendent of Prospect Park. Member of the Knights of Pythias. A Republican. Belongs to the Methodist Episcopal Church. Retired engineer on the Baltimore & Ohio Railroad, and farming.

657. GEORGE WILLIAM GAIL - b. 8 Jul. 1828 in Hesse-Dramstadt, Germany, s/o George Philip and Susanna (Busch) Gail. Father, b. in same place, had tobacco factory. Grandfather, George Christian Gail, and great-grandfather, also b. in Hesse-Darmstadt. George m. Mary S. Felgner, of Balt. in 1854, and had five children, four daughters, and George W. Mary d. in Mar. 1891. George m. (2) Emma Landmann, in Germany, Oct. 1892, and had one child, George Philip, b. 28 Jan. 1894. A Democrat. Manufactured smoking tobacco.

658. FRED REESE - b. in 1867 in Biron, Germany, s/o Michael and Ida (Ballingsmat) Reese. Father, b. in Germany, blacksmith, d. in 1867, leaving wife and five children. Mother lives in Balt. Children of Michael and Ida: Jacob, engineer; John, with Spring Garden Brewing Company; Annie, lives in Germany; Annie, w/o George Langfiler, in Balt.; and Fred. Fred m. Maggie Getz in 1889, and had one child, Dora, at school. Members of the St. Mark's Lutheran Church. Dealer in fish and cheese at No. 2215 East Monument street and the Bel Air Market.

659. AUGUST HENRY LANGE - b. 6 Jan. 1857 in Balt., s/o Henry and Elizabeth (Westerman) Lange. Father, b. 18 Sep. 1818, in Germany, ship carpenter, came to Balt. in 1846, member of Emanuel Lutheran Church, belonged to St. Peter's Lutheran Church, of Balt. Co., d. 29 Feb. 1896. Mother, b. in Prussia, d/o Gerhard H. and Margaret (Meyer) Westerman. Henry and Elizabeth, m. in

Balt. 24 Apr. 1848, and had six children: Elizabeth B., w/o Henry Deemer, of Balt.; Robert H., d. at three months; Hannah, d. at twelve years; August H.; Mattie, w/o Simon J. Martenet, of Gardenville, Balt. Co.; and Cynthia, m. Dr. J. F. Martenet, and d. in Balt. August m. Anna E., d/o George Kahl, in Balt. in 1884, and had a daughter, Florence E. Anna, b. in Columbus, Ohio. Member of the Seventh Ward Republican Club. Belongs to the Faith Lutheran Church. Manager of H. Lange & Son's Coal Company, wholesale and retail dealers of coal, at East Chase street.

660. BENJAMIN F. JORDAN - b. 5 Nov. 1823 in York Co., PA, s/o Archibald S. and Rebecca (Turner) Jordan, both of PA. Archibald and Rebecca had fourteen children: John S. and James P., both d.; Benjamin F., Mary J., Rachel A., Harriett R., Margaret A., Thomas R., Dr. Edward C., Samuel M., and four d. in infancy. Family founded in America by great-grandfather, John Jordan, of Ireland, settled in Cecil Co., MD, before the Revolutionary war, a farmer. Grandfather, Thomas Jordan, b. in Cecil Co., farmer. Maternal great-grandfather Turner, b. in Ireland, came to America during colonial days, locating near Oxford, Chester Co., PA. Maternal great-grandfather Thomas Campbell, a Scotchman, came to Ameica, settled in Lycoming Co., PA. Mary, d/o Thomas Campbell, m. James Turner, of Chester Co., PA, settled in Muncy, Lycoming Co. Benjamin m. at age of twenty-eight, Julia E. Anderson, b. in the seventh district, and had ten children: 2 d. in infancy; Archibald S., Benjamin F., Jr., John L., Mary S., Harriett R., Rachel A., James P. and Otho. Julia, d. Feb. 1886, age fifty-nine. Member of the Mt. Moriah Lodge No. 116, A.F.&A.M., of Towson. A Democrat. Belongs to the Presbyterian Church of Stewartstown, PA. Farmer of the seventh district.

661. PHILIP EDWARDS - b. in 1849 in Wales, s/o George and Ann (Davis) Edwards, also of Wales. Father, came to America in 1857, settled in Canton, Balt., d. in 1885. George and Ann had: John, merchant at Marsh Market, Balt.; William, d. in childhood; Sarah Ann, d.; Ella, d. in Canton; Mrs. Mary Davis, of Wales; and Philip. Philip m. Temperance Rebecca Biddison, (see sketch of her parents), in 1875, and had seven children: George Olivet, Philip Franklin, Edwin Ernest, William R., Nevet Ocean, Ella B. and Grace E., all at home. Member of the Knights of Pythias. A Republican. Belongs to the Methodist Episcopal Church. Farmer of the twelfth district.

662. JOHN BIEN, JR. - b. in 1874 in Balt., s/o John and Margaret (Otto) Bien, Sr. Father, b. in Germany, settled in Balt., established a meat market in 1866. Mother b. in Germany. John and Margaret had: John, Jr.; Conrad, student; Lizzie, m. John Zeeflie, grocer in Balt.; Barbara, m. William Schwartz, of Balt.; and Maggie, w/o John Schumann, of Balt. John m. Annie, d/o Henry Weber, in 1894, at St. Marcus' Church, and had two children: Arthur and Eva. Members of St. Marcus' Lutheran Church. Proprietor and manager of wholesale and retail meat market on McElderry street.

663. JOHN EDWARDS - b. in Wales, s/o George and Ann (Davis) Edwards. (see sketch on Philip Edwards) John m. Elizabeth Ann Biddison, (see sketch on George Thomas Biddison), and had three children: George Thomas, works with father; John V., attending school; and Anna Rebecca, w/o George Earle, farmer on Bird river in the twelfth district. Member of the Knights of Pythias, the Sons of Temperance, and the Masons. Engaged in the commission business at Marsh Market, and is an agriculturist in the twelfth district.

664. OBADIAH G. TOWSON - b. 23 Aug. 1825 in Balt., s/o James W. and Sarah (Root) Towson. Great-grandfather, William Towson, b. in Germany, moved to London, m. Catherine Allen, came to America, settled in Balt. Co., village of Towsontown sprang up around him; had three sons: Obadiah, William and Roland; William had son, Gen. Nathan Towson. Grandfather, Obadiah, blacksmith near Towson, now Lock Raven. Father, blacksmith in Balt., d. of cholera in 1832. Mother, b. in Berks Co., PA, d. at sixty-five. James and Sarah had: Margaret, Mrs. Deaver; John; Frances, Mrs. Helm; Obadiah G.; Mary, Mrs. Ward; and John W. Obadiah m. Lydia, d/o Tracy Richards in CT and had five children: Mary, Mrs. DeMuth, of Balt.; Jame O., machinist in Balt.; Charles, head secretary of the Young Men's Christian Association, at Norfolk, VA; Rev. Emory S., Episcopal minister of Bristol, TN; and one who d. Lydia b. in CT. Tracy Richards, merchant of Preston City. Members of the Baptist Church. Old-line Whig, now Republican. Retired tobacco manufacturer and lime manufacturer.

665. THOMAS B. TODD - b. 1 Feb. 1834 at Todd's Inheritance, on North Point, s/o Thomas J. and Mary (Trotton) Todd. First of family to come to Balt. Co., Thomas Todd, of Toddsbury, Gloucester Co., VA., in 1664. Son of Thomas Todd, Thomas Todd, Jr., b. in VA, d. in Balt. Co. in 1725. Thomas, son of Thomas Todd, Jr., had son Thomas, the great-grandfather of Thomas B., of this sketch. Grandfather, Bernard Todd, b. on homestead, m. Mary Green, sister of Josiah Green. Father, b. on homestead, farmer, old-line Whig, d. Mar. 1843. Mother, b. on Sparrows Point, d/o Luke Trotten, d. in 1882. Great-grandfather, Luke Trotten, Sr., merchant of Balt., of English descent. Thomas and Mary had four children: George W., at home; John T., in commission business in Balt.; Sarah Frances, widow of William Ruskell; and Thomas B. Subject m. Sarah R., d/o Joshua Todd, 1 Feb. 1866, and had three children: Thomas B., m. Mary, d/o Alexander Morrison; Ella Merryman and Clara Ridgely, at home. Joshua Todd, farmer of Cockeysville, Balt. Co. Member of the Grange. A Democrat. Attends the Methodist Episcopal Church South. Agriculturist of the twelfth district.

666. REV. JUDSON C. DAVIDSON - b. in 1849 in Appomattox Co., VA, s/o J. T. and Martha (Osborn) Davidson. Paternal great-great-great-grandfather, b. in Scotland, settled in VA. Father, b. in Appomattox Co., VA, contractor and builder, a Democrat, member of the Sons of Temperance, attended the Baptist Church, d. in 1886, at seventy-four. Grandfather, Samuel Davidson, of same neighborhood as father. Maternal grandfather, wealthy planter of VA.

Mothers family originally from Ireland. J. T. and Martha had six children: John W., farmer in VA; T. O. and Samuel, farmers in VA; Catherine, w/o Capt. J. W. Carson, d.,leaving six sons; Emma, single, lives in VA; and Judson. Judson m. Lizzie, d/o George Diuguid, of Lynchburg, VA, in Jan. 1878, and had three children: George D., Mabel and Grace. Member of the Masonic order, and the Winchester Lodge No. 21, A.F.&A.M. A Democrat now Prohibitionist. Pastor of the Grace Baptist Church.

667. CHARLES W. BAILEY - s/o Anthony and Martha (Smith) Bailey. Great-grandfather, b. in France, settled on the Hudson, a wagon and coach maker. Grandfather, Nathaniel Bailey, b. in Ulster Co., lived there all his life. Father, b. in Ulster Co.,a wagon and coach-maker, blacksmith, then pilot on the Hudson, then in hotel business, then contracting and building at Marlboro, where he d. in 1891. Mother, b. in same area as father, d/o William Smith, of CT, and great-granddaughter of Cornelius Smith, who located in Ulster Co. Grandfather of Martha, John Smith, farmer. Mother, lives in Marlboro, age eighty. Anthony and Martha had four children. Charles m. Eliza Nash in Balt. Eliza, b. and d. in Balt. Charles m. (2) Martha, d/o Jacob Wilson, and had one child, Harriet. Martha, b. in Balt. Co. Jacob Wilson, blacksmith, d. at seventy-eight. Grandfather of Martha, Samuel Wilson, d. at ninety-eight. Member of the Carroll Lodge No. 9, K.P, and the Marine Engineers' Beneficial Association of Baltimore, Division No. 5. Chief engineer on the Columbia.

668. JAMES E. EVANS - b. 1 Jan. 1831 on the Isle of Bermuda, s/o James H. and Catherine (Roberts) Evans. Father, b. same place. in Bermuda in 1838 at thirty-eight. Mother, b. in Bermuda, d/o John Roberts, d. at eighty-six. Grandfather, Capt. Edward Evans, b. in Wales, m. twice, d. on Isle of Bermuda. Great-grandfather, John Harley, went from London to Bermuda, built first house there for the English government, d. at ninety. Wife of John Harley, Harriett Wade, d. at one hundred and four. Grandfather, John Roberts, b. on Bermuda, d. there at eighty-six. Great-grandfather, John Roberts, Sr., from England. James and Catherine had four children. Subject m. Sarah Leverick, d/o William Cornelius Gauntlett, in Bermuda, in 1853, and had ten children: William S., Walter Harley and Stephen Humphrey, painters with father; Mrs. Emma Catherine Stevens, of Balt.; Sarah Melissa; Mary; Mrs. Ellen E. Dukehart, of Balt.; and three who d. A Royal Arch Mason. Member of the Madison Square Methodist Episcopal Church. A Democrat. Contractor in painting and decorating at No. 847 Park avenue.

669. PROF. E. MILLER REID, M. D. - b. 15 Nov. 1844 near Lancaster, Fairfield Co., OH, s/o Thomas N. and Keturah (Miller) Reid, both of MD. Great-grandfather, George Reid. Father, one of oldest real-estate brokers of the city. Maternal grandfather, Elijah Miller, one of the largest real-estate owners of the city and county. Subject m. Mary A., d/o John Allen, 9 Nov. 1887, and had four children, all deceased. Member of the American Medical Association, the Medical-Chirurgical Faculty of Maryland, the Baltimore Medical and Surgical Society, the Baltimore Clinical

Society, and the Baltimore Medical Association. Physician and surgeon at Nos. 904-906 North Fremont street, and professor of diseases of the nervous system and of the throat and chest, Baltimore University School of Medicine.

670. HON. FREDERICK R. BYE - b. 8 Feb. 1840 near Oxford, in Chester Co., PA, s/o Howard and Sarah (Woollens) Bye, also of that county and members of the Society of Friends. Paternal great-great-grandfather, Enoch Bye, also member of the Society of Friends, came from Scotland, located in Berks Co., PA, reared two sons, Enoch and Kiah. Enoch d. soon after moving to Chester Co., leaving two sons, Albert, d. at ninety-two leaving large family, and Amos, the grandfather of Frederick. Grandfather, Amos Bye, b. in Berks Co., settled in Chester Co. Maternal grandfather, Jesse Woollens, lived in Chester county, owned and operated a mill, member of the Society of Friends, wife, Margaret Erp. Father, farmer and school teacher, d. at fifty-six. Frederick m. Martha E., d/o Henry Bennett, at Elkton, and had seven children: Mrs. Emma Handy, of Balt.; Lillie, at home; Mrs. Roberta Gootee, of Balt.; Clara, at home; Henry Howard, veterinarian in Balt.; Mortimer, artist; and Clarence. Martha, b. in Elkton. Henry Bennett, b. in Elkton. Grandfather of Martha, Col. Henry Bennett. Member of Wilson Post No. 1, G.A.R., the Young Men's Republican Club, the Nineteenth Ward Republican Club, and the Columbia Club. A Republican. Engaged in the livery business at No. 219 North street.

671. CAPT. CHARLES W. J. SPENCE - b. 6 Aug. 1860 in Queen Anne Co., s/o John F. and Martha Jane (Jones) Spence. Paternal grandfather, William T. Spence, b. in Scotland, came to America with parents when very young, locating in Queen Anne Co., MD, m. Lavina Starkey, of Queen Anne Co. William, m. (2) Mrs. Gibbs, of Balt. Father, b. in Queen Anne Co., blacksmith, then had shop near Easton, Talbot county, member of the Methodist Church, d. at forty-four. Mother, b. in Queen Anne Co., d/o Joseph Charles and Priscilla (Perkins) Jones who were b., reared and m. in same county. Joseph, a farmer, d. at eighty-two, and Priscilla d. at seventy-eight. Joseph and Priscilla had twenty children, two now living, Mrs. Spence and Joseph H., who lives in Caroline Co., MD. John and Martha had fifteen children: William T., carriage maker; Rev. Joseph H., United Brethern minister in Parkersburg, WV; James E., blacksmith in Williston, Caroline Co., MD; John F., employed by Baltimore, Chesapeake & Atlantic Railroad Company; and Charles W. J., the youngest; and ten now deceased. Charles m. Eliza, d/o Col. Edward Randall, of Balt., 17 Apr. 1888, and had one daughter, Mildred B. Eliza d. 26 Sep. 1890. Charles m. (2) 28 Jun. 1892, Sarah Catherine, d/o F. W. and Mary A. Lowe, of Queen Anne Co., and had two children, Willard Francis Lowe and Charles Woodland. Member of the Warren Lodge No. 71, I.O.O.F., Potacon Tribe No. 58, I.O.R.M., of Baltimore, Carroll Lodge No. 27, Shield of Honor, and Iris Lodge No. 47, A.O.U.W. A Methodist. Master of the steamer Cambridge, owned by the Baltimore, Chesapeake & Atlantic Railroad.

672. HON. JAMES J. LINDSAY - b. 31 Aug. 1859 in Balt. s/o

Anthony and Annie (Clark) Lindsay. Family originated in Ireland. Paternal great-grandmother was a Miss Gibbons, who came from same county of Ireland as Cardinal Gibbons, of Balt. Father, b. in County Mayo, came to United States and settled in Balt. in 1846, had a grocery business, then farm near Towson, d. 13 Mar. 1897. Anthony and Annie m. at St. Patrick's Catholic Church, Balt., by Rev. James Dolan, 30 Jun. 1858, and had three children: James; Mary C., w/o James Kelley, in insurance business in Towson; and Annie Teresa, w/o Peter J. Dengler, farmer in Balt. Co. Mother, b. in County Mayo, Ireland, d. on home farm 10 Aug. 1893. James m. Catherine T. R. Padian, in St. Francis' Catholic Church of Towson, 29 Oct. 1891, by Rev. Matthew O'Keefe, and had three children, Mary Regina, James J., Jr., and Annie. Catherine, b. in Balt. Co., d/o John Padian. A. Democrat. Attorney to the school board of Balt. Co. Retired from the senate.

673. EDWARD S. CHOATE - b. 2 Jul. 1842 in the second district, s/o Richard and Ann J. (Pearse) Choate. Father, b. in same district. Grandfather, Rev. Edward Choate, came to America from Scotland about 1790, farmer, d. in 1842 at eighty-five. Mother b. in Balt. Co. Maternal grandparents, Richard and Elizabeth Pearse, natives of England, came to America about 1796. Richard and Ann, both b. in 1804, had four children: Mary E., w/o William E. Fite, d. about 1867; Richard, farmer in the second district, and twin Georgia, w/o George P. Prough, of Carroll Co., MD. Edward m. Maggie A., d/o Charles Shipley, of Balt., in 1873, and had five children: Anna Mabel, Edward Stephen and Georgia Pearse. Member of the Masons and the Knights of Pythias, the Baltimore County Grange, and the Wheatland Grange. A Democrat.

674. AUGUST SCHRADER - b. 5 Mar. 1854 in Bad-Salzdetfurth, Germany, s/o Lewis and Betta Schrader, both of Germany. Father, manufacturer of jewelry, now seventy-six. Mother d. in Germany 13 Jun. 1879. Lewis and Betta had five children: August, the eldest; Frits, a painter in Germany; Edward, druggist in Balt.; Lewis, Jr., painter in Vienburg; and Alvina, lives with father in Germany. August m. Amelia, d/o Peter Rost, in 1880, and had two children, Louisa and Katie. Member of the Royal Arcanum and Shield of Honor. Identified with the German United Evangelical Church. Engaged in the drug business at No. 2920 Elliott street.

675. FRANK C. WACHTER - b. 16 Sep. 1861 in Balt., s/o August and Clara Emilia (Fraske) Wachter, he b. in Hanover, and she b. in Bremen. Paternal grandfather, August Wachter, farmer and school principal. Maternal grandfather, Henry Fraske, tax collector. August and Clara, came to America on their wedding tour, settled in Balt. in 1850, and had eight children, five living: Charlotte; Dr. J. C.; Dr. C. H.; Frank C., and Hannah H. Frank m. Sophia Helen, d/o John Mainz, and had two children, Edmund J. and Hattie C. Sophia b. in Balt. John Mainz, wholesale cigar manufacturer. A Republican. Engaged in the clothing business at No. 211 West German street.

676. JOSEPH VAN NEWKIRK - b. 5 Apr. 1844 in Balt., s/o Joseph and Mary (Jemes) Newkirk, he b. of Balt., and she of England.

Father, b. in 1818, a painter, a Democrat, d. in 1889, age sixty-nine. Mother d. in 1870. Joseph and Mary had ten children: John W., d. in early life; Samuel, lives in Balt.; James and William, live in Cumberland, MD; Boygar, d. at four; and four daughters d. quite young. Subject m. Mary L., d/o Charles Eagleston, in 1867, and had four sons: Charles L, with the Pennsylvania Railroad at Union Station in Balt.; Joseph J., living in Balt.; George E., pilot on the Chesapeake bay; and John T., at home. Charles Eagleston, butcher and bacon dealer, in Balt. Co. A Democrat. Attends the Episcopal Church. Painter, hunter, and served on the police force.

677. HENRY W. LAUMANN - b. 28 Jan. 1867 in Balt., s/o Adam and Elizabeth (Dannenfelser) Lauman. Grandfather, Henry Laumann, b. in Germany, merchant tailor, settled in Balt. Father, b. in Messel, Hesse-Darmstadt, came to America at eight, a Republican. Mother, b. in Einseldum, Germany, d/o Jacob Dannenfelser, farmer. Adam and Elizabeth had ten children. Henry m. Ada Virginia, d/o James Brown, in Balt., and had four children: Charles Harrison Morton, d. at seventeen months; Henry W., William Owens and Ada Virginia. James Brown and daughter Ada, b. in Balt. Member of the Active Republican Club, the Government Loyal Republican Club, the Wellington Republican Club, the Pacific Lodge No. 63, I.O.O.F., the Mt. Ararat Encampment No. 13, the Steuben Lodge No. 87, K.P., the Harmony Lodge No. 33, Shield of Honor, and the Francis Scott Key Council No. 20, J.O.A.M.. Connected with First German Lutheran Church of Baltimore. Councilman from the second ward.

678. GEORGE H. CAIRNES, M. D. - b. 1 May 1838 in Harford Co., MD, s/o Isaac H. and Anna (Watt) Cairnes, both of MD. Grandfather, George Cairnes, b. in MD, a farmer, m. Miss Hope. Parents of George Cairnes came from Ireland. Maternal grandfather, William W. Watt, b. in Md, of Welch and English extraction, a farmer, m. Miss Streett. Great-grandfather, William, and his son, Col. John Streett, soldier of the Revolution. Father, farmer, Democrat. Mother d. at fifty-nine. Isaac and Anna had four children: Mary V., Mrs. Jarrett, of Jarrettsville, MD; Dr. George H.; Robert T., superintendent of the farm at the Maryland Insane Asylum; and C. F., physician in New Market, MD, d. in Oct. 1895. George m. Mrs. Catharine V. Tarman, d/o William Reside, of Balt., in Woodberry, in 1873. A Democrat. Physician of Balt.

679. HON. CHARLES M. NASH - b. 11 Aug. 1837 in Balt., s/o Ephraim and Elizabeth Ann (Young) Nash, he of Balt., she of Queen Anne Co., MD. Family originated in Wales, settled in MD. Thomas Nash, grandfather, farmer, d. in Queen Anne Co. Maternal grandfather, John Young, b. in MD, a planter. Father, ship-calker, then in transfer business, d. at over eighty. Ephraim and Elizabeth had ten children. Elizabeth d. at sixty-five. Ephriam m. a second time and had three children. Charles m. Louisa Crispence, in Balt. and had: Elizabeth, Mrs. Bogelman; Catherine, Mrs. Turner; James A., Balt. fire man; William H., oysterman; Robert E., farmer and merchant on Kent Island; John H. and Arthur; Louisa, b. in Hesse-Darmstadt, Germany. Member of the

Knights of Pythias. Attends the Episcopal Church. A Republican. Member of the firm of Armiger & Nash, oyster commission merchants, at the corner of Cheapside and Pratt streets.

680. EDWARD W. JANNEY, M. D. - b. 30 Jun. 1838 in Loudoun Co., VA, s/o Dr. Daniel and Elizabeth A. (Haines) Janney, he of Loudoun Co. and she of Jefferson Co., VA. Father, physician in Loudoun Co., of Quaker stock. Mother, from one of the F.F.V.'s. Daniel and Elizabeth had eight children: Dr. Nathan H., physician of Loudoun Co., killed by a runaway horse in prime of manhood; Albert, farmer of Loudoun Co., accidentally killed by kick from a horse; Dr. Daniel, physician in Winchester, VA; Mayo, d. in Washington, D.C. in 1895; Eli H., inventor, lives near Alexandria; Hugh W., farmer near Winchester, VA; Annie Maria, w/o Herman Greg, miller. Founder of family in America came from England, settled in VA. Edward m. Hettie S. Corse, of Balt. in 1863 and had six children: Edward W., Jr, with the firm of Shoemaker & Co., of Philadelphia; Daisy C., nurse in Philadelphia; Rawley C. at home; and three d. young. Member of the Legion of the Red Cross. A Republican. Physician at Highland.

681. JOHN G. MILLER - b. 16 Feb. 1852 in Bavaria, Germany, s/o Conrad and Barbara (Sirgel) Miller. Family came to America when John was an infant. Father, wheelwright in Balt., moved to Arlington, MD, d. in 1863. Mother lives in Balt. Conrad and Barbara had: Margaret, single, lives with mother; Mary, w/o Henry Hirsch, of Balt.; Kate, school teacher in Balt., d. a few years ago; and John G. John m. Barbara Schmidt, in 1876, and had five children: Kate A., Carrie M., John Henry, Annie and Louisa. Barbara, b. in Germany, came to America as a child with parents. Member of the Odd Fellows, the Shield of Honor and the Legion of the Red Cross. A Republican. Attends the Abbott Memorial Presbyterian Church. Engaged in the dairy business on the corner of Third and Lombard streets.

682. SAMUEL ROBINSON - b. 18 Apr. 1851 in Balt., s/o George W. and Mary Elizabeth (Buck) Robinson. Great-grandfather, came from England, settled in Balt. Co., planter. Grandfather, George Robinson, b. in Balt., had sons: George W., Lewis H. and Joseph J. Father, b. in Balt. in 1805, brick manufacturer, d. in 1888, age eighty-three. Mother, d in 1890 at eighty-three. George and Mary had fourteen children, six living, all in Balt.; Emily, Mrs. Cullen; Joseph J., brick manufacturer; Elizabeth, w/o Nathan G. C. Turner; Almira, Margaret and Samuel. Samuel m. Mary W., d/o Lewis H. Dungan, in Balt., and had three children: Emily C.; Morris B. and James D. Lewis Dungan, b. in Balt., wholesale fish dealer. Mary b. in Balt. Member of the Baltimore Coal Exchange. A Republican. Wholesale and retail dealer in coal on Central avenue.

683. REV. THOMAS MORYS - b. 29 Dec. 1872 in Silesia, German-Poland, s/o Martin and Mary Anne Morys, both of German-Poland. Father, farmer, now seventy. Mother now sixty-six. Martin and Mary had nine children, Thomas only one not in native land. Ordained 29 Jun. 1896, by Rt. Rev. Bishop Van Den Branden de

Reeth. Priest of St. Stanislaus' Roman Catholic Polish Church.

684. JACOB H. MEDAIRY - b. 6 Jan. 1822 in Balt., s/o John and Rachel (Russell) Medairy, also of Balt. Grandfather, Jacob Medairy, b. in MD, d. at about eighty-four, wife d. at fifty-five. Jacob and wife, members of the Methodist Episcopal Church, had eight children. Maternal grandfather, Alexander Russell, m. twice, had twenty children, Rachel from first marriage, Methodists. Father, an engraver in Balt., d. in 1857, at sixty-three. Mother d. at eighty-three. John and Rachel, member of the Methodist Episcopal Church, had twelve children, three living: Nicholas B., John W. and Jacob H. Subject m. Caroline, d/o John Kriel, of Balt., in 1844, and had thirteen children. Members of the Mt. Vernon Methodist Episcopal Church. Has store selling general line of stationery, blank books, school books, etc.

685. E. H. RITTER - b. 1 Sep. 1844 in the second district, s/o Thomas Ritter, Jr. Father, b. in the third district, Balt. Co., d. at sixty-six. Mother d. at sixty-four. Thomas and wife had twelve children: Mary A., w/o J. Miller; John T., d.; Harriet, w/o John Schock, of the fourth district; Howard T., d.; George O., lives at Spring Grove, MD; Emily D., and Miranda E., both d.; Clementine V., w/o Washington Crook, of Balt.; Hiram A., lives on old homestead; E. H.; Blenna S., w/o George W. Mellon, of Balt.; and one d. in infancy. E. H. m. Mrs. Mary (Workington) Shipley, widow of Samuel T. Shipley, in 1875. Agriculturist of Balt. Co.

686. J. WALTER GUNTS - b. 11 Apr. 1862 in Balt., s/o John P. and Mary E. (Thompson) Gunts, both of Balt. Of German extraction. Father, glass-blower, lives in Balt. Subject m. Medora Miller of Balt. in 1888, and had three children, Ada I., Anna B. and Robert T. Member of the Masons, the Junior Order of American Mechanics and the Improved Order of Heptasophs. Chief engineer at the power house of the City & Suburban Street Car Company of Balt.

687. FRED B. HALSTEAD - b. in 1871 in New York City, s/o Egbert and Nora Halstead, natives of Columbia Co., N.Y. Grandfather, Ezra Burrows, a NY builder. Grandfather, Joseph Halstead, native of CT, of German descent, moved to Columbia Co., NY, as a young man. Father, in hotel business, a Republican, one of six children, others being: Sarah, m. Hyde Frost; Joseph, prospector of North Carolina and Georgia; Elias, retired in Dutchess Co., NY; Samuel, d.; and John, with the New York Central & Hudson River Railroad. Egbert and Nora had son, Ezra W, d. in boyhood. Member of the Sharon Lodge No. 182, F.&A.M., at Arlington. Proprietor of the Halstead Hotel in Arlington.

688. J. WILLIAM JUNKINS - b. 3 Oct. 1850 in Portland, ME, s/o Oliver and Elizabeth (Arnold) Junkins. Maternal ancestors of English descent, and lived for several generations in Providence, RI. Father, b. in Portland, a cabinet-maker, a Democrat, d. in 1888. Mother also d. in 1888. Oliver and Elizabeth had three children; George F., in real-estate business in Portland; Charles E., salesman in wholesale house in Balt.; and J. William. Subject m. Alice V., d/o John Davis, 6 Sep. 1877, and had three

children: Edith Arnold, Mabel Davis, and Florence Wilson. John Davis, d. in Balt. when Alice was small child. Member of the Orders of American Mechanics and the Golden Chain. Belongs to the Baptist Church. A Republican. Engaged in pickle and preserving industry at Gay and Hoffman streets.

689. ELLIS C. GAREE, M. D. - b. 8 Aug. 1860 in Marion, VA, (now WV), s/o John S. and Nancy A. (Hayhurst) Garee, he of PA, and she of VA. Paternal great-grandfather, Job Garee, of England, d. at one hundred and four. Grandfather, also Job Garee, had farm in Westmoreland Co., PA, d. at ninety-nine. Maternal grandfather, Benjamin Hayhurst, farmer and blacksmith in VA, d. at ninety-six. Father, b. 9 Mar. 1807, farmer, justice of the peace and judge, reared a Friend, became connected with the Episcopal denomination of his wife, d. 14 Jun. 1884, at seventy-seven. Mother, d. 1 Oct. 1897, at seventy-nine. John and Nancy had six children: Benjamin C., d. at twenty from small-pox; Sarah A., m. Henry C. Boggs, farmer and stock-raiser of Roanoke Co., VA, and had fifteen children; Mary P., w/o Isaac Boggs, lives next to Henry; John S., farmer in Braxton Co., WV; Ida M., m. Joseph A. Pierson, of Braxton Co. Ellis m. Grace, d/o Amos and Saccharissa Gorrell, 13 Nov. 1886. Grace, of Braxton Co., WV, but native of Pleasant Co., WV. Amos and Saccharissa, members of the Sutton Presbyterian Church of Braxton Co. Members of the Westminster Presbyterian Church. Physician at No. 830 Columbia avenue.

690. A. KINGSLEY LOVE - s/o Philip G. and Josephine (Bond) Love. Father, b. in St. Mary Co., farmer and merchandiser in St. Mary Co., an Episcopalian, a Mason, d. in 1892 at sixty-seven. Grandfather, Charles K. Love, b. in Prince George Co., MD, d. at twenty-seven. Father of Charles Love, b. in Scotland, located in St. Mary Co. Maternal grandfather, Benedict Bond, of St. Mary Co., farmer and merchant. Brothers of A. Kingsley, Benedict and Bernard, merchants of St. Mary Co. Subject m. Nora, d/o R. B. Tippett, 18 Apr. 1894, and had two children, Melvin and Mary. Member of the Catholic Benevolent Legion. A Democrat. Lawyer at No. 108 East Lexington street.

691. HERMAN R. LINTHICUM - b. 26 Sep. 1831 in Middletown, MD, s/o Thomas F. and Catherine (Reineker) Linthicum, b., reared and m. in MD. German on the paternal side. Father, teamster, d. at sixty-six. Mother d. at sixty. Thomas and Catherine had eleven children, six d. Herman m. Mary C. Hill, of Sharpsburg, MD, and had two children: Frank, passenger engineer on the Philadelphia, Wilmington & Baltimore Railroad; and Mary C., w/o John A. Cockley, passenger engineer between Philadelphia and Washington. Member of the American Protective Association. Connected with the Monument Street Methodist Episcopal Church. A Republican. Foreman of the locomotives on the Northern Central Railroad.

692. W. S. GILROY, M. D. - b. in Baltimore, s/o John and Laura (Fisher) Gilroy. Father, b. in Scotland, came to America a young man, located in Balt., in the grocery business. Mother, b. and d. in Balt. Maternal grandfather, John Fisher, of German descent, had large farm in MD. Maternal grandmother, Susan

Perry, b. in England, and sister of Col. William Perry. W. S. m. Carrie Everett, b. in Balt. Member of the American Medical Scoiety, the Medical & Chirurgical Faculty of Maryland, and the Medical & Surgical Society of Baltimore. Belongs to the Third English Lutheran Church. Physician in Balt.

693. JAMES CAMPBELL - b. in 1848 in Paterson, NJ, s/o Robert and Nancy (Dunlap) Campbell, he of NY, she of Balt. Father, farmer, came to MD in 1851, a Republican. Robert and Nancy had twelve children: James; John, with the Steelton Company at Sparrows Point, MD; Robert, lives in the ninth district; Thomas, with the City & Suburban Street Railway Company; William, in the employ of a gas company of Philadelphia, PA; one brother d. when young; Hugh, carpenter; Mary and Maggie live in Canton; Annie lives in Philadelphia; Ella, lives in Canton; and other sister, d. James m. Martha M. Kyle, of Philadelphia, PA, in 1869, and had two children: Mary Ann, w/o John Keller; and Ella, Mrs. Van White, of Cecil Co., MD. Martha d. some years ago. Member of the Junior Order of American Mechanics. Belongs to the Methodist Episcopal Church. A Republican. Farmer of the twelfth district.

693. JOHN WATERS - b. 22 Nov. 1940 near Carlisle, Cumberland Co., PA, s/o Jesse and Elizabeth (Lynch) Waters, he of NJ, and she of Cumberland Co., PA. Paternal grandfather, farmer in NJ. Father, settled in Cumberland Co. as a young man,, moved to Balt. Co. in 1843, farmer, d. in Balt. at ninety-three. Maternal grandfather, b. in Londonderry, Ireland, came to America in early manhood, settled in Cumberland, PA, m. Mary Webb of Balt. Mother, d. in 1882, age seventy-six. Jesse and Elizabeth had ten children. John m. Mary Elizabeth, d/o Capt. Rawlings, of Balt., and had two children: Ida Grace, and Mary, w/o Dr. Clarence Busey, of Balt. Member of the Pimlico Driving Club, of Baltimore, the Maryland Agricultural Society, and the City Democratic Committee. Contractor and builder.

695. LEWIS M. BACON - b. 1 Jul. 1848 in the eighth district, s/o John and Pamela F. (Cole) Bacon. Grandfather, Martin Bacon, b. on old homestead that has been in family since 1740. Father, b. on family homestead in 1816, dairyman, a Democrat. Maternal grandfather, Lewis R. Cole, of Cole's Cavalry in war of 1812. John and Pamela had two sons, Lewis M. and George C., a Methodist minister in Hagerstown, MD. Lewis m. Anna M., d/o Rev. John J. C. Dosh, in 1876, and had three children, John Dosh, Lewis M., Jr. and Anna M. Member of the Masons, Knights of Pythias, Royal Arcanum, the Farmers' Market Company and the Farmers' Agricultural Club. A Democrat. Clerk of Balt. Co.

696. MELCHOR HOSHALL - b. in the sixth district, s/o Nicholas and Betsy A. (Matthews) Hoshall, of same district. Mother, m. (1) Mr. Hampsher, and had four children, Nancy, Diana, Johanna and George. Paternal grandfather, Jesse Hoshall, b. in the sixth district. Nicholas and Betsy had four children: Melchor, Hester R.; and Howard and Martha, both d. Melchor m. Ella Miller, b. in the sixth district, at twenty-six, and had four children, Clarence E., Althea B., Bessie L. and Helen. A Democrat. A

165

Baptist. Farmer of the sixth district.

697. JOHN C. KRANTZ - b. 7 Dec. 1866 in Balt., s/o George and Margaret (Buchheimer) Krantz. Father, b. in Germany, came with the grandfather to America, locating in Balt., in real-estate business, a Master Mason, d. in 1870, at thirty-one. Mother, b. in Balt., d/o John and Barbara (Weitzel) Buchheimer, natives of Hesse-Darmstadt, Germany; John d. in Balt. at seventy-five, Barbara d. 2 days later. George and Margaret had four children, Mrs. Barbara Gralley, Elizabeth, John C. and George H. John m. Mrs. Hannah Ortman, of Balt., d/o William and Catherine Steinmann, and had one child, Janet Taylor. William Steinmann, cigar merchant in Balt. Member of the Royal Arcanum. A Republican. Druggist.

698. GEORGE L. BARKELY - b. 1 Oct. 1835 in Balt., s/o Edwin and Hannah C. (Knorr) Barkley, he of Scotland and she of Balt. Father, came to America in early manhood, first in Philadelphia, then Balt., a cooper, old-line Whig, d. 31 Oct. 1846, at thirty-five. Mother, d. 1 Jan. 1892, at seventy-nine. Maternal grandfather, William Knorr, b. in Germany, came to America in early life, rope maker in Balt. til death, in 1861. Edwin and Hannah had three children; George L; Marcus C., chief engineer in Balt. city waterworks; and Laura J., w/o James Collins, who d. several years age, leaving wife and daughter. George m. Anna R., d/o William Grant, 24 Feb. 1857. William Grant, came from Scotland to Balt., m. lady of that city, manufactured screens and wires, moved to Cincinnati, d. in 1851. Members of the Methodist Church. Retired from the provision business at Lombard and Regester streets to a farm in the twelfth district.

699. REV. HENRY DALHOFF - b. 1 May 1863 in northern part of Germany, s/o Ernst and Frederica (Schulte) Dalhoff. Father, musician, d. in 1877 at sixty-three. Mother, d. in 1891, at sixty-seven. Ernst and Frederica had five children: Rudolph, orchestra leader in Germany; Dena, lives in Germany, w/o Adolph Sonnenbaum; Marie, in Germany, w/o Berthold Woertz; Fritz, orchestra leader in Germany; and Henry. Henry m. Elizabeth, d/o Rev. Christian Kirschmann, of Balt., 12 Apr. 1890, and had four children, Henry, Freda, William and Hans. Christian, b. in Wurtemberg, Germany, 20 May 1832, d. 16 Oct. 1894, came to America in 1857. Mother, of Elizabeth, Elizabeth, d/o William and Elizabeth (Summerlatt) Geiger, he of Germany and she of PA. Christian and Elizabeth m. 14 Jun. 1860 and had: Emma, lives with mother; Paul, organist and music teacher in Johnstown, PA; Henrietta, d. at six; Mary, musician and teacher and organist at Rev. Dalhoff's church; Mrs. Dalhoff; Christian, motorman; Martha; Salome; Gustav; and Eugene. Rector of the German Evangelical United Christ Church.

700. WILLIAM DULANY THOMAS, M. D. - b. 4 Jul. 1865 in Balt., s/o Joseph A. and Martha M. (Redgrave) Thomas, he of Balt. and she of Wayne Co., NY. Father, attorney in Balt. Joseph and Martha, identified with the Lafayette Square Presbyterian Church, had five children: Ettie C., Frank B., William Dulany, and 2 d.

Member of the Maryland State Homeopathic Society. Attends the Lafayette Square Presbyterian Church. Physician and surgeon at No. 611 North Carrolton avenue.

701. HON. JOHN A. JANETZKE - b. 4 Aug. 1858 in Dantzic, Germany, s/o August R. and Emily (Natchtigall) Nightingale) Janetzke, also of Prussia. Father, wheelwright, came to America in 1868, family came in 1871, a Republican. August and Emily had two children: John A., and Otto F., in the post-office of Balt. John m. Caroline, d/o Nicholas and Barbara Herman, of Balt., and had two children, John A., Jr., and Nicholas W. Member of the Independent Order of Mechanics, the Shield of Honor and the Heptasophs. A Republican. Attends the Evangelical Lutheran Church. Police magistrate for the eastern district of the city of Balt.

702. REV. WILLIAM KESSELL, C. SS. R. - b. 23 Sep. 1853 in Hamburg, Germany, s/o Philip and Sophia (Steinhauser) Kessel. Philip and Sophia also had: Fred, of New York, and Philip, of Buffalo. Family came to America in 1867, settled in Buffalo. Father, stone cutter, d. in 1877, age fifty-four. Mother, member of St. Ann's Catholic Church. Ordained in 1883 by Cardinal Gibbons. Rector of St. James' Catholic Church.

703. JUDGE ANDREW DORSEY - b. 7 Feb. 1836 in Howard Co., MD, s/o James A. and Susanna (Brooks) Dorsey. James and Susanna had eight children: Nicholas, James P., Caleb, Andrew, Susanna, Emily, Virginia, and Susanna (2d). Father, settled near Woodstock College when Andrew was eight, d. in 1849. Mother, d. in 1883, age seventy. Andrew m. Frances S. Key, descendent of Francis Scott Key, in 1879. A Democrat. Identified with the Catholic Church.

704. REV. HOWARD O. KEEN - b. 3 Apr. 1870 in Canton, MD, s/o William J. and Sarah E. (Mitchell) Keen. Grandfather, George Keen, b. in England,, came to America, settled in Balt. Co., farmer. Father, b. on old homestead, moved to Harford Co., a farmer, a Republican, member of the Junior Order of American Mechanics. Maternal grandfather, Isaac Mitchell, miller, had five sons, all millers. Mitchell family settled in Balt. Co. in the seventeenth century. William and Sarah, Methodist Protestants, had nine children: William Frank, in lumber business in Bel Air; Sarah Virginia, w/o Samuel T. Walker, of Waverly; Margaret Ann, schoolteacher at Fountain Green, near Bel Air; Harry C., works in hardware store in Bel Air; Lutine Mitchell, Walter, Nelson and Fannie, at home; and Howard. Member of the Junior Order of American Mechanics. Pastor of Keen Memorial Church in Baltimore.

705. GEORGE B. REYNOLDS, M. D. - b. 26 Oct. 1846 in Cumberland Co., VA, s/o James W. and Julia Ann (Carter) Reynolds. Father, b. in Cumberland Co., owned large plantation, Mt. Aery farm. Grandfather, John O. Reynolds, of Cumberland Co., attorney-at-law. Maternal great-grandfather, King Carter. On maternal side, connected with the Lees, the Carters and the Pages, of VA. Mother d. about 1878. James and Julia had four children, George

the eldest. George m. Ada Campbell, d/o Charles B. and Mary E. (Bender) Fiske, in Balt., and had four children: Charles Carter, Mary Elizabeth, Stanley Meade and Julia Ann Carter. Ada, b. in Washington, DC, granddaughter of Major Bender of the United States Army. Father of Major Bender, George Bender. Charles Fiske, civil engineer, planned the Chesapeake & Ohio Railroad, and the Chesapeake & Ohio Canal. Member of the Masons, the Royal Arcanum, the Heptasophs, the Ancient Order of United Workmen, the American Medical Association, the Medical and Chirurgical Faculty, the Baltimore Clinical Society, the Baltimore Medical Association, and the Baltimore Surgical Association. Attends Grace Episcopal Church. Physician in general practice in Balt.

706. FRANCIS GEORGE - b. 25 Jul. 1854 in Balt., s/o Francis J. and Roscena (Welsbach) George, both of Germany. Father, paint contractor in Balt. Mother, b. in Berlin, d. in Balt. Francis and Roscena had four children, Francis being second oldest. Subject. m. Rebecca. d/o John Strickland, in Balt., and had one child, Francis Barry. Rebecca, b. in Prince George Co., MD. John Strickland, farmer in Prince George Co. Member of the Eighth Ward Republican Club. Contractor, painter, and frescoer at No. 1204 Greenmount avenue.

707. ROBERT MAGRUDER - b. in 1856 in Washington, DC, s/o Thomas J. and Sarah (Boteler) Magruder. Father, b. in Prince George Co., MD, ran a boot and shoe house, a Democrat. Grandfather, Edward Magruder, b. in Scotland, a Presbyterian, came to MD before the Revolutionary war. Mother, of English descent. Thomas and Sarah had: Lyttleton; Edward B.; Robert; Alice, Mrs. L. D. Passano, of Balt.; May, widow of H. A. Cooper; Ella, Mrs. John L. Rodgers; and Minnie, Mrs. Jasper M. Berry, Jr. Robert m. Elizabeth, d/o James P. and Elizabeth R. (McGee) Thomas, in 1877, and had five children: Hamline, Herbert, Ethel, Robert, Jr., and Donald. Member of the Knights Templar. Attends the Methodist Episcopal Church South. President of The Union Credit Company.

708. HENRY R. CRANE - b. in 1845 in Richmond, VA, s/o James C. and Isabella (Steel) Crane. Descendant of English ancestors who came from London to New Haven, CT in 1638. Jasper Crane, moved to Newark, NJ. Father, b. in Newark about 1803, moved to Richmond in 1819, had wholesale hide and leather business, a Baptist. Grandfather, Rufus Crane. Maternal grandfather, George Steel of Philadelphia, connected with the Bank of North America. James and Isabella had six children. Henry m. Clara, d/o Micajah Merryman, 29 Nov. 1871, and had five children: Laura M., Edith C., Clara I., Helen Bond, and one who d. Member of the Sons of the Revolution, the Society of the Army and Navy of the Confederate States, in Maryland. Secretary of the Maryland Life Insurance Company, No. 10 South street.

709. HARRY TYLER CAMPBELL - b. 30 Jun. 1859 near Warrenton, Fauquier Co., VA, s/o Alexander Spotswood and Mary Ann Tyler (Horner) Campbell, of VA. Father, lawyer, then farmer, a Whig, d. 10 Sep. 1890. Alexander and Mary m. 17 Apr. 1844, and had eight children: John Wilson, d. single; Mary Horner, d. in

infancy; William Horner, single, lives near Warrenton;; Mildred Moore, Mrs. Inmon Evans, d.; Robert Richard, an attorney-at-law, lives in Warrenton, VA, m. d/o Col. John S. Mosby; Josephine Horner, m. Albert Windmill, lives in VA; Alexander Spotswood and Harry Tyler. Through father, descendant from Sir Alexander Spotswood, Sir Alexander's eldest daughter, Mildred, being his great-great-grandmother. Through mother, who is only child of Robert Richard Horner, he is descended from the Brown family of Charles Co., MD. Ann Brown m. Richard Horner, of Warrenton, VA. Campbell family descended from Duncan Campbell, who left Scotland for Ireland in 1700 with three sons, Dougald, Robert and John. Three sons of Robert: Hugh, John and Charles, settled in Augusta Co., and from John Campbell, Harry Tyler Campbell descended, being his grandfather. Harry m. Florence, d/o William and Susan (Blackman) Muller, 2 Jan. 1888, and had three children, Harry Guy, Bruce Spotswood and Florence Susan. William Muller, came to America from England in 1873, lived near Warrenton, til d. Florence Muller, b. in London, England. Members of the Episcopal Church. Contractor for railroad work and other corporations in the state with office on Lexington street.

710. WILLIAM SCHLUDERBERG - b. 29 Sep. 1839 near Hessen, Germany, s/o Daniel Schluderberg. Father, farmer, d. when William was three. Mother m. (2) Conrad Miller, came to America about 1851. Daniel and wife had six children: George, Balt. business man; Henry, butcher in Balt., d. in 1893; Conrad, in meat business in Balt.; Willmenia, w/o Capt. John Rau; Mary, single, d. in 1891; and William. William m. Sophia Falk, of Germany, in 1858, and had nine children: Kate, w/o Clayton Emerich, in hotel business in Washington, DC; George, in business with father, m. Maggie Marsh and had three children, Henry, Amolia and Conrad, all d.; Lillie, at home; Wilhelmina, Annie and Lizzie d. in childhood, and others in infancy. Member of the Butchers' Association. Belongs to two churches, the Reformed Church on Canton avenue and the Canton German Lutheran Church. A Republican. Engaged in wholesale and retail beef and pork business in Highland.

711. WILLIAM REYNOLDS - b. in 1842 in Balt., s/o William and Rosanna (Ewell) Reynolds. Descendant of John Reynolds, who came to America from the north of Ireland about 1735. William, s/o John, captian in the PA colonial service during Indian wars, d. before the Revolution. William (2d), s/o Capt. William Reynolds, a farmer in PA. His eldest son, William Reynolds, father of William of this sketch. Father, b. in PA, came to Balt. in 1817, wholesale grocer, a Whig, a Mason, attended the Central Presbyterian Church, d. at Newville, PA in 1873. Mother, of Prince William Co., VA, descendant of English ancestors, who settled in America in latter part of the seventeenth century. William and Rosanna had seven children: William; James, stock-broker in NY, then in grain business in Peoria, IL; Hugh Williamson, in lumber business in Peoria; Samuel D., lives in Peoria; Sophia D., lives in Peoria; Rose E., d., single. William m. Nora M. Lightfoot, of Mobile, AL in 1876, and had two children, Eleanor and Nora. Mr. Lightfoot, a Virginian, moved to AL, owned large plantation.

Member of the University Club. An independent Democrat. Attends
the First Presbyterian Church. Attorney-at-law at No. 216 St.
Paul street.

712. J. FUSSELL MARTENET, M. D. - b. 10 Jul. 1858 in Balt., s/o
Simon J. and Philena (Fussell) Martenet of Balt. Maternal grandfather, Jacob Fussell, a Quaker. Paternal grandfather, Simon
Jonas Martenet, b. in Switzerland, came to Balt. when son, Simon,
was almost four. Father, b. 13 Apr. 1832, surveyor and civil
engineer, d. in Balt. 6 Nov. 1892, at sixty. Mother d. in 1894.
Simon and Philena m. August 1853, and had nine children, four
living: Jefferson, civil engineer, d. at thirty; Simon J., in
insurance business in Balt., lives at Gardenville; William H.,
veterinary surgeon in Balt.; and Clarissa F., m., lives in Balt.
Subject m. (1) Cynthia, d/o Henry Lange, in Balt. in 1880;
Cynthia d. two years later. Subject m. (2) Ella R. Reed, M.D.,
of Arlington, VA in Mar. 1896; Ella d. in Aug. 1896. Member of
the Landmark Lodge No. 127, the St. John's Chapter No. 19,
R.A.M., the Monumental Commandery No. 3, K.T., the Boumi Temple,
Mystic Shrine, the Shield of Honor, the Golden Chain and the
Junior Order of American Mechanics. A Republican. Identified
with the Orthodox Society of Friends. Physician at No. 1701
North Caroline street.

713. JOHN HURST MORGAN - b. 25 Apr. 1866 in Balt., s/o DeWitt
Clinton and Sarah Berry (Hurst) Morgan. Father, b. 2 Mar. 1830
in Rockingham Co., VA. DeWitt and Sarah m. 11 May 1865. Paternal grandparents, Rev. Gerard Morgan and Rosannah Brown.
Rosannah, d/o Maj. John Brown, of Augusta Co., VA. Rev. Gerard
Morgan, s/o Nicholas Morgan and Mary Butler. Nicholas Morgan,
s/o John Morgan and Annetje Van Cortlandt. John Morgan, s/o
Charles Morgan, of Newport, Wales, who settled in Monmouth Co.,
NJ about 1650 and m. Catalyntje Huyberts, of Harlem. Sarah Berry
Morgan, b. at Balt., 25 Sep. 1842, d/o John Hurst and Susan L.
Berry. John Hurst, s/o Samuel Hurst. Susan L. Hurst, d/o Col.
John Berry and Sarah Duke Jackson. Col. Berry, s/o Benjamin
Berry, Jr., and Eleanor Lansdale. Benjamin Berry, Jr. b. 1768,
d. 1815, s/o John Berry and Eleanor Bowie Clagett. Eleanor Bowie
Clagett Berry, d/o Edward Clagett and Eleanor Bowie. Edward
Clagett, s/o Richard Clagett and Deborah Ridgely, nee Dorsey.
Richard Clagett, s/o Capt. Thomas Clagett, who settled in MD
about 1680. Capt. Thomas Clagett, s/o Col. Edward Clagett and
Margaret Adams, d/o Sir Thomas Adams, of London. Deborah
Ridgely, widow of Charles Ridgely, and d/o Hon. John Dorsey and
Pleasance Ely, who settled on the Severn about 1660. Eleanor
Bowie Clagett, d/o John Bowie and Mary Mullikin. John Bowie
settled in Prince Georges Co. about 1685. Subject m. May C.,
d/o George R. Vickers, Esq., 28 Janurary 1897. Member of the
Society of the War of 1812, the Sons of the Revolution, and the
Maryland Club. A Democrat. Member of the Balt. bar.

714. MARTIN J. REESE - b. 27 Apr. 1858 in Balt., s/o Charles A.
and Mary E. (Hich) Reese. Father, b. in Melsing, Germany, came
to America at twenty-eight, settled in Baltimore, a Democrat.
Mother, b. in Germany, came to America as a young lady with her

brothers. Charles and Mary had five children: Martin J.; John, in the harness business; Joseph, d. at twenty-one; Mary, w/o Casper Dennis, of Balt.; and Lizzie, w/o Harry Downs. Charles m. (2) Mary Brand, and had two children: Peter, plumber and tinner; and Frederick, merchant. Charles m. (3) Miss Hoot. Martin m. Kate A. Pfrom , in 1875, and had seven children: Mamie, Charles A., Katie E. and Martin J.; and Johnnie, Joseph and Eva, d. young. Ancestors of Kate are from Germany. Member of the Shield of Honor, Junior Order of the Legion of the Red Cross, and the Centennial Butchers' Association No. 1. Politically an independent. Attends the Lutheran Church. Wholesale and retail butcher at Highlandtown.

715. CAPT. COLUMBUS W. LEWIS - b. 12 Nov. 1838 in Montgomery Co., MD, s/o Arnold T. and Elizabeth (Watkins) Lewis. Father, b. in same county, farmer, Democrat, d. in 1884 at seventy-three. Maternal grandfather, Joseph Watkins, farmer of Montgomery Co. Arnold and Elizabeth had twelve children, five living: R. C., business man of Washington, DC; A. T., business man of Washington, DC; Ellen, w/o William Purdum, farmer of Frederick Co., MD; and Annie, w/o James Burdett, farmer of Montgomery Co. Columbus m. Rosa R. J., d/o David and Mary Gamble, in spring of 1863, and had a son, William J. A Democrat. Inclined to Methodism, attends the Presbyterian Church. Superintendent of Bay View Asylum.

716. PROF. DAVID STREET, M. D. - b. 17 Oct. 1855 in Harford Co., MD, s/o Corbin Grafton and Nancy Streett, both of Harford Co. Father, b. in 1812, contractor and builder, d. Mar. 1878. Mother, now eighty-two, a Presbyterian, lives with David. Corbin and Nancy had eight children. Three brothers, David, Thomas and John (or William) came from England, landed in Balt. about 1770. Last named went north, David settled on the eastern shore, where descendants spell name Streets, and Thomas settled in Harford Co. David m. (1) an English lady, m. (2) Sarah, b. in Wales, David d. in 1822. Subject m. Sadie, d/o W. H. B. Fusselbaugh, in 1882, and had three children: William F., d. in infancy; Anna R. is fourteen; and David Corbin is ten. Member of the Landmark Blue Lodge, St. John's Chapter, Concordia Council and Crusade Commandery, the Mystic Shrine, Maryland Academy of Sciences, the Medical and Surgical Society of Baltimore, the Baltimore Medical Association, the Medical and Chirurgical Faculty of Maryland, and the American Medical Association and Clinical Society of Maryland. A Democrat. Dean of the Baltimore Medical College.

717. GILMAN P. EVANS, M. D. - b. 28 May 1857 in Jefferson Co., NY, s/o Gilman and Mary A. (Kelsey) Evans, he of NH and she of NY. Paternal grandfather, Tallman Evans, from New England. Maternal grandfather, James Kelsey, b. in the Mohawk Valley, in NY state, a farmer. Both sides of family of Welsh ancestry, very long-lived. Father, farmer, a Presbyterian, d. in 1875, age seventy-one. Mother d. in 1894. Gilman and Mary had four children: S. Ellen, w/o C. C. Eddy, farmer in Theresa, NY; Alice M., w/o col. Edward Stirling, farmer of Huron, SD; Ada, w/o A. B. Huntington, of Watertown, NY; and Gilman. Physician at No. 1019

North Fulton avenue.

718. FREDERICK J. SCHNEIDER - b. 22 Nov. 1852 in Coblentz, Rhenish Prussia, on the Rhine, s/o Philip and Philapena (Wentz) Schneider. Father, a weaver, came to America from Germany about 1858, settled in Balt. Co., a Democrat, d. in 1874. Mother d. in Sep. 1891. Philip and Philapena had five children; Frederick J.; Philip H., blacksmith; Catherine, m. William H. Rever, works in the emigration department; Amanda, w/o John Holler, foreman of the work train of the Baltimore & Ohio Railroad Company; and Mary, drowned when a child. Frederick m. Agnes Louisa, d/o John Kurtz, in 1879 and have two children living, William J. and Edward. A Republican. Identified with the Lutheran Church. Engaged in the mercantile business on the Philadelphia road.

719. GEORGE T. SHOWER, M. D. - b. 20 Aug. 1841 in Manchester, Carroll Co., MD, s/o Adam and Mary Ann (Geiger) Shower. Grandfather, John Adam Shower, b. in Carroll Co. which was at that time Balt. Co., farmer, d. at fifty-nine. Great-grandfather, John Shower, b. in Germany, and early settler of Carroll Co. Father, b. in Carroll Co., conducted a foundry in Manchester, MD, now eighty-two. Maternal grandfather, Rev. Jacob Geiger, of Lehigh Co., PA, minister of the German Reformed Church, d. in 1849, age fifty-two. Paternal grandfather of Jacob Geiger, surgeon, came to America with French army during the Revoluntionary war. Maternal grandmother, Catherine Seltzer Geiger, of Balt., MD, member of the Reformed Church, d. in 1878, at fifty-eight. Adam and Mary had twelve children, eight living: George T.; Mary C., lives in York, PA; Dr. Edmund G., physician in Balt.; Charlotte E., w/o Dr. J. W. Dehoff, of York, PA; William H., runs the foundry at Manchester; Catherine Amelia, music teacher in Balt.; Dr. John Adam, physician in York, PA; and Leonora Virginia, lives with George. George m. Ida M. Leslie, of Loudoun Co., VA, 5 Dec. 1890. Ida d. 25 Sep. 1895. Member of the Homeopathic Medical Society, and the Baltimore Investigating Club of Materia Medica. Belongs to the Trinity Reformed Church of Woodberry. Physician at No. 421 Roland avenue.

720. ALEX LAUF - b. 12 Aug. 1863 in New York City. Member of the Sincerity Lodge No. 181, A.F.& A.M., the Mohawk Tribe of Red Men, the Hiawatha Shield of Honor, the Fraternal Legion, the Steuben Lodge, K.P., and the Uniformed Rank Knights of Pythias. A Republican. Proprietor of Alex's Exchange.

721. CAPT. HENRY C. SMYSER - b. in 1832 in York Co., PA, s/o Jacob and Elizabeth (Diehl) Smyser. Father, b. in York Co., farmer, then contractor and builder, d. at forty-four. Mother, b. in York Co., of an old family of German origin, d. in 1875, m. (1) had five children, one living, m. (2) Jacob and had eleven children, five living. Henry m. Rebecca, d/o Thomas Jenkins, in Balt., and had one child, Elizabeth, now Mrs. Parsons, of Balt. Thomas Jenkins, a coach-builder. Member of the Masons, the Custer Post No. 6, G.A.R. Belongs to the Franklin Square Baptist Church. A Republican. Contractor and builder.

722. DIETRICH HERMAN RADECKE - b. 19 Dec. 1807 in Hanover, Germany. Came to America in 1831, settled in Balt. Dietrich m. Sophia Margaret Wedeman, of Hanover, 26 Jul. 1835 in Zion Church, and had nine children: John, eldest, owns factory father had; Anna C., w/o Otto Duker; Harmon Henry, retired on old homestead; Sophia Ann, d. in 1892; Margaret A., w/o Charles Gunther; Mary Sophia, w/o Ernest Sack, lives in Balt. Co.; Louisa Margaret, w/o George Stoll, farmer at Snow Hill, Anne Arundel Co.; Henry F. and Philip, own and live on the homestead, (see sketches on them). A Democrat. Retired business man. Dietrich d. 15 March 1886.

723. CHARLES GUNTHER - b. 17 Feb. 1840 in Balt. Co., s/o Otto and Christina Louisa Gunther, both of Germany. Otto and Christina had seven children: Wilhelmina, widow of Peter Murray; Louisa, w/o George E. Coxen; Fredricka, single; Charles; Attilla, single; and Caroline, w/o Frank Hammond. Charles m. Margaret S., d/o Dietrich H. and Sophia M. (Wedeman) Radecke, 17 Oct. 1866, and had six children: Charles O., with Otto Duker & Co., m. Susie Harrisburg and had two children, Margaret Anna and Mildred; Emma Sophia, w/o Thomas C. Biddison, and have one child, Edna Margaret; Anna Louisa, Mary Ella and Herman Henry d. in infancy; and Bertha Margaret, student. Member of Zion Lutheran Church of Baltimore. Farmer of the twelfth district. Charles d. 8 Sep. 1882.

724. EDWARD M. DUNCAN, M. D. - b. 8 Nov. 1860 in Balt. Co., s/o John D. C. and Catherine E. (Jones) Duncan. Father, of same locale, merchant. Grandfather, William Duncan, b. in northern part of Ireland, old blue-Presbyterian, came to United States a youth. Maternal grandfather, Charles Jones, of Balt. Co. John and Catherine m. in 1854, and had six children: Frank I., attorney in Balt. Co.; George C., in merchandising in Cockeysville, m. Ella Shipley; Albert E., single, lives in Cockeysville; Nellie G. and Bettie B., at home. All are members of the Methodist Episcopal Church. Edward m. Roberta, d/o Rev. R. W. Block, in 1886, and had three children, Roberta, Edward G. and J. Elizabeth. Member of the Knights of the Golden Eagle, the Royal Arcanum and the Ancient Order of United Workmen. Physician in Govanstown.

725. JAMES H. LIVINGSTON - b. 27 Jun. 1845 in Balt., s/o Seth F. and Nancy A. (Dobbins) Livingston. Grandfather, William Livingston, b. in Worcester Co., MD, of Scotch descent, a farmer. Father, b. near Snow Hill, Worcester Co., shoemaker, d. at seventy-two. Mother, b. in Balt., d/o William Dobbins, of English descent, d. at sixty-five. Seth and Nancy had three children: William E., d.; Mrs. Sarah E. Smith, of Washington, DC; and James H. James m. Anna E. Kellum of Balt. and had four children: E. Latrobe, in the office of the Baltimore Traction Railroad Company; Anna Keene, Mrs. Mahler, of Balt.; Mrs. Ida V. McComas, of Balt.; and James H., works with father. Member of the Legions of the Red Cross, the Knights of the Golden Eagle in Baltimore, the Shield of Honor, the Ancient Order of United Workmen, the Heptasophs, the Junior Order United American Mechanics, the United States Benevolent Fraternity, and the Essenic Order. A Republican. Belongs to the Emanuel Reformed Episcopal

Church. Engaged in wholesale and commission business.

726. HARRY SENIOR - b. 1 Jan. 1859 in Maytown, IL, s/o Squire and Louisa (Vandergrift) Senior, he of England and she of IL. Father, cloth weaver, settled first at Maytown, IL, then Philadelphia about 1864, d. in Philadelphia at seventy-four. Squire and Louisa had two sons: William, of Philadelphia, and Harry. Harry m. Caroline F., d/o Christian M. Fagley, in Philadelphia, and had one child, William, d. at four years. Caroline, b. in Mifflintown, Juniata Co., PA. Member of the Concordia Lodge No. 13, A.F.&A.M., the Iris Lodge No. 16, of the Golden Chain, and the Marine Engineers' Beneficial Association No. 5, of Baltimore. Caroline attends the Presbyterian Church. Chief engineer of the Atlanta, of the York River Steamboat Company.

727. CHARLES W. HATTER - b. 17 May 1840 in Balt., s/o Martin and Fredericka (Leinsz) Hatter. Father, b. in 1815, in Hesse-Darmstadt, Germany, crossed the Atlantic in 1829, settled in Balt., confectioner, a Lutheran then Mennonite, d. in 1877. Paternal grandfather, came to America in early nineteenth century, a farmer. Mother, b. in Germany, came to America about same time as Martin, d. in 1879, at fifty-nine. Maternal grandfather, Daniel Leinsz, soldier under Bonaparte, d. at eighty-two. Martin and Fredericka had six children, Charles the eldest. Charles m. Anna, d/o Hugh Porter, and had five children: C. W., Jr., bookkeeper; Emma, at home; Anna, teacher; Frank and Eleanor, students. Member of the Masons, Warren Lodge, A.F.&A.M., the St. John's Chapter No. 19, R.A.M., the Jerusalem Council, R.&S.M., and the Crusade Commandery No. 5, K.T. A Republican. President of Oldtown Fire Insurance Company.

728. EDMOND JONES WILLIAMS, M. D. - b. 16 Aug. 1841 in Cumberland Co., NC, s/o William L. and Sarah Ann (McKellar) Williams. Grandfather, John C. Williams, Scotch-Irish, spent entire life in NC, a farmer. Father, d. in 1856, at fifty. Mother, b. in NC, d. at home in 1896. Maternal family founded in NC in 1774 as part of the Cross Creek Colony. William and Sarah had nine children: Henrietta, w/o Dr. McCoy, of NC; William L, farmer of NC; John C., in insurance business in Harrisburg, PA; Peter McKellar, in turpentine business in GA; Martha, w/o Charles Purcell, farmer of NC; Henry M., d. during the war; Louis D., in insurance business in Harrisburg, PA; Benjamin J., commercial traveler; and Edmond. Edmond m. Ellen Sumors Wootton, of VA, in 1875, and had seven children: Jesse Wootten, student; Thomas Bayard, student; William L, student; Edmond Jones, d. in infancy; Augustus Schrader and Sarah McKellar, at home; and Henry Martin, d. in infancy. Member of the Masons, the Shield of Honor, and the Ancient Order United Workmen. A Democrat, like paternal ancestors, maternal ancestors being old-line Whigs. Raised Presbyterian, belongs to the Baptist Church. Physician in Canton.

729. WILLIAM H. H. ANDERSON - b. in 1841 in Harper's Ferry, s/o William and Susanna (Hall) Anderson. Father, b. in VA, settled in MD in 1847, d. in Anne Arundel Co., in 1877, at eighty. Grandfather, John Anderson, VA planter, of English descent.

Maternal grandfather, Everett N. Hall, of Prince George Co., MD. William and Susanna had two children, William H. H. and Susanna, w/o John Bowie, of Prince George Co. William m. Cornelia M., d/o Robert L. Brockett, in 1868. Cornelia, b. and reared in VA. Robert Brockett, president of Lynchburg College. A Mason. A Democrat. Belong to the Episcopal Church. Attorney at No. 5 East Lexington street.

730. ISRAEL J. WOODWARD, A. M., D. V. S., M. D. - b. 10 Feb. 1870 in New Egypt, now Oakford, Ocean Co., NJ, s/o Dr. Charles Edmund and Aeliza (Templeman) Woodward. Abner Woodward and wife came to America from England, settled in NJ. Grandfather, Israel J., farmer in NJ. Father, b. in NJ. Mother, b. in Georgetown, DC. Maternal grandfather, Richard Templeman, b. in America of English parents, d. in Washington, DC. Charles and Aeliza had six children, five living: Charles P., M.D., lives on old homestead; Israel J.; George G., student; William K. and Frances A., at home. Israel m. Barbara F. Panetti, in Balt., and had one child, I. J., Jr. A Republican.

731. EDWARD FLAYHART - b. 12 May 1820 in what is now Kalmia Park, s/o John Flayhart. Father, b. in Harford Co. in 1794, had three brothers and two sisters: Joshua, d. in Balt., at ninety-seven, blind; William, carpenter and builder, of Harford Co.; James, d. in Frederick Co.; Mary, m. Mr. Burkins, of Harford Co.; and Ann, m. Solomon Wheeler. Grandfather, John Flayhart, b. in Harford Co., ancestors came to America from Ireland and settled in York Co., PA. Mother, b. in Balt., d. in 1881. Maternal grandfather, Richard Dunphy, came here from Ireland. Maternal grandmother, came England. Richard Dunphy had seven children: John, Thomas, Richard; Ann, m. Benjamin McCullough; Margaret, single; Elizabeth, m. John Hall; and Mrs. Flayhart. John and wife had six children: Edward; John, d. in childhood; Joshua, d. in Balt. at thirty-five; Sarah, m. Thomas Whittle; Eliza, m. James H. Boyd; and Margaret, m. (1) Frank Phoebus, a painter, and m. (2), a cousin, Thomas, s/o Joshua Flayhart. Edward m. Margaret, d/o Joseph Yost, in 1843, and had thirteen children: Mary, d. at fourteen; Sophia, d. at sixteen; Charles M., m. Mary C. Curry, of Balt., a painter, d. in Balt., at forty-two, leaving four children (William H., m. Belle Welsh, and had one son; Charles R., John Edward, and Susie); John Edward, b. 14 Aug. 1853, member of the Methodist Episcopal Church, and the Epworth League, m. Emma W. E., d/o Adam H. Krout, d. in 1886, has son John Howard; William Henry, b. 3 Dec. 1854, a printer, m. Kate Ruby, of York, PA, and had two children, Ada May and Walter Finch, a Methodist; others d. in infancy. Former school teacher and justice of the peace.

732. FRANCIS BEASTON LAURENSON - b. 10 Aug. 1818 in Balt., s/o Philip and Margaretta (Whelan) Laurenson. Father, b. in shire of Essex, England, came to the United States after finishing school. Philip and Margaretta had six children: Mary A. and Laura, nuns in England; Margaretta, m. Francis W. Elder, of Balt.; Elizabeth, w/o James Beatty, Jr., of Balt.; Philip, d. in San Francisco, CA, a young man; and Francis B. Francis m. Elizabeth Carroll, 30

Apr. 1839, and had twelve children, following survive: Sarah, w/o
Dr. J. C. Monmonier, of Wetheredville; Margaretta, m. Milford R.
Lackey, of Washington, and has three children; Elizabeth, Mrs.
Edwin F. Abel; Laura R., m. Dr. B. J. Byrne, of Ellicott City;
Julia L., Mrs. Thomas R. Myer; Nora R., w/o William S. Myer; and
C. Philip, m. Elizabeth P. Beatty in 1878, she d. in 1892 leaving
three children, Charles R., Augusta M. and Philip. Elizabeth
Carroll, granddaughter of Daniel Carroll. Retired farmer.

733. REV. WILLIAM LAWRENCE JORDAN - b. 9 Aug. 1840 in West
Balt., s/o Henry J. and Mary C. (McFaden) Jordan. Father, b. in
England, came to America at twenty-two, returned to England, then
back to America, d. in 1858. Mother, living in Balt., age
eighty-six. Henry and Mary had: William Lawrence, Henry F.,
Charles, Edward, John Joseph, Thomas and Mary E., w/o Henry H.
Ostendorf. Ordained 28 Jun. 1865. Pastor at St. Bridget's
Church of Canton.

734. PHILIP A. PANETTI, M. D. - b. in Dec. 1869 in Balt., s/o
Ernest and Barbara (Gamier) Panetti. Paternal great-grandfather,
native of Italy, moved to France in early life, a physician, had
brother that was a cardinal in the Roman Catholic Church in
Italy. Grandfather, Dr. Panetti, b. in France, went to Germany
after the war, d. in Germany. Father, a D.D.S., b. in Amsbach,
Germany, d. in Balt. at fifty-four. Mother, family name now
spelled Gammar, b. in Balt. Maternal grandfather, Jacob F.
Gamier, of French descent, a merchant in Balt. Ernest and
Barbara had seven children, six living; Rev. J. M., Episcopal
clergyman, d. soon after graduation; Jacob F., professor in
Balt.; Ernest F., musician; Philip A.; O. F., pharmacist in
Balt.; Barbara, w/o Dr. I. J. Woodward; and Marguerite, w/o James
McKnight, of Balt. Attended Trinity Episcopal Church. Physician
in Balt.

735. JOSEPH C. OHLENDORF, JR., M. D. - b. 7 Sep. 1862 in Balt.,
s/o Joseph C. and Mary T. (Eschback) Ohlendorf. Father, b. in
Hanover, Germany, came to Balt. 1846, pharmacist, retired to
York, PA, came back to Balt., member of St. James' Roman Catholic
Church, now sixty-nine. Mother, b. in Balt., now about fifty-
three. Joseph and wife had thirteen children, six living: Mary
T., w/o James Westerfield, of Balt.; Katie, lives in Chicago;
Agnes, at home; Maggie, lives with Joseph; Ignatius, with father;
and Joseph C. Joseph m. Anna, d/o Mrs. Shapiro, of Balt., 17
Aug. 1892, and had one child, Anna Ida, b. 7 Sep. 1892. Anna
reared in the Hebrew faith, Joseph in the Catholic. Maternal
grandfather, John Eschbach, b. in Germany, contractor, d. in
1888, nearly ninety-three. Maternal grandmother, d. at forty-
seven, with typhoid fever, had twenty-two children, Mary T., the
third. Member of the Maryland Medical and Chirurgical Faculty,
the Improved Order of Heptasophs, the Order of the Golden Chain,
the Lord Baltimore Council, Catholic Benevolent Legion No. 192,
the Improved Order of B'Nai B'rith. A Republican. Physician in
Balt.

736. RICHARD M. DUVALL - b. 1 Nov. 1857 near Annapolis, s/o

Richard I. and Rachel (Waring) Duvall. Father, b. in Prince George Co., MD, moved, at about twenty-five, to Anne Arundel Co., near Millersville, m. (1) Sally Duvall, his cousin, had a number of children, five lived to majority: James Monroe, Philip Barton, Samuel Fulton, Daniel Clayton and Sally Duvall. Richard m. (2) Rachel Waring, who d. in 1865, leaving six children: Richard Mareen and Marius Turner (twins), Everett, Herbert, Barton Lee, and Frances C., d. in infancy. Richard m. (3) Mary A. Mitchell, of Prince George Co., MD, in 1869 and had one child, Hannah L. Family descended from Mareen Duvall, a French Hugeunot, fled his native Normandy, came to America, settled in what is now Prince George Co., MD, about 1640, a civil engineer. Great-grandfather, Samuel Duvall. Grandfather, Barton Duvall. Maternal grandfather, Frank Waring, b. in Prince George Co. Waring family descended from Sampson Waring, who came to America with Leonard Calvert before 1640, settled in St. Mary Co., MD. Basil Waring, s/o Sampson, m. (1) Mary Marsham, d/o Sir Richard Marsham, member of the H. M. Privy Council. Basil m. (2) Sarah Hayne. Basil, s/o Basil and Mary, m. Martha, d/o Thomas Greenfield, also of H. M. Privy Council. Basil, s/o Basil and Martha, m. Cassandra McGregor, and had James Waring, father of Frank Waring and grandfather of Richard M. Duvall. James Waring m. Elizabeth Hilleary. Richard m. Nannie Yerbury, d/o Dr. John Schley Goldsborough, of Frederick, 30 Oct. 1895. Member of the Balt. bar.

737. A. W. MACDONALD, M. D. - b. in 1865 in County Inverness, Nova Scotia, s/o John and Mary (Gilles) Macdonald. Descended from the lords of the Isle of Skye, off the coat of Inverness, Scotland, where grandfather, John Macdonald, Sr., was b. Moved to Nova Scotia, originally Ardacia, when father was about fifteen. Grandfather, farmer, m. Catherine Ross, d. at ninety-nine. Mother, b. in Nova Scotia. Maternal grandfather, Archibald Gilles, b. on the Isle of Skye, farmer of Nova Scotia. John and Mary had thirteen children, eleven living, A. W., being the eighth. Member of the Baltimore Medical and Surgical Society. Physician at No. 1041 North Broadway.

738. GEORGE D. MUDD, M. D. - b. 20 Nov. 1826 in Charles Co., MD, s/o Theodore and Dorothy (Dyer) Mudd, both of Charles Co. Father, farmer, d. in MO while visiting daughter, Clarissa, w/o Dr. Hilary P. Mudd, and his sons, Henry T., Alexander and Dr. James Marcellus Mudd. Mother, d. in 1861, at sixty-eight. Theodore and Dorothy, both Catholics, had ten children, three living: Anna, in a convent in Balt.; Alexander, lives in MO; and Dr. George D. George m. Rosalie, d/o Edward D. Boone, of Charles Co., 25 Oct. 1853, and had three children, one living, F. DeSales, lives in Charles Co. Dorothy, a Catholic, d. in 1858, at twenty-three. George m. (2) Catharine M., d/o John E. Turner, in 1871, and had three children: M. Anna, at home; George D., clerk in Central Savings Bank, of Balt.; and Fannie T., has government position in civil service commission at Washington. George is uncle of Hon. Sydney E. Mudd, whose father, d. leaving three sons, Sydney, Oscar J. and Robert Lee. A Republican. A Catholic. Physician and surgeon, and coroner for the southwest district of Balt.

739. D. CALDWELL IRELAND, M. D. - b. 4 May 1844 in Annapolis, MD, s/o Thomas and Elizabeth (Nichols) Ireland. Father, b. in MD, merchant of Annapolis, a Whig then Republican, d. in 1877, at seventy-seven. Mother, b. in Anne Arundel Co., d. at sixty-nine. Maternal grandfather, William Nichols, farmer. Thomas and Elizabeth had four children: William, retired merchant, d. in Balt. in 1895; Mrs. D. McKune Cook, lives in Cincinnati, OH; D. Caldwell; and John, lawyer in Annapolis. Subject m. M. E., d/o Rev. David Henderson, in Balt. Members of the Methodist Episcopal Church. A Democrat. General practitioner and surgeon of Balt.

740. GEORGE JESSOP - b. 6 Jul. 1803 in the eighth district of Balt. Co., s/o Charles Jessop. Father, b. in Sheffield, England, came to the United States, settled at Ridgely's Forge, a wheelwright and millwright, joined the Methodist Episcopal Church. George m. (1) Elizabeth, d/o Joseph Ashton, of near Bel Air, Harford Co., MD, and had seven children, one being George Jessop, Jr., b. 3 Sep. 1848, in the eight district, m. Bettie, d/o John Bosley, of Williams, 21 Feb. 1883, and had three children, John B., George and William H. After death of Elizabeth, George m. (2) her sister, Ellen Ashton, and had three children: Dr. Charles A. and Nettie, d.; and Elizabeth, m. Pietro Palagano, lives in Ashland, Balt. Co., and had two children, Nettie J. and Maria A. George Jessop, Jr., a Democrat, member of the Junior Order of American Mechanics, an Episcopalian. Agriculturist of the eighth district. George d. 3 Apr. 1887.

741. F. ALBERT KURTZ - b. 5 Oct. 1854 in Balt., s/o T. Newton and Julia (Grafton) Kurtz. Father, b. in 1822 in Balt., d. in Balt. 9 Janurary 1881. Grandfather, Benjamin Kurtz, D.D., LL.D., b. in Harrisburg, PA, a Lutheran, m. Ann Snively of PA. Great-grandfather, John Kurtz, a tanner, of German descent. Father, publisher and bookseller of Balt., m. Julia Grafton, of Balt., 2 Oct. 1845. Maternal grandfather, Mark Grafton, a merchant, of Scotch lineage, b. in Balt. Co. Maternal grandmother, Keziah Hall, b. in Balt. Co., of English descent. Mother, d. 23 Mar. 1897 age seventy-three. T. Newton and Julia had five children, F. Albert the youngest. Subject m. Abbie, d/o Henry W. and Mary C. Gambrill, 11 Apr. 1882, and had a daughter, Edna L. Abbie d. in Sep. 1890. Henry W. Gambrill, of the firm of Gambrill, Sons & Co., manufactured cotton ducks, etc. Member of the Young Men's Republican Club. State insurance commissioner of MD.

742. REV. ANDREW ANTHONY DUSZYNSKI - b. 30 Nov. 1866 in province of Posen, Germany, s/o Simon and Catherine Duszynski, natives of same area, of Polish descent. Father, farmer, d. 19 May 1873, age fifty-two. Simon and Catherine, both Catholics, had six children, Andrew being the youngest. Mother, after death of Simon, brought her children to America in 1881, settled in South Bend, IN. Ordained 21 Jun. 1894 by His Eminence James Cardinal Gibbons. Rector of St. Athanasius' Catholic Church, at Curtis Bay, Anne Arundel Co..

743. GEN. JAMES E. WHITEFORD, M. D. - b. 24 Jun 1848 in Harford

Co., MD, s/o James W. and Nancy Nelson (Ramsay) Whiteford. Father, b. on the Fox's Den Farm, Harford Co., farmer, d. in 1854. Grandfather, Michael Whiteford, native of the Emerald Isle, located in Harford Co. at an early day, farmer. Sons of Michael: James W.; Michael, sheriff of Harford county; and Hugh E., member of the house of delegates. Mother, b. in York county, PA, d. in Balt. at eighty-two. Maternal grandfather, Robert Ramsay, b. in Ireland, located in Balt., a ship chandler, then farmer in York Co., PA, then ran the Ramsay Hotel at Ramsay Cross Roads. James and Nancy had seven children, among whom Robert H. killed at sixteen, Michael N., connected with a hotel in Harford Co., and Mrs. Sally Jennie Barry, lives in Balt. Subject m. Leonora Porter, of Ellicott City, Howard Co., MD, 4 Aug. 1875. Member of the Medical and Chirurgical Faculty of Maryland, the Medical and Surgical Society of Balt., the Knights of the Golden Eagle in Maryland, the Red Lyon Castel No. 1, Junior Order United American Mechanics, and Baltimore Council No. 2, Legion of the Red Cross. A Democrat. Physician in Balt.

744. JOHN HOOD - s/o Colonel Joshua and Matilda Ann (Haughey) Hood. Great-grandfather, Benjamin Hood, b. in England, located at Bowling Green, now in Howard Co., MD. Grandfather, Benjamin, b. at Bowling Green, farmer and minister of the Methodist Church, d. at Bowling Green, age sixty. Father, b. near Freedom, Carroll Co., farmer, commission broker and horse dealer til death, in November 1890, age eighty-seven, old-line Whig, then Democrat. Mother, b. in DE, d. in 1867 at fifty-nine. Great-grandfather Haughey, b. in Scotland, early settler of DE. Joshua and Matilda, both Methodist Episcopalians, had: Sarah, Mrs. Van Zant, d. in Balt. 1897; Mary, Mrs. Waters, widow living in Balt.; Emily, Mrs. S. T. Walker, d. in Balt.; B. Franklin, horse dealer, d. in 1890; Amelia, Mrs. B. F. Walker, d.; James, farmer, d. in 1895; Joshua, with local express company of Balt.; John; and Ella, Mrs. Baxley, of Howard Co. John m. Mary F., d/o Henry Smith, in Union Square Methodist Episcopal Church, Balt., and had three children: Stella, Mrs. Bull, of Balt.; Mamie, Mrs. William Jones, of Balt.; and Carrie. Henry Smith, a tobacconist of Balt. Member of the Independent Order of Odd Fellows, the Knights of Pythias, the Golden Chain, the Royal Aracnum and the Expressmen's Mutual Benefit Association. Belongs to the Methodist Church. A Republican. Messenger for the Adams Express Company at Balt.

745. HON JAMES H. PRESTON - b. 23 Mar. 1860 in Harford Co., MD, d/o James Bond and Mary A. (Wilks) Preston. Grandfather, James Bond Preston, planter of Harford Co. Father, b. in Harford Co., a Democrat, a Mason, and Episcopalian. Mother d. in 1874. Maternal grandfather, James K. Wilks, wholesale hardware merchant of Balt. Great-grandfather, James Wilks, b. in Scotland, had hardware business in Balt. James and Mary had two sons, James and Hon. Walter Wilks Preston, attorney of Bel Air. Subject m. Helen, d/o Col. Wilber F. Jackson, in 1894, and had two children, James and Alice Wilks. Col. Jackson, business man and president of the Continental Bank. Member of the Masons, and the Maryland Club. A Democrat. Attorney-at-law, of Balt., and ex-member of the state legislature.

746. EDWARD BAUM, M. D. - b. 4 Jul. 1869 in Knoxville, Tenn., s/o Charles and Barbara (Ritz) Baum. Father, of German birth and parentage, connected with the German Lutheran Church, car builder in Knoxville, still living at sixty-eight. Mother, b. in Switzerland, came to America with parents in girlhood. Charles and Barbara had ten children: John, d. at nineteen; Charles L, florist in TN, m. Mattie A. Gallyon, and had three children; Frederick Wilhelm, machinist in Knoxville, m. Anna Lever, of England, and had three children; Anna, m. John A. Dobson, of Knoxville, and had two children; Edward; Katie, singer; Rose, m. 10 Jun. 1897 to Homer G. Price, of Knoxville; Albert G., with the Southern Railroad; Minnie, singer; and Mary E., student. Member of the Baltimore Alumni Association, the Baltimore Medical College, the Medical Society of Baltimore Medical College, and the Knights of Honor. Reared in the German Lutheran faith, inclines to the Presbyterian Church. Physician and surgeon at No. 1209 Presstman street.

747. JOHN B. MULLINS, M. D. - b. in 1867 in Princess Anne Co., VA, s/o Col. John and Emily (Garrison) Mullins. Father, b. in 1832 in Mississippi, cadet at West Point, farmer, d. 1 Oct. 1891. Mother, b. in Princess Anne Co., d. 28 Jun. 1885. Maternal grandfather, James S. Garrison. John and Emily had three children: James G., d. 30 Dec. 1896; Mrs. Dr. Meredith, lives in Norfolk; and John B. John m. Annette B., d/o W. F. Kennedy, in Brunswick, MO, and had a daughter, Virginia Annette. W. F. Kennedy, of the Chariton County Exchange Bank. Member of the Millington Lodge No. 166, A.F.&A.M., of Baltimore, the Druid Chapter No. 28, R.A.M., and the Alumni Association of the University of Maryland. A Democrat. Physician on Augusta avenue and Frederick road.

748. LOUIS CHARLES HORN, SR., M. D. - b. 2 Jun. 1840 in Braunfelds, Germany, s/o Balthasar and Augusta (Kloch) Horn. Family came to America in 1855, settled in Balt. Father, attorney in Germany, d. in 1885, age seventy-three. Mother, d. in 1894, age seventy-six. Balthasar and Augusta, both Lutherans, had six children, two living, Louis C. and Lena, w/o Henry Smith. Grandfather, Dr. Philip Horn. Louis m. (1) Frances, d/o John Bender, of Balt., in 1863, and had four children: Louis C., druggist, m. Mary Striewig; August, M.D., partner of father, m. Maggie Striewig, 13 Mar. 1895; Amanda; and Minnie, w/o Harry Kirby of Balt. Francis, a Lutheran, d. in 1871, age twenty-eight. Louis m. (2) Anna R. Romoser in 1872. Member of the Maryland Lodge, A.F.&A.M., Eureka Lodge, K.P., the Knights of Honor and the Ancient Order of United Workmen. Physician and surgeon , and proprietor of the drug store at the corner of Mulberry street and Myrtle avenue.

749. HOWARD BRYANT - b. 21 Jul. 1861 in Queen Anne Co., MD, s/o Col. J. W. and Sarah H. (Cook) Bryant. Maternal grandfather, Clinton Cook, attorney at Centerville, d. at forty-seven. Father, b. 22 Jul. 1837 at Ellicott Landing, in Anne Arundel Co., a Democrat. Grandfather, Joshua Bryant, in the iron business at Havre de Grace. Brother and sister, Linnie T. and Mark, live on

father's farm in Caroline Co. Howard m. Alice A., d/o Charles O. Harris, of Zanesville, OH, 13 Jul. 1887, and had two children, Allen H. and Charles Harris. A Democrat. Attorney, and instructor at the Baltimore School of Law at Brown Hall, No. 210 North Calvert street.

750. REV. JOSEPH A. LIETUVNIKAS - b. 25 Jan. 1865 in the province of Lithuania, s/o Matthew and Anna Lietuvnikas. Father, farmer, now eighty. Mother, now seventy. Matthew and Anna had seven children, six living, five in Russia. Came to America 4 Mar. 1884, to New York City, Shenandoah, PA, Shamokin, PA, and then Balt. Ordained 23 Dec. 1893 by Cardinal Gibbons. Priest of St. John the Baptist's Catholic Church, on Lloyd street.

751. WALTER SCOTT CARSWELL, M. D. - b. in Dec. 1874 in Balt., s/o Lockhart Scott Carswell. Father, b. in Balt., in oil refining business. Grandfather, John Scott Carswill, b. in Paisley, Renfrewshire, Scotland, 8 Jan. 1807, left homeland for Canada in 1827, then came to Balt. and established oil refining business. Great-grandfather, George Carswill, citizen of Paisley. Lockhart had two children, Walter, and H. Charlotte, at home. Member of the Neurological Society, the Maryland Surgical Society, the Medical and Chirurgical Faculty of Maryland, the University Club and the University Alumni. Physician at the corner of North Charles and Twenty-fifth streets.

752. ALBERT NORMAN WARD - b. 27 Nov. 1871, at Shawsville, Harford Co., MD, s/o John and Elizabeth (Mellor) Ward. Father, b. in Harford Co., in wholesale grocery business in Balt. City, moved to Harford, Republican then Prohibitionist. Grandfather, William Ward, b. in Harford Co., farmer, old-line Whig. Great-grandfather, farmer in Harford Co. Great-great-grandfather, Joseph Ward, farmer. Family originally from England, settled in New England prior to 1630. Maternal grandfather, Joshua Kaye Mellor, b. in Royton, England in 1806, came to America in 1827, settled in Catonsville, MD, a Whig then Democrat, m. Miss Wolfenden, d. in Catonsville, in 1877. Maternal great-grandfather, Edmund Mellor, s/o James Mellor, of a titled family of England. John and Elizabeth had seven children: William M., business man in Harford Co.; Joshua B., farmer in Harford Co.; T. Harry, in firm of Jarrett & Ward; Mary E., w/o William Roe, of Forest Hill, Harford Co.; Hattie and Maud, at home; and Albert N. Member of the Pythagoras Lodge No. 123, A.F.&A.M. Pastor of the Mt. Royal Avenue Methodist Protestant Church in Baltimore.

753. HENRY WULFERT - b. 29 Nov. 1828 in Germany, s/o Henry and Elizabeth (Stratenberg) Wulfert, Sr. Father, b. in Germany, a cabinet-maker, came to America in 1858, settled in Suffolk Co., NY, a Lutheran, d. in 1893. Mother, d. in Germany in 1837. Henry and Elizabeth had four children: Wilhelmina, lives at the old home in Germany; Dietrich, living in Columbia, MO; Fred, d. about 1883; and Henry. Father m. again and had five daughters, all m. Henry m. (1) Mollie Kretchman, of Saxony, Germany, in 1855, and had five children: three d. in infancy, Henry at ten, and Emma at eighteen. Mollie d. in New York in 1865. Henry m.

(2) Caroline Hagg, of Germany, in 1866, and had seven children: two d. in infancy and Julia d. at eighteen; Julius, manager of hotel; Bertha, Carrie, Gussie and Harry. Member of the Odd Fellows, the Red Men, Knights of Pythias, Washington Lodge No. 3, A.F.&A.M., St. John's Chapter No. 19, R.A.M., Baltimore Commandery No. 2, K.T., and the Mystic Shrine. A Republican. Proprietor of the Hotel National, of Balt.

754. T. ALVAH MERRITT - b. 28 Feb. 1844 in Anne Arundel Co., MD, s/o John and Eliza C. (Stewart) Merritt, of same county. Father, b. in 1806, mother, b. in 1811. Merritt family originated in Cornwall, England. Stewart family came to America from Scotland during early colonial days, settled in MD. Maternal grandfather, Stephen Stewart, ship inspector. John and Eliza had eleven children, T. Alvah being the fifth. Subject m. Sallie E., d/o Richard Todd, 8 Dec. 1869, and had five children: George W., in business for self; Alvah R. and Richard Todd, at home; Walter and Eliza Stewart, at school. Member of the Royal Arcanum, Shield of Honor and Patrons of Husbandry. A Democrat, now Prohibitionist. Farmer of the twelfth district.

755. REV. JOHN J. MURRAY - b. 31 Jan. 1864 in Balt., s/o Patrick and Bridget (Feehely) Murray. Patrick and Bridget had seven children: John; three sons d.; Mary Ann, w/o Joseph Sweeney, of Balt.; Agnes, w/o Thomas Sweeney, of Balt.; and Elizabeth, lives in Balt. with father. Mother d. in 1884. Father, now over seventy. Pastor of St. Luke's Catholic Church at Sparrows Point.

756. WILLIAM T. MARSHALL - b. in 1850 in Accomac Co., VA, s/o Thomas and Caroline (Gillett) Marshall. Great-grandfather Marshall came from England with two brothers, one settling in VA, one in MD, and one in DE. Father, b. in Accomac Co., farmer, d. in 1854, less than fifty years old. Grandfather, William Marshall, b. in Accomac Co., farmer. Mother, b. in VA, d. in 1857, about fifty years old. Maternal grandfather, Suthey Gillett, farmer in VA. Thomas and Caroline had four children, two living. William m. Sadie, d/o Rev. Samuel Johnson, in Balt., and had two children, Edgar and Howard. Rev. Johnson, minister in the Methodist Episcopal Church. Member of the Marine Engineers' Beneficial Association No. 5, of Baltimore. Belongs to the South Baltimore Methodist Episcopal Church. A Prohibitionist. Chief engineer of the Josephine Thompson.

757. JOHN SEYMOUR T. WATERS - b. 7 Aug. 1864 in Balt., s/o William S. and Sarah Lindsay Waters, he of Somerset Co., MD, and she of King George Co., VA. Father, lawyer on eastern shore, then Balt., a Democrat, d. in Sep. 1873. Maternal grandfather, John Seymour Taliaferro. Maternal great-grandfather, John Taliaferro, of King George Co., VA. Maternal great-grandfather, Governor James Barbour. Sister, w/o Charles F. Penniman, of Asheville, NC; half-brother, from father's first marriage, William S., attorney in Los Angeles, CA, and half-sister, w/o William T. Penniman, of Asheville, NC. John m. Mary I., d/o Dr. Francis Donaldson, of Balt., in 1894, and had one child, Lindsay T. Member of the Baltimore Bar Association, the University Club

of Baltimore and the American Bar Association. Belongs to the Episcopal Church. Lawyer in Balt.

758. RICHARD EMORY, M. D. - m. Agnes S., d/o Thomas W. Hall, of Harford Co., and had one child, Thomas Hall Emory, b. in Jul. 1874. Member of the Masons and Knights Templar. A Democrat. Belonged to the Epicsopal Church. Richard d. 11 Jun. 1895. Physician and surgeon of Balt. and Harford Counties.

759. GEORGE JENKINS - b. in 1810 in Balt. Co., m. Lydia, d/o David Armour, at Jackson, TN, and had twelve children: Elizabeth, m. Brooke Pleasants, of Balt.; Mary, Mrs. William H. Saxton, d.; Annie M.; Lycurgus and George, d. in infancy; Josephine, m. William H. Saxton; R. Hillen, m. Mary Josephine Jenkins, of Harford Co., live in Balt.; Frances L., w/o Jacob P. White, of Balt.; Talbot W., m. Matilda Banks; W. Armour, in business with older brother in Balt.; Corinne, w/o farmer in the eleventh district; and Lydia, lives on old homestead. David Armour, b. in Scotland, came to America at early age, settled in Balt., m. (1) Mary Hillen, m. (2) Mary Winchester, having children by both. George d. Dec. 1882. Business man of the eleventh district.

760. CAPT. JAMES H. BULL - b. 5 Dec. 1844 in Accomac Co., VA, m. Annie Forrest, and had four children, one living, Edna, b. 20 May 1882. Annie, b. in Balt., reared in Richmond, VA. Member of the Masons, Joppa Lodge No. 32, A.F.&A.M., the Phoenix Chapter No. 7, R.A.M, and Beauseant Commandery, K.T., and the American Mechanics Society. A Republican. Attends the Lutheran Church. Master of the steamer McLane, in the state service.

761. LEWIS H. VOGT - b. in 1844 in Balt., s/o F. E. Vogt, of Germany. Father, came to America in 1836, settled in Balt., a mechanic, d. in 1855, at fifty-four. F.E. had eleven children, Lewis being the eighth. Member of the Junior Order of American Mechanics and the Independent Order of Odd Fellows, Concordia Lodge No. 13, Jerusalem Chapter No. 9 and Maryland Commandery No. 1. Chief engineer of the steamer Glouster, of the Merchants and Miners' Transportation Company.

762. EDWARD CARY EICHELBERGER - b. 1 Nov. 1850 in Winchester, VA, s/o Dr. Lewis and Penelope Lynn L. B. J. (Hay) Eichelberger. First of family in America was Philip Frederic Eichelberger, who came from Germany, 4 Sep. 1728, settled in York County, PA, then moved to MD. Capt. Adam Eichelberger, s/o Philip, officer is the Revolution. Grandson of the captain, Rev. Lewis Eichelberger, D. D., of the Lutheran Church, b. in Frederick Co., MD, d. in VA in 1859. Lewis m. (1) Mary, d/o John M. Miller, of Winchester, VA, and had four children: Rev. John M., attorney and minister in the Lutheran Church, d. in St. Louis, MO, in 1857; Dr. Henry S., physician in Staunton, VA, m. Susan Baylor, d/o Col. William Baylor, and had three children, Gilbert (lawyer in Staunton), Charles P. (physician), and Kate, and d. in 1891; Charles F., merchant of Winchester, d. in Jan. 1895; and Margaret, m. John Bushnell, of Winchester, had two children, Rev. John E. Bushnell of CA. and Ella who m. William Sperry. Margaret d. 1862. Lewis

m. (2) Penelope Lynn L. B. J., d/o John Hay, of Glenmore, VA, and had Edward Cary and William Hay, a railroad civil engineer in the west and south. John Hay, clerk of the court and judge of Clarke Co., s/o William and Elizabeth (Cary) Hay, she d/o Miles Cary of VA. Subject m. Julia H., d/o Thomas Sanderson, and had: Julia P., Annie Lynne, Lewis Hay, Edward Cary, Jr., and Francis Maury, all at home. Thomas Sanderson, farmer of Balt. Co. Julia, granddaughter of Joseph Pierson, fur dealer in Balt. Member of the West Boundary Improvement Association of Walbrook, the Ben Franklin Lodge of Masons, the Royal Arcanum, Golden Chain, American Mechanics, Bar Association of Baltimore, and the State Bar Association of Maryland. A Democrat. Lawyer at No. 114 East Lexington street.

763. JOHN H. DINNEEN - b. 29 Jun. 1853 in Berryville, VA, s/o Michael and Mary Dinneen. Michael and Mary, Catholics. Member of the Catholic Knights of America and of the Catholic Club of Baltimore. John m. Mary G., d/o Dr. M. H. Houston, in 1881, and had five children. Dr. Houston, formerly of Wheeling , WV, then Richmond. Lawyer in Balt.

764. HON. GEORGE W. PADGETT - b. 1 Feb. 1858 in Balt., s/o W. H. and Easter (Rankin) Padgett. Grandfather, Richard Padgett (see sketch of R. J. Padgett). Mother, b. in Ireland, brought to America by parents at eight years, d. in 1865, age thirty-four. Father, merchant tailor in Frederick Co., MD, then in retail fish business at Bel Air, Richmond and Balt. City, d. in 1889 at sixty-four. George m. Theresa F., d/o William H. Schoolden, in Nov. of 1878, and had eight children, following living: William H., Florence May, Robert Garfield, Grace Easter and Blanche Ethel. William Schoolden, native of Manchester, England, an ironworker, member of the G.A.R., d. in Balt. Mother of Theresa, Catherine McConnell, b. in Manchester, England, d/o Patrick and Mary (Hall) McConnell, who moved from Ireland to England, then America. Member of the Masons, the Knights of Pythias, the Independent Order of Odd Fellows, the Ancient Order of United Workmen, the National Union and the U.R.K.P. A Republican. Member of the state legislature.

765. GRAFTON MARSH BOSLEY, M. D - b. 8 Mar. 1825, s/o Amon and Rebecca (Marsh) Bosley. Founder of Bosley family in America, Walter Bosley, barrister-at-law, came from England about the middle of the seventeenth, settled in Balt. Co., MD. Walter had five sons: Joseph, James, William, John and Charles. From James, the grandson of Walter, descended James, the paternal grandfather, of Dr. Bosley. James m. Temperance Marsh, and had nine children, one being Amon Bosley, b. 27 Feb. 1779, near Towson. Amon, farmer, m. Rebecca Marsh, 27 Apr. 1813, and had ten children: Joshua M., m. Penelope Merryman; Temperance Ellen, m. Edward C. Talbott; Sarah, d.; James Walter, d.; Rebecca, m. Nicholas H. Merryman; Grafton Marsh; Ann Elizabeth, m. Joshua F. C. Talbott; E. Sophia, m. Walter Shirley; Elizabeth M., d.; and Nicholas M., m. Emily Hooper. Father, d. 23 Aug. 1838, at home place. Mother, d. 25 Sep. 1853. Founder of Marsh family in Maryland, Thomas Marsh, settled in Balt. Co. about 1675. Capt. Joshua

Marsh, s/o Thomas, m. Temperance Harryman, and their daughter Rebecca was Dr. Bosley's mother. Grafton m. Margaretta M., d/o Isaac L. and Caroline Nicholson, nee Cook, 5 May 1857. Arthur L., surviving child of Grafton and Margaretta, owner of Frederick Electric Light and Power Company of Frederick, MD, m. May A. Turner, of Philadelphia, d/o Dr. William Mason Turner of VA, and Hannah A. Turner, nee Ford, of Philadelphia, and had two children, Beatrice and Marguerite Bosley. Margaretta d. 17 Jul. 1885, age fifty-one. A Democrat. An Episcopalian. Retired physician of Towsontown.

766. THOMAS P. AMOSS - b. in Balt., s/o Alfred P. and Elizabeth B. (Clark) Amoss, Jr. Old Quaker family, founded in America by two brothers, came from England, settled in Harford Co. Father, b. in Harford Co., business man. Maternal grandfather, Thomas S. Clark. Alfred and Elizabeth had two children, Thomas P. and Minnie B. Thomas m. Bessie C., d/o Francis Demmead, of Balt., in 1887, and had three children: Bessie; Marguerite; and son, d. in 1896. Belongs to the Episcopal Church. Real-estate operator in Balt.

767. DR. HERMAN VOLTZ - b. 17 Sep. 1857 in Hessian Germany, s/o Richard and Mary Voltz. Father, b. in Germany, d. in Germany in 1895, age fifty-seven. Mother, b. in Germany, now fifty-eight. Richard and Mary had ten children, Herman only one to come to America. Came to America in 1877, settled in New Brunswick, NJ, then Balt. Herman m. Mary, d/o John Presser, of Balt. in Nov. 1879, and had three children: William, Minnie and George. Member of the Knights of Pythias, Uniform Rank. Veterinary physician and surgeon on the southeast corner of Hanover and Cross streets.

768. AUGUSTUS D. CLEMENS, JR. - b. in 1845 in Balt., s/o Augustus D. and Henrietta M. (Bryden) Clemens. Clemens family originated in France. Great-grandfather, Augustus Ducas Clemens, b. in France. Father, b. in Balt. in 1818, in real-estate business, now seventy-nine, a Democrat. Mother, now eighty-four. Maternal grandfather, Capt. William Bryden, sea captain. Maternal grandmother, Elizabeth Bryden. William and Elizabeth, both buried in Westminster churchyard. Augustus and Henrietta had three children: William Bryden, d. in Leavenworth, KS, in 1859; Augustus; and Mary J., w/o Jacob H. Aull, of Balt. Subject m. Mary, d/o William C. and Amelia Bordley, in 1881, and had three children: Lennox Birkhead, Henrietta Amelia and Augustus Ducas. Bordley family from the eastern shore. Member of the Maryland Historical Society, the St. Andrew's Society and Concordia Lodge No. 13, A.F.&A.M. Wife belongs to St. John's Episcopal Church. Engaged in the real-estate business.

769. FRANK P. HUTCHINSON - b. 15 Jul. 1857 in Balt., s/o John T. and Julia (Sutton) Hutchinson. Father, business man in Balt., d. at army headquarters during the war. Mother, from Northumberland Co., VA. Frank m. Mollie E., d/o James and Miranda (Colburn) Marvel, of Seaford, Sussex Co., DE. Member of the Marine Engineers' Beneficial Association No. 5, of Baltimore, the Improved Order of Heptasophs, and Victory Council No. 447. Wife belongs

to the William Street Methodist Episcopal Church. Assistant engineer on the Easton.

770. JOHN H. COOK - b. in 1864 in Balt., s/o Joseph B. and Medora S. (Roelkey) Cook. Descendant of German ancestors. Father, learned undertaking business from his father, d. in Balt., May 1889. Joseph and Medora had four children, John being second. John m. Adelia V. Bankerd, of Balt. 25 Apr. 1885. Funeral director with office on the northwest corner of Baltimore and Stricker streets, and proprietor of a livery establishments at No. 131 West North avenue, No. 1204 West Baltimore street and Nos. 1715, 1721, 1730 West Baltimore street.

771. WILLIAM H. SALTER - b. 26 May 1854 in Balt., s/o Theodore and Harriet A. (Yearley) Salter. Four Salter brothers came to America from Germany in an early day, settling in NJ, then PA, then MD. Grandfather, Theodore Salter, b. in Philadelphia, PA, a painter. Father, b. in Balt., a painter. Mother, d/o John W. and Elizabeth (Hatten) Yearley, one of eight children. Theodore and Harriet had seven children: William; John E., in business in Govanstown; Harriet, Mrs. James Sanders, lives in Balt.; Mary E., Mrs. Edward Lucy, d. in 1894; Aquilla, works in sash mill in Balt.; Albert, plumber; and Washington Irving, musician in Balt. William m. Alice Cory, of NJ, in 1875, and had six children: Theodore, musician; James, Harriet, William, Virginia and Alice, at home. Member of the Masons, the Odd Fellows, the Knights of Pythias, Golden Chain and Improved Order of Red Men. A Democart. Wife identified with the Presbyterian Church. Plumber in connection with hardware business in Pikesville.

772. WILLIAM WISE - b. in the seventh district, s/o John and Ann (Hunter) Wise. Grandfather, John Wise, Sr., b. in Germany, came to America, settled in Harford Co., then Balt. Co., founding Wiseburg, a farmer. Father, farmer and hotel keeper of Wiseburg, b. in the seventh district. Mother b. in seventh district. John and Ann had nine children, three living: Elizabeth, William and Mary F. William m. Miranda Hicks, of Balt. Co., and had five children, three living: Dorcas A., w/o William Bosley, of Balt. Co., had four children; Charles H., single, has general store at Whitehall; and Lorenia,, w/o William Carr, of Balt. Co. Wife, member of the Methodist Episcopal Church at Wiseburg. An Independent. Engaged in the manufacture of paper, and a farming.

773. CHARLES E. BRACK - b. 7 Jul. 1831 in Schmalkalden, Kur-Hessen, Germany, s/o John Conrad and Fredericka (Heisse) Brack. Father, b. in Herleshausen, Kur-Hessen, member of the Reformed Church, d. at Rauschenberg at eight-four. Mother, b. in Rothenburg, d/o Dr. Heisse, d. at forty-five. John and Fredericka had eleven children: Fredericka, d. at Schmalkalden, Germany, age seventy-two; Dr. Wilhelm, physician, d. in LA; Rev. Ernst, minister of the Reformed Church, d. in Germany in 1892; Caroline, lives in Hamburg, Germany; Ferdinand, farmer, d. in Heimback, Germany, age twenty-nine; Frederick, d. while mayor of Schmalkalden; Louisa, lives in Chicago, IL; Charles E.; Albert, d. in Balitmore; Matilda, lives in Hesse-Cassel, Germany; and

Sophia, d. in Schmalkalden. Charles m. Henrietta, d/o John Melchior Treulieb, in Balt. in 1864, and had six children: Dr. Charles Emil, physician in Balt.; William Rudolph, machinist of Balt.; George P., machinist of Balt.; Elsie, Edward and Anita, at home. John Treulieb, b. in Germany, located in Balt. at an early day, an iron worker. Henrietta d. 22 Sep. 1897. Member of the Germania Lodge No. 160, A.F.&A.M., Knights of Honor, Germania Maennerchor, Harmonie Club, the Germania Club, the Baltimore College of Pharmacy, and the National Pharmaceutical Association. Attends Zion Lutheran Church. A Republican. Member of the Kriegerbund. Pharmacist at No. 520 Forrest street.

774. FRED H. TAFT - b. in 1848 in West Bloomfield, NY, s/o Alfred S. and Laura H. (Brown) Taft. Taft family came to America from England, settled in VT, then NY. Grandfather, Robert Taft, b. in NY. Father, b. in West Bloomfield, NY, moved to Prince George Co., MD, d. in 1872, age fifty-six. Mother, of West Bloomfield, d. 1 Apr. 1897 in OH, age eighty. Fred m. Sarah J., d/o Samuel Meakin, in 1880, and had three children, A. Samuel, Laura L. and M. Rena. A Republican. Identified with the Methodist Church. Connected with the pension bureau of the interior department.

775. CAPT. JOHN H. MASINGO - b. in 1838 in Prince George Co., MD, s/o John and Elizabeth (Action) Masingo. Descendant of the French family of Mozingo. Father, b. in Westmoreland, VA, s/o a farmer, d. at fifty. Mother, b. in Prince George Co., of English descent, d. there in 1850. John m. Amanda A. Hutchinson, in Balt., and had one child, John H., an insurance collector in Balt. Member of the Masters & Pilots' Association of Baltimore. Attends the Methodist Episcopal Church. Captain of the steam boat Samson.

776. JOHN C. GILL - b. 11 Feb. 1845 in the fifth district, s/o Didymus and Annie (Ambrose) Gill. Didymus and Annie had eight children: William F., lives in the fourth district; John C.; Thomas E., lives in Mantua Mills, fourth district, merchandiser and miller; Mary E., w/o Benjamin Kneteber, of the third district; Joseph N., of Fairview, fourth district; Stephen R., of Arcadia, fourth district; and Barbara and another, d. Father, farmer, d. in 1883, age seventy-three. John m. Mary M. Holthebner, in 1885, and had son, William P., now ten. Members of the Methodist Church. Farmer of the fifth district.

777. GEORGE W. REVER - b. in Feb. 1843 in Balt., s/o Henry Garrett and Lucinda Rever. Father, b. in Hanover in Sep. 1797, came to America in 1831, settled in Balt., carried on a grocery, became a machinist, then farmer, a Democrat, d. in 1873, age seventy-six. Mother, b. in Germany, came to America in girlhood, d. in 1848, age thirty-four. Ferdinand, s/o Henry and Lucinda, in grocery business in Balt. Henry m. (2) and had Lewis, d. in 1884; William H., interpreter for German emigration port of Locust Point; Elizabeth, w/o Henry Friend, of Balt.; and Catherine, w/o Ferdinand Sharer, of Balt. Henry m. (3) and had two sons, William F., farmer, and John H., with Henry Smith &

Son, of Balt. George m. Caroline, d/o of Jacob Klinger, in 1872, and had: Carrie, m.; Ida, d. in 1895; Sophia, Katherine, George W., Jr., William B. and Harry J., at home. A Democrat. Proprietor of a hotel in the twelfth district.

778. GEORGE SCHNEIDER - b. 7 Nov. 1844 in Balt., s/o George and Christine (Eidel) Schneider. Father, b. in Hesse-Darmstadt, Germany, settled in Balt. about 1831, an iron worker, then dealt in milk, d. at seventy-six. Mother, b. in Germany, lives in Balt., now seventy-eight. Both grandfathers came to America, lived in Balt. Maternal grandfather, d. in 1861. George and Christine had twelve children, six living. Subject m. Catherine, d/o George W. Beck, in Balt., and adopted two children, Sadie and Catharine. George W. Beck, b. in Wurtemberg, Germany, came to America in 1848, in dairy business. Member of the G.A.R., the Legion of Honor, The Knights of Pythias, and the Improved Order of Heptasophs. A Republican. Belongs to the German Lutheran Church. Proprietor of a hotel at No. 1001 Eastern avenue.

779. JAMES T. TUCHTON - b. 24 Dec. 1833 in the ninth district of Balt. Co., s/o Henry and Eliza (Wood) Tuchton, he of Balt. Co., and she of Harford Co. Paternal grandfather, Henry Tuchton, Sr., b. in France, came to America in early manhood, settled in Balt., a miller. Father, a miller, d. in Harford Co. in 1837, age thirty-three. Mother d. in 1863. Henry and Eliza had five children: Nathan, d. in childhood; John, d.; Theodore, engineer; Annie, d. in girlhood; and James. Mother m. (2) and had a son, lives with James. James m. Sarah R. Dover, of Harford Co., in 1859 and had five children: Sarah, d. in girlhood; Henry F., farmer in the ninth district; Mary E., m. Christian Lawrence, of Balt. Co.; Effie E., Mrs. George Johnson, d. at twenty-nine, leaving a child; and James, d. in boyhood. A Republican. Identified with the Methodist Episcopal Church. Farmer of the twelfth district.

780. ELIJAH T. BENSON - b. 1 Jun. 1835 near Mt. Carmel, in the fifth district, s/o Elijah Benson. Father and grandfather, b. same place. Subject m. Cornelia Byerly in 1862, and had two children: Jacob T.; and Ella E., w/o Henry Pitts, farmer of the ninth district. Cornelia d. in Feb. 1892. Elijah m. (2) Rebecca Fowble. Member of the Independent Order of Odd Fellows, the Knights of Pythias, and the Senior Order of American Mechanics. A Lutheran, wife, a Methodist. Retired agriculturist of the fifth district.

781. GEORGE W. SEIPP - b. 26 May 1844 in eighth district of Balt. Co., s/o Conrad and Elizabeth (Sparks) Seipp. Father, b. in Hesse-Darmstadt, Germany, came to America at seventeen, settled in Balt., in the shoe business, d. in 1883. Mother, b. on eastern shore. Conrad and Elizabeth had twelve children: Mary, m. Elijah Fishpaw, Balt. Co. farmer, d. leaving two children; Charles A., m. Florence Osburn, in supply department of the Northern Central Railroad; James, m. Anna Hook, works in Wright's bleaching works; Selina J., m. Charles E. Justus, d. leaving three children; B. Frank, m. Ada Simmons, connected with the City

Passenger Company; Ella, d. at twenty; and Anna B., lives with Charles, connected with a wholesale millinery house. George m. Elizabeth Ann, d/o James and Jane (Akehurst) Goodwin, in Dec. 1864, and had seven children: Emma Jane, m. Clarence McMaster, d. at twenty-six; George Wilson, printer, d. at twenty-nine; Henry H. and Albert, d. in boyhood; Warren, m. Minnie Held, of Towson, instructor at Polytechnic Institute of Baltimore; M. Florence and Anna G., at home. James and Jane Goodwin had five children: Elizabeth, Emma Jane, James R., Herbert Henry and Edward, only one living. Elizabeth, member of the Towson Chapter of the Epworth League and the Towson Methodist Episcopal Church board, d. 25 Mar. 1897. Member of the Odd Fellows' Lodge No. 79, at Towson, the Ridgely Encampment No. 15, I.O.O.F., the Wilson Post No. 1, G.A.R., the Encampment No. 109, Union Veteran Legion, the Knights of Pythias, the Junior Order United American Mechanics and the Ancient Order of United Workmen. A Democrat. Court crier for Balt. Co.

782. WALTER H. STEWART - b. 29 Dec. 1843 in Balt., s/o Joseph J. and Eliza (Burgan) Stewart. Great-grandfather Stewart came to America from Scotland, located at Brandywine, DE. Grandfather, James Stewart, b. at Brandywine, miller. Father, b. in 1793 at Brandywine, moved to Balt. in 1812, miller, then grocer, d. in 1880, age eighty-seven. Mother, b. in Balt. Co., d. in 1884, age seventy-nine. Joseph and Eliza had: William A., jurist, d. in Jul. 1892; Joseph J., member of Spanish claims commission, d.; Robert, killed in Civil war, Confederate; Walter H.; Samuel G., in business in Philadelphia; and Mary E., of Balt. Maternal grandfather, descended from French Huguenots who settled in Balt. Co. very early. Maternal grandmother belonged to the Sindall family of English descent. Walter m. Isabella, d/o Albert Lombard, in 1865, and had four children: Walter L., dealer in leaf tobacco; Howard E., teller in National Union Bank of Baltimore; William A., clerking for eldest brother; and Joseph J., at school. Isabella b. in Balt. Albert Lombard, b. in Springfield, MA, business man in Balt. Mother of Isabella, Mary A. C. Jones, of Balt., b. in 1820, d. in 1897. Member in the Holy Innocents Protestant Episcopal Church. City councilman.

783. GEORGE D. BAUER - b. in 1868 in Balt., s/o Frederick and Augusta (Hubbe) Bauer, both b. in Germany. Father, came to America in early manhood, kept a restaurant in Balt., a Democrat, d. in Balt. in 1890. Mother came to America a very young child. Frederick and Augusta had three children; John Frederick, clerk in hardware store of Geroge D. Bauer; Mary Louisa, w/o Albert Wagner, Jr.; and George D. George m. Marie, d/o Frederick J. Ruth, in 1893. Frederick Ruth, oyster packer in Balt. Member of the Knight Templar in the Masonic fraternity, and the Royal Arcanum. A Republican. Proprietor of a hardware store in Canton.

784. FREDERICK C. COOK - b. in 1849 in Balt., s/o Frederick C. and Julia A. (Bevan) Cook. Grandfather, George Adam Cook, business man. Father, b. in Balt., banker and broker, d. at thirty-one. Frederick and Julia had three children: Frederick

C., Jr., George Bevan, and Margaret Clark. Maternal grandfather, Thomas H. Bevan, head of Bevan & Sons, building and monumental stone company. Frederick m. Margaret P., d/o Joseph S. Heuisler, and had five children: Victor J., M. Alice, Joseph S., Matthew L. and Julia A. Joseph S. Heuisler, criminal lawyer. Lawyer in Balt.

785. A. SHELMON WARNER, M. D. - b. 30 Mar. 1856 in Carroll Co., MD, s/o Peter and Rachel (Fair) Warner. Father, minister of the English Lutheran Church, d. in York Co., PA, in 1882. Descended from Swiss ancestors. Mother b. in Balt. Co. Maternal grandfather, John Fair, Carroll Co. farmer. Peter and Rachel had ten children: Rev. Adam N., Lutheran minister; Albert, works for the Pennsylvania Railroad; Martin Luther, PA farmer; John Calvin, railroad man, lives in NM; William Henry, lives in Topeka, KS; A. Shelmon; Kate, w/o Samuel Kaufman, of PA; Margaret, w/o Jonathan Minnich; Ella, w/o Edward Heisler; and Lizzie, m. Subject m. Florence Nightingale Eisenberger, and had two children: Augustus and Sarah Wynne, both at school. Florence, b. in PA. Member of the Knights of Pythias, the East Baltimore Medical Society, and the Medical and Chirurgical Faculty of Maryland. Belongs to the Abbott Memorial Presbyterian Church of Highlandtown. Physician in Highlandtown.

786. DAVID MARION NEWBOLD, JR. - b. 3 Feb. 1873 in Balt., s/o David M. and Eliza (Boyd) Newbold. Father, business man in Newbold & Sons, ancestors settled in NJ and MD about 1660. Maternal grandfather, William A. Boyd, tobacco merchant in NY City and Balt. A Republican. Member of the law firm of Paca & Newbold.

787. PROF. HAMPSON H. BIEDLER, M. D. - b. 26 Aug. 1854 at Page View, Page Co., VA, s/o Ambrose M. and Sarah E. (Keyser) Biedler. Father, b. in PA, merchant farmer, a Baptist, d. at fifty-seven. Mother, Baptist, d. in 1894, at sixty-seven. Ambrose and Sarah had ten children, six living: Charles E. and Frank R., live in Balt.; William T., d. 8 Jul. 1867, at fifty-one; A. J., lives in Washington; Ashely L. in New York; and Anna M., w/o Rev. William C. Bitting, D.D., of Mt. Morris Baptist Church, New York City. Member of the Medical and Chirurgical Faculty of Maryland, the Clinical Society of Maryland, the American Medical Association, and Baltimore Medical Association. Secretary of Baltimore University, professor of principles and practice of surgery and clinical surgery in its medical department.

788. JOHN A. SHERIDAN - b. in 1851 in Balt. Co., s/o John and Miranda (Tredwell) Sheridan. Father, b. in Harford Co., MD, in 1828, farmer in Balt. Co., a Democrat. Mother b. in Balt. Maternal grandfather, Stephen Tredwell, farmer, a Whig, d. in Balt. Co. at ninety. John and Miranda had eleven children, four living: John A.; Nellie, w/o Robert Metzel, of Washington, DC; Asbury, commission merchant of Balt.; and Wesley, in the laundry business in New York City; others d. in childhood. John m. Fannie Bella Gale, of Anne Arundel Co., MD, in 1878. A Democrat. Members of the Methodist Episcopal Church. Contractor and

builder with a mercantile store in Chase, in the twelfth district.

789. GEORGE M. STECK, D. V. S. - b. 16 Nov. 1861 in Balt., s/o Charles A. and Elizabeth (Lorenz) Steck, both of Baden, Germany. Maternal grandparents, b. in same province, first to locate in Balt. at old family homestead. Father, came to Balt. a young man, blacksmith and farrier, d. at sixty-eight. Mother d. at sixty. Charles and Elizabeth had twelve children, four living. Member of the Alumni Association of the American Veterinary College. Veterinary surgeon at the corner of Broadway and Orleans street.

790. WILLIAM H. WILHELM - b. 27 Jun. 1867 in Balt., s/o William and Rebecca (Feldman) Wilhelm. Grandfather, William Wilhelm, manufacturer of pottery ware, came to America from Germany, settled in Balt. Co., farmer, lives in Richmond, VA at eighty-eight. Father, William, b. in Hesse-Darmstadt, Germany, had meat business in Bel Air market, Balt. Mother, b. in Aldenbruch, Germany in 1840. Maternal grandfather, Herman Feldmann, roofing contractor, d. in Balt. William and Rebecca had nine children: John H., Balt. merchant; William H.; Otto A., lives in Philadelphia; Frederick A. and Harry, with William; Mrs. Kate Johnson, of Balt.; and Minnie, Anna and Lillie, of Balt. Member of the Beefsteak Club, the Old Town Merchants and Manufacturers' Association, Baltimore Lodge No. 107, Order of Elks, and the Legion of the Red Cross. Wholesale and retail dealer in meat at No. 611 Forrest street.

791. HON. J. MORRISON HARRIS - b. in 1818, s/o David and Sarah (Montgomery) Harris. Father, b. in PA, merchant in Balt. Maternal grandfather, Colonel Montgomery. David and Sarah had four children. Subject m. Sidney C., d/o B. W. Hall, in 1881, and had one son, William H. Member of Friendship Lodge, A.F.&A.M., and the Odd Fellows. Whig, turned American, now Republican. Lawyer in Balt.

792. JOHN S. WILSON - b. 9 Feb. 1846 in Balt., s/o James Wilson. Great-grandfather, John Wilson. Father d. in Balt. 21 Dec. 1854. John m. Rebecca M. Minnick, in 1877, and had three children: Charles E., bookkeeper for father; H. Bertram and Mary Ethel. Member of the Masons, Providence Lodge No. 116, I.O.O.F., the Sons of the American Revolution and the Society of the War of 1812. A Democrat. Deals in Lumber, building materials, coal and agricultural implement under the firm name of John S. Wilson & Co.

793. CAPT. CHARLES H. DIXON - b. in New York City, s/o Hiram Dixon. Father, b. in Rhinebeck, NY, sea-farer. Charles m. Sarah E., d/o Cyrus Gault, and had one child, Charles H., physician in Balt. Cyrus Gault, of NH, manufacturer of brick and dealer in stone and granite, in Balt., w/o Cyrus, Margaret Atkinson, d/o Captain Atkinson. Member of the Naval Veterans' Association, and Rescue Harbor No. 14, American Association of Masters and Pilots, the Masons, the Benevolent Protective Order of Elks, the Ancient

Essenic Order and Monumental City Lodge No. 12, Knights of the Golden Chain. Captain of the Isaac Emerson's steam yacht Nydia.

794. WILLIAM WYMAN - b. in 1825 in Balt., s/o Samuel and Hannah D. (Mayo) Wyman. Wyman family settled in MA. Father, b. near Boston, MA, moved to Balt., had wholesale dry-goods house, d. in New York City in 1865. Samuel and Hannah had three children: Elizabeth W., w/o Herman D. Aldrich, of New York City; Samuel, in New York; and William. William m. Amanda Sanderson, of MA. in 1853, and had one daughter, Helen. A liberal.

795. PROF. FRANK T. BARRINGTON - b. 12 Mar. 1828 in Balt., s/o John and Catherine (Baker) Barrington, he of Ireland, she of Philadelphia, PA. Paternal grandfather, b. on the other side of the Atlantic, of English and Irish lineage. Father, d. in Philadelphia, in 1840. Mother, d. in Balt., 23 Mar. 1866. Frank m. Mary W. Taylor in York, PA. Member of the Waverly Episcopal Church. Director of music in the Maryland School for the Blind.

796. JOHN PHILPOT - b. in Sep. 1801 in Balt. Co., s/o Brian and Elizabeth (Johnson) Philpot. Grandfather, Brian Philpot, Sr., b. in Stamford, England, in early part of eighteenth century, orphaned quite young, came to America. Great-grandfather, Philip Philpot. Brian and Elizabeth had six children: Brian, Mary Ann, John, Elizabeth, Clara and Edward. John m. Susan Isabella Stewart, his cousin, 21 Apr. 1829, and had: Mary D.; Thomas, d.; Elizabeth Buchanan, w/o Maj. Richard T. Allison; Catherine Stewart; and Anna Isabella. Son, Thomas, b. 15 Oct. 1840 at Hereford, Balt. Co., d. 29 Nov. 1896, near Phoenix, buried in the Episcopal cemetery at the Manor. Lawyer of Balt.

797. WILLIAM T. ROBERTS - b. in 1846 in Balt., w/o William and Eliza (Mottu) Roberts. Father, b. in Manchester, England, came to America in boyhood, had boot and shoe business in Balt., a Democrat, member of the Odd Fellows, belonged to the Methodist Episcopal Church, d. in 1883, at seventy-two. Grandfather, Rev. Dr. Roberts, b. in Manchester, England. Great-grandfather, William Roberts, penman and lawyer. Mothers ancestors were French-Huguenots, family came to America during the revolution in France. Mother d. in 1855. William and Eliza had: William; John N., merchant in Idaho; Maria A., single; and Alice, w/o Thomas Wood, farmer in NY. William m. Georgia, d/o William R. Glen, in 1865, and had two children: William Collins, bookkeeper with Baltimore & Ohio Railroad, and Claude, at home. Member of the Odd Fellows and the Heptasophs. Belongs to St. Paul's Methodist Episcopal Church. Lawyer.

798. REV. ARTHUR H. THOMPSON - b. in 1859 in Washington, DC, s/o Andrew J. and Sarah A. (Clampitt) Thompson. Father, b. in Balt., brickmason, a Baptist, an Odd Fellow, buried in Loudoun Park Cemetery. Mother, of English parentage. Andrew and Sarah had: Arthur H., and George G., in insurance business in Jamaica, West India Islands. Arthur m. Maggie M., d/o James Gamble, in 1884. Member of the Royal Arcanum. Pastor of Bennett Memorial Methodist Episcopal Church.

799. GOTTLIEB STENGEL - b. 19 Apr. 1842 in Balt., s/o Christian and Barbara (Beihler) Stengel. Father, in meat business in Balt., then farming. Christian and Barbara had four sons: 2 d.; Gottlieb; and Christian, ranchman in Sonoma Co., CA. Mother and father d. when Gottlieb was eight. Gottlieb m. Elizabeth Augusta Tarbert, of Balt. Co., 16 Aug. 1866, and had six children: Lewis C., in CA; Charles R., in implement and seed business; Mattie, w/o Albert Putts, of Balt.; Harry, employed in the city; Gottlieb, Jr., at home; and Elizabeth, at school. A Republican.

800. THE OFFUTT FAMILY - Thomas Z. Offutt, M.D., physician of the second district, b. 25 Dec. 1829, in Montgomery Co., MD, s/o Zadoe and Elizabeth Offutt. Thomas m. Elizabeth E., d/o Lemuel and Maria Offutt, in Jul. 1856, and had seven children: Milton W., Thomas W., Virginia, Anna B., Noah E., James P. and Mary A. Lemuel and Maria Offutt, of Balt. Co., Zadoe and Elizabeth of Montgomery Co., no relation. Col. Milton W. Offutt, b. 14 May 1857 in Balt. Co., admitted to the bar in Jan., 1881, m. (1) Nannie Parr who d., m. (2) Mary Emily, d/o Dr. Felix Jenkins, of Balt., in 1894, and had one child. Thomas W. Offutt, b. 16 Nov. 1868, m. Colgate Cockey, she d. few months later. Virginia Offutt, m. Richard W. Hagen. Anna B. Offutt, single, lives with parents. Noah E. Offutt, b. 22 Jul. 1873, m. Mrs. Comfort Sudler, d/o Joshua F. Cockey, 26 Aug. 1897. James P., b. 12 Feb. 1876. Mary A., with sister in TN.

801. WILLIAM T. HIGGINS - b. 15 Jun. 1849 in Balt., s/o John F. and Martha (Adair) Higgins. Father, b. in Holland, came to America, d. near Leonardtown, St. Mary Co., MD, age forty-five. Mother, b. in Virginia, descendant of first white family that settled in VA, d. at forty-two, two days after husband, William was about eight. William m. Margaret A. Seward, of Balt., and had three sons, all d. William m. (2) Margaret A. Kallfues, of Balt. and had one daughter. Member of the Hiram Lodge No. 107, A.F.&A.M., of Baltimore, the Grand Lodge, K.ofP., Wilson Post, G.A.R., Association of Navy Veterans and Shield of Honor, and Marine Engineers' Beneficial Association. Belongs to the Methodist Protestant Church. A Republican. Chief engineer of the steamer Gov. R. M. McLane, police patrol boat.

802. CHARLES T. COCKEY - b. 6 Dec. 1829 near Reisterstown, in Worthingtons Valley, Balt. Co., s/o Edward Augustus and Uratt C. (Owens) Cockey. Father, b. 19 Oct. 1791 at Prospect, the homestead in fourth district. Grandfather, Charles Cockey, b. 14 Feb. 1762, same place, farmer, had two sons and one daughter. Older son of Charles, Thomas Beal, b. 1787, m. Mary Ann Worthington 9 Apr. 1816. Great-grandfather, Thomas Cockey, b. 1724 in Green Spring Valley, d. in 1784. Maternal grandfather, Samuel Owens, of Green Spring Valley, farmer, d. 21 Aug. 1834, had six children. Subject m. Susannah D., d/o William and Ann Brown, of Carroll Co., in Mar. 1852, and had six children. A Democrat.

803. CAPT. OCTAVIUS W. HUDSON - b. 22 Jul. 1853 in Northumberland Co., VA, s/o Joseph W. and Mary Ann (Pridham)

Hudson. Descendant of Hendrick Hudson. Father, b. in Brooklyn, NY, trans-Atlantic captain, d. in 1893, at eighty-five. Grandfather, Rev. John Hudson, Methodist Episcopal minister in NY and VA. Mother, b. and m. in VA. Maternal grandparents, Fleet and Melinda (Harrison) Pridham, of English descent, had nine children. Octavius m. Rosa, d/o James and Mahala (Lewis) Winstead, in VA, and had three children: Ella Estelle and Julia Etta, both d., and Harry Gilmore. Rosa, b. in Northumberland Co., VA. James and Mahala, farmers, of English descent. Member of the Washington Lodge No. 3, A.F.&A.M., the Junior Order of United American Mechanics, Brantley Council No. 119, the Pilot Association, Rescue Harbor No. 14, and the Alpha Conclave No. 1, Improved Order of Heptasophs. A Democrat. A Methodist. Superintendent and master of the Rock Creek Steamboat Company.

804. EDWARD A. DAY - b. in 1833 in Balt. Co., s/o William Y., and Charlotte M. (Orso) Day. First of family in Balt. Co. was Edward Day, m. Avarilla Taylor in 1722. Great-grandfather, Edward Day, Jr., m. (2) Mrs. Cleggit, d/o John Young, and had John Y. Day, grandfather, b. in the eleventh district in 1772. John Y. m. Agnes, of Balt. Co., and had three sons, William Y., Edward A. and John Y., Jr. Grandfather d. in early nineteenth century. Maternal grandfather, Jean Baptist Orso, of New Orleans, LA, of French extraction. William and Charlotte had: Agnes, d. in childhood; Edward A.; Charlotte B.; and John Orso, m. Rachel Drake, of New York, d. in Kansas City, MO, leaving two children, Halleck D. and Agnes L., w/o John Mason, of Kansas City. Subject m. Laura C., d/o Capt. Edward and Mary (Ogle) Oldham, in Oct. 1859, and had one child, Mary Forman. A Democrat. An Episcopalian. Agriculturist of the eleventh district.

805. FRANK H. DEANE - b. 3 Jan. 1842 in Dorchester Co., MD, s/o John and Josephine (Ennalls) Deane. Father, native of eastern shore, carpenter and builder, farmer, owner of hotel, member of the I.O.O.P., a Methodist Episcopalian, d. at fifty-six. Maternal grandfather, Joseph Ennalls, spent life on eastern shore. John and Josephine had four sons: James, killed when young; John, mechanic on eastern shore; Charles, farmer and miner in Walla Walla, WA; and Frank. Frank m. Emma Fooks, of eastern shore, in 1866, and had ten children: two d.; Estelle, dressmaker in Balt.; Margaret J., w/o Holly Moore; Sallie M., travels for Armstrong & Co.; James F., a clerk; Frank Harry, Jr., with the Automatic Telephone Company; Emma May, John E. and Annie E., at home. Member of the Ancient Order of United Workmen. A Republican. Contributes to the Methodist Episcopal Church. Pension lawyer and magistrate for the city of Balt.

806. HON. HARRY NETHERCLIFT ABERCROMBIE - b. 4 Apr. 1871 in Balt., s/o John and Elizabeth (Daniel) Abercrombie. Father, b. in Edinburgh, Scotland, came to America at five with parents, settled in Balt. Mother, b. in Ontario, Canada, on maternal side descended from the Netherclifts, an old English family. John and Elizabeth had seven children, some: David T., oldest, business man of New York City; and Dr. John R., physician of Balt. City. Republican. Member of the Second Presbyterian Church of

Baltimore. Lawyer at Nos. 622-624 Equitable Building.

807. JOHN F. HOFFMAN - b. 4 Apr. 1823 in Balt. Of German descent. Grandfather came to Balt. at early age, leather merchant. John m. Sarah Ann, d/o William H. Collins, in 1846, and had one daughter, Laura V. William H. Collins, Balt. tailor. A Republican. Member of the Third Reformed Church. Retired from commercial pursuits.

808. WILLIAM E. JEWELL - b. 28 Dec. 1860 near Chestertown, Kent Co., MD, s/o Samuel and Ruthess Jewell, he of Kent Co., she of Chester Co., PA. Father, farmer. Samuel and Ruthess had four sons: Samuel, engineer; T. Morgan and John, machinists and engineers; and William. Grandfather, Samuel Jewell, b. in England, early settler of Kent Co., farmer. Maternal grandfather, John Ruthven, b. in PA, farmer of Kent Co., MD, of Scotch-Irish stock, d. at ninety-four. Maternal grandmother, Rebecca, of a Quaker family. William m. Miss Amelia, d/o John Weber, of Balt. John Weber, merchant on Gay street. Member of the Marine Engineers' Beneficial Association of Baltimore. Attends the German Lutheran Church. A Democrat. Chief engineer of the City of Philadelphia, a coasting vessel.

809. FRANCIS JAMES DASHIELL - b. 9 May 1845 near Princess Anne, Somerset Co., MD, s/o James A. and Charlotte (Dashiell). Dashiells originally French-Huguenots, went to England, then America, settled in Somerset Co., MD. Grandfather, James W. Dashiell, b. in Somerset Co., farmer. Father, b. at the head of Wetipquen creek, lumber manufacturer, d. at Snow Hill, on the Pocomoke, at seventy-nine. Mother, b. in Somerset Co., very distant relative of her husband, d. at forty-four. Maternal grandfather, Haste W. Dashiell, cabinet maker. James and Charlotte had two children: Francis, and Erastus S., dentist of Snow Hill. Francis m. Miss Harriett, d/o James Broughton, at Temperanceville, Accomac Co., VA, and had one child, Frances M. Harriett, b. in Balt. Member of the Royal Arcanum, and Evergreen Lodge No. 153, A.R.&A.M., of Snow Hill, MD. An Episcopalian. A Democrat. Chief engineer of the Enoch Pratt.

810. CAPT. LEVIN CHANCE - b. 14 Oct., 1824 in Leesburg, Cumberland Co., NJ, s/o Capt. Spencer and Elizabeth (Peterson) Chance, of same place. Paternal grandfather, William Chance, extensive land owner, farmer. Maternal grandfather, Squire Peterson, farmer and justice of the peace, of Swedish descent, fought in Revolutionary war. Father, d. at Linwood Station, Delaware Co., PA, at sixty-five. Mother d. at sixty-one. Spencer and Elizabeth had six children, Levin being the second. Levin m. Miss Mary A. Bartow at the old Swedish Church in Philadelphia, and had five children, three living: Theodore Peterson, in transfer business in Balt.; Mrs. Clara G. Roemer and Mrs. Laura V. Bangs, both of Balt. Mary, b. in Linwood, PA, d. on the Martha Stevens, returning to Balt. from New York. Levin m. (2) Miss Mary Murphy, of MD, and had two children: Willie R. and Ethel G. Member of the Justice Lodge No. 186, I.O.O.F., of Philadelphia. A Republican. Master of the William Woodward.

811. HENRY A. DAVIS - b. 1 Mar. 1860 in Pikesville, s/o Henry and Alice B. (Mittam) Davis. Father, b. in Hesse-Cassel, came to America with parents, settled in Hanover, PA, blacksmith, d. in 1893, a Democrat, member of the Knights of Pythias and the Odd Fellows, a Baptist. Grandfather, John Davis, farmer in PA, then manager for Samuel Shoemaker in Balt. Co. Grandmother, Martha Catherine Davis. Henry m. Alice B., d/o Joseph and Ruth Mittam, and had six children: John Joseph, farmer in Balt. Co.; Alice B.; Kate R., d. at twenty-eight; Bertha E., w/o William R. Coughlan; Escaville M. and Henry A. Joseph and Ruth Mittam, both b. in England. Member of the Odd Fellows the Masons, and the Knights of Pythias. A Baptist. Postmaster of Pikesville.

812. CHARLES W. LANTZ - b. 16 Jun. 1864 at Edgewood Station, Harford Co., MD, s/o Jacob and Ann Sophia Frederica (Immorda) Lantz, he of Hesse-Cassel, and she of Hanover, Germany. Father, b. in 1821, came to America with parents at age four, baker in Balt. for twenty-three years, then farmer in Harford Co. til death, 12 Aug. 1882, a Democrat. Mother, b. in 1820, came to America with parents at thirteen, settled in Balt., d. in 1895 at seventy-five. Jacob and Ann had eight children: George C., in dairy business in Balt.; John J. Fred, has canning factory in Magnolia, Harford Co.; Jacob, d. at twenty-two from kick of horse; John, d. at twenty-seven, in Edgewood, Harford Co.; Ann Elizabeth, w/o Daniel Digel; Dora, d. in girlhood; Mary A., w/o Alexander P. Norris, Harford Co. farmer; and Charles. Charles m. Miss Caroline, d/o Henry Volz, Sr., 10 Mar. 1889, and had four children: Mary F.; Jacob H., d. in childhood; Wilhelmina Elizabeth and Amelia C. Member of the Ancient Order of United Workmen. A Democrat. Belongs to the Zion Evangelical Church. Wheelwright at Golden Ring.

813. HON. HENRY D. HARLAN - b. 23 Oct. 1858, at family homestead in Churchville, s/o Dr. David and Margaret Rebecca (Herbert) Harlan. Descendant in the fifth generation of Michael Harlan, who with brother George, came to America in 1687, settled near Kennet (now Pennsbury), PA. Next in line was David Harlan, owned much land and several mills in Chester Co., PA, member of the Society of Friends. Grandfather, Jeremiah Harlan, moved to Harford Co., MD, from London Township, Chester Co., PA, in the last quarter of the eighteenth century, bought Strawberry Hill farm from Reuben Stump in 1812, m. Esther, d/o Henry and Rachel (Perkins) Stump in 1800, and had seven children, David being the fifth. Father, surgeon in United States navy, m. Margaret R., d/o James B. and Mary A. (Baker) Herbert, 3 Mar. 1846, and had five children: Oleita, d. 25 Jul. 1866; Dr. Herbert Harlan, professor at University of Maryland; David E., civil engineer at Lima, OH; W. Beatty, lawyer in Bel Air; and Henry. Father, d. at home in Churchville, 12 Jul. 1893. Mother, b. 25 Jun. 1826. Maternal grandfather, James Beatty Herbert, s/o Capt. John Herbert, and brother of Dr. William Paul Herbert. Maternal great-grandfather, Capt. Jeremiah Baker, of Cecil Co., d. in May 1814, age seventy-four. Jeremiah Baker, m. Rebecca Maulden, and had Jeremiah, Mary (mother of Margaret Rebecca) and Charlotte. Maternal great-grandmother, Margaret (Beatty) Herbert, d. at

ninety-eight. First of Herbert family in America was Capt. John Herbert and wife, who came from Ireland in 1794, settled on large estate at Churchville. Henry m. Helen, d/o Henry and Hannah (Eyre) Altemus, of Philadelphia, 19 Dec. 1889, and had two children Helen and Henry Altemus. Member of the Balt. Club, the University Club. A Democrat. Belongs to the Episcopal Church. Chief justice of the supreme bench of Balt.

814. EDWIN HIGGINS - b. 30 Apr. 1841 in Montgomery Co., s/o Jesse T. and Margaret Rebecca (Waters) Higgins. Father, b. in Montgomery Co., moved to Balt. after the war, in the commission business, d. in Balt. in 1885. Grandfather, James B. Higgins, farmer of Montgomery Co. Great-grandfather, James Higgins, served on the first grand jury impanelled in Montgomery Co. in 1776. Maternal grandfather, Richard R. Waters. Maternal great-grandfather, Dr. Richard Waters, surgeon in Revolutionary war. Jesse and Margaret had three sons: Rev. Jesse Higgins, an Episcopal minister in Philadelphia; James R., a hatter at Tucker & Co., in Balt.; and Edwin. Edwin m. Rebecca S., d/o Robert Ould, 1 Nov. 1866, and had five children: Jesse, eldest, member of Higgins & Waters; Robert, proprietor of Crown Hand Laundry; Margaret; and 2 who d. Robert Ould, lived in Georgetown, educator. Assisted in organization of Prohibition party. Lawyer in Balt.

815. GEN. FERDINAND C. LATROBE - b. in Balt., s/o John H. B. and Charlotte B. (Claiborne) Latrobe. Grandfather, Benjamin H. Latrobe, b. near London, England, came to America a young man, locating in Washington, then Balt., an architect, d. in New Orleans. Great-grandfather, Isaac Hazelhurst, of Philadelphia. Father, b. in Philadelphia, patent rights lawyer, a Mason, belonged to the Episcopal Church, d. in 1892. Mother, b. in MS, living in Balt., age eighty-two. John and Charlotte had: Henry; Ferdinand C.; Osmun, of Balt.; R. Stuart, Balt. attorney; John, an attorney, drowned; Virginia, of Balt., m. Judge Andrew Coggswell, of NJ; and Lydia, w/o Dr. Frank Loring, physician of Washington. Maternal grandfather, Gen. Ferdinand Leigh Claiborne, lineal descendant of William Claiborne, of an old English family. Ferdinand m. Louisa, d/o ex-Gov. Thomas Swann, of MD, and had one son, T. Swann, who d. in Balt. in 1894, at twenty-five. Ferdinand m. (2) Miss Ellen, d/o John R. Penrose (deceased), of Philadelphia, and had three children: Ferdinand C., Charlotte and Virginia. Member of the Fidelity Lodge, the St. John's chapter, R.A.M., the Maryland Commandery, K.T., and the Franklin Lodge, I.O.O.F. A Democrat. Retired mayor of Balt.

816. HON BARNES COMPTON - b. 16 Nov. 1831 at Port Tobacco, Charles Co., MD, s/o William Penn and Mary Clarissa Bond (Barnes) Compton. Father, merchant in Balt., then merchant and planter in Charles Co., d. at about forty-seven. Grandfather, Dr. Wilson Compton. Grandmother, Elizabeth (Penn) Compton. Great-grandfather, Wilson Compton, came to America from England, settled in Charles Co., named estate Wilton, after Compton home in England. Great-grandmother, d/o William Penn, who owned estate called Laidloes on the Potomac. Mary Clarissa, d/o John and Mary (Key)

Barnes, he a clerk of the court of Charles Co. til he d. at seventy-four. Father of John, Richard Barnes, clerk of the circuit court of Charles Co. Mary Barnes, d/o Philip Key, also the lineal ancestor of Francis Scott Key. Father of Philip, also Philip, came from England, s/o Richard and Mary Key, of Havengorden, London. Philip, father of Mary, b. in St. Mary Co., a founder of the Episcopal Church in Chaptico, St. Mary Co., m. (1) Rebecca Joel Sothoron, m. (2) Miss Hall, granddaughter of Robert Morris. Subject m. Miss Margaret Holliday, d/o Col. John Henry Sothoron, in St. Mary Co., and had six children: Mary Barnes; John Henry, cashier of the Baltimore & Ohio Railroad; Key, agent of the Bay line at Norfolk; William Penn, medical practitioner in Washington, D.C.; Elizabeth Somerville, Mrs. Rees; and Barnes, Jr. Member of the Sons of the American Revolution. A Democrat. Naval officer of the port of Balt.

816 JAMES C. TUCHTON - b. 24 Dec. 1833 in the ninth district of Balt. Co., s/o Henry and Eliza (Wood) Tuchton, he of Balt. Co. and she of Harford Co. Paternal grandather, Henry Tuchton, St., b. in France, came to America in early manhood, settled in Balt. Co., a miller. Father, also a miller, d. at thirty-three. Mother d. in 1863. Henry and Eliza had five children: Nathan, d. in childhood; John, engineer, d.; Theodore, engineer; Annie, d. in girlhood. Mother, m. a second time and had a son, who lives with James and is a brakeman on the Delaware Railroad. James m. Sarah R. Dover, of Harford Co., in 1859, and had five children: Sarah, d. in girlhood; Henry F., farmer in the ninth district; Mary E., m. Christian Lawrence, of Balt. Co.; Effie E., Mrs. George Johnson, d. at twenty-nine, leaving a child; and James, d. in boyhood. A Republican. Identified with the Methodist Episcopal Church. Farmer and runs mercantile business in Chase.

818. WILLIAM H. KLINE - b. in 1846 in Balt., s/o Frederick and Elizabeth Kline. Father, farmer in the ninth district, d. in 1877. Mother, b. in Balt., d. when William was eleven months old. Frederick and Elizabeth had six children: George, John, Elizabeth, Julia, Fannie, and William. William m. Miss Margaret, d/o Amos and Elizabeth Armacost, in 1868, and had five children: Thomas H. H., head bookkeeper for father; Edgar, manager of the teams in the coal business; Maggie and Ida, at home; and Bessie, m. George W. Smith and lives in the twelfth district. Member of the Sixth Ward Club and the Young Men's Republican Club. A Republican. Coal merchant at No. 19 North street.

819. JOHN McPHERSON DENNIS - b. 23 Feb. 1866 in Frederick, MD, s/o Col. George R. and Fannie (McPherson) Dennis. About 1664 Damrock Dennis came from the south of England to MD, settled in Somerset Co., an attorney. Father, b. in Somerset Co., moved to Frederick Co. in 1852, an Episcopalian, now seventy. Maternal great-great-great-grandfather, Col. John McPherson of Frederick, s/o Col. Robert McPherson, who came from Scotland in 1738 with wife, Janet, and settled on Marsh Creek, York Co., PA. Grandmother, Frances Russel Johnson, granddaughter of Thomas Johnson, who was grandson of Thomas Johnson who came to America from Yarmouth, England in 1690. George and Fannie had six children:

John McPherson; Ann Graham, w/o Dr. Franklin B. Smith, of Frederick; George R., Jr., an attorney, lives in Frederick; Archibald R., lives in Indianapolis, IN; Elizabeth U. and Thomas Jennings, at home. Member of the Commonwealth and Pimlico Clubs, and the Chillicothe (Ohio) Commandery No. 8, K.T., and Moolah Shrine, of St. Louis. Full partner in the grain commission and export business of Tate, Muller & Co., office in the Chamber of Commerce.

820. HON. WILLIAM L. MARBURY - b. 26 Dec. 1858 at Wyoming, Prince George Co., s/o Fendall and Catherine (Marshall) Marbury, he of Wyoming, MD, and she of Warrenton, VA. Maternal grandfather, Alexander J. Marshall. Fendall and Catherine had: William L.; Fendall, Jr., d.; and A. Marshall, of Prince George Co. After death of Catherine, Fendall m. (2) Miss Sallie C., d/o William I. Berry of Prince George Co., and had one son, Dr. Charles C., of Washington, DC. Father, a Democrat, d. 17 Nov. 1896. Paternal grandfather, William L. Marbury, b. in MD, a planter. Great-grandfather, William Marbury, soldier of war of 1812. Great-great-grandfather, Luke Marbury, Revolutionary soldier. Marburys came from Cheshire, England, became planters in MD, original homestead was at Wyoming. United States district attorney for Maryland.

821. CAPT. W. ASBURY THOMAS - b. 22 Aug. 1844 near Hurlock, in Dorchester Co., s/o Joseph Thomas. Grandfather, Thomas Thomas, lived in Dorchester Co. Father, also b. in Dorchester Co., farmer, d. at seventy-six. Mother, b. in Dorchester Co., d. at seventy-seven. Maternal grandfather, Edmund Andrews, tanner, retired in Dorchester Co. Subject m. Miss Emma Sarah E., d/o John Edward Brumwell, of Dorchester Co., in Balt., and had four children, Willie E., Maud, Minnie Lillian and Albert. John Brumwell, carpenter and contractor. Emma, member of the Independent Methodist Episcopal Church, d. in 1891. A Republican. Captain of the steamer John W. Garrett, of the New York & Baltimore Transportation Company.

822. HON. HARRY WELLES RUSK - b. 17 Oct. 1852 in Balt., s/o Jacob Krebs and Catherine Olivia (Lane) Rusk, he of Balt., and she of Washington, DC. Paternal grandfather, George W. Rusk, b. in Balt., s/o John Rusk, of England. John came to America, settled in the vicinity of Balt., farmer. Paternal grandmother, Mary Krebs, d/o Jacob Krebs. Jacob of German descent, first brick manufacturer of Balt. Father, in wholesale and retail leather business, an Odd Fellow. Maternal grandparents, b., reared and m. in Ireland. Maternal grandmother, d/o Cornelius Ryan. Jacob and Catherine had; Dr. G. G., physician and surgeon of Balt.; Harry Welles; J. Krebs; and J. Stewart, attorneys. Harry m. Belle W., d/o John Q. Adams, of Balt., and had one child, Harry Welles, Jr. Member of the Calumet Club. A Democrat. Attends the Methodist Episcopal Church. Former member of the Maryland house of delegates and the state senate. Attorney in Balt.

823. CAPT. NICHOLAS TEGGES - b. 29 Jun. 1841 in Homberg,

Germany, s/o Frederick and Gertrude (Happel) Tegges. Father, hotel owner in Homberg, d. at fifty-six. Mother, d. in 1885, in Homberg, at seventy-two. Frederick and Gertrude had: Henry, came to America in 1846, a Balt. butcher; Frederick, hotel keeper in Germany; Nicholas; and four children who d. Nicholas m. Miss Margaret, d/o John and Mary Miller, of Balt. in 1864, and had six children: John F., in business with father; Louisa, w/o Charles Maasch; Maggie, Annie, Nicholas, Jr., and Marie, at home. Member of the Knights of Pythias, and the Masons. A Democrat. Attends St. Matthew's Lutheran Church. Butcher in the Lexington market and on Pratt street.

824. ISAAC FREEMAN RASIN - b. 11 Nov. 1833 in Kent Co., MD, s/o Robert Wilson and Mary Rebecca (Ringgold) Rasin. Of French extraction. Father, farmer, then moved to Balt., a real-estate broker. Paternal grandfather, Philip Freeman Rasin, merchant of Kent Co. Great-grandfather, William Rasin, settled in Kent Co. in 1669, captain in the Revolutionary war. Philip Freeman Rasin m. Phoebe, d/o George and Susan (Holliday) Wilson, he s/o George and Margaret (Hall) Wilson, of Castle Cary, Kent Co., MD; his parents were George and Mary (Kennard) Wilson, and his parents were James and Catherine Wilson. James Wilson came to America from England, settled in MD in 1700, d. in 1732. Susan (Holliday) Wilson, d/o James and Margaret (Cook) Morris, and James was s/o Anthony Morris, of St. Dunstan, England, b. 23 Aug. 1654, m. Mary Jones 30 Jan. 1676, d. 24 Oct. 1721. Mother m. (1) William Ringgold, her first cousin, d. in 1816; father of William was Thomas Ringgold, s/o William and Rebecca Ringgold, who d. in 1790; maternal grandfather, Edward Ringgold, planter on Kent Island, Kent Co., m. (1) his first cousin, m. (2) Rebecca Smith, d. in Chestertown, Kent Co., MD, 10 Dec. 1854, age eighty. Maternal great grandparents, Thomas and Elizabeth (Sudler) Ringgold, Thomas, s/o Josiah Ringgold and grandson of James Ringgold, of Talbot Co., MD, s/o Maj. James Ringgold, who m. Mary, d/o Capt. Robert Vaughn, of Kent Co. Maj. Ringgold d. in 1686. Father of Maj. Ringgold, Thomas, Lord of Huntingfeld, progenitor of the family in America, settled on the Isle of Kent with two sons, James and John in 1650. Isaac m. Miss Julia A., d/o Capt. John Claypoole, and had: Martha Anne, b. in 1863 and d. in 1865; Genevieve R., b. in 1865 and d. in 1877; Howard D., b. in 1866 and d. in 1868; John F., Balt. insurance man; Morris C., b. in 1872, d. in 1880; Gertrude, Julia, Helen, Carroll and Alice. Capt. John Claypoole, descendant of James Claypoole; father of Capt. John, Adam Claypoole, m. Dorothea, d/o Robert Wingfield and Elizabeth (Cecil). Maternal grandfather of Julia Claypoole, Edward Browne, of Kent Co.; Julia can trace ancestry back to Princess Elizabeth Plantagenet and Edward I, King of England. A Democrat. Retired state insurance commissioner for Maryland.

825. HENRY M. WALKER - b. 18 Mar. 1869 in Pikesville, MD. s/o Patrick Henry and Rosa B. (Mittnacht) Walker. Grandfather, Noah Walker, b. 23 Jan. 1796 in Carroll Co., MD, d. 3 Feb. 1874 at Dumbarton, in Balt. Co. Great-grandfather of Noah, Henry Walker, founder of the first Baptist Church in MD. Wife of Noah, Sarah

Ann, d/o Patrick Caughy, b. 17 Oct. 1812, d. 30 Sep. 1842, leaving two sons: Patrick Henry and Noah Dixon, b. 17 May 1834, d. 3 May 1863 at Chancellorsville, VA. Father, b. 7 Mar. 1833, a Democrat, d. 27 Oct. 1886 in Balt. Mother, b. 9 Dec. 1836, d. 26 Mar. 1891. Patrick and Rosa had six children: Noah, the eldest; George, d. at eighteen; Dixon Chancellorsville, m. Georgia Hoops, lives in Frederick Co., MD, raises horses and cattle; Sarah T., m. (1) Charles Shelton, m. (2) James B. Councilman; Henry M.; and Hamilton C., lives in London. Maternal grandfather, George H. Mittnacht, b. 4 Jul. 1804 in Lemberg, Germany, m. (1) Katherine Schwartz, came to Balt. in 1832, had six children, m. (2) Abigail Lyal Armitage, and had three children: one, Laura B., m. I. H. Caughy, cousin of P. H. Walker. Henry m. Alice T., d/o James McMahon, in 1890. A Democrat.

826. REV. W. H. H. POWERS, D. D. - b. 13 Jun. 1849 in Staunton, VA, son Rev. Pike and Delia Skipworth (Harrison) Powers. Father, principal of boarding school at Staunton til sixty, then entered the ministry, now rector of St. Andrew's Episcopal Church of Richmond, VA. Richard Powers, brother of Pike. Mother, member of the Saunders family of VA, d. in 1867. Pike and Delia had seven children. Maternal grandfather, Edward Harrison, planter at The Oaks, in Amelia Co., VA, first cousin of William Henry Harrison. Subject m. d/o Judge H. W. Sheffy, of Staunton, VA, in Oct. 1872, and had seven children. Rector of Trinity Episcopal Church of Towson.

827. MICHAEL HOFFMAN - b. New Year's day, 1820 in Balt. Founder of this branch of the Hoffman family in America was great-grandfather, Michael, b. 26 May 1718 in Germany, settled in PA, farmer, d. in Aug. 1798. Grandfather, Jacob Hoffman, b. in Lancaster Co., PA, came to Balt., established a leather house. Father, b. in Balt., in business with father, worker in the German Lutheran Church. Mother, Mary Hoffman, not a relative, but from another branch of the family. Maternal grandfather, Jacob Hoffman, made guns and swords, d. in Philadelphia at advanced age. Father of Jacob, a German, d. at one hundred four years. Mary and her husband had fourteen children: five d. in early childhood; Jacob V., in the leather business, d. ten years since; George L., was in leather business; John Frederick, (see his sketch) inspector of leather; Albert H., d. long ago, leather merchant, then in postoffice; Isaac R., dealer in leather; Washington S., invalid; Susanna, w/o Dr. George Powell, d. leaving one child; Julia M., died young. Michael m. at twenty-eight, Rosetta, d/o Thomas Bissett, of VA, and had: William Albert, employed by A. F. Brown & Co.; Thomas M., partner of father; Mary Hannah, w/o William H. Garrett, lives in Philadelphia, has nine children. Michael m. (2) Ann Rebecca Ellicott, of VA. Member of the German Reformed Church. Owner and proprietor of a large preserving company in Balt.

828. HON. EDWARD D. FITZGERALD - b. 8 Oct. 1858 in Balt., s/o Capt. John and Catherine Fitzgerald. John and Catherine had two sons: John, in the shipping business, d. in 1883, age twenty-three; and Edward. Edward m. Miss Lillie, d/o Dennis Robinson,

in Washington, DC, and had five children: Elsie M., Edward D., Jr., John R., Lillie and Catherine. A Democrat. Lawyer of Balt.

829. CHARLES E. FORD - b. in 1856 in Balt., s/o John T. and Edith B. (Andrews) Ford. Father, a Democrat, had stock company and theater. Mother, of Hanover Co., VA, had ten children, Charles E., being the eldest son. Charles m. Annie, d/o Addison Hardcastle, of St. Louis, in 1876 and had three children: Mabel, w/o P. P Dunan, of Balt.; Charles E., Jr., student; and Edith Octavia. Member of the Order of Elks. Owner and manager of Ford's Grand Opera House, in Balt. and Washington, DC.

830. CHRISTOPHER C. SPEED - b. in 1840 near Bangor, Penobscot Co., ME. Grandfather, Joseph Speed, b. in ME, of Scotch-Irish parentage, shipbuilder, d. at eighty-four. Paternal grandmother, Patience Rogers Speed, of Kennebec. Father, b. in Penobscot Co., farmer, d. in 1892 at ninety-two. Mother, Mary Reeves Speed, b. in Penboscot Co., ME, had fourteen children, six served in the Union army during the Civil war: James, lives in Penobscot Co., ME, member of the Twenty-second Maine Infantry; John, member of the First Maine Heavy Artillery for two years, wounded at the battle of the Wilderness, lives in Piscataquis Co., ME; Charles, member of the First Maine Heavy Artillery, wounded at the battle of the Wilderness, d. in ND; William H., member of the Sixteenth Maine Infantry. Maternal grandfather, James Reeves, b. in Kennebec, ME, farmer, soldier in war of 1812. Maternal grandmother, Lucy Trask Reeves. Father of James Reeves, b. in England, founder of family in America. Christopher, member of Company E, Eleventh Maine Infantry. Subject m. Miss Mary E., d/o Elias Magers, in 1864 in Balt., and had four children: William G., attorney; Fletcher B., capitalist; Mary E., at home; and Bertie L., w/o John McAllister, of Balt. Member of the Warren Lodge No. 51, A.F.&A.M., St. John's Chapter, R.A.M., Monumental Commandery, K. T., the Knights of Honor, the Royal Arcanum, and Custer Post No. 6., G.A.R., the Union Veteran League. A Republican. Belongs to the Methodist Episcopal Church. President of the Catonsville Water Company.

831. HON. FRANK BROWN - s/o Stephen Thomas Cockney Brown. Founder of family in America, great-grandfather, Abel Brown, came from Dumfries, Scotland, settled near Sykesville, Carroll Co., MD. Father, b. in Nov. 1820, agriculturist, Presbyterian, founded Springfield Church, d. in Dec. 1876. Hon. Elias Brown, uncle of Abel Brown. Mother, a Miss Patterson, sister of Madame Jerome Bonaparte (formerly Miss Elizabeth Patterson), w/o the brother of the famous Napoleon. A Democrat. Ex-Governor of MD.

832. WILLIAM R. BARNES - b. 31 Oct. 1864 in Balt., s/o Hanson P. and Katherine A. (Weyrauch) Barnes. Father, b. in 1831 in Cumberland, Allegany Co., MD, came to Balt. at about eighteen, a Democrat, a Knight of Pythias. Mother b. in Balt. Hanson and Katherine had: William R.; Charles E., in commission business with father; Hanson P., Jr., d. in 1885; Jacob S., with father; and Emma K., w/o John Hannibal. William m. Lillian L. Peat in 1885 and had three children: Martha E., William Lenos, and Janet

K. Member of the Royal Arcanum and the Loyal Legion. Belongs to the Methodist Episcopal Church.

833. HON. ROGER BROOKE TANEY, LL. D. - b. 17 Mar. 1777 in Calvert Co., MD. Family of English descent, came to this country about the middle of the seventeenth century, paternal ancestor settled on the Patuxent in 1656. On maternal side, Robert Brooke and family came to America six years earlier and settled on the Patuxent, about twenty miles up the river. Subject m. Anne Phoebe Key, sister of Francis Scott Key, in Frederick, in 1806, d. 12 Oct. 1864. Chief justice.

834. HON. THOMAS J. SHRYOCK - b. 27 Feb. 1851 in Balt., s/o Henry S. and Ophelia (Shields) Shryock. Paternal grandfather, Jacob Shryock, b. in VA. Mother and father both of prominent old Virginia families. Father, Revolutionary soldier, d. in 1881, a Republican, a Baptist. Shryocks of German origin. Maternal grandfather, Thomas Shields, merchant in VA, a Mason, of Irish descent. Mother, had eleven children, d. in 1882. Thomas m. Miss Maria Mann, in Balt., and had five children. Maria d. Thomas m. (2) Catherine B. Miller, of Syracuse, NY, in 1887, and had two children. Member of the Masons. A Republican. State treasurer of Maryland.

835. JOHN B. HART, M. D. - b. 20 Jun 1862 in Balt., s/o Thomas A. and Eliza (O'Brien) Hart. Grandfather, Thomas R. Hart, b. in Manchester, England, came to America with wife, manufactured cloth in Boston til 1824, came to Balt., a hand-loom weaver, then cloth manufacturer, d. on the York road at sixty-five. Paternal grandmother, Harriet Barber Hart, b. in London, England, member of the Episcopal Church, d. at seventy. Thomas and Harriet had ten children. Father, b. 27 Nov. 1820 in Boston, MA, a Democrat, contractor and builder. Mother, b. in Ireland, came with parents to America during early girlhood. Thomas and Eliza had ten children. John m. Miss Mamie, d/o Nicholas Rogers, in Balt., and had one child, Bessie LeRoy. Mamie, b. in Balt., d. John m. (2) Mrs. Birdie Rouse, of Woodstock, VA, d/o A. B. Miller, of NY. Member of the Medical and Chirurgical Faculty of Maryland and the State Clinical Association. A Democrat. Engaged in general practice of medicine and surgery.

836. JOHN J. CALDWELL, M. D. - b. 28 Apr. 1836 at Oak Hill, in Newcastle Co. DE, s/o Col. John Sipple and Rebecca (Baker) Caldwell. Of French-Huguenot ancestry, name originally spelled Colville. John Caldwell, son of Sir David Caldwell, who lived in the north of Ireland, came to America in the eighteenth century, settled in DE. Sons of John, Capt. Jonathan, Capt. Joseph and Rev. James, were in Revolutionary war. Great-grandfather, Capt. Jonathan Caldwell, served in Col. John Haslett's regiment, from Kent Co., DE . Grandfather, Jabez, lived in Talbot Co., MD. Father, farmer in DE, NY, PA and MD, an Episcopalian, d. in 1878 at about sixty-eight. Father and mother m. 10 Jun 1835, and had twelve children: John J.; Caroline, widow of Albert Osterhoudt, of NY; Rebecca, w/o Richard U. Clark, a secretary of the NY Life Insurance Company; Catherine, widow of Augustus Hull, who lived

in NY, and was with the Chicago & Rock Island Railroad Company; Ella, w/o Charles H. Benner, of the firm of Benner, Brown & Pinkney, of NY; Gertrude, w/o Hon. Samuel Stevenson, of Montreal, Canada; Virginia, d. in Jun, 1897, w/o Albert Isaacson, of Montreal; James, of Chicago, assistant manager of the Wagner Palace Car Company; Richard Baker, d. in Cuba in 1886; Alexis Dupont, d.; Leonora, Mrs. Mindus Frailey, of NY; and Elizabeth, w/o Charles H. Corliss, of Troy, NY. Mother, d/o Richard and Rebecca (Webb) Baker who lived near Brandywine, a Quaker, one of twelve children, d. about 1890, age eighty. Great-grandfather of Rebecca Caldwell, Jehu Harlan, member of the Society of Friends, one of original settlers of PA, with William Penn. Subject m. d/o R. Horace and Mary W. Love, direct descendent of Sir Richard Johns, of England, 4 Jan. 1864, and had five children: Maud Worthington, m. Bareda Turner, grain merchant, manufacturer of wire tacks and nails, and clerk of the circuit court of Balt., had three children, Robert, Bessie and Dorothy; Ridgely Love, electrician of Balt.; Edgar Calhoun, partner of R. L.; Marianne, d. in Brooklyn when two; and Adele, d. in Balt. at seven. Member of the Baltimore Medical Society, the State Faculty of Maryland, the Medical and Surgical Society of Baltimore, the Toxicological and Medico-Legal Society of New York. A Republican. An Episcopalian. Physician at No. 808 Fulton avenue.

837. MICHAEL J. CONWAY - b. 21 May 1869, s/o Daniel and Mary (McVeigh) Conway. Father, b. in Ireland, wholesale tea merchant in Philadelphia for ten years, returned to Ireland, came back to America several years later, landing in Balt. in Mar., 1879, wholesale grocer, a Democrat, d. 12 Dec. 1896. Mother, d/o Patrick McVeigh of Cappagh, County Tyrone, Ireland. Daniel and Mary had four children: Michael J.; Dr. J. H. Conway, lives in Balt.; Catherine, at home; and Mary, sister of mercy in St. Agnes' Convent, Mount Washington, MD. Michael m. Margaret, d/o John P. Harrington, of Erie, PA, and had a son, who d. in Jul., 1897. Member of the Ancient Order of Hibernians, the Catholic Benevolent Legion, Knights of Columbus, the American Catholic League, and the Baltimore Athletic Club. A Democrat. Lawyer at No. 9 St. Paul street.

838. ROBERT H. CAMPBELL, M. D. - b. 1 Oct. 1866 in Portsmouth, VA, s/o Dr. James B. and Martha E. (Tatum) Campbell. Descendant of Dougall Campbell, who with brothers John and Samuel came to America, settled in VA., John settled in PA, Samuel d. in Berkeley Co., leaving no children. First will ever probated in the clerk's court of Berkeley Co. was of Dougall Campbell, descendent of original Dougall. Father, b. in Martinsburg, Berkeley Co., VA, (now WV), in 1830, surgeon during civil war, a Mason, d. at Portsmouth in 1891. Mother, b. in Portsmouth in 1833, of English ancestors, d/o Robert H. Tatum, owner of Hermitage, at Tatum, VA. Physician at No. 2121 Maryland avenue.

839. JOHN W. WALTER - b. 29 Jul. 1845 in Balt. Father, b. in Adams Co., PA, in Mar., 1819, owner of Olive Flouring Mills, on Herron Run, retired to Harford Co., MD, a Democrat, d. in Mar., 1887. Grandfather, farmer in Adams Co., PA. Brothers of father,

Dr. John Walter, of Hanover, PA, and Michael, a farmer. Mother and father, had nine children: John W.; Rev. J., Methodist Episcopal minister in MD; Joseph Edward, manufacturer and merchant, d.; William O., farmer in Harford Co.; Lewis Albert, dairyman in Harford Co.; Charles S., miller in Harford Co.; George Thomas, killed by insane man, Franklin Wettaker, who was about to kill George's father; Harry A., operates a flour mill; Laura, widow of John Judd, resident of Delta, PA; and Alice, w/o George T. St. Meyer, of Aberdeen, MD. Subject m. Mary E. C., d/o Aaron Rambo, in 1870, and had two children: Edmond Andrew, paperhanger, and Alvin Wesley, farmer and miller in York, PA. Aaron Rambo, owner of Rambo Mills. Mary d. John m. (2) Cecilia, s/o Samuel D. Franklin, 6 Feb. 1891,and had three children: John D., Samuel D. and Mary Cecilia. Samuel Franklin, contractor. Member of the Odd Fellows, the Junior Order of American Mechanics, and the State Temperance Society. A Democrat. Belongs to the Memorial Evangelical Church. Lawyer in Balt.

840. REV. GEORGE SCHOLL, D. D. - b. 22 Apr. 1841 near Connersville, IN, s/o Jacob and Elizabeth (Reed) Scholl. Ancestors came from Germany about 1750, settled in Schuylkill Co., PA, moved to IN in 1833. Grandfather, John Jacob Scholl, head of group that moved to IN, d. in 1869, at ninety-seven, leaving eleven children, forty-seven grandchildren, eighty five great-grandchildren, and one great-great grandchild. Father, b. in 1804, d. at ninety. Parents, founders of the Lutheran Church in central IN. George m. Miss Barbara Emma Barr, of Springfield, OH, 1 1869, and had four children: Maud Isabelle, w/o Rev. James Cattanach, of Taneytown, MD; George Barr, student; and two d. Member of the Foreign Missionary Board. Corresponding secretary of the Foreign Missionary Board.

841. MICHAEL A. GARRETT - b. 28 Jun 1852 in Balt. Co., s/o Michael Garrett. Father, b. in Ireland in 1818, came to America in manhood, settling in MD, connected with the Baltimore & Ohio Railroad. Michael and wife had six children: William; P. J., m. Miss Bertha Browning, s/o Senator Browning; Thomas J. and Mary E., live on old Garrett farm in Garrett Co., MD; Annie, w/o Peter Kane, farmer and merchant in WV; and Michael A. Member of the Elks and the Shield of Honor. A Republican. Superintendent of the John W. Garrett estate in the ninth district.

842. REV. A. FRED STERGER - b. 4 Nov. 1856 in Baden, Germany, s/o Henry and Mary Sterger. Father, d. in 1883. Mother, now sixty-three. Subject m. Lizzie, d/o Valentine Pfiermann, of Falmouth, KY, 25 May 1879, and had three children: Josephine, Fred and Henry. Member of the Masons and the Arabic order of Mystic Shrine. Pastor of Trinity German Lutheran Church, Trinity street, Balt.

843. WILLIAM F. WELLER - s/o Joseph and Susan Matilda (Reifsnider) Weller. Descendant of John Weller, who settled in Mechanicstown in 1736, a member of a group of German emigrants who came from Wurtemberg to America in 1730 and located in NJ, later moved to Reading, PA, then Frederick Co., MD. There were

two distinct families, one settled at Graceham, the other at Mechanicstown (now Thurmont). Great-grandfather, Jacob Weller, b. 26 Oct. 1752 in Mechanicstown, a blacksmith, m. Anna, b. 24 Jan. 1754, 20 Apr. 1774, and had ten children. Grandfather, Jacob Weller, m. Anna Margaret Weller, of the Graceham family, and had five children. Family connected with German Reformed Church, later Jacob became interested in the United Brethren Church. Father, second son, b. 10 Sep. 1807, merchant in Balt. and later Reisterstown, d. in 1875. Mother, of Frederick Co., now eighty-eight. Great-grandfather had general store in Mechanicstown. Ancestors on mother's side came to America at same time as paternal ancestors and moved to Reading, PA. Maternal grandparents, John and Catherine (Krider) Reifsnider, moved to Taneytown about 1794, he a hat manufacturer. Great-grandfather, William Reifsnider, also hat manufacturer, d. in Reading, PA. Joseph and Susan had six children: Edwin A., William F., Dr. Joseph M., Morris W., Virginia O. and Maria L. William m. d/o William M. Berryman, farmer of Reisterstown, and had eight children. Engaged in merchandising, farming and carrying on extensive granite quarries and works.

844. NOAH WALKER - b. Mar. 1861, s/o Patrick Henry and Rosalie B. (Mittnacht) Walker. Grandfather, Noah Walker, clothier in Balt. and Washington, DC. Brother of Patrick, Noah, killed at Chancellorsville. Father, b. in Balt. Patrick and Rosalie had six children: Sarah A., w/o James B. Councilman, of the third district; Noah; George, d. at eighteen; Dixon C., lives on large farm at Urbana, Frederick Co., MD; Hamilton C., now in Europe; and Henry M. (see sketch). Noah m. Katharine Zachary, of Washington, DC in 1895. Father of Katharine, b. in Balt. Grandfather of Katharine, Alexander Zachary, soldier of war of 1812, d. eighteen years age, wife living at eighty-six.

845. JOHN R. BAILEY - b. in 1844 in Dorchester Co., MD, s/o William and Ann (Richardson) Bailey. Paternal grandfather, John Bailey, farmer of York Co., PA. Maternal grandfather, William T. Richardson, of Dorchester Co., MD. Father, b. in York Co., of English descent, and Quaker stock, moved to Balt. at sixteen, learned trade of merchant tailor, moved to Church Creek, Dorchester Co., a Republican, a Presbyterian, d. at seventy-six. Mother, b. in Dorchester Co., of English descent, lives in Baltimore, now eighty. William and Ann had twelve children, five living. Maternal grandmother, Ellen, d/o Zachariah Fooks. John m. Addie, d/o William G. Weber, in Norfolk, VA, and had six children: Inez A., d. at three; Lottie U., Mrs. J. M. King, of Balt.; Sallie W., d. at six months; William W., in silk business; Susie M. and J. Maurice. Addie, b. in Maine; William Weber, provost-marshall of Norfolk. Member of the Grand Army of the Republic, the Royal Arcanum, the Knights of Pythias. A Republican. Belongs to Grace Methodist Episcopal Church. Warden of Baltimore city jail.

846. PINKNEY L. DAVIS, M. D. - b. 5 Apr. 1860 in Carroll Co., MD, s/o Henry S. and Drusilla (Dade) Davis. Father, b. in 1808 in what is now Carroll Co., MD, member of state legislature, a

Democrat, farmer, member of the Baptist Church, d. in 1885.
Paternal grandparents, Thomas and Amelia (Shipley) Davis, he of
Frederick Co. and she of Howard Co., MD. Other children of
Thomas and Amelia Davis: Elizabeth and Samuel, twins, d.,
unmarried; George, of Balt., now eighty-nine, father of Dr.
Charles Davis of Balt.; and Dr. Frank, d. in St. Joseph, MO.
Mother, now seventy-six, d/o Col. Robert Townsend Dade, of Montgomery
Co., MD. Henry and Drusilla had eight children: three d.
in infancy; George, farmer, school examiner of Carroll Co.; Henry
S., in commission business in Balitmore with cousin, Louis W.
Davis; Harvey, owns much property in Richmond Co., VA; and Ruth
Amelia, w/o Christopher Raborg, who works for the Merchants and
Miners' Transportation Company, of Balt. Subject m. Florence,
d/o James H. Steele, of Carroll Co., in 1882, and had three
children, Henry, Emily and Florence. Florence, b. 13 Aug. 1858,
an Episcopalian, d. 29 1885, at twenty-seven. Subject m. (2)
Grace, d/o Richard Dorsey Armstrong, in 1889, and had one son,
Dorsey. A Democrat. Physician at No. 913 North Fulton avenue.

847. FRANK C. BRESSLER, M. D. - b. in 1859 in New York City, s/o
Frank Bressler. Grandfather, well-to-do citizen of Bavaria,
Germany. Father, b. in Frankenthal, Bavaria, came to America,
locating in New York, member of the Grand Army of the Republic,
d. at Wilkes Barre, PA, at fifty-nine. Mother, Miss Kohl, of
Weisenheim, Germany, d. in 1862, leaving two children: Frank C.,
three years of age; and Mrs. Lena Gregory, of Athens, PA. Father
m. (2) Miss Elizabeth Reudelhuber, of Lambsheim, Bavaria, and had
one son, Melvin, of Athens, PA. Frank m. Miss Emma A., d/o J. G.
Gehring, Sr., in Balt., and had one child, Mary Gertrude. Emma,
b. in Balt.; J. G. Gehring, prominent jeweler. Member of the
Arcana Lodge No. 110, A.F.&A.M., the Reform League of Baltimore,
the Civil Service Reform Association, the Medical and Chirurgical
Faculty of Maryland, the Clinical Society, and the Baltimore
Medical and Surgical Society. Physician in East Balt.

848. GEORGE R. WILLIS - b. 31 Oct. 1851 in Balt., s/o John E.
and Virginia (Green) Willis. Paternal grandfather, Levin N.
Willis, farmer, on the eastern shore, moved to Frederick Co.
Father, b. 8 Aug. 1826 in Balt., Balt. merchant, a Democrat, d.
in 1871. Mother, descendant of English ancestors who were among
the very early settlers of MD, lives with George R. Maternal
grandfather, Josias Green, business man of Balt. George m. Miss
Mary, d/o Col. Joseph Haskins, in 1881, and had two children,
Luther M. R. and Mary. A Mason. A Democrat. Attorney-at-law at
No. 213 Courtland street.

849. WALTER WALTON WHITE, M. D. - b. 5 Jun. 1843 in Oxford,
England, s/o John W. and Ann White. Descended from two old and
honored families of the old world, the Whites of English and the
Waltons of Scotch origin. Father, mother and five children,
sailed on the John A. Westervelt, landed in New York, settled in
Balt. Father, manufacturer of furniture, d. at sixty-two.
Mother, d. at eighty-three. John and Ann, Episcopalians, had
five children: John Walton, physician of Glyndon, Balt. Co.; Ann
W., d. in Balt.; Walter Walton; Mrs. Harriet M. Blankfard, of

Balt.; and Mary A., d. in Balt. Walter m. Elizabeth Grace, d/o Arthur Ewens, and had three children: Walter Walton, Jr., physician in Balt.; William Kelso, student; and Grace E., student. Elizabeth, b. in Wales; Arthur Ewens, b. in England. Member of the Masons, the Medical and Surgical Society of East Baltimore, the Baltimore Medical Society and the Medical and Chirurgical faculty of Maryland. A Democrat. Physician and surgeon at No. 1101 North Broadway.

850. CAPT. OSWALD T. WEST - b. 23 Sep. 1856 in Balt. Oswald m. Miss Minnie Shafer, of Balt., and had three children: John R., Willie H. and Louisa M. Member of the St. John's Lodge No. 34, A.F.&A.M., of Balt. and the Independent Order of American Mechanics. A Democrat. Belongs to the Lutheran Church. Commander of the dredge Baltimore, of the Baltimore Dredging Company.

INDEX

ABBOTT Isabel Marion 85
  John 85
ABEL Edwin F. 176
  Elizabeth 176
ABELL Arunah S. 4
  Edwin Franklin 4
  George William 4
  Susie 9
  Walter Robert 4
ABERCROMBIE David T. 194
  Elizabeth 194
  Harry Netherclift 194
  John 194
  John R. 194
ABEY Joseph W. 11
  Sarah Louise 11
ABRAHAM Mary 145
ABURN Charles 101
  Melvina 101
ACKLER Hugh H. 90
  Louise T. 90
  Margaret A. 90
  Mary 90
  Robert 90
  William F. 90
ACTION Elizabeth 187
ADAIR Martha 193
ADAMS Belle W. 199
  John Q. 199
  Margaret 170
  Thomas 170
ADLER Virginia 121
ADY Annie E. 67
  Benjamin W. 67
  Bessie 67
  Caroline 67
  Cassandra M. 67
  Christiana 67
  Elizabeth 67
  Francis 66
  Francis H. 67
  Francis M. 67
  Henrietta 67
  Jennie M. 67
  Laura 67
  Solomon 66
  William H. 67
AHERN Regina 118
AINSLIE Jane Patterson 125
  Peter 125
AIREY Annie 50
  George 50
AITKEN Alexander 141
  Annette 141

AKEHURST Amanda 89
  Charles 89
  David 89
  Edward 89
  Elizabeth 89
  Emily 89
  Emma 89
  George W. T. 89
  Henry 89
  James 89
  Jane 189
  Louisa 89
  Mary 89
  Mary J. 89
ALBERT Augustus James 106
  Jennie 106
  Martha Jane 106
  Melinda 62
ALBEY Besty A. 129
  Judge 129
ALDRICH Elizabeth W. 192
  Herman D. 192
ALDRIDGE Elizabeth 91
  Hattie 47
  John 91
  Julia 113
ALER Eliza J. 105
  Elizabeth 105
  George F. 105
  George Washington 105
  John M. 105
  Pauline 105
  Reuben A. 105
  Roxana 105
ALEXANDER Amanda 69
ALFORD Mary 40
  William 40
ALGER James 30
  Sallie 30
ALGERE George 96
  Henry 96
  Kate 96
  Mary 96
ALGIRE Henry 84
  Nancy 84
ALLEN Amanda 51
  Amy 34
  Ann 51
  Annie 51
  Catherine 51, 157
  Charles 51
  Elizabeth 82, 137
  Elizabeth Ann 11

  George 51, 137
  Herschel 34
  Hugh 11
  James 11, 51
  John 158
  Louis 34
  Maria 51
  Mary A. 158
  Matilda 51
  Newton D. R. 34
  Patience 139
  Peter 34
  Robert 34
  Robert William 11
  Rosa 34
  Samuel 51
  Sarah 34, 51, 82
  Sarah Ruth 34
  Solomon Columbus 51
  Wendell Dewitt 34
  William 51
ALLISON Amy 153
  Edgar 153
  Elizabeth Buchanan 192
  Ella 153
  Frank 153
  James 153
  James S. 152, 153
  Lillian 153
  Margaretta L. 153
  Mary 153
  Richard T. 192
ALMOCK Catherine 93
ALMOND Audry 139
  Family 138
  William 139
ALMONY Albert 33
  Albert J. B. 32
  Catherine 32
  Charles 32
  Eliza 32
  Ephraim B. 32
  Franklin T. 32
  Harriet 59
  Henry D. 32
  John 32
  John W. 32
  Kezia 32
  William 33
  William H. 32
ALMY Annis 139
  Audry 139
  Captain W. C. 138
  Christopher 139
  Deborah 139

INDEX

Eliza 139
Elizabeth 139
Frances 138, 139
Holder 138, 139
Hope 139
Joseph 139
Patience 139
Sarah 139
William 139
ALOFF Bernadena 103
Catherine 103
Elizabeth B. 103
Joseph 103
Margaret 103
Mary 103
Pelina 103
Wentling 103
ALQUIST Batel 147
Olivia 147
ALTEMUS Hannah 197
Henry 197
ALTVATER Ann 50
Annie 50
Baruch 50
Cassandra 50
Edward 50
Edward Williams 50
Frances 50
Garrett 50
George Barney 50
John 50
John H. 50
Louisa 50
May Josephine 50
Morris 50
AMBROSE Annie 187
AMEY Rosa 114
William 114
AMOS Anna R. 29
Benjamin F. 29
Charles 29
Eliza A. 29
George W. 29
Izah 29
John W. 29
Susan 49
William 29
AMOSS Alfred P. 185
Bessie 185
Bessie C. 185
Elizabeth B. 185
Marguerite 185
Minnie b. 185
Thomas P. 185
ANDERSON Abbie 43
Charles E. 43

Cornelia M. 175
Elizabeth 43, 47
Elizabeth B. 43
Fannie 128
George Lucas 47
George O. 43
Isaac 43
Isaac C. 43
Isaac T. 43
James H. 43
Jesse E. 43
John 174
John D. 43
John F. 43
John I. 43
Julia E. 156
Laura 43
Lavinia 47
Lydia E. 43
Mary 28, 43
Miss 63
Morris W. 43
Robert 43
Sargeant H. 43
Susanna 174, 175
William 43, 174
William H. H. 174, 175
William T. 43
ANDRE Delaware Clayton 153
James R. 153
Loma M. 153
Margaret 153
William E. 153
ANDREWS Edmund 199
Edith B. 202
Sarah 78
ANNISON Eliza 94, 97
John 94
ANTHEY Lavina 46
Samuel 46
ARDMAN Mary A. 65
ARMACOST Adam 104
Amos 198
Amos H. 104
Carrie 68
Edna Pear 68
Elijah 104
Elizabeth 49, 68, 198
Emory 68
George 104
Georgia A. 104
Grace 68
James G. 128

Janey A. 105
John 105
John Adam 104
Johnnie 68
Kate S. 128
Keziah 104
Lissie 68
Lucinda 104
Margaret 104, 198
Mary E. 104
Mary E. A. 154
Melchor 68
Rachel 89
Susan 104
Susanna 104
Thomas 68
William M. 68
ARMITAGE Abigail Lyal 201
ARMOUR David 183
Lydia 183
Mary 183
ARMSTRONG C. V. 104
Frederick 20
Grace 207
Harriet 20
J. W. 104
Mary A. 82
Richard Dorsey 207
Sarah 26
ARNOLD Charlotte 135
Elizabeth 163
Jane 135
William 135
ASCUE Ellen 111
ASHLEY James 127
Mary 127
ASHTON Elizabeth 178
Ellen 178
Fannie 87
Joseph 178
ASSHETON Eleanor 102
Eleanor L. 102
Elizabeth 102
Evelyn 102
Juliet 102
Ronald 102
Walter 102
William 102
William Herbert 102
ATHINGTON Elizabeth 37
ATKINSON A. C. 85
A. S. 95
Captain 191
Frieda 96
Kate 95

INDEX

Margaret 191
W. G. 95
AULD Dawson 108
　Elizabeth 108
　Susan 108
AULL Jacob H. 185
　Mary J. 185
AULTHER Jacob 61
　Loretta 61
　William 61
AYLER Henry 15
　Sarah 15
AYRES Amanda 74

BACHMAN Ann 108
BACK George W. 188
BACKMAN Rachel 72
BACON Anna M. 165
　George C. 165
　John 139, 165
　John Dosh 165
　Lewis M. 139, 165
　Martin 165
　Pamela F. 165
　Pamelia F. 139
BADEN Elizabeth 85
　J. A. 85
　Jeremiah 85
　Richard 85
　Maria C. 85
BAGLEY Clara A. 59
　Dr. 59
　John O. 59
BAILEY A. Hamilton 26
　Addie 206
　Ann 206
　Anthony 158
　Charles W. 158
　Eliza 158
　George W. 33
　Harriet 158
　Ida 62
　Inez A. 206
　J. Maurice 206
　John 206
　John R. 206
　Lottie U. 206
　Margaret 26
　Martha 158
　May 107
　Nathaniel 158
　Salie W. 206
　Sarah A. 33
　Susie M. 206
　Thomas 62

William 206
William W. 206
BAKER Barbara 55
　Barnabas 139
　Charlotte 196
　Edward 3
　Frances 138, 139
　Hester Ann 65
　Isaiah 65
　Jane 3
　Jeremiah 196
　Keturah 88
　Mary 196
　Mary A. 196
　Rebecca 196, 203, 204
　Richard 204
BALARD Barbara 28
　George W. 28
BALDWIN Abraham S. 55, 56, 58
　Alice 56
　Amy 58
　Blanche 56
　Charles 58
　Charles A. 58
　Charles W. 51
　Charlotte 55, 58
　Clarence 56
　Eleanor L. 70
　Elizabeth 51, 56
　Ella L. 51
　Emma 56
　Harry Streett 58
　Harry W. 58
　Ida J. 51
　J. Morris 51
　James 51, 55, 58
　James W. 51
　John 51, 55, 58
　John R. 58
　John S. 56, 58
　Leon 58
　Lottie 58
　Margaret E. 142
　Martha E. 56, 58
　martha Elizabeth 56
　Mary 58
　Mary A. 51
　Mary E. 56, 58
　Mary Margaret 58
　Olivia 56
　R. Cora 58
　Rachael 80
　Rachel C. 58
　Rachel E. 58

Samuel 51
Sarah E. 51
Silas 51, 55, 56, 58
Silas E. 58
Thomas 56, 58
Thomas C. 58
William 51, 55, 58
BALL Sallie 30
BALLARD Ada 39
　Donald Dunan 39
　Edwin K. 39
　Wilson Turner 39
BALLINGHAM Anna 36
BALLINGSMAT Ida 155
BALTES Ferdinand 30
　Isabella 30
BAMBER Eliza Jane 44
BANAM Maria 116
BANGS Laura V. 195
BANKARD Henrietta 28
　John 28
BANKERD Adelia V. 186
BANKS Annie 136
　Daniel B. 136
　Matilda 183
　Robert T. 20
BARABASZ Cecilia 3
　John 3
　Julia 3
　Mary 3
　Mieczyslaw 3
　Stephanie 3
BARBER Lizzie 26
　Mary M. 69
　Philip 26
BARBOUR James 182
BARKELY Anna R. 166
　Edwin 166
　George L. 166
　Hannah C. 166
　Laura J. 166
　Marcus C. 166
BARKER Anna B. 125
　Ruth 82
BARNES Alice Lynn 101
　Charles E. 202
　Clara 101
　Ellen A. 31
　Emma K. 202
　Flossie M. 101
　Hanson P. 202
　Hellen Lynn 101
　Henrietta 101
　Jacob S. 202
　Janet K. 202

211

INDEX

John 101, 197
Judge 142
Katherine A. 202
Lillian L. 202
Mamie 101
Martha E. 202
Mary 197, 198
Mary Clarissa 197
Mary Clarissa Bond 197
Miss 142
Nancy 101
Nettie 101
Oneida 41
Richard 198
Ruth C. 68
William 68
William L. 31
William Lenos 202
William R. 202
William W. 101
BARNETT George 90, 91
Hannah 90
BAROOH Joseph 99
Mary 99
BARR Barbara Emma 205
BARRINGTON Catherine 192
Frank T. 192
John 192
Mary W. 192
BARROLL Ann Ellen 137
Elizabeth 137
Frederick 137
James W. 137
BARRON Andrew 53
Catherine 53
Edward F. 53
Edward T. 53
Eliza C. 50
Elizabeth Ann 53
Elizabeth M. 53
Helen 53
John 53
John T. 53
Julia 50
Julian Paul 53
Margaret 53
Marie 53
Mary 53
Prescott 50
Thomas 53
Thomas Francis 53
William Julian P. 53
BARRY Sally Jennie 179
BARTLESON Caroline 87
William 87

BARTLETT Daniel Webster 12
Florence E. 44
John M. 145
John Milton 145
John W. 44
Jonathan P. 145
Joseph T. 145
Mary 145
Rebecca T. 145
Sallie A. 145
Sarah Ann 145
Sarah Augusta 12
William E. 145
BARTON Asa 92
Captain 92
Elizabeth 92
Mary J. 141
BARTOW Mary A. 195
BATES Sarah 72
BATTENFIELD Daniel 114
Lizzie 114
BATTY Anna C. 3
Annie C. 130
Annie M. 130
Ella M. 130
George 130
George J. 130
J. F. 130
Joseph 3
Joseph W. 130
Walter L. 130
BATZ Augusta 154
Bertha 154
Elizabeth 154
Henry 154
Hilda 154
Louisa 154
Philip 154
Philip Daniel 154
Philipine 154
Valentine 154
William 154
BAUER Anna Elizabeth 45
Augusta 189
Barbara 14
Frederick 189
George D. 189
John Frederick 189
Marie 189
Mary Louisa 189
BAUM Albert G. 180
Anna 180
Barbara 180
Caroline 46

Charles 180
Charles L. 180
Edward 180
Frederick Wilhelm 180
John 180
Katie 180
Mary E. 180
Mattie A. 180
Minnie 180
Peter 46
Rose 180
BAUMANN Margaret Gertrude 18
BAUMGARTNER Elizabeth 45
BAXLEY Eliza 153
Ella 179
Francis 153
Mary 153
BAXTER Sarah 23
BAYARD Ethel 106
BAYLEY Ellen 46
Levi 46
BAYLOR Susan 183
William 183
BAYLY Eunice Butler 39
John Frederick 39
Marcus B. 39
Nathan Rogers 39
BAYNE Rebecca 37
BAYNES Alice P. 87
Joseph 87
Sarah 87
BEACHAM George 103
Margaret 103
BEAL Alexander 143, 144
Charles B. 143, 144
Ellen 144
Harry 144
Lindsey 144
Nell 144
Sallie 144
BEALL Margaret 103
BEANS Edward 153
Margaretta L. 153
BEATTY Elizabeth 175
Elizabeth P. 176
James 175
Margaret 196
BECK Ann Steener 102
Annie M. 153
Catherine 188
Charles R. 153
Edward L. 127
Elijah 127
Elizabeth 127

INDEX

Lemuel 127
Margaret 127
Mary 127
William 127
William R. 127
BECKER Erna 96
BECKETT John 47
Mary H. 47
BECKLEY Elizabeth 91
Margaret 88
BEDFORD Ann 40
BEHLER Ketherine 33
BEIHLER Barbara 193
BELL Eliza 32
 Eliza Ann 115
 Elizabeth 69
 Frederick 112
 George 88
 Hester 88
 John 61
 Margaret A. 61
 Martha 88
 Mary 112
 Percy B. 88
 Susan 110
 Thomas 69
 William A. 88
 William Morris 88
BELT Adeline 45
 Alva G. 93
 Amos 93
 Bayard O. 93
 Caroline 93
 Catherine 93
 Charles 93
 Charles E. 114
 Darby 93
 Denton O. 93
 Elijah 93
 Ephraim 93
 George W. 93
 Goldo F. 93
 Henry E. 93
 Irene 114
 Jackson 93
 John 93
 Keziah Cordelia 93
 Leonard 93, 114
 Lizzie 114
 Mary F. 93
 Mary J. 93
 Mary W. 93
 Nolan E. 93
 Sarah A. 114
 Thomas 93

Truman 45
Vesta I. 93
William 93
BENDER Frances 180
 George 168
 John 180
 Major 168
 Mary E. 168
BENDLER Lizzie 91
 Minnie 91
 Sophia 91
 William H. 91
BENNER Charles H. 204
 Ella 204
BENNETT Charlotte 42
 George W. 140
 Georgia C. 140
 Henry 159
 Martha E. 159
BENSON Alijah 96
 Annie G. 101
 Annie N. 154
 Benjamin R. 154
 Beulah M. 154
 Carroll P. 154
 Clarence I. 154
 Cornelia 188
 Cullom Stewart 154
 E. Belle 101
 Edna Luella 154
 Edward Hayes 154
 Elijah 100, 108
 Elijah T. 97, 188
 Ella E. 188
 Emory W. 154
 Helen Levering 154
 Ida V. 101
 Jacob T. 188
 James 100
 Jesse 89
 John W. 100
 Joseph K. 12
 Joshua E. 154
 Joshua F. 100
 Joshua L. 154
 Katie Cobert 154
 Lillian 101
 Margaret 96, 100
 Mary E. A. 154
 Mattie E. 154
 Melchor A. 100
 Peggy 100
 R. Seymour 101
 Rachel J. 154
 Rebecca 97, 188

Ruth A. 89
Sylvania 100
BERRIDGE John 3
 Mary A. 3
BERRY Anne F. 87
 Benjamin 170
 Eleanor Bowie 170
 Jasper M. 168
 John 170
 John F. 87
 Mary 52
 Minnie 168
 Mrs. N. O. 15
 Sallie C. 199
 Susan L. 170
 William I. 199
BERRYMAN William M. 206
BESS James H. 6
BETTS Dr. B. F. 112
 Lucy C. 77, 112
 Prof. B. F. 77
BETZOLD Barbara 24
 George A. 24
 Michael 24
BEVAN Julia A. 189
 Thomas H. 190
BEVANS Amanda 89
 Family 135
BEYER Charles A. 56
 George L. 56
 Howard W. 56
 Marguerite A. 56
 Mary A. 56
 Mary E. 56
 Mary Ethel 56
 Sarah R. 56
 William L. 56
BIBBY James 146
 Susie 146
BICKINGHAM Eliza A. 43
BIDDISON Abram 26
 Alice 26, 144
 Benjamin 144
 Bessie 26
 Clara 144
 Edna Margaret 173
 Elizabeth Ann 144, 157
 Emma Sophia 173
 Eva 26
 Florence 144
 George Thomas 144, 157
 Helen 26
 John S. 26
 Julia 26
 Lizzie 26

213

INDEX

Martha 26
Mary 26
Mary Ellen 144
Rebecca 144
Samuel J. 144
Stella 26
Susan 26
Susanna 26
Temperance Rebecca 144, 156
Thomas C. 26, 173
William 26
BIDEN Edward 12
Eugenia M. 12
BIEDLER A. J. 190
Ambrose 190
Anna M. 190
Ashely L. 190
Charles E. 190
Frank R. 190
Hampson H. 190
Sarah E. 190
William T. 190
BIEN Annie 156
Arthur 156
Barbara 156
Conrad 156
Eva 156
Jennie 20
John 156
Lizzie 156
Maggie 156
Margaret 156
BIGERMAN John 103
Pelina 103
BILLINGSLEY Elizabeth 65
Ella 65
Ruth C. 117
William 65
BING Caroline 33
Catherine 45
Conrad 33
George J. 33
Katie 33
Lizzie 33
Mary 33
Sophia 33
BINGHAM Ann Sophia 15
Charles 15
BIRD Clark 102
Eleanor L. 102
Harold 102
Harold Assheton 102
Helen Wilson 102

BIRT John 25
Mary 25
BISHOP Susie Ann 37
BISSETT Rosetta 201
Thomas 201
BISSON Cecelia V. 4
William 3
BITTING Anna M. 190
William C. 190
BIXLER Mary C. 97
BLACKBURN Mildred 77
BLACKMAN Susan 169
BLADES Elizabeth 127
Thomas 127
BLAKENEY Abel 30
Albert A. 30
John D. 30
John W. 30
Sarah 30
BLAND Benjamin F. 49
C. T. 49
Jack 11
James E. 49
John R. 49
Louisa A. 49
Lucy M. 49
Mary Ann 49
Mary C. 49
Mary O. 49
Robert 49
Thomas Jackson 49
Virginia B. 49
William Boyd 49
William F. 49
BLANKFARD Harriet M. 207
BLOCK Charles E. 150
Edward 150
Emily D. 150
Marie R. 150
Mary 150
William H. 150
BLOOM David 62
Edith 62
Emma 62
Ida 62
Isaac 62
Jennie 62
Maggie M. 62
Mary 62
Melinda 62
Millard P. 62
Thomas 62
Thomas G. 62

BLOUNT Elizabeth Mutter 22
Thomas H. 22
BLUBAUGH Mary A. 104
BLUNT Agnus 34
Albert S. 34
Alexander W. 34
Amanda 34, 132
Attwood 34, 132
Bradley T. D. 34
Eleanor 34
Elizabeth 34
Harriet W. 34
Maria 34
Samuel 34
Sarah 34
William 34
BOAL Elizabeth I. 54
George Y. 54
BODDY Ann 82
BOEDEN Hope 139
BOGELMAN Elizabeth 161
BOGGS Henry C. 164
Isaac 164
Mary P. 164
Sarah A. 164
BOHANNON Alice 125
Anna B. 125
Christopher A. 125
Columbia 125
Cornelius 125
Eliza 125
Jane Patterson 125
Joseph 125
Joseph Edgar 125
Kate 125
W. J. 125
Wickliffe J. 125
BOISSEAU Annie A. 63
BOKLAGE Bernadena 103
BOLINGER Annie 31
BOLTZ Maggie 154
BOMME Mollie 60
BOND Anniel L. 44
Benedict 164
Bertie 43
Caroline V. 43
Charles C. 43
Charlotte 93
Eda E. 58
Edward 43, 78
Elizabeth 64, 93
Emma 43
Eugene 43
Florence E. 43

INDEX

George 78
George Morris 102
Harriet 78
Harry 93
Irving Monroe 44
Jane E. 78
Jemima 78
John R. 78
Joseph 43, 107
Josephine 164
Josiah 43
Lottie A. 78
Margaret 102
Mary 99, 107
Mary Jane 78
Mary L. 43
Mollie C. R. 78
Porter Terry 93
Ross 78
Sadie 43
Sallie 43
Sarah 106
Smith B. 78
Theresa 93
Virrena J. 78
Walter 44
William 44, 93, 99
William C. 93
William D. 43, 44
William Sewell 44
William T. 58
BONOVEL Elizabeth 69
BONSAW Ann Maria 61
John 61
BOON Elizabeth 107
Sarah R. 149
BOONE Elizabeth A. 142
William M. 151
BOOTH Clara B. 38
Edward M. 38
Eliza 38, 47
Emma A. 38
Harry W. 38
J. Albert 38
John 38
John G. 38, 47
Katherine 38
Mary M. 38
Rachel 38
Robert 38
Walter 38
Walter F. 38
William 38
BORDLEY Amelia 185
Mary 185
William C. 185

BOSLEY Amon 36, 184
Ann Elizabeth 184
Arthur L. 185
Beatrice 185
Bertha 55
Bettie 47, 178
Catherine E. 60
Catherine Elizabeth 60
Charles 184
Daniel 7, 22, 54, 119
Daniel W. 54, 55
Dorcas A. 186
E. Sophia 184
E. Stanton 119
Edgar Winthrop 119
Eleanor G. 54
Elizabeth 119
Elizabeth M. 184
George 119
Georgie 119
Georgie Price 119
Grafton Marsh 184
James 36, 184
James C. 47
James Walter 184
John 178, 184
John A. 60
John G. 36
John H. 119
Joseph 54, 184
Josephine 55
Joshua G. 54, 55
Joshua M. 184
Laura Talbott 36
M. Louisa 54
M. Rebecca 55
Marguerite 185
Martha 54
Mary Ann 7
Mary E. 55
Mary Elizabeth 36
Mary Parker 119
May A. 185
Nicholas M. 184
Orville Mason 119
Penelope 184
Rebecca 184
Samuel Parker 119
Sarah 119, 184
T. Ellen 36
Temperance 64, 184
Temperance Ellen 184
Thomas C. 54
Walter 184

William 60, 184, 186
Zebulon 119
BOSTON Esther 23
BOSWELL Sallie 71
Susie 20
Thomas 20
Thomas T. 71
BOTELER Sarah 168
BOULDIN Alexander J. 14
Alexina 14
Arianna 14
BOUNDS George W. 126
Levin 135
Minnie 126
Sarah A. 32
Virginia 135
BOWEN --- 61
Alexander P. 37
Alice E. 57
Ann Maria 57, 61
Annette Stitt 57
Benjamin 57
Benjamin W. 37
Celia Ann 61
Charles B. 57
Charles Wesley 57
Clara Belle 57
Clara F. 57
Edgar Howard 57
Elijah 37
Elizabeth 37, 45, 61
Elizabeth Marcella 45
Ella 53, 62
Emily 37
Emma 64
Esley 37
Fannie 57
Fernandis 61
Frances 57
George C. 57
George V. 56, 57
Gerand 61
Grace E. 37
Harriet Loretta 62
Henry L. 61
Hettie 92
Ida 57
James 74
James P. 37
John 37
John E. 37
John Franklin 57
John M. 64
John N. 37
John R. 57

215

INDEX

Joseph G. 37
Joseph Gorsuch 57
Josiah S. 45
Julia 37, 57
Laura Isabella 57
Laura V. 57
Levi K. 139
Loretta 61
Mark 53
Martha 45
Martha Ellen 74
Mary 62
Mary Ann 57, 62
Mary Frances 57
Minnie P. 57
Polly 37
Rebecca 37, 45
Rebecca Jemima 57
Robert H. 57
Ruth 37, 61
Ruth Ann 57
Sarah 37
Sarah E. 37
Solomon 37, 61
Sophia 139
Sophronia Helen 37
Temperance 37, 57
Walter 57
Wilks 45
William 37, 57, 61
William Rice 57
BOWIE Ada 98
 Adaline 98
 Amelia 98
 Blanche 98
 Cecelia 98
 Clarence K. 98
 Eleanor 170
 Henry B. 98
 John 170, 175
 Mary 98, 170
 Mary B. 98
 Reginald 98
 Robert A. 98
 Susanna 175
 Walter 98
 Walter William Wims 98
BOWMAN Anna 95
 Anneda 95
 Catherine 95
 Charles 95
 Elwood E. 95
 Henry C. 95
 John 95
 Lula 46

Nannie R. 95
 Sarah 95
BOXLEY Elizabeth A. 22
BOYD Caroline E. 134
 Eliza 175, 190
 Frances 134
 J. J. 134
 James 116
 James H. 175
 James T. 49
 John 49
 Louisa A. 49
 Mary Ann 49
 Mattie 20
 Temperance 116
 William A. 190
 William L. 20
BOYLE Charles Bruce 1
 Daniel Scott 1
 Emily 36
 Henry 1
 John B. 1
 John Brooke 1
 Joseph B. 1
 Junius J. 36
 Norman Bruce 1
BOYSE Lydia 35
 W. W. 35
BRACK Albert 186
 Anita 187
 Caroline 186
 Charles 187
 Charles E. 186
 Edward 187
 Elsie 187
 Ernst 186
 Ferdinand 186
 Frederick 186
 Fredericka 186
 George P. 187
 Henrietta 187
 John Conrad 186
 Louisa 186
 Matilda 186
 Sophia 187
 Wilhelm 186
 William Rudolph 187
BRACKEN Cecilia A. 68
 John 68
BRADDOCK Clarinda 73
 Jesse N. 73
BRADEN Janet 67
BRADFORD Catherine 150
 Susannah 6
BRADY Benjamin F. 57

Bessie 57
 Helen 57
 Jefferson 57
 John W. S. 57
 Margaret 35, 57
 Martha A. 57
 Mary 57
 Mary P. 57
 Samuel 35, 57
 Samuel P. 57
 Thomas S. 57
 Upton S. 57
BRAND Mary 171
BRANFORD Augustine D. 150
 Elizabeth 150
 Lulu 150
 Martha 150
 Thomas 150
BRANNAN Charles H. 149
 Charles H. S. 149
 Clarence W. 149
 Edith 149
 Harry N. 149
 John B. 149
 Maggie 149
 Margaret M. 149
 Martin C. 149
 Sarah R. 149
 William 149
BRANNON Ella 79
 Henry 79
BRASHARES Annie M. 82
 Frank B. 82
BRASHEARS Hannah 13
BRAY Columbia 125
BRAYTON William 120
BRECKENRIDGE Robert J. 21
 Sarah 21
BRENNAN Nellie 122
BRENT Julian 41
 Mary 41
BRESEE Abigail Patterson 48
BRESSLER Elizabeth 207
 Emma A. 207
 Frank 207
 Frank C. 207
 Lena 207
 Mary Gertrude 207
 Melvin 207
BREVITT Catherine 100
 Edwin W. 100
 Elenora I. 100
BRIAN Alexina 30
 James 29, 30

INDEX

Nicholas M. 30
Sallie S. 30
Stansbury 30
BRINKER Jennie M. 67
  Samuel W. 67
BRINKMYER Annie D. 132
BRINTON Alban H. 17
  Clara M. 17
  Mary E. 17
BROCK Beulah 113
  William 113
BROCKETT Cornelia M. 175
  Robert L. 175
BRODIE Agnes 115
  Robert 115
BRODY Abbie 43
  John 43
BROGDEN Margaret 52
BROMWELL Hester 88
  John 88
BROOKE Emme Cathernie 67
  Robert 203
BROOKS Allen G. 110
  Augusta 70
  Benjamin 110
  Charles 56, 110
  Helen 110
  John R. 6
  Landon 110
  Margaret 110
  Mary 56
  Mary P. 110
  Nanie E. 110
  Nanny 46
  Peter 70
  Ruth 56
  Ruth T. 110
  Susanna 167
  William 56, 110
  William C. 46, 110
BROUGHTON Harriett 195
  James 81, 195
BROWN Abel 202
  Abraham 40
  Ada Virginia 161
  Albert M. 62
  Alberta 62
  Alexander 106
  Alexander E. 62
  Andrew 71
  Andrew J. 71
  Ann 169, 193
  Annie S. 28
  B. R. 58
  Benjamin R. 82

Bertha 55
Captain 133
Carrie 133
Charles E. 62
Edward 71
Elias 202
Elisha 84
Elizabeth 40, 84
Ellen 62
Esther A. 46
Fannie Mactier 106
Fletcher S. 62
Frank 202
Garrett 62
George 28, 106
George F. 62
Grace 28
Helen 26, 133
James 161
Jane B. 71
Jane Shields 28
Jennie 71
John 18, 71, 72, 133, 170
John H. 71
Julia 62
Laura H. 187
Luke 46
Margaret 18
Margaret F. 71
Martin W. 133
Mary 58, 62, 71, 84
Mary E. 71
Mary H. 62
Mary L. 28
Mrs. A. D. 60
Nancy 84
Percy Howard 62
Robert P. 28
Robert Patterson 28
Rosa 28
Rosannah 170
Salina 72
Sallie 71
Sarah 84, 139
Sarah C. 28
Septimus 62
Stephen Thomas
Cockney 202
Susan 127
Susan L. B. 82
Susannah D. 193
T. W. 26
Thomas 62, 84
Thomas H. 62

William 193
William H. 62
William J. 84
William Stewart 71
BROWNE Edward 200
  Henry Elliott 68
  Holland Lee 68
  Margaret 68
BROWNING Bertha 205
  Senator 205
BRUMFIELD Georgiana 27
  William 27
BRUMWELL Emma Sarah E. 199
  John Edward 199
BRUNE Maria Frederica 39
  Thomas 39
  Wilhelmina 39
  Wilhelmina Sophia 39
BRUSH Delia A. 79
  Edward N. 78
  Florence 79
  John 79
  Lavinia 79
  Myra 78
  Nathaniel 79
  Nathaniel H. 78
BRUSHER Jeannette 15
  John 15
BRUTON Emma J. 143
  Mr. 143
BRYAN Anna I. 19
  Anna R. 1
  Benjamin A. 1
  Ida M. 1
  J. Frank 1
  Joel 19
  John 1
  Joshua 1
  Martha 92
  Richard 1
  Richard Moffett 1
  Thomas H. 1
BRYANT Alice A. 181
  Allen H. 181
  Charles Harris 181
  Col. J. W. 180
  Howard 180
  Joshua 180
  Linnie T. 180
  Mark 180
  Sarah H. 180
BRYDEN Elizabeth 185
  Henrietta M. 185
  William 185

217

INDEX

BUCHANAN Anna 51
BUCHHEIMER Barbara 166
  John 166
  Margaret 166
BUCHHOLZ Dora 96
  Frederick 96
  Heinrich 96
  Henry 96
  Mina 96
BUCK Carrie 25
  Catherine 141
  Jane A. 143
  Mary Elizabeth 162
  Rebecca 111
BUCKINGHAM Georgiana 70
BUCKLES Alma 66
BUCKLESS William 66
BUCKLEY Ann 60
  Edward 127
  Ella V. 143
  John 142
  John Lee 143
  John T. 142
  Larua M. 127
  Samuel 60
BUCKWATER John 95
  Sarah Ann 95
BUDEKE Anthony Wahl 113
  Clara 113
  George H. 113
  George Milton 113
  Henry 113
  Julia 113
  Wilhelmina 113
BUFFINGTON Abraham 75
  Eliza 74
BUHLER Julia 148
BULL Annie 183
  Edna 183
  Elisha 58
  James H. 183
  Mary 58
  Rachel C. 58
  Stella 179
BURDETT Annie 171
  James 171
BURGAN Eliza 189
  Elizabeth 26
  John L. 26
  Joshua 51
  Mary Elizabetjh 51
BURIER John 75
  Maggie 75
BURK Minnie 91
BURKE Ida 151

BURKHEAD Elizabeth 47
  Samuel 47
BURKINS Mary 175
BURNETT Grace 79
  Helen 79
  Joseph P. 79
  Lizzie 79
  Mary M. 79
  Ruth 133
  Solomon 79
BURNHAM Edith M. 134
  John B. 134
  Virginia 134
BURNS Bridget 73
  Clara 130
  Thomas 42
  William F. 130
BURROUGHS Mary J. 27
  William F. 27
BURROWS Ezra 163
BURTON Amelia 143
  C. Owen 67
  Charles 68
  Edmond A. 67
  Eliza 68
  Eliza R. 67, 68
  Elizabeth 55
  Ellen 67
  George Henry 68
  Harry 67
  Horatio 67
  James 67, 68
  James A. 67
  James Woolf 68
  John 64, 67, 68
  John Eugene 68
  John W. 67
  Mary 64
  Oliver 67
  Robert 68
  Sarah Elizabeth 74
  Sarah J. 67
  Thomas 74
  Uriah 67
  William 143
BURWELL Elizabeth 9
  Nathaniel 9
BUSCH Susanna 155
BUSEY Anna 51
  Clarence 165
  Mary 165
BUSH McLane 64
  Zipporah A. 64
BUSHEY Clara 128
  Florence 129

  Lena 128
  Mary 128
  R. H. 128
  Rachel 128
  Simon 128
BUSHIA Family 128
BUSHNELL Ella 183
  John 183
  John E. 183
  Margaret 183
BUSSEY Anna V. 124
  Bennet F. 124
  Bennete F. 124
  Charles R. 124
  Clement 51, 124
  Dr. B. F. 55
  Fannie Julia 124
  Henry Greene 124
  Mary 51
  Mary R. 124
  Rachel A. 124
  Robert H. 124
  Sallie E. 124
  Thomas C. 55, 124
BUSSIE August 112
  Lizzie 112
BUTLER Alford 39, 40
  Beulah 149
  Elizabeth 40
  Eunice 39
  Hannah 40
  John 67, 107
  Marcella 106
  Maria Frederica 39
  Mary 40, 170
  Mary M. 75
  Mercy 40
  Ormond 40
  Peter 40
  Samuel 39
  Sarah 67, 149
  Thomas M. 149
BUXTON Jane 23
  John H. 23
BYE Albert 159
  Amos 159
  Clara 159
  Clarence 159
  Emma 159
  Enoch 159
  Frederick R. 159
  Henry 159
  Howard 159
  Kiah 159
  Lillie 159

INDEX

Martha E. 159
Mortimer 159
Roberta 159
Sarah 159
BYERLY Cornelia 188
BYRNE Dr. B. J. 176
Laura R. 176

CABLE Mrs. 80
CADWALLANDER Elizabeth 43
CAIN John 142
John J. 142
Kate 142
Mary 142
CAIRNES Anna 161
C. F. 161
Catharine 161
Frank 11
George 161
George H. 161
Isaac H. 161
Mary V. 161
Robert T. 161
CALBFLEISH Margaret 41
CALDWELL (Colville) Adele 204
Alexis 204
Caroline 203
Catherine 203
David 203
Edgar Calhoun 204
Elizabeth 204
Ella 204
Gertrude 204
Jabez 203
James 203, 204
John 203
John J. 203
Jonathan 203
Joseph 203
Leonora 204
Marianne 204
Maud Worthington 204
Rebecca 203, 204
Richard Baker 204
Ridgely Love 204
Virginia 204
CALLIS Anna 110
Charles 110
Daniel 110
George 110
Harry 110
James 110
James H. 110
Susan 110
Thomas 110

CALLOWAY James B. 150
Martha 150
CALTON Edward Wade 102
Evelyn 102
CAMERON Daniel W. 76
Elizabeth 76
Evaline 76
George H. 76
Hugh 76
James 76
Mary 76
Sarah 76
William 76
CAMPBELL Ada 168
Alexander Spotswood 168, 169
Annie 112, 165
Bruce Spotswood 169
Charles 169
Dougald 169
Dougall 204
Duncan 169
Edward S. 77, 112
Elizabeth 78
Ella 165
Florence 169
Florence Susan 169
Harry Guy 169
Harry Tyler 168, 169
Hugh 165, 169
James 54, 165
James B. 204
John 54, 112, 165, 169, 204
John Wilson 168
Josephine Horner 169
Maggie 165
Margaret 10
Marion 54
Martha E. 204
Martha M. 165
Mary 8, 156, 165
Mary Ann 165
Mary Ann Tyler 168
Mary Horner 168
Mary W. 77, 112
Mildred Moore 169
Nancy 72, 165
Robert 165, 169
Robert H. 204
Robert Richard 169
Samuel 204
Sarah 21
Thomas 156, 165
William 165
William Horner 169

CANNON Bartina 50
Bertha M. 50
Laura 143
William 143
CARBACK Annie 153
Cassie 153
Elisha 153
Elizabeth 148, 153, 155
Elizabeth Ann 153
John 136, 148, 153
John Wesley 153
Temperance 136
CARL Louisa 137
Mary 39
William 137
CARLIN Maria E. 74
CARLISS Mary 2
CARLTON Dovie 77
William A. 77
CARMADY Isabella V. 46
CARMAN Carrie May 29
Clarence Grafton 29
Elisha 29
Elizabeth 29
Harry Lee 29
Ida 29
Perry 29
Roy R. 29
Stanley C. 29
William H. 29
CARR Amelia 138
Dabney 10
John 84, 138
John J. 84
Julia 84
Lorenia 186
Mary 84
Robert 84
Sarah 84
William 186
CARROLL Bridget 138
Captain 37
Charles R. 42
Daniel 176
Elizabeth 175, 176
Elizabeth H. 106
Henry 106
John 138
Margaret 106
Mary 42
Ruth 37, 61
Sarah Jane 106
Susanna 152
CARSON Captain J. W. 158
Catherine 158

INDEX

CARSWELL H. Charlotte 181
  John Scott 181
  Lockhart Scott 181
  Walter 181
  Walter Scott 181
CARTER Allen L. 77
  Carrie 77
  Cecelia 77
  Desman 77
  George 36
  Julia Ann 167
  Kate H. 36
  Mary 80
  Mary A. 56
CARUTHER I.H. 56
  Mollie 56
CARVER Annie M. 106
  Joseph 106
CARY Anne 9
  Elizabeth 184
  Miles 184
  Wilson 9
CASPAR Bauer 14
CASSIDY Bernard 144, 145
  Catherine 144, 145
  Charles B. 145
  Francis 145
  Joseph H. 145
  Margaret 145
CATHCART Jemima 56
  Mary 56
  William 56
CATOR Joseph E. 46
  Mary J. 46
CATTANACH James 205
  Maud Isabelle 205
CAUGHY I. H. 201
  Laura B. 201
  Patrick 201
  Sarah Ann 201
CAVE James 133
  Mary 133
  Mary E. 133
CECIL Elizabeth 200
CHABOT Eleanora 4
  G. H. 4
  G. Henry 4
  Julia 4
  Lawrence J. 4
  William H. 4
CHAIMS Cecelia 72
  Charles 72
  Clara 72
  George S. 72
  Lizzie 72

Mary 72
Morris 72
Rachel 72
Sadie 72
CHAMBERLAIN Mary 61
CHAMELON Susanna S. 16
CHANCE Clara G. 195
  Elizabeth 195
  Ethel G. 195
  Laura V. 195
  Levin 195
  Mary 195
  Mary A. 195
  Spencer 195
  Theodore Peterson 195
  William 195
  Willie R. 195
CHANEY Celone 74
CHANT Louis 20
  Mary 20
CHAPMAN Christopher 136
  Elizabeth 136
  General A. A. 72
  Joseph R. 77
  Mary A. 72
  May Josephine 50
  Rose B. 77
  Walter 50
CHARLES Allie 134
  James H. 134
  James L. 134
  Mary E. 134
  Michael 134
  Samuel 134
  William Lawrence 134
CHASE A. B. 26
  Ellen 26
CHASON Mary M. 79
CHENNOWORTH Lillie R. 22
CHENOWETH Absalom B. 111
  Amy 111
  Arthur 111
  David 111
  Edna 111
  Elizabeth 55
  Ellen 111
  George 111
  Harriet 111
  Horace 111
  Jemima 111
  John 111
  Joshua 111
  Louis N. 111

Mary 111
Mary Florence 111
Priscilla 55
Richard 55, 111
Rixton 111
Robert 111
Sarah E. 111
William 111
CHENOWITH Ann R. 92
  Richard 92
CHESGREEN Eliza 23
  William 23
CHESTNUE Calvin 5
  W. Calvin 5
CHILCOAT Ada 39
  Anna 39
  Aquilla 39
  Edward 39
  Elizabeth 39, 56
  Ella 39
  Ensor 56
  George 39
  George B. 56
  George R. 110
  James 56
  John 56
  Julia 56
  Louis 39
  Mary 39, 56
  Matilda 39
  Mollie 56
  Rachel 39
  Ruth 56
  Ruth T. 110
  Theodore 39
  Thomas 56
  William 39
CHILD Mary W. 107
  Robert D. 107
CHITTENER Annie 84
  Elizabeth 84
  Thomas 84
CHIVERAL Emma Jane 45
CHOATE Ann J. 160
  Anna Mabel 160
  Edward 160
  Edward S. 160
  Edward Stephen 160
  Georgia 160
  Georgia Pearse 160
  Laura 33
  Maggie A. 160
  Mary E. 160
  R. P. 33
  Richard 160

INDEX

CHRIST Anna M. 99
CHURCH Elizabeth J. 75
  Jane 76
  John 76
CLAGETT Deborah 170
  Edward 170
  Eleanor 170
  Eleanor Bowie 170
  Margaret 170
  Richard 170
  Thomas 170
CLAGGETT Ellemora Bowie 110
CLAIBORNE Charlotte B. 197
  Ferdinand Leigh 197
  William 197
CLAMPITT Sarah A. 192
CLARK Anne E. 124
  Annie 160
  Archibald 83
  Arietta 12, 13
  Augustus 55
  Clement S. 124
  Elizabeth 47, 151
  Elizabeth B. 185
  Hannah 83
  Harry 83
  Henry 12, 13
  Isaac 83
  J. B. 124
  J. Clement 124
  John Wesley 83
  Joshua P. 83
  Laura J. 29
  Lemuel B. 151
  Mary 7, 13, 124
  Mary J. 55
  Rebecca 203
  Richard 47
  Richard U. 203
  Rosanna 83
  Sallie S. 30
  Thomas S. 185
  Wilbur 83
CLARKE Cecelia G. 71
  George F. 71
  Jane 71
  M. Manly 71
  Martin 71
CLAYPOOLE Adam 200
  Dorothea 200
  James 200
  John 200
  Julia A. 200

CLAYTON Annie 124
  Henry 124
CLEGGIT Mrs. 194
CLEMENS Augustus D. 185
  Augustus Ducas 185
  Henrietta M. 185
CLEMM Virginia 121
CLEMMENCY Charles 3
  Henry 3
  Susan A. 3
CLENDENIN Joseph 2
CLEWELL Anna 130
  Augustus A. 130
  Christina 130
  David 130
  Dorothy 130
  Edward 130
  Frank 130
  John H. 130
  Margaret E. 130
  Mary A. 130
CLIFFORD Alberta 68
  John 68
CLINTON Ann Rebecca 64
  Elijah 64
CLOMAN Annie 78
  Henry 78
CLOUD Benjamin 98
  Isabel 98
  Sarah J. 98
  William 98
COALE Duscomb R. 64
  Charles H. 64
  Elizabeth Ann 64
  Ellen Isabel 64
  Emma 64
  Frank W. 93
  George B. B. 64
  George H. 64
  Grace M. 64
  Hettie 92
  Jessie E. 64
  John W. 64
  Joseph 93
  Joseph M. 92
  Laura V. 64
  Louisa E. 93
  Mary Emma 64
  Mary L. 93
  Myra 64
  Philemon 92
  Samuel Amos 64
  Samuel Carroll 64
  Samuel W. 64
  Sarah 37

Susan 112
Walter I. 93
William 92
Zipporah A. 64
COCHRAN Sarah A. 95
COCKEY Albert 51
  Anna 51
  Anna V. 124
  Annie 51
  Charles 193
  Charles T. 193
  Colgate 193
  Comfort 51, 193
  Edward Augustus 193
  Elizabeth Frances 132
  Fannie 51
  Henrietta 50
  John G. 36
  John Thomas 51
  Joshua F. 50, 51, 96, 124, 193
  Laura 53
  Laura Bell 36
  Mary Ann 193
  Mary R. 124
  Penelope 96
  Penelope C. D. G. 41
  Samuel 53
  Sarah J. 51
  Susannah D. 193
  Thomas 193
  Thomas Beal 193
  Thomas D. 51, 124
  Uratt C. 193
COCKLEY John A. 164
  Mary C. 164
CODD Col. M. V. 53
  Elizabeth M. 53
CODORI Catherine 144
  John A. 144
  Nicholas 144
COE Benjamin 55
  Elizabeth 55
  Laura V. 50
  William 50
COGGSWELL Andrew 197
  Virginia 197
COHEN Della 144
  Edwin 144
  Elizabeth 144
  Johan 144
  Joseph 144
  Lee 144
  Minoli 144
  Sol 144
  William 144

221

INDEX

COLBURN Miranda 185
COLE Abram 68, 139
  Alice A. 7
  Bettie 96
  Edith 139
  Eleanor 98
  Elizabeth 68
  Emily 98, 139
  Estella 139
  Fannie 139
  Florence G. 97
  Frank 98, 139
  George 139
  George H. 98
  Helen 139
  J. Irving 139
  James H. 96
  Lewis R. 139, 165
  Lewis S. 98, 139
  Louisa 97
  Mary A. 4
  Mary F. 98
  Pamela F. 165
  Pamelia F. 139
  S. Howard 98, 139
  Samuel 44
  Susan 44
  Thomas 97
  William P. 98, 139
COLEMAN John 25
  Margaret 127
  Pleasance 25
  Rebecca Ridgeley 25
  Thomas 127
COLES Albion 101
  Nettie 101
COLGATE Family 72
  Richard 101
COLLENBERG George W. 51
  Kate 51
  Louise T. 90
  Theodore 90
COLLINGS Annie 34
  C. Harris 35
  Eliza 34
  Henry 34
  Lydia 35
  Matilda 34
  Samuel 34
  William 34
  William S. 35
COLLINS Ida 29
  James 166
  Laura J. 166
  Lt. 29
  Sarah Ann 195
  William H. 195
COLLISON Annie M. 82
  Benjamin 82
  Charlesanna 95
  David W. 82
  Elizabeth 82
  George 82
  John R. 95
  Laura P. 82
  Mary Elizabeth 82
  Myrtle C. 82
  Nicholas 82
  Nicholas George 82
  Paul G. 82
  Roy A. 82
  Ruby S. 82
  Sarah C. 82
  Susan 82
  Susan L. B. 82
  Thomas E. 82
COMBS Elizabeth 84
  Nathaniel 84
COMPTON Barnes 197
  Elizabeth 197
  Elizabeth Somerville 198
  John Henry 198
  Key 198
  Margaret 198
  Mary Barnes 198
  Mary Clarissa Bond 197
  William Penn 197, 198
  Wilson 197
CONARD Annie C. 112
  Calvin 112
CONLEY Dixon 33
  Ella M. 33
  Ida 33
  John W. 33
CONRAD Annie C. 77
  Calvin 77
CONWAY Catherine 204
  Daniel 204
  Dr. J. H. 204
  Edith Stockton 140
  Margaret 204
  Mary 204
  Michael J. 204
COOK Adelia V. 186
  Alice Elizabeth 107
  Caroline 185
  Charlotte 41
  Clinton 180
  D. McKune 178
  Deborah 139
  Eliza M. 107
  Frederick C. 189
  George Adam 189
  George Bevan 190
  John H. 186
  Joseph B. 186
  Joseph S. 190
  Julia A. 189, 190
  M. Alice 190
  Margaret 200
  Margaret Clark 190
  Margaret P. 190
  Martin 107
  Matthew L. 190
  Medora S. 186
  Sarah H. 180
  Victor J. 190
COOKE Adolphus A. 13
  Arietta 13
  Edgar S. 13
  Fannie E. 13
  Israel 12, 13
  Marquerite 13
  Mary 13
  Mary J. 13
  O. W. 13
  Sarah B. 13
  Sophie 13
  Theodore 12, 13
  Virginia M. 13
COOPER Abraham B. 104
  Abraham S. 104
  Barbara 104
  Diana 104
  Elizabeth 104
  Emma S. 104
  Frances 88
  Frances L. 29
  H. A. 168
  Henry 104
  Henry Richard 104
  Henry S. 104
  Laura M. 104
  Margaret 104, 126
  Margaret G. 108
  Mary E. 104
  May 168
  Nancy 88
  Nelson 56
  Samuel S. 104
  Samuel W. 104
  Thomas 88
  William 104

INDEX

William J. 126
William S. 104
COPPENHAVER Elizabeth 151
CORBETT Annie 27
  Catherine 27
  Elizabeth 27
  John 27
  Kate 27
  Margaret 27
  Mary 27
  Robert 27
  Timothy 27
CORBIN Nathaniel P. 71
  Rachel F. 71
  Rebecca 71
  William 71
  William W. 71
CORDES Louisa 87
CORDORI Blanche 97
  John A. 97
CORKRAN Edna Brown 36
  Frank 36
  Montgomery 36
  Nellie 36
CORKRIN Charlesanna 95
  George Cowell 95
  James R. 95
  Kitty Iola 95
  Sarah A. 95
  William H. 95
CORLISS Charles H. 204
  Elizabeth 204
CORNELIUS Annie E. 44
  Daniel 13
  Mary J. 13
  Nicholas 44
CORNELL Elizabeth 139
CORNES Amanda 51
CORNTHWAIT Deborah 62
CORRIE Eliza A. 5
CORSE Annie C. 77, 112
  Caroline 77
  Carrie 77
  Carrie D. 112
  Deborah 77
  Deborah S. 112
  Ella S. 77
  Esther S. 112
  Frank E. 77, 112
  George F. 77, 112
  Henry C. 112
  Hettie S. 77, 162
  John 112
  Laura S. 77
  Lucy C. 77, 112
  Mary W. 77, 112
  Rachel S. 112
  Robert 77
  Robert S. 112
  Sallie H. 112
  Sarah 77
  Susan 77, 112
  Susan C. 112
  William 77, 112
  William J. 77, 112
CORY Alice 186
COSGROVE Kate 16
COSKERY Allen 42
  Arthur B. 42
  Campbell 42
  Claude 42
  Elizabeth 42
  Felix S. 42
  H. J. 42
  Harry M. 42
  Lawrence 42
  Paul 42
COSTON Laura 69
COTTON John 40
COUGHLAN Bertha E. 196
  William R. 196
COUNCILMAN George 32
  James B. 201, 206
  John 155
  Martha A. 32
  Mary 155
  Sarah A. 206
  Sarah T. 201
COWAN Annie 135
  Beulah 135, 144
  Charles 151
  Charles D. 135
  Elizabeth 151
  Fielding 135
  Horace F. 151
  James 135
  James S. 135
  Jane 135, 151
  John 135, 144
  Joshua 135
  Kate 135
  Lemuel C. 151
  Martha L. 135
  Mary 151
  Rebecca S. 151
  Sophia J. 135
  William 135, 151
  William L. 151
COWLES Almira 85
  Margaret 85
  William 85
COX Alice Lynn 101
  Dr. D. A. 101
  Ella G. 52
  Emory 52
  Florence 52
  John 53
  Martha 53
  Mr. 52
  Sophia C. 56
  Susan 53
COXEN George E. 173
  Louisa 173
CRAIG Adam 26
  Carrie B. 26
  Dr. 54
  Elizabeth 26
  Fannie 26
  Florence 26
  Hannah 26
  James 26, 48, 54
  John A. 26, 48
  Lawrence Ennels 48
  Margaret 26
  Mary 81
  Mary Armstrong 26
  Sallie 48
  Sarah 26, 54
  William 81
  William P. 26
  William Pinkney 48
CRAIGHILL Anne F. 87
  Annie 87
  Nathaniel R. 87
  William E. 87
  William Nathaniel 86
CRANE Clara 168
  Clara I. 168
  Edith C. 168
  Helen Bond 168
  Henry R. 168
  Isabella 168
  James C. 168
  Jasper 168
  Laura M. 168
  Micajah 168
  Rufus 168
CRAWFORD Andrew 71
  Andrew J. 135
  Elizabeth 116
  Mary 71, 135
  Robert 116
CREIGHTON Delilah 74, 75
CRENSHAW Martha 40
CREUTZBERG Clara 101
  Herman 101

INDEX

CRISPENCE Louisa 161
CROCKER Elizabeth 35
  Letitia 35
  Samuel G. 35
  William Griffiths 35
CROCKETT Captain H. 129
  Ellery 129
  Elsie 129
  John 129
  Josephus 129
  Marvin H. 129
  Minna 129
  Myrtle Virginia 129
CROOK Clementine V. 163
  Washington 163
CROSS Annie N. 154
  Arabella 118
  Betsy A. 129
  Fielder 118
  George R. 105
  Henry Winter Davis 118
  John 129
  Joseph 118
  Maria 30
  Mary 151
  Mary Ann 105
  Samuel 151
  Sarah J. 29
  Thomas A. 118
CROSSMORE Alfred 66
  Alice 66
  Carrie 66
  Cornelia 66
  Jennie 66
  George 66
  Jacob 66
  John 66
  Martha 66
  Mary 66
  Minnie 74
  Oliver 66
  Theodore 66
  Wade H. 66
  William 66
  William S. 74
CROTHER Florence 58
  James B. 58
CROUCH Anna 27
  Anna R. 28
  Blanche 98
  David 151
  Frank T. 28
  Georgiana 27
  Helen F. 28
  John 27

John M. 27
John W. 27
Margaret 151
Margaret P. 28
Mary J. 27
Rebecca L. 27
Robert M. 28
Sarah 151
CROW Henry 127
  Mary 127
CUDDY Clarence Eugene 117
  James B. 117
  John P. 117
  John Preston 117
  Laura 118
  Laura C. 117
  Professor J. W. C. 117
  Rebecca 117
  Ruth C. 117
  Sarah E. 117
CUGLER John 26
CULLEN Emily 162
  Hezekiah 74
  J. K. 74
  John W. 74
  Margaret 74
CULLISON Caroline 93
  Joshua 93
  Mary w. 93
CUMMINS Florence 36
  George D. 36
  Lizzie 36
  Maud 36
CUNNINGHAM Margaret 76
CURRY Jackson 33
  Mary c. 175
CURTIS Amanda 29, 63
  Annie 63
  Charles A. 22
  Charles H. C. 63
  Charles Roscoe 23
  Daniel 63
  Eli 63
  Eliza 63
  Elizabeth 63
  Estelle 63
  Florence C. 23
  George W. 23
  Georgiana 23
  Ida Frances 23
  James A. 23
  Jane 22, 23
  John R. 22

John S. 63
Joseph 23, 63
Levi 63
Lillie 23
Luella 63
Mary 31
Mary M. 23
Matilda 63
May 63
Minerva 23
Nancy 63
Rachel 63
Roscoe C. 63
Sarah 23
Sarah C. 23
Thomas 63
William 31, 63
William H. 23, 63
CURTON Eliza 147
CUSTIS Miss 135
CUTHRIE Eleanor 144
  George 144
CUTLER E. Waldo 36
  Mabel 36

DABLO Fredericka 14
DADE Drusilla 206
  Robert Townsend 207
DAILEY Sarah 152
DAILY Belle V. 35
  Elizabeth 35, 59
  Emma S. 35
  Florence L. 35
  Grace 35
  Harry N. 35
  Jacob 59
  Jesse 35, 59
  Jesse N. 35, 59
  Jesse W. 35
  Lydia S. 35
  Mary E. 35
  Mary Elizabeth 59
  Susan 59
  Viola D. 35
DALHOFF Dena 166
  Elizabeth 166
  Ernst 166
  Freda 166
  Frederica 166
  Fritz 166
  Hans 166
  Henry 166
  Maria 166
  Rudolph 166
  William 166

INDEX

DALLAM Mary 150
  Samuel 150
DAMER Anna 129
  Anna Mary 129
  Charles 129
  Elenore 129
  Sebastian A. 129
DANCE Elizabeth 92
  Milton 92
  Rachel 38
DANEKER Charles W. 151
  Charles William 151
  David 16
  David George 151
  David H. 151
  Elizabeth 151
  Henry B. 151
  Henry Baker 151
  Henry W. D. 151
  Ida 151
  India 151
  John Jacob 151
  Mary Barbara 151
  Mary E. 16, 151
  Sallie 151
  Sarah 151
DANIEL Elizabeth 194
DANNENFELSER Elizabeth 161
  Jacob 152, 161
  Magdelene 152
DASHIELL Charlotte 195
  Erastus S. 195
  Frances M. 195
  Francis James 195
  Harriett 195
  Haste W. 195
  James A. 195
  James W. 195
DAVIDSON Catherine 158
  Emma 158
  George D. 158
  Grace 158
  J. T. 157
  John W. 158
  Judson C. 157
  Lizzie 158
  Mabel 158
  Martha 157
  Matilda 52
  Rosa 28
  Samuel 158
  T. O. 158
DAVIES Betty 83
  Solomon 83

DAVIS Alice B. 196
  Alice V. 163
  Amelia 207
  Amy 111
  Ann 138, 156, 157
  Bertha E. 196
  Caroline A. 70
  Charles 70, 72, 207
  Daniel 72
  Daniel M. 72
  Dora E. 35
  Dorsey 207
  Drusilla 206
  Eleanor 35
  Elizabeth 35, 82, 207
  Emily 207
  Fannie Anne 73
  Florence 72, 207
  Frank 207
  George 207
  George Gibson 35
  Georgiana 70
  Grace 35, 207
  Harvey 207
  Henry 196, 207
  Henry A. 196
  Henry S. 206, 207
  Ida 35
  James L. 72
  James Morgan 35
  Jesse 70
  John 72, 73, 138, 163, 196
  John Joseph 196
  Joseph 70
  Joseph J. 111
  Joseph P. 70
  Kate R. 196
  Letitia 35
  Louis W. 207
  Louisa 81
  Margaret 143, 151
  Martha Catherine 196
  Mary 70, 156
  Mary Florence 111
  Matthew 6
  Milton C. 142
  Minnie 72
  Miriam 65
  Morgan James 35
  Mollie Edith 142
  Pinkney L. 206
  Ruth Amelia 207
  Salina 72
  Samuel 207

  Sarah 72
  Thomas 65, 70, 138, 207
  Walter 72
  Warren W. 70
  William 72
  William Marshall 70
  Winnie 72
DAWES Eudocia 24
  William 24
DAWSON Elmira 47
  Francis 144
  Laura P. 82
  Leah 144
  Lewis 47
  Nancy 144
  Thomas K. 82
DAY Agnes 194
  Agnes L. 194
  Avarilla 194
  Charlotte B. 194
  Charlotte M. 194
  Edward 194
  Edward A. 194
  Halleck D. 194
  John Orso 194
  John Y. 194
  Laura c. 194
  Mary 194
  Rachel 194
  William Y. 194
de FORD Lilla 106
De HARENDT Frederick 149
  Wilhelmina 149
  William F. 149
De RUSSY Edward 9
De SHIELDS Charlotte 81
  Erastus S. 81
  Frances M. 81
  Francis 81
  Francis James 81
  Harriett 81
  Haste W. 81
  James A. 81
  James W. 81
DEAN Catherine E. 88
  J. P. 88
  John L. B. 88
  Margaret 88
DEANE Annie E. 194
  Charles 194
  Emma 194
  Emmay May 194
  Estelle 194
  Frank H. 194
  Frank Harry 194

INDEX

James 194
James F. 194
John 194
John E. 194
Josephine 194
Margaret J. 194
Sallie M. 194
DEAVER Margaret 157
DEBENDOFFER Amos 46
Matilda 46
DECATUR Commodore 20
DECKART Julius 103
Mary 103
DECKER Charles 97
Charles C. 97
Elizabeth 155
Frank 155
Frederick 97
Frederick William 97
Louisa 97
Margaret 97
Mary L. 97
Matthias 97
DEEMER Elizabeth B. 156
Henry 156
DEEMS Grace 130
Jacob 130
DEHOFF Charlotte E. 172
Dr. J. W. 172
DEITRICH Henrick 97
Margaret 97
DELLA Laura V. 152
DELVES Louisa 89
DEMAREE Ernestine 52
Annstina 53
DEMMEAD Bessie C. 185
Francis 185
DEMPSEY Ida 61
DEMSEY Amanda 155
John 148, 155
Melvina 148
DEMUTH Mary 157
DENGLER Annie Teresa 160
Peter J. 160
DENISON Charles Carroll 42
Edward 42
Elizabeth 42
Mary 42
Mary Carroll 42
Rebecca Carroll 42
Robert M. 42
DENMEAD Elizabeth A. 80
Rachael 80
Sarah J. 51
William 51, 80

DENNIS Ann Graham 199
Archibald R. 199
Caroline 152
Casper 171
Elizabeth U. 199
Fannie 198
George R. 198, 199
John McPherson 198, 199
Mary 171
Thomas Jennings 199
DENNISON Ellen J. 17
John R. 17
Nellie R. 17
DENT George 9
William 9
DERING Christopher 87
Katie Anna 87
DETRICHT Hammond 26
Susan 26
DEVINE George William 139
DICKMYER Anna 55
Barbara 55
Christian 55
Dorothy 55
Eleanora 55
Frederick 55
Henry 55
Wilhelmina 55
DIDIER Hester H. 28
DIEDRICH Albert 89
Alexander J. 89
Annie 90
Emma 90
Martin 89
Menno 90
Millard 90
Sophie M. 89
DIEGEL Mary 100
William 100
DIEHL Elizabeth 172
DIETER Annie K. 125
DIETSCHLER Henry 154
Louisa 154
DIETZ Annie M. 121
Bernhard 121
Mary 121
DIGEL Ann Elizabeth 196
Daniel 196
DIGGS Charles F. 107
Edward R. 107
Mary W. 107
DILLAHEY Lettie 127
DILLEHUNT Mollie M. 61

DILWORTH Albert 61
Annie 60
Anthony 61
Carrie 61
Catherine E. 60
Florence 61
George 61
Harry 61
Jesse 60, 61
John 61
Joseph 60, 61
Lillie 61
Mary 61
Paul 61
Robert 60, 61
Susan 61
William 61
DINNEEN John H. 184
Mary 184
Mary G. 184
Michael 184
DITTMAN Elizabeth 141
DIUGUID George 158
Lizzie 158
DIVERS Mary 58
DIXON Ann 25
Charles H. 191
Ellen 111
Hiram 191
Isaac 149
John 25
Margaret M. 149
Sarah E. 191
DOBBINS Nancy A. 173
William 173
DOBSON John A. 180
DODD Sallie 105
DOHLER Rosa 154
DOHONEY Bridget 23
DONALDSON Catherine W. 140
Esther M. 122
Frances 122
Francis 182
Fred 122
Fred R. 122
Joseph H. 122
Lewis 122
Margaret 122
Maria 122
Mary I. 182
Nellie 122
Susan H. 122
Theodore 122
Waller A. 122

INDEX

William 140
William E. 122
DONGER C.C. 23
  Sarah 23
DONOVAN Ann 16
  Mary 1
  Valentine 1
DORRETT Emma 43
  William 43
DORSEY Andrew 167
  Caleb 167
  Chloe 36
  Deborah 170
  Elizabeth 25
  Emily 167
  Enoch 36
  Frances S. 167
  Henry 25
  James A. 167
  James P. 167
  John 170
  Mary A. C. 41
  Milcah 25
  Napoleon 41
  Nicholas 167
  Pleasance 170
  Susan 36
  Susanna 25, 167
  Virginia 167
  William 25
DOSH Anna M. 165
  John J. C. 165
DOSTER Lissie 60
DOTTERWEICH Francis 106
  Sophia 106
DOUGLAS Colonel 124
  James M. 11
DOVALL Alice 61
DOVER Sarah R. 188, 198
DOWD Ellen 102
DOWELL Catherine 96
  Eliza 96
  Jane 96
  Jesse 96
  Samuel 96
  Sarah 96
  Thomas 96
  Virginia 96
DOWNING Jacob 137
  Mary 137
DOWNS Harry 171
  John N. 51
  Lizzie 171
  Mary 51
DRAKE Rachel 194

DRINKAUS Anna 129
  Henry 129
DRYDEN Emily 69
Du HAMEL Elizabeth A. 13
DUBBS Angeline 46
  Caroline 46
  Daniel 46
  Ellen 46
  Elmira 46
  George B. 46
  Henry 46
  Jesse 46
  John Stambaugh 46
  Lavina 46
  Lilly May 46
  Lucy Ann 46
  Miller 46
  Sarah 46
  Warren 46
  William 46
DUCKER Catherine D. 88
  Henry 89
  Julia C. 89
  Mary E. 115
DUERING George S. 53
  Mary 53
DUFFIELD Edith 146
DUKE George 5
DUKEHART Ellen E. 158
DUKER Anna C. 173
  Annie C. 122
  Otto 19, 122, 173
  Sophia M. 19
DUNAN Mabel 202
  P. P. 202
DUNCAN Albert E. 112, 173
  Bettie B. 112, 173
  Catherine E. 112, 173
  Charles H. 112
  Clara 112
  Edward G. 173
  Edward M. 112, 173
  Eliza 112
  Ella 173
  Ella M. 42
  Ellen 112
  Frank I. 112, 173
  George C. 42, 112, 173
  George H. 112
  J. Elizabeth 173
  Jackson L. 112
  James A. 112

John D. C. 112, 173
  Martha 112
  Mary 127
  Nathaniel J. H. 127
  Nellie F. 112
  Nellie G. 173
  Roberta 173
  William 112, 173
DUNGAN Fannie 14
  Lewis H. 162
  Mary W. 162
DUNKLE Martin 100
  Mary A. 100
DUNLAP Nancy 165
DUNN Francis 108
  Hannah 108
  J. E. 85
  Rachel 108
DUNNING Arthur G. 47
  Beverly W. 47
  Edward E. 47
  Edward Waugh 47
  Elizabeth 47
  John 47
  John M. 47
  Lulu 47
  Margaret A. 47
  Margaret E. 47
  Norris W. 47
  Robert S. 47
DUNNINGTON Helen 87
DUNPHY Ann 175
  Elizabeth 175
  John 175
  Margaret 175
  Richard 175
  Thomas 175
DURHAM Martha L. 100
  Sarah Catharine 4
  William 4
  Zaccheus 100
DUSZYNSKI Andrew Anthony 178
  Catherine 178
  Simon 178
DUTTON Susan 6
DUVAL Maria E. 20
DUVALL Arabella 118
  Barton 177
  Barton Lee 177
  Daniel Clayton 177
  Dennis 118
  Emily 73
  Everett 177
  Frances C. 177

INDEX

Hannah L. 177
Herbert 177
James Monroe 177
Marius Turner 177
Mary A. 177
Nannie 177
Philip Barton 177
Rachel 176, 177
Richard I. 176
Richard M. 176
Richard Mareen 177
Sally 177
Samuel 177
Samuel Fulton 177
William B. 73

EAGLESTON Charles 161
Mary L. 161
EARHART Elizabeth 93
EARL Florence 144
John 61
Margaret 61
EARLE Anna Rebecca 157
George 157
EASSON Alexander 131
Isabella 131
John 131
Thomas C. 131
Thomas Chalmers 131
EASTON Lord 8
EATON Thomas 8
EBAUGH Conrad 96
Elisha 38
Emma V. 38
Sevena 96
EBELING Flora 44
George W. 44
Henry 44
Herman 44
Maria 44
Mary 44
Wilhelm 44
ECKELS Anna 21
August 21
Caroline 21
Frederick W. 21
Henry F. 21
Louis 21
Mamie 21
Margaret 21
Philip 21
Powell 21
William 21
EDDY C. C. 171
S. Ellen 171

EDWARDS Alice 65
Ann 156, 157
Anna Rebecca 157
Edwin Ernest 156
Elizabeth Ann 144, 157
Ella 156
Ella B. 156
George 156, 157
George Olivet 156
George Thomas 157
Grace E. 156
Isabella N. 51
John 144, 156, 157
John V. 157
Mary 156
Nevet Ocean 156
Philip 156
Philip Franklin 156
Sarah Ann 156
Temperance Rebecc 144, 156
W. Henry Harrison 65
William 144, 156
William N. 51
William R. 156
EFFORD Alice 117
Charles 117
George W. 117
Harry 117
Margaret 117
Mollie 117
Zachariah 117
EHLERS Amelia 99
Justus Henry 99
Lewis 99
Louisa 99
Sarah R. 99
William H. 99
EHRHARDT Alice 69
Charles P. 69
Dora 69
William 69
EICHELBERGER Adam 183
Annie Lynne 184
Charles F. 183
Charles P. 183
Edward Cary 183, 184
Francis Maury 184
Gilbert 183
Henry S. 183
John M. 183
Julia H. 184
Julia P. 184
Kate 183
Lewis 183

Lewis Hay 184
Margaret 183
Mary 183
Penelope Lynn L. B. J. 183, 184
Philip 183
Philip Frederic 183
William Hay 184
EICHNER Annie 64
John C. 64
EIDEL Christine 188
EIGENRAUG Augusta 154
Frederick 154
EISENBERGER Florence Nightingale 190
ELBINDER Susan 82
ELDER Francis W. 175
Gertrude 149
Margaretta 175
Zachariah 149
ELGERT Andrew L. C. 146
Charles 146
Elizabeth 146
Henrietta 146
Henry 146
John Adam 146
Kate 146
Kunigunchen 146
Lillie 146
Lizzie 146
Maggie 146
ELINE Celia 113
Joseph F. 113
ELLICOTT Ann Rebecca 201
Charles L. 37
David B. 37
John 128
Lindley 37
Mary 37
Mary M. 37
Nancy P. 37
Sarah 37
Sarah P. 37
Thomas 37
Thomas P. 37
William M. 37
William Miller 37
ELLIOTT Abraham 76
Abraham J. 76
Eliza E. 76
Elizabeth 76
George 76
George W. 76
Keziah 76
Margaret 76
Mary Ellen 120

228

INDEX

Robert 76
Ruth 131
S. Florence 76
Sarah 29
Thomas 29
ELY Pleasance 170
EMERICH Clayton 169
Kate 169
EMERY Almira 153
J. S. 153
EMICH Charles C. 62
Charlotte C. 62
Harris C. 62
Harrison 62
Harrison Holliday 62
Henry F. 62
Mary Sophia 62
Nanie Hiser 62
Nanie R. 62
Nicholas 62
EMMEL John 83
Rosanna 83
EMMERT C. Frank 52
Clara V. 52
EMORY Agnes S. 183
Anna 83
Bessie 116
Griselda 116
Mary Rogers 116
Richard 83, 116, 183
Thomas Hall 183
Thomas Lane 116
ENNALLS Joseph 194
Josephine 194
ENNALS Elizabeth 26
ENNIS Jennie 71
ENSOR Abraham 42
Alice 73
Andrew 2, 73
Anna R. 44
Caroline L. 2
Catherine 58
Daily 42
Delila 43
Delilah 37
Eliza 42
Elizabeth 42, 56
Florence A. 2
Frances 147
Frances R. 81
George 42, 56, 81
George B. 2
George H. 42
George S. 37
Howard 37

James B. 2
John 37, 42
John B. 42
John C. 37
John E. 42
John H. 42
John S. 2
John T. 2
Joseph 42
Josephine 37
Julia 56
Luke 42, 44
Luke E. 44
Luke G. 42
Mary E. 43
Nathan 58
Nellie 37
Noah F. 44
Orick M. 37
Peter W. 44
Rachel 37, 42, 44
Rebecca 90
Ruth Ann 42
Sarah 42
Temperance 57
Thomas 42
W. O. 56
William 42, 44
EPER Elizabeth 154
EPPES Fannie 26
EPPLER Ellen 107
Herman 107
ERDMAN Anna 48
Barbara E. 65
Charles 65
Clarence Elmer 8
Ella 8
Francis S. 65
Frederick 65
Gottlieb H. 65
Harry 8
Harry S. 65
Henry L. 65
James M. 8
John 65
John G. 8
Letitia 8
Mary A. 65
Mary L. 8
Mathias 54
Peter 65
Peter F. 8
Peter G. 8, 65
Rose 65
Susan 52

Susanna 54
Virginia S. 8
William 8
Willilam Kenneth 8
ERP Margaret 159
ESCHBACH John 176
ESCHBACK Mary T. 176
EVANS Ada 171
Alice M. 171
Annie 135
Bessie 26
Catherine 158
Clara B. 8
Edward 158
Ellen E. 158
Emma Catherine 158
Families 37
George 71, 135
Gilman 171
Gilman P. 171
H. E. 135
Inmon 169
James E. 158
James H. 158
John W. 26
Mary 158
Mary A. 171
Mildred Moore 169
Olivia 152
Rachel F. 71
S. Ellen 171
Sarah 158
Sarah Melissa 158
Stephen Humphrey 158
Tallman 171
Thomas 8
Walter Harley 158
William M. 135
William S. 158
EVERDING Catherine E. 48
Herman B. L. 48
Herman H. C. 48
EVEREST Zoe 37
EVERETT Carrie 165
EVERHART Catherine 121
David 120
Elizabeth 120
Eve Elizabeth 120
George 120
George H. 120
George Philip 120, 121
Mary 120, 121
Mary Almeda 121
Mary M. 120
Paulus 120
Rachel 120

229

INDEX

EWELL Rosanna 169
EWENS Arthur 208
  Elizabeth Grace 208
EWING Alexander 134
  Eleanor 134
  Esther 134
  James 134
EYRE Hannah 197

FAGLEY Caroline F. 174
  Christian M. 174
FAIR John 190
  Rachel 190
FAIRALL Achsah 142
  Alfred 142
  Annie R. 142
  Effie E. 142
  John B. 142
  Margaret E. 142
  Mollie Edith 142
FAIRBANKS Almeda J. 132
  James A. 132
FALK Sophia 169
FARMER Cora A. 11
FARNSWORTH Almira 153
FARRELL Jane 71
FASTIE Annie 64
  Arthur 64
  Eliza 64
  George 64
  George J. 64
  Howard 64
  Isa 64
  John 64
  Julia 64
  Lillie 64
  Mary 64
  Maus 64
  Minnie 64
  Theodore 64
  Walter 64
  Washington 64
  William F. 64
FAUCETT Family 141
FEAST Martha L. 100
FECHTER Capt. C. H. 75
  Fredericka 75
FEEHELY Bridget 182
FEFFEL Mary E. 93
FELDMAN Herman 191
  Rebecca 191
FELGNER Mary S. 155
FELTER Catherine 65
  George 65
  George L. 65

  Helen C. 65
  Irene 65
  John 65, 137
  John C. 65
  Margaret 137
  Robert E. 65
FELTMAN Rebecca 145
FENBY Mary 62
FENTON Martha J. 106
FERGUSON Adam 78
  David B. 92
  Edna 78
  Elizabeth 78, 92
  Ellen 94
  Emma J. 78
  Ethel 78
  Harry 78
  Keziah B. 92
  Levi 92
  Mamie 78
  Oliver 78
  W. J. 94
  William 92
  William J. 78
FERNSNER Johannetta 138
  Lewis 138
FESSENDEN Cora J. 31
  Edwin A. 31
  Justina E. 31
FICCHER Grace 28
  P. L. C. 28
FIFE Rebecca J. 38
FILLMORE Maria 122
  Rev. 122
FINK Mrs. Charles E. 1
FINNEY Dora C. 78
FISH Henry 118
  Mary 118
FISHBAUGH John 46
  Sarah 46
FISHER Alberta 73
  Augusta 126
  Catherine 70, 137
  Charles 126
  Elizabeth 66, 73
  Frederick 126
  Isabella 30
  J. Henry 126
  Jesse 73
  John 164
  Laura 164
  Margaret Mary 126
  Mary 132
FISHPAW Elijah 188
  Mary 188

FISKE Charles B. 168
  Mary E. 168
FITE Achsah 33
  Annie 33
  Elizabeth R. 33
  Emma 33
  Georgiana 33
  Henry 33
  Israel 33
  J. Albert 33
  Jacob 33
  Laura 33
  Mary E. 160
  Oliver 33
  Sarah 33
  William 33
  William E. 33, 160
FITZELL Annie 112
  George 111
  James 111
  John 111
  Lizzie 112
  Mary A. 112
  Mollie 112
  Rebecca 111
  Richard 112
  Samuel 112
  Thomas R. 111
  William 111
FITZGERALD Catherine 201, 202
  E. H. 121
  Edward 201
  Edward D. 201, 202
  Elsie M. 202
  John 201
  John R. 202
  Lillie 201, 202
  Mary Almeda 121
FITZHARRIS Martha M. 40
FITZSIMMONS Bessie 73
  Bridget 73
  Christopher 73
  Christopher E. 73
  Edward 73
  Ella 73
  Gertrude 73
  John Francis 73
  Mary 73
  Mary Elizabeth 73
  Michael P. 73
  Thomas 73
  Thomas Joseph 73
  William Henry 73
FLAHARTY James 123
  Mary 123

INDEX

FLANNERY Ella 79
  Frank 79
  Frank J. 79
  John 79
  Loretta 79
  Mamie E. 79
  Mary 79
  Thomas J. 79
FLARITY Miss 50
FLAYHART Ada May 175
  Ann 175
  Charles M. 175
  Charles R. 175
  Edward 175
  Eliza 175
  Emma W. E. 175
  James 175
  John 175
  John Edward 175
  John Howard 175
  Joshua 175
  Margaret 175
  Mary 175
  Sarah 175
  Sophia 175
  Susie 175
  Thomas 175
  Walter Finch 175
  William 175
  William H. 175
  William Henry 175
FLEMING Margaret 106
FLETCHER Robert 14
FLOYD James 21
  Mary 21
FOARD Aaron H. 69
  Kate 69
  Miss 29
FOGARTY Dr. 128
  Mary 128
FOOKS Ellen 206
  Emma 194
  Zachariah 206
FOOS Bertha 136
  Christian 136
  Elizabeth 135
  Frederick 136
  Frederick E. 135
  William 135, 136
FORD Annie 202
  Charles E. 202
  Edith B. 202
  Edith Octavia 202
  Hannah A. 185
  John T. 202
  Mabel 202

FORE A. W. 115
  Martha J. 115
FOREMAN Elizabeth A. 104
  James 104
FOREST Callie 58
  Elmer B. D. 58
  John 144
  Sallie 144
FORESTER Gottlieb 83
  James 26
  Kate 83
  Mary 26
FORREST Annie 183
  Emma C. 85
  J. L. 85
FORRESTER Joseephine 152
FORSTBURG Jennie 150
  John 150
FOSTER Angeline 32, 137
  Anna F. 41
  Annie 137
  Charles Taylor 137
  Edward Rider 41, 137
  Elizabeth 68
  William R. 32, 137
  William T. 137
FOTSCH Lydia 5
  Martin 5
FOWBLE Alfred 96
  Charlotte 96
  Charlotte C. 98
  Charlotte G. 97
  Eliza 109
  Elmo 109
  Florence G. 97
  Florence T. 97
  Irene 97
  J. M. 37
  Jacob 96
  John 96
  John T. 97, 109
  Joseph I. 97
  Josephine 37
  Joshua 96
  Joshua A. 97
  Joshua V. 96
  Kate 96
  Louisa 97
  Maggie 109
  Margaret 96
  Mary 96
  Mary C. 97
  Milliker 96

  Nelcor 96
  Ollie E. 109
  Penelope 96
  Peter 96
  Phoebe 97
  Rebecca 97, 188
  Sarvena J. 97
  Selina 97
  Sevena 96, 109
  Stephen M. 97
  Susan 96
  Thomas 96
  Wilbur 97
FOWLER Annie 146
  Charles E. 146
  Charles Henry 146
  Edith 146
  Elizabeth 148
  John 148
  Julia 127
  Lydia 146
  Peggy 100
  Vera Rose 146
  William 146
  William Arnold 146
FOX Charles J. 14
  Families 37
  Harriet Damby 14
  Hazel Annie Bell 14
  Henry W. 14
  John 14
  John Morris 14
  John Sidney 14
  Marbury Brewer 14
  Martina B. 7
  Mary 25
  Susanna 25
  Thomasine M. 14
FRAILEY Leonora 204
  Mindus 204
FRANCIS Charles 55
  Edwin 55
  Elizabeth 55
  Ellen 55
  Florence 55
  George W. 55
  Grace 55
  John C. 55
  Marie 55
  Mary J. 55
  Priscilla 55
  R. Lewis 55
  Richard C. 55
  Robert 55, 78
  Sadie 78

INDEX

Samuel 55
Sarah Eliza 55
Thomas 55
FRANK Mary 31
FRANKLIN Cecilia 205
  Mary 98
  Samuel D. 205
  Thomas 98
FRASER Alexander 10
  Dorothy Campbell 10
  General 17
  Marie Helen 10
  Martha W. 17
  William 10
FRASKE Clara Emilia 160
  Henry 160
FRAZIER Mary 60
  Mr. 60
FREDERICK Ann M. 88
  Anna 58
  George 28, 58, 88
  Hannah 88
  Jacob 56
  James N. 88
  Jennie 88
  John 88
  John T. 88
  Maggie 28
  Mary E. 56
  Morris 88
FREELAND Sarah J. 46
FRESSENJAT Elizabeth 67
FREUND Jacob 53
  John W. 53
  Lewis 53
  Louisa 53
  Magdelena 53
  Mary 53
FRICK Charles 42
  Mary Carroll 42
FRIEND Elizabeth 187
  Henry 187
FRITSCH Bertha 5
  Carl 5
  Edward 5
  Emil 5
  Frederick 5
  John 5
  Leonie 5
  Wilhelm 5
FROELICH Mary E. 45
FROST Hyde 163
  Sarah 163
FULLER Mary 77
  Stella 69
  William 77

FULTZ Catharine 29
  Charles E. 29
  Edna M. 29
  Frances L. 29
  George C. 29
  George M. 29
  Jennie M. 29
  John 29
  Lucetta 29
  Nancy 29
  Nellie M. 29
  Sarah J. 29
FUSSELBAUGH Amanda M. 1
  Ann 16
  Harriet Newell 16
  John 1
  John Henry 1
  Liston P. 1
  Sadie 171
  W. H. B. 171
  William 1, 16
  William H. B. 1
FUSSELL Jacob 170
  Philena 170
  Ruth Ann 57
FUSTING Margaret E. 66

GABEL Erma 135
GAIL Emma 155
  George Christian 155
  George Philip 155
  George William 155
  Mary S. 155
  Susanna 155
GAINES Sarah 84
GALE Fannie Bella 190
GALLEN Isabell 8
  James 8
  John 8
  Joseph A. 8
  Mary 8
  Patricius 8
GALLOWAY Moses 99
GALLYON Mattie A. 180
GALT Cyrus 191
GAMBLE David 171
  James 192
  Maggie M. 192
  Mary 171
  Rosa R. J. 171
GAMBRILL Abbie 178
  Abigail 65
  Adaline 65
  Alice 65
  Augustus 65

  B. Franklin 65
  Edward 65
  Eli 65
  Elizabeth 65
  Ella 65
  Elmira 65
  Henry W. 178
  Hester Ann 65
  John 65
  Juliet 65
  Louisa 65
  Mary C. 178
  Melville 65
  Miriam 65
  Nelson 65
  Robert 65
  William 65
GAMIER (Gammar) Barbara 176
  Jacob F. 176
GAMPHOR Eliza 64
GANSTAR Laura May 12
  N. C. 12
GARDNER Arthur 114
  James 113
  Joseph 113
  Myrtle 114
  Rosa 114
  Sarah 114
GAREE Benjamin C. 164
  Ellis C. 164
  Grace 164
  Ida M. 164
  Job 164
  John S. 164
  Mary P. 164
  Nancy A. 164
  Sarah A. 164
GARRETT Annie 205
  Mary E. 205
  Mary Hannah 201
  Mary O. 49
  Michael 205
  Michael A. 205
  P. J. 205
  Thomas J. 205
  William 205
  William H. 201
GARRETTSON Ann 50
  Job 50
GARRISON Emily 180
  Hannah 83
  James S. 180
  Miss 55, 58
GARTBERRY Jane 90

INDEX

GARY E. Stanley 61, 94
James A. 61, 94
James S. 61
Mary 94
GASKINS Frances 73
GATCH Ann T. 96
Anna Maria 152
Anna W. 30
Arthur C. Turner 152
Ashby Fred Albert 152
Belle Xenia 152
Benjamin 96, 152
Benjamin W. 30, 152
Eleanor M. 152
Elizabeth 127, 152
Frank Ray 152
Godfrey 152
Gordon G. 152
Harry L. 152
John M. 152
Joseph A. 152
Josephine 152
Nicholas 152
Nicholas B. 152
Sarah 23
Thomas B. 152
GAULT Margaret 191
Sarah E. 191
GAUNT John 30
Sarah 30
GAUNTLETT Sarah Leverick 138
GEBB Amelia 41
Charlotte 41
Conrad 41
Elizabeth 41
George 41
Henry 41
Margaret 41
Philip 41
Wilhelmena 41
GEER Annie 22
Bettie 22
Edwin 22
Elizabeth M. 22
Mary 22
Sallie 22
GEHRING Emma A. 207
J. G. 207
GEIGER Catherine Seltzer 172
Elizabeth 166
Jacob 172
Mary Ann 172
William 166
GELLER Catherine 104
GEMMELL Robert 142
Sarah 142
GEMMILL Agnes J. 46
Gladys E. 46
James L. 46
James Stephen 46
John 46
Lula 46
Margaret 46
Martha E. 46
Mary 46
Sarah J. 46
Sarah L. 46
Vernon A. 46
William T. 46
GENGNAGEL George 149
George W. 148
Henry 148
Jacob 148, 149
Julia 148
Sophia 148
Theodore E. 149
GENNESS May 12
GEOGHEGAN Celone 74
Charles M. 74
Roberta 74
Stewart K. 74
Susan A. 74
William 74
William C. 74
GEORGE Anna 125
Francis 168
Francis Barry 168
Francis J. 168
John S. 52, 125
Mary F. 52
Rebecca 168
Roscena 168
GERMAN Annie 104
Celia Ann 62
Charles S. 104
Christian 104
Clara 104
Edith 104
Elizabeth A. 104
Emory 104
George Edwin 104
George Israel 103
James Oscar 104
John Wesley 62, 104
Joseph 103, 104
Lilian May 104
Mary 104
Mary A. 103, 104
Mary Elizabeth 104
Rachel 104
Randolph 104
Rosa 104
Solomon 104
Theodore 104
Thomas 104
GERRY Agnes 66
C. N. R. 66
Charles F. 66
James L. 66
Joseph P. 66
Lillie A. 66
N. R. 66
Philip 66
GETTEMULLER Amelia 124
Anna 124
Anna Maria 124
Annie M. 18
Bertha 124
Eleanore B. 18
Fred 124
H. J. 18, 124
Herman 124
Herman H. 18
J. F. 124
J. Fred 18
Mabel E. 18
Mamie 125
Mary Ann 18
William 124
GETTY Frances 77
GETZ Fannie 57
Maggie 155
GIBBONS Dr. L. 36
James Cardinal 3
Miss 160
GIBBS Mrs. 159
GIBNEY Mary V. 141
GIBSON Annie E. 122
Annie K. 92
Ella May 81, 147
Estelle 92
Eugenia 94
Frances R. 15
G. T. M. 94
James F. 15
John Norman 92
John W. 92
William 147
William L. 81
William S. 81
GILBERT David 114
Ephpraim 46
Mary 46
Sarah A. 114

INDEX

GILBREATH Major E. C. 77, 112
  Susan 77
  Susan C. 112
GILD Dr. 31
  Mary 31
GILES Alfred B. 140
  Catherine W. 140
  Donaldson 140
  George Stewart 140
  Georgia C. 140
  Jacob Washington 149
  Martha 149
  Sarah 140
  Stewart 140
  William F. 140
  William Fell 140
  William Gell 149
GILKES Ellen 27
  Malin 27
GILL Agnes Rebecca 89
  Andrew J. 90
  Annie 187
  Barbara 187
  Catherine A. 90
  Charlotte 96
  Didymus 187
  Eliza 109
  Elizabeth 89
  Florence E. 89
  George W. 90
  Harrison 90
  John 90
  John C. 187
  John G. 90
  Joseph 89, 90
  Joseph N. 187
  Julia Edna 89
  Mary E. 187
  Mary J. 93
  Mary M. 187
  Miss 97
  Nicholas 90
  Nicholas A. 90
  Rebecca 90
  Richard 109
  Robert O. 89
  Samuel 90
  Stanley H. 89
  Stephen 90, 96
  Stephen R. 187
  Susan 53
  Thomas E. 187
  William F. 187
  William P. 187
GILLES Archibald 177
  Mary 177
GILLESPIE Elizabeth 155
  William 155
GILLETT Caroline 182
  Suthey 182
GILLINGSLEY John 65
GILMORE Agnes Virginia 72
  James 72
  John Campbell 72
  Nancy 72
GILROY Carrie 164
  John 164
  Laura 164
  W. S. 164
GISSEL Christoph 114, 115
  Maggie 114
  Mary Sophia 115
  Paul 114
GIST Eleanor R. 68
  Joseph 68
GITTINGER Mary 84
GITTINGS Henry W. 139
  Nannie E. 139
GLACHER Lewis 73
GLADDEN Miss 50
GLASS George 36
  Rebecca 36
GLEASON Mary 79
GLEN Georgia 192
  James 140
  Mary 140
  William R. 192
GLYNN Mary 66
GODDESS Charles Wesley 35
  Grace 35
GODWIN Alice 136
  Ann 25
  Anna 136
  Annie 136
  Austin 25
  Cornelius 25
  Elizabeth 25
  Esther 25
  Frank 136
  Henry 25
  Lionel 25
  Lyde 25
  Margaret 136
  Mary 25
  Nathaniel 25
  Peter 25
  Pleasance 25
  Rachel Lyde 25
  Rebecca W. 136
  Robert 25
  Sarah 136
  Susanna 25
  W.F. 136
GOERCKE Martha 129, 130
  Maurice 130
GOGEL Charles 95
  Jane 95
  Kate 95
GOLDEN Emma 132
  John H. 132
GOLDSBOROUGH John Schley 177
  Nanie 177
  Sarah 48
GONTRUM Ann Catherine 24
  Ann Margaret 24
  Anna Catherine 24
  Anna Maria (Barbara) 24
  Caroline 24
  Christopher 24
  Emma 24
  John 24
  John F. 24, 26
  Mary 26
  Matilda 24
  Peter 24
GOODWIN Bertha Cordelia 45
  Bertha Frost 45
  Charles Thomas 45
  Edward C. 45
  Eliza 45
  Eliza Jane 44
  Elizabeth Ann 189
  Emma 45
  Etta Jet 45
  F. P. 55
  Florence Holbrook 45
  George Franklin 45
  George W. 45
  George Wesley 44
  Hannah Elnora 45
  Henrietta 101
  James 44, 45, 101, 189
  James Frederick 45
  James Herbert 45
  James Roland 45
  Jane 189
  John 37
  Josephine 55
  Layton Wesley 45

INDEX

Lyde 50
Mary Blanche 45
Mary E. 45
Mary P. 110
Robert Henry 45
Sarah 50
Temperance 37
William Herdman 45
GOOTEE Roberta 159
GORDON Eliza 13
  J. S. 153
  Lydia 153
GORE A. Washington 86
  Albert 86
  Charles W. 86
  Elijah 86
  George 86
  Hugh C. 86
  Katie 86
  Martha J. 86
  Mary Belle 86
GORRELL Amos 164
  Grace 164
  Saccharissa 164
GORSUCH Abram B. 43
  Alexander R. 43
  Ann 95
  Ann T. 96
  Annie Pamelia 14
  Bettie 96
  Captain 54
  Charles 14, 95
  Charley 31
  Dickinson 138
  Elizabeth A. 43
  Ellen 95
  Gertrude Louisa 14
  Helen Virginia 14
  James F. H. 14
  James V. 43
  John 31
  John H. 43
  Joseph 57, 95
  Lawrence E. 43
  Luther 95
  Luther M. 14
  Malinda 31
  Martha 54
  Mary E. 43, 95, 96
  Mary Frances 57
  Nicholas 95
  Rachael 31
  Ruth Ann 57
  Sarah Ann 95
  Sarah E. 14

Susan 95
Thomas 95, 96
Thomas R. 43
Wesley 95
William 43
William P. 43
GOSNELL Israel 13
  Martha Ann 110
  Ruth 13
GOURLEY Annie E. 122
  Helen 122
  James 122
  James David 122
  Mariette 122
  Mason W. 122
  Sadie Smith 122
GOVER Samuel 47
  Temperance 47
GRACE Aaron Boyer 99
  Carval James 99
  E. M. 119
  E. P. 119
  George Washington 99
  John 99
  John T. 99
  John W. 119
  Joseph A. 99
  Mary 99, 119
  Mary A. 119
  Mary Alice 99
  Mary Margaret 99
  Sarah 99
  Wallace Eugene 119
  Wilhelmina 119
  William 119
GRACEHAM Family 206
GRAEFE Caroline 60
  Charles 60
  Edward 60
  Frederick 60
  Henry 60
  Mary 60
  Minnie 60
  Mollie 60
  William 60
GRAF Johannes 80
GRAFTON Delia 29
  Elizabeth 29
  Hannah 29
  Harry 29
  Jennie 29
  John H. 29
  John Hanna 29
  Julia 178
  Mark 178

Mary 29
Mary Ann 29
Rebecca 29
GRAHAM Andrew 117
  Catherine 28
  Eliza 13
  Elizabeth 151
  Ellis C. 13
  George 13
  George R. 13
  Gertrude 37
  Hannah 13
  Henry G. 13
  Ignatius 13
  John 127
  Laura 13
  Laura C. 117
  Maria 13
  Mary 13
  Ruth 13
  Sallie 127
  Samuel 28
  Thomas I. 37
  William J. 13
GRAIGHILL James M. 86
  Mary A. 86
  William P. 86
GRALLEY Barbara 166
GRANNISS Annie M. 26
GRANT Anna R. 166
  Archibald 66
  Calules S. 66
  General 9
  Isabella 66
  Isabella R. 66
  Jane A. 66
  Julia Dent 9
  Mary L. 66
  William 166
  William M. 66
GRAPE George 80
  Georgia 80
GRAVES Aberilla C. 95
  Edward 86
  Katie 86
  Mary A. 65
GRAY Anna 21
  Daniel C. 55
  Jennie 66
  John 106
  Lena 106
  Rev. J. F. 66
  Sarah Eliza 55
GREANER Daniel 143
  Margaret 143
  William 143

INDEX

GREAVES Mary 83
  Rosamond 83
  Sarah 83
GREBLE Louisa E. 93
GREEN A. H. 50
  Abigail 65
  Caroline 50
  Charles H. 70
  Edith R. 70
  Eleanor 109
  Eleanor L. 70
  Eleanor Ruth 109
  Elisha 70, 142
  Elizabeth 83
  Ella L. 51
  G. W. 83
  Ida May 70
  John S. 51, 70
  Joshua R. 70
  Josiah 109
  Josias 207
  Julia B. 50
  Laura V. 109
  Lillian 109
  Lillie May 70
  Margaret 142
  Marilla 95
  Mary E. 70
  Maurice B. 70
  Miss 131
  Moses 70
  Phoebe V. 142
  R. Corville 70
  Rev. John 142
  Sarah R. 70
  Vincent 109
  Virginia 207
  William H. 50
  William J. 109
GREENFIELD Martha 177
  Thomas 177
GREENWELL Elizabeth 85
  Thomas 85
GREER Laura 124
  Mary 124
  Robert 124
GREG Annie Maria 162
  Herman 162
GREGG Alexander 116
  Athalinda 116
  David 116
  Dr. J. 136
  Elizabeth 136
  James 116
  John 116

  Martha Jamison 116
  Mary 116
  Narcissa 136
  Gregory Lena 207
GREGWIRE Emma Melvina 133
  Lee 133
GREIDER Abraham 23
  Lillie 23
GREMPLER A. Edward F. 130
  Clara 130
  Doretta 130
  Edward 130
  Godfrey J. 130
  Grace 130
  Grace C. 130
  Gustav 130
  Henry 130
  Karl 130
  Karl Freckerick 130
  Louisa 130
  Paul 130
  Walter Edward 130
  William 130
GRIFFIN Bertha S. 46
  Felix 16
  John B. 16
  John R. 46
  Kate 16
  Mary 16
  Michael 16
  Michael T. 16
  Theresa 16
GRIFFITH Curtis C. 77
  Edward 58
  Elizabeth Josephine 39
  Frederika 77
  Louis 39
  Penelope 58
GRIFFITHS Elizabeth 35
  William 35
GRIMELL Bertha 143
GRIMES Charlotte B. 75
  Elias 75
  Elias Oliver 75
  Eliza 74, 75
  Franklin A. 75
  George 75
  George Washington 74
  John H. 74, 75
  Margaret 75
  Mary M. 75
  Robert Harold 75

  S. Butler 75
  William S. 75
GROFF Abraham 80
  Benjamin Franklin 80
  Clara Denmead 80
  Elizabeth A. 80
  Guy B. 80
  Mary Ray 80
  William Denmead 80
GROSS Carrie M. 146
  Edgar Allen 144
  Elizabeth 145
  Ella M. 144
  Elsie Augusta 146
  Frederick Raymond 146
  George 145
  George W. 145
  Harry Archer 144
  Helen V. 144
  Howard Milton 146
  Jacob 145
  Jacob J. 144
  Jacob Harvey 144
  James Percy 144
  John H. 145
  John Henry 146
  Joseph 145
  Julia 145
  Maggie 145
  Mary Ellen 145
  Maud Alberta 144
  Walter Kroeber 146
GROTHAUS Wilhelmina 113
GROVE Alberta 73
  Alice 73
  Benjamin F. 73
  Beulah 73
  Blanche Newman 19
  Charles 73
  Emma Jane 73
  Fannie 73
  Fannie Anne 73
  Frances 73
  Herbert 73
  Howard 73
  Jacob 73
  Jesse 73
  John Edgar 73
  Leonard Ellsworth 73
  Lewis Jewett 73
  Martin 22
  Mary 22
GROVER Charles 106
  Charles G. 106
  Minnie 91
  Susanna 106
  William 91

INDEX

GRUBB Alexander D. 49
  Virginia B. 49
GRUNEWALD Elizabeth 93
GUENTHER Augusta 126
GUITEAU Sarah B. 13
  Sheridan 13
GUNDRY Catherina A. 68
  Jonathan 40
  Martha M. 40
  Richard 40
  Richard F. 68
GUNN Edith 41
GUNTHER Anna Louisa 173
  Annie 63
  Attilla 173
  Bertha Margaret 173
  Caroline 173
  Charles 122, 173
  Charles O. 173
  Christina Louisa 173
  Elizabeth 41
  Emma Sophia 173
  Fredericka 173
  Herman Henry 173
  Louisa 173
  Margaret A. 122, 173
  Margaret Anna 173
  Margaret S. 173
  Mary Ella 173
  Mildred 173
  Otto 173
  Susie 173
  Wilhelmina 173
GUNTS Ada I. 163
  Anna B. 163
  J. Walter 163
  John P. 163
  Mary E. 163
  Medora 163
  Robert T. 163
GUTHERIGE Mattie 118
  William 118
GUTHRIE Beulah 135
  Beulah 144
  Charles E. 135, 144
  Freedom 144
  Mary A. M. 5
  Nancy 144
  Philip 144
  Sherman 144
  William Wade 144
GWYN Fannie R. 63
  John T. 63

HACKETT Edith 84
  Henrietta 84
  William T. 84
  Cecelia Maryland 84
  Charles 84
  Elizabeth 84
  Henrietta 84
  Emma 84
  James M. 84
  John P. 84
  Joseph P. 84
  Mary Kate 84
  Reese 84
  Stella 84
  William P. 84
HAGEN Charles J. 150
  Mamie 150
  Richard W. 193
  Virginia 193
HAGER Susanna 104
HAGERTY John 119
  Sarah 119
HAGG Caroline 182
HAHN Edward 65
  Kate 65
HAINES Anna Catherine 24
  Elizabeth A. 162
  Henry 24
HAK Elizabeth 70
HALE Anna 23
HALL Agnes S. 183
  Albert 47
  Almira 85
  B. W. 191
  Caroline G. 85
  Caroline T. 85
  Cecelia 85
  Charles 62
  Delila 85
  Delila J. 85
  Elizabeth 175
  Ellen 62
  Emily 85
  Everett N. 174
  Frances S. 60
  Jane 76
  John 85, 175
  John W. 85
  Keziah 178
  "Long" John 76, 85
  Maggie 47
  Margaret 85, 200
  Mary 184
  Miss 198

  Nathaniel 76, 85
  Rebecca 115
  Sarah 85
  Sarah J. 98
  Sidney C. 191
  Susanna 174
  Thomas W. 183
  Vernon 47
  William A. 47, 85
HALLOWELL Ann 87
HALSTEAD Egbert 163
  Elias 163
  Ezra W. 163
  Fred B. 163
  John 163
  Joseph 163
  Nora 163
  Sarah 163
HAMILL Alexander 19
  Ann J. 123
  Blanche Newman 19
  Blanche Rosalie 19
  Eliza 34, 123
  Eva Pauline 19
  George W. 19
  R. J. W. 109
  Robert 123
  Sylvia C. 19
  William J. 19
HAMILTON Allen McClain 26
  Augustus 108
  Elizabeth 67
  Emma 108
  Florence 26
  George 107
  Mary 107
  Sarah 107
  Thomas 107
  William 67
HAMMEL John G. 145
  Laura R. 145
HAMMETT James S. B. 151
  Rebecca S. 151
HAMMOCK Amelia 105
  William 105
HAMMOND Amanda 74
  Augusta 74
  Caroline 173
  Clause 74
  Dominick 74
  Edward Clinton 74
  Ella M. 74
  Francis 74
  Frank 74, 173
  J. Dominick 74

INDEX

Joshua 74
Martha 74
Minnie 74
Roscoe 74
Sarah Elizabeth 74
HAMPSHER Betsy A. 165
  Diana 165
  George 165
  Johanna 165
  Nancy 165
HAMPSHIRE Johanna 33
HAMSEN John 23
  Mary M. 23
HANCOCK John 71
  Miss 71
  Rebecca 71
  Sarah 85
HAND Alice 144
HANDY Amelia 143
  Charles Curtis 143
  Charles E. 143
  Clarence 143
  Edward Henry 143
  Edward J. 143
  Emma 159
  Emma J. 143
  Estella Curtis 143
  Harry J. 143
  Isaac 143
  Laura 143
  Maggie May 143
  Margaret 143
  Rachel J. 143
  William G. 143
  William R. 143
HANNA Elizabeth 29
HANNIBAL Emma K. 202
  John 202
HANSON Abbralia 21
  Miss 50
HANWAY Sarah E. 51
  Washington 51
HAPPEL Gertrude 200
HARDCASTLE Addison 202
  Annie 202
HARDIN Dorothy 55
  Mary 118
HARDY Amanda 2
  Anna M. 4
  Elmira 153
  Nicholas 2
HARE Annie 31
  Emory 31
  Harry 31
  Jennie 31

John 31
Lawrence 31
Lee 31
Mary 31
Milton 31
Royden 31
Virgil 31
William F. 31
William W. 31
HARGADINE Mary 23
HARGEST Andrew Jackson 71
  Augusta 72
  Catherine E. 72
  Charles Franklin
  Marion 72
  E. Tupper 72
  Edward Everett 71
  Elizabeth 51
  George Washington 71
  James Monroe 72
  Mary Elizabeth 72
  Mr. 73
  Thomas 71
  Thomas Jefferson 71
  Urith Ann 71
  William Henry
  Harriston 71
HARLAN David 196
  David E. 196
  Esther 196
  George 196
  Helen 197
  Henry Altemus 197
  Henry D. 196
  Herbert 196
  Jehu 204
  Jeremiah 196
  Margaret R. 196
  Margaret Rebecca 196
  Michael 196
  Oleita 196
  W. Beatty 196
HARLEY Annie E. 107, 142
  Charles T. 133, 142
  Charles W. 142
  Elizabeth 107
  Elizabeth A. 142
  Harriett Wade 158
  Harry F. 142
  Ida 133
  Ida L. 142
  John 158
  Joseph 142

Joseph L. 107, 142
William M. 142
HARMON Betsey 133
HARP Ellen 126
  Hezekiah 126
  Sarah Ann 126
HARRETT James H. S. 67
HARRINGTON John P. 204
  Margaret 204
  Mary 104
HARRIS Charles O. 181
  David 191
  Isaac 128
  J. Morrison 191
  Rachel 128
  Sarah 191
  Sidney C. 191
  William H. 191
HARRISBURG Susie 173
HARRISON Ann 23
  Annie A. 63
  Annie B. 63
  Annie R. 142
  Delia Skipworth 201
  Dr. H. T. 54
  Edward 201
  Edward H. 23
  Eliza 23
  Emily 85
  Fannie R. 63
  George L. 23
  J. Arthur 23
  James 23
  James C. 23
  John W. 63
  Marion 54
  Mary 23
  Mary Carrey 63
  Mary Ellen 23
  Mary Jane 23
  Matilda Ann 23
  Melinda 194
  Olivia G. 23
  Peyton 54
  Richard M. 63
  Sarah 23
  Sarah J. 23
  William H. 63, 142
  William Henry 23, 201
  William Shipley 23
HARRYMAN Temperance 185
HARSHBERGER Mary 138
HART Bessie LeRoy 203
  Birdie 203
  Eliza 203

238

INDEX

Harriet Barber 203
John B. 203
Julia 143
Mamie 203
Mary 51
Thomas A. 203
Thomas R. 203
HARTLEY Annie 62
 Deborah 62
 Elizabeth 62
 Joseph 62
 Phineas 62
 Samuel 62
 Wilbur 62
HARTMAN Alice J. 47
 Andrew 11
 Florence 6
 George A. 11
 Joseph 47, 87
HARTZELL Irene 65
 Leonard 65
HARVEY Alice 126
 Andrew 126
 Andrew E. 126
 Annie E. 126
 Annie H. 145
 John K. 99
 Mary 126, 142
 Merrill 126
 Minnie 126
 Sarah R. 99
 William G. 126
HASKINS Joseph 207
 Mary 207
HASLUP John S. M. 32
 Mary 32
 Sophia 91
HASSINGER Jacob 154
 Philip 154
 Philipine 154
 William 154
HASSON Alice 102
 Ann Steener 102
 Annie 102
 Charles 102
 Edward 102
 Ellen 102
 Hugh 102
 Isabel 102
 Joseph 102
 Malcolm 102
 Mary 102
HASTINGS Addie 39
 Clara W. 39
 D. H. 39
 R. J. 39

HATCH Margaret B. 41
 William J. 41
HATTEN Elizabeth 186
HATTER Anna 174
 Charles W. 174
 Eleanor 174
 Emma 174
 Frank 174
 Fredericka 174
 Martin 174
HAUER Catherine 121
 Daniel J. 121
 Henrietta 121
 Jacob 121
 Mary 120, 121
HAUGHEY Edith 128
 Homer K. 128
 Matilda Ann 179
 W. T. 128
 Williametta 128
HAVENNER Franck 44
 Mary L. 44
HAVERN Ella S. 81
HAWKINS Dr. 58
 Ella 58
 James 66
 Martha 66
HAWLEY Delia A. 79
 E. S. 79
HAX Ella M. 130
HAY Alexander 39
 Annie 39
 Eleanor 39
 Eliza 27, 41
 Elizabeth 184
 John 184
 Margaret 39
 Penelope Lynn L. B.
 J. 183, 184
 William 39, 184
HAYDEN Alfred C. 13
 D. F. 13
 Edward G. 13
 Elizabeth A. 13
 Holliday H. 13
 Isaac 13
 Lloyd T. 13
 Mary 127
 Sarah C. 13
HAYES John s. 5
 Katie Cobert 154
 Miss 1
 Phoebe 5
 Rutherford B. 1
HAYHURST Benjamin 164
 Nancy A. 164

HAYNE Sarah 177
HAYS Edward 75
 Eliza 126
 Ella S. 75
HAZELHURST Isaac 197
HAZELTINE Elizabeth A. 38
 Silas W. 38
HEARD Alice 9
 Charles A. 9
 George H. 9
 J. E. 9
 James E. 9
 Joseph 9
 Mills A. 9
 Robert 9
 Roland E. 9
 William D. 9
HEARN N. R. 135
 Rosa E. 135
HEATHCOTE Rosa 34
HEBB Anna 5
 Elizabeth 5
 Henry J. 5
 John W. 5
 Richard 5
 Thomas 5
 Thomas A. 5
 William 5
HEBRANK Annie 106
 Bernidene 106
 Christina 106
 Henry 105, 106
 Joseph 105, 106
 Lena 106
 Lizzie 106
 Mary 106
 Max 106
 Michael 106
 Sierlies 106
 Sophia 106
 Teresa 105
HEBRON Almira 85
HEILIG Addie 39
 Charles 39
 Clara W. 39
 John C. 39
 Mary 39
 May V. 39
 William M. 39
HEIM Frederick 7
HEINLE Agnes 155
 Elizabeth 155
 Frank 155
 John 155
 Joseph 155

INDEX

Kate 155
Mary 155
Michael 155
Tracy 155
HEINZ Bertha 136
George 136
HEISER Theresa 93
HEISLER Edward 190
Ella 190
HEISSE Belle 117
Dr. 186
Edwin W. 117
Fredericka 186
J. Fred 117
John F. 117
Rebecca 117
HELD Minnie 189
HELLEN Caroline 152
Charles Loudon 152
George E. 152
Henry J. 152
John H. 152
Joseph H. 152
Margaret J. 152
Mary A. 152
Sarah 152
HELM Beil 110
Ella 110
Frances 157
HELWIG Annie M. 47
Barbara 47
Christian 47
Christian A. 46
Godfried 46
Lizzie M. 47
Louis G. 47
Maggie 47
Theresa 47
William 47
HEMPEL Mary Sophia 115
HENDERSON Archibald 95
David 178
Laura 38
M. E. 178
Sabra E. 38
Sarah E. 14
Susan 95
HENGST Anne Leah 100
Benjamin 100
Charles D. 100
John Edwin 100
Louis Alfred 100
Martha L. 100
Mary A. 100
Michael 100

Samuel 100
William F. 100
HENNING Mary 2
HENRY A. C. 85
Camilla L. 128
Emma C. 85
Fannie 128
George A. 128
James 85
John 128
John B 85
Joseph E. 128
Katie 85
Lucy 85
Maggie 128
Martha 85
Mary S. E. 128
Ora 85
Patrick 128
Robert J. 128
Robert S. 128
Sallie 48
Samuel H. 128
William 85
William F. 85
HERBERT Ezekiel R. 40
Gideon 40
James B. 196
James Beatty 196
John 196, 197
Margaret 196
Margaret R. 196
Margaret Rebecca 196
Mary A. 40, 196
Mary E. 40
William Paul 196
HERGET Andrew 154
Mary M. 154
HERMAN Barbara 167
Capt. 22
Caroline 167
Elizabeth I. 54
Emanuel W. 54
Grace 54
Margaret 22, 54, 59
Nicholas 167
Sallie M. 54
Sarah 54
HERRING Laura 43
HERRMANN Albert 51
Amelia 51
Edward J. 51
Elizabeth 51
Emma A. 51
Frederick 51

John P. 51
Kate 51
Mary 51
Peter 51
Ruth 51
Tabitha 51
Tina 51
Walter 51
HERTON Susan 96
William 96
HESS George 47
Margaret E. 47
HESZLER Charles F. 52, 53
Sophia 53
Sophia P. 52
HETTINGER Susan 123
HEUISLER Joseph S. 190
Margaret P. 190
HEWITT Agnes 132
HICH Mary E. 170
HICKMAN Laura J. 1
William 1
HICKS Eliza E. 76
Miranda 186
HIGGINS Edwin 197
James 197
James B. 197
James R. 197
Jesse 197
Jesse T. 197
John F. 193
Margaret 197
Margaret A. 193
Margaret Rebecca 197
Martha 193
Rebecca S. 197
Robert 197
William T. 193
HILDEBRAND Susan 49

INDEX

HILL Amelia 48
  Caroline Toole 6
  Charles A. 6
  Charles Geraldus 6
  Charles Irving 6
  D. S. 6
  Daniel S. 6
  Florence 6
  Frederick 48
  Geraldus Toole 6
  Gladys 6
  Green 6
  Isabella 6
  James J. 6
  Louisa 6
  Madeline 6
  Mary C. 164
  Milton P. 6
  Paulina 6
  Susan Rebecca 6
  William I. 6
HILLEARY Elizabeth 177
HILLEN Ann 137
  Charles 105
  Elizabeth 59
  Louisa 105
  Mary 183
HILYARD Charles 111
  Mary 111
HIMES Kate 135
  Mary 135
  Nicholas 135
HINDLE Catharine 60
HINES Catherina A. 68
HINKEL Charles 26
  Susanna 26
HINTZ Philip P. 51
  Tina 51
HIPKINS Eleanor 91
  Mary 91
  Richard 91
HIRSCH Henry 162
  Mary 162
HIRSCHMANN Mary Elizabeth 124
HISER Mary Sophia 62
HISS Ann Elizabeth Lee 127
  Bettie S. 127
  Christiana 127
  Elizabeth 127
  Hester Ann 127
  Jacob 24, 127
  Jesse 127
  Joseph 127
  Mary 127
  Nicholas 127
  Philip 127
  Providence 127
  Sally 127
  Susan 64, 127
  Susannah 127
  Thomas 127
  Valentine 127
  William 64, 127
  William J. 127
HOBOURG Clara L. 37
HODDINOTT Mary A. 65
  Simon 65
HOECK Catherine 75
  Henry 75
  John 75
  Joseph 75
  Kate 75
  Maggie 75
  Margaretta 75
HOEN Alma 66
  George 66
  Gerhardt 66
  Henry 66
  John 66
  Josephine 66
  Mary 66
HOENER Frederick G. 87
  Frederick W. A. 87
  Katie Anna 87
  Lizzie W. 87
  Mattie 87
HOERR Alexander 135
  Anna Margaret 135
  Dora Mary 135
  Ella M. 135
  Emma Louisa 135
  Erma 135
  Frederick C. C. 135
  Henry Alexander 135
  John 135
  John P. M. 135
  Lucy Augusta 135
  Margaret 135
  Margaret J. R. 135
  Martin Louis 135
  Rev. J. H. W. 135
  William A. 135
HOFFMAN Aaron 118
  Albert H. 201
  Ann Rebecca 201
  Catherine 48
  Charles E. 118
  Daniel 118
  Daniel M. 118
  Eliza 49
  Eliza M. 107
  Elizabeth 49
  George 49
  George F. 49
  George L. 201
  George M. 118
  Hannah 49
  Isaac R. 201
  Jacob 201
  Jacob V. 201
  Jane 49
  Johanna 49
  John 118
  John F. 195
  John Frederick 201
  Joseph 49
  Julia M. 201
  Laura V. 195
  Lillie M. 118
  Lizzie 68
  Lucinda 49
  Mary 49, 118, 201
  Mary E. A. 118
  Mary G. 92
  Mary Hannah 201
  Mattie 118
  Michael 201
  Naomi 118
  Peter B. 48, 49
  Rosalba 118
  Rosetta 201
  Salema 49
  Sarah 49
  Sarah Ann 195
  Susan 49
  Susanna 201
  Susie 49
  Washington S. 201
  William Albert 201
  William D. 49
  William S. 118
HOFSTETTER Annie 24
  Aug. 41
  Catherine 24, 122
  Edward 24, 122
  Elizabeth 41
  Frank 24
  George 24, 41
  Harmon 41
  Henry 41
  John 24, 41
  Joseph 24
  Kate 41

INDEX

Lawrence 24
Louisa 24
Mary 24
Mary C. 24
William Henry 24
HOGAN Edith 41
  Edward 41
  Mary 41
HOGARTH Abbralia 20
  Alice 20
  W. A. 20
HOLBROOK Amelia 99
  Oliver 99
HOLDEN Anne 133
  Edward 115
  James P. 133
  Lillie 115
  William 133
HOLDERMAN Mary A. 112
HOLLAND Carrie 61
  Henry 127
  John G. 61
  Laura M. 127
  Sarah 60
  Sophia Suter 68
HOLLER Amanda 172
  John 172
HOLLIDAY Susan 200
HOLLINGSWORTH Jesse 25
  Rachel Lyde 25
  Sarah 152
HOLMES D. R. 115
  Elizabeth 71, 116
  Ella 115
  Gabriel 116
  Griselda 116
  James 116
  Jane 116
  John B. 58
  John G. 116
  Temperance 116
  Victoria 58
  Victor 116
  William 116
HOLTHEBNER Mary M. 187
HOMBURG Lena 107
  Martin 107
HONNEMAN Catherine E. 48
HOOD Amelia 179
  B. Franklin 179
  Benjamin 179
  Carrie 179
  Ella 179
  Emily 179
  James 179

John 179
Joshua 179
Mamie 179
Mary 179
Mary F. 179
Matilda An 179
Sarah 179
Stella 179
HOOK Anna 188
  Elizabeth 65
  Elizabeth Marion 34
  Lydia A. 60
  Rachel 60
  Richard 65
  Thomas 60
HOOPER Emily 184
HOOPS Georgie 201
HOOT Miss 171
HOOVER Susan 103
HOPE Miss 161
HORDEY William Harvey 52
HORN Amanda 180
  Anna R. 180
  August 180
  Augusta 180
  Balthasar 180
  Francis 180
  Lena 180
  Louis C. 180
  Louis Charles 180
  Maggie 180
  Mary 180
  Minnie 180
  Philip 180
HORNER Mary Ann Tyler 168
  Richard 169
  Robert Richard 169
HOSHALL Althea b. 165
  Bessie L. 165
  Besty A. 165
  Clarence E. 165
  Clarence M. 33
  Elizabeth 89
  Elizabeth O. 89
  Ella 165
  Ellen 89
  Florence S. 89
  Frederick R. 89
  Hester R. 165
  Howard 165
  Jacob 97
  Jesse 89, 165
  Jesse M. 89

Johanna 33
Martha 165
Melchor 165
Minnie B. 89
Nelson 33
Nicholas 165
Phoebe 97
Sarah A. 89
HOSMER Fannie Albert 106
  James Ray 106
  Jennie 106
HOUCK Maggie 115
HOUSE Agnes 106
  Charles 106
  Ida 57
HOUSTON Dr. M. H. 184
  Mary G. 184
HOWARD Elizabeth 38, 44
  Ellen 62
  Frances 44
  Margaret 102
  Mary 58
  Robert 62
HOY Alice 26
  Harry 26
HOYT Margaret 120
  Thomas 120
HUART Frank 150
  Rosa 150
HUBBARD Alan H. 42
  Sarah 42
HUBBE Augusta 189
HUBER Edward 87
  Emma 87
  Frederick 87
  John Ulrich 87
  Louisa 87
  Margaretta 87
  Ulrich 87
HUCKELMANN Clara 113
HUDSON Calvin 82
  Calvin T. 107
  Clarkson 82
  Elizabeth 82
  Ella Estelle 194
  Harry Gilmore 194
  Hendrick 82, 194
  John 194
  John L. 82, 107
  Joseph W. 193
  Julia Etta 194
  Lewis 82
  Margaret Ann 105
  Mary A. 82
  Mary Ann 193

INDEX

May 107
Mazie 107
Octavius W. 193
Rosa 194
Sarah 82
Susan 82
William 82, 105
HUFFER Catherine 123
Daniel N. 123
David 123
Eliza 123
George C. 123
J. Dawson 123
Jacob M. 123
John 123
Joseph L. 123
William E. 123
HUGHES Alexander 155
Amanda 155
Ann 148
Charles D. 155
Clemantha 38
Elisha H. 148, 155
Elizabeth 148, 155
Elizabeth Ann 148
Frances A. 155
Frances Ann 148
Henry 148, 155
James 155
James Wesley 148
Jane 155
John 141
John Henry 148
John W. 148, 155
Louisa 148
Margaret Ann 155
Martha Ann 155
Melvina 148
Mrs. J. 135
Sophia J. 148
Thomas 155
Thomas H. 155
Virginia E. 141
William 155
William C. 155
William Henry 148, 155
William James 148, 155
Willimina 56
Zenue 56
HULL A. K. V. 31
Abbie V. 31
Augustus 203
Catherine 203
HUMMER Annie R. 7
Braden E. 7

Earnest E. 7
George W. F. 7
J. C. 7
Washington 7
HUMRICHAUSE Maggie 128
HUNT Sylvia C. 19
HUNTER Andrew 98
Ann 186
Elizabeth 98
Jennie 88
Sarah J. 98
Thomas 88
HUNTINGTON A. B. 171
Ada 171
HURST Ellen 89
John 170
Samuel 170
Sarah Berry 170
Susan L. 170
HURTT Annie E. 98
Charles R. 98
Edward W. 98
Emma G. 98
Linda E. 98
Mabel 98
Martha 98
Mary E. 98
Mary L. 98
Robert M. 98
Sarah E. 98
William N. 98
HUSS Susan 127
HUTCHINS Emily 15
Florence E. 89
Mary J. 36
Nicholas T. 36
William 15
HUTCHINSON Amanda 56
Amanda A. 187
Frank P. 185
John T. 185
Julia 185
Mollie E. 185
HUTTON Dovie 77
Elizabeth 25
Emily 76
George H. 76
Giralda 77
Julia 77
M. Dora 77
Robert E. 77
Rose B. 77
William 25
Mildred 77
HUYBERTS Catalyntje 170

HYATT Alpheus 102
Amelia 102
HYDE Maria Louise 1
HYLAND Absalom 119
Wilhelmina 119
HYMAN Abbie 146
Christopher 146
George W. 146
George W. 146
Lillian Gertrude 146
Susie 146
William H. 146
HYNSON Annie M. 34
Benjamin 34

IGLEHART Helen 52
Eleanor 52
Elizabeth 52
Helen 52
John W. 52
Mary 52
Matilda 52
ILER George Washington 105
John 105
John Highland 105
Maggie 105
Margaret Ann 105
Mary Ann 105
Sarah 105
Sarah R. 105
Stephen 105
Tolbart Stephen 105
IMMLER Caroline 138
George 138
IMMORDA Ann Sophia
Frederic 196
IMWOLD Adaline 28
Anna 28
Caroline W. 28
Carrie 28
Catherine 28
Charles F. 28
Frank 28
Henry 28
John A. 28
John B. 28
Mary 28
Samuel 28
Samuel G. 28
INGHAM Alberta E. 88
Anna R. 88
Charles W. 88
Emily 88
Erma 88

INDEX

Grace 88
Henrietta 88
John W. 87
Lucy S. 88
Mary 88
Milton W. 88
Sarah 88
Sereptha J. 88
Virginia B. 88
INLOWS Mary 145
IRELAND D. Caldwell 178
 Elizabeth 178
 M. E. John 178
 Thomas 178
 William 178
IRONS Anna Rowe 9
 Edward Pontney 9
 James 9
 Rebecca 9
ISAAC Amy P. 63
 Andrew J. 63
 Eleanor 63
 Elizabeth 63
 Ella 63
 George W. 63
 Gertrude 63
 John 63
 Mary Ann 63
 Mary R. 63
 Mary W. 63
 Randolph Moore 63
 Thomas J. 63
 William Moore 63
 Williams 63
 Zedekiah Howard 63
 Zedekiah Moore 63
ISAACSON Albert 204
 Virginia 204

JACKSON Andrew C. 136
 Benjamin 100
 Elisha 80
 Emily J. 80
 Helen 179
 J. Wesley 80
 John H. B. 80
 Julia 37
 Julia Ann 80
 Margaret A. 47
 Robert Royston 80
 Sarah Duke 170
 Sylvania 100
 Temperance 136
 Thomas 80
 Thomas D. 80

Wilber F. 179
William 47
JACOBS Emily T. 137
 Johan 144
 M. L. 144
JACOBSON Barbara 152
JAMES Alfred 12
 Margie 94
 Norman 94
 W. Armstrong 12
 William M. 12
JAMISON Charles E. 94
 Edward C. 94
 Ellen 94
JANNEY Albert 162
 Annie Maria 162
 Daisy C. 162
 Daniel 162
 Dr. E. W. 77, 112
 Edward W. 162
 Eli H. 162
 Elizabeth A. 162
 Esther S. 112
 Hettie S. 77, 162
 Hugh W. 162
 Mayo 162
 Nathan H. 162
 Rawley C. 162
JARBOE James A. 9
JARRETT Asbury 10
 Brooke Lessig 67
 Emma W. 11, 66
 Francis W. 11
 Hon. J. H. 67
 J. H. S. 11
 James H. 10, 11, 66
 Jesse 10
 Joshua W. 11
 Julia H. 11
 Lillie 67
 Luther M. 10, 11
 Martin L. 11
 Mary V. 161
 Sarah E. 11
 Thomas B. 11
 William B. 11
JASPER Anna 55
JEAN Anna A. 5
 David 5
 Susan Bowen 61
JEFFERS Ann 12
 George W. 12
 John G. 12
 Naomi Emily 12
JEFFERSON Thomas 10

JEFFRESS Ann Bedford 40
 Jennings 40
 Jennings M. 40
 Margaret Bedford 40
 Thomas 40
JEMES Mary 160
JEMMISON Rachel 57
JENETZKE August R. 167
 Caroline 167
 Emily 167
 John A. 167
 Nicholas W. 167
 Otto F. 167
JENIFER Bettie 54
 Charles W. 54
 Daniel 54
 Eleanor T. 54
 Eliza Campbell 54
 Elizabeth 54
 Emily B. 54
 Florence C. 54
 H. Courtney 54
 John 54
 John B. Morris 54
 Margaret A. 54
 Marion 54
 Mary R. 54
 Nannie C. 54
 Robert Moore 54
 Sarah 54
 T. C. Risteau 54
 Thomas 54
 Thomas R. 54
 Walter 54
 Walter H. 54
JENKINS Albin 137
 Alfred 59
 Alice Julia 137
 Ann 59, 136, 137
 Ann Ellen 137
 Ann Maria 136, 137
 Annie M. 59, 183
 Arthur 137
 Austin 59
 Bessie 59
 Captain R. A. 130
 Charity A. 59, 137
 Clara 59
 Corinne 183
 Edward 59, 136, 137
 Edward F. 59
 Eleanor 137
 Elizabeth 59, 136, 137, 183
 Elizabeth Hillen 137

244

INDEX

Ellen 59, 137
Elsie H. 137
Emma 112
Eugene 137
Felix 193
Frances L. 183
George 59, 136, 183
Harriet 59
Helen 59
Henry 136
Henry C. S. 137
Hillen 59, 137
Ignatius 136, 137
James 136
James Willcox 137
Jane 136
John 59
John Hillen 137
John W. 137
John Willcox 136
Joseph Willcox 137
Josephine 183
Josiah 59, 137
Josias 137
Lycurgus 183
Lydia 183
Margaret E. 130
Mark 136
Mark Willcox 137
Mary 136, 137
Mary A. 136, 151
Mary Augusuta 59
Mary Emily 193
Mary Josephine 59, 183
Mary L. 59
Matilda 183
Michael 59, 136, 137
R. Hillen 183
Rebecca 137, 172
Robert 60
Sarah 59
Sarah Catherine 59
Talbot W. 183
Thomas 59, 136, 172
Thomas C. 137
Thomas Courtney 136, 137
Thomas Meredith 59
W. Armour 183
William 59, 136, 137
William Spaulding 59
JENNESS Althine 12
Bessie 12
C. K. 12
E. K. 12
Ida 12
J. F. 12
Mattie 12
JESSOP Bettie 178
Charles 178
Charles A. 178
Charles M. 38
Elizabeth 178
Ellen 178
Emma A. 38
George 178
John B. 178
Keziah B. 92
Nettie 178
William H. 178
JESTER Mary 102
JEWELL Amelia 195
Charles 84
Gertrude 149
John 195
Mary Irene 149
Ruthess 149, 195
Samuel 195
Samuel A. 149
Samuel R. 149
T. Morgan 195
William E. 195
JIMISON Absalom 114
Elizabeth 114
Elsie 114
Howard W. 114
Jane E. 114
John C. 114
Mary 114
Matilda 114
Samuel T. 114
JOHNS Richard 204
JOHNSON Annie 91
Annie M. 110
Captain J. D. 115
Catherine 96
Daisy 115
Edward 115
Edward A. 91
Effie E. 188, 198
Elijah 90
Elizabeth 91, 192
Elmer 91
Emma 115
Frances Russel 198
Frederick 115
George 115, 188, 198
George B. 90
George E. 110
George H. 91
Gladys M. 64
H. C. 63
Hannah 90
Henrietta A. 4
Henrietta M. 103
Henry 115
James 81, 115
James W. Pegram 116
Jennie 31
Jethro 63
Joab 31
John 115
Julia 64
Kate 191
Katie 115
Laura 64
Lena 115
Lizzie 115
Lizzie L. 115
Maggie 115
Margaret 18
Mary 115
Mary E. 91
Peter 116
Philip G. 91
Priscilla 116
Rachel 63
Rev. H. S. 64
Sadie 182
Samuel 182
Sarah 114
Sarah C. 81
Sarah Lund 3
Thomas 198
Virginia 116
Virtue 31
W. W. 63, 64
William 115
William H. 5
Wilmot 10, 18
JONES Alice Elizabeth 107
Annie 146
Annie H. 145
Annie J. 153
Benjamin 153
Benson 107
Bertie 107
Catherine E. 112, 173
Charles 107, 112, 173
Charlotte Abbott 145
David 84
David W. 117
Edgar 142
Edity Wynne 145

INDEX

Elizabeth 117, 119, 142, 145, 153
Ellen 111
Estella 142
Garland 6
Harriet 111
Harriet Sterrett 106
Harvey Llewellyn 145
Helen 107, 145
Helena May 145
Henry 146
Howard 142
J. Wynne 145
James 111
James A. 111
Jenkin 145
John S. 106
John W. 117
Joseph Charles 159
Josiah 107
Maggie 105
Maggie A. 58
Mamie 179
Margaret Catherine 142
Martha Jane 159
Mary 107, 112, 117, 200
Mary A. C. 189
Mary V. 133
Milton 142
Minnie 55
Nettie 107
Priscilla 159
R. B. 105, 142
Rebecca 111
Robert H. 142
Sidney 142
Taylor 107
Thomas 112, 145
William 107, 179
Worthington Luke 107
JORDAN Archibald S. 156
Benjamin F. 156
Charles 176
Edward 176
Edward C. 156
Harriett R. 156
Henry F. 176
Henry J. 176
James P. 156
John 156
John Joseph 176
John L. 156
John S. 156
Julia E. 156
Margaret A. 156
Mary C. 176
Mary E. 176
Mary J. 156
Mary S. 156
Otho 156
Rachel A. 156
Rebecca 156
Samuel M. 156
Thomas 156, 176
Thomas R. 156
William Lawrence 176
JUDD John 205
Laura 205
JUNKINS Alice V. 163
Charles E. 163
Edith Arnold 164
Elizabeth 163
Florence Wilson 164
George F. 163
J. William 163
Mabel Davis 164
Oliver 163
JUSTUS Charles E. 188
Selina J. 188
KAHL Anna E. 156
George 156
KAHLER Annie 100
August 100
Charles 100
Charles 100
Christina 100
George 100
Jack 100
Jacob 100
John 100
Joseph 100
Kate 100
Maggie 100
Mary 100
Philipine 7
Ricka 100
KAHLOR Susanna 141
KAISER Anna 28
KALAL Annie 99
KALLFUES Margaret A. 193
KALMEY Anna Maria 124
Annie M. 18
KAMMER Anna 45
William 45
KANE Allen 78
Annie 205
Frances 77, 78
Irving 78
James 77
James G. 77
Jane 116
Lenore 78
Marjorie 78
Mary A. 77
Nathan 116
Peter 205
Robert J. 77
Wallace 78
KAREW Katie 9
KARR Elisha 29
Hannah Perry 29
Rebecca 29
KASTNER Susan 152
KATTER Cecelia 72
KAUFMAN George J. 20
John G. 20
Kate 190
Lena 20
Samuel 190
KAUSMALL Barbara 103
KEABNEY Ellen 27
John 27
KEARNS Ella 23
Thomas 23
KEDWELL Jane 96
KEEN Fannie 167
George 167
Harry C. 167
Howard 167
Howard O. 167
Lutine Mitchell 167
Margaret Ann 167
Nelson 167
Sarah E. 167
Sarah Virginia 167
Walter 167
William Frank 167
William J. 167
KEENE Abigail Patterson 48
Ann Hall 48
Charles Ridout 48
Elizabeth Dorsey 48
Frances Cook 48
Jane 48
John Henry 48
Laura Eleanor 48
Mary Hollingsworth 48
Robert Goldsborough 48
Sallie 48
Samuel Yerbury 48
Sarah 48
Sarah D. 48
William C. 48

INDEX

KEENEY Harvey 57
 Sarah 57
KEETCHUM Charlotte M. 36
KEHS L. W. 47
 Lizzie M. 47
KEIDEL Charles 44
 Henry 44
 Lewis 44
 Maria 44
KEISER George 31
 Jennie 31
KEITH James 1
KELLER John 165
 Mary Ann 165
KELLEY Isabel 98
 James 160
 Mary C. 160
KELLUM Anna E. 173
 Custes 111
 Eliza R. 111
KELLY Celia R. 4
 J. T. 58
 John G. 43
 Julia E. 4
 Mary Jane 43
 May 58
 Thomas 4
KELSEY James 171
 Mary A. 171
KEMP Diana 104
 Francis S. 132
 Howard 104
 Lillian 132
 Shedwick 104
 Susan 104
 Williametta 128
KENLY Albert C. 110
 Annie 34
 Annie M. 34
 Daniel 34
 Davis L. 110
 Douglas C. 110
 Edward 34, 110
 Edward G. 110
 Edward Marion 34
 Elizabeth 34
 George T. 34
 George Tyson 34, 110
 Guy 34
 John R. 110
 John Reese 34
 Laura Hook 34
 Maria 34, 110
 Maria Reese 34
 Martha Emily 34

Priscilla 34, 110
 Richard 34
 Ritchie G. 34
 Roberta Martin 34
 William L. 34, 110
 William Lacy 34
 William W. 110
KENNARD Catherine 140, 141
 George W. 140, 141
 Henrietta 141
 John R. 141
 Mary 200
 Mary J. 141
 Richard 140, 141
 William w. 141
KENNEDY Annette B. 180
 John 151
 Mary A. 151
 W. F. 180
 William 151
KEPHART Susan 89
KERCHNER Anton 99
 Mary Rosina 99
KERL Catharine 24
KERSHBAUM Elizabeth 144
KESMODEL Christina 130
KESSELL Fred 167
 Philip 167
 Sophia 167
 William 167
KEESLER Lena 20
KETCHUM Elmer Leroy 36
 Frederick M. 36
 Kate H. 36
 Kate Helen 36
KETTERING Elizabeth 2
 Mary 2
KEY Anne Phoebe 203
 Frances S. 167
 Francis Scott 131, 167, 198, 203
 Mary 197, 198
 Philip 198
 Rebecca Joel 198
 Richard 198
KEYSER Sarah E. 190
KIDD Temperance 64
KIMMEY Margaret 74
KINDERVATTER Elizabeth 117
 Frederick 117
 Hanna 117
KING Abraham 44
 Anderson B. 115

Cecelia G. 71
 David 44
 Elizabeth 44
 Emma 46, 115
 Esther A. 46
 Isaac 46
 Isabella V. 46
 J. A. 206
 James 111
 Jemima 46
 Jemima E. 46
 Joshua M. 46
 Joshua McKinley 46
 Lottie U. 206
 Mary 46
 Mary E. 44
 Matilda 46
 Priscilla 111
 Rachel 46
 Sarah 46
 Thomas 46, 71
KINLEY Newton 110
KINSLE Caroline 24
 Jacob 24
KIRBY Harry 180
 Minnie 180
KIRKLAND Ann L. 83
 Bessie Green 83
 Elizabeth 83
 John Thornton 83
 Margaret Calvert 83
 Mary Clara 83
 Ogden 83
 Ogden A. 83
 Samuel Maxwell 83
KIRSCHENHOFER Anton 14
 Barbara Bauer 14
 Charles 14
 Fredericka 14
 George 14
 Kate 14
 Mary 14
KIRSCHMANN Christian 166
 Elizabeth 166
 Emma 166
 Henrietta 166
 Mary 166
 Paul 166
KIRWAN Annabel 19
 Nellie R. 19
 Sarah A. 19
 William B. 19
 William Benjamin 19
 William H. 19

247

INDEX

KISER Allen 50
  Mary 50
  Newberry A. S. 50
KISNER Conrad 118
KLAWITTER Anna 151
KLEIN Joseph 100
  Mary 100
KLIMA Caroline 99
  Joseph 99
KLINE Bessie 198
  Edgar 198
  Elizabeth 198
  Fannie 198
  Frederick 198
  George 198
  Ida 198
  John 198
  Julia 198
  Maggie 198
  Margaret 198
  Sophia 129
  Thomas H. H. 198
  William H. 198
KLINK Alexander 16
  Helen Knight 16
KLOCH Augusta 180
KLUTH Augusta 70
  Charles 70
  Elizabeth 70
  Emma 70
  Frederick 70
  Harry 70
  Herman 70
  Lizzie 70
  Mina 70
  Tena 70
  William 70
KNELL John J. 129
KNETEBER Benjamin 187
  Mary E. 187
KNIGHT Ann L. 83
  Gertrude 27
KNOCH Family 52
KNOEBEL Anna 60
  Annie 60
  Catherine E. 60
  Henry 60
  Henry W. 60
  Mary 60
KNOEFLER Anna 138
KNORR Captain 17
  Deborah M. 17
  Elizabeth 17
  Hannah C. 166
  William 166

KNOTTS William H. 91
KNOX Annstina 53
  Bessie 54
  Charles H. 52, 53
  Charles R. 52
  Ernestine 52
  Eugene 54
  Hazel 52
  John P. 53
  John W. 54
  Julius W. 52, 53
  Katherine 38
  Louis Peter 52
  Lulu 54
  Margaret 64
  Peter 52
  Sophia 52, 53
  Sophia P. 52
  Stevenson Arthur 54
  Susan 52
  Susanna 54
  Teresa 52
  William 52
  Winchester 54
KOHL Miss 207
KONE Elizabeth 36
KRACH Annie Elizabeth 122
  August 103
  Barbara 103
  Elizabeth 103
  Ernest 103
  George C. 103
  George Caspar 103
  Jacob P. 103
  John J. 103
  John P. 103, 122
  Leonard 103
  Lillie 103
  Mary 103
  Philip J. 103
  Robert T. 103
KRAMER A. M. 129
  Caroline 28
  Frederick 28, 129
  Mary A. 129
KRANTZ Barbara 166
  Elizabeth 166
  George 166
  George H. 166
  Hannah 166
  Janet 166
  John C. 166
  Margaret 166
KRASH Jaco 65
  Lizzie 65

KRATZ Conrad 33
KREBS Jacob 199
  Mary 199
KRETCHMAN Mollie 181
KRIDER Catherine 206
KRIEL Caroline 163
  John 163
KROEBER Carrie M. 146
  Frederick 146
KROH Sarah A. 89
KROUT Adam H. 175
  David 57
  Emma W. E. 175
  Martha 57
KUKEL Johanna 48
KUNKE John N. 99
KUNKEL Anna M. 99
  Casper 99
  Francis F. 99
  Frederick J. 99
  John A. 99
  John Adam 99
  Joseph A. 99
  Margaret 99
  Mary R. 99
  Mary Rosina 99
  Mary Theresa 99
  Nicholas 99
  Nicholas A. 99
  William F. 99
KURTZ Abbie 178
  Agnes Louisa 172
  Alice J. 126
  Ann 178
  Anna V. 126
  Benjamin 178
  Catherine 52
  Edna L. 178
  Eliza 126
  F. Albert 178
  France P. 126
  George J. 126
  Harriet C. 52
  Harry J. 126
  John 52, 172, 178
  John Jacob 126
  Julia 178
  Nettie A. 126
  Sherman L. 52
  T. Newton 178
  Thomas 52
  William F. 52
KUSZMAUL Laurence 129
  Mary A. 129
  Sophia 129
KYLE Martha M. 165

INDEX

LACKEY Margaretta 176
  Milford R. 176
LAIB Alice J. 126
LAINE Nora Latrobe 123
LAMBERT Elijah 16
  Maria 16
LAMDIN Robert P. 14
  Thomasine M. 14
LAMLEY Barbara E. 65
  Jacob 65
  Mary E. 78
LAMPKIN Elizabeth 116
  Griffin 116
LANDMANN Emma 155
LANE Catherine Olivia 199
LANG Henry 76
  Kunigunchen 146
  Mary 76
LANGDON Wilhelmina 141
  William G. 141
LANGE Anna E. 156
  August H. 156
  August Henry 155
  Cynthia 156, 170
  Elizabeth 155
  Elizabeth B. 156
  Florence E. 156
  Hannah 156
  Henry 155, 170
  Mattie 156
  Robert H. 156
LANGFILER Annie 155
  George 155
LANGHENRY Emma 90
LANGKAM Elizabeth Anna 55
LANSDALE Eleanor 170
LANTZ Amelia C. 196
  Ann Elizabeth 196
  Ann Sophia Frederica 196
  Caroline 196
  Charles W. 196
  Dora 196
  George C. 196
  Jacob 196
  Jacob H. 196
  John 196
  John J. Fred 196
  Mary A. 196
  Mary F. 196
  Wilhelmina Elizabeth 196
LANZER Caroline 21
LAOCOMPT Lydia 146
LARRIMORE Annie 150
  Robert 150
LATCHFORD Mary 126

LATROBE Benjamin H. 197
  Charlotte 197
  Charlotte B. 197
  Ellen 197
  Ferdinand C. 197
  Henry 197
  John 197
  John H. B. 197
  Louisa 197
  Lydia 197
  Osmun 197
  R. Stuart 197
  T. Swann 197
  Virginia 197
LATZ Anna B. 55
LAUDER Mary A. 103, 104
LAUF Alex 172
LAUMANN Ada Virginia 161
  Adam 151, 152, 161
  Annie 152
  Barbara 151, 152
  Charles Harrison Morton 161
  Elizabeth 152, 161
  George S. 152
  Henry 151, 161
  Henry W. 152, 161
  Louis D. 152
  Mary 152
  Simon 152
  Susan 152
  Susanna 152
  William Owens 161
LAURENSON Augusta M. 176
  C. Philip 176
  Charles R. 176
  Elizabeth 175, 176
  Francis B. 175
  Francis Beaston 175
  Julia L. 176
  Laura 175
  Laura R. 176
  Margaretta 175, 176
  Mary A. 175
  Nora R. 176
  Philip 175, 176
  Sarah 175
LAVENBURG Daniel 147
  Sarah A. 147
LAWLER John P. 8
LAWRENCE Christian 188, 198
  Mary E. 188, 198
  Sarah D. 48

LAWSON Ida 137
  John 137
LAWTON Cyril 30
  Susan 30
LAWYER Caspar 21
  Martha E. 22
  Christian 21
  Clarence 22
  Dr. 21
  Edwin J. 21
  Martin 21
  Mary 22
  Philip 21
  Susan 21
  Susanna 21
  William 21, 22
LAYTON Emma Jane 45
  Florence Holbrook 45
  James Holbrook 45
Le BRUN Ambrose 132
  Annie 132
  Emma 132
  George 132
  Henry 132
  John A. 132
  Joseph 132
  Josephine 132
  Julia A. 132
  Louis 132
  Mary Elizabeth 132
  Mary J. 132
  Nicholas Deshields 132
LEACH Urith Ann 71
LEAGUE Anna P. 28
  Joshua 28
  Margaret P. 28
LEATHERWOOD Miss 107
LeBARON Charles 13
  Mary 13
LeCOMPTE Esther A. 45
LEDLEY Augusta 74
  Isaac 74
LEE Elizabeth 61
  Ella 143
  Ella V. 143
  Emma . 66
  J. Wesley 66
  James H. 66
  John 143
  John R. 82
  Julia A. 66
  Margaret I. H. 68
  Marguerite 66
  Martin L. 66
  Mary Elizabeth 82

INDEX

Myra 64
Sophia Suter 68
William 61, 68
William A. 11, 64, 66
LEE (Leigh) Alexander
  Nisbet 101
  Cassandra O. 101
  Frank M. 101
  Frank M. 101
  Susan Palfrey 101
  Thomas Jefferson 101
  Thomas Nisbet 101
  William 101
LEECH Blanche 131
  Clara E. 131
  G. Eddie 131
  George F. 131
  George T. 131
  Mary A. 131
  Ruth 131
  Susan S. 131
  Thomas 131
  Wilbur R. S. 131
LEEF Henry 65
  Juliet 65
LEES Alice 4
LEESE James P. 27
  Mrs. James P. 27
LEESON Alfred Bradford 150
  Catherine 150
  Richard 150
LEIDSHUH Agnes 155
  Daniel 155
LEILLECK Fredericka 123
LEINSZ Daniel 174
  Fredericka 174
LEISENRING Eliza H. 27
  George Washington 27
  Georgiana 27
  John G. Morris 27
  L. Morris 27
  Mary Helen 27
  Mrs. G. Morris 41
LEMMERT Anna 138
  August 138
  Bertha 138
  Caroline 138
  Emma 138
  George 138
  Johannetta 138
  John R. 138
  Ruth 138
LEONARD Annie 150
  Annie Nora 150

Arianna 150
Carrie 28
Clifford B. 150
Colonel 53
Edmund T. 150
Helen 53
Helen E. 150
Howard E. 150
John 28
Joshua 150
Robert 150
Robert Hall 150
LERCH Charles 81
  Elizabeth 81
  Sophia 91
LESLIE Ida M. 172
LESSIG Emma Catherine 67
  George B. 67
  Lillie 67
LEUTZ Catherine 52
LEVER Anna 180
LEVY Abby 25
LEWIN Sarah C. 23
LEWIS A. T. 171
  Anna 93
  Annie 171
  Arnold T. 171
  Columbus W. 171
  Elizabeth 171
  Ellen 171
  George C. 148
  George S. 148
  George W. 122
  Henrietta J. 148
  John 82
  Julia Etta 148
  Mahala 194
  R. C. 171
  Rosa R. J. 171
  Sarah 82
  Susan H. 122
  William J. 171
LIDEN Elizabeth 150
LIEBNOW Charles 70
  Mina 70
LIESENER Wilhelmena 18
LIETUVNIKAS Anna 181
  Joseph A. 181
  Matthew 181
LIGHTFOOT Nora M. 169
LILLY Austin Jenkins 59
  Edward Joseph Jenkins 59
  George Cromwell 59

Helen 59
Henry J. 59
Josephine Jenkins 59
Margaret Jenkins 59
Mary 59
Mary Edith 59
Mary Loretta 59
LINDSAY Annie 160
  Annie Teresa 160
  Anthony 160
  Catherine T. R. 160
  James J. 159, 160
  Mary C. 160
  Mary Regina 160
LINK Kate 65
  Mary 65
  Peter 65
LINTHICUM Annie S. 12
  Catherine 164
  Elizabeth V. 12
  Frank 164
  G. Milton 12
  Herman R. 164
  J. Charles 12
  James S. 12
  Mary C. 164
  Seth Hance 12
  Sweetser 12
  Thomas F. 164
  Wade Hampton 12
  William 12
LINTNER Fredericka
  Henrietta 128
LIPP James 75
  Lottie E. 75
LIPPINCOTT Lydia 73
LIPSCOMB Miss 24
LIST Anna Elizabeth 45
  Catherine 45
  Christopher 45
  Elizabeth 45
  J. Adams 45
  J. Philip 45
  John 45
  John P. 45
  Katie 45
  Louisa 45
  Mary 45
LITCHFORD James A. 17
  Mollie 17
LITSINGER Ellen 112
  Joseph 112
LITTLE Daniel 73
  Emma Jane 73
LITTLETON Mary Kate 84
  William 84

INDEX

LITZINGER Harriet 15
  Joseph 15
LIVAS Jane 22
LIVINGSTON Anna E. 173
  Anna Keene 173
  E. Latrobe 173
  Ida V. 173
  James H. 173
  Nancy A. 173
  Sarah E. 173
  Seth F. 173
  William 173
  William E. 173
LLOYD A. Parlett 19, 20
  Anna 48
  Annie E. 20
  Benjamin MacDonald 20
  Eugene D. 20
  Eugenie 19, 20
  Eugenie U. 20
  Henry L. 20
  John 19
  John H. 19
  Josiah E. 48
  Lillie 48
  Madison E. 48
  Mattie 20
  Samuel E. 48
LOANE Annie E. 20
  George J. 20
LOCKARD G. W. Aler 105
  Roxana 105
  William 105
LOEWER John 109
  Martha E. 109
LOMBARD Albert 189
  Isabella 189
LONG Annie 118
  Caroline 118
  Conrad 118
  Elizabeth 137
  Frank 118
  George 118
  John 118, 137
  Katie 118
  Lina 118
  Lizzie 118
  Mary 118
  Michael 118
  Nicholas 6
  Rebecca 6, 118
  Regina 118
  Rose 118
  William 118

LONGNECKER Ann 108
  Annie S. 108
  Betsy 108
  David 108
  David S. 108
  Edwin B. 108
  Emma 108
  Frank 109
  John G. 109
  John H. 108
  John S. 108
  Lizzie 108
  Mabel 109
LORD Bessie 116
  Charles Robbins 116
LORENZ Elizabeth 191
LORING Frank 197
  Lydia 197
LORT Amanda 21
  Joseph 21
LOVE A. Kinglsey 164
  Benedict 164
  Bernard 164
  Charles K. 164
  Josephine 164
  Mary 164
  Mary W. 204
  Melvin 164
  Nora 164
  Philip G. 164
  R. Horace 204
LOVELL Elizabeth A. 21
  Martha 86
LOWE Alfred 88
  Amos 88
  Ann Rebecca 47
  Asenath 88
  Elizabeth 90
  F. W. 159
  Jacob E. 47
  Jane 88
  Jeremiah 88
  Julia A. 134
  Keturah 88
  Mary A. 159
  Merab 88
  Nicholas 88
  Ralph 88
  Sarah Catherine 159
LOWNAN Mary 65
LUARD Eleanor L. 102
  Lawrence Shirley 102
  Montague 102
  William Sidney 102

LUCAS Basil 61
  Earnest N. 61
  Edward 91
  Emma B. 61
  George L. 61
  Henry W. 91
  James 61
  John 61
  John A. 61
  John Deaver 61
  Lucia 91
  Margaret 116
  Mary 61
  Mary Vickery 61
  Mollie M. 61
  Sarah E. 61
  Sophia 91
  Thomas 61
  William 91
LUCE Honora 118
  William 118
LUCY Edward 186
  Mary E. 186
LUKENS Julia A. 22
LUMBERSON Catherine 148
  E. L. 148
  Emeline 148
  John 148
  Margaret 148
  Mary 148
  Naomi 148
  Philip 148
LUTHER Caroline 119
LUTZ Catherine 24
  Elizabeth 145
  Mary C. 122
  Mary Christina 24
  Mary Ellen 140
  Nicholas 140
  Valentine 24
LYDE Ann 25
  Ann Maria 25
  Cornelia 25
  Cornelius 25
  Elizabeth 25
  James 25
  John 25
  Lionel 25
  Martha 25
  Mary 25
  Rachel 25
  Roger 25
  Samuel 25
  Sarah 25
  Susanna 25

INDEX

LYNCH Alice 147
  Alice R. 81
  Anna 125
  Annie C. 130
  Benjamin 125
  Blanche 125
  Catherine 141
  Charles Edwin 141
  Edmund 81
  Edwin 141
  Eliza 106
  Elizabeth 165
  Ella May 81, 147
  Ellen 81
  Frances 81, 147
  Frances R. 81
  George 81, 125
  George E. 125
  George L. 106
  Helen Virginia 141
  Howard 81
  Howard Milton 147
  Hugh 125
  James 81
  James B. 141
  Jane 155
  Jennie Vernon 81
  John 155
  John E. 81
  John H. 81, 147
  John T. 81, 147
  John Thomas 147
  John W. 125
  Joseph 81
  Joseph M. 81
  Joshua 81, 103, 130
  Laura 81
  Lewis 81
  Margaret 125
  Mary S. 103
  Patrick 99, 141
  Richard 81
  Richard H. 81, 147
  Richard Hardesty 147
  Ross 125
  Sarah 81, 99
  Sarah Elizabeth 147
  Vernon 81
  Wilhelmina 141
  William 99, 125, 141
  William P. 141
LYONS Mary Luella 17
  William J. 17
LYTLE Charity 75
  Elizabeth O. 38
  Julia P. 75
  Thomas 75

MAASCH Charles 200
  Louisa 200
  Sophia 149
MACABEE Susan 36
MacDONALD A. W. 177
  Catherine 177
  Eugenie 19
  John 20, 177
  Mary 177
MACE C. Ross 103
  Carville V. 5
  Charles Ross 5
  Dr. S. V. 103
  Elizabeth M. 5
  Ella Corrie 5
  Florence Virginia 5
  Henrietta M. 103
  Rebecca Newbold 103
  S. Veirs 4
  Sue N. 103
  William H. 4, 103
  William Johnson 5
  William Ross 103
MACGILL C. G. W. 94
  Charles 94
  Eugenia 94
  J. Charles 94
  Louisa 94
  Louisa R. 94
  Margie 94
  Mary Ragan 94
MACKENHAMER Laura J. 109
MacKENZIE Cassandra 100
  Catherine 100
  Colin B. 100
  Cosmo T. 100
  Edward E. 100
  Elenora B. 100
  Elenora I. 100
  Mary E. T. 100
  Thomas 100
MACKLIN John 94
  Mary A. 94
MADDOCK Edward 148
  Edward E. 155
  Frances A. 155
  Frances Ann 148
MAGERS Elias 202
  Mary E. 202
MAGNESS Mary A. 148
MAGRUDER Alice 168
  Donald 168
  Edward 168
  Edward B. 168

  Elizabeth 168
  Ella 168
  Ethel 168
  Hamline 168
  Herbert 168
  Lyttleton 168
  May 168
  Minnie 168
  Robert 168
  Sarah 168
  Thomas J. 168
MAHLER Anna 173
MAINLEY Mary 119
  William 119
MAINZ John 160
  Sophia Helen 160
MALLANEE Achsah 142
MALLONEE Anna B. 43
  Eliza A. 43
  Emma Florence 43
  Ephraim 43
  George 43
  Gertrude 43
  Hezekiah 43
  Hezekiah Tipton 43
  John 43
  John Ephraim 43
  John T. 43
  Josiah 43
  Lewis 43
  Mary Jane 43
  Sallie 43
  Sarah Ann 43
  Thomas O. 43
  Thomas W. 43
  Wallace W. 43
  William 43
MALLORY Margaret F. 71
MALONEE Hezekiah 43
  John 43
  Keturah 43
  Shade 43
MALSTER Jeremiah 105
  Sarah R. 105
  William T. 105
MANLY Anna 27
  William 27
MANN B. F. 146
  Eliza 32
  Henrietta 32
  James 32
  Lina Amelia 146
  Maria 203

INDEX

MANNING Elizabeth Carroll 106
  General 106
  Richard Irwin 106
MANSFIELD Margaret 52
  Mrs. 52
  Richard 52
MARBURY A. Marshall 199
  Catherine 199
  Charles C. 199
  Elenora B. 100
  Fendall 199
  Luke 199
  Ogle 100
  Sallie C. 199
  William 199
  William L. 199
MARKERET Catherine 95
MARKEY Jane 78
MARKS Ellen 15
  Worrall W. 15
MARQUETT Mary J. 132
MARR James 13
  James Donelan 13
  James H. 13
  Sarah A. 13
MARRIOTT Sarah 85
MARSH Clara V. 5
  Ellen 47
  Joshua 185
  Maggie 169
  Rebecca 184, 185
  Temperance 184, 185
  Thomas 185
MARSHALL Alexander J. 199
  Caroline 182
  Catherine 199
  Edgar 182
  Estelle 63
  Howard 63, 182
  Margaret Catherine 142
  Sadie 182
  Solomon 142
  Thomas 182
  William 182
  William T. 182
MARSHAM Mary 177
  Richard 177
MARTELL Alexander H. 81
  Alexander Harrison 81
  Catherine 81
  Charles 81
  Elizabeth 81
  Ella S. 81
  Emma S. 69

J. Scott 81
John S. 69
Justus 80
Louisa 81
Lucinda 81
Margaret 81
Mary 81
Mary Martha 81
Peter 80
Peter H. 81
Sarah C. 81
MARTENET Clarissa F. 170
  Cynthia 156, 170
  Dr. J. F. 156
  Ella R. 170
  J. Fussell 170
  Jefferson 170
  Mattie 156
  Philena 170
  Simon J. 156, 170
  Simon Jonas 170
  William H. 170
MARTIN Charlotte M. 36
  Helen 133
  Isaac 36
  Jennie 26
  John 133
  Josephine 132
  Juilian 132
  Julia 16
  William D. 26
MARTINDALE Harry 107
  Nettie 107
MARVEL James 185
  Miranda 185
  Mollie E. 185
MASE Charles Ross 5
MASEMORE Elizabeth 35
  Jemima A. 22
  Zedekiah 22
MASINGO (Mazingo)
  Amanda A. 187
  Elizabeth 187
  John 187
  John H. 187
MASK Mary 70
MASMORE Elizabeth 59
MASON Agnes L. 194
  Allen 41
  Deanie M. 41
  E. C. 8
  George H. 8
  John 194
  Rosa Lillian 8

MATHEWS Carrie B. 26
  Edward 31
  George 26
  John D. 112
  Julia 31
  Nancy 88
  Richard 68
  Sallie H. 112
  Sarah C. 68
MATHYAS Eva 107
MATTFELDT Charles L. 76
  Mary 76
  Wilhelmina 76
MATTHEW Anna R. 45
  George 45
MATTHEWS Alonzo 116
  Amos 47
  Andrew Aldridge 47
  Bell 47
  Betsy A. 165
  Captain W. W. 116
  Clara 77
  Clyde V. 47
  Col. D. M. 38
  Dennis M. 47
  Eleanor M. 47
  Eli 49, 77
  Eliza 38, 47
  Ellen 47
  Enoch 141
  Harry 49
  Hattie 47
  J. Marsh 47
  James G. 47
  Joshua M. 47
  Laura S. 77
  Leroy 116
  Maria 116
  Mary 47
  Matilda 39
  Mordecai 47
  Oliver J. 77
  Priscilla 116
  Rachel 141
  Sarah A. 49
  Stphen 116
  Temperance 47
  Willietta Montrue 116
MATTOX Maggie 149
MATTSON Asa 102
  Rebecca 102
MAUGHT Mary A. B. 136
MAUL Mary J. 134
  Rebecca Jane 134
  Upton R. 134

253

INDEX

MAULDEN Rebecca 196
MAX Lillie 146
   Nicholas 146
MAXWELL Marion 54
MAY August 124
   Pauline 124
MAYES Bertha S. 46
   Elizabeth 46
   Jeremiah 46
   Margaret A. 46
   Nanny 46
   Thomas T. 46
   William McGee 46
   William Rowen 46
MAYO Hannah D. 192
MAYS Charles H. 76
   Elizabeth A. 59
   G. Albert 59
   James 25
   John 59
   John E. 76
   John F. 59
   John P. 59
   Martha 25
   Martha E. 59
   Mary 59
   Mellor 59
   Nannie E. 110
   Rachel A. 59
   Rowan 110
   S. Florence 76
   Sarah R. 59
   Sterling 59
   Walter H. 76
   William 59
   William M. 59
MAYZE Martha 64
McALLISTER Bertie L. 202
   John 202
McANDREW Mary Ann 4
McATEE Ann 67
   Clement 67
   Elizabeth 67
   Elizabeth A. 67
   Francis 67
   George 67
   George I. 67
   Henrietta Maria 67
   Henry 67
   Ignatius 67
   Jane 67
   Leonard 67
   Lewis 67
   Mary 67
   Mary A. 67

   Mary Ann 67
   Samuel 67
   Sarah 67
   Sylvester 67
   Teresa 67
McBURNEY Margaret Ann 155
McCABE Aileen 27
   Caroline 27
   Catherine 27
   Cora 27
   Dorothy 27
   Ellen 27
   Ernest 27
   Frank B. 15
   Gertrude 27
   Henry 27
   James F. 27
   James P. 27
   John 27
   Kate 27
   Lawrence B. 27
   Lawrence P. 27
   Mary 15, 27
   Patrick 27
   Richard 27
   Rosanna 27
McCALL Sarah J. 95
McCAULEY Giddeon 26
   Julia 26
McCLEAN Ann Sophia 15
   Charles B. 15
   Ellen 15
   Hannah 15
   Jeannette M. 15
   Mary 15
   Oliver O. 15
   Olivia 15
   Sophia 15
   William 15
McCLUNG Mary 29, 56
   Robert 56
   Ruth 77
McCOLGAN Charles 16
   Edward 16
   James 16
   John 16
   Mary 16
   Patrick 16
McCOMAS Charity 75
   Charles 134
   Charles H. 134
   Clarence B. 134
   Elva 134
   George 134

   George Upton 134
   Ida V. 173
   James B. 134
   Joshua 134
   Marion E. 134
   Mary Edith 134
   Rebecca Jane 134
   William M. 134
McCONKEY George 32
   Rebecca S. 32
McCONNELL Catherine 184
   Mary 184
   Patrick 184
McCORMICK Alexander 32
   Charles J. 32
   Edward S. 32
   George Carvill 32
   Harry Clifton 32
   Joseph 32
   Maria K. 32
   Martha A. 32
   Mary A. 69
   Nelson F. 32
   R. Howard 32
   Samuel 32
   Thomas A. 32
   William Clarence 32
   William J. 32
McCOU Lizzie 60
McCOY Dr. 174
   Henrietta 174
McCREADY George 95
   John E. 95
   Lillian 95
   Marcella 95
   Margaret E. 95
   Marilla 95
   Mary E. 95
   Samuel E. 95
   Sarah J. 95
McCREARY Harry 50
McCRONE John 153
   Margaret 153
McCUBBINS George W. 31
   Sarah R. 31
McCULLEN Florence C. 23
   Joseph 23
McCULLOUGH Ann 175
   Benjamin 175
   David 52
   Helen 52
   Jane 52
   Sereptha J. 88
McCULLY Jonathan 12

INDEX

McDONALD Abraham 78
  Elizabeth 84
  Jane 78
  Lambert R. 69
  Mary E. 69
  Mary Jane 78
McELROY Robert 74
McELVAINE Mary 49
McENDREE Eugenia 94
  John H. 94
  Louisa 94
McFADEN Mary C. 176
McFEELY Rosanna 27
McGEE Elizabeth R. 168
  Mrs. Ellen 60
McGILL Mary Janet 76
  Thomas 76
McGINN Elizabeth 60
  R. C. 60
McGLONE Fannie Julia 124
  H. B. 124
McGOWEN Harry 99
  Lee 99
  Mary Margaret 99
McGRAHAM Catherine E. 60
  Robert 60
McGREGOR Cassandra 177
McINNES Mary 5
McINTOSH Alexander 116
  David Gregg 116, 117
  James 116
  James II. 116
  John 116
  Margaret 116
  Martha 116
  Martha Jamison 116
  Virginia 116
McKELLAR Sarah Ann 174
McKENZIE Jennie 29
McKEY Jennie 111
McKNIGHT James 176
  Marguerite 176
McLAUGHLIN Cora J. 31
  George E. 31
McMAHON Alice T. 201
  James 201
McMASTER Clarence 189
  Emma Jane 189
McNEIR Alice A. 97
McNORTON Mary 121
McPHERSON Fannie 198
  Janet 198
  John 198
  Miss 15
  Robert 198

McVEIGH Mary 204
  Patrick 204
McVICAR Alexander 5
  Alexander G. 5
  Alice Marion 5
  Charles Morrison 5
  Donald 5
  Donald Malcolm 5
  Guthrie James 5
  Ian Douglas 5
  Innes Mary 5
  Juliet Stewart 5
  Lewis Stewart 5
  William Archibald 5
MEADES Mary L. 38
  Thomas J. 38
MEAKIN Samuel 187
  Sarah J. 187
MEDAIRY Caroline 163
  Jacob 163
  Jacob H. 163
  John 163
  John Kriel 163
  John W. 163
  Nicholas B. 163
  Rachel 163
MEEK Ann 133
  Betsey 133
  David B. 133
  Emma Melvina 133
  Ida 133
  Ida L. 142
  John 133
  John S. 133
  Louisa 133
  Ruth 133
  William D. 133
MEEKINS Elizabeth 151
  Susan 120
  Thomas H. 151
  William 151
MEEKLEY Angeline 46
  Jacob 46
MEISNER Agnes 119
  Caroline 60, 119
  Carrie 119
  Christopher 119
  Harry Albert 119
  Henry 119
  John 119
  Minnie Florence 119
MELLIMONY Miss 127
MELLON Blenna S. 163
  George W. 163

MELLOR Edmund 181
  Elizabeth 181
  James 181
  Joshua Kaye 181
  Mark 59
  Martha E. 59
MEREDITH Ann 95
  Dr. 180
  Thomas 95
MERREY Amanda 21
  Clifton Lort 21
  Florence W. 21
  George 21
  George E. 21
  Isaac J. 21
  James 21
  James F. 21
  Mary 21
MERRIMAN Eliza 68
  Harvey 68
MERRITT Abbie 95
  Aberilla C. 95
  Alvah R. 182
  Boyd 95
  Eliza C. 94, 182
  Eliza Stewart 182
  George W. 182
  John 79, 94, 182
  Leah Z. 79
  Levering 95
  Lillie 95
  Maggie 95
  Richard Todd 182
  Sallie E. 182
  Stephen 95
  Stephen S. 94
  T. Alvah 182
  Walter 182
MERRYMAN Anna Maria 152
  Clara 168
  Ella 157
  Micajah 168
  Nicholas H. 184
  Penelope 184
  Rebecca 184
METCALF Robert 1
METTAM Alice 83
  George de Brimington 83
  Joseph 82
  Katharine Louisa 82
  Mary 83
  Robert 83
  Rosamond 83
  Ruth 82
  Sarah 83

INDEX

METZEL Nellie 190
  Robert 190
MEYER Albert G. 75
  Carl 75
  Charles H. A. 75
  Edith 75
  Fredericka 75
  John 75
  John D. 75
  John F. 75
  Lottie 75
  Lottie E. 75
  Margaret 155
MEYERS Nancy 29
MICHAELS David 46
  Elizabeth 46
MICHAU Agnes 119
  Henry 119
MICHENER Carrie 133
MIDDENDORF Alice 27
  J. William 27
MIDDLETOWN Isabella 66
MILBURN Ellen 144
MILES S. Irene 133
MILLENNER Frank 97
  Irene 97
MILLER A. B. 203
  Albert A. 79
  Anna 79
  Annie 79, 162
  Barbara 162
  Bessie 91
  Betha A. 109
  Birdie 203
  Carrie M. 162
  Catherine 81
  Catherine B. 203
  Charles 79
  Conrad 162, 169
  Dr. J. S. 58
  E. Olivia 58
  Edward 79
  Elizabeth 79, 91
  Ella 165
  Ella J. 24
  Franklin 79
  George 109, 155
  Hannah A. 101
  Hattie H. 58
  Henry F. 109
  Herman 79
  Ida E. 58
  Irving 91
  J. 163
  James 108

  John 79, 200
  John G. 162
  John Henry 162
  John M. 183
  Joseph 79, 104
  Kate 155, 162
  Kate A. 162
  Keturah 158
  Leonard J. 79
  Lily M. 109
  Lizzie 108
  Louisa 162
  Lydia L. 109
  Mabel F. 58
  Margaret 79, 100, 104, 162, 200
  Margaret Mary 126
  Maria 34
  Martha E. 109
  Mary 11, 37, 58, 79, 162, 183, 200
  Mary A. 163
  Mary Melletta 58
  Medora 163
  Nellie L. 109
  Nimrod 79
  Rachel J. 154
  Robert 154
  S. Elmer 58
  S. Francis 34
  Samuel 58
  Sarah S. 109
  Stephen 79
  Thomas 100
  Thomas J. 58
  Victoria 58
  Wilhelmina 149
  William 91
  William T. 91
MILLIS Eliza Ann 30, 31
MILLS Laura M. 127
  Lieutenant 127
  Mary E. 134
MINNICH Jonathan 190
  Margaret 190
MINNICK Rebecca M. 191
MIRCH Jane E. 114
MITCHELL Alexander 138, 140
  Alexander R. 138, 140
  Amelia 138
  Charles Edwin 15
  Charles H. 15
  Clarence L. 138
  E. Madison 141

  Eliza 141
  Eliza Campbell 54
  Elizabeth 138
  Emily C. 138
  F. Dorsey 138
  Frank 101
  Frederick G. 138
  Harriet 15
  Henrietta H. 141
  Hugh 54
  Ida R. 15
  Ida V. 101
  Isaac 167
  Jennie S. 140
  John 141
  John H. 54
  Josephine 140
  Josiah H. 15
  Mary A. 177
  Mary D. 140
  Mary E. 138
  Mary R. 54
  Mary V. 138, 141
  Sarah 141
  Sarah E. 167
  Spencer 138
  Thomas D. 15
  Thomas Parkison 15
  Virginia E. 141
MITTAM Alice B. 196
  Joseph 196
  Ruth 196
MITTNACHT George H. 201
  Katherine 201
  Laura B. 201
  Rosa B. 200
  Rosalie B. 206
MOALE Augusta 10
  John 10
  Samuel 10
MOBRAY Anne E. 124
  Joseph 124
MOFFETT Emily 108
  Family 131
MONDUR Ann Maria 86
MONEYMAKER Celia 113
MONKENMEYER Emma 138
  Henry 138
MONMONIER Dr. J. C. 176
  Sarah 176
MONTELIUS John 147
  John A. 147
  John L. 147
  Maggie 147
  Olivia 147
  Rt. Rev. 147

INDEX

MONTGOMERY Acal 78
  Annie 78
  Birkhead E. 78
  Colonel 191
  Edward A. 78
  Elijah B. 78
  Eliza E. 78
  Gen. 78
  Harriet A. 78
  Henry 78
  Issac 78
  James L. 78
  Katie 78
  Mary E. 78
  May 78
  Sadie 78
  Sarah 78, 191
  William B. 78
MOORE Alexander 143
  Anderson 77
  Bertha 143
  Eleanor 33
  Elizabeth 63
  George 143
  Harry E. 143
  Holly 194
  John 143
  Julia 77, 143
  Margaret A. 54
  Margaret J. 194
  Maria 153
  Mary 143
  Rachel 63
  Robert 33, 54
MORAN Alice 97
  Alice A. 97
  Blanche 97
  Edwin 97
  Florence 97
  Ira 97
  James Avan Gibbons 97
  Richard G. 97
  Richard Thomas 97
  William J. 97
MORELAND A. A. 3
  Alonzo Gordon 3
  Annie C. 130
  Geraldine Cecelia 3
  Jabez 3
  Joseph Foster 3
MORGAN Annetje 170
  Benjamin H. 127
  Catalyntje 170
  Charles 127, 170
  Charles E. 152
  Charles H. 152
  Cora E. 152
  DeWitt Clinton 170
  Elizabeth 127
  Emily D. 152
  Emma 46
  Eugenia 94
  George H. 127
  George W. 127
  Gerard 170
  Hamilton 67
  Jennie 127
  John 170
  John Hurst 170
  Julia 67, 127
  Laura V. 152
  Lettie 127
  Mary 127, 170
  May 127
  May C. 170
  Nicholas 170
  Peter 127
  Peter H. 127
  Robert L. 127
  Rosannah 170
  Sarah Berry 170
  Thomas 127
  William R. 127
MORRICE Ada 98
  Professor 98
MORRIS Annie 141
  Annie Hay 27, 41
  Anthony 143, 200
  Catherine 141
  Eliza 27
  Elizabeth 104
  Georgiana 27
  Israel 143
  James 200
  John 104, 141
  John G. 27, 41
  M. Hay 41
  Margaret 200
  Miss M. Hay 27
  Panola 96
  Robert 198
  Susan E. 143
  Tacie 53
  William 143
  William Hugh 143
MORRISON Alexander 157
  Alexander Martin 21
  Clara E. 131
  Comfort 51
  Douglas 21
  Elizabeth A. 21
  Elizabeth M. 21
  Emmor 143
  Esther R. 21
  Florence 143
  George 21
  George C. 143
  George Clarence 143
  Hans 21
  Henry 21
  Hugh 21
  J. Ralph 143
  Jane A. 143
  John 21
  Mansel 143
  Margaret 21, 143
  Margaret Lovell 21
  Mary 157
  Mary A. 143
  Neal 21
  Professor F. D. 143
  Robert 21
  Sarah 21
  Selina 57
  Susan 143
  Susan E. 143
  William Douglas 21
MORROW Ann 148
  Martha Ann 155
  William 148, 155
MORSELL James S. 87
  Mary A. 86
MORTON John 6
  Sarah 6
  William Waller 116
MORYS Martin 162
  Mary Anne 162
  Thomas 162
MOSBY John S. 169
MOSELEY Almira 153
  David C. 153
  Elizabeth 153
  Elmira 153
  Isaac 153
  Lydia 153
  Margaret Bedford 40
  T. Benton 153
MOSELY Ann 40
  Hilary 40
MOSS Henry 41
  Mary 41
  Wilhelmena 41
MOST Frank 62
  Jennie 62

INDEX

MOTTS Diedrich 28
  Jane Mary 28
MOTTU Eliza 192
MOUNT Elizabeth 82
MOWBRAY Edwin 32
  Rachael 32
MOWELL Emily C. 138
  George R. 138
MUDGE A. B. 35
  Louis Hastings 35
  Mary S. 35
MUELLER Anna 60
  John 60
MULLER Charles 66
  Florence 169
  Herman 66
  Josephine 66
  Mary 66
  Mary C. 24
  Mina 96
  Susan 169
  William 169
MULLIKIN Mary 170
MULLINDORE Catherine 123
  John 123
MULLINS Annette B. 180
  Emily 180
  James G. 180
  John 180
  John B. 180
  Virginia Annette 180
MULVAHILL Sarah 73
MUNKENBECK Christiana 130
  John 130
  Matilda M. 130
MUNOZ Antonia 108
  E. A. 108
  Joseph 108
MURDOCK Emma E. 133
  James H. 133
MURPHY Hedgeman 96
  John 150
  Mary 73, 195
  Naomi 118
  Samuel 118
  Sarah 96
MURRAY Agnes 182
  Annie M. 106
  Bridget 182
  Carrie C. 106
  Elizabeth 106, 182
  Elizabeth G. 106
  Fannie E. 18
  James 23
  John 106

John F. 106
John J. 182
Julia Ann 80
Martha J. 106
Mary 23
Mary Ann 182
Mary O. 106
Patrick 182
Peter 173
Wilhelmina 173
William 80
MUSE Bernard Purcell 117
  Florence 117
  Marie Lorena 117
  Mary Louise 117
  S. W. 117
  Samuel William 117
MYER Julia L. 176
  Nora R. 176
  Thomas R. 176
  William S. 176
MYERS Abraham 17
  Charles Evers 101
  Charles H. 17, 18
  Christian 17
  Daniel 93
  Doretta 130
  Edna C. 18
  Elizabeth 93
  Emma C. 18
  Esther V. 93
  Fred 101
  George 93
  Harriet 93
  Henry W. 101
  Ida M. 93
  Isabella 18
  Jane 93
  John 101
  John G. 18
  Johnzey E. 93
  Keziah 104
  Laura 93
  Louisa 101
  Mabel 101
  Martha 93
  Mary A. 17
  Mary E. 86
  Mary E. A. 118
  Mary Iola 18
  Melvina 101
  Nelson 17
  Oliver 17
  Otto P. 18

Polly 93
Rachel 93
Samuel 18, 93
Sarah 93
Sophia 101
Stephen 17
Susan 93

NACE Mary 24
NAIMASTER Amelia 51
NASH Arthur 161
  Catherine 161
  Charles M. 161
  Eliza 158
  Elizabeth 161
  Elizabeth Ann 161
  Ephraim 161
  James A. 161
  John H. 161
  Louisa 161
  Robert E. 161
  Thomas 161
  William H. 161
NASLLE Charles 96
NATCHTIGALL Emily 167
NAUMANN Gebhardt 135
  Margaret 135
  Rose 135
NAYLOR Bertha Perrie 35
  Dr. H. L. 57
  Henry A. 35
  H. Louis 35
  James 35
  Joshua S. 35
  Julia 35
  Llewellyn 35
  Maggie 35
  Margaret 35, 57
  Martha W. 35
  Mary 35
  Mary Helen 35
  Mary S. 35
  Susan 35
  Thomas K. 35
NEEL Hugh 115
  John A. 115
  Joseph 115
  Martha J. 86, 115
  Mary 115
  Mary E. 115
  Rebecca S. 115
  Samuel 115
  Thomas 115
NEEPER Mary 115

INDEX

NEIDHARDT Annie Elizabeth 122
  Annie Estella 122
  Catherine 122
  Cynthia M. 122
  Frederick 122
  George 122
  John 122
  John F. Carpenter 122
  Katie M. 122
  Mary 122
  Sophia 122
  Theresa 122
NELSON Benton 11
  Charles 124
  Charles W. 124
  Frederick 124
  Gardner 124
  George W. 124
  Joseph 124
  Mary 117
  Mary Elizabeth 124
  Pauline 124
  Pauline May 124
  William 124
NESBITT John C. 7
NEWBERRY Louisa 50
NEWBOLD David M. 190
  David Marion 190
  Eliza 190
NEWCOMER Margaret 148
NICE Emma E. 133
  George M. D. 133
  George V. 133
  John H. 133
  Maggie 133
  Maggie Jane 133
  Mary E. 133
  Sadie 133
NICHOLAS Ann White 10
  Augusta Campbell 9
  Blanche 41
  Cary Anne 9, 10
  George 9
  George Stevenson 10
  Harry Ingerson 10
  Jane 9, 10
  John 35
  John Patterson 10
  John Smith 9, 10
  Maggie 35
  Margaret 9, 10
  Mary Buchanan 9, 10
  Mary Patterson 10
  Robert Carter 9
  Samuel Moale 10
  Sarah Elizabeth 9, 10
  Sidney 9, 10
  Thomas Jefferson Randolph 10
  Wilson C. 9
  Wilson Cary 9, 10
NICHOLS Alpheus 120
  Annie 120
  Clarence 120
  Edith 120
  Edward 120
  Elizabeth 178
  Eva 26
  Flora 120
  Frank 120
  Harry 120
  John 120
  Mary 120
  Mary Ellen 120
  William 178
  Winfield 120
NICHOLSON Caroline 185
  Fennie Estelle 51
  Isaac L. 185
  Jacob K. 51
  Margaretta M. 185
NICKERSON Amelia 107
NICKLE Captain A. C. 73
  Clarinda 73
  John 73
  Lydia 73
NISBET Alexander 101
  Anne 101
  Cassandra O. 101
  Charles 101
  Mary 101
  Mary C. 101
  William 101
NITZEL August 137
  Elizabeth 137
  Margaret 137
NITZEN Anna E. 8
NOE Louisa 76
NOLTE Maggie 109
  William J. 109
NORMAN Annie 69
  Annie K. 92
  Henry 69
  John T. 92
  Martha 92
NORRIS Alexander P. 196
  Alice 56
  Aquilla 6
  Benjamin 6
  Chester 6
  Edward 56
  Emma J. 22
  Hannah 88
  Hazel 6
  Jacob D. 6
  Jacob Dimmitt 6
  James 57
  James H. 6
  Jessie 6
  John 6
  Lester 6
  Lloyd A. 6
  Mary 6
  Mary A. 196
  Mary J. 134
  Nellie 6
  Rachel S. 112
  Rhesa M. 6
  Sarah 57
  Susan 6
  William H. 22
NORWOOD Giles 70
  Harriet Rebecca 70
NUTWELL Mary L. 80

O'BRIEN Eliza 203
O'CONNOR Julian 53
  Mary 53
O'DONNELL Bridget 73
  Ella 73
  Frank 73
  James 73
  John 73
  Joseph 73
  Mamie 73
  Patrick F. 73
  Sarah 73
  Thomas 73
  William 73
  William H. 73
O'DONOUGHUE F. H. 4
  James 4
O'KEEFE Matthew 138
O'LAIGHLIN Mary Ann 1
O'REILLY Catherine 144
ODELL Georgiana 33
  William C. 33
OESTERLA Adam 64
  Emma 64
  Laura 64
OFFUTT Agnes 132
  Amanda 132
  Amanda F. W. 34
  Anna B. 193

INDEX

Colgate 193
Delia 132
Dorsey W. 132
Elizabeth 132, 193
Elizabeth E. 193
Elizabeth Frances 132
Fannie 51
James 132
James F. 132
James P. 193
James W. 132
John W. S. 42
Lemual 193
Lemuel 132
Lillian 132
Mamie O. 42
Maria 193
Mary A. 193
Mary D. 42
Mary E. 132
Mary Emily 193
Milton W. 193
Nannie 193
Noah E. 193
Norah 42
Thomas W. 193
Thomas Z. 132, 193
Virginia 193
Zadoe 193
OGIER Andrew C. 51
Annie 51
Charles Stewart 51
Edna B. 51
Elizabeth 51
Emma Lillie 51
Fannie Estelle 51
Florence Virginia 52
George 51
George B. 51
Harry Clinton 51
India Belle 51
Isabella N. 51
James Edwin 51
James H. 51
John 51
John B. 51
John S. 51
Martha 51
Mary 51
Mary Elizabeth 51
Mary J. 51
Myrtle Helen 51
OGLE Mary 194
OHLENDORF Anna 176
Anna Ida 176

Ignatius 176
Joseph C. 176
Katie 176
Maggie 176
Mary T. 176
OHN Elizabeth 135
OLDHAM Edward 194
Larua C. 194
Mary 194
OLER Elizabeth 64
Mary 121
ONION James 79
Lizzie 79
ORAM Eleanor 91
Franklin H. 91
James D. 91
James F. 91
John 91
John w. 91
Margaret A. 91
Mary L. 91
Nellie Olivia 91
Olivia A. 91
William B. 91
ORMOND David 23
Sarah M. 23
ORSO Charlotte M. 194
Jean Baptist 194
ORT George 103
Mary 103
ORTH A. M. 129
Elizabeth 129
G. F. 129
George P. 129
J. P. 129
Mary E. 129
William H. 129
ORTMAN Hannah 166
OSBORN Martha 157
OSBORNE Margaret
Frances 40
OSBURN Charles A. 188
Florence 188
OSGOOD John 14
Martha 14
OSTENDORF Henry H. 176
Mary E. 176
OSTERHOUDT Albert 203
Caroline 203
OTIS Christina 100
OTTA Johanna 132
OTTAWACO Margaret 104
Theodore 104
OTTISON Nettie A. 126

OTTO Albert 65
Barbara 65, 103
Elizabeth 103
Henry 65
John 65, 103
John W. 65
Leonard 65
Lizzie 65
Margaret 156
OULD Rebecca S. 197
Robert 197
OURSLER Almeda J. 132
OUSSLER John 99
Louisa 99
OWEN Elizabeth 112
Isabella 18
OWENS Achsah 33
Ann 133
Ellen 26
Israel 33
Miss 50
Ruth E. 37
Samuel 133, 193
Uratt C. 193
OWINGS John 101
mary 101
Thomas 14
OYIMAN Ann Margaret 24
Robert T. 24

PACKARD Family 27
PADGETT Ann J. 123
Blanche Ethel 184
Easter 184
Florence May 184
George W. 184
Grace Easter 184
Grace M. 123
Lillie May 123
Mary 123
Nora 123
R. J. 184
Richard 123, 184
Robert Garfield 184
Robert J. 123
Theresa F. 184
W. H. 184
William 123
William H. 184
William R. 123
PADIAN Annie 2
Catherine T. R. 160
James 2
John 160
Maria 2

INDEX

Michael 2
Peter 2
Richard 2
William 2
PAINTER Charles 6
 Harry C. 6
 Isabella 6
 Mabel 6
PAPAGANO Elizabeth 178
 Maria A. 178
 Nettie J. 178
 Pietro 178
PALMER Mary A. 130
PANETTI Barbara 176
 Barbara F. 175
 Dr. 176
 Ernest 176
 Ernest F. 176
 Jacob F. 176
 Marguerite 176
 O. F. 176
 Philip A. 176
 Rev. J. M. 176
PARKER Elizabeth 90, 119
 Mary A. 22
 Nicholas 22, 36
 Rachel Lyde 25
 Richard 25
 Susan 36
PARKISON Christopher 15
 Ida R. 15
PARKS Adoline 58
 Blanch 58
 Charcillia C. O. 58
 Charles 58
 Cornelia 25
 Effie 58
 Florence 58
 J. Linwood 58
 John 58
 Margaret 58
 Mary Ann 62
 May 58
 Penelope 58
 Peter 58
 Samuel E. 25
 William 58
 William G. 58
PARLETT Ada F. 29
 Anna R. 29
 Annie E. 67
 Charlotte 64
 Elizabeth 64
 Elizabeth A. 29
 Gertrude 29

Grace L. 29
James G. 29
John T. 29
John T. B. 64
Julia A. 29
Margaret 64
Mary J. 64
Massey 29
Matilda 64
May M. 29
Minnie E. 29
Morris H. 29
Moses 64
Temperance 64
Thomas 29, 67
W. Howard 29
William 64
William J. 29
William J. B. 64
PARR Nannie 193
PARRISH Clemantha 38
 Edward 38
 Edward M. 38
 Elizabeth O. 38
 Laura 38
 Maggie B. 38
 Nicholas M. 38
 Norris B. 38
 Sabra E. 38
 Thomas L. 38
PARSONS Elizabeth 172
 Joseph 147
 Sarah 81
 Sarah Elizabeth 147
PARVIN Sarah 34
PASSANO Alice 168
 Charlotte C. 62
 Joseph 62
 L. D. 168
PATRICK Mary A. 143
 Samuel 143
PATTERSON Eleanor 39
 Elizabeth 202
 Harry 92
 John 10
 Lenore 78
 Lorenzo 78
 Mary E. 92
 Sarah A. 95
PAYNE Alice 56
 Amanda 56
 Benjamin 56
 Benjamin N. 56
 Charlotte 56
 Frank 56

Frank H. 56
Harry B. 56
Jemima 56
Jemima C. 56
John 56
Josiah 56
Lillie 56
Lillie C. 56
Mary 56
Nettie 56
Nettie A. 56
Ruth 56
Sophia C. 56
Stella 75
William 56
Willimina 56
PEABODY George 136
PEARCE Adam 7
 Anna 75
 Bettie 25
 Beulah 26
 Bosley 7
 Cassie 25
 Charles M. 75
 Daniel 7
 Elizabeth 7
 Elizabeth A. 25
 Ella 25
 Ella S. 75
 Elmer 26
 Fannie 7, 26
 Goldie 26
 John 25
 John B. 75
 Joseph W. 25
 Josiah S. 25
 Katie M. 25
 Lida A. 75
 Maggie R. 25
 Silas W. 25
 Stella 75
 Thomas C. 7, 26
 Thomas E. 25
 Thomas Lytle 75
 Virgie 26
 Wilbur M. 7
 William 7, 25
 William H. 75
PEARSE Ann J. 160
 Elizabeth 160
 Richard 35, 160
 Susannah 35
PEAT Lillian L. 202
PECH Frances 99

INDEX

PEEBLES A. B. 36
  Anna 36
  John 36
  Lizzie 36
  M. B. 36
  Mabel 36
  T. C. 36
  T. C. D. 36
  T. Chalmers 36
  Waldo Cutler 36
  William B. 36
PEGRAM John 117
  William I. 117
PEIRSON Eliza 63
PELTIER Louise 113
PENN Elizabeth 197
  William 197
PENNIMAN Charles F. 182
PENNINGTON Col. H. 84
  Henrietta 84
  Robert 105
  Sarah 105
PENROSE Ellen 197
  John R. 197
PENTZ Anna M. 3
PERCY --- 61
PERINE William J. 37
PERKINS Priscilla 159
  Rachel 196
PERRIE Hugh 35
  Mary 35
PERRY Captain 148
  Charles 113
  Comodore 29
  David F. 113
  Fannie 113
  Georgia 113
  Georgia Alice 113
  Harriet V. 148
  Harry Oscar 113
  Mary 113
  Nancy 113
  Nathan 113
  Rosa L. 41
  Sarah A. 113
  Susan 165
  William 113, 165
  William Henry H. 113
  William Henry Harrison 113
PETERMAN Clara A. 7
  Eliza 7
  Harry E. 7
  James H. 7
  Jeremain 7

PETERS Mary J. 40
PETERSON Elizabeth 195
  Squire 195
  Tillie B. 94
PETEZOLD Joseph 112
  Mollie 112
PETTY Sarah C. 82
  Thomas E. 82
PEW Elizabeth 79
PFAU Mary Ann 18
PFIERMANN Lizzie 205
  Valentine 205
PFROM Andrew 154
  Annie 154
  Annie C. 154
  Catherine 154
  Elizabeth 154
  Henry 154
  Henry Wischhusen 154
  John M. 154
  John Martin 154
  Kate A. 171
  Lillie 154
  Sophia 154
PHILBIN Albert F. 92
  Francis 92
  Katie C. 92
  Magdelene 92
PHILLIPS Ella 63
  Martha 149
PHILPOT Anna Isabella 192
  Brian 192
  Catherine Stewart 192
  Clara 192
  Edward 192
  Elizabeth 192
  Elizabeth Buchanan 192
  John 192
  Mary Ann 192
  Mary D. 192
  Philip 192
  Susan 192
  Thomas 192
PHIPPS Elizabeth J. 57
  Harry 57
  Joseph F. 57
  Ruth Ann 57
PHOEBUS Frank 175
  Margaret 175
PICKERING Anna J. 2
  Charles F. 2
PIERCE Henrietta J. 148
  Mary A. 60

PIERSON Ida M. 164
  Jemima 46
  John 63
  Joseph 184
  Joseph A. 164
PIETSCH Emma C. 18
  Otto 18
PIKE A. H. 31
  Elmira B. 31
  Elvira 31
  Lewis 30
  Lomira G. 31
  Maria 30
  Melintha 30
  Oliver 30
  Philetus 31
  Viola A. 31
PINES Mollie 117
  William 117
PINKERTON Eleanor L. 50
  Samuel 50
PINKNEY William 62
PITTS Ella E. 188
  Henry 188
PLEASANTS Brooke 183
  Elizabeth 183
  Honor Hampden 9
  Samuel S. 9
PLOWMAN Emma 62
POCOCK Jemima 78
POE David 121
  Edgar Allen 121
  Virginia 121
POLK Jane 151
POOLE Julia 62
POPE Andrew 25
  Martha 25
PORTER A. W. 15
  Alberta 69
  Amanda 69
  Anna 174
  Caroline 152
  Emma 69
  Horace 140
  Hugh 140, 174
  James 140
  Leonora 179
  Mary 69, 140
  Mary E. 69
  Rose 69
  Sophia 15
  Sophia E. 140
  William 140
  William F. 69
  William H. 69, 140

INDEX

PORTS Florence 98
  Wesley 98
POSEY John V. 9
  Nina L. 9
POTEET Mary J. 36
  Susan 36
  Susannah 35, 36
  Thomas 35, 36
  Zephaniah 35, 36
POULTNEY Ann 37
  Sarah 37
  Thomas 37
POWELL George 201
  Susanna 201
POWER Margaret 39
POWERS Delia Skipworth 201
  Pike 201
  Rev. W. H. H. 201
  Richard 201
PRATT Adeline 45
  Enoch 1
  Phineas 1
PRENTISS Annette 141
  Captain H. G. 141
  Harry G. 141
  Susanna 141
PRESSER John 185
  Mary 185
PRESTON Alice Wilks 179
  Bertie 108
  Edward D. 108
  Elizabeth 108
  Ellen 108
  George C. 108
  Helen 179
  James 179
  James Bond 179
  James H. 179
  Mary A. 179
  Mary R. 108
  Rachel 108
  Susan R. 108
  Walter Wilks 179
  William 108
PRICE Alice A. 49
  Anna 57
  Anna R. 45
  Annie 138
  B. F. 138
  Bertha C. 49
  Betty 138
  Catherine 45
  Charles H. 45
  Charles M. 49

  Charles W. 49
  Edward 22
  Edward R. 49, 77
  Elizabeth 64, 119
  Ella 49, 138
  Elmer W. 49
  George 119
  Georgie 119
  Homer G. 180
  J. Richardson 49
  Jarrett 49
  Joseph R. 146
  Joseph Richardson 146
  Lina Amelia 146
  Mamie 138
  Mary 49, 138, 146
  Mary A. 98
  Mary Ellen 77
  Mary R. 49
  Mattie 138
  Miss 50
  Nora 138
  Oliver 77
  Penelope 22
  Penelope H. 49
  Penelope R. 49
  R. Oliver 49
  Robert 58, 146
  Robert Harry 146
  Robert Wright 146
  Rose 180
  Samuel 49
  Samuel M. 45
  Sarah 33, 88
  Sarah A. 49
  Skelton 49
  Susan 49
  Susan A. 49
  Susie 77
  Thomas 138
  William 49, 64, 119, 138
  William T. 49
  Zachariah 49
PRICHARD Elizabeth 112
  Emma 112
  Harry F. 112
  Henry E. 112
  Hugh J. 112
  John E. 112
  John W. 112
  Magdaline 112
  Mary 112
PRIDHAM Fleet 194
  Mary Ann 193
  Melinda 194

PRIGEL Dora 91
  William 91
PRINCE Matilda 63
  William 63
PROCTOR Sarah R. 56
  Thomas 56
PROUGH George P. 160
  Georgia 160
PULK Martha 88
  Mr. 88
PUMPHREY Anna Catherine 12
  Capt. W. F. 17
  Lizzie E. 17
PURCELL Charles 174
  Martha 174
  Mary Louise 117
PURDUM Ellen 171
  William 171
PUTNAM Israel 14, 19
  John 14
  Rufus 14
PUTTS Albert 193
  Mattie 193

QUADE Agnes 151
  Anna 151
  August 151
  Edward 151
  Edward L. 150
  Michael 151
QUATMANN Minnie 150
QUICK Edward 73
  George 73
  George Peter 73
  Jacob 73
  Louisa 73
QUINBY Emma 56
  James H. 56
QUINN Rose 8
QUISTORP Emma 130

RA Henry 7
RABORG Christopher 207
  Ruth Amelia 207
RACH Lizzie 154
  Otto 154
RADCLIFFE Aleda Grace 110
  Annie M. 110
  Carrie 110
  Charles C. 110
  Ella 110
  George Worth 110
  Leah Susan 110
  Martha Ann 110

INDEX

Rutledge Winfield 110
Samuel E. 110
Samuel J. 110
Thomas Brent 110
William Austin 110
William W. 110
RADECKE Anna c. 173
Annie C. 122
Dietrich Harmon 122
Dietrich Herman 172, 173
Harmon H. 122
Harmon Henry 173
Henry 122
Henry F. 173
John 122, 173
Louisa 122
Louisa Margaret 173
Margaret A. 122, 173
Margaret S. 173
Mary 48, 122
Mary Sophia 173
Philip 122, 173
Sophia 122
Sophia A. 122
Sophia Ann 173
Sophia M. 122, 173
Sophia Margaret 173
William 122
RADLEY Andrew 112
Magdaline 112
RAMBO Aaron 205
Mary E. C. 205
RAMESBURG Eliza 123
William 123
RAMSAY Nancy Nelson 179
Robert 179
RAMSEY James W. 9
Mary 61
RANDALL Anna 32
Edward 159
Eliza 159
Julia A. 132
Mattie 113
RANDOLPH Thomas Jefferson 10
RANKIN Easter 184
Luella L. 142
Margaret 142
Mary M. 142
Moses 142
Moses E. 142
Phoebe V. 142
Robert G. 142
Sarah 142
Sarah R. 70

RAPHEL Alexis 67
Amedee 67
Anna Teresa 67
Elizabeth 67
Eugene 67
Eugene F. 67
Eugene Fressenjat 67
Florence 67
Henry 67
Janet 67
Joseph Alexis 67
Mary A. 67
Noble 67
Stephane 67
Stephen 67
Stephen Amedee 67
Stephen Joseph 67
RASIN Alice 200
Carroll 200
Genevieve R. 200
Gertrude 200
Helen 200
Howard D. 200
Isaac Freeman 200
John F. 200
Julia 200
Julia A. 200
Martha Anne 200
Mary Rebecca 200
Morris C. 200
Philip Freeman 200
Phoebe 200
Robert Wilson 200
William 200
RATCLIFFE Leah S. 38
Maggie 147
William W. 38
RATTEL Elizabeth 153
RAU Adam 48
Annie 7
Beate 48
Christiana 48
George D. 7
John 7, 169
John C. 7
Kate 7
Mary 7
William 7
Willmenia 169
RAWLINGS Captain 165
Mary Elizabeth 165
RAWLINSON David 14
Eleanor Annie 14
Ethel Rose 14
F. H. 14

Frank Joseph 14
H. J. 14
Herbert Howard 14
Joseph 14
Percy 14
Rebecca 14
Rev. D. J. 14
Sarah A. 14
RAY Alfred 152
Eleanor M. 152
Rosa 104
RAYNOR Allen 5
Charles B. 6
Elijah 6
George A. 6
George Allen 5
Henry 6
James E. T. 6
RAZER Elizabeth Ann 153
READ Mrs. K. C. 90
RECKORD D. Burnett 22
Edward 22
Grace 22
Henry 22
Janet 22
John H. 22
Julia A. 22
Lillie R. 22
Milton H. 22
Raymond 22
Walter P. 22
William H. 22
RECKWART Elizabeth 51
Julius 51
REDECKE Dietrich H. 173
REDGRAVE Martha M. 166
REECE Susan 15
REED Ann M. 17
Elizabeth 205
Ella R. 170
Emily 15
John 31
John O. 17
Lomira G. 31
Martha W. 17
William 31
REES Elizabeth 198
REESE Andrew 81
Annie 155
Charles A. 81, 170, 171
David 81
Dora 155
Eva 171
Frances D. 81
Fred 155

INDEX

Frederick 171
Ida 155
Jacob 155
John 81, 148, 155, 171
John B. 81
John E. 50
John R. 81
Johnnie 171
Joseph 171
Kate 171
Katie E. 171
Lizzie 171
Maggie 155
Mamie 171
Maria 34, 110
Martin J. 170, 171
Mary 50, 117, 171
Mary E. 170
Mary L. 81
Michael 155
Naomi 148
Peter 171
Rebecca 81
Thomas 34
REEVES Hannah 26
James 202
Lucy Trask 202
REGESTER Elizabeth 2
Ella 2
Esther 21
John 2
Joshua 21
Margaret 21
Nicholas 2
Samuel 2
Sebastian 2
REICHE Barbara 28
Carolina 73
Caroline 73
Christian 73
Conrad 28
Emily 73
Fannie 73
John 28
Louise 73
Magdalena 28
Maggie 28
Mary 28, 73
R. H. 73
REID George 158
Keturah 158
Mary A. 158
Professor E. Miller 158
Thomas N. 158

REIER Adam 91
Annie 91
Antoine 91
Carl 91
Catharine 91
Conrad 91
Dora 91
Eleanor 91
George 91
Henry 91
Marie 91
Mary E. 91
Minnie 91
Paul 91
REIFSNIDER Catherine 206
John 206
Susan Matilda 205
William 206
REILEY Asbury 134
Asbury Roberts 134
Eleanor 134
Esther 134
James 134
Julia A. 134
Toabias 134
Tobias 134
REILLEY Amanda M. 1
REINEKER Catherine 164
REINHART Elizabeth 120
REINICKER Mr. 8
REITER Bettie 22
George C. 22
RENNOLDS Georgia 80
Henry T. 80
Lindsay H. 80
Mary 80
Mary L. 80
Virginia R. 80
William Lindsay 80
REPSON Henry A. 150
Jennie 150
Kate 150
Mamie 150
Minnie 150
Peter 150
Rosa 150
RESIDE Catharine V. 161
William 161
RETTBERG Amelia 124
Anna 124
REUDELHUBER Elizabeth 207
REUTER John 122
Sophia 52
Sophia C. 122

REVER Carrie M. 114
Catherine 172, 187
Elizabeth 187
Ferdinand 187
George W. 114, 187
Henry Garrett 187
John H. 187
Lewis 187
Lucinda 187
William F. 187
William H. 172, 187
REYNOLDS Ada 168
Charles Carter 168
Edward 87
Eleanor 169
George B. 167
Harriett 87
Helen 87
Helen Dunnington 87
Hugh Williamson 169
James 169
James W. 167
John 169
John O. 167
Joseph 87
Julia Ann 167
Julia Ann Carter 168
Mary Elizabeth 168
Nora 169
Nora M. 169
Rachel 87
Rosanna 169
Rose E. 169
Sarah Brice 87
Sophia D. 169
Stanley Meade 168
Thomas 87
William 169
William Augustus 87
RHEINHART Charles 14
Fredericka 14
Mary 14
RHODES Bessie C. 117
John 117
Maria K. 32
Matilda E. 117
William 32
RICE Abbie V. 31
Alonzo 30
Arvilla Lucretia 31
Asher 30
Charles 104
Chester Curtis 31
Daniel 30
David 30

INDEX

David Hazelton 31
Duane H. 30, 31
Duane Ridgely 31
Eliza Ann 30, 31
Elizabeth 116
Ellen A. 31
Elvira 31
Emma S. 104
Ephraim 30
Ephraim Emerson 31
Esther 30
Florence A. 31
Frank 145
George 31
George Emory 30, 31
Griffin D. 116
Hazelton 30
Henry E. 31
Hiram 30
Hosea Johnson 31
J. B. 116
Justina E. 31
Levi Henry 31
Lewis 30
Lewis Clark 31
Margaret 145
Maria 30
Mary 145
Maude E. 31
Melina 30
Melintha 30
Nancy 30
Perez 30
Rhoda 30
Richard 116
Sallie 30
Sarah R. 31
Sherman Delos 31
Susan 30
Virtue 31
William Clark 31
RICHARD Frederick 45
Rosa 45
RICHARDS Ann Bedford 40
Annie 141
David 141
David John 141
Elizabeth 72, 141
John 41, 72
John W. 55
John Young 40
Joseph 69
Lydia 157
Mary 41, 141
Mary W. 55
Millicence 41
Rachel 141
Rosa J. 40
Sarah 69
Susie 105
Thomas 141
Tracy 157
William 40
RICHARDSON Alberta 22
Ann 206
D. Virginia 22
Elizabeth A. 22
Emma J. 22
James K. 22
Jemima A. 22
John F. 22
John Pearce 22
Joshua 22
Joshua K. 22
Mary 22
Mary A. 22
Mary C. 77
Mary E. 22
Penelope 22
Penelope H. 49
Rebecca B. 22
T. Monroe 22
Thomas 22, 49
Thomas V. 22
William 22, 77
William T. 206
RICHMOND Agnes 115
Annie 74, 115
Belle 115
Bessie 74
Daniel 74, 115
Daniel Walker 115
Eliza 74
Eliza Ann 115
Ella 115
John 115
Lillie 115
Mabel 74
Mary 74, 115
Matthew 74, 115
Mattie 74, 115
May 115
Samuel 74, 115
RICHSTEIN Alberta 68
George 68
RICKARD Margaret 27
RIDDEL John A. 126
Margaret 126
Mary Ellen 126
Sarah Ann 126
William W. 126
RIDDLE Annie Pamelia 14
RIDER Abram 31
Angeline 137
Anna R. 32
Edward 31, 32, 59, 137
Eliza 32
Elizabeth 22, 32, 59
Ella 32
Florence 32
Harrison 31
Howard 31
John G. 31
Mary 32
Rachael 31, 32
Rebecca S. 32
Richard 31
Sarah Jane 32
Thomas 31
William B. 32
William G. 31
William J. 31
RIDGELEY Achsah 25
Charles 25
Pleasance 25
RIDGELY Charles 170
Clara 157
Deborah 170
Mary 51
RIDGLEY Charles 50
Ida 50
Julia 50
Mary E. 132
William 132
RIECKE Anna 60
RINGGOLD Edward 200
Elizabeth 200
James 200
Josiah 200
Mary 146
Mary Rebecca 200
Rebeca 200
Thomas 200
Thomas C. 146
William 200
RINGROSE Rev. 149
Sarah R. 149
RIPPLEMEYER C. H. 10
Marie 10
RISON Martha E. 127
RISTEAU Ann B. 54
Elizabeth 54
Thomas C. 54
RISTEN Charlotte 56
Jesse 56

266

INDEX

RITTER Alice 61
  Blenna S. 163
  Clementine V. 163
  E. H. 163
  Emily D. 163
  George O. 163
  Harriet 163
  Henry T. 61
  Hiram A. 163
  Howard T. 163
  Ida 61
  Jacob 61
  John T. 163
  Letitia Alice 61
  Margaret 61
  Margaret A. 61
  Martha 61
  Mary 163
  Mary A. 163
  Mary Martha 81
  Miranda E. 163
  Thomas 61, 163
  William 81
RITZ Barbara 180
ROACH Florence 97
  Mary 141
  Vincent 97
  William 141
ROBB E. Tupper 72
  James D. 72
  Mary Elizabeth 72
ROBBINS Mary E. 120
ROBERTS Alice 192
  Amelia 8
  Annie E. 44
  Catherine 158
  Clara S. 17
  Claude 192
  Eliza 192
  Essie 116
  Florence E. 44
  George B. 44
  Georgia 192
  John 158
  John N. 192
  Louis 44
  Louis J. 44
  Margaret 117
  Maria A. 192
  Mary E. 126
  Mary F. 44
  Mary L. 44
  Rev. Dr. 192
  Robert R. 44
  Sarah 95
  Susan 44
  Thomas 117
  Wilber S. 44
  William 192
  William Collins 192
  William T. 192
ROBERTSON Anna F. 41
  Augusta 41
  Brooks 40
  Charles Henry 40
  Christopher 40
  Deannie M. 41
  Emmett Henry 41
  Grayson Woods 41
  Henry 40
  John Young 41
  Lenora 41
  Margaret B. 41
  Margaret Frances 40
  Martha 40
  Mary H. 41
  Mary L. 41
  Mortimer O. 41
  Oneida 41
  Reps Osborne 40
  Richards Osborne 41
  Rosa 41
  Rosa J. 40
  Rosa L. 41
  Rosa Perry 41
  William Edwin 40, 41
ROBEY Mary L. 11
ROBINSON Almira 162
  Beulah 113
  Burke 113
  Charles Edward 8
  Charles Russell 9
  Clara B. 8
  Dennis 201
  Elizabeth 162
  Emeline Rebecca 136
  Emily 162
  Emily C. 162
  Fradus A. 113
  George 162
  George W. 162
  Hannah 40
  Harry 113
  Harry F. 8
  J. Frank 8
  James D. 162
  John 40, 113
  Joseph J. 162
  Julia 113
  Leah E. 8
  Leslie 113
  Lewis H. 162
  Lillie 201
  Louise 113
  Margaret 162
  Mary Elizabeth 162
  Mary W. 162
  Mattie 113
  Morris B. 162
  Nannie R. 95
  Narcissa May 136
  Nicholas 113
  Roger R. 9
  Ruth 9
  Samuel 162
  Thomas 8
  William 113
ROBSON A. W. 20
  Juliette M. 20
ROCHE Alice 23
  Annie J. 153
  Annie M. 153
  Bridget 23
  Captain 92
  Edward 153
  Ella 23
  George Benjamin 153
  George J. 153
  Harry S. 153
  Johanna 23
  John J. 23
  Katie C. 92
  Kittie 23
  Maria 153
  Mary E. 23
  N. Annie 23
  Patrick T. 23
  Samuel 23
  Samuel F. 23
  Sarah M. 23
  Sylvester J. 23
  Sylvester James 23
  William 23
  William L. 153
RODENMEYER Frank 93
RODENMYER Mary L. 93
RODEWALD Eliza M. 28
  Henry 28
RODGERS Ella 168
  John L. 168
ROE Bessie Payne 56
  John D. 56
  Lillie 56
  Mary E. 181
  Thomas 7
  William 181

INDEX

ROELKEY Medora S. 186
ROEMER Clara G. 195
ROGERS Annie 39
  Bertha Cordelia 45
  Bridget 73
  Charles A. 11
  Charles B. 39
  Charles Butler 39
  Eliza Butler 39
  Emily butler 39
  Emma 11
  Eunice 39
  Eunice Butler 39
  James Power 39
  John Power 39
  Mamie 203
  Nathan 39
  Nicholas 203
  Sally 127
  Samuel Butler 39
  Thomas 39
  Timothy 45
  William 127
  William Hay 39
ROHRBAUGH Clara 128
ROLFE A. F Nelville. 85
ROMOSER Anna R. 180
ROOP Rebecca 81
ROOT Sarah 157
ROSER Daniel 46
  Lucy Ann 46
ROSS Joseph 64
  Laura V. 64
  Maria 13
  Mary A. 131
  Philip 13
  Sohia E. 140
ROST Amelia 160
  Peter 160
ROTH Catherine 75
  Joseph 75
ROTHEN Benjamin 88
  Martha 88
ROUSE Birdie 203
ROUSE (La Rue) Ann R. 92
  Edwin Wells 92
  Fannie C. 92
  Francis W. 92
  Hattie M. 92
  Mary G. 92
  Susan 92
ROWE Annabel 19
  Daniel 34
ROYSTON Alice 77
  Augusta 77
  Blanche 77
  Caleb 77
  Cecelia 77
  Clara 77
  Clara L. 77
  Cora Estelle 77
  Edward Price 77
  Elizabeth 77
  Ella 49
  Emily J. 80
  Emma 77
  Emma Grace 77
  Frederika 77
  George R. 77
  Horace Wesley 77
  J. Marion 49, 77
  John 77
  Joshua 77
  Joshua Marion 77
  Margaret 77
  Mary 22, 29, 77
  Mary C. 77
  Mary E. 77
  Mary Ellen 77
  Matilda 34
  Robert 29, 80
  Ruth 77
  Susan A. 49
  Susie 77
  Thomas 77
  W. A. 22
  Wesley 49, 77
  Wesley A. 77
  William 77
  William A. 77
RUBY Kate 175
RUDISILL Mary M. 142
  Rev. A. W. 142
RUDKIN Rebecca 82
RUDOLPH Elizabeth 121
  Harry 121
  John Harmon 121
  Joseph 121
  Lawrence 121
  Lizzie 121
  Martin 121
  Martin V. 121
  Mary 121
  Virginia 121
  William 121
RUE Allie 134
RUHL Margaret E. 57
RUPP Bertha 115
  Mary E. 104
  Nicholas 115
RUSH Frederick 84
  Sophia 84
RUSK Belle W. 199
  Catherine Olivia 199
  Dr. G. G. 199
  Fannie T. 16
  George w. 199
  Harry Welles 199
  J. Krebs 199
  J. Stewart 199
  Jacob Krebs 199
  John 199
RUSSELL A. H. 89
  Alexander 163
  Allen 26
  Annie D. 26
  Annie M. 26
  Cecelia 85
  Charles 26
  Charles Wesley 85
  Delphia Anne 26
  Edith 89
  Elizabeth 84, 89
  Ellen 26
  Emma May 26
  Fannie 52
  Frank Donaldson 85
  George 89
  Grace 89
  Henry H. 89
  Isabel Marion 85
  James S. 89
  Jennie 26
  Jeremiah D. 89
  Julia C. 89
  Margaret 75
  Mary 85
  Millie L. 26
  Rachel 163
  Raymond 89
  Reister 88
  Reister K. 89
  Samuel Owens 26
  Susan 89
  Thomas 84, 123
  Wallace 52
  Walter 89
  William 89
  William L. 26, 84
  Willie Nathaniel 85
RUTH Frederick J. 189
  Marie 189
RUTHVEN John 195
  Rebecca 195

INDEX

RUTLEDGE Elizabeth 38
  Elizabeth A. 38
  John 102
  John F. 38
  Leah S. 38
  Leah Susan 110
  Mary 102
  Mary L. 38
  Rebecca J. 38, 110
  Rufus F. 38
  Sarah G. 38
  Thomas 38
  Thomas G. 38, 110
RUTTER Edward 70
  Edward J. 70
  Harriet Rebecca 70
  Harry 70
  Isabella Alexander 70
  Maud 70
RYAN Cornelius 199
  Johanna 23

SACK Adam 48
  Amelia 48
  Beate 48
  Charles 48
  Ernest 48, 122, 173
  Frederick 48
  George 48
  Helen 48
  Johanna 48
  John 48
  Lizzie 48
  Maggie 48
  Mamie 48
  Mary 48, 122
  Mary Sophia 173
SADLER C. C. 57
  Comfort 51
  Mary 57
  Warren 51
SADLEY Elizabeth 44
  Frances Howard 44
  Thomas 44
SAHM Mary A. B. 136
  Peter 136
SALES Judge 58
SALFNER Adolphus 23
  Minerva 23
SALISBURY Eliza 132
  Matthew 132
SALTER Albert 186
  Alice 186
  Aquilla 186
  Harriet 186

Harriet A. 186
  Irving 186
  James 186
  John E. 186
  Mary E. 186
  Theodore 186
  Virginia 186
  William 186
  William H. 186
SAMPSON Mary Ann 105
  Samuel 105
SANDBORN A. M. 58
  George 58
  Mary 58
SANDERS Bushrod 108
  Emily 108
  Harriet 186
  James 186
  Rachel 108, 132
  Rachel R. E. 131
SANDERSON Julia H. 184
  Thomas 184
SASTLER Barbara 65
SAUER Ambrose C. 12
  Andrew J. 11, 12
  Francis A. 12
  George P. 12
  Joseph L. 12
  Linus J. 12
  Margaret H. 12
  William F. 12
3AUL Noah 44
SAUNDERS Abram 94
  Captain 94
  Family 201
  J. B. 94
  James 94
  James S. 94
  John T. 94
  Mary A. 94
  Mary E. 94
SAVAGE George 16
  Mary C. 49
  Mary E. 16
  Susanna S. 16
  Thomas K. 49
SAXTON Josephine 183
  Mary 183
  William H. 183
SCALLAN Anne 133
SCARF Hannah 23
  William 23
SCARFF Elizabeth 51
  Henry 11
  Joshua H. 11
  Julia A. 10

SCHAEFFER John 21
  Susanna 21
SCHAFERMAN Mamie 48
SCHAIBLE Mary J. 43
SCHARF Mary A. 140
SCHARFF Joshua H. 51
SCHAUER John 121
SCHETLICH Lizzie 91
SCHILLING Frank 2
  Frank A. 2
  George 2
  George A. 2
  Mamie 2
  Michael 2
  Peter 2
  William H. 2
SCHIPPER Emily d. 150
  John F. 150
SCHLUDERBERG Amelia 169
  Annie 169
  Conrad 169
  Daniel 169
  Elmira 7
  George 169
  Henry 169
  Kate 169
  Lillie 169
  Lizzie 169
  Maggie 169
  Mary 169
  Sophia 169
  Wilhelmina 169
  William 7, 169
  Willmenia 169
SCHMEISER Andrew Herget 154
  Christian 154
  George 154
  Henry 154
  John 154
  Lissie 154
  Lula 154
  Maggie 154
  Mary 154
  Mary M. 154
  Reda 154
  Rosa 154
SCHMELZ Amelia 8
  Philip 8
SCHMIDT Adam 128
  Alvan 128
  Anna 128
  August 128
  Barbara 162
  Blanche E. 133

INDEX

Frederick 128
Fredericka Henrietta 128
Georgianna 128
H. Louis 128
Harry 28
Jennie 128
Julius 128
Katie 128
Lecetta 128
Mary 28
Minnie 128
Tillie 128
SCHNEIDER Agnes Louisa 172
  Amanda 172
  Catherine 172, 188
  Christine 188
  Edward 172
  Frederick J. 172
  George 188
  Philapena 172
  Philip 172
  Philip H. 172
  Sadie 188
  William J. 172
SCHOCK Harriet 163
  John 163
SCHOENING Anna 18
  Margaret Gertrude 18
  Matthias 18
SCHOFIELD Carrie M. 114
  Catherine J. 114
  Edward 114
  J. Calvin 114
  James F. 114
  Myrtle 114
  Robert K. 114
  William 114
  William H. 114
  Zella 114
SCHOLL Barbara Emma 205
  Elizabeth 205
  George 205
  George Barr 205
  Jacob 205
  John Jacob 205
  Maud Isabelle 205
SCHONE Harmon 24
  Henry 24
  Louisa 24
  Mary C. 24
SCHOOLDEN Theresa F. 184
  William H. 184

SCHRADER Amelia 160
  August 160
  Betta 160
  Edward 160
  Frits 160
  Katie 160
  Lewis 160
  Louisa 160
  Susan 57
SCHUBERT Jerome H. 43
  Mary L. 43
SCHUCKHARDT Mary L. 97
SCHUESSLER Frank Joseph 76
  Frank W. 76
  Herbert Franklin 76
  Ida M. 76
  Louisa 76
SCHULTZ Frederica 166
SCHULTZ Charles 45
  Clara 144
  Dorothy 130
  Henry 45
  Louisa 45
  Mary 45
SCHUMANN John 156
  Maggie 156
SCHUMK Jacob 109
  Laura V. 109
SCHUYLER Margaret 10, 18
SCHWARTZ Barbara 156
  Eliza 96
  Elizabeth 45, 129
  Frederick 45
  Katherine 201
  William 156
SCHWATKA August 108
  John 108
  John A. 108, 131
  John B. 132
  John Bushrod 108
  John Bushrod Herdman 132
  Margaret G. 108
  Margaret V. 108
  Rachel 108
  Rachel R. E. 131
  Rosa P. 132
  William 132
  William H. 108, 131
SCHWIENSBURG Wilhelmina 76
SCHWIND Johanna 132
  John G. 132

Mary 132
Philip 132
SCOTT Abram C. 68
  Achsah 25
  Alberta 68
  Annie 69
  Arianna H. 68
  Cecilia A. 68
  Daisy 69
  Eleanor R. 68
  Eli 68
  Eliza 68
  Elizabeth 25, 68, 69
  Elizabeth Ann 68
  Elizabeth M. 1
  Ella 69
  Frank 55
  Gretchen 151
  Jennie 69
  John 1, 25, 68, 69
  Julia D. 68
  Laura 69, 151
  Lewis C. 68
  M. Rebecca 55
  Mary 69, 151
  Mary A. 69
  Ruth C. 68
  Sarah C. 68
  Thomas 68
  Thomas M. 68
  William 69
  William J. 69
  Winfield 151
SCOVILLE Andrew 89
  Sarah I. 89
SCULLY Catherine 27
  Peter 27
SEABREASE Alphonse 11
  Edward 11
  Frank 11
  Harry 11
  Laura 11
  William 11
SEAGER James R. 16
  Sarah Elizabeth 16
SEEGAR Lenora 41
SEIPP Albert 189
  Anna B. 189
  Anna G. 189
  B. Frank 188
  Charles A. 188
  Conrad 188
  Elizabeth 188
  Elizabeth Ann 189
  Ella 189

INDEX

Emma Jane 189
George 8
George W. 188
George Wilson 189
Henry H. 189
James 188
Kate L. 8
M. Florence 189
Mary 188
Minnie 189
Selina J. 188
Warren 189
SEITZ Joseph 46
  Rachel 46
SELBY Celia 113
  Edwin D. 113
  Mary E. 113
SELIG John 155
  Tracy 155
SELLMAN Margaret 52
SENIOR Caroline F. 174
  Harry 174
  Louisa 174
  Squire 174
  William 174
SENTZ George 61
  Letitia Alice 61
SETCK Charles A. 191
  Elizabeth 191
  George M. 191
SEWARD Edith 120
  Margaret A. 193
  Thomas J. 120
SEWELL Ann Rebecca 9
  Anniel L. 44
  Colonel 44
  James 44
  Thomas H. 9
SHAFER Minnie 208
SHAMBURGER Clara 112
  Joseph 112
SHANKLIN Elizabeth 89
  Samuel 89
SHANNON Anna 17
  Deborah M. 17
  Edmond L. 17
  Elizabeth 17
  Esther K. 17
  George C. 17
  George E. 17
  Isabel 102
  Jared 17
  Jesse 17
  Joseph 17
  Mary 17

Mary Luella 17
Nellie R. 17
Samuel 17
Samuel D. 17
Thompson Mitchell 17
SHAPIRO Anna 176
SHARER Catherine 187
  Ferdinand 187
SHARMAN Caroline 57
SHARP Sarah C. 28
SHAUL Benjamin 44
  Benjamin L. 38
  Bessie O. 38
  Clay 38
  Emily 139
  Emma V. 38
  Estella 38
  John 38
  Joseph 38, 44
  Joseph W. 38
  Julia A. 38, 44
  Nancy 38, 44
  Noah 38
  Rachel 38, 44
  Rachel F. 38
  Reason W. 38, 44
  Samuel 139
  Sophia 139
SHAVER Barbara 104
SHAW Alice 1
  Alice Julia 137
  B. 1
  Eleanor 98
  Emily 98
  Nancy 101
  T. Darrah 137
SHEFFY Judge H. W. 201
SHEHAN Mary 84
SHELDON Elizabeth 142
  J. M. 142
SHELLMAN Catherine 121
SHELLY Blanche 77
  William 77
SHELTON Charles 201
  Sarah T. 201
SHENTON Fannie 83
  Harry Worth 83
  James 83
  James Frank 83
  Kate 83
  Mary 83
  Moses 83
  William 83
  William Franklin 83
SHEPPARD Miss 63

SHERIDAN Asbury 190
  Fannie Bella 190
  John 190
  John A. 190
  Miranda 190
  Nellie 190
  Wesley 190
SHERWOOD Eliza J. 18
  Fannie E. 18
  Helen 18
  Henry 145
  Henry A. 18
  Irvin 18
  John P. 18
  Rebecca L. 27
  Sallie A. 145
SHIBLEY Elizabeth 45
  Matthew 45
SHIELDS Ophelia 203
  Thomas 203
SHIMANEK Annie 99
  Anton 99
  Caroline 99
  Frances 99
  Francis 99
  John 99
  Joseph 99
  Joseph F. 99
  Lizzie 99
  Mary 99
  Wenceslaus 99
SHIPLEY Amelia 207
  Annie M. 47
  Brice 42
  Charcillia 58
  Charles 160
  Charlotte 42
  Dora 42
  E. C. 42
  Edna 111
  Ella 173
  Ella M. 42
  Harry B. 42
  Harry V. 42
  Howard B. 42
  John F. 42, 58
  Joshua 47
  Luther 12
  Maggie A. 160
  Mary 163
  Mattie 115
  Roger 42
  Samuel 115
  Samuel T. 163
  Sarah 42

INDEX

V. T. 42
Walter V. 42
SHIRLEY E. Sophia 184
  Walter 184
SHOEMAKER Jane 20
  Samuel 196
SHORTER Sarah A. 19
SHOWER Adam 172
  Anna Elizabeth 121
  Catherine 121
  Catherine Amelia 172
  Charlotte E. 172
  Edmund G. 172
  George T. 172
  Ida M. 172
  John 172
  John A. 121
  John Adam 172
  John Adams 121
  Leonora Virginia 172
  Mary Ann 172
  Mary C. 172
  William H. 172
SHRYOCK Catherine B. 203
  Henry S. 203
  Jacob 203
  Maria 203
  Ophelia 203
  Thomas J. 203
SHUNK Mary 76
SHUPPERT Catharine 24
  Ella J. 24
  George 24
  George Walter 24
  J. Adam 24
  John 24
  John H. 24
  Mary 24
  Mary A. 24
  Rebecca J. 24
SICKLE Mary E. 129
SICKLES Elizabeth 136
SIDWELL Eliza M. 18
  Joseph 18
  Levi 18
SIEBRECHT Henry 21
  Margaret 21
SIECH Henry f. 33
  Katie 33
SILVER Eliza 141
SIMERING Annie 84
  Annie Elizabeth 84
  John Thomas 84
  Sophia 84
  William F. 84

SIMMONS A. H. 4
  Ada 188
SIMON Henrietta 146
SIMPSON Eliza Ann 140
  Thomas B. 140
SINCLAIR Deborah S. 112
  Deoborah 77
  Robert 77, 112
SINDALL Family 189
SINGEL Mary 118
SINNOTT Bridget 138
  Catherine 138
  John T. 138
  Patrick 138
  Robert P. 138
SIRGEL Barbara 162
SITLER Elizabeth 42
  Morris 42
SKINNER Blanche E. 133
  Clifford Scott 133
  Eliza 132
  James 132
  John 132
  Louisa 133
  Mary V. 133
  S. Irene 133
  Thomas 132
  Wiiliam 132, 133
  William J. 132
  Zachariah 132
SKRETNY Adalbert 3
  Amy 3
  Anthony 3
  Joseph 3
SLACK Martha 45
SLADE Abraham 74
  Ann 74
  Asbury 74
  Belinda T. 69
  Bettie W. 74
  Carl 74
  Christ 74
  Christopher 74
  Columbus C. 74
  Creighton 74
  Delilah 74, 75
  Ella 75
  Ezekiel 74
  H. M. 69
  John 74
  John R. 74
  John T. 74
  John V. 38
  Julia P. 75
  Lida A. 75

Maria E. 74
Marion F. 75
Mary 74
Minerva 59
Sally A. 86
Sarah G. 38
W. A. 69
William 74, 75
Zipporah 74
SLINGLUFF Dr. F. K. 118
  Helen 57
  Upton 57
SLOCUM Mary 83
SMEDLEY Jane 95
SMINK A. C. 43
  Adolphus 43
  Mary J. 43
SMITH Albert 7
  Alexander 15
  Allen W. 37
  Andrew 37
  Ann Graham 199
  Ann Rebecca 64
  Anna 55
  Anne Donnell 28
  Annie 48
  Augusta 77
  Bessie 198
  Charlotte 64
  Cornelia 25
  Cornelius 158
  Eleanor O. 37
  Elizabeth 64, 119
  Ella M. 33
  Emma B 15
  Esther 30
  Frances R. 15
  Franklin B. 199
  Franklin Howard 15
  Frederick 25, 64, 119
  Frederick J. 64
  George A. 64, 97
  George W. 198
  Gertrude 37
  Harriet 78
  Harry 25, 33
  Henry 15, 179, 180
  Henry C. 137
  Hettie 26
  Holly 81
  Ida 33
  Jacob 64
  James 12, 64
  James H. 15
  Jane A. 5

INDEX

Jennie 147
Jennie Vernon 81
John 9, 10, 28, 33, 158
John Jackson 33
John S. 37
John T. 64
John W. 33
Joseph M. 15
Katherine 33
Laura E. 12
Lee 69
Lena 180
Louisa 64
Margaret 9, 64, 81
Martha 25, 61, 64, 158
Mary 33, 46, 62, 64, 147
Mary E. 69, 95, 179
Mary J. 64
Nellie 37
Oliver S. 64
R. Percy 37
Rebecca 64, 137, 200
Robert 28
Roy 25
Ruth E. 37
Samuel 10, 28
Samuel W. 28
Sarah 15
Sarah E. 15
Sarvena J. 97
Susan 64
Susannah 127
W. Gill 25
W. O. 15
Wallace 33
Walter 147
William 62, 64, 77, 81, 158
William B. 25
William H. 33
William L. 37
William R. 33
SMITHSON Amelia 40
SMYSER Elizabeth 172
Henry C. 172
Jacob 172
Rebecca 172
SNIVELY Ann 178
SNOT Jeannette 30
Juliet 30
SNOW Annette 30
Fayette 30
Henriette 30
Levi 30
Nancy 30

SNOWDEN Adaline 98
Kate 27
SNYDER Annie 66, 79
Catherine 66
Elizabeth 66
Helen 66
Henry 51
John 66, 79
Joseph 66
Joseph H. 66
Josephine 66
Mary A. 66
Mary J. 51
Mary L. 66
SOLLERS Thomas 14
SONNENBAUM Adolph 166
Dena 166
SOTHORON John Henry 198
Margaret Holliday 198
Rebecca Joel 198
SPANGLER Mary E. 98
SPARKS Alice J. 47
Ann Rebecca 47
Anna Elizabeth 79
Annie E. 131
Benjamin D. 79
Benjamin I. 79
Benjamin R. 79
Bettie 47
C. Anna 79
Caroline 79
David H. 79
Edward A. 47
Edward E. 79
Elijah 47
Elijah B. 47
Elizabeth 8, 47, 79, 188
Elmira 47
Emma F. 103
Francis M. 103
George A. 103
Hannah Elizabeth 79
John 47, 131
John H. 47
John W. 79
Laban 131
Laura M. 104
Lavinia 47
Leah Z. 79
Margaret P. 79
Mary E. 103
Mary Louisa 79
Mary M. 79
Mary Martha 79

Mary Melvina 79
Mathida P. 79
Matilda 79
Rachel E. 47
Reverdy B. 131
S. G. 131
Sarah Elizabeth 79
Sarah Ethel 79
Sarah M. 103
Shadrach D. 131
Squire W. C. 103
Susan 103
Susannah 131
T. C. 104
Theodore E. 103
Thomas 131
Walter H. 103
William 47
William E. 79
William H. 103
SPAULDING Ann 59
SPEED Bertie L. 202
Charles 202
Christoher C. 202
Fletcher B. 202
James 202
John 202
Joseph 202
Mary E. 202
Mary Reeves 202
Patience Rogers 202
William G. 202
William H. 202
SPEISMOCHER Magdelene 152
SPENCE Charles W. J. 159
Charles Woodland 159
Eliza 159
James E. 159
John F. 159
Joseph H. 159
Lavina 159
Martha Jane 159
Mildred B. 159
Sarah Catherine 159
Willard Francis Lowe 159
William T. 159
SPENCER Allen 111
Allen D. 111
Eliza R. 111
Ella I. 111
Jennie 111
Priscilla 111
William 111
SPERRY Ella 183
William 183

INDEX

SPOTSWOOD Alexander 169
  Mildred 169
SPOTTSWOOD Julia A. 11
  William 11
SPRACKET Honor 20
SPRAGUE Aggie 147
  Arthur A. 147
  Eliza 147
  George 147
  George H. 147
  George W. 147
  Helen 147
  James 147
  Jennie 147
  Louis 147
  Reese 147
  Walter 147
ST. MEYER Alice 205
  George T. 205
STABLER Ann 7
  Carrie 25
  Christian 25
  Daniel 7
  Henry 25
  Katie M. 25
  Margretta 7
STACK Mary 120
  Mary Ellen 120
STAGGERS Mary 66
STANLEY James 14
STANSBURY Abraham 30
  Abram 109
  Alexina 30
  Alice M. 19
  Ann Mary Proctor 57
  Annie E. 107, 142
  Annie Louise 107
  Arcana 86
  Caleb 33
  Catharine 86
  Catherine Elizabeth 60
  Charles B. 86
  Charles E. 103
  Charles Vernon 107
  Charles W. 107, 142
  Christiana 19, 24
  Colonel 6
  Darius 30, 86, 103
  Dixon 116
  Eleanor 109
  Elijah 96
  Elizabeth 49, 116
  Elmer 107
  Eudocia 24
  Frank P. 86

George 103
George L. 103
Hammond 86
Hannah A. 86
Isaac 49
John 24
John E. 19, 86
John Thomas 24
Mary 107
Mary Ann 6
Mary E. 96, 103
Mary Elizabeth 19
Mary J. 103
Mary S. 103
Nathaniel 86
Percy 86
Rebecca 33, 82
Richard C. 107
Ruth 33
Sara A. 19
Sarah 82, 107
Thomas 24, 33
Tobias 86
William E. 19, 24, 49
William Mondur 86
STARK Ella 118
  Henry 118
  Honora 118
  Maggie May 119
  Walter 6
  William 118
  William H. 118
STARKEY Lavina 159
STARR Campbell 68
  Charles Howard 140
  Eliza Ann 140
  George W. 140
  Harry Lee 140
  Henry 140
  Julia D. 68
  Mary A. 140
  Mary Ellen 140
  Mary Virginia 140
  William H. 140
STEEL George 168
  Isabella 168
STEELE Florence 207
  James H. 207
STEINFELT Elizabeth 79
STEINHAUSER Sophia 167
STEINMAER Maggie 114
STEINMANN Catherine 166
  Hannah 166
  William 166

STENGEL Barbara 193
  Charles R. 193
  Christian 193
  Elizabeth 193
  Elizabeth Augusta 193
  Gottlieb 193
  Harry 193
  Lewis C. 193
  Mattie 193
STEPHEN Aquilla 88
  Benjamin 88
  Frances 88
  Francis D. 88
  Silas C. 88
STEPHENSON Matilda 114
STERGER A. Fred 205
  Fred 205
  Henry 205
  Josephine 205
  Lizzie 205
  Mary 205
STERLING Eliza 74
  Elizabeth A. 59
  Harriet 59
  William 59
STEVENS Alexina 14
  Ebenezer 14
  Emma Catherine 158
  Flora 120
  Francis Alexander 14
  Francis Putnam 14
  Leah C. 134
  Martha 14
  Morris Putnam 14
  R. H. 120
  Samuel Small 14
  Susan S. 131
STEVENSON Allen 22, 59
  Anna W. 30
  Annie Belle 30
  Caroline 13
  Charles Lee 30
  Edmond 30
  Elizabeth 22, 32, 59
  Esther 9
  George Pitt 9
  Gertrude 204
  H. Burton 22, 54, 59
  Isabella 30
  John M. 22, 32, 59
  John Metzgel 59
  John W. 30
  Joshua 30
  Josias 30
  Margaret 22, 54, 59

INDEX

Martha Lee 30
Samuel 204
Thomas G. 30
Urath 30
Washington 30
STEWART Agnes 106
C. J. 95
Caroline G. 85
Eliza 189
Eliza C. 94, 182
Elizabeth 71
Howard E. 189
Isabella 189
James 189
Jane 71
Jane B. 71
John 71
Joseph J. 189
La Fayette 85
Margaret 106
Mary E. 71, 189
Richard B. 131
Robert 106, 189
Samuel 13
Samuel G. 189
Sarah 106
Sarah A. 13
Stephen 95, 182
Susan Isabella 192
Susanna 106
Susannah 131
W. 71
Walter H. 189
Walter L. 189
William 106
William A. 189
STIEBER Annie 53
Carrie 53
John G. 53
STIEGLER Eleanora 91
George 91
Mary E. 91
STIEMKE A. L. T. 18
A. L. Timothy 18
Anna 18
Augusta 18
Charles A. 18
Clara 18
Edward 18
Henry 18
Lydia 18
Martin 18
Paul 18
Rudolph 18
Wilhelmena 18
Zachariah 18

STINCHCOMB Alice 126
Wesley 126
STIRLING Alice M. 171
Edward 171
STOCKETT Charles
William 20
George S. 20
Howard Duval 20
Jonathan S. 20
Joseph Nobel 20
Juliette M. 20
Maria E. 20
Robert P. 20
Sophia 20
Thomas 20
Thomas Noble 20
STOCKSDALE Estella 139
George 139
STOKES Caroline 2
STOLL George 122, 173
Louisa 122
Louisa Margaret 173
STOLLERS Arcana 86
STONE Alice M. 17
Clara M. 17
Clara S. 17
Clarence 17
Elizabeth 17
Ellen 81, 107
Fannie T. 16
Harriet 16
Harriet Newell 16, 17
Harvey 16, 17
Helen 17
Jacob H. 106
James Harvey 16
Jerusha 16
John L. 106
John T. 17
Jonas 16
Marcella 106
Maria 17
Mary 16, 17, 111
Mary E. 17
Newell 16
Rhoda 30
Ruth 17
Sarah Elizabeth 16
William 17
William F. 17
William H. 106
Wilmer T. 17
STORMS Annie 89
STOVER Ellen 55
Jacob 55

STRAHAN Ebenezer 36
Eliza M. 36
Nellie 36
STRATENBERG Elizabeth 181
STRAWBRIDGE Isaac 52
Louisa 52
STREET (Streett, Streets)
Anna R. 171
Corbin Grafton 171
David 171
David Corbin 171
John 171
Nancy 171
Sadie 171
Sarah 171
Thomas 171
William 171
William F. 171
STREETT Charlotte 55, 58
John 55, 58, 161
Miss 161
Shadrach 42
William 161
STRICKLAND John 168
Rebecca 168
STRIEWIG Maggie 180
Mary 180
STROHMER Michael 118
Rosalba 118
STUMP Alice 27
Christopher 27
Edward 26
Ellen 27
Ernest 27
Esther 196
Henry 196
Margaret 26, 27
Mary 27
Norman 27
Rachel 196
Reuben 26, 27, 196
Samuel 26
William S. 27
STURGEON Mary S. E. 128
W. R. 128
STUVEN Alfred 41
Amelia 41
SUDLER Comfort 193
Elizabeth 200
SULLIVAN Artemus 47
Kate 142
Maggie Jane 133
Rachel E. 47
SUMMERLATT Elizabeth 166

275

INDEX

SUNDERLAND Benjamin C. 63
  Florence 117
  Gertrude 63
  William H. 117
SUTHERLAND A. B. 127
  Albion 127
  Anna D. 128
  Carlton M. 127
  Catherine 128
  D. Cameron 127, 128
  Dr. J. B. 127
  Edward Paul 128
  Kate S. 128
  Laura M. 127
  M. H. 127
  Martha E. 127
  Sadie V. 128
  Sallie 127
  Samuel 127
  Samuel W. 127
SUTTON Elizabeth M. 77
  James L. 77
  Julia 185
  Sarah 77
SWAIN W. M. 4
SWANN Louisa 197
  Thomas 197
SWARTZ Margaret 58
SWEENEY Agnes 182
  Catherine 138
  Joseph 182
  Mary Ann 182
  Michael B. 138
  Thomas 182
SWOMLEY Annie 123
  Daniel 123
SWORD Jennie 127
SYLVA Lord 3

TAFT A. Samuel 187
  Alfred S. 187
  Fred H. 187
  Laura H. 187
  Laura L. 187
  M. Rena 187
  Robert 187
  Sarah J. 187
TALBERT Hannah 29
  William 29
TALBOTT Adam D. 51
  Ann Elizabeth 184
  Annie 51
  Edward C. 36, 184
  Eliza M. 36
  J. Fred C. 36
  Joshua F. C. 184
  Laura Bell 36
  Mary Elizabeth 36
  Rebecca 36
  T. Ellen 36
  Temperance Ellen 184
TALIAFERRO John 182
  John Seymour 182
TALLMAN Eliza 125
TAMES Amelia 105
  Annie Catherine 104
  Charles 105
  George W. 105
  John 104
  John H. 104, 105
  Kate 105
  Sallie 105
  Samuel 105
  Susie 105
  Theresa 47
TANEY Roger Brooke 203
TARBERT Elizabeth
  Augusta 193
TARMAN Catharine V. 161
TATE Anna 57
TATTERSALL Alice M. 4
  James C. 4
  John 4
  Samuel H. 4
  Samuel Leslie 4
  Sarah 4
TATUM Martha E. 204
  Robert H. 204
TAY Mercy 40
TAYLOR Anna 23
  Anna R. 1
  Annie 34
  Annie L. 90
  Annie McEldowney 33
  Avarilla 194
  Benjamin F. 45, 46
  C. B. 34
  Caleb 83
  Caleb Stansbury 33
  Caroline Cator 46
  Christiana 19, 24
  Edmund 90
  Edvina V. 76
  Effie E. 90
  Eleanor 33
  Elijah 19, 23
  Elijah G. 24
  Eliza Marsh 33
  Elizabeth 24, 45, 75, 152
  Elizabeth Ruth 33
  Esther A. 45
  Fannie 83
  Frances 135
  Franklin 1
  George F. 75, 76
  George McGill 76
  George W. 46
  H. E. 135
  Hannah 23
  Harry C. 90
  Herbert Douglass 76
  Isaac 23
  J. Zachary 135
  Jacob 23
  Jacob H. 24
  James 90, 145
  James E. 145
  James J. 46
  James W. 90
  Jane 90
  Jesse 75
  Jesse Church 76
  John Wesley 135
  Joseph 23, 24
  Joseph C. 46
  Maggie 145
  Martha Adele 46
  Mary 23, 24, 90, 135
  Mary C. 24
  Mary Ellen 145
  Mary F. 44
  Mary J. 46
  Mary Janet 76
  Mary W. 192
  Mary Wesley 135
  Miss 20
  Nathan 46
  Page 135
  Paul 135
  Pearl 135
  Rebecca 23, 33
  Richard 23, 33
  Robert 45
  Robert Alexander 46
  Robert Moore 33
  Rosa E. 135
  Ruth 33
  Samuel 23
  Sarah 23, 33
  Sarah R. 23
  Thomas 23, 33
  Thomas F. 90
  Thomas H. 33
  Thomas Wesley 46

INDEX

Virginia 135
Virginia M 90
Walter E. 90
Wilkerson 33
William 90
William A. 90
TEGGES Annie 200
Frederick 200
Gertrude 200
Henry 200
John F. 200
Louisa 200
Maggie 200
Margaret 200
Marie 200
Nicholas 199, 200
TEMPLEMAN Aeliza 175
Richard 175
TENNANT Edward 3
Emily I. 3
THACKERY Mary 143
Robert 143
THEILL Anna 55
William H. 55
THOMAS Albert 199
Alfred W. 133
Benjamin Marvin 53
Bessie Jennie 53
Bruce 126
Caroline 57
Carrie 53
Charles 53
Charles Edward 53
Edna Agnes 53
Elizabeth 168
Elizabeth R. 168
Ettie C. 166
Fletcher 126
Frank B. 166
George 53
George Albert 53
Grace 126
Harry 57, 126
Harvey 57
Henry 57
Henry S. 57
Howard 126
Ira 89
James P. 168
John 57
Joseph 199
Joseph A. 166
Julia 57
Julia A. 57
Laura 53

Lewis 57
Lizzie 57
Louisa 57, 89
Maggie 133
Margaret E. 57
Martha 53
Martha M. 166
Mary 56, 57
Mary A. 57
Mary E. 126
Maud 199
Millie 57
Minnie Lillian 199
Rudolph 57
Ruth Anna 53
Sarah 57, 126
Sarah E. 199
Seabrook Stieber 53
Susan 57
Thomas 199
Virginia M. 53
W. Asbury 199
Wesley 126
William 57, 126
William Dulany 166
Willie E. 199
THOMPSON Andrew J. 192
Arthur H. 192
Elizabeth 67, 102
Elmira 65
George G. 192
George T. 67
James R. 85
Louisa 94
Maggie M. 192
Maria C. 85
Martha 109
Mary E. 163
Miss 23
Reuben 61
Sarah A. 192
Sarah E. 61
Sarah L. 46
Susan 61
Thomas 65
Virginia M. 90
William T. 46
THORN John 103
Mary 103
THORNBURGH Joseph 68
THORNE Alice 20, 21
Alice J. 21
Betsey 20
Christopher 20
Grace 20

Harriet 20
Helen 20
Henry 20
James 20
Jane 20
Job 20
John 20
Louis 20
Mark 20
Martha 20
Mary 20
Nathaniel 20
Samuel 20
Susie 20
Walter 21
Walter H. 20
Walter Henry 20, 21
William 20
William Emory 21
TIDINGS Anna 32
Edwin R. 32
Henrietta 32
Richard E. 32
William Henry 32
TILLMAN Anna 75
TIMANUS Andrew 52
Ann 52
Charles 52
Clara V. 52
Ella G. 52
Ernest L. 52
Ethan 52
Fannie 52
Florence 52
George 52
George E. 52
Israel 52
Jacob 52
Jane 52
Jesse 52
John 52
John J. 52
Louisa 52
Luther 52
Margaret 52
Mary 52
Mary F. 52
Mary J. 52
Mollie 52
Nathan 52
Richard H. 52
Selena 52
William J. 52
TIPPETT Nora 164
R. B. 164

INDEX

TIPTON Keturah 43
  Mary E. 113
  W. S. 113
TITTER Curtis 97
  Edward 97
  Eliza 94, 97
  George 97
  George B. 94
  Harry 97
  Harry R. 97
  Isaac 94, 97
  John 97
  Milton 94
  Tillie b. 94
TODD Anna Elizabeth 79
  Benjamin G. 79
  Bernard 157
  Clara 157
  Ella 157
  Ella M. 144
  George W. 157
  James 144
  John T. 157
  Joshua 157
  Mary 157
  Richard 182
  Sallie E. 182
  Sarah Frances 157
  Sarah R. 157
  Thomas 157
  Thomas B. 157
  Thomas J. 157
TOLSON E. F. 151
  Edward F. 16
  Edwin F. 16
  John A. 16
  Maria 16
  Mary A. 77
  Mary E. 16, 151
  Rebecca 16
  William H. 77
TOMPKINS Coles 18
  Eliza M. 18
  J. M. 18
  Margaret 18
  Noah 18
TOOLE Geraldus 6
  Susan Irving 6
TOWNEY George 39
  Matilda 39
TOWNSEND Anna 19
  Anna I. 19
  Eleanor 19
  Elizabeth T. 11
  Guy 19

  Joseph Benson 35
  Julia 35
  Mathias B. 11
  Miss 35
  Perry 11
  Richard 19
  Sophia M. 19
  Susan 35
  Sylvanus 19
  W. Guy 19
  Walter R. 11
  William 35
  Wilson 11
TOWSON Catherine 157
  Charles 157
  Emory S. 157
  Frances 157
  James O. 157
  James W. 157
  John 157
  John W. 157
  Lydia 157
  Margaret 157
  Mary 157
  Nathan 147, 157
  Obadiah 157
  Obadiah G. 157
  Roland 157
  Sarah 157
  William 157
TRACEY C. Melvin 98
  Charlotte C. 98
  Emory C. 98
  Florence 98
  George C. 98
  Jonathan 98
  Laura V. 98
  Mary A. 98
  R. W. Price 98
  Richard C. 98
  Samuel J. 98
TRACY Catherine 137
  George 137
  Susan 59
TRAIG Teresa 105
TRAVERS George 132
  Martha 3
  Rosa P. 132
  Susan A. 74
TREDWELL Miranda 190
  Stephen 190
TRESSEL Ephrain L. S. 8
  George 8
  Samuel 8
  Walter E. 8

TREULIEB Henrietta 187
  John Melchior 187
TRIPLETT Amos 90
  Catherine 105
  Clarence W. 90
  Edward 90, 105
  Elizabeth 90, 105
  Ellen 90
  Elmire V. 90
  Emma L. 90
  Ephraim J. 90
  Ernest 90
  Jefferson 90
  John 90
  Margaret 90
  Mary 90
  Ollie E 90
  Raymond W. 90
TRIPP Elizabeth 54
TROGLER Esther 23
  George L. 23
  Sarah J. 23
TRONE Lewis 70
  Lizzie 70
TROWBRIDGE Mrs. M. L. 27, 41
TROXEL Ann a Elizabeth 121
TRUITT Asa Mattson 103
  Bertha 103
  Captain J. H. 102
  Elisha 102
  John 102
  Mary 102
  Rebecca 102
TRUMBO Susan 71
  William A. 71
TRUMP Susan Van 5
TUCHTON Annie 198
  Effie E. 188, 198
  Eliza 188, 198
  Henry 188, 198
  Henry F. 188, 198
  James 188, 198
  James C. 198
  James T. 188
  John 188, 198
  Mary E. 188, 198
  Nathan 188, 198
  Sarah 188, 198
  Sarah R. 188, 198
  Theodore 188, 198
TUCKER Anna 110
  Zachariah 110
TURBERT Gertrude 43
TURFORD Joseph 4

INDEX

TURNER Bareda 204
  Bessie 204
  Captain J. 119
  Catherine 161
  Charles 78
  Dorothy 204
  Elizabeth 162
  Ella Elizabeth 118
  Emma J. 78
  Hanna A. 185
  James 156
  Joseph 145
  Mary Vickery 61
  Maud 204
  May A. 185
  Nathan G. C. 162
  Rebecca 156
  Robert 204
  Sarah Ann 145
  Smith Fancher 61
  William Mason 185
TUTTLE Albert Vinton 115
  Alfred 115
  Bertha 115
  Charles 115
  Rebecca 115
TWEEDIE Anne 101
  Thomas 101
TWINING Albert 87
  Alice P. 87
  Ann 87
  Barclay 87
  Caroline 87
  D. Hallowell 87
  David 87
  David Hallowell 87
  Fannie 87
  Frank 87
  Horace B. 87
  Isaac 87
  Joseph 87
  Martha 87
  Mary 87
  Robert B. 87
TYSON Laura 124

UHRICH Annie 86
  I. T. 86
  Lizzie 86
  Martha 86
  Mary 86
  Nettie M. 86
ULLRICH Caroline E. 134
  John H. 134
  Leah C. 134
  Seth S. 134

UMPHREY Elizabeth 154
  Louis 154
UNGER Mary 132

VALENTINE Emily T. 137
  George 137
  Mary 137
  Robert 137
  Thomas 137
VALIANT Louisa 133
Van BUSKIRK Blanche W. 96
  Elma 96
  Panola 96
  Panola M. 96
  Thomas J. 96
Van CORTLANDT Annetje 170
Van der WEER Jacob 123
Van HORN Clara L. 37
  Cornelius L. 37
  Sarah E. 37
  Sophronia 37
  William 37
  William H. 37
  Zoe 37
Van NEWKIRK Boygar 161
  Charles L. 161
  George E. 161
  James 161
  John T. 161
  John W. 161
  Joseph 160
  Joseph J. 161
  Mary 160
  Mary L. 161
  Samuel 161
  William 161
Van RENSSELAER Margaret 18
  Stephen 10, 18
Van TRUMP Samuel N. 103
  Sue N. 103
Van WACHTER Family 121
Van WHITE Ella 165
Van ZANT Sarah 179
VANDERGRIFT Louisa 174
VANDIVER Alice 123
  Annie 124
  Dorothy 124
  Ellen 124
  George T. 123
  Jacob 123
  Martha 123
  Mary 123
  Murray 123

  Robert M. 124
  Robert R. 123
VAUGHN Mary 200
  Robert 200
VEASEY Austin Henry 69
  Elizabeth 69
  Emily 69
  H. James 69
  Isaac N. 69
  James 69
  Laura 69
  Louise 69
  Marion T. 69
  Sadie 69
  Sarah 69
  Thomas J. 69
  William F. 69
  William H. 69
VENDERBURY Catherine E. 60
  Ed. L. 60
VICKERS Arianna 150
  Clement 150
  George R. 170
  May C. 170
VOGT Anna Mary 129
  F. E. 183
  Lewis H. 183
VOGTS Eliza E. 78
  Henry 78
VOLKER Margaret 55
  Martin 55
VOLTZ George 185
  Herman 185
  Magdalena 28
  Mary 185
  Minnie 185
  Richard 185
  William 185
VOLZ Caroline 196
  Henry 196
Von der WETTERN A. 96
  Caroline 96
  Dora 96
  Erna 96
  Frieda 96
  Otto 96
  Tillie 96
  William 96
Von FREINSEIN Wilhelmina Sophia 39
Von KAPFF Amelia 28
  Anne Donnell 28
  Annie S. 28
  Bernard 28
  Eleanor Donnell 28

INDEX

Eliza M. 28
Frederick 28
Henrietta 28
Henry C. 28
Hester H. 28
J. F. C. 28
Jane Mary 28
John B. 28
Samuel W. 28
Von SOMMER Caroline 73
Vonder HAFF Louisa 101
WAAG Joseph 10
WACHTER August 160
  Charlotte 160
  Clara Emilia 160
  Dr. J. C. 160
  Dr. C. H. 160
  Edmund J. 160
  Frank C. 160
  Hannah H. 160
  Hattie C. 160
  Sophia Helen 160
WADDELL Ann Maria 86
  Eleanor 35
  Hannah A. 86
  Henry M. 86
  Letitia 8
  Louisa 64
  Nancy 113
  William 35
WADE Delia 132
  George B. 72
  H. B. 72
  J. Perrcy 72
  James T. 72
  John J. 72
  Mary A. 72
  Wallace 132
  Walter S. 72
  William A. 72
WAGGONER Rachael 82
WAGNER Albert 189
  Carl 135
  Emma Louisa 135
  John 135
  L. W. 135
  Margaret 135
  Martha E. 22
  Mary Louisa 189
WAGONER C. V. 104
  Carroll 104
  Frederick 104
  Hilton H. 104
  Jacob 104
  Mary A. 104

Mildred 104
P. H. 7
WAHL Julia 113
WAILES Annie M. 47
  Annie Shipley 47
  Edwin Early 47
  Elizabeth 47
  John B. 47
  John P. 47
  John Shipley 47
  Joseph B. 47
  Joseph C. 47
  Mary B. 47
  Mary H. 47
  Susie 47
  Theodore Cook 47
  Thomas 47
WAINWRIGHT Matilda 39
WALKER Alice T. 201
  Amelia 179
  B. F. 179
  Daniel 76
  Dixon C. 206
  Dixon
    Chancellorsville 201
  Ellen 95
  Emily 179
  George 201, 206
  Georgia 201
  Hamilton C. 201, 206
  Henry 200
  Henry M. 200, 201, 206
  Katharine 206
  Mattie 115
  Noah 200, 201, 206
  Noah Dixon 201
  Patrick Henry 200, 201, 206
  Rachel 78
  Rosa B. 200
  Rosalie B. 206
  S. T. 179
  Samuel T. 167
  Sarah 76
  Sarah A. 206
  Sarah Ann 201
  Sarah T. 201
  Sarah Virginia 167
  Thomas 95
WALL Catherine J. 114
  John 114
WALLACE Maggie B. 38
  Mary H. 41
WALNAU Della 144
  Leopold 144

WALSH Mary 48, 83
WALTER Alice 205
  Alvin Wesley 205
  Anna 55
  Anna B. 55
  Cecilia 205
  Charles S. 205
  Conrad 55
  Edmond Andrew 205
  Edward 55
  Elizabeth Anna 55
  George 55
  George Thomas 205
  Harry 55
  Harry A. 205
  Henry 55
  James 184
  John 55, 205
  John D. 205
  John W. 55, 204, 205
  Joseph Edward 205
  Laura 205
  Lewis 55
  Lewis Albert 205
  Ludwig 55
  Margaret 55
  Mary 64
  Mary Cecilia 205
  Mary E. C. 205
  Mary W. 55
  Michael 205
  Rev. J. 205
  Samuel D. 205
  Sarah 184
  Sena 55
  William F. 55
  William O. 205
WALTHER Augusta 70
WARD Adaline 65
  Albert Norman 181
  Annie E. 126
  Elizabeth 181
  Hattie 181
  John 181
  Joseph 181
  Joshua B. 181
  Laura V. 50
  Mary 157
  Mary E. 181
  Mary Theresa 99
  Maud 181
  Miss 34
  P. J. 99
  T. Harry 181
  V. Hance 126
  William 181
  William M. 181

INDEX

WARE Asbury 63
  Caroline L. 50
  Catherine 105
  Charles R. 50
  E. Tyson 50
  Eleanor L. 50
  Elias 63
  Eliza C. 50
  Eliza V. 50
  Fannie 50
  Henry 63
  Isa 50
  Julia B. 50
  Margaret 90
  Mary 63
  Mary R. 63
  Nathan 50
  Nathan H. 50
  Randolph R. 50
  Robert 50
  Robert P. 50
  Valverda A. P. 50
  Wallace T. 50
  William B. 50
WARFIELD Anna 83
  Betty 83
  Daniel 83
  Douglas Robinson 83
  H. M. 42
  Henry M. 83
  Henry Mactier 83
  J. 47
  Mary B. 47
  Mollie 6
  Rebecca 42
  Richard Emory 83
  S. B. 47
  S. Davies 83
  Sarah 126
  Susie 47
WARING Basil 177
  Cassandra 177
  Elizabeth 177
  Frank 177
  James 177
  Martha 177
  Mary 177
  Rachel 176, 177
  Sampson 177
  Sarah 177
WARNECKE Louisa 12
WARNER A. Shelmon 190
  Adam N. 190
  Albert 190
  Augustus 190
  Ella 190
  Florence Nightingale 190
  Henrietta 121
  Henry 121
  John Calvin 190
  Kate 190
  Lizzie 190
  Margaret 190
  Martin Luther 190
  Peter 190
  Rachel 190
  Sarah Wynne 190
  William Henry 190
WARREN Myra 78
WARRENBERGER Albert 71
  Catherine 70
  Clara 71
  Ella 71
  George W. 70, 71
  Mabel 71
  Peter M. 70
  Susan 71
WASHINGTON George 148
  William 50
WATERS Annie 66
  Araminta 95
  Elizabeth 165
  Ida Grace 165
  Jesse 165
  John 165
  John Seymour T. 182
  Lindsay T. 182
  Margaret Rebecca 197
  Mary 165, 179
  Mary Elizabeth 165
  Mary Wesley 135
  Richard 197
  Richard R. 197
  Sarah Lindsay 182
  Sophie 13
  Sophie Marguerite 13
  William S. 182
WATKINS Annette Stitt 57
  Charles Beale 59
  Clara A. 59
  Colonel 34
  Eliza R. 67
  Elizabeth 171
  Ellemora Bowie 110
  Ellen 67
  Gassaway 110
  Harry Guyton 59
  Isaiah S. 67
  John 59
  John B. 59
  Joseph 171
  Maurice 57
  Ninerva 59
  Priscilla 34, 110
  Samuel 59
  Samuel M. 59
  Sophia 20
  Thomas 153
WATT Anna 161
  William W. 161
WATTS Albert Sydney 82
  Ann 82
  Benjamin 82
  Benjamin P. 148
  Bushard M. 148
  Catherine 148
  Edward 82
  Harriet V. 148
  John 82
  John Marion 148
  Katharine Louisa 82
  Lister Turner 82
  Mary A. 148
  Mattie Adele 82
  Nathaniel 82
  Philip 82
  Philip Bartley 82
  Rachael 82
  Rebecca 82
  Ruth A. 82
  Samuel 148
  Sarah 82
  Walter D. 148
WAUGH John 47
  Lulu 47
WAY Edward 118
  Isaac 79, 81
  Lizzie 118
  Lucinda 81
  Mary M. 79
WEAKLEY Charles 29
  Eugenia 29
WEAVER Elizabeth 120, 146
  George 146
  Mariette 122
  Philip 120
WEBB Cornelius Harrison 37
  Elisha 111
  Euphemia 37
  Henry 37
  Jacob J. 37
  James 111

INDEX

Josephine I. 37
Mary 165
Mary A. 40
Mary Ann 37
Mrs. William B. 145
Rebecca 204
Sarah Jane 37
Sophronia Helen 37
WEBER Addie 206
Amelia 195
Annie 156
Frederick 79
Henry 156
John 195
Mary 79
William g. 206
WEBSTER Anna 93
Bertha May 93
Caroline 13
Clara Olivia 93
Emma Elizabeth 93
George W. 68, 93
H. W. 13
Harry 13
Henry 93
John 120
John H. 93
Margaret I. H. 68
Mary E. 93
Mary Ellen 120
Sophie 13
WEDEMAN Sophia M. 122, 173
Sophia Margaret 173
WEEGE Lizzie W. 87
WEEMS Rachel 87
WEGNER R. T. 109
WEHR Alberta 69
Peter 69
WEIGEL Louis A. 2
WEIL Augusta 41
WEIS August 137
Augustus E. 137
Catherine 137
Conrad 137
Elizabeth 137
Henry 137
Jennetta 137
Lillie 137
Louisa 137
Lulu 137
Margaret 137
Robert 137
William Carl 137
WEISER Sallie M. 54

WEISSER Adeline 10
Anthony 10
August J. 10
Caroline 10
Frank 10
Gabriel 10
John 10
Philomina 10
WEITZEL Barbara 166
WELCH Amelia 98
Thomas W. 98
WELD Calvin 31
Elmira B. 31
WELLER Anna 206
WELLER Anna Margaret 206
Edwin A. 206
Jacob 123, 206
John 205
Joseph 205
Joseph M. 206
Maria L. 206
Mary 123
Morris W. 206
Susan Matilda 205
Virginia O. 206
William F. 205
WELLINGFIELD Lizzie 2
WELLS Caroline V. 43
Elizabeth Ann 68
Harriet A. 78
John M. 68
Susan 92
WELSBACH Roscena 168
WELSH Belle 175
Charles 29
Delia 29
WELTNER Adaline 28
Catherine 28
Henry 28
WENGEL Barbara 151
WENIG Amelia 107
Caspar 107
Eva 107
George 107
Lena 107
WENTWORTH Abbie 146
Thomas 146
WENTZ Philapena 172
WEST Eunice 39
John 40
John R. 208
Louisa M. 208
Oswald T. 208
Willie H. 208

WESTERFIELD James 176
Mary T. 176
WESTERMAN Elizabeth 155
Gerhard H. 155
Margaret 155
WETTAKER Franklin 205
WETTERN Louisa 130
William V. D. 130
WEYLER John F. 105
Louisa 105
WEYRAUCH Katherine A. 202
WHALEY Annie A. 7
WHEELER Ann 175
Belinda 31
Benjamin 31, 67
Caroline 67
Catherine A. 90
Charity A. 137
Charles 109
Charles G. 31
Clarence E. 109
Edward 31
Eliza 112
Ella 31
Elsie May 109
F. I. 112
Francis I. 67
George Thompson 109
Grafton 31
H. S. 39
Harry Howen 109
Henrietta maria 67
Ida Grace 109
Ignatius 67
Joseph 109
Joseph Lewis 109
Julia 31
Kate 31
Laura J. 109
Lillie 31
Lizzie 31
Malinda 31
Martha 109
Mary 31
Mary Ann 67
Rachel 39
Salica 31
Sallie 31
Solomon 175
Teresa 67
Thomas 31, 109
William E. 109
WHEELWRIGHT Juliet 102
WHELAN Margaretta 175
Mary 53

INDEX

WHER Miss 96
WHITAKER Addie E. 50
  Bertha Jennie 50
  Bertha M. 50
  Bertie 50
  Elizabeth 49
  Eugenia 50
  Henry 112
  Isaac 49
  John E. 50
  Joseph 50
  Lloyd D. 49, 50
  Martha 50, 112
  Thomas 49
  Wesley 49, 50
  Wesley R. 49
WHITE Alice 69, 147
  Ann 10, 207
  Ann W. 207
  Catherine 140
  Dora 69
  Edwin C. 147
  Elizabeth Grace 208
  Emma 69
  Emma S. 69
  Ethel 69
  Frances L. 183
  George W. 69
  Georgia 69
  Grace E. 208
  Harriet M. 207
  Jacob P. 183
  James 69
  John W. 207
  John Walton 207
  Joseph 8
  Kate 69
  Mary 69
  Mary A. 208
  Mary E. 8, 69
  Mary M. 69
  Milton 69
  Stella 69
  Walter Walton 207, 208
  William 69
  William Kelso 208
WHITEFORD Aloysius X. 125
  Annie K. 125
  Charles R. 125
  Hugh E. 179
  James E. 178
  James V. 125
  James W. 179
  John M. 125
  Leonora 179

  Lingart I. 125
  Mary A. 125
  May Irene 125
  Michael 179
  Michael N. 179
  Nancy Nelson 179
  Robert A. 125
  Robert H. 179
  Sally Jennie 179
  William 125
  William T. 125
  William T. G. 125
WHITELOCK Mary 138
WHITMORE James S. 89
  Susan 89
WHITTLE Sarah 175
  Thomas 175
WHYTE William Pinkney 62
WICKER Ambrose 17
  Anne M. 17
  James Caldwell 17
  John J. 17
  Lizzie E. 17
  Lizzie Pumphrey 17
  Mollie 17
WICKERSHAM Eliza 153
WIEGAND Emma C. 85
WIEMACK Caroline 96
  Henry 96
WIGHT Alpheus 102
  Amelia 102
  James 102
  John H. 102
  John J. 102
  Margaret 102
  Richart 102
  William H. 102
  William J. 102
WILCOX Daniel B. 152
  Eliza 139
  Margaret J. 152
  Sarah 152
WILFE Susan 93
WILHELM Anna 191
  Caroline 36
  Carrie 36
  Charles 53
  Chloe 36
  Cora 53
  Daniel 53
  Daniel S. 53
  Daniel W. 36
  David 58
  Dora E. 35

  Edith 53
  Eliza 96
  Elizabeth 36, 53
  Elizabeth Ann 57, 58
  Ella 53
  Emanuel 96
  Frederick A. 191
  George Bowen 53
  George W. 36
  Harry 191
  Henry 36, 58
  Jacob N. 35
  Jennie 7, 53
  Jeremiah 36
  John H. 145, 191
  Joshua 53
  Julia A. 36
  Kate 191
  Laura R. 145
  Lillie 191
  Mary E. 36
  May 36
  Minnie 191
  Otto A. 191
  Peter B. 36
  Rebecca 145, 191
  Samuel 53
  Sophronia 58
  Tacie 53
  Webster 53
  William 145, 191
  William H. 191
WILKINSON Cassie 153
  Elizabeth 136
  Emeline 136
  Emeline Rebecca 136
  James 99, 136
  James H. 136
  Mary Alice 99
  Mary Ellen 144
  Narcissa 136
  Narcissa May 136
  Nina 136
  Rebecca 144
  Samuel 136
  Samuel J. 136
  Susan L. 136
  Temperance 136
  William 136, 144
WILKS James 179
  James K. 179
  Mary A. 179
WILLARD Russell 31
  Viola A. 31
WILLCOX Ellen 137

INDEX

WILLIAMS Annie 48
  Augustus Schrader 174
  Baruch 50
  Benjamin L. 174
  Catherine 48
  David S. H. 48
  Delila 85
  Dorsey McCubbin 39
  Dr. 127
  Edmond Jones 174
  Elizabeth 43
  Ellen Sumors 174
  Emily Butler 39
  Henry M. 174
  Henry Martin 174
  Henryetta 174
  James 90
  James W. 39
  James Wright 39
  Jesse Wootten 174
  John 41
  John C. 174
  Joshua Barney 50
  Kate 125
  Louis D. 174
  Louisa 50
  Martha 174
  Mary 90, 91, 141
  Nathan 85
  Nathan Rogers 39
  Olivia A. 91
  Peter McKellar 174
  Providence 127
  Richard 91
  Robert 43
  Sarah 85
  Sarah Ann 174
  Sarah McKellar 174
  Thomas Bayard 174
  Wilhelmina 41
  William L. 174
WILLINGER Annie 106
  Bernidene 106
  L. J. 106
WILLINGHAM Mary A. 125
WILLIS George R. 207
  John E. 207
  Levin N. 207
  Luther M. R. 207
  Mary 207
  Virginia 207
WILLS Grace 20
  Jane 20
  Joseph 20
  Thomas 20

WILLSTON Sallie A. 145
  William E. 145
WILSON Alice 77
  Amanda 29, 63
  Andrew 29
  Benjamin 50
  Benjamin K. 50
  Beryl G. 86
  Caleb 50
  Catherine 200
  Charles E. 191
  Christopher 26
  Clara F. 57
  Daniel S. 35
  David 27
  Eleanor Donnell 28
  Elizabeth 42, 50, 106
  Emily 15
  Eugenia 29
  Eugenie U. 20
  Frances Howard 44
  George 200
  Goodwin 50
  H. Bertram 191
  Henry 50
  Hettie 26
  Ida 35
  Jackson 29, 63
  Jacob 158
  James 29, 191, 200
  James Armstrong 42
  James H. 86
  James Henry 29
  James W. 28
  Jane Shields 28
  John 191
  John C. 29
  John S. 191
  Joseph R. 15, 20
  Julia 143
  Lydia S. 35
  Margaret 26, 125, 200
  Martha 158
  Mary 27, 29, 50, 116, 200
  Mary E. 44
  Mary Ethel 191
  Mary Parmelia 29
  Michael 29
  Miss 59
  Olive 86
  Philip 125
  Phoebe 200
  Rebecca 50
  Rebecca M. 191

  Rev. T. 15
  Robert 29, 57, 77
  Robert S. 44
  Sally A. 86
  Samuel 158
  Sarah 29, 50, 140
  Stephen 44
  Stephen Haven 44
  Susan 15, 200
  William W. 50
  Young Owens 15
WIMBISH Delphia Anne 26
  J. A. 26
WINAND John 27
  Kate 27
WINCHESTER Alexander 106
  Elizabeth Carroll 106
  Fannie 106
  Fannie Mactier 106
  Henry Carroll 106
  Mary 183
  Samuel 106
  Samuel Mactier 106
  Sarah Jane 106
WINDMILL Albert 169
  Josephine 169
WINEHOLT George F. 60
  George G. 60
  Irwin 60
  Leander J. 60
  Lizzie 60
  Nellie 60
  Zachariah 60
WING Maggie 146
WINGFIELD Dorothea 200
  Elizabeth 200
  Robert 200
WINHOLT Catharine 60
WINSTEAD James 194
  Mahala 194
  Rosa 194
WISCHHUSEN Annie C. 154
  Henry 154
WISE Ann 186
  Caroline 5
  Charles H. 186
  Corinna J. 147
  Dorcas A. 186
  Elizabeth 186
  George 147
  Henry A. 147
  John 186
  Lorenia 186
  Mary F. 186
  Miranda 186

INDEX

Sarah A. 147
William 186
WISER Rachel 44
WISNER Abraham 89
  Annie 89
  Christian 89
  Christopher 89
  Emily 37
  George H. 105
  George W. 89
  Henry 89
  Isaac 89
  J. H. 105
  Jacob 37
  Janey A. 105
  John 89
  John Arthur 105
  John H. 89
  Joshua 89
  Katie 89
  Margaret 89
  Mary 89
  Mathias 89
  Nancy 89
  Nellie J. 105
  Rachel 38, 89
  Rachel B. 105
  Ruth A. 89
  Sarah I. 89
  Susan 89
WISTLAND Augusta 72
WITKE Emma 130
  James 130
  John S. M. 129
  Martha 129, 130
  Matilda M. 130
  Peter 130
  Samuel 129, 130
WITTLE John 55
  Mary 55
  Priscilla 55
  Sarah 55
WOERTZ Berthold 166
  Marie 166
WOLF Charles M. 123
  Christian 123
  Edward 123
  Fredericka 123
  George 123
  Jacob 123
  John 123
  Julia 57
  Lewis 123
  Mary 123
  Mitchell 123
  Susan 123

WOLFE Belle 117
WOLFENDEN Miss 181
WOLFORD Miss 94
WOMACK Benjamin F. 12
WONDERER Louis 23
  Matilda Ann 23
WOOD Alice 192
  Eliza 188, 198
  Isabella 131
  John 148
  Louisa 148
  Thomas 192
WOODARD Emanuel 23
  Mary Jane 23
WOODEN Annie M. 130
WOODER Rebecca 64
WOODLAND Cassandra 50
  Louisa 50
  William 50
WOODS Elizabeth 121
  Mary A. 152
WOODWARD Abner 175
  Aeliza 175
  Alexander 16
  Amon 16
  Barbara 176
  Barbara F. 175
  Charles Edmund 175
  Charles P. 175
  Dr. I. J. 176
  Edith 16
  Emma 115
  Frances A. 175
  George P. 175
  Helen Knight 16
  Israel J. 175
  James M. 16
  James S. 16
  Joseph M. 115
  Julia 16
  Marcellus 115
  Mary E. 16
  Meddie 115
  William K. 175
WOOLF Eliza R. 68
  James 67, 68
  Mary 122
  Massey 29
  Sarah J. 67
WOOLLEN Martha A. 57
  Richard H. 57
WOOLLENS Jesse 159
  Margaret 159
  Sarah 159

WOOTTON Ellen Sumors 174
WORKINGTON Mary 163
WORLEY Alexander 32
  Angeline 32
  John 32
  Mary 32
WORTCHE Henry 128
  Lena 128
  Mary 114
WORTHINGTON Blanche 41
  Elizabeth 41
  Henrietta 50
  John 41
  Joshua F. C. 41
  Mary A. C. 41
  Mary Ann 193
  Mary D. 41
  Noah C. 41
  Noah H. 41
  Penelope C. D. G. 41
  Rezin 41
  Thomas 41
WRIGHT Ada 139
  Amelia 40
  Ann 60
  Anna 57, 58
  Blouis 40
  Callie 58
  Callie G. 58
  Catherine 58
  Daniel S. 40
  Eliza J. 18
  Elizabeth 40, 60
  Elizabeth A. 25
  Elizabeth Ann 57, 58
  Ella M. 58
  Ellen 60
  Emily 40
  Fannie 113
  Frances S. 60
  Frank H. 60
  Harry 58
  Harry Ellsworth 58
  Helen E. 60
  Johanna 40
  John 40, 57, 60
  John A. 60
  John W. 40
  Joshua W. 40
  Lydia 60
  Lydia A. 60
  Mabel D. 58
  Maggie A. 58
  Martha 57
  Mary 40, 58, 60

INDEX

Mary Ann 60
Mary E. 40, 60
Mary J. 40
Mary O. 58
May 115
Pearl L. 58
Rachel 57
Richard 57
Robert 58, 60
Robert E. 60
Robert J. 57, 58
Sarah 57, 60
Sarah A. 40
Sena 55
Sophronia 58
Sylvester 58
Thomas 57, 60
Thomas C. 60
Thomas Henry 57
William 40
Willis 113
WULFERT Bertha 182
Caroline 182
Carrie 182
Dietrich 181
Elizabeth 181
Emma 181
Fred 181
Gussie 182
Harry 182
Henry 181
Julia 182
Julius 182
Mollie 181
Wilhelmina 181
WUNDER Jennie 20
WYKE Alice 81
E. D. 81
WYMAN Amanda 192
Elizabeth W. 192
Hannah D. 192
Helen 192
John B. 60
Mary Ann 60
Samuel 192
William 192

YATES Cora 9
YEARLEY Elizabeth 186
Harriet A. 186
John W. 186
YEATMAN Blanche 131
YELLOTT Coleman 25
George 25
George W. 139
Jeremiah 25
John 25
John I. 25
Nannie E. 139
Rebecca Ridgeley 25
YERBURY Nannie 177
YERKES Mr. 141
Susanna 141
YORK Charles A. 85
Delila J. 85
Elizabeth 153
George 153
YOST David G. 138
Elizabeth L. 138
Joseph 175
Margaret 175
Mary E. 138
YOUNG Agnes Virginia 72
Amanda 78
Ariel B. 78
Bessie 78
Beulah 78
Daniel 78
Dora C. 78
Elizabeth 120
Elizabeth Ann 161
James 120
James B. 78
James M. 78
John 78, 161, 194
John Andrew McKay 120
Joseph 78
Laura 120
Mabel 78
Margaret 120
Mary E. 120
Millicence 41
Pearl 78
Rachel 78
Ruth 78
Sallie 78
Smith 41
Susan 120
Thomas 120
Thomas J. 120
William 120

ZACHARIAS Eve Elizabeth 120
ZACHARY Alexander 206
Katharine 206
ZEEFLIE John 156
Lizzie 156
ZEHNER Magdelena 53
ZELL Miss 67
ZENCKER Elizabeth 53
ZEPP Charles 54
M. Louisa 54
ZIEGLER Benjamin 3
Charles Benjamin 3
Edith 3
Helen 48
John E. 3
John M. 3
Margaret 3
William 48
ZIMMERMAN Henry 17
Laah 17
Lizie L. 115
Peter 115
Rev. L. M. 17
ZOUCK Edith E. 86
George P. 86
H. Blanche 86
Harry M. 86
Mary E. 86
Peter G. 86
Rebecca N. 86

www.ingramcontent.com/pod-product-compliance
Lightning Source LLC
Chambersburg PA
CBHW071423150426
43191CB00008B/1022